T0305319

Managing Credit Risk

Founded in 1807, John Wiley & Sons is the oldest independent publishing company in the United States. With offices in North America, Europe, Australia, and Asia, Wiley is globally committed to developing and marketing print and electronic products and services for our customers' professional and personal knowledge and understanding.

The Wiley Finance series contains books written specifically for finance and investment professionals as well as sophisticated individual investors and their financial advisors. Book topics range from portfolio management to e-commerce, risk management, financial engineering, valuation and financial instrument analysis, as well as much more.

For a list of available titles, visit our Web site at www.WileyFinance.com.

Managing Credit Risk

The Great Challenge for the Global Financial Markets

Second Edition

JOHN B. CAOUETTE
EDWARD I. ALTMAN
PAUL NARAYANAN
ROBERT NIMMO

John Wiley & Sons, Inc.

Published by John Wiley & Sons, Inc., Hoboken, New Jersey.
Published simultaneously in Canada.

For general information on our other products and services or for technical support, please contact our Customer Care Department within the United States at (800) 762-2974, outside the United States at (317) 572-3993 or fax (317) 572-4002.

Wiley also publishes its books in a variety of electronic formats. Some content that appears in print may not be available in electronic formats. For more information about Wiley products, visit our Web site at www.wiley.com.

Library of Congress Cataloging-in-Publication Data:

   Managing credit risk : the great challenge for global financial markets /
John B. Caouette . . . [et al.]. – 2nd ed.
        p.   cm. – (Wiley finance series)
   Rev. ed. of: Managing credit risk / John B. Caouette, Edward I. Altman,
Paul Narayanan. c1998.
   Includes bibliographical references and index.
   ISBN 978-0-470-11872-6 (cloth)
      1. Credit–Management.   2. Risk management.   3. Derivative securities.
I. Caouette, John B., 1944–   II. Caouette, John B., 1944– Managing credit risk.
   HG3751.C32   2008
   332.7–dc22   2007047647

10   9   8   7   6   5   4   3   2   1

We dedicate this book to our wives, Judy Caouette, Elaine Altman, Vasantha Narayanan, and Linda Jensen.

Contents

About the Authors

J **ohn B. Caouette** is Chairman of Channel Capital Group, a European-based credit derivative products company. He is also a nonexecutive director of Picture Financial Group, a specialty finance company based in Wales.

He was Founder, Chairman, President, and CEO of CapMAC Holdings and its principal subsidiary, Capital Markets Assurance Corporation, a triple-A rated financial guarantor that focused on the global market for structured finance.

He was an independent director of LCH Clearnet Group, Ltd., a British/French central clearinghouse, and non-executive chairman of Asia Ltd. Singapore, a consortium owned by Asian Financial Guarantee Company.

He was Vice Chairman of MBIA Insurance Corporation, where he oversaw the company's international financial guarantee business and new business development from London. He was also Senior Vice President and General Manager at Foreign Exchange & Money Market Division, Continental Grain Company; and with Citibank for many years, serving in a variety of capacities including Executive Director of the Asia Pacific Capital Corporation in Hong Kong, and Vice President and General Manager in the Swaps and Eurosecurities Department in New York.

Mr. Caouette is an advisory board member to the Haas School of Business, University of California at Berkeley, where he teaches corporate entrepreneurship in the graduate school.

Edward I. Altman is the Max L. Heine Professor of Finance at the Stern School of Business, New York University, and Director of the Credit and Fixed Income Research Program at the NYU Salomon Center.

Dr. Altman has an international reputation as an expert on corporate bankruptcy, high-yield bonds, distressed debt and credit risk analysis. He was named Laureate 1984 by the Hautes Etudes Commerciales Foundation in Paris for his accumulated works on corporate distress prediction models and procedures for firm financial rehabilitation and awarded the Graham & Dodd Scroll for 1985 by the Financial Analysts Federation for his work on default rates and high-yield corporate debt.

He was inducted into the Fixed Income Analysts Society Hall of Fame in 2001 and elected President of the Financial Management Association (2003) and a Fellow of the FMA in 2004.

In 2005, Dr. Altman was named one of the "100 Most Influential People in Finance" by *Treasury & Risk Management* magazine.

Dr. Altman is an advisor to many financial institutions, including Citi, Concordia Advisors, Equinox (Italy), Investcorp, KPMG, Miller-Mathis, and SERASA (Brasil). He serves on the Board of Trustees of Franklin Mutual Series Funds and was on the Investment Advisory Committee of the New York State Common Retirement Fund and on the Board of Automated Trading Desk. He is also Chairman of the Academic Advisory Council of the Turnaround Management Association and serves as an Associate Editor of several risk-related scholarly and practitioner journals.

Paul Narayanan is Director of Credit Portfolio Analytics at American International Group, Inc., New York. His responsibilities include credit portfolio risk issues, structured finance, reinsurance credit risk, measurement and management of exposure and limits, and the development of an economic capital allocation system for the firm. Previously, he was the principal algorithm architect for trade credit insurance in the development and deployment of a system that underwrites and sets credit limits for any public or private enterprise in 18 countries by utilizing credit information from a variety of sources.

Narayanan has been involved credit risk management for more than two decades and in the development of analytical solutions for credit issues as an executive in major institutions, which have included the predecessors of JPMorgan Chase, Bank of America, and Mellon Bank. His work has included failure prediction models of which ZETA (Z-score) model is the best known. He helped build ZETA with Dr. Edward Altman. He has developed and implemented credit and portfolio models in the entire asset spectrum—corporate debtors, residential real estate, financial institutions, and consumer loans.

For several years he was consultant to banks and insurance companies on credit and portfolio management. His clients have included Zeta Services, CASA, Citigroup, Enhance Financial Services, Asian Development Bank, and Banco Provincia de Buenos Aires. Paul has published, taught, and delivered talks on credit and portfolio risk in many forums, including the Society of Actuaries, the Wharton School of the University of Pennsylvania, NYU Stern School, Drexel University, Fundacao Getulio Vargas, IACPM, and the Central Bank of Argentina.

Robert W. J. Nimmo has enjoyed a 37-year-long international banking career in a number of different roles and countries. He started with 24 years at Citigroup, serving in both line and risk management. He was a member of the Groupwide Credit Policy Committee, based in Tokyo, and served with Citigroup in the United States, Hong Kong, the Philippines, and Japan.

Later he was with Westpac Banking Corporation in Sydney, Wachovia NA in Charlotte, North Carolina, and Barclays Bank in London. In all three companies he was the Group Chief Risk Officer.

Mr. Nimmo is a graduate of Stanford University and the Thunderbird School of International Management. He was born in Brisbane, Australia and currently resides with his wife in Portland, Oregon.

ABOUT THE ASSISTANTS

Elizabeth Jacobs kept the authors on their writing schedules and organized delivery of the manuscript to the publisher. Elizabeth has been administrative secretary to John Caouette for nearly two decades.

Jaime Pozuelo-Monfort graduated from Universidad Politecnica de Madrid in 2000 with a master's and a bachelor's in telecommunications engineering. Subsequently, he earned master's degrees in business administration from Collège des Ingénieurs in Paris, in financial economics from Universidad Carlos III de Madrid, in financial engineering from the University of California at Berkeley, and in economic development from the London School of Economics. He currently pursues a master's in public administration at Columbia University. He has worked in the technology sector in Madrid, Stuttgart, and Paris, and in the financial industry in New York City and London. His interests lie in the interaction between financial economics and economic development.

Introduction

Credit risk is the oldest form of risk in the financial markets. If credit can be defined as "nothing but the expectation of a sum of money within some limited time," then credit risk is the chance that this expectation will not be met. Credit risk is as old as lending itself, which means that it dates back as far as 1800 BCE.[1] It is essentially unchanged from ancient Egyptian times. Now as then, there is always an element of uncertainty as to whether a given borrower will repay a particular loan. This book is about how financial institutions are using new tools and techniques to reshape, price, and distribute this ancient form of financial risk.

Ever since banks as we know them were organized in Florence 700 years ago, they have been society's primary lending institutions.[2] *Managing Credit Risk* has formed the core of their expertise. Traditionally, bankers and other lenders have handled credit evaluation in much the same that tailors approach the creation of a custom-made suit—by carefully measuring the customer's needs and capacities to make sure the financing is a good fit. When we originally wrote this book in the late 1990s, it was accurate to say that the approaches taken then did not differ fundamentally from the one used by the earliest banks. This is not necessarily the case today, although the changes we will comment on later in the book still vary from institution to institution, and certainly there are major differences between money center institutions, regional banks and banks in emerging markets. Meanwhile the first decade of the twenty-first century has seen the credit markets become the focus of a whole new category of lender including hedge funds, private equity firms, and other institutional players who are bypassing the traditional credit methodologies in favor of the new ways of credit risk management. Thanks to the creation of credit derivative products, market participants can take or shed credit risk on any entity anonymously, that is, without entering into any legal credit arrangement with that entity or lending to it. This is one of the reasons you find a bank in Germany taking credit risk on a subprime home mortgage in Kansas without ever seeing either the borrower or the property. This used to be the preserve of the local Kansas bank.

It is easier to design a suit for a customer you already know. Because of the very nature of this approach, banks historically have been drawn to *relationship banking.* This led to a pattern where they were more concerned about their relationship with a customer than they were about the profitability of a specific loan or about the effect a given transaction may have on their overall loan portfolio. As long as a borrower met the credit criteria, the bank did not pay much attention to concentrations that were building up. Citibank's buildup of construction loans and the effect they had on the institution when these loans went sour in the late 1980s is a case in point. At the time of the publication of the first edition of *Managing Credit Risk,* the banking industry had begun to recover from a crisis that had emerged nearly a decade earlier. There was widespread recognition within the industry that the traditional approach to lending had led to unacceptable results and that banks had done a rather poor job of pricing and *Managing Credit Risk.*

In some ways the banking crisis of the day was just what you would expect from an industry that was adapting to a more limited role in the provision of credit. In other ways, it reflected an evaluation that the traditional banker/client roles needed some updating if not revolutionary change. Those who read our first edition would not have had to look hard to find a decidedly negative view of how banks were dealing with credit risk at the turn of the century. Less than a decade later, things look a lot different. Later in this introduction, we list the 10 major changes that are shaping the management of all risk, credit included. Those changes are significant and banks are at the cutting edge of the change. So we take a more generous view of the way banks are managing credit and portfolio risk and in many places you will see us holding many of them up as examples of excellence in the management of this risk. They are better, but as we can now see in the subprime mortgage crisis at the end of 2007, they are still capable of major missteps.

The first decade of the twenty-first century has seen the credit markets transformed by several institutional developments. First, the markets mirror their environment: They have become global, highly innovative, and of critical importance to the global economy. The top market players have developed into universal *megabanks.* There are a handful of such organizations, which were formed from the top ranks of what was once the top tier of commercial or investment banks. Now they do both investment and commercial banking as well as many other types of investment related services and lending. The names are familiar—-Citicorp, JPMorgan Chase, Goldman Sachs, Morgan Stanley, UBS, Merrill Lynch, Deutsche Bank, Credit Suisse, Bank of America, and so on. These organizations are on the cutting edge of credit risk management and are a proving ground for "best practices" within the industry. Secondly, *real* credit risk has been embraced by the capital markets and this has fueled the development of whole new categories of lenders including structured finance lenders, hedge funds, private equity firms, and others who, for the most part, are finding new ways to approach credit risk management. Thirdly, credit risk management has evolved into total enterprise risk management. Best practice for the major players is to include market, operational, and reputation risk alongside the management of credit. Finally, the shape and day-to-day operations of the credit risk markets in this new millennium are heavily influenced by regulators who are setting the rules (e.g., Basel II and Solvency II) for most of the players in a much more sophisticated way, and by the rating agencies whose rating practices have set the market standard of credit risk measurement—especially with respect to securitized products.

The counterpart to credit risk is market risk—the chance that an investment's value will change in price as a result of marketplace forces such as interest rates, commodity prices, and currency levels. Market risk has affected financial institutions ever since markets were created. Techniques for managing market risk have undergone a radical change. Anyone who tours a large trading floor at a bank or an investment bank can see that the management of market risk has been the focus of tremendous technological development. Major breakthroughs have turned this aspect of risk management into something of a science—one that is applied to both equities and debt instruments. Market risk developments were an important precedent for our focus on credit risk management. Some have commented that the 1980s were a period when market participants focused on how to manage market risk. This led to the Basel Committee introduction in 1995 of a system that allowed banking institutions to set capital requirements based on market risk levels calculations using the models the banks had developed. This focus on models and other mathematical analysis by the Basel Committee continued as they turned to the management of credit risk in Basel I and II.

This is not to suggest that market risk has been eliminated. In the case of America's savings and loan associations, for example, an entire industry quaked because of bad bets made on commercial real estate asset values during a period when deregulation was increasing the risks in the financial markets. Periodically, we learn of major losses experienced by trading firms that are the result of "rogue traders" who are identified—after the fact and accused of misappropriating the firm's capital. Sometimes the problem is that a firm does not really understand what it is doing (despite a great pedigree such as with Long Term Capital Management) and bets the ranch on a losing idea.

Despite its shortcomings in anticipating systemic events and overcoming the actions of some individuals, the science of managing market risk does nevertheless reflect late twentieth-century knowledge and technology. For example, banks have adopted the concepts of gap management, duration, and even the theory of contingent claims. Major banks have created huge markets for interest rate and currency swaps.

By contrast, in 1998, when we first published *Managing Credit Risk*, the management of credit risk at banks was, to a substantial degree, a kind of cottage industry in which individual leading decisions were made to order. As befitted a cottage industry, there was, for the most part, no common credit language. Practitioners, academics, and regulators heatedly debated fundamental measurements such as default timing, default events, workout costs, and recoveries. There was a dearth of reliable quantitative data on financial and nonfinancial variables as well as on recovery rates following failure. There was, however, at the time, a considerable effort underway to improve the situation. Many studies were initiated by Edward Altman and the rating agencies on default levels and recovery rates, but they were all a work in progress and not yet internalized by many leading institutions. Ten years later things look a lot different. Credit risk is still a tougher risk to master than market risk. There are many more variables to consider. However, we now have many more tools, much more information and some important new players who are willing to take credit risk, expect to be fairly compensated for it, and are demanding more transparent market pricing.

TOP 10 CHANGES IN THE CREDIT MARKETS IN THE LAST DECADE

- New product innovations, particularly in the credit derivative and structured finance areas and the standardization of older innovations.
- The growing sophistication of the major players in the credit markets in terms of techniques and strategies.
- The increased use of scientific and mathematical models (e.g., credit scoring models for residential mortgage lending and correlation models to price basket credit default swaps).
- The New Basel accords, which have directly shaped the banking markets and indirectly influenced market participants in general (often called *regulatory capital arbitrage*).
- The ready availability and easy delivery of reliable credit information on a global basis, 24/7 through the Worldwide Web.
- The phenomenal growth in technology and systems capabilities at affordable prices leading to better reporting and modeling.
- Huge changes in the markets themselves, in terms of size, liquidity, and globality.

- The emergence of hedge funds as major investors in the markets.
- The growing influence of the rating agencies.
- Lower levels of loss and higher levels of liquidity led to constantly reducing credit spreads, which reached their historical lows in June 2007. This market frenzy was a vortex dragging more people into what turned out to be poor credit choices.

Creating this list was the first thing we did after deciding upon a revision of this book. We knew that many changes have taken place over the past decade, and it seemed like an important first step to try to capture them in a list that we could agree on and refer to as we made changes. Everyone might not agree with our 10 and certainly others might wish to emphasize or describe things somewhat differently. However, we doubt that we would have a substantially different list if we polled everyone who is working in the credit markets of Europe and the United States. Nevertheless, the list is our own and forms the basis for all the changes that will appear in the second edition of *Managing Credit Risk*.

EVOLUTION OF CREDIT RISK IN THE ECONOMY

Credit risk is a consequence of contracted and/or contingent financial transactions between the providers and users of funds. To understand how it has evolved in modern times, we have to look at the private corporation as the vehicle of economic growth. In precapitalist societies, family and sovereign wealth were the primary bearers of credit risk. Subsequently, the formation of joint stock corporations created entities that were able to pool resources, bear economic risk, borrow money, and exist beyond the natural lives of the owners. Financial intermediaries were created to pool savings and provide them to the users of funds. Even before interest expenses were given preferential tax treatment, corporations (for example, railroads and utilities) used the debt market to raise funds from distant investors, using corporate assets or a government guarantee to secure their borrowing. The bond markets and banks were the dominant providers of debt capital (see Baskin and Miranti 1997).

As markets grew, other providers of funds gradually took market share away from banks. Junk bonds, asset-based securities, and commercial paper displaced conventional bank financing to a significant extent. A primary reason for this was economics. According to Bryan (1993), the total cost of intermediating a security over the life of an asset is under 50 basis points, whereas the cost of bank intermediation is well over 200 basis points.

A NASCENT SCIENCE OF CREDIT RISK MANAGEMENT

In the mid-1980s and early 1990s, the United States experienced record defaults on bank loans and corporate bonds. When junk bond defaults jumped to over 10 percent in the years 1990 and 1991, many observers argued that both junk bond and the leveraged bank lending markets were likely to disappear. The high-yield bond markets recovered, however, and reached record volumes later in the decade.

Prompted in large part by very poor performance in their portfolios in the mid-1980s, practitioners of credit risk management became increasingly interested in new techniques. However, the heightened concern about credit management that emerged did not evolve into a pervasive drive to create and deploy new evaluation techniques. Nor did banks embrace portfolio management, believed to be much needed for them. Instead, this period saw the development of a few standalone models, continued refinement of some relevant default databases (first established in the late 1980s), and a spate of surveys be regulators and consultants on existing techniques. The latter invariably reached the conclusion that in most financial institutions, credit culture and lending strategies needed to be rethought and possibly redesigned (for example, see Bryan 1988).

Paradoxically, interest in new approaches to credit risk management exploded during a period when the credit markets themselves were exceptionally benign. Although same economists are now predicting a recession for the United States in early 2008, the U.S. economy has been strong for much of the last decade and most of the world's stock markets have been booming for a substantial period, reflecting impressive corporate growth and low interest rates. With a few conspicuous exceptions such as Argentina, Japan, Indonesia, Thailand, Malaysia, and South Korea, credit markets in most parts of the world have been well behaved. Indeed, for the last seven years (2000–2006), well under 1 percent of total bank loans have been non-performing, compared to an average of close to 4 percent in 1988 through 1993. Default rates on leveraged loans and junk bonds were likewise well under 2 percent for the last three years, in contrast to the 4.2 percent average for junk bonds in 1991 through 2006. Given these positive credit market statistics, the surge of interest in new techniques for managing credit risk during the early years of the new millenium is surprising. Even more surprising was how little this seems to have helped avert the latest credit crisis—and worse yet, may have contributed to its creation. What is the reason behind the renewed focus on credit?

The answer, we believe, may be found in the changes that have occurred in both the lending institutions and others such as hedge funds which have fueled a huge increase in market liquidity. Lending institutions have reached a stage of development where they no longer want or need to make (buy) a loan and hold it to the end of its natural life (maturity, payoff, or charge-off). The reasons undoubtedly include pressures from regulators, the emergence of dynamic trading markets for loans, and the pursuit of internal objectives for return on equity. Today, banks are increasingly willing to consider shifting their credit exposure through transactions with counterparties. The markets in which banks can sell their credit assets (other than residential mortgages and consumer loans) are still fairly small and illiquid, and they are inefficient in comparison, say, with the Treasury market. Nevertheless, the market for bank loans has grown in size and liquidity. Consequently, banks and their counterparties are invested heavily in processes for gathering credit information and the analytical foundation necessary to value bank loans by a meaningful risk/return standard. Increased competition, the drive for diversification and liquidity, and regulatory changes such as risk-based capital requirements created by Basel I and II have thus stimulated the development of many innovative ways to manage credit risk. Banks realized (yet again) from the real estate default experience of 1989 to 1991 that concentration was a critical issue. Out of this realization arose portfolio management. The contagion of the financial crisis in the Asian economies in 1997 signaled that credit risk correlation, if anything, was yet to be well understood.

Around the world, the experiences in the U.S. banking system are being repeated. European countries such as Switzerland and Sweden have gone through a similar real estate crisis. European and Japanese banks have been hurt more than the U.S. banks by concentration in lending to the Asian economies. Domestic financial institutions in the damaged Asian economies, including Japan, are looking to improve their systems for managing credit by building a new credit culture and moving toward an improved market-driven discipline. Thus, just as portfolio management appears to have arrived in U.S. and European banks, the need for credit culture is being acutely felt in the emerging economies.

INNOVATIVE PRODUCTS AND STRUCTURES

Many innovative products and structures have been developed to manage credit risk. The following are some important examples:

- *Structured finance transactions such as collateralized mortgage obligations and asset-backed securities.* These instruments pool assets and transfer all or part of the credit risk borne by the originator to new investors and, in some cases, to one or more guarantors as well. By means of the secondary market, investors can, if necessary, transfer the risk to yet any other party.[3]

- *Exchanges and clearinghouses.* By introducing a structural hub, these entities minimize the need for every pair of contracting parties to create a separate mechanism for managing their counterparty credit risk exposure.

- *Credit derivatives, which can be layered to modify the credit risk profile of an underlying asset.* Although it is still young and currently being challenged, the credit derivative market is growing at an explosive pace. A lender who does not want to continue to assume the credit risk from an asset no longer has to sell the asset outright. Financial instruments are being devised—some simple and some complex—that create a kind of insurance mechanism for transferring the risk of default, and, in some instances, of credit migration. For the first time ever, it is now possible to go short on credit. Furthermore, the credit risk to be bought or sold may be tailored as to amount, period, and the type of credit event. The credit derivative market will transform the business of borrowing and lending in a way that was quite inconceivable just a few years back.

CREDIT RISK IS LIKE MILK

As financial innovation has progressed, credit risk has changed in many ways. In the case of senior/subordinated securities, for example, credit risk has been segmented and redistributed. To avoid the possibility that an entire issue will be downgraded because of poor performance in an isolated segment, these structures are partitioned into separate classes (Myerberg 1996). In the dairy, milk from a cow is first separated into components and then reconstituted into various grades to suit the consumer tastes: low fat, high fat, light cream, and so on. Similarly, financial innovation has decomposed risk and repackaged it into parts that appeal to different types of investors. In this way, a single issue can attract multiple investor classes. This approach to credit risk has turned it from a *defensive* concern to an *offensive* opportunity—understanding the credit risk has made it possible to open up new channels of funds flow. The new generation of finance companies that are funded by asset-backed commercial paper are a prime example of this trend. Debt obligations are pooled and recast as super-senior, senior, mezzanine, and equity tranches. The mezzanines themselves are later pooled to create what has come to be called CDO-squared. Similar structures have been created in the *synthetic* space, where there are no cash flows per se, but the holder of a synthetic tranche will get a credit spread income. In exchange, this layer will absorb credit loss caused by the default of an entity in the underlying pool.

The number of entities participating in a credit-related transaction has grown. A structured finance transaction, for example, may include an originator, a seller/servicer, a trustee, and a guarantor. Each of these entities faces exposure from or represents exposure to some other participant. This does not mean *total* credit risk has increased. However, because multiple parties are involved, it does mean that credit risk must now be assessed from more than one perspective. Credit risk of the underlying obligor has now been exchanged for counterparty financial institution risk and, in many instances, for market risk.

Financial engineering has created instruments with various embedded options and dependencies, each of which may expose participants to both market risk *and* credit risk. In the case of an interest rate swap, for example, potential counterparty exposure is not fixed. In some cases, it begins at zero, then increases over time, then gradually returns to zero at the maturity of the swap. Derivative transactions such as swaps require new forms of financial disclosure and accounting, and they also raise legal issues regarding enforceability. On one pretext or another, some counterparties may simply refuse to honor contractual commitments. For these reasons, rapid growth in the derivatives markets means an overall increase in credit risk.

THE GLOBAL RATE OF CHANGE IS TRULY UNPRECENDENTED

Credit risk has grown exponentially against the backdrop of dramatic economic, political, and technological change around the world. In decades past, geopolitical boundaries and government regulation restricted the mobility of capital. Ever since exchange rates were allowed to float in the early 1970s, financial markets have witnessed a steady progression of deregulation. This has led to increased competition between financial institutions and a blurring of the boundaries separating banks, investment banks, insurance companies, and investment companies. There have been major changes in the geopolitical arena as well: the breakup of the USSR, the reunification of Germany, and the introduction of free-market approaches in China and the Eastern European countries. The bipolar tension between capitalism and communism has faded and with it much of the pressure for oversized military budgets. However, geopolitical issues continue, in the form of nuclear proliferation, terrorism, and world poverty. The spotlight is today, however, on economic growth and an improved standard of living. China and India are leading examples of this paradigm shift.

Around the world, liquidity has increased. This represents an opportunity in the sense that new sources of capital have appeared. It represents a challenge, too, because new uses and users of this capital have emerged around the globe as well. Transactions take place involving currencies and entities of unprecedented variety. In many instances, credit risk must now be analyzed where parties have little or no credit history. In all, credit risk has grown more complex. At the same time, the ability of governments to guarantee and offer bailouts has diminished and the velocity with which a major credit crisis can cast its shadow globally has increased.

Superimposed on these geopolitical developments is the powerful force of information technology. Today, it is easier than ever before to gather, pool, and retrieve data from far-flung regions of the globe. Techniques such as genetic algorithms, neural networks, and optimization models are within reach of any analyst equipped with a personal computer. Newer models and databases are leading to a better understanding of the expected financial behavior of any particular asset and its relationship to other assets. This improved knowledge may well further increase the importance of securities markets at the expense of banks. However, markets do not have the same commitment to a credit relationship that a bank may have: When the source of funds dries up overnight, a borrower cannot renegotiate the terms of the loan as easily as with a bank. Borrowers will have to manage financing sources as a portfolio of choices, each with a different price-availability profile, and learn to tolerate greater volatility in the financing arena.

Many of the techniques developed to measure and control market price risk are being applied to credit risk. But as in the case of market risk, tools for *Managing Credit Risk* will not, by themselves, make the world a safer place. Any analytical tool is a child of the human intellect attempting to model the real world through a limited set of variables. These tools employ estimation and optimization techniques that are also inventions of the human mind. A model may capture a large proportion of the reality being modeled, but it must nonetheless omit some important aspects of it. Furthermore, a model's very existence may alter market behavior over time, rendering it less and less useful. For these reasons, participants in the financial markets will need to pay great attention to the issue of *model risk*. It appears that model risk of this type was one of the causes of the subprime crisis.

As we explain in the chapters that follow, the new financial tools are, in themselves, works in progress—useful but still imperfect. If they are accorded unwarranted authority or if they are handled without proper care and judgment, they can actually amplify and not minimize an institution's exposure to credit risk. In the end, the effectiveness of these tools depends absolutely upon the skills, motivations, and attitudes of the people using them. That is why participants in the credit markets must pay close attention to the selection and training of their professionals, to the incentives they create for them, and to the attitudes that pervade their organizations. All of these are critical elements of a firm's risk culture. Over the coming decades, success will go to those firms that employ the right tools *and* create the right kind of culture. So is there still a challenge in the management of credit risk? The answer is, yes. But it is a very different kind of challenge. Our skills as an industry are much better and we have many more tools to work with, but the environment and the scale of things all have changed and have created new challenges to manage. The market is much more fragmented. A world where derivatives outweigh physicals by a factor of 10 or more will create unintended consequences that we are only now just beginning to understand.

When we wrote the first edition of *Managing Credit Risk,* the challenge we saw was quite different from what it looks like only 10 years later. In the late 1990s, banks were still struggling to move past the credit problems that emerged a decade earlier. Most of the new tools, innovations, and methods for managing credit risk had been developed at that time, but it was not clear then whether a lot of these new ideas would come into practical use in banks. Ten years later, the outcome is clear. Motivated by a strong survival instinct and some direction from regulators, the world's banking industries are now much better at managing risk and they have incorporated most of the concepts we discuss into their risk management systems. So what are the challenges today? Today's challenges arise from the growing sophistication of the markets. The megabanks we discussed earlier in this introduction and are now the central core of the credit markets have successfully turned themselves into experts in managing, packaging and selling off risks to the global financial markets. The challenge now is whether the full range of players in the system has the intellectual foundations and proper risk capitalization to handle the range of risks that are now routinely moved around the globe. If they do not, the cost to the global economy could be high.

The first six chapters of this book describe the institutional setting for credit risk: banks, insurance companies, pension funds, exchanges, clearing-houses, and rating agencies. The chapters that follow introduce and discuss the tools, techniques, and vehicles available today for managing credit risk. The concluding chapters integrate the emerging trends in the financial markets and the new tools and techniques in the context of credit culture. Throughout the book, we place our primary emphasis on *practice,* introducing insights provided by *theory* as needed. Our goal is to present state-of-the-art credit risk solutions along with the perspectives of leading experts in the field who have successfully implemented them. The appendix lists the sources of hard copy and electronic information on credit risk available to the practitioner.

REFERENCES

Altman, E. I. 2007. Global Debt Markets in 2007: New Paradigm or the Great Credit Bubble?, *Journal of Applied Corporate Finance* 19, no. 3, Summer 2007.

Altman, E. I., and S. Ramayanam. 2007. *The High-Yield Bond Default and Return Report: Third-Quarter 2006 Review*, NYU Salomon Center Special Report.

Baskin, J. B., and P. J. Miranti, Jr. 1997. *A History of Corporate Finance.* New York: Cambridge University Press.

Bryan, L. L. 1988. *Breaking up the Bank: Rethinking an Industry Under Siege.* Homewood, Ill.: Dow Jones-Irwin.

———. 1993. The Forces Reshaping Global Banking. *McKinsey Quarterly* 2:59–91.

de Roover, R. 1963. *The Rise and Decline of the Medici Bank.* Cambridge, Mass.: Harvard University Press.

Guttmann, R. 1994. *How Credit-Money Shapes the Economy: The United States in a Global System.* Armonk, N.Y.: M. E. Sharpe.

Homer, S., and R. Sylla. 1996. *A History of Interest Rates,* 3d ed. New Brunswick, N. J.: Rutgers University Press.

International Monetary Fund. 1997. *World Economic Outlook: Interim Assessment.* Washington, D.C.: International Monetary Fund.

Myerberg, M. 1996. The Use of Securitization in International Markets. In *A Primer on Securitization,* edited by L. T. Kendall and M. T. Fishman. Cambridge, Mass.: MIT Press.

Sasson, J. M., ed. 1995. *Civilizations of the Ancient Near East.* New York: Charles Scribner's Sons.

CHAPTER 1

Credit Risk

The Great Challenge For The Global Economy

Moderate leverage undoubtedly boosts the capital stock and the level of output ... the greater the degree of leverage in any economy, the greater its vulnerability to unexpected shortfalls in demand and mistakes.
—Alan Greenspan, Board of Governors of the Federal Reserve System, 2002

In recent decades, credit risk has become pervasive in the United States and throughout the world. The U.S. Treasury borrows to keep the federal government afloat, and local water districts borrow to construct new treatment plants. Corporations borrow to make acquisitions and to grow, small businesses borrow to expand their capacity, and millions of individuals use credit to buy homes, cars, boats, clothing, and food. The dramatic growth in U.S. borrowing by all segments of the society is illustrated in Figure 1.1, which suggests the scale of this credit explosion.

An element of credit risk exists whenever an individual takes a product or service without making immediate payment for it. Telephone companies and electric utilities accept credit risk from all their subscribers. Credit card issuers take this risk with all their cardholders, as do mortgage lenders with their borrowers. In the corporate sector, businesses in virtually every industry sell to customers on some kind of terms. Every time they do so, they accept credit risk. The credit risk assumed may be for a few hours or for a hundred years.

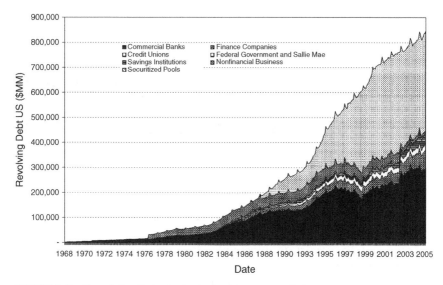

FIGURE 1.1 Revolving Debt in the United States, 1968–2006
Source: Federal Deposit Insurance Corporation (2006).

Meanwhile, the use of credit became a major factor of other countries as well. Europe has seen a significant increase in leverage by corporations and individuals, particularly in Britain where the patterns are similar to those in the United States. Emerging markets have also joined the bandwagon as both countries and their corporations and individuals have come to see credit as a powerful tool for economic progress. Meanwhile the capital markets have provided many more ways for these institutions and individuals to borrow.

CHANGING ATTITUDES TOWARD CREDIT

The credit explosion has been accompanied—and accelerated—by a dramatic shift in public attitudes. When Shakespeare's Polonius advised his son, "Neither a borrower nor a lender be," he was voicing the wisdom of his time. He reasoned that "loan oft loses both itself and friend, and borrowing dulls the edge of husbandry." Such advice—whatever its merits were in the Elizabethan age—has been drowned out by the contrary opinion. And Polonius may have been wrong about friends, too. Banks continue to court borrowers who caused them to lose money in the past! And if borrowing dulls the edge of husbandry, no one seems to mind. Any shame that once attached to the use of credit has vanished.

Even the words we use to describe credit reflect a major shift in attitude. The word *debtor* still carries connotations of misery and shame—an echo of Dickensian debtors' prisons. The word *borrower,* likewise, may still call to mind a pathetic figure going hat in hand to a powerful and possibly scornful banker. But today, we no longer need to see ourselves as debtors or borrowers. We can think of ourselves as people using *leverage*—a word with entirely different connotations. *Leverage* suggests that we are clever enough and skillful enough to employ a tool that multiplies our power. And using leverage leaves the rest of our identity intact—we do not become *leveragors* in the same way that we become debtors. Using leverage is something to boast about, not something to conceal. Today many people see credit as an entitlement.

From many directions, in fact, Americans are bombarded with invitations to increase their borrowing. Automobile manufacturers attract buyers with low rates on auto loans and offer leases with easy terms to customers who cannot afford a down payment. Retailers entice consumers to open charge accounts by offering discounts on their first purchases. Credit card issuers cram Americans' mailboxes with competing offers. Even credit-impaired individuals—those who once sought the protection of the bankruptcy court—are soon viewed as good credit risks because they are now debt free (*Philadelphia Inquirer* 1996, D-1). Indeed, if there is still shame in any type of consumer transaction, it currently attaches to cash. Many may have seen recent commercials from Visa regarding the use of cash by a customer as slowing down the progress of purchasing in a busy market circumstance. The merchant who insists that you pay for a purchase in cash may well be impugning your integrity.

This shift in attitude is just as visible in the commercial sphere. CEOs and CFOs are paid handsomely to find other people's money for their companies to leverage. The stock market, which shows little taste for underleveraged companies, exerts steady pressure on public companies to put an appropriate level of debt on their balance sheets. Meanwhile, pension funds and insurance companies are the major investors in hedge funds and private equity firms who vie with one another to lend money to finance leveraged buyouts.

High-yield (or junk) bonds have existed for decades, but they were once symptomatic of "fallen angels"—formerly prosperous companies whose fortunes had declined. Today, however, issuing junk bonds is seen as a perfectly respectable strategy for companies lacking access to lower-cost forms of credit.

Even bankruptcy—at least the Chapter 11 variety—has lost much of its sting. Once avoided as a shameful and potentially career-ending debacle, bankruptcy is now widely accepted as a reasonable strategic option. Many companies have sought Chapter 11 bankruptcy as a way to obtain financing for growth, to extricate themselves from burdensome contractual obligations, or to avoid making payments that they deemed inconvenient to suppliers, employees, or others. Meanwhile, individuals who choose personal bankruptcy know that their credit can be resurrected in a mere 10 years—or as little as three to five years if they have completed a repayment plan under a Chapter 13 filing (U.S. Courts, *Bankruptcy Basics*). Meanwhile in the United Kingdom, the Enterprise Bill 2002 enables a first-time bankruptcy to be discharged after only one year.

The spectacle of Orange County's financial woes suggests that attitudes toward bankruptcy have changed in the public sphere, too. Neither the county's population nor its leaders showed much embarrassment or sense of urgency when it defaulted on its obligations in 1994 because of losses exceeding $1.6 billion that it had suffered in derivative "investments." Apart from front-page stories like this, credit quality, as assessed by the rating agencies, has followed a downward trend in the public finance market. At the same time, state and local government entities have accessed the public debt market in growing numbers over the past 35 years. Seventeen states had a triple-A credit rating in 1970. Just nine states could lay claim to this distinction in 2006 (Moody's and S&P reports). The causes for the erosion of municipal credit quality—taxpayer revolts, mismanagement, and, in the cities, declining tax revenues and inflexible labor costs—may be endemic to the municipal arena, but the decline is in keeping with trends visible in the corporate market, too.

Attitudes towards the use of credit and the importance of maintaining a reputation as a conservative and careful borrower have changed. For example, California, our largest state, and the world's sixth largest economy, is a particularly interesting case. Triple-A rated in the early 1990s, the state's GOs (general obligations) began a drop in the mid-1990s to AA and then into freefall in 2001–2003 to reach Baa before a more recent uptick to A1. Similar attitudes in the corporate sector are evident such as when U.S. Air went bankrupt simply to renegotiate long-term leverage uses of aircraft.

MORE NATIONS BORROW

The appetite for borrowing is truly global in scope. Sovereign obligors have come to the international financial markets in ever-greater numbers. Figure 1.2 shows the growth in rated sovereign borrowers in the period 1975–2006.

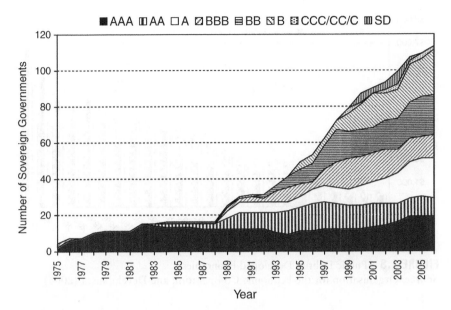

FIGURE 1.2   Sovereigns Rated by Standard & Poor's, 1975–2006
Source: Standard & Poor's *The Future of Credit Ratings* (2006).

What is particularly interesting in this table is the growth in the number of countries that now are rated by the global rating agencies. This is a clear indication of the importance of access to the capital markets by countries all over the world. As Figure 1.3, Figure 1.4, and Figure 1.5 show, developed countries have increasingly relied on public and private debt.

A new trend in many other developed and developing countries is privatization. Traditionally, infrastructure projects such as roads or bridges were financed by the government. This is changing rapidly. In the United Kingdom, for example, under the Private Finance Initiative, major projects, and even defense-related activities, are being shifted to private sector operators under long-term contracts remunerated by service charges. This trend has accelerated into the European Union, Australia, and in the United States.

Deregulated domestic financial institutions and corporations in emerging markets have been able to tap into foreign capital to finance domestic growth.

In emerging economies, the growth in borrowing is not limited to corporations and governments. Consumers in many regions are quickly learning how to pay with plastic. In developing countries from Argentina to Thailand, credit card debt is rapidly expanding.

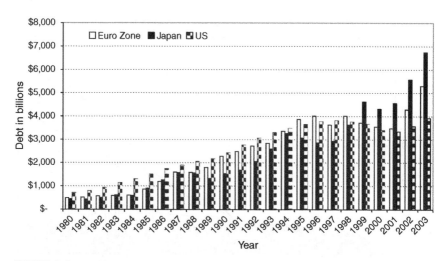

FIGURE 1.3   Public Debt in Developed Economies
Source: Organisation for the Economic Co-operation and Development (2006).

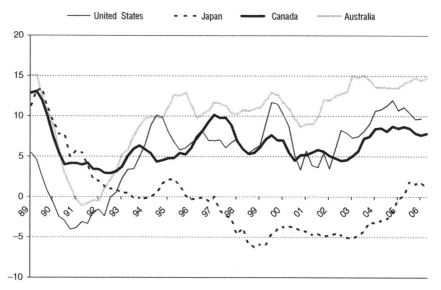

FIGURE 1.4   Credit Growth (private domestic credit)
Source: Bank for International Settlements, *Annual Report 2007*.

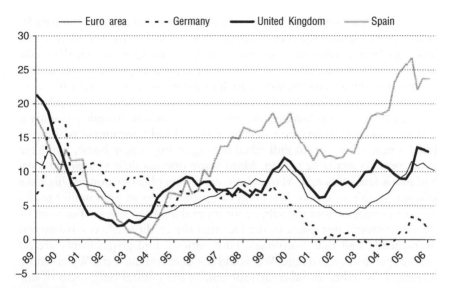

FIGURE 1.5 Credit growth in Europe (private domestic credit)
Source: Board of Governors of the Federal Reserve System (2006).

MORE LEVERAGE, MORE OPPORTUNITY, AND MORE RISK

Without question, the availability—and acceptability—of credit facilitates modern life and fuels the economy. Credit enables individuals of even modest means to buy homes, cars and consumer goods, and this, in turn, creates employment and increases economic opportunity. Credit enables businesses to grow and prosper. Governmental agencies all over the world use credit to build infrastructure that they cannot fund from annual budgets. In the United States, the municipal bond market is huge, allowing states, cities, towns, and their agencies the meet the public's needs for schools, hospital, and roads.

Hermando de Soto in his book *The Mystery of Capital* has argued that the ability to leverage for both individuals and commercial enterprises is the most important factor in understanding why some economies are developed and others are not. In the United States, we have taken this leveraging concept to new levels and Europe is not far behind. The economies in the United States and in Europe have become both large and diversified. This means that leverage is needed to marshal the investment required to operate the economy and to develop new products and services. The diversification of the economies—which is a huge change from what existed 100 or even 50 years earlier—makes the economies much more stable and therefore much less risky from a systemic basis. So it should be no surprise that the credit markets in the developed world have grown to massive proportions and that countries in the developing world are looking for ways to emulate it.

The credit markets clearly have grown. We are more leveraged than we used to be. Credit facilities are on offer everywhere. Whether you are a treasurer looking to finance a new business, a local government wishing to build a new school or an individual hoping to buy a new home, you have many options available to you. Many more options than you would have had just a few years ago. Many observers of this phenomenon see big risks inherent in this situation. Warnings of upcoming doom are familiar topics in our newspapers and the subject for more than a few books. But most of the doomsayer's just point to the fact that the credit markets have grown dramatically and that consumers, corporations, and governments are all more dependent on leverage. We would not question the facts. We are more leveraged. Whether an inherent problem, or the natural outgrowth of our capitalist economic system, it poses an interesting question. One thing for sure is that we need excellent credit management skills to help us operate in this environment.

To understand whether this increase is leverage is bad or good requires an analysis about how it has come about. Credit can grow rapidly for three reasons:

1. *Financial deepening.* This occurs when credit is extended to those who were not eligible before, or when those who are eligible use the credit markets more extensively to invest in inventory or capital equipment. Examples of the former would be the extension of the mortgage markets, credit cards, and auto finance to many people who probably were ineligible in the past. Another example would be in small business credit, or when borrowers in less developed economies gain access to the global capital markets. At the grass roots level, microfinance in emerging markets is yet another example of financial deepening. Most of the aggregates we see in the expansion of credit levels are the result of financial deepening and are a good thing for the most part.
2. *Normal structural upturns.* More growth in the global economy means more credit gets expended. We have experienced an unprecedented growth period over the past few decades, so it is natural that credit would have grown along with it. There is also a multiplier effect, because of financial deepening credit actually grows faster than GDP, normally by a factor of 1.75 times according to research done by S&P.

3. *Excessive structural movements.* This is where the credit expansion becomes a credit boom that is potentially destabilizing. Asset prices get magnified—stock prices shoot up, real estate prices boom, and banks are tempted to lend more against inflated asset values. This is what often is referred to as a *bubble*. Much of the popular press today would argue that this is exactly the situation currently faced by the United States and most of the global economy.

What we know for sure is that credit has been expanding at a rapid pace. We can also observe that this expansion is happening at a time when credit management tools have improved and information sources are significantly better than they were just a few years ago. Attitudes toward debt, amongst both borrowers and lenders have changed, also probably for the better as many of the players are approaching the markets with a much higher level of sophistication. The main lenders are much more skillful than they were when we wrote the first edition of *Managing Credit Risk*.

In the early months of 2007 it appeared that the credit markets were in some sort of new paradigm driven by the improvement of credit management tools coupled with a stable economic situation. At the end of 2007 we appear to be on the edge of a precipice, a few additional missteps away from a major global recession created by a crisis in the credit markets. How this will play out is hard to say with any certainty. However, what is certain is that the higher levels of leverage do make individual players and the economy as a whole, more vulnerable to some kind of systemic back up. It may be that the high levels of diversification, the fact that there are many more risk takers in the markets, and everyone has more information, may make this current credit downturn more limited in the end. But we can now see very clearly that we have not seen the last of credit cycles.

Before we leave the discussion of more debt and more risk, there is one additional risk that has arisen from the new credit markets. Credit has always been a personal idea. At the core of most good credit guidelines is the idea that the lender needed to know the borrower. Banks only lent to their good customers. Customers they nurtured over long periods of time. From this came a familiarity and trust between lender and borrower. When things changed and the borrower needed some adjustments to their credit line, or more money, or more time—the adjustment often took place with a minimum of stress. All of this was not good, of course. Relationship banking brought a lot of damage to the banking systems in many countries. But it did provide stability and a clear path for individuals and corporations when they faced some problem. They called their banker and had a discussion. Today it is not so simple. Few banks hang on to the loan that they make. When problems arise it is not so easy to make adjustments. If major problems occur things could get even more difficult. Who do you turn to then?

THE GOLDEN AGE OF BANKING

The decade of 2000 was beginning to look more and more like a golden age in global banking until the recently escalating subprime crisis. Even the low profit and relatively higher risk banking markets of Japan and Germany have rebounded from low payments earlier in the decade. We believe that structural improvements—resulting from global consolidation, improved risk management, tightening of costs, and lighter regulation—position the industry well to ride out a number of future risk scenarios such as a sharp rise in long-term interest rates or external systemic shocks.

While the banking industry has made great adjustments from the 1990s, credit risk is still a serious challenge today, but for other reasons. Major lending institutions such as commercial banks and insurance companies are no longer the dominant source of credit to the global economy. They still have a critical part to play, particularly in the creation of credit instruments but they no longer dominate the field by holding on to the credit instruments. This means that there is a disconnect between the creator of the debt from the holder of the debt from the debtor. This disconnect is a growing concern to regulators and major participants in the credit markets as it may produce much more volatility when the credit cycle becomes more challenging.

Despite the significant improvements made by banking institutions over the past decade, the events of the not-too-distant past have demonstrated that the judgment of bankers is far from infallible. American banks have made serious errors in lending from time to time. While several factors converged to produce the recent bank crises, an inadequate credit policy and/or process was surely one of the most important. In lending to Latin American countries in the 1970s and to commercial real estate developers in the 1980s, banks based their decisions on their traditional credit methodology: They evaluated individual risks, and they focused on lending to customers with whom they had longstanding business relationships. These techniques failed them badly. In Latin America, as in the commercial real estate market, banks got into trouble because they selected the wrong sector, not because they chose the wrong individual risks. Some of the problems may be blamed on poor bank management, but even good management by itself does not make credit risk go away.

The collapse in the Asian economies (Thailand, Indonesia, Malaysia, and South Korea) was reminiscent of the way Latin American borrowing grew in the early 1980s, the causes of the financial crises in these two instances were different. In the Latin American case, according to Jack Guenther, formerly senior vice president of, Country Risk at Citibank, many of the difficulties experienced by those countries were due to external shocks, such as sharp declines in world commodity prices and high interest rates following the restrictive monetary policy pursued by the United States to control inflation at home. With the Asian economies, the problems were caused, on the one hand, by an asset bubble in real estate, and, on the other, by excessive investment in productive capacity and decline in export growth. Moreover, the collapse itself was accelerated by pessimistic sentiments in the financial markets and the flight of short-term foreign capital. The Asian countries with one or two exceptions (e.g. Philippines) have by and large rebounded from this crisis.

CREDIT RISK PRICING IS NOW MARKET-DRIVEN

When the first edition of *Managing Credit Risk* was published in 1998, it was easy to make the case that credit risk was underpriced. There was clear evidence that U.S. banks had systematically underpriced credit risk to their commercial customers. And the pricing policies of these banks looked sensible in comparison to what was happening elsewhere in the world. It seemed like a great time to be a borrower from one of these institutions. The reasons for inadequate pricing were varied: Banks in many countries viewed themselves as a type of utility—their job was to funnel the nation's savings into economic development, not necessarily to make money on the process. Many banks treated commercial loans as a "loss leader" that induced customers to purchase other, more lucrative products from them. Exacerbating the problem was that these institutions lacked good default and recovery data regarding their own lending experience. In the absence of knowledge and information, they did what they could.

Ten years later the situation could'nt be more different at the major global lending institutions. Much more data is available and the major banking regulators have created a risk-based capital system that makes it very clear to banks what the capital consequences are when making a loan to their customers. All evidence would suggest that the markets are much more sophisticated than they were a decade earlier. It also seems that there is more systemic risk to worry about. So what happened to credit spreads in this new world of finance? They collapsed. Spreads became tighter than ever and reached a low in the summer of 2007. So was credit risk underpriced then? Maybe it was, but perhaps not.

It can be said that there is a whole new paradigm at work here. Ten years ago the banking systems were the primary sources of long-term credit provision. That is no longer the case, no matter which market you look at. So we have new lenders, with new economic models to work from and even quite different motivations. In some respects, credit risk should be similar to any other commodity service. Pricing of any commodity is a function of three things:

1. The cost of providing the service.
2. Expected and unexpected losses associated with the provision of the service.
3. An acceptable return on the capital required.

So what is the new paradigm? Whereas credit spreads used to be set by bankers based on a mixture of cost analysis, customer relationships, and some good old-fashioned "country windage," they are now set by the market. By June 2007, we had gone through a long period of low defaults, some distinct changes in the flow of funds, and huge surpluses of liquidity from traditional and nontraditional sources. There were many new savers (such as the Chinese who are believed to hold almost a trillion dollars of U.S. Government obligations) and new managers of the savings. Cash, which used to sit in a bank deposit, is today in a mutual fund or in a hedge fund. Credit risk had essentially "followed the money." The new players have a completely different cost base (mostly lower), smaller capital requirements (if any) and a limited and largely more positive experience to price from. So it was not surprising that credit spreads in mid-2007 would be dramatically lower than they had been in some time. Indeed, in some markets, for example, in the U.S. high-yield bond market, spreads were the lowest ever. However, new information regarding the riskiness of the market began to become apparent to all participants in the summer and fall of 2007. The market processed this new information and spreads rocketed predictably. By the fall of 2007, many market players were no longer interested or willing to participate in the market and market spreads increased from record lows to above average in just five months! This repricing of credit risk, while painful to many, was cheered by those who felt that despite the "new paradigm" of market structures, the basic risk assessment of credit was out of line in June 2007. The message was quite clear. The new market paradigm is that credit spreads are now a function of market supply and demand pressures as well as fundamental default and loss expectations. They incorporate information on credit as well as the fears and expectations of the participants. As a result, we can expect market pricing for credit risk to be highly volatile going forward.

Market participants are now much more sophisticated when it comes to pricing credit risk. In recent times, many lenders could see that the market was underpricing credit. Their response was to continue to originate credit but not to hold it. That wasn't illegal or improper, it was just smart business.

CREDIT MANAGEMENT IS IMPORTANT TO THE GLOBAL ECONOMY

Every major economy and most developing countries have experienced credit problems in their banking systems, which have had a negative effect on economic growth and financial market stability. Previously, we referred to the U.S. problems of the past 30 years that arose from real estate lending and other problems. European banks have experienced banking crises comparable to those in the United States. Major banks in France, Spain, and the United Kingdom have come close to failure in recent years. The German banking system is in a turmoil served up by systemic credit failures. Elsewhere the story is not much better. Problems in the Japanese banking system dominated the financial press for nearly a decade and set off a long period of deflation and recession for the Japanese economy. Table 1.1 shows the profitability of major banks in the industrialized nations of the world for the period 2002–2004.

Serious problems in the economies of Thailand, Korea, Malaysia, and Indonesia were a direct result of problems in their credit markets. So it is no wonder that the central bankers of these countries have come together to set rules designed to insure that good credit practices and adequate capitalization is a feature of the banking systems.

NEW TRANSACTIONS, NEW RISKS

The emergence of new kinds of financial transactions has also created greater awareness of credit risk. Financial derivatives such as interest-rate or currency swaps represent the unbundling of market risk and credit risk. An interest rate swap, for example, is typically a transaction between the following two parties: (1) a highly rated issuer that prefers floating rate obligations but can raise fixed rate debt at a relatively low rate; and (2) a lower-rated issuer that prefers fixed rate obligations but can raise only floating rate funds. Thus, a major share of the more innovative swap deals actually turns on credit risk, and it is by accepting credit risk that swap sellers derive a great proportion of their revenues.

Derivatives expand the concept of credit risk to include counterparty risk. Suppose, for example, that automaker A agrees to swap currencies

TABLE 1.1 Profitability of Major Banks, 2002–2004

| | Number of Reporting Banks | Percent of Total Average Assets | | | | | | | | | | | |
| | | Pretax Profits | | | Provisioning Expenses | | | Net Interest Margin | | | Operating Costs | | |
		2002	2003	2004	2002	2003	2004	2002	2003	2004	2002	2003	2004
United States	12	1.89	2.10	1.99	0.84	0.47	0.36	3.45	3.21	3.12	3.28	3.16	3.48
Canada	5	0.61	1.00	1.19	0.58	0.23	0.06	2.07	1.99	1.92	2.75	2.78	2.77
Japan	11	−0.55	−0.47	0.29	1.14	0.75	0.56	1.13	1.21	1.11	1.20	1.35	1.12
Australia	4	1.49	1.49	1.46	0.26	0.21	0.17	2.16	2.13	2.05	2.04	2.30	2.55
United Kingdom	9	1.06	1.22	1.15	0.37	0.33	0.23	2.15	1.96	1.56	2.26	2.04	2.07
Switzerland	5	0.12	0.59	0.68	0.15	0.03	−0.01	1.02	0.97	0.82	2.55	1.96	1.65
Sweden	4	0.69	0.77	0.98	0.09	0.10	0.03	1.48	1.44	1.35	1.44	1.37	1.24
Austria	2	0.46	0.53	0.69	0.39	0.36	0.31	1.80	1.71	1.80	1.92	1.85	1.84
Germany	9	−0.01	−0.12	0.09	0.48	0.30	0.15	0.80	0.81	0.71	1.37	1.26	1.35
France	7	0.45	0.59	0.09	0.15	0.17	0.08	0.62	0.80	0.72	1.49	1.50	1.41
Italy	6	0.67	1.03	0.67	0.91	0.68	0.49	3.07	2.82	2.24	3.33	3.22	2.73
Netherlands	3	0.46	0.65	1.03	0.26	0.20	0.10	1.62	1.62	1.53	1.98	1.85	1.82
Spain	5	1.01	1.29	0.72	0.50	0.44	0.35	2.73	2.45	2.17	2.36	2.13	1.79

Source: Bank for International Settlements, *Annual Report 2007*, and Fitch Ratings.

with bank B at some future time. On the basis of this agreement, automaker A then signs a contract to purchase parts from offshore supplier C. If bank B subsequently fails to uphold its end of the currency swap bargain, offshore supplier C may suffer the consequences of settlement delays or worse, even though it had no direct relationship with bank B. If automaker A is able to stop its payment to the bank in time, then its principal would not be at risk. Nevertheless, this company would have to absorb any losses due to an adverse market move. In this way, counterparty risk adds a new dimension to credit risk. Companies now have exposure to third parties with whom they may never have entered into formal credit relationships. As society becomes increasingly interdependent, counterparty risk expands exponentially.

This is not to say that total financial risk in the economy has increased simply because there are derivative transactions; after all, derivative transactions are a zero-sum game. But derivatives entail additional financial contracting and, therefore, additional exposure to be monitored and managed by the contracting parties. Adequate standards for disclosure regarding creditworthiness have become increasingly important, and investments have had to be made in credit evaluation and monitoring structures. There are also additional risks in the interpretation and enforcement of financial contracts (see Mason 1995, 181). Default by a counterparty with a substantial aggregate exposure could lead to a chain reaction affecting many other institutions.

In fairness to derivatives, it may be argued that these systemic risks are nothing new. For example, the failure of Drysdale Securities in 1982 caused more than $300 million in losses to Chase Manhattan Bank and others in a repo transaction; at that time the Federal Reserve had to act to avert disruptions in the financial markets (see Greider 1987, 487–489). However, derivatives transactions differ from more traditional financial interactions in one key respect: They are off-balance sheet. As a result, their true risks are often not visible to outsiders or, for that matter, even to insiders. It is very difficult, if not impossible, to assess a complex institution's derivative risk exposure solely from the disclosures it has made in its financial statements and the accompanying notes. In the final analysis, while derivatives may pose no incremental risk to the financial system as a whole, they do pose significant risks to participants who have not made adequate investments in people, analytics and technology.

The emergence of asset-backed securities, like that of financial derivatives, forces market participants to focus more sharply on credit risk. Securitization entails systematically grading and segmenting these risks. The typical asset-backed transaction involves a large number of variables, and understanding the correlations among them may require a high level of analytic sophistication. As securitization technology spreads to new jurisdictions and as more institutions begin to invest in residential and commercial mortgage-backed securities and asset-backed securities, financial professionals need to know more about managing the credit risk of an obligor as it evolves over time. They also need to know more about managing *correlated* credit risk—the risk associated with separate assets that show a collective tendency to change in credit quality in the same direction.

NEW LENDERS

A new set of lenders has become increasingly important in the United States. After 1945, banks held 70 percent of the country's money, insurance companies 20 percent, and everyone else the remaining 10 percent. Since then, as is clear from Table 1.2 and Figure 1.6, banks and insurance companies have lost market share to institutional investors—pension funds in particular—which accounted for 25 percent of assets as of 1995. This shift has accelerated in recent years.

Pension funds, mutual funds and endowments have enormous amounts of money to invest/lend, but their preferences differ appreciably from those of banks. Banks take in short-term deposits and have a natural predilection for making short-term loans. Institutional investors, by contrast, take in long-term money and are inclined to lend for the longer term. To a growing degree, a borrower's timeframe determines whether a bank or an institutional investor will be the better source of debt capital. This bifurcation of the market is another reason why credit risk needs to be better understood.

As the global economy becomes a reality, the distance between debtor and creditor is likely to grow. It is already possible, for example, for receivables from a credit card issued in Indonesia to be purchased by a fund in New York and then sold to a private banking client in Zurich. Evaluating credit risk is a matter of gathering and interpreting information, and as the distance between the borrower and the ultimate lender increases, this becomes more difficult to do.

NEW APPROACHES TO CREDIT RISK

American bankers who survived their industry's crises of the 1980s and 1990s recognized that their approach to credit risk had been deeply flawed. Today, all of the major global financial institutions and many of the second-tier institutions are creatively pursuing effective techniques for managing credit risk. This is a requirement of the banking regulators particularly as a

TABLE 1.2 Relative Shares of Total Financial Assets, 1950–2005

	1950	1960	1970	1980	1990	1995	2000	2005
Monetary authority	9.18%	1.12%	5.43%	1.04%	1.55%	1.23%	2.43%	1.21%
Depository organizations	50.51%	55.03%	58.15%	46.70%	−5.46%	26.55%	31.91%	37.21%
Insurance companies and pension funds	30.10%	27.65%	18.37%	27.94%	38.19%	16.73%	−2.70%	8.90%
Capital markets investors	3.57%	4.47%	11.20%	19.26%	62.92%	43.70%	54.10%	37.06%
Finance and mortgage companies	6.63%	11.73%	6.85%	5.07%	2.81%	11.80%	14.26%	15.62%
Total	100.00%	100.00%	100.00%	100.00%	100.00%	100.00%	100.00%	100.00%

Source: Board of Governors of the Federal Reserve System (2006).

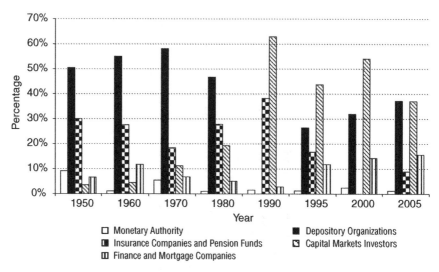

FIGURE 1.6   Relative Shares of Total Financial Assets, 1950–2005.

part of the Basel II Accords. These days all major institutions have developed global credit exposure information systems that are updated continuously so that exposure and pricing may be monitored in real time. Moving away from the traditionally held view that judging credit is fundamentally an "art," many banks are adopting new approaches.

The banking system's general creditworthiness has vastly improved as a result of the following:

1. Consolidation and globalization, which has helped to spread best practices and to diversify their business such that they become less vulnerable to a single country or economic sector.
2. Most major banking institutions have actively developed diverse activities which have reduced their dependency on interest income and led to better balance in their businesses.
3. Enhanced risk management techniques are now widely accepted. This includes statistical portfolio management, securitization, and active hedging using derivatives markets, all of which facilitate better disposal of credit risk in their portfolios. Further, the implementation of Basel II should reinforce the trend of improvement, particularly among those institutions below the top tier.

TECHNOLOGY TO THE RESCUE

Technology has already changed the credit markets. The lender community has changed, the debtor community has changed and the circumstances of lending have also changed radically over the past 10 years. The process of granting credit has also changed although the way commercial loans are made today is not terribly different from the way they were done in the past; however, the consumer finance market has been heavily influenced by new technology. Technology has helped make the market more flexible and is an important part of the reason that the credit markets have all grown so rapidly in recent years. New approaches are particularly evident amongst the new players such as hedge funds and specialty finance companies in the consumer market. Technology has particularly influenced what happens after the original loan has been made. Instead of making loans and holding on to them, most financial institutions now make the loan with the expectation that it will be sold. Hedging is much more commonplace and portfolio management is now a reality at a growing number of financial institutions.

While technology is providing many solutions and new techniques for the management of credit risk, there are challenges that arise from the use of technology. The current turmoil in the subprime mortgage market is an example of what happens when technology goes awry. The subprime markets exist because of the ability to model and manage credit risk using mathematical models. However, when the models do not produce the expected outcome, industry participants are left with substantial losses and some very bad publicity, which is causing many of them to pull back from this marketplace.

And the technical story is a work in progress. In contrast to market risk, credit risk is, by nature, the kind of low probability/high impact risk that is challenging to hedge, or even in some cases to fully understand. Although information is now much more readily available, good information on credit risk is not always available, isn't always reliable and a serious academic study of it in all its aspects has a limited history.

In at least one respect, however, modern society is well equipped to deal with this challenge. Information technology and related analytic tools have evolved at a remarkable pace in the last 20 years. We can gather, analyze, compare, and interpret information more rapidly than any prior generation. Indeed, it is the availability of this technology that has made it possible for lenders to provide credit as widely as they have. It is realistic to expect that additional analytic tools will be developed in the years ahead, and that they will enable us to manage credit risk that is both more complex and more extensive than that of the present.

Some new risk-management approaches have already been applied, and others are still on the drawing board. However, the evolution of new techniques for managing credit risk has been uneven, and significant gaps still remain. The decade ahead should be a period of ferment, innovation, and experimentation, as new approaches are devised, tested and put into use.

REFERENCES

Ahern, K., R. A. Clark, and R. Swanton. 2006. "Lonely at the Top: Why So Few 'AAA' U.S. Life Insurers Remain." *Standard and Poor's Research*, 7 April.

Beers, D. T. 2004. "Credit FAQ: The Future of Sovereign Credit Ratings." *Standard and Poor's*, 23 March.

———. 2004. "Sovereign Credit Ratings: A Primer." *Standard and Poor's*, 15 March.

Daly, K. 2006. "Sovereign Ratings History Since 1975." *Standard and Poor's Research*, 1 December.

DeStefano, M. T. 2003. "The Major U.S. Banks: Why No 'AAA's?" *Standard and Poor's Research*, 17 November.

Federal Deposit Insurance Corporation, 1997. "The Banking Crises of the 1980s and Early 1990s." Federal Deposit Insurance Corporation Division of Research and Statistics.

Ganguin, B., J. M. Six, and R. Jones. 2006. "It's All a Game of Snakes and Ladders for the Top 50 European Corporate Entities." *Standard & Poor's*, 2 November.

Greenspan, Alan. 2002. "Testimony before the Committee on Banking, Housing, and Urban Affairs, U.S. Senate." *Federal Reserve Board's Semiannual Monetary Policy Report to the Congress*, March 7, 2002. www.federalreserve.gov/BoardDocs/HH/2002/march/testimony.htm.

Greider, W. 1987. "Slaughter of the Innocents." Chapter 13 in *Secrets of the Temple: How the Federal Reserve Runs the Country*. New York: Simon and Schuster.

Hitchcock, D. 2007. "California's Fiscal 2008 Budget Proposal Offers Both Risks and Rewards." *Standard and Poor's Research*, 5 February.

International Monetary Fund. 2004. "Are Credit Booms in Emerging Markets a Concern?." In *World Economic Outlook*, Chapter 4. April.

———. 2005. "Development of Corporate Bond Markets in Emerging Market Countries." In *Financial Stability Report*, September.

———. 2006. "Structural Changes in Emerging Sovereign Debt and Implications for Financial Stability." In *Financial Stability Report*, April.

———. 2006. "Household Credit Growth in Emerging Market Countries." In *Financial Stability Report*, September.

Ivaschenko, I. 2003. How Much Leverage Is Too Much. IMF Working Paper, January.

Jones, S., R. Conforte, D. Fanger, C. Manoyan, L. Muranyi, P. Nerby, A. G. Reid, A. Tischler, G. W. Bauer. 2003. "Aaa U.S. Banks: Characteristics and Likely Candidates." *Moody's Special Comment*.

Kraemer, M. 2005. "In the Long Run We Are All Debt: Aging Societies and Sovereign." *Standard and Poor's Research*, 18 March.

Mason, S. P. 1995. *The Allocation of Risk in the Global Financial System*. Boston: Harvard Business School Press.

Moody's Investors Service. 2006. "Country Credit." In *Moody's Statistical Handbook 2006*. New York.

———. 2006. "Default and recovery rates of corporate bond issuers 1920–2005". In *Moody's Special Comment*. January.

———. 2006. *Moody's Statistical Handbook 2006*. New York.

Philadelphia Inquirer. 1996. "The Debtor's Great Escape: Bankruptcy." 29 December.

Samolyk, K. 2004. "The Future of Banking in America." *FDIC Banking Review* 16, no. 2:

Standard & Poor's. 2006. "Global Banking Golden Age," *Credit Week*, 8 November.

Standard & Poor's. 2007. "25 Years of Credit." *Credit Week*, 28 February.

CHAPTER 2

Credit Culture

Captain Renault: I am shocked, shocked to find that gambling is going on in here.
Emil: Your winnings, Sir.
Captain Renault: Oh, thank you very much.
—Casablanca (1942)

Captain Renault exhibits two interesting traits in the 1942 film *Casablanca*. He feigns surprise at a transgression in which he has participated willingly all along, and he does not hesitate to take credit when the game has gone his way. These traits are not uncommon in the business world. Senior lenders often look the other way when rules are broken, and they frequently mistake luck for skill in risk taking. These can be fatal mistakes in a world where leverage and risk can combine to make markets highly volatile.

Since every kind of business entails some degree of risk, every company must decide just how much risk it is prepared to take and to be brutally honest about how they are faring in the market at all times. Senior management must establish a comfort zone for risk taking and ensure that people within the organization understand it and remain within it. Outside this zone, the potential consequences of losing are more severe than the potential satisfaction from winning. Establishing a comfort zone and—more importantly—staying within it are not as simple as they may at first appear. The quest for profitable growth often puts businesses on a collision course with their risk boundaries. A few lucky companies may for a time grow rapidly without experiencing major losses. Most, however, must make tough choices among competing interests and priorities. Will the organization aim, above all, to maximize market share, asset quality, or profitability? What level of losses will it tolerate? How predictable must its performance be? How should it maximize shareholder wealth?

Businesses can learn to be comfortable—and profitable—with levels of risk that may seem high to outsiders. An author of this book, active in the derivatives market at an earlier stage of his career, shares his observations:

> *On one occasion, I explained what I did to an oil executive who was seated next opposite me at a dinner. "You do interest rate swaps and credit derivatives? That's risky stuff. How do you sleep at night?" The oil executive asked.*
>
> *"And your company spends hundreds of millions of dollars drilling holes in the bottom of the ocean," I replied. "You bet money on what your geologist tell you, and they don't know exactly what's down there!"*
>
> *The oil executive was not alarmed by this seemingly high-risk activity. It fell within his company's comfort zone. His entire organization was culturally attuned to this risk, which was viewed as a normal aspect of its business. My own derivatives organization, likewise, was comfortable with the risks that it was taking.*

A cultural attitude toward risk is critical in the credit-granting organization. P. Henry Mueller (1997, 8) defined bank credit culture in the following terms at the end of the century:

> *Credit behavior has its own cycle, ranging from defensive conservatism to irresponsible aggressiveness. Overlaying each credit system is a stratum of linked attitudes, responses, and behavioral patterns emanating from the CEO and infiltrating the organization. Institutional philosophies, traditions, priorities and standards are additional factors to consider. Personalities of line officers play a role, as do their personal attributes—knowledge, abilities, and biases, together with frailties. These are the seeds from which credit cultures grow, and it is bank culture that influences individual lending behavior. The CEO and the board of directors are its designated guardians.*

Mueller's view was that bank credit cultures were formed over long periods of time and reflected the history, traditions and personalities of the banks and their bankers. Senior management's role was to nurture and, to some degree, to shape the culture. While much of what he wrote has relevance today, it does seem like today's financial institutions are too big and too diversified to have such a passive approach to the development of a risk culture for their organization. What is needed now is a tangible, specific set of rules of the road that are fully understood and accepted throughout the organization. As we will see in the interviews discussed later in this chapter it seems like this is exactly what may be happening at most of the universal megabanks which are at the forefront of good practices.

Senior management must begin by deciding what the company's risk profile ought to be—taking into account the realities of the businesses they are in. Anyone who is uncomfortable drilling holes far off the beaten track probably does not belong in the oil exploration business. Similarly, anyone who is unprepared to take credit risk in complex ways should not be a banker. In both businesses, there are, of course, gradations of risk. As there are very speculative drilling opportunities, there are speculative credit opportunities. Calibrating the amount of risk organization will take is a fundamental strategic issue that must be resolved directly by its CEO. Having established a strike zone for risk taking, senior management must then explain the dynamics and parameters of the zone to people throughout the firm. If the firm is to be a low-risk player, the CEO needs to identify low-risk places to place. Similarly, if higher risk activities are a part of the game plan, then the conditions of play need to be explicit and consistent with the skills and experience of the organization.

Inconsistent signals and vague statements about what is permitted, and what is not, generally do more harm than good. Either the policy will be so loosely interpreted such that it lacks any teeth; or senior management will have to be consulted for its input every step of the way.

An organization may establish complicated policies and procedures as checks and balances to control its risk taking, but if it lacks a strong cultural core, these will be of little avail. If drivers on a highway simply do not believe in the speed limit, the police can never succeed in enforcing it. But if the drivers basically accept the speed limit, then the job of the highway patrol becomes the manageable one of preventing rogue individuals from causing harm. Institutions generally fail not because they lack credit systems, policies, and procedures, but because they have a prevailing credit culture that makes the deployment of these systems, policies, and procedure meaningless. In some organizations, credit culture is an integral part of a risk culture and is facilitated by a strong and clear sense of purpose. Interestingly, money management firms frequently have a very specific and client oriented culture. Here is Howard Rubin, director at Standish, Ayer and Wood, a fixed income money manager in a 1997 interview with one of the authors

> *We seek to enhance return to the client over time ... everything*
> *we attempt is related to adding value to a specific portfolio relative*
> *to client objectives. Taking less of a big picture look, we roll up*
> *our sleeves and get very much into the individual security selection.*
> *Utilizing a team approach beings people with different skills to the*

*table. Using the collective wisdom of the team creates a portfolio
with a very favorable risk-reward return to the client.*

*We have built a culture where taking risk is accepted and where
people can feel comfortable taking risks within their individual specialized area without, for example, the penalty that if you are wrong
you are going to be reprimanded. Unless, of course, you are sloppy
or outside of the boundaries that have been agreed. We have nurtured this risk-taking attitude. You are still being prudent, still doing
the research, and the collective judgment will be supportive of the
decision that has been reached.*

If a credit culture has truly entered an organization's bloodstream, it
is readily apparent to those inside the firm—and just as frequently to its
customers, shareholders, and suppliers. In this chapter, we look at how some
organizations have attempted to instill the right culture and how others have
integrated culture with supporting policies and procedures to create a strong
and vibrant risk management system.

A MODERN RISK MANAGEMENT FRAMEWORK

Barclays, working together with Marakon Associates, an international management consulting firm, developed a simple but useful framework to capture the essence of a modern approach to risk culture and strategy that is
summarized in Figure 2.1.

The framework builds on the premise that excellent risk management
in a financial services company is essential and carries a major impact on
the performance of the company, for both better and worse. Because of
the stakes involved and the way in which risk permeates financial businesses, risk management must be the responsibility of all employees in
the firm.

Risk management must be effective, must be efficient, and it must contribute decisively to the control environment within the business. To judge
if, in fact, it does this is best evaluated against two benchmarks. Does it
provide value for money (the *cost of risk management*); and does it result in
a *cost of risk* that is within the business's capacity to absorb and within the
parameters established by the board and management?

Cost of risk, in this sense, includes the explicit costs of losses such
as credit losses and increased provisions and also the opportunity cost
of risk arising from maintaining standards that are unrealistic and not
commercial.

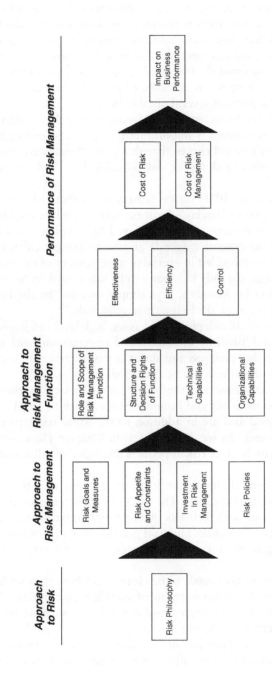

FIGURE 2.1 Modern Risk Management Framework
Source: Barclays Bank Plc.

To get these desirable results, businesses need to create the right context for their risk management activities by making some fundamental, explicit choices. Together these make up the culture of the organization.

First of all, management and the board of directors need to determine the *risk philosophy* of the firm, and decide how they want to approach risk management. There is a wide range of possible choices as expressed in the 2006 annual reports of several notable firms.

Goldman Sachs states that "Management believes that effective risk management is of primary importance to the success of Goldman Sachs."

JPMorgan Chase believes that the firm's "ability to properly identify, measure, monitor and report risk is critical to both its soundness and profitability."

Barclays, in its 2006 annual report, notes that risk management "is a fundamental part of Barclay's business activity and an essential component of its planning process. This is achieved by keeping risk management at the centre of the executive agenda and by building a culture in which risk management is embedded in everyday management of the business."

Wells Fargo, the only U.S. bank to be rated AAA by Standard & Poor's (S&P) and Aaa by Moody's, says simply that to "be the best in financial services we have to be the best at managing risk."

Once the overall risk philosophy is set, high level *risk goals and measures* need to be established by the board and management with objectives that are explicit so that progress and status can be clearly demonstrated. If there are shortfalls, then these can be corrected.

Then management and the board need to articulate their *risk appetite* and the key constraints and boundaries they wish to set. These constraints are self imposed and are in addition to the usual regulatory requirements that must be met. As we discuss later, in Chapter 18, a common way for leading firms to describe risk appetite is through their allocation of economic capital.

Management should identify the investment that they are willing to commit to risk management. The extent of their resource allocation should be commensurate with their risk management ambitions and appetite. In the high velocity and complex financial markets that operate on a global basis, 24/7, staffing, tools and systems all need to be of a very high caliber to be successful.

Management also needs to be clear about how they wish risk management to be implemented in terms of their key *risk policies*. These policies go beyond legal requirements and cover issues such as the avoidance of risk concentrations, minimizing new product or illiquid risks, aggregating exposures to related parties, and avoiding all conflicts of interest. It is these policies in particular that allow management to stamp their imprimatur on risk management behaviors in their firm. It is what makes their firm unique.

Once the board and management have determined their approach to risk management, they then need to decide what roles they want to assign to their *risk management function* and what they want to assign to other management areas.

So, they need to start with the role and scope of the risk management function.

They need to determine the structure and decision rights of the risk function as compared to the senior managers of the constituent businesses within the firm. Some firms have separate chains of command that come together only with the chief executive; others have intermediate points where control functions and line business functions come together. And they need to decide the technical and organizational capabilities they wish to allocate to the risk function.

All of these decisions about the risk function need to be consistent with the firm's approach to risk and approach to risk management generally. There should not be disconnects between the resourcing allocated and power delegated to the risk function and the expectation about how it will influence the performance of the firm.

CREDIT CULTURE AT WORK

> We have grown a lot in the last 20 years. We were 3,000 people when I started, we are close to 30,000 now. Our risk culture has always been good in my view, but it is stronger than ever today. We have evolved from a firm where you could take a little bit of market risk and no credit risk, to one where we could take quite a reasonable amount of market risk and no credit risk, to a place that takes quite a bit of market and credit risk in many of our activities. However, we do so with the clear proviso that we will only take on risks that we understand, can control and are being compensated for.
>
> —Craig Broderick, Goldman Sachs (2007)

The chapter on credit culture was high on our priority list when approaching the revision of *Managing Credit Risk*. There were two reasons for this. For the first edition we featured two strong cultures at banks where we interviewed several people about how those bank cultures worked. Morgan Guaranty Trust was an example of how a culture could be built around tradition, consistency in recruiting, and a focused business plan. Banc One represented a firm dominated by a family management and a belief in taking only small-sized risks. Ten years later these two firms have merged, along with Chase and First Chicago to form the new megabank, JPMorgan Chase. We could not wait to get a chance to see how the new culture evolved and how different it might be from the old Morgan or Banc One version. The second reason we were looking forward to this revision was that it seemed like the size, complexity, and scope of the big universal megabanks made them a wonderful case study of how risk was managed and the extent that corporate culture was an important ingredient in this effort. As Chuck Powis, managing director of fixed income at the Royal Bank of Canada said, "The only firms that have distinguished themselves in a positive way in the current crisis are Goldman Sachs and JPMorgan" (2007).

GOLDMAN SACHS: MANAGING THROUGH CREDIT CULTURE

Our first stop was at Goldman Sachs, which has an extraordinary record of accomplishment, and the language they use in their business is based on innovation, excellence, and success. Whenever we spoke to people in the markets about this project, we were directed to Goldman Sachs as a firm that successfully balanced risk and opportunity. The world of investment banking has its ups and downs, and Goldman Sachs has been able to avoid more of the downs than most. Culture is important at Goldman Sachs. On Goldman's web site, the Business Principles page section defines the Goldman Sachs culture as 14 business principles:

1. *Our clients' interests always come first. Our experience shows that if we serve our clients well, our own success will follow.*
2. *Our assets are our people, capital and reputation. If any of these is ever diminished, the last is the most difficult to restore. We are dedicated to complying fully with the letter and spirit of the laws, rules, and ethical principles that govern us. Our continued success depends upon unswerving adherence to this standard.*
3. *Our goal is to provide superior returns to our shareholders. Profitability is critical to achieving superior returns, building our capital, and attracting and keeping our best people. Significant employee stock ownership aligns the interests of our employees and our shareholders.*
4. *We take great pride in the professional quality of our work. We have an uncompromising determination to achieve excellence*

in everything we undertake. Though we may be involved in a wide variety and heavy volume of activity, we would, if it came to a choice, rather be best than biggest.

5. We stress creativity and imagination in everything we do. While recognizing that the old way may still be the best way, we constantly strive to find a better solution to a client's problems. We pride ourselves on having pioneered many of the practices and techniques that have become standard in the industry.

6. We make an unusual effort to identify and recruit the very best person for every job. Although our activities are measured in billions of dollars, we select our people one by one. In a service business, we know that without the best people, we cannot be the best firm.

7. We offer our people the opportunity to move ahead more rapidly than is possible at most other places. Advancement depends on merit and we have yet to find the limits to the responsibility our best people are able to assume. For us to be successful, our men and women must reflect the diversity of the communities and cultures in which we operate. That means we must attract, retain and motivate people from many backgrounds and perspectives. Being diverse is not optional; it is what we must be.

8. We stress teamwork in everything we do. While individual creativity is always encouraged, we have found that team effort often produces the best results. We have no room for those who put their personal interests ahead of the interests of the firm and its clients.

9. The dedication of our people to the firm and the intense effort they give their jobs are greater than one finds in most other organizations. We think that this is an important part of our success.

10. We consider our size an asset that we try hard to preserve. We want to be big enough to undertake the largest project that any of our clients could contemplate, yet small enough to maintain the loyalty, the intimacy and the esprit de corps that we all treasure and that contribute greatly to our success.

11. We constantly strive to anticipate the rapidly changing needs of our clients and to develop new services to meet those needs. We know that the world of finance will not stand still and that complacency can lead to extinction.

12. We regularly receive confidential information as part of our normal client relationships. To breach a confidence or to use

confidential information improperly or carelessly would be un-thinkable.

13. *Our business is highly competitive, and we aggressively seek to expand our client relationships. However, we must always be fair competitors and must never denigrate other firms.*

14. *Integrity and honesty are at the heart of our business. We expect our people to maintain high ethical standards in everything they do, both in their work for the firm and in their personal lives.* (Goldman Sachs 2008)

Goldman Sachs' Risk Objectives, Philosophy and Culture

We were delighted when the head of Credit, Market, and Operational Risk at Goldman Sachs, Craig Broderick, agreed to meet with us. It was immediately clear that he and the senior management of Goldman Sachs thought about risk culture a lot. Broderick provided us with the following list. It was part of a presentation that he had made at a recent management meeting. It became even clearer as we talked through the material that Goldman Sachs used both the language and tools of culture to manage their business.

Risk Culture at Goldman Sachs
- Sophisticated, detailed understanding of risks by senior management.
- Culture of overcommunication: multiple formal and informal forums for risk discussions coupled with a constant flow of risk reports.
- Escalation, escalation, escalation.
- Cooption of business unit professionals into the risk management process.
- Accountability.
- Long history of promoting each business unit's best risk managers.
- Intolerant of lack of control focus.
- Learn from past mistakes.
- Predilection to "run a little paranoid," especially when things are going well.

The roots of Goldman Sachs go back to when it had mostly a trading orientation and 100 members of management who also owned the firm. Partners got to be partners by demonstrating an ability to be good stewards and to understand the risks of the markets as well as the opportunities they provided. That tradition has continued such that Goldman Sachs attempts to identify and promote people who have a demonstrated ability to get the risk/reward balance right. This means that the key management roles are filled with senior managers who understand risk taking from both a qualitative and quantitative point of view. And they are engaged. The Risk Committee meets every week. It invites the heads of different units to come and talk about market developments and the risks that need to be managed, or just accepted. According to Broderick (2007), "There is a very strong focus on risk, and the level of sophistication and depth of understanding is pretty impressive. Our senior people have been in risk-taking roles in the past and they got to where they are by being effective in taking and managing risk. The risk of unexpected losses diminishes considerably when senior management engages in an informed, honest, and open dialog about the risks that are being taken."

The message is pretty clear at Goldman Sachs. Opportunities come with their own set of risks. It is okay to take risk as long as you know what it is, know how you can manage it and the rewards are commensurate to the risk you are taking. Goldman Sachs has stocked its organization with a lot of talent, but they know that no one is talented or experienced enough to make good decisions all the time. So they have built a number of checks and balances into the system and have embraced the concept of good communications, particularly when something is new, particularly risky or not doing what was expected. No surprises. No covering up. No pretending you were not involved in something that goes awry. Such is the stuff of a strong risk culture.

JPMORGAN: MOLDING A NEW CULTURE FROM A GRAND AND VARIED TRADITION

JPMorgan is an amalgamation of organizations with rich traditions in the banking industry. We have already mentioned the merger that brought together Banc One and JPMorgan and Chase. But this is really just the tip of the iceberg. Banc One grew from its base in Columbus, Ohio by acquiring small regional banks all over the United States. In 1994, it owned 88 separate banks, which operated semiautonomously except in credit, where all credits over $10 million had to be approved in Columbus by John B. McCoy, the second McCoy to serve as Chairman-CEO of the firm his father built from modest midwestern roots. "What John wants" shaped everyday business decisions at Banc One and sustained a strong and cohesive credit culture. The McCoys dominated their organization. They believed in a strong customer orientation and they had a big preference for small exposures. "The philosophy articulated from day one by McCoy is that wants us to be a middle-market lenders," said Chief Underwriting Officer Jim Lavelle in an interview. "We avoid extremely large exposures where you have the problem of event risk." When customers such as The Limited or Wendy's grew beyond a certain size, Banc One happily passed them along to money center banks such as Morgan Guaranty Trust. Meanwhile, to avoid diluting its own culture, Banc One had a policy of not acquiring any bank more than a third of its size to ensure that it would be the dominant partner. In 1998, John McCoy decided to abandon this practice when he agreed to merge with First Chicago Corporation, a big Chicago money center bank with a long history of involvement in commercial lending. Clearly the "small is beautiful" culture needed to change.

Meanwhile, in New York, the banking industry was in the middle of a major consolidation. In 1991, the Chemical Bank, with a strong legacy in middle market lending, joined together with Manufacturers Hanover Trust. "Manny Hanny" was known for its big ticket lending and as a leading player in correspondent banking, the provision of banking services to banks around the world. The "new" Chemical Bank proved to be a powerhouse, quickly gaining market share in many new markets, particularly the lending for acquisition financing. In 1995, Chemical acquired Chase Manhattan Bank, long the leading Corporate Bank in New York and changed its name to Chase. Those who were involved, however, would claim that Chase's name was on the door, but Chemical's culture was in its soul. Nevertheless, included in the acquisition came the Chase credit training tradition, a rigorous one-year training program that formed the core of a strong risk management culture at Chase. In 2000, Chase bought JPMorgan, the holding company for Morgan Guaranty Trust. Morgan was the second bank culture that we featured in the first edition of *Managing Credit Risk*. JPMorgan could not have been more different than Banc One. Here big was good, and teamwork was essential. To call the Morgan culture, cult-like is probably too strong, but it certainly was a culture steeped in tradition, experience, and doing things the "Morgan way." You could only succeed at JPMorgan by putting in your time and by staying with the program. It was a strong culture, but remarkably informal in the sense that there was few explicit rules to be followed. The formula was pretty simple—lend to the best firms and don't take too much risk.

In 2004, JPMorgan Chase bought Banc One, which brought together all of these traditions. Just to make it more interesting, the new Chairman and CEO is Jamie Diamond, who rose to this position on the basis of a career at Travelers and Citicorp. So to say this reflects a mix of cultures is to understate the case.

To find out what the new culture looks like after two years, we met with John Hogan and Ken Phelan. John is the Chief Risk Officer for JPMorgan (the investment banking arm of JPMorgan Chase) and Ken was at the Corporate Center, involved in policy relating to risk. In an hour-long-plus interview, we learned that culture was an important tool, just like we had found at Goldman Sachs. At JPMorgan Chase, however, there was a clear understanding that the culture needed to be reworked and shaped to fit the needs of this new enterprise, which was now bigger, more diversified, and much more complex than any of the organizations from which it was formed. So a new culture was needed and, according to Hogan and Phelan, was already in place. "The first thing we needed to do was to make everyone aware that there is no reward without risk," said Hogan. According to Phelan, "We want to make sure that everyone, our managers as well as the people on the line, understand the notion of risk versus reward and that they develop a control philosophy to balance their pursuit of opportunities." They described a culture where contrarian's views were encouraged and supported. "We want folks to ask the next question, think about the unexpected, and focus on the downsides, including the way a particular action might look in the aftermath of the deal."

The old "buy and hold" mentality that was a big part of commercial banking is not a part of the new JPMorgan culture. "There should be a market clearing price for credit; we want everyone to think about credit decisions in that context. This is probably the main difference from a decade ago," said Hogan. "The blurring of market and credit risk has happened to the point that both are viewed as 'risk' and organizationally we are looking at things in this way," added Phelan. They discussed an approach that involved looking at opportunities in market risk terms, thinking about what the market clearing terms would be before deciding to do anything. "We are not a hold culture. We like to say that we are a partnership that has distinct lines of businesses where the individual business management owns the risk. We want everyone to make, and live with, market oriented decisions," said Hogan.

Clearly this is now a culture that has more of a trading orientation. They still have relationship bankers in their commercial banking areas, but the role seems to have changed to a combination of customer leadership combined with industry and company credit specialization. "The coverage banker together with the credit manager are making the decisions to acquire risk, the portfolio guys are deciding how much to keep," said Phelan.

The importance of the CEO in the establishment of a strong culture was evident. Both Phelan and Hogan mentioned the role that Jamie Diamond was playing in the development of the new culture. "Jamie came in with the idea that the old culture needed reworking. He felt the Banc One had suffered culturally from the merger between themselves and First Chicago and he was determined to establish a strong culture at JPMorgan Chase" said Phelan. "Taking ownership of your business and thinking like an owner is a big part of what we want our culture to be." We also want this to be a no-surprises culture." Diamond is involved at all levels of the business and encourages an open and honest dialog about everything.

"Every Tuesday from 12 noon to 2 P.M. there is a management meeting, which brings together the CEO, the heads of each of the businesses, the heads of the risk functions. It is a disciplined forum for a robust dialog about both opportunities and risks. Think of an Italian family dinner."

WHAT MAKES CREDIT CULTURE WORK?

In the real world, financial service organizations cannot afford to make risk management their sole priority. If a bank, finance company, or insurance company were always to put its own interest first, its customers would soon realize what was happening and move on to other providers of the service. In a successful organization, customer service and profitability must also occupy an important place within the culture. It seems that this is the case at Goldman Sachs and JPMorgan; the challenge for senior management at other organizations is to strike the right balance between them.

Problems arise when risk management takes a back seat to other priorities. Senior management may say, "We're focused on our customers—we're going to do what they need us to do." This attitude may be admirable as far as customer relations are concerned, but it sends a message to people throughout the organization that customer service is the highest priority of all. In the long run, putting risk management in second or third place behind customer service or short-term profitability can be extremely hazardous. The history of banking is full of names and organizations that no longer exist because they got this mixture wrong. Generally the good risk managers were the acquirers of those who weren't.

A good credit culture also means avoiding a one-size-fits-all view of the world. Things are too fluid for that and every organization needs to shape what works for their unique business and strategy. Risk management should go hand in hand with product pricing; it is an ingredient of pricing and not just something to protect the organization from unexpected loss.

As we can see from the approach at both Goldman Sachs and JPMorgan Chase, the CEO has a special role to play in credit culture. The culture of the firm reflects the people who run it. If the CEO declines to take personal responsibility for establishing and maintaining a strong risk culture, it will undoubtedly suffer and break down—even if there is a long history in the firm. For a time in the 1980s and early 1990s, it became fashionable to think that senior bank executives needed, above all, to be managers and that they could delegate the credit function to people below them. It probably did not make sense then, but it really doesn't make sense today in a world where leverage and volatility have created markets, which require balance and sophistication. Today, more than ever, every individual in the credit-granting chain needs to understand a firm's credit culture:

> *The behavior of lenders within a strong credit culture is connected with the value of the bank. The behavior of bank personnel must exemplify the bank's risk-taking attitudes and its commitment to excellence.* (Mueller 1994b, 81)

Managers' actions often speak louder than their words:

> *Management must not only firmly believe in the culture it wishes to achieve, it must live and breathe it. Management establishes the credit culture through its behavior, attitudes, responses, verbal and nonverbal signals, and the heroes it creates. These signals, no matter how inconsequential or inadvertent, are assimilated by loan managers and lenders and dictate their behavior* (Morsman, 1994, 21)

A firm's compensation system is one of the most effective tools it has for shaping its culture. Employees pay attention to what their leaders say, but they generally pay even closer attention to what their leaders do—constantly trying to discern what the senior team *really* cares about. If employees, who find business without regard to risk, get paid well, if risk management people get paid less than new business people, if compensation gets front-ended while risk tails are ignored, then messages are sent throughout the organization. Similarly, if someone who breaks the rules but succeeds is subsequently rewarded, this also sends a message. People in the organization conclude that as long as you win, everything else is okay.

It takes a strong culture to reward individuals who spot a high risk and protect the firm against it. In many cases, dodging a bullet also means avoiding a revenue opportunity. Far too many organizations actually penalize people for doing this by reducing or eliminating their annual bonus, and other employees are quick to notice this aspect of their company's culture. An incident, from the career of one of the authors, illustrates this point:

> *I was a senior manager in an organization that was considering transactions in a real estate market that was overheating. At the time, some of our competitor's underwriting standards were hard to understand, let alone justify. Deals were getting done on the assumption that they could be refinanced the future—not because of their intrinsic value. Most transactions provide no second way out—a violation of a fundamental banking rule.*

We had plenty of opportunities to look at and we had a big budget for the year. Turning deals down wasn't easy. But the manager of our real estate department felt the market was just too risky. She said, "I just don't think this is a place we want to be right now. We probably shouldn't be playing in this market." We accepted her recommendation and turned down everything we saw.

At that time, our company was a subsidiary of a larger firm that was focusing primarily on its earning's growth and market share. When the end of the year arrived, I wanted to reward our real estate department head for making the tough call and keeping us out of trouble. But our parent company was very reluctant to pay bonuses for anything other than revenue. We had a big fight, and finally a small bonus was agreed, but far less than was deserved. Within 24 months after our decision, we knew with absolute certainty that she had saved us a great deal of money.

Another good test of an organization's credit culture is the way it handles transactions that lie outside its normal comfort zone. In the 1776, in the *Wealth of Nations*, Adam Smith wrote:

Though the principles of the banking trade may appear somewhat abstruse, the practice is capable of being reduced to strict rules. To depart from these rule, in consequence of some flattering speculation of extraordinary gain, is almost always extremely dangerous, and frequently fatal to the banking company which attempts it (Smith [1776] 1976).

While it is easy to recommend that banks and investors think long and hard before approving deals outside of their comfort zone, today's market innovations make this a hard rule to live by. The reality is that most credit assuming organizations see new products and opportunities all the time. P. Henry Mueller offered advice that still seems fresh today:

Determine the purpose of the credit and the quality of the risk. Is the transaction an appropriate use of the bank's funds? How will it be repaid? Should the funds be obtained for sources other than a bank?

1. *Concentrate on the underlying economics of the deal. Is the structure appropriate? Does the transaction and its terms make sense for the bank as well as for the borrower?*

2. *Evaluate risk and reward. Is it worth it to the bank to make an exception to time-tested policies? Is there more than one way out? Can the bank better employ its funds elsewhere?* (Mueller 1994b, 82)

Credit culture, then, is the collection of principles, actions, deterrents, and rewards that exist within a lending organization. The CEO sets the table and must serve as a primary example of these principles:

1. A person cannot innovate or take risks unless he or she is disciplined.
2. All employees must know the boundaries of acceptable risk.
3. The firm must take a consistent approach to quantifying and pricing that can generate an adequate return on the shareholder's risk capital.

As we discuss at length in later chapters, advances in the technology of credit risk management are providing banks and other lenders with much better tools of the trade. These new tools and information technology are transforming the credit markets. Effective as they are, these tools and information sources must be used in concert with a sound credit culture. Learning from the lessons of the 1980s and 1990s, senior managers in most lending institutions are paying close attention to the design, establishment, maintenance, and, when necessary, transformation of risk culture.

REFERENCES

Broderick, C. 2007. Personal interview, conducted by authors in New York, NY, 24 January.

Goldman Sachs. 2008. "The Goldman Sachs Business Principles." *GoldmanSachs. com.* http://www2.goldmansachs.com/our-firm/about-us/business-principles. html. (29 January 2008).

McKinley, J. E. 2002, Linking: Credit Culture and Risk Management Strategy. *RMA Journal* (February).

McManus, T. H. 2004, The Importance of Effective Credit Cultures at Community Banks. *Federal Reserve Bank of Philadelphia, SRC Insights, 1st Quarter.*

Morsman, E. 1994. "Analyzing Credit Culture." In *Credit Culture.* Philadelphia: Robert Morris Associates.

Mueller, P. H. 2001. Risk Management and the Credit Culture: A Necessary Interaction. *RMA Journal* (December).

Muller, P. H.1994a, "Notes on the Credit Culture." In *Credit Culture.* Philadelphia: Robert Morris Associates.

———. 1994b. "Risk Management and the Credit Culture—A Necessary Interaction." In *Credit Culture.*Philadelphia: Robert Morris Associates.

————. 1997. "Cycles and the Credit Culture," *Journal of Lending and Credit Risk Management* Vol. No (June) 6–12.

Samuelson, R. J., The End of America's Credit Culture?. *San Diego Union-Tribune*, 23 August.

Smith, A. [1776] 1976, *An Inquiry into the Wealth of Nations.* Chicago: University of Chicago Press.

Strischek, D. 2002. "Credit Culture Part I: Defining Credit Culture." *RMA Journal* (November).

————. 2002. "Credit Culture Part II: Types of Credit Cultures." *RMA Journal* (December)

————. 2003. Credit Culture Part III: Changing Direction and Implementing A New Credit Culture. *RMA Journal* (March).

CHAPTER 3

Classic Industry Players

Banks, Savings Institutions, Insurance Companies, Finance Companies, and Special Purpose Entities

Accidents that arise from common causes will continue to happen with their expected frequency and variations until the system is corrected. The split is possibly 99 per cent from the system and 1 per cent from carelessness.
—W. Edwards Deming, *Out Of the Crisis* (1982)

Credit markets in the United States are dynamic, changing, and growing. In this chapter, we look at what we have termed the traditional industry players, who are typically active lenders as well as investors in credit instruments. In Chapter 4, we look at the portfolio managers, who are primarily investors, and at hedge funds. Our focus is on the role all these participants play in the management of credit risk. The principal participants are shown in Table 3.1.

Malcolm Knight, General Manager of the BIS (Bank for International Settlements) categorized several major changes over the last 10 years in a speech delivered in early 2007. He referred (Knight 2007) to the "atomization of risk," by which he meant the "major advances in financial know-how and information technology," which "have resulted in a quantum leap in the ability to create new financial products" where "risk is deconstructed into its constituent elements and recombined in a variety of ways." He referred to the "emergence of new financial players, outside traditional intermediation channels," such as hedge funds and private equity firms. And he referred to "the growing symbiosis between markets and financial

TABLE 3.1 Principal Participants in Credit Markets

Sector	Assets Held	Funding Sources
Lenders/Intermediaries		
Commercial banks	Business loans, consumer loans and mortgages, securities	Deposit accounts, borrowings
Savings institutions	Home mortgages, securities	Deposit accounts, borrowings
Insurance companies	Securities, mortgages	Contingent liabilities to claims holders
Finance companies	Business loans and leases, consumer loans, mortgages and leases	Commercial paper, borrowings
Government-sponsored enterprises (GSEs), agency and GSE-sponsored mortgage pools; ABS issuers	Home mortgages, consumer loans, securities	Commercial paper, bonds
Broker/dealers	Securities	Repurchase agreements, commercial paper, bank loans
Investors		
Investment managers, mutual funds, pension funds	Corporate bonds, commercial paper, U.S. governments and agency securities, state and local government securities, structured securities	

Source: Federal Deposit Insurance Corporation, amended by authors.

institutions." Markets now rely on both old and new financial firms for the supply of securities, market-making services and backup liquidity lines. Conversely, financial firms increasingly rely on markets for their profits and above all, for their risk management activities."

Total direct liabilities outstanding in the U.S. financial system at the end of 2006 were approximately $98 trillion, of which approximately $45 trillion were in so-called "credit market debt instruments" (Federal Reserve Board 2007). Our focus for Chapters 3 and 4 is going to be on these credit market instruments.

All holders of broadly defined liabilities, of course, are exposed to credit risk. Although liabilities that are not in the form of credit market instruments involve very significant exposures, with few exceptions (such as SDRs[1]), they are not tradable and consist of bilateral transactions such as repurchase agreements, deposits with financial institutions, mutual fund shares, and life insurance company and pension fund reserves.

Most of the credit instrument debt is owed by households, businesses, and government at various levels (which are collectively called the *domestic nonfinancial sector*) with approximately $29 trillion and by the financial sector with approximately $14 trillion. The balance is owed by foreign entities (approximately $1.7 trillion). Most of the credit instrument debt is held by the financial sector (approximately $33 trillion) with foreign entities (approximately $6.5 trillion) and the domestic nonfinancial sector, principally households, owning a relatively small amount of these instruments (approximately $5.1 trillion).

Table 3.2 shows the profile of credit market debt identifying the principal borrowing and lending sectors.

BANKS AND SAVINGS INSTITUTIONS

The financial sector is the largest holder of credit market instruments, and the banks (including savings banks) are by far the largest players within this sector. Banking has grown to become an enormous industry, central to the functioning of modern economies. They owned approximately $9.5 trillion in credit instruments as of the end of 2006, compared with $6.8 trillion at the end of 2002. Approximately 60 percent of all bank assets are in loans and leases and 20 percent are in securities (FDIC 2007).

Since the origin of modern banking in medieval Europe, the distinguishing characteristic of a bank has been its deposit-taking function. To this day, most banking regulations continue to define a bank by this function. Thanks in large part to deposit insurance and their dominant role in the payments systems, deposits continue to flow into banks.

The earliest bankers often charged customers a fee for warehousing their funds. It was not long, however, before bankers recognized that by lending the proceeds of these deposits to others, they could create a profitable business. Bankers paid one fee to depositors, charged a higher fee to borrowers, and then earned their profits from the spread between the two fees. The unique ability of banks to attract deposits and savings has made them central players in providing liquidity to modern financial markets and in lending.

TABLE 3.2 U.S. Credit Market Sectors and Participants, 2002–2006 (amounts in USD billions)

	2002	2003	2004	2005	2006
Total Credit Market	31,722	34,607	37,695	41,000	44,549
Debt Owed by:					
Domestic Nonfinancial Sectors	20,593	22,310	2,432	26,602	28,699
Households	8,460	9,450	10,565	11,804	12,816
Corporate business	4,742	4,853	5,018	5,263	5,697
Local/state/federal government	5,084	5,601	6,078	6,556	6,891
Other	2,307	2,406	2,662	2,979	3,295
Rest of World	1,072	1,244	1,425	1,466	1,720
Financial Sectors	10,057	11,052	11,947	12,932	14,129
Banks/savings institutions	874	929	1,072	1,173	1,285
Finance companies	884	995	1,130	1,109	1,145
Government-sponsored entities and agency and GSE mortgage pools	5,509	6,083	6,201	6,252	6,599
ABS issuers	1,878	2,075	2,407	3,071	3,603
Other	912	970	1,137	1,327	1,497
Assets Held by:					
Domestic Nonfinancial Sectors	3,889	4,275	4,607	5,037	5,139
Rest of World	3,737	4,169	4,981	5,640	6,465
Financial Sectors	24,096	26,162	28,106	30,323	32,944
Banks/savings institutions	6,782	1,254	8,028	8,806	9,520
Insurance companies	2,866	3,140	3,360	3,634	3,664
Private/government pension funds	1,274	1,360	1,391	1,409	1,472
Mutual funds	3,056	3,135	3,141	3,268	3,681
Government-sponsored entities and agency and GSE mortgage pools	5,482	6,049	6,148	6,217	6,540
ABS issuers	1,790	1,993	2,326	2,971	3,478
Finance companies	1,082	1,205	1,420	1,537	1,630
Other	1,764	2,026	2,292	2,481	2,959

Source: Federal Reserve Board, *Federal Reserve Statistical Release Z.1: Flow of Funds Accounts of the United States*, 8 March 2007, amended by authors.

As discussed in Chapter 7, banks have managed the credit risk in their lending activities by adopting procedures for credit analysis over a very wide range of customers and a broad set of different types of loan products. Credit analysis focuses on two distinct but interrelated issues: the borrower's willingness and ability to repay a loan. Analyzing willingness to pay is essentially a matter of investigating the borrower's character. Analyzing the ability to pay is a matter of investigating the borrower's economic prospects.

In addition to developing techniques for credit analysis, bankers also learned how to manage their risks through such mitigation techniques as down payments, structuring, and collateral, again customized to the borrower.

COMPETITION, CONCENTRATION, AND CHANGE

By any measure, banking is a mature industry in the United States and other industrialized countries. However, the last 25 years in the United States have been extraordinarily eventful. Industry experience over this time period is a sober reminder that banking is a heavily regulated industry and demonstrates the serious problems that can be caused when economic changes, market competitive forces, and outdated regulations collide. These resulted in an enormous upsurge in the number of bank failures, such that between 1980 and 1994 there were more than 1,600 failures, far more than in any other period since the early 1930s (see Figure 3.1). The cumulative effect of these failures was such that in 1988 the Federal Deposit Insurance Corporation (FDIC 1997) needed to be recapitalized to meet the depositor claims. The cause of these failures resulted from a concurrence of various forces working together:

- First, there were significant changes in the economic and financial market environment. Intrastate banking restrictions were lifted, allowing new players to enter once sheltered markets, and competition increased from several different direction: within the U.S. banking industry itself, and from thrift institutions, foreign banks and the commercial paper and junk bond markets. In an environment of high interest rates, the development of money market funds and the deregulation of deposit interest rates increased interest expenses and squeezed profit margins. The banking industry's market share of loans to large business borrowers declined, partly because of market innovations and partly because the banks were unable to be price competitive.
- Second, there were a series of severe regional (Southwest, New England, and Midwest) and sectoral recessions (oil and gas, commercial real

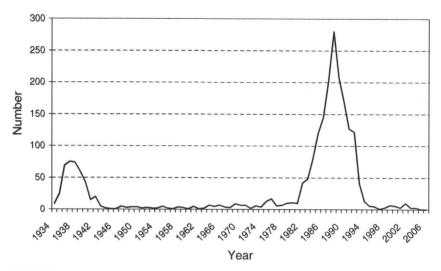

FIGURE 3.1 Number of Bank Failures, 1934–2006
Source: Federal Deposit Insurance Corporation. 1997. The Banking Crisis of the
1980s and 1990s: Summary and Implications.

estate, agriculture) that hit banks in a number of different markets and
led directly to their demise.

- Third, many banks shifted to higher risk loans. For most, this involved
commercial real estate lending and for the large banks lending to less-
developed countries and for leveraged buyouts. The banks had neither
the skills, tools, nor culture to prudently undertake these activities.
- Fourth, the regulatory authorities did not understand that banks were
taking on these excessive risks and acted inadequately in effectively
overseeing and restraining the industry. (FDIC 1997)

Bankers who had been trained to manage their way through more typical
credit cycles, with their characteristic boom, bust, recession, and recovery
phases were poorly positioned strategically to handle the stresses of this
period. Some observers at the time believed that the banks, especially the
money center banks, were in secular decline and that their roles would
be assumed by others. The *price earnings ratios* (P/Es) of banks relative to
the S&P 500 Index declined gradually over this period to the point that, by
the early 1990s, bank P/Es were less than 50 percent of the S&P 500 index.
Price-to-book value per share for all banks struggled to stay above 100
percent in the 1980s and, for the money center banks, only briefly exceeded
100 percent in the 1980s before falling to 50 percent in 1990 (FDIC 1997).

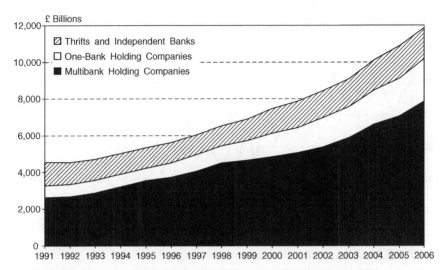

FIGURE 3.2 Assets of FDIC-insured Banking Organizations 1990–2006
Source: Federal Deposit Insurance Corporation, *Annual Reports* 1990–2006.

Despite this pessimism, however, the banking industry was able to recover strongly by the mid-1990s and has developed new managerial strengths and strategic capabilities. Banks have continued to perform well. They have adapted to the changes in regulation that initially caused them problems. They have benefited from new regulation such as the lifting of the Glass-Steagall Act (an act originally passed by the U.S. Senate in 1932 as a reaction of the Stock Market Crash of 1929) restricting their ability to underwrite corporate securities, which has given them new competitive opportunities.

As shown in Figure 3.2, the assets of U.S. banks have grown substantially over the last 15 years, especially the large multibank holding companies. At the same time there has been a significant amount of consolidation. The numbers of banks and savings institutions have shrunk over this same period from about 12,000 to less than 9,000 continuing a long decline in their numbers. The large banks have become significantly more efficient (Figure 3.3) and have been able to diversify their revenue streams such that for the larger banks over 40 percent of their net operating revenue is now noninterest income. The industry has become increasingly concentrated, with the largest 25 banks controlling almost 60 percent of total industry assets, and the top 10 banks themselves approximately 45 percent of assets.

The financial results for this more streamlined and competitive industry have been impressive with high *returns on assets* (ROA) and on *equity* (ROE)

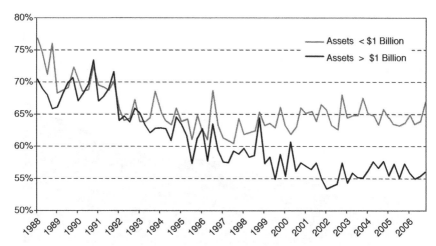

FIGURE 3.3   Annual Efficiency Ratios, 1996–2006
Source: Federal Deposit Insurance Corporation, *Annual Reports* 1996–2006.

as shown in Figure 3.4. In 2006, the industry reported $145.7 billion in net income, the sixth consecutive year of record earnings.

These results have been achieved in a relatively benign period for credit risk as shown in the annual net charge-off rates on loans experienced by the industry (Figure 3.5). Indeed, at the end of 2006, the industry's ratio of loan

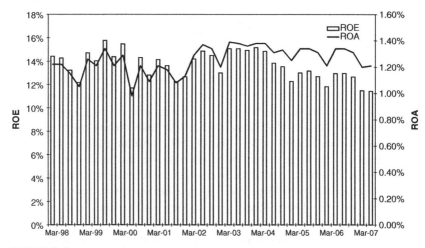

FIGURE 3.4   Quarterly Returns on Assets and Equity Annualized, 1997–2006
Source: Federal Deposit Insurance Corporation, *Annual Reports* 1997–2006.

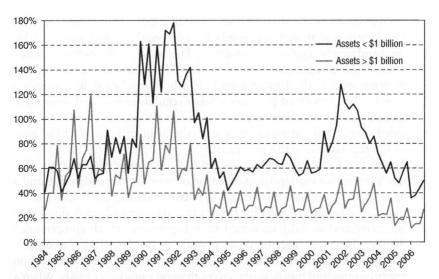

FIGURE 3.5   Annual Net Charge-off Rates on Loans, 1984–2006
Source: FDIC, *Annual Reports* 1984–2006.

loss reserves to total loans and leases declined to 1.07 percent, the lowest level of coverage since mid-1985.

SOME LESSONS WERE LEARNED

The question for bankers and their regulators going forward is whether the risk management lessons from the 1980s and 1990s have been learned. There have been testing environments already. In 1997–1998, there were significant country credit problems (Russia, Argentina, Indonesia, Thailand, and Korea) and the collapse of a very large hedge fund (Long Term Capital Management) to contend with. In 2000–2001, problem loan exposures to U.S. corporate borrowers caused banks to increase their loan loss reserves in the third quarter of 2001 by $11.3 billion, the largest increase in reserves since the fourth quarter of 1990. However, none of these problems have come during a period of extreme stress, so we have to wait and see just how durable and effective the changes have been. The principal lessons from the earlier period were as follows:

- First, the regulatory environment had been allowed to deteriorate so that the banks were in an uncompetitive position. When changes were made, the initial impact made the situation worse, not better, and neither the regulators nor the bankers were able to cope with the consequences. The lesson is that in a necessarily heavily regulated industry, enlightened and timely regulation is essential. This is especially so in the United States, where regulation is "rules based" as opposed to other jurisdictions such as the United Kingdom, where regulation is "principles based." The benefit of principles-based regulation is that it allows the industry more flexibility to adjust to different market conditions provided they remain in accordance with the principles, without the need by the regulator to write new rules.

■ The second lesson was the essential role that strategic planning and culture play in risk management. Because of poor strategic planning and a misunderstanding of their competitive environment, the banks continued to lend heavily to risky borrowers in real estate and lesser-developed countries and actually increased their exposures, which compounded their problems during the crisis periods of the late 1980s and early 1990s. Senior executives at many large banks were more focused on opportunities and business objectives than on questions of risk. When a CEO says, "We're going to earn a billion dollars from commercial real estate lending," the message travels throughout an organization. If the financial target has been risk adjusted, and if it is within the organization's capabilities, then it may be appropriate. If not, then the message the organization receives is "Just do it! Find a way!"

■ Third, these banking crises illustrated the severe problems that occur when organizations lacked the appropriate skills and tools to manage the risks in their businesses. Banks were lending into markets that were inherently much riskier than those for which their traditional techniques had been designed. Their analysis and structuring were often inadequate and the traditional approach—built around customers and relationships—had an inherent tendency to produce concentrations of risk. Exposures were aggregated by borrower with little thought to the correlations that existed between the borrowers, whether these were companies in the same industry or countries with similar economic profiles. There was also little understanding of the loss severities that could occur when some of these borrowers defaulted so that the extent of loss was frequently underestimated.

In many of these areas, there have been major changes and improvements. The new Basel II regulations are introducing much more sophisticated risk-based insights and constraints on risk taking than was available previously. The regulations require banks to understand categorize and report their risks (credit, operational, and market) fully, and they establish a clear linkage between a bank's risk profile and its capitalization. The industry has also demonstrated a great deal of initiative and creativity in developing new sources of business. In particular, they have taken the competitive threat of asset disintermediation, where borrowers were going directly to the capital markets and adopted these techniques themselves. As investors the large banks in particular have adopted new approaches to credit risk management and portfolio management, which should contribute to improved performance. They have learned the value of diversification from W. Edward Deming's observation that "accidents that arise from common causes will continue to happen with their expected frequency and variations until the system is corrected" (Deming 1986, 479).[2]

LIQUIDITY: A RESOURCE UNIQUE TO BANKS

Banks have a unique ability to provide liquidity to their customers and to the financial markets generally. This comes as a result of their access to cheap and plentiful deposits (that benefit from the protection of government provided deposit insurance) and from their access to the discount window of the Federal Reserve. Historically, liquidity has been a major concern for the industry. Throughout the Great Depression, banking crises invariably revolved around liquidity. Bad publicity would prompt depositors to withdraw their funds, causing a run on the bank. Bankers and regulators have therefore focused on liquidity management and it has become a source of strength and business opportunity.

Banks use their liquidity primarily in two ways. First, they provide standby facilities to a whole range of customers across a broad spectrum of different products from letters of credit in trade transactions, to unused loan commitments for corporations, to revolving credit transactions for consumers and businesses, to standby liquidity facilities to backstop commercial paper borrowings, whether for corporate- or asset-backed conduits. As of 2006, these facilities totaled $7.6 trillion for the universe of FDIC-insured banks, up from $2.2 trillion in 1995. This compares to $11.9 trillion in on balance sheet assets in 2006 for these same banks. This just serves to underline further the critical role that banks play in the credit markets. Of that $7.6 trillion, $4.2 trillion were for credit card lines and $700 billion for consumer home equity lines of credit (revolving lines secured by residential real estate). Also included in these facilities were $524 billion in letters of credit for performance and standby credit purposes and $29 billion for trade transactions. There were also $223 billion in liquidity backstops for asset backed commercial paper conduits (FDIC 2006).

Banks also use their liquidity strengths to trade extensively in the financial markets (Table 3.3). As shown in the Table 3.3, all FDIC-reporting

TABLE 3.3 2006 Derivative Exposures of all Depository Institutions (amounts in USD 000s)

	2006
Total derivative exposures	$132,177,091,293
Interest rate contracts	107,429,328,447
Foreign exchange contracts	12,564,211,404
Credit derivatives (notional amount)	9,019,299,143
Bank as guarantor	4,495,902,904
Bank as beneficiary	4,523,396,539
Contracts and other commodities and equities	3,164,252,299

Source: FDIC Statistics on Repository Institutions Report, amended by authors.

institutions had exposure to derivatives outstanding of $132 trillion as of 2006. Essentially, all of these exposures involve commercial banks. While the amounts are very large, they are all expressed in notional amounts, which are far larger than their underlying fair value. For example, the $9 trillion in credit derivative exposure has a fair value of $31.5 billion. Additionally, because these are all trading exposures, there are two-way flows of exposure that will probably offset each other to some degree. For example, with credit derivatives, the fair value exposure of $31.5 billion, where the banks are acting as guarantors is offset by the fair value of derivative contracts of $32.7 billion in which the banks are the beneficiaries. These trading exposures are growing at high rates. Overall they grew on average at 30 percent in 2006 over 2005. Some components are growing at even higher rates, for example the notional value of equity derivatives grew at 81 percent, commodity derivatives at 62 percent, and credit derivatives at 55 percent over this period (FDIC 2007).

INSURANCE COMPANIES

Insurance companies are the next largest active institutional players in the credit markets, with $3.7 trillion in total credit instrument holdings as of year-end 2006. The life insurance companies are the largest players ($2.9 trillion) in this sector with the balance held by property and casualty companies. A number of the biggest insurance companies are active in both life insurance and property and casualty. For insurance companies, corporate securities, especially bonds are the largest investment type ($2.2 trillion followed by agency- and GSE-backed securities [$502 billion] and municipals [$368 billion]).

Life insurers offer products based on life expectancy and health. They absorb mortality risk for a fee, which becomes their primary source of earnings. They offer retirement products such as single-premium deferred annuities and guaranteed investment contracts. They also sell products such as life annuities that combine investment and insurance features. Their long-term, fixed income products—annuities and life insurance policies—have historically provided them with predictable cash flows. Consequently, they have specialized in long-term, fixed rate investments. Since they do not have access to the Federal Reserve discount window, they do not offer liquidity products.

All these products require an insurer to forecast cash flows accurately. They also expose the insurer to the risk that the expected return will not be earned, whether through changes in earnings rates or through unexpected credit losses. The credit process at life insurers has traditionally been a disciplined one. Very little of their investing is done on a relationship basis so that they do not face the conflicts that banks often do. Credit problems that the life industry has faced historically have originated with having a costly distribution infrastructure, which diminished their returns and caused them to seek higher-yielding investments, particularly in the high-yield markets. This, combined with a strong buy-and-hold orientation and no requirements to mark their credit exposures to market, led them to experience significant investment underperformance.

Property and casualty insurers have a different set of risks for which they provide cover, most commonly against damage to property arising from accidents, fires, natural causes, or malfeasance. Cash flows from premiums fluctuate more widely and claim activities are much more unpredictable. The investment bias is consequently oriented toward liquidity rather than absolute returns. The investment portfolios of *property and casualty* (P&C) insurers have therefore had a different and lower risk profile with a particular bias to tax-exempt securities.

Over the last 15 years, these industries have been placing as much emphasis on strengthening their credit processes and portfolio management skills as they placed previously on their risk underwriting, marketing, and distribution with good effects. Insurers have moved away from primarily buy-and-hold strategies, where carrying values of securities for management purposes were the same as their accounting values and towards managing on a total return basis The regulatory environment for insurers has also strengthened and improved. In 1993, the National Association of Insurance Commissioners (NAIC) introduced risk-based capital requirements. The

Securities Valuation Office of the NAIC, while not a nationally recognized statistical rating organization, does categorize investment instruments in a standard manner so that all U.S. insurance companies can have a uniform frame of comparison for their investment portfolios.

The life insurers in particular went through a stressful period in 2001 and 2002, when issuers of $24.3 billion in bonds and preferred securities they held went into bankruptcy proceedings. Enron filed in December 2001 and, in 2002 according to Moody's, a record number of companies as ranked by assets went into Chapter 11 such as WorldCom, Conseco, UAL, Global Crossing, and Adelphia.

FINANCE COMPANIES

Finance companies held $1.6 trillion in credit market instruments at year-end 2006. These were fairly evenly divided between consumer real estate mortgages ($599 billion), consumer credit for vehicle loans and leases ($534 billion), and vehicle loans and leases for businesses ($98 billion).

Finance companies are basically lending institutions without deposits. Unable to raise low cost funds by taking deposits they do not try to compete with banks in what the latter have traditionally viewed as their core customer base—prime commercial clients and consumers with FICO scores of 720 and above. And lacking access to the Federal Reserve discount window, they do not offer liquidity products. Instead, finance companies specialize in higher risk/higher return forms of lending, which they have generally managed quite well.

Generally, finance companies fall into three categories. There are *consumer finance companies* that are direct lenders to consumers on both a secured and unsecured basis, often with a branch network. There are *sales finance companies* that are indirect lenders, purchasing retail and wholesale loans and leases from automobile and mobile home manufacturers, retailers, and other consumer and capital goods companies. And there are *commercial finance companies* that make loans and lease equipment to manufacturers and wholesalers on both a direct and indirect basis.

The traditional business of a finance company was in consumer finance, lending to working class individuals and small entrepreneurs. The interest rates were higher than the banks, but their terms were more flexible.

Over time the industry has changed. There has been consolidation, just as in with depository institutions.

A number of banks have extended their activities into the industry. Wells Fargo, the fifth-largest U.S bank, has mostly grown organically in the consumer finance arena with Wells Fargo Financial. Citigroup and HSBC have grown their consumer finance activities both organically and through acquisition—Citi in 2000 by buying Associates and HSBC in 2003 through the purchase of Household Finance.[3] In commercial finance, Citicorp has long been a major player through CitiCapital focusing on specialty financing and equipment leasing as has Wells Fargo.

A number of the largest sales finance organizations are also large manufacturing companies such as General Motors with General Motors Acceptance Corporation (GM having a majority interest sold in 2006 to a private equity consortium), Ford Motor Credit, and IBM. General Electric Capital Corporation, which has its origins back in 1932 financing GE products, is the largest finance company with assets of $544 billion at the end of 2006. Its businesses are divided into three separate groups—commercial finance, consumer finance, and equipment services—making GECC a massive and extremely profitable financial services supermarket.

While both banks and finance companies have grown at strong rates over the last several years, the growth rates of their portfolios have been affected by the even greater growth in the *asset-backed securities* (ABS) market. A large proportion of these ABS issues are sponsored by banks and finance companies for which the ABS market represents simply an alternative method of financing. However, over the last 15 years there has been a substantial growth in the number of small finance companies that warehouse principally consumer loans, especially mortgages, through the financing of banks and broker-dealers, and then package and sell these loans as ABS. For these companies, this is the only way in which they can be competitive because they have no other means of financing their operations.

Finance companies are heavily reliant on banks and securities markets for their funding. Over time their performance has been quite sound with occasional large problems, usually caused by asset quality deterioration. One strength the industry has is the specialization of companies; but this can lead to crisis if their area of specialization gets into trouble. The most substantial example of this was Conseco, which filed for bankruptcy in December 2002, the third-largest bankruptcy filing ever. Conseco's problems started with the acquisition in 1998 for $6 billion of Green Tree Financial Corporation, whose main business was lending money for the purchase of mobile homes. The purchase price was broadly criticized at the time as being excessive; but the real problem was the quality of the loan portfolio that deteriorated over the ensuing years until the bankruptcy.

In 2006 and 2007, we are seeing problems with subprime home loans portfolios that have caused the failure of several smaller finance companies and significant problems in the portfolios of larger companies.

SPECIAL PURPOSE ENTITIES

This category of lenders primarily consist of *government-sponsored enterprises* (GSEs[4]), the mortgage pools backed by the GSEs and various government agencies and ABS issuers. Taken together they have a major impact on the credit markets not just because of their size, but because they act in almost equal volumes as investors in the markets ($10 trillion) and as borrowers ($10.2 trillion).

The GSEs benefit from extremely strong credit ratings and have significant financial flexibility. As direct borrowers, they had $2.6 trillion outstanding at year-end 2006, which they invested in securities, loans, and mortgages. There was an additional $4.0 trillion in securitized mortgage pools backed by the GSEs and agencies.

In the ABS market, there was $3.6 trillion outstanding in credit instruments, consisting mostly of mortgages ($2.5 trillion), and consumer credit ($671 billion). Approximately 20 percent of the mortgages were *commercial mortgage-backed securities* (CMBS), and the balance *residential mortgage-backed securities* (RMBS). By the end of 2005, the volume of ABS issues had exceeded the volume of corporate bonds outstanding, and the gap has widened since then. We discuss the ABS markets further in Chapter 23.

All of the borrowings of these special purpose entities rest on the assumption that the financial performance of the borrowers based on their underlying cash flows and asset values can be readily and accurately estimated. This has proven to be largely true and the performance of structured finance transactions that have been rated by the rating agencies have been as good or better than their corporate bond equivalents in both default and loss frequencies. However, as Malcolm Knight (2007) noted;

> The financial system has been going through an extraordinarily tranquil phase. Financial firms have made steady and strong profits, the few episodes of stress have been easily absorbed, interest rate spreads have been very thin across a broad range of asset classes, and implied volatilities have been unusually low ... Based on these market signals, risk is hard to detect, or at least appears quite low. Do these market prices provide an accurate reading of the potential risks—the range of possible outcomes that lie ahead—or do they offer an overly sanguine picture of risks?

His conclusion was that while the financial system overall is more resilient than it was before, more complexity, more innovation, and vastly increased volumes of debt require high levels of caution to prevent a false sense of security.

REFERENCES

Deming, W. E. 1986. *Out of the Crisis*, Cambridge, Mass.: MIT Press.

Federal Deposit Insurance Corporation (FDIC) 1997. *History of the Eighties—Lessons for the Future: An examination of the banking crises of the 1980s and early 1990s*. Washington, D.C.

———. 1997. *The Banking Crisis of the 1980s and 1990s: Summary and Implications*. Washington, D.C.

———. 2006. *Annual Report*. Washington, D.C.

———. 2007. *Statistics on Banking*. Washington, D.C.

Federal Reserve Board. 2007, March 8. *Federal Reserve Statistical Release Z.1: Flow of Funds Accounts of the United States*. Washington, D.C.

Knight, M. D. 2007. Speech to the Eighth Annual Risk Management Convention of the Global Association of Risk Professionals, New York City, February 27–28.

Samolyk, K. 2004. "The Future of Banking in America: The Evolving Role of Commercial Banks in U.S. Credit Markets." *FDIC Banking Review* 16, no. 2: 29–65.

CHAPTER 4

The Portfolio Managers

Investment Managers, Mutual Funds, Pension Funds, and Hedge Funds

Even if you put all your eggs into different baskets, as long as you are long in eggs you cannot escape systemic risk.
—Not attributed to Harry Markowitz

There has been an enormous increase in the amount of pension-related savings over the last 15 years driven by demographic trends in the United States and other industrialized nations, especially Japan, as the Baby Boom generation prepares for retirement. It is a trend expected to continue well into the future. Across all OECD (Organisation for Economic Co-operation and Development) countries, pension fund assets have increased rapidly in size and totaled almost $18 trillion in 2005, up from $13 trillion in 2001. (OECD 2006, 3). Collectively, these assets represent approximately 88 percent of the annual GDP of these countries.

The United States has a major influence in these trends. In 2005, U.S. pension fund assets amounted to $12.3 trillion, up from $9.7 trillion in 2001, representing 99 percent of GDP, up from 96 percent in 2001 (OECD 2006, 3).

Unlike many other OECD countries that primarily invest in bills and fixed income securities, the United States just has approximately 15 percent of its pension fund assets in these credit instruments (approximately $1.8 trillion), and almost 65 percent in mutual funds and equities (OECD 2006, 7). These credit instrument assets are spread between the public sector local, state, and federal pension funds (collectively $750 billion at the end of 2005), the private sector pension plans ($659 billion) and life insurance pension plan reserves (Federal Reserve 2007).

In addition to these pension-related credit instrument assets, as we showed in Table 3.1, professionally managed investment funds such as mutual funds, money market mutual funds, closed-end funds, and exchange-traded funds controlled another $3.7 trillion in credit instrument assets. Clearly these portfolio managers have an influential role to play in the credit markets.

FIXED INCOME PORTFOLIO STRATEGY

As trillions of dollars have accumulated in pension funds and mutual funds, an entire industry has sprung up to manage and invest this money. Professional money managers compete with one another on the yields that they can produce for investors as well as on the price of their services. In both respects, the differences between individual managers may be quite small.

Money managers can invest in a wide range of instruments from equities to real estate, but they really have just two basic ways to make money. To the extent that they are able to buy low and sell high, they can earn money through price appreciation. To the extent that they are able to lend money at a reasonable rental, they can earn money by taking credit risk. The latter strategy places them in a position very similar to that of a bank, finance company, or insurer.

It is in their approach to handling credit risk that professional money managers differ dramatically from the cottage industry players such as banks and insurance companies. While a bank or insurer focuses primarily on the individual risk, a money manager focuses on *both* individual risk and portfolio risk—constructing a diversified group of investments and trying, as quickly as possible, to sell any holdings that are not performing well or are not expected to perform well. This approach is generally known as total return portfolio management. While some money managers select securities through a fundamental value/bottom-up process, others combine a top-down view of the economy with a bottom-up view of relative values.

Money managers make use of industry and company research in attempting to select the best investments possible. Let us take for example, Standish, Ayer and Wood, a successful investment management firm based in Boston. This firm is historically known for its successful track record in sector/security selection (65 percent of its historic returns are attributed to security selection and the other 35 percent to the firm's interest rate outlook). In its investment approach, Standish, Ayer and Wood balances classic credit analysis, collective credit judgment, and constrained optimization. It looks, in particular, for companies whose credit rating may be upgraded.

As Howard Rubin, director at Standish, Ayer and Wood explains in an interview with the authors:

> *From a sector perspective, we are comfortable in all sectors of the marketplace and do not base our decisions on just a select few. Based on the perceived relative value of these broad sectors, we buy the cheapest securities, hoping their value would be recognized by the market place and enhanced—thereby filtering down in terms of performance to the client.*

Here is how David Stuehr, another of the firm's directors interviewed, describes the bond acquisition process:

> *The initial theory can come from many sources. It can be triggered from the trading desk—say, an A-rated bond is trading like a BB. . . . There is always some reason things are trading out of whack. Another example is the current tobacco litigation. How is that going to affect the billboard companies used by the tobacco companies? The idea could come out of screening from our data warehouse. Here we maintain company financials, yield spreads, and company analyses such as ratings and S&P plus, minus, and watch list. We can slice and dice company data coming from many diverse sources. Any of this gets you focused on a fundamental idea.*
>
> *We look at the financial ratios such as traditional interest coverage and free cash flow. Are they improving? We construct a pro forma model. We want to know what the downside is. We try to relate the company to the overall state of the economy. In some cases, such as a paper company, the management will tell you the sensitivity of their revenue streams to external variables so we can come up with our own scenario. For others, such as a conglomerate, this is more difficult. Take Koppers, for example. As a conglomerate, that company is into many things: treating railroad ties and telephone poles, supplying industrial coke for steel. You cannot even talk about sector sensitivity with their management; they may not know it. In this case, we try to assess the revenue and profit impact of a 5 to −10 percent recession.*
>
> *We also look at market capitalization. We learned early that the equity analyst knows the company better than the bond analyst. It is not that they are smarter than bond analysts, but just that they have to follow the companies more closely and have fewer companies to follow. We then rate the companies based on the chances that*

they will get upgraded. We set sector limits based on qualitative and subquantitative judgment.

We then assess the credit positives and the credit negatives for the company, including its size and leverage, both financial and operational. Then we analyze relative value; sometimes you will find that the security is not available at the price that was indicated. . . . The individual analyst will set up the idea and then build support for it. We build consensus and once it is reached, the decision has our collective support.

The decision to buy/hold/sell does not stop there. Every security has to satisfy what Howard Rubin calls "the capital rationing criterion." That is, is the investment in the security the best use of capital? Securities in each rating tier are continually ranked according to spread, duration, and potential for a credit quality upgrade. Collaborative decision making does not seem to slow the process. Caleb Aldrich, director at Standish, Ayer and Wood, notes in the interview:

But we will not hesitate to challenge each other. Over time, we have built up a level of mutual confidence and respect as we have sought to enhance return to the client. It is understood that everything that we attempt is related to that. For this reason we will not hesitate to challenge each other if necessary to maintain the leading edge we have. That does not mean that we will dismiss ideas out of hand, but we do turn down an idea if it does not fit in with our risk/return perspective.

Professional investment management firms operate with far less manpower than do banks, and, in general, they have less confidence in their ability to select the right borrowers. Disciplined selling is therefore a critical aspect of their approach. The practitioners of total return portfolio management measure their success not only by the skill with which they identify good investments, but also by the speed with which they recognize and jettison bad ones. As Caleb Aldrich observes, "We do have the benefit of having liquidity and marketability on our side. We can afford to make mistakes because we can exit quickly—before the market realizes that it is a mistake. In a lending situation, a bank does not always have that option."

For the vast majority of professional portfolio managers, diversification is the key to managing credit risk. Following the precepts of modern portfolio theory, money managers try to structure a portfolio that is diversified by every conceivable variable—sector, geography, duration, and type of instrument. In doing so, they are careful to avoid excessive portfolio concentrations. If any one security should begin to lose value, it will be counterbalanced by a great many others that have retained their value.

As a corollary to the diversification axiom, money managers generally stay invested in all segments of their chosen market. If they do not like the immediate prospects, say, for mortgage-backed securities, they will lighten their allocation to this segment rather than exiting from it altogether. Professional managers generally stay within the context of the market in which they are investing, observing the relative weightings of its various segments in the index against which their performance is measured. When, for example, they decide to overweight a portfolio in corporate bonds, they regard the decision as a conscious bet on this sector. Their focus is on relative rather than absolute performance: The primary objective is to outperform the index—and other money managers.

Although the benefits of diversification have, by now, been well documented, it does remain true that, in diversifying, a manager typically passes up some investment opportunity in order to reduce risks, and he or she may invest in some things that he or she probably would not select in an undiversified pool. At the extremes, a few money managers, such as hedge funds, may ignore the principles of diversification in an effort to maximize returns. However, the experience of professional investment managers has generally been quite good. It is demonstrably true that modern portfolio theory helps to mitigate investment risk and to dampen portfolio volatility.

Practitioners of total return management effectively avoid one of the fundamental flaws of the banking industry—the tendency to hold on to bad loans for too long. When a borrower gets into trouble, a banker may well take the time to hear the company explain its situation and plan of action. Under some circumstances, a bank may even agree to lend additional money. They do this because bank loans have generally been hard to sell in the public markets. If a loan deteriorates in quality, a bank may have few alternatives to participating in its restructuring. A portfolio manager, by contrast, will generally try to get out of a deal at the earliest sign of weakness. As a result, pension funds and mutual funds have rarely suffered the kinds of large losses that banks experienced in recent decades.[1] While banks emphasize their relationship with the customer through good times and bad (with varying results), fixed income portfolio managers never lose sight of where they stand relative to the investment that they have made.

Money managers are able to take this tack because they do not allow portfolio concentrations to become so great that the liquidity and marketability of their securities would be affected. Selling any one holding will cause only a small loss, and the proceeds of the sale can then be used to purchase other securities. Portfolio managers typically have no interest in learning how a stressed credit plans to get back on its feet. Such loyalty to the borrower would make little strategic sense. A fixed income security provides a relatively small stream of interest income. Investing in such securities at 100 cents on the dollar is an activity that offers relatively little upside. Typically, a fixed income manager has few opportunities to recover a large loss. It is therefore more rational to sell distressed securities as quickly as possible. At the right price, there will always be buyers. Other investors will be willing to pay 60 or 70 cents on the dollar for such bonds because there is an upside for them—a chance to see their investment appreciate.

Fixed income portfolio managers differ from bankers in other important respects as well. They invest in publicly rated securities for which there is generally a liquid market, and they are required to mark their investments to market. When a credit deteriorates, a portion of their portfolio will decline in value. This market discipline strengthens a money manager's motivation to sell. Bankers, by contrast, do not mark loans to market; as long as they continue to receive current payments, they classify a loan as performing—even if the borrower is barely staying afloat.

Banks and pension funds also operate under different regulatory regimes. Indeed, society looks to them to serve somewhat different purposes. While both kinds of institutions are expected to safeguard people's savings, banks are also expected to provide financing to meet the legitimate needs of businesses and individuals. For many people, banks are, above all, a source of liquidity, mortgages, and working capital loans. When banks tighten their credit policies and slow the flow of financing, some Americans promptly contact there representatives in Congress to complain about the resulting credit crunch. By contrast, virtually no one expects pension funds to carry the burden of financing American enterprises. When a pension fund declines to buy a particular company's bonds, the firm's executives do not call Congress to complain. Indeed, under the terms of the Employee Retirement Income Security Act of 1974 (ERISA), pension plans are legally bound to put the interests of their participants first. If the officers of a plan allow other interests to intrude, they may be guilty of breaching their fiduciary responsibility to plan participants.

Despite the generally positive record, some professionally managed, fixed income funds have encountered problems. In the case of certain junk bond funds and real estate funds, for example, diversification has been ineffective because the portfolios were too concentrated within a specific segment of the market. Economic problems affecting the entire segment caused large losses. Funds that are highly concentrated in a particular geographic region (such as country funds) have also experienced sizable losses.

More generally, it should be noted that portfolio diversification has largely been a matter of intuition and common sense rather than of hard science. To date, relatively little serious analytic work has been done on the correlations among different industries and among various types of securities. Lacking these tools, portfolio managers have been unable to realize all the potential benefits of diversification. Pension funds, mutual funds, and unit trusts may therefore gain a great deal from future advances we expect to see in portfolio theory. These are discussed at length in Chapters 17 through 22.

A second problem for portfolio managers derives from the security selection process itself. Most money management firms are overmuscled in portfolio theory and undermuscled in security selection. This is evidenced by the number of analysts they employ relative to the size of the marketplace that they have to address on a name-by-name basis. As a result, they are liable to purchase securities that may potentially lose value because of declining credit quality. While disciplined selling generally protects them against catastrophic losses, fixed income funds may nonetheless be accepting an unnecessary volume of small losses.

To address this problem and also to take advantage of investment opportunities in the growing market for bank loans, high-yield corporate debt, and the debt of emerging countries—all of which involve credit risk (and yield) of higher than customary magnitude—some large investment firms have begun to incorporate credit skills that are normally associated with banks. Companies such as Fidelity Investments have begun hiring professionals trained at banks to help them design credit systems that combine individual credit analysis with portfolio management skills. Banks, meanwhile, are acquiring some of the portfolio skills normally associated with money managers. Whether in the hands of a bank or a money manager, the combination of the two approaches should lead to much more effective management of credit risk.

HEDGE FUNDS

Any discussion of credit instrument portfolio managers and the credit markets today needs to include the role of hedge funds because of their significant impact and influence. When the first edition of *Managing Credit Risk* was published in 1998, there were approximately 3,000 hedge funds, up from approximately 600 in 1990, but many less than the 9,228 now estimated to be in operation (Wastler 2006).

To a significant degree over the last 10 years, many of the changes in the credit markets and improvements in terms of innovation, liquidity, and risk dispersion have been driven by the hedge funds. They are estimated to manage approximately $1.6 trillion (FSF 2007, 8)[4] but they are responsible for a much higher share of turnover in many markets, in particular the credit derivatives market. "In 2005 the consulting firm Greenwich Associates estimated that while hedge funds accounted for 15% of trading volumes in the U.S. fixed income markets, this proportion rose to 45% of trading in emerging market bonds, 47% in distressed debt, and 58% in credit derivatives." (FSF 2007, 8) Movement between the funds is very dynamic, with the launch of some 1,518 in 2006 and the liquidation of 717 in 2006. Their growth has been a global phenomenon, still concentrated primarily in the United States, which has 65 percent of the assets under management, compared to Europe with 24 percent and Asia with 8 percent as of 2006, but down from 2002 when the United States had 80 percent of assets. As we have seen with other financial organizations, there has been a trend towards concentration, with the 100 largest funds representing 65 percent of the industry total compared to 54 percent in 2003. The very largest global fund groups now manage $20 to $30 billion each or more (FSF 2007, 8).

William White, Economic Adviser and Head of the Monetary and Economic Department at BIS, in a speech in early 2007, commented that "unlike the hedge funds of the 1940s, today's hedge funds are far from hedged. Rather, operating with a very few investment restrictions, but different "styles" (principal investment strategies), they commonly take speculative and leveraged positions in the pursuit of absolute target rates of return to which the manager's compensation is generally related. Whereas, hedge fund investors were originally wealthy individuals, in recent years hedge funds have attracted the interest of institutional investors, including pension funds and insurance companies. This has led to the greater professionalism and "institutionalization," especially of larger hedge funds" (White 2007).

Unlike the portfolio investors we have discussed previously in this chapter, who seek to create efficient portfolios through careful analysis and diversification, hedge funds are outright risk takers seeking only commensurate or better rates of return for the exposures they take on. In doing so, they help reduce and spread systemic risk but in the process they create their own sets of risks. As organizations they themselves are highly leveraged and they tend to focus on complex and illiquid products and markets where the technical challenges of risk measurement and management are high. As we saw with Long-Term Capital Management in 1998, even the very best management and trading teams with substantial capital can be fatally damaged if there is sustained high stress and adversity. In William White's words, they have contributed much of the "grease," which has helped to grow the financial system so successfully but care must be taken so that the hedge funds under extreme events do not become the "sand."

REFERENCES

Employee Benefit Research Institute (EBRI). 2003. *EBRI Data Book 2003*. Washington, D.C.

Financial Stability Forum (FSF). 2007. Update of the FSF Report on Highly Leveraged Institutions, May 19.

Organisation for Economic Co-operation and Development (OECD). 2006. *Pension Markets in Focus*, Issue 3 (October).

Wastler, A. 2006. "Hedge Fund Apocalypse . . . Not," *CNNMoney.com*. 26 October. money.cnn.com/2006/10/26/commentary/wastler/index.htm.

White, W. R. 2007. "Hedge Fund Flurries: Introductory comments by Mr William R. White, Economic Adviser and Head of the Monetary and Economic Department of the BIS, to Session 3 of the Bellagio Meeting, London, 19–20 January 2007." *BIS Management Speeches, 25 January*, <http://www.bis.org/speeches/sp070125.htm>.

CHAPTER 5

Structural Hubs

Clearinghouses, Derivative Product Companies, and Exchanges

The synthesizing of custom financial contracts and securities is for financial services what the assembly-line process is for the manufacturing sector. Options, futures and other exchange-traded securities are the raw "inputs" applied in prescribed combinations over time to create portfolios that hedge the various customer liabilities of financial intermediaries.

—Robert C. Merton (1992)

Banks, derivative dealers, and other financial institutions that engage in a high volume of transactions with each other take on credit risks in the course of their daily interactions. Clearinghouse, exchanges, and derivative contracts are structural means of mitigating theses risks.

Although derivatives have attracted a great deal of public attention in the last two decades, they are not a new phenomenon. For many years, traders have bought and sold pieces of paper representing pork bellies, corn, gold, or oil rather than buying and selling the commodities themselves.[1] Whenever a standard unit of trade can be established, an instrument can be created to reflect this basic transaction. Derivatives are easier to deal with than the physical goods. While most futures contracts are closed out in cash before the maturity date, on occasion goods are actually delivered in accordance with the terms of the contract.

It is financial derivatives, which represent rights or options in a variety of financial instruments, that have made headlines in recent years. The overall

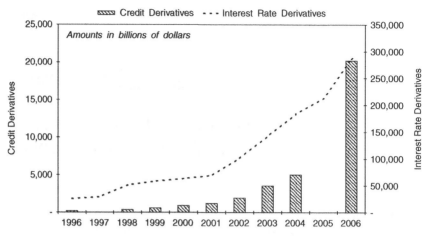

FIGURE 5.1   Growth in Financial Derivatives
Source: British Bankers Association (2006) and ISDA Market Survey (2007).

volume of trading in financial derivatives has increased from $618.3 billion in 1986 to over $285 trillion in 2006 (see Figure 5.1). The growth of interest rate derivatives has been high for some time now; more recently credit derivative growth has also started to accelerate, although still from a much lower base.

This explosive growth has created substantial risks of several kinds: counterparty risk, settlement risk, and systemic risk, to name a few. Someone buying a stock option from a dealer depends upon the dealer to make good on what it has sold. At the same time, the seller depends upon the buyer to make the payment agreed upon.

Derivative dealers are specially organized companies that are typically affiliated with a commercial bank, or more recently, one of the megabanks. A sizable portion of their business involves trades with other dealers. As a result, in addition to having exposure to the credit risk of their customers, these organizations are also exposed to the credit risk of other dealers. Since the total number of dealers is limited, these risks may become quite concentrated.

When the financial derivatives market was in its infancy, dealers knew one another and felt comfortable that there was little risk of nonperformance. Growth in the derivatives markets, concentrations in the banking market because of consolidations, and the rapid demise of a series of major trading institutions such as Barings, Enron, and Long-Term Capital Management (LTCM) have combined to create sharper awareness of counterparty risk. Market participants who trade over-the-counter derivatives such as swaps, options, swaptions, caps, and collars are increasingly concerned about managing these risks. Indeed, the management of such counterparty risk is one of the major themes of the financial markets for the past two decades.

EXCHANGES

An exchange is an institutional means of reducing counterparty risk. As trading has expanded in size and scope, more of that trading has been done on exchanges. The reason for this is that the exchange can set standards for participation and monitor the ongoing creditworthiness of its customers. In fact, smaller participants typically do not participate directly on the exchange but mostly through larger participants usually subsidiaries of the banks, investment banks, and megabanks. Listing on an exchange—whether stock, bond, options, futures, metals, chemical, oil, and so on helps to create liquidity in the listed instrument and is one of the key factors in the huge increase in trading we have seen in recent years.

Anyone buying a contract on a futures exchange—whether an individual or an institution—is required to put up margin. Because the buyer has posted margin, the seller knows that money will be available to pay for the contract. Since the seller is likewise obliged to post margin, the buyer has the same assurance about receiving the purchased goods or their monetary equivalent. The margin requirement effectively eliminates most counterparty risk between buyer and seller. The only remaining credit risk is for very short term—intraday or overnight movements in the traded instrument—where the counterparty may not be able to make the next margin call. When this occurs, a player relinquishes any rights to margin or to the underlying contract. The margin requirement allows small players such as individual investors or small investment firms to trade on an equal basis with the megabanks. Many participants consider this equality of access one of the great advantages of an exchange. Another advantage of an exchange is that it standardizes the terms of contracts, thereby reducing the transaction costs.

While the calculation of margin requirements and the posting of collateral seem like relatively simple administrative functions, when this needs to be done thousands, even millions of times daily, a focused and specialized organizational response is required. For this reason, all major exchanges have established dedicated clearinghouses to manage these functions.

Many investment banks are joining forces to create private exchanges (typically called *trading systems*) in which private placements can take place. This would allow the trading of unregistered U.S. securities. The advantage of such system could be phenomenal for companies outside the United States. Many international companies view the current system as cumbersome and intrusive. An unregistered electronic exchange could be quite attractive to such companies allowing access to the financial markets in North America avoiding the need to deal with the SEC regulations.

CLEARINGHOUSES

Clearinghouses are the major credit managers of the capital markets. They exist to manage the counterparty risk between institutions that do a lot of business with each other. They position themselves between buyer and seller, thereby guaranteeing that the trade will be completed. Clearinghouses set standards for membership in the clearinghouse (which can be more stringent than membership in the exchange), approve new members, set margin requirements that reflect the volatility of the traded instrument, and carefully monitor the creditworthiness of the institutional players. They have massive trading systems that allow them to process every trade done on the exchange, record the buyer and seller, and book the required margin. For the major clearinghouses in the United States and Europe, this means millions of trades every day. The clearinghouses also are big players in the short -term investment markets as they have huge sums to invest on an overnight basis. This system has been very effective in virtually eliminating credit risk from the exchange-traded markets.

Banks have also used clearinghouses to manage risk between them. New York banks, for example formed a clearinghouse to clear checks and other obligations they have to one another. Instead of exchanging millions of bits of paper and billions of dollars in cash, the banks use a clearinghouse as a central place to meet and sort out their transactions electronically as shown in Figure 5.2.

An associated clearinghouse is an important component of an exchange. It can be a dedicated clearinghouse or one that serves a variety of markets. LCH.Clearnet Group Limited is the prime example of a *horizontal model clearinghouse,* which handles most of the trading activities in London, Paris, and several other European financial centers. As can be seen in Figure 5.2, LCH.Clearnet clears a wide variety of markets and instruments including equities, derivatives of all types, swaps and commodities, and energy. Institutionally, the credit risk of LCH.Clearnet substitutes for the credit risks of the multiple counterparties transacting business on the various exchanges listed in the Figure 5.2. Every trade executed on one of these exchanges spawns two trades: one between the buyer and LCH.Clearnet and the other between LCH.Clearnet and the seller. At the end of the day, LCH.Clearnet has a

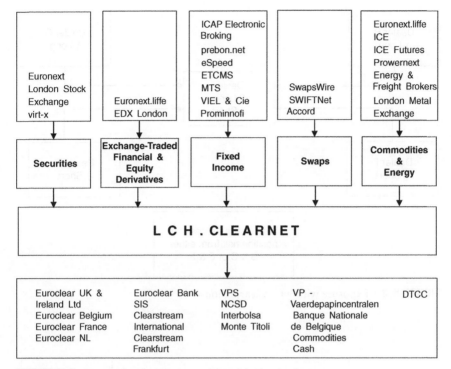

FIGURE 5.2 Example of a Horizontal Model Clearinghouse
Source: London Clearinghouse (2007).

perfectly matched book of contracts and thus incurs no market risk. However, LCH.Clearnet is now exposed to the risk of their clearing members, who in turn are exposed to the counterparty risk of their own customers. Figures 5.3 and 5.4 illustrate how a clearinghouse provides a structural hedge for a member.

Figure 5.3 depicts of the operation of the trading in the absence of the clearinghouse. Dealer A is long two contracts with dealers B and F, and short two contracts with dealers C and E. Because the short positions exactly offset the long positions, dealer A is market neutral, that is, immune to changes in the market value of the positions. But dealer A is exposed to the credit risk of either B and C or E and F because one of these pairs will owe money to A if there is a market move up or down. In Figure 5.4, dealer A is again in market neutral, but a clearinghouse has been interposed between A and the other dealers. In this case, the clearinghouse assumes the credit risk of the counterparties: If the market moves against B and C,

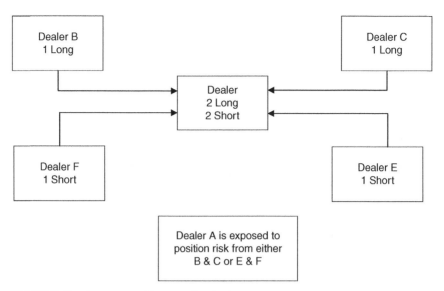

FIGURE 5.3   Exposure without a Clearinghouse

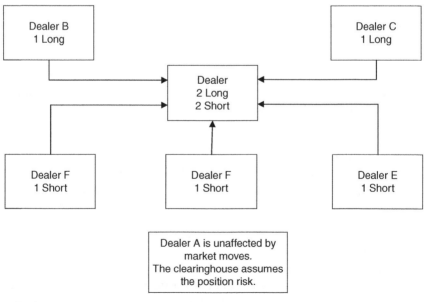

FIGURE 5.4   Exposure with the Clearinghouse

the clearinghouse covers the position as far as A is concerned. By serving as a hub, the clearinghouse eliminated the crisscrossing of credit exposure between every dealer and every other dealer. Since the exposure of the clearinghouse to each dealer is net of that dealer's long and short positions in an instrument, the existence of the clearinghouse enlarges the liquidity of the market—enabling dealers to execute trades in greater number and dollar volume. Since the clearinghouse monitors the credit of each dealer and sets standards for their participation in the system, the dealers themselves no longer need to monitor one another. This is a more efficient arrangement.

NETTING, COLLATERAL, AND DOWNGRADE TRIGGERS

Netting—the practice of setting off payments in one direction against those in the opposite directions—is the primary risk management technique of a clearinghouse or exchange. Netting enables market participants to get an accurate view of their exposure to other players. In reality, the flows between particular institutions are not even. Most players are comfortable accepting each other's credit up to a certain point, but beyond this limit, they want some form of reassurance before they will engage in further business.

Reassurance typically comes in the form of collateral. If dealer A is uncomfortable when its exposure to dealer B exceeds a given threshold, dealer A may ask dealer B is post collateral as a condition for continuing to trade together. Under some circumstance, dealer B's collateral will remain at dealer A on a permanent basis. Dealer B may also insist on collateral from dealer A. Collateralization has become a major part of derivatives trading, both on exchanges and over-the-counter markets.

The collateral requirement creates a kind of handicapping system that effectively sets limits for trading. Clearinghouses and exchanges provide the recordkeeping needed to track and mitigate counterparty risk through collateralization.

Since the value of derivatives may be highly volatile, time is a critical aspect of counterparty risk. Exchanges and clearinghouse require participants to mark their portfolios to market, using the market price at the close of the business day to determine the value of each instrument they hold. In this way, margins and collateral can be adjusted on a daily basis. In recent years, in high-volume markets, this requirement has been increased to be intraday, with margin calls being made two to three times during the trading day. Knowing the value of an instrument on any given day, or part of a day focuses both buyer and seller on their responsibilities to one another. In addition, clearinghouses and exchanges have membership requirements including minimum capital, surety bonds, credit surveillance, and monitoring of members.

Clearinghouses also invest in huge processing systems to assure high reliability and to support massive volumes of trades. They develop procedures to deal with default by a member and with market emergencies, and establish financial resources to withstand stresses from major disruptive events. They maintain relationships with regulatory bodies (who generally view them as critical components of the capital markets) and may arrange for government support in times of financial distress. They create systemic linkages with other clearinghouse to manage the risk exposures connect with them. Should their resources be depleted as a result of losses sustained, some clearinghouses have the power to impose an assessment on their members.

Time can affect counterparty's creditworthiness. That is why structural hedgers make use of downgrade triggers. A contract between dealers typically specifies that if the credit of one party is downgraded beyond a certain point, that party must post collateral in order to continue trading. This assures other players that money will be available to satisfy the downgraded company's obligations.

The combination of these structural hedges—netting, margins, collateralization, marking to market, and downgrade triggers with good old fashion close surveillance—has proven to be highly effective. The record at clearinghouses and among dealers has been outstanding: The megabanks, clearinghouses, and exchanges have all lost very little money because of their exposure to credit risk related to trading activities. And some very large bullets have been dodged in recent years—Barings, LTCM, Enron, Worldcom, Parmalat, and Amaranth are recent examples of high-volume, high-profile disasters that did not result in credit losses at clearinghouses in the United States or Europe. Even where many small players are involved, clearinghouses and exchanges have seen very few losses attributable to credit risk.

CREDIT DERIVATIVE PRODUCT COMPANIES

Credit derivatives have not yet become exchange traded. Nor have any clearinghouses been created for these instruments. However, without doubt the credit derivative market has been the most innovative sector within the financial markets. The bespoke nature of the contracts, the length of the contracts and several other factors have made stymied efforts to trade credit derivatives on exchanges or to clear the trades using clearinghouses. Still the amount of credit being transferred by dealers in an increasing number of products is huge and is increasing rapidly. These products tend to be complex and there has been some difficulty finding investors whose interests and mentality is to "buy and hold" the risk over the period of the transaction. Today, when the markets create opportunities, it is not long before we see an innovation focused on what is needed. *Credit derivative product companies* (CDCPs) are relatively new and as yet niche segment within the credit derivatives space.

While CDCPs will use some of the structural hedging tools developed elsewhere in the marketplace, they are somewhat different breed. They may hedge their exposures, but they are a typically taking a long position in the credit. Since they are providing protection to the major dealers, they will normally have a triple-A rating from the rating agencies and will need to keep their ratings at this level. The protection they provide is executed in a swap format using international Swaps and Derivative Association (ISDA) documentation.

The *derivative product company* (DPC) concept is not a new one. Indeed, DPCs can trace their origins back to the early 1990s, the focus back then was on interest rate and currency swaps. At that time, DPCs were developed a means for lower-rated banks to increase their swaps positions. As the banks improved their creditworthiness and more trading moved into clearinghouses, it seemed that the time for DPCs had passed. In 2002, however, the technology was applied to credit derivatives for the first time with the launch of Primus Financial Products LLC. Since then, only four more vehicles have been launched, two of which started in 2007. Nevertheless, the concept seems to have caught on—in January 2007 Moody's stated that it was in the process of rating 24 new CDCPs.

LIMITATIONS OF STRUCTURAL HUBS

There are significant limitations on the application of structural hedging techniques. To begin with, they require the existence of a market sufficiently large and liquid that the value of items in every player's portfolio can be marked to market. Prices are posted daily for corn and silver, for example, but not for corporate loans. Banks, in fact, generally resist proposals to mark their loans to market because it would make holding them in their portfolio difficult and expose their income statements to a lot of volatility. To a degree, the credit derivative market is making this issue less relevant, since prices for most big corporate names are readily available in the derivative markets. But even if the credit derivative market has provided more information, prices are still somewhat unrelated to what a loan could be purchased for in the cash markets.

In addition, netting is meaningful only where there is two-way flow between parties, in the loan market, where the bank is always the lender;

netting may be relevant only to the limited extent where there is a right of offset. Some degree of netting might become possible where a company has money on deposit at the same bank from which it has taken a loan. However, the situation is inherently more complicated than that between two derivatives settling trades with one another.

Structural hubs are inflexible systems that work best for standardized products that are traded in volume. Consequently, they will probably grow in importance as the markets mature. For some less-common types of derivatives, for example, these techniques may turn out to be more trouble than they are worth. In addition, transparency is critical to the establishment of clearinghouses or exchanges: Every aspect of a transaction must be perfectly visible to regulators and other players. Transparency quickly leads to commodity-like pricing and a focus on cost efficiencies.

Clearinghouses and exchanges are complex organizations that cannot be developed overnight. It is only when concerns about credit risk exceeding a fairly high threshold that the establishment of such an institution becomes feasible. However, once an exchange has been created, it is comparatively easy to add new products and new types of players. That is why a number of futures exchanges have expanded in recent years.

Structural hubs are powerful techniques with a proven record of success. In all probability, the coming years will see them applied to many areas where they have never been used before. As Merton (1992) notes, structural hubs are the key element in the construction of special purpose, risk-management structures out of general-purpose components. Recently we have seen this applied with CDPCs in the credit derivatives markets. We will undoubtedly see more in the future.

REFERENCES

Akorecki, A., and F. Guerrera. 2003. "Clearing House Shake-Up Proposed." *Financial Times*, 3 April.

Barrett, R., and J. Ewan. 2006. *Credit Derivatives Report 2006*. London: British Bankers Association.

Bliss, R., and C. Papathanassiou. 2006, 8 March. *Derivatives Clearing, Central Counterparties and Novation: The Economic Implications*. Frankfurt am Main: European Central Bank.

Cameron, D. 2006. "Investors 'Miss Importanace of Clearing System'." *Financial Times*, 29 November.

Cohen, N. 2007. "UK Treasury Signs Up for Clearing House Membership." *Financial Times*, 29 March.

The Economist. 2000. "One World, Ready or Not,"18 May.

———. 2000. "European Stock Exchanges: The X Files." 13 July.

———. 2001. "European Clearing and Settlement: Werner's Silo." 13 December.

———. 2001. "Securities Exchanges: After Liffe." 1 November.

———. 2003. "Exchanges, Clearing and Settlement: All for One, or One for All." 23 January.

———. 2003. "European Clearing and Settlement: The American Dream." 10 April.

———. 2003. "Derivatives Exchanges: Clear for Take-Off." 24 April.

———. 2003. "Exchanges: Banks Beaten." 12 June.

———. 2005. "Stock-Exchange Mergers: Three-Dimensional Chess." 4 August.

———. 2006. "Securities Trading: Only Connect." 31 July.

———. 2007. "Euro Payments: Untangling Europe's Wires." 29 March.

European Central Bank. 2006, March. *Payment and Securities Settlement Systems in the European Union and in the Acceding Countries*. Frankfurt am Main.

Guadamillas, M., and R. Keppler. 1999. *Securities Clearance and Settlement Systems: A Guide to Best Practices*. Washington, D.C. The World Bank

Hardy, D. 2006. "The Case for a Single European Clearing House." *Financial Times*, 6 June.

International Monetary Fund (IMF). 1997. *International Capital Markets: Developments, Prospects, Key Policy Issues*. Washington, D.C.: International Monetary Fund.

Kroszner, R. S. 1999. "Can the Financial Markets Privately Regulate Risk?." *Journal of Money, Credit and Banking*, November.

Merton, R. C. 1992. "Financial Innovation and Economic Performance." *Journal of Applied Corporate Finance* 4, no. 1:12–22.

Moody's Investors Service. 1995. *Credit Risks of Clearinghouses at Futures and Options Exchanges*. New York.

Russo, D., T. Hart, M. C. Malaguti, and C. Papathanassious. 2004, October. *Governance of Securities Clearing and Settlement Systems*. European Central Bank Occasional Paper Series, No. 21.

Simonian, H., and N. Cohen. 2006. "Swiss Clearing House Issues Challenge to LCH.Clearnet." *Financial Times*, 2 June.

Teweless, R. J., and F. K. Jones. 1987. *The Futures Game*, 2d ed. New York: McGraw-Hill Book Co.

U.S. House. 1996. Committee on Banking ad Financial Services. *Hearings on Committee on Banking and Financial Services*. 104th Cong., 13 March.

CHAPTER 6

The Rating Agencies

All that glitters is not Gold;
Often have you heard that told.
                —William Shakespeare, *The Merchant of Venice* (II, vii)

Rating agencies specialize in evaluating the creditworthiness of debt securities issued by corporate, financial, structured finance, municipal, and sovereign obligors, and by evaluating the general creditworthiness of the issuers themselves. It is the job of the agencies to inform investors about the likelihood that they will receive all the principal and interest payments as scheduled for a given security. In other words, what is the probability of repayment?

The agencies are tremendously influential around the world today, covering in excess of $34 trillion in securities around the world, and in excess of $750 billion in loans and their businesses are growing at double digit rates (Moody's Investors Service 2007). Jochen Sanio, president of Germany's financial regulator BaFin, said the rating agencies do a good job but they nevertheless have become "uncontrolled world powers" (Klein 2004).

In some markets—the United States for example—the capital markets have replaced banks as the primary source of debt capital; and ratings agencies have assumed enormous importance in the management of credit risk. The agencies make no recommendations about buying, selling, or holding a particular security or about suitability for a particular investor. Their ratings express nothing more than informed opinions about creditworthiness; although the agencies stress that the opinions are independent, objective, and produced through a transparent and high-quality analytic process. However, these ratings have achieved very widespread acceptance with investors who have confidence in their accuracy and like their convenience and low cost.

For borrowers credit ratings are critical because they affect their access to markets and the cost of their borrowings.

Increasingly regulators have permitted use of ratings from certain of the rating agencies, designated in the United States as *nationally recognized statistical rating organizations* (NRSROs) in evaluating the quality of loan and investment portfolios and the equity capital needed to support the risk in these portfolios. Examples of some of the primary regulatory uses in the United States of rating agency information are summarized in Table 6.1. In the Basel II Agreement, finalized in June 2004, the Basel Committee of the Bank for International Settlements (BIS), whose membership consists of the major central banks in the world (including the United States, Japan, Germany, and the United Kingdom), has also raised the profile of the agencies, described as *external credit assessment institutions* (ECAIs), again highlighting their role in providing the basis for capital adequacy calculations.

AGENCIES AROUND THE WORLD

The three major U.S. rating agencies are Moody's Investors Service, Standard and Poor's (S&P), and Fitch Ratings. Moody's has been an independent, publicly owned company since 2000. Since 1966, S&P has been a subsidiary of McGraw-Hill Companies, Inc. which is a large, publicly owned publishing group. Fitch is majority owned by a French conglomerate FIMALAC SA, which has diverse global operations and whose shares are traded on the Paris Bourse, with some 64 percent owned by one individual. In addition, there are several other notable agencies in the United States and internationally (shown in Table 6.2), but the market shares on a revenue basis of the majors are highly concentrated, with S&P estimated to have 40 percent share, Moody's 39 percent, Fitch 15 percent, and A.M. Best 3 percent. Market shares can also be computed on a coverage basis, which tends to give a larger weighting to smaller agencies, and Fitch in particular, given the structure of fee levels between agencies. In this chapter, we focus mostly on the big three companies.

Ratings agencies developed in the United States when John Moody began initiating bond ratings in 1909 for U.S. railroads. Credit reporting agencies also developed in the United States during the middle of the nineteenth century, when two of the foremost were founded, namely R.G. Dun Company and John Bradstreet Company. They merged in 1933 to form Dun and Bradstreet, which, in 1962, acquired Moody's Investors Service, the company originally founded by John Moody. Moody's is the only pure play rating agency listed company. At the beginning of 2007, it had a market capitalization of US $19 billion, although by early December 2007 this had declined to US $10.3 billion as concerns about the future role and profitability of the agencies have risen.

TABLE 6.1 Uses of Ratings by the Regulators

Regulator	Examples
SEC	NRSRO ratings are included in a number of key SEC regulations including the Securities Act of 1933, the Exchange Act, and the Investment Company Act of 1940.
	For example:
	— Calculations of broker-dealer net capital requirements are based on the ratings of securities held.
	— The rating from an NRSRO may be included in the registration without obtaining the written consent of the NRSRO.
	— Exemption from certain reporting requirements on rated securities transactions.
	— Eligibility for investment by taxable money market funds, including aggregate risk limits, single risk limits, and downgrades linked to NRSRO ratings.
OTS/OCC/FDIC Federal Reserve	NRSRO ratings are used in a number of key federal and state banking regulations governing domestic banking and thrift institutions and foreign institutions operating in the United States.
	For example:
	— The assets with highest ratings qualify as liquid assets.
	— There is additional capacity to lend to highly rated borrowers which receive a favorable risk rating for capital purposes.
	— Eligibility for investment by FDIC-insured banks.
	— Capital calculations of state-chartered banks.
	— Eligibility and valuation of assets to be pledged by foreign banks whose deposits are insured by FDIC.
	— Investment eligibility of assets and valuation for capital determination, and margining requirements are based on agency ratings.
NAIC	Valuation of securities held for investment purposes, for reserve requirements and for capital adequacy.
DOL	Eligibility for pension fund investments.
States	Eligibility for investment by state-regulated entities such as insurance companies, public retirement funds, state chartered banks, and thrift institutions.
Other	Self-regulatory organizations such as the New York Stock Exchange (NYSE) and Nasdaq set margin requirements based on the type of security pledged to secure a loan.

TABLE 6.2 Selected Ratings Agencies around the World

Agency Name	Year Founded	Market Orientation	Short-term Rating Symbols	Long-term Rating Symbols
A.M. Best	1999	Global	A-1+ to D	A++ to S
Canadian Bond Rating Service (S&P)	1972	Local	A-1 to A-4	A+ + to D
Dominion Bond Rating Service (DBRS)	1976	Global	R-1 to U	AAA to C
Agence d'Évaluation Financière (S&P)	1986	Local	T-1 to T-4	AAA to D
Credit Rating Services of India Ltd.	1988	Local	P-1 to P-5	AAA to D
Egan Jones Rating	1995	Local	A-1+ to D	AAA to D
European Rating Agency	—	Local	S-1 to S-4	AAA to D
Japan Bond Research Institute	1979	Local	—	—
Japan Credit Rating Agency	1985	Local	J-1 to J-5	Aaa to D
Mikuni & Co.	1975	Local	N/A	AAA to D
Nippon Investors Service	1985	Local	A-1 to D	AAA to D
Korean Investors Service	1985	Local	A-1 to D	AAA to D
Fitch Ratings	1922	Global	F1+ to D	AAA to D
Moody's Investors Service	1909	Global	P-1 to P-3	Aaa to C
Standard & Poor's	1916	Global	A-1+ to D	AAA to D

Standard & Poor's grew out the publishing venture established by Henry Varnum Poor to print financial and operating information about U.S. railroads after the Civil War. Poor's Publishing Co. turned to bond ratings in 1916 and merged with Standard Statistics, another financial publishing and rating company in 1941.

The ratings agencies started out strongly and flourished into the 1930s. By the 1960s the agencies had become much less important as well as small and quite moribund. The U.S. bond markets were very safe, dominated by government debt and investment-grade corporates. Banks were the dominant medium-term corporate capital providers, and the markets in the rest of the world generated very little business.

However, starting from the 1970s, there were several major changes that together have caused the activity of the agencies to grow very strongly. Corporates began to diversify their funding bases and the volumes of debt issuance have exploded over the decades since, taking share from the banking system. Some major bankruptcies, notably Penn Central in 1970, shook the markets and heightened concerns about credit quality. In 1973, the first SEC securities rule was established that formally incorporated credit ratings into securities regulations and gave official status initially to a select group of four NRSROs. Over time, mergers reduced the number of NRSROs to three by 2002, after which two additional NRSROs were added. There are currently five NRSROs, namely S&P, Moody's, Fitch, A.M. Best and Dominion Bond Rating Services.

Over time the agencies innovated with their business model and in the 1970s switched their revenue base from subscription-paying investors to fee-paying issuers. They also greatly broadened their services to cover the entire spectrum of instruments and obligors, including asset-backed securities, commercial paper, municipal bonds, counterparty risk, the claims-paying ability of insurance companies, and credit risks of all kinds (Moody's Investors Service 2007).

GROWTH IN ISSUES RATED

The importance of the ratings agencies is reflected in the rapid increase in the number of ratings that they provide. In 2005, for example, Moody's rated a total of 5,423 corporate bond issuers—substantially above the 2,522 in 1990 and 885 in 1960 (see Figure 6.1). The breadth of their ratings is wide,

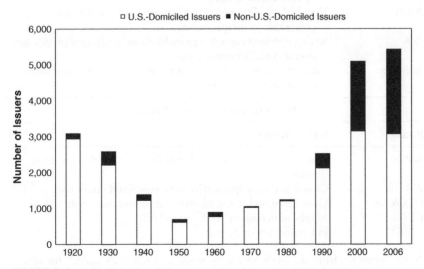

FIGURE 6.1 Moody's-Rated Corporate Bond Issuers, 1920–2006
Source: Moody's Investors Service (2007).

with Moody's following over 100 sovereigns, 11,000 corporates, 25,000 public finance issuers, and 70,000 structured finance issuers' obligations. Structured finance for all the agencies has been a major source of growth. In 2005, Moody's earned 41 percent of its revenue from these issuers, rating $2.4 trillion in issuance up from $632 billion in 2005.

In rating long-term debt, each agency uses a system of alphanumeric letter grades that locate an issuer or issue on a spectrum of credit quality from the very highest (AAA/Aaa meaning an extremely strong capacity to meet financial commitments) to the very lowest (C/D meaning there has been a payment default). Each letter grade has three notches (Fitch and S&P use + and − modifiers, Moody's uses numerical modifiers 1, 2, 3) within it (see Table 6.3).

The lower the grade the greater the risk that principal and interest payments will not be made. All debt rated BBB/Baa or above is considered to be of investment-grade quality, while issues rated BB/Ba or below are viewed

TABLE 6.3   Long-Term Senior Debt Rating Symbols

Investment Grade Ratings	
Rating	Interpretation
AAA/Aaa	Highest quality; extremely strong, highly unlikely to be affected by foreseeable events.
AA/Aa	Very high quality; capacity for repayment is not significantly vulnerable to forseeable events.
A/A	Strong payment capacity; more likely to be affected by changes in economic circumstances.
BBB/Baa	Adequate payment capacity; a negative change in environment may affect capacity for repayment.
Below Investment Grade Ratings	
Rating	Interpretation
BB/Ba	Considered speculative with possibility of developing credit risks.
B/B	Considered very speculative with significant credit risk.
CCC/Caa	Considered highly speculative with substantial credit risk.
CC/Ca	Maybe in default or wildly speculative.
C/C/D	In bankruptcy or default.

Note: Summary from the main rating agencies. Consult each agency for specific details on their grades.

as speculative or noninvestment grade. The agencies each use a different grading system for short-term debt obligations.

Since the credit quality of an obligor can change dramatically over time, ratings are subject to revision. As a part of their commitment to transparency, agencies update and publish their credit outlook for most issuers on a continuing basis. When they issue ratings, they indicate whether the rating outlook is *positive*, meaning it the rating may be raised, *negative*, meaning it the rating may be lowered, *stable* indicating a neutral outlook for rating changes, or *developing/evolving*, meaning it may change up or down. To do so they maintain contact with issuers they have rated and review not only their periodic earnings releases but also other relevant financial and economic data. When there is an important development whose rating impact has not yet been determined, an agency notifies both the issuer and the market of this fact—S&P by placing the issue on its Credit Watch, Moody's doing the same on its Rating Review WatchList and Fitch through a news release and posting on its web site.

The switch in payment arrangements from subscribers to issuers remains a point of some controversy, raising concerns about the independence of the agencies. It certainly has not changed the willingness of the regulators to incorporate ratings from NRSROs into their prudential oversight of financial institutions, which they are doing with more frequency.

In truth, although they are paid for their services, the agencies generally behave more like academic research centers than businesses. Analysts are engaged in pure analysis and their position is far from that of a bank lending officer or an investment banker who are always constrained by budgets. The International Organization of Securities Commissions (IOSCO) published a *Code of Conduct Fundamentals for Rating Agencies* in December 2005, which codifies guidelines for the agencies and is designed to promote sound practices.

Policies vary from agency to agency regarding which securities they will rate. Both S&P and Moody's, for example, will rate nearly every taxable security in the U.S. market that has been registered with the SEC—whether or not that issuer has requested a rating. Agencies may also assign ratings at their own initiative, often described as unsolicited or agency-initiated ratings. Generally, such ratings represent only a small minority of the larger agencies' coverage, and the agencies maintain that such ratings are assigned on the same basis as compensated ratings. Disclosure of unsolicited ratings varies. Both Moody's and Fitch disclose agency-initiated ratings in press releases accompanying the initial rating assignment, and both have some form of regular disclosure regarding issuer participation in the rating process. S&P discloses uncompensated ratings in each press release, but does not otherwise indicate the level of issuer participation. Where ratings are either initiated by the agency, or maintained by the agency without compensation, each of the large agencies offers to meet with the issuer concerned and provides issuers with the same opportunity to appeal their ratings afforded to other issuers if they feel that factual errors have been made or material new information has not been considered.

THE RATING PROCESS

In evaluating credits issuers and obligations, the rating agencies use many of the same tools normally applied by equity analysts; but their approach is focused on a longer time horizon than short-term earnings and performance forecasts. Moody's indicates that they are looking at a variety of horizons depending on the maturity of the instruments being rated and the nature of the issuer. Equity analysts approach their work understandably from the perspective of shareholders, while the agencies are looking out for the interests of bondholders, other creditors and counterparties, and, in the case of insurance companies, policyholders. Figure 6.2 illustrates that there are a variety of approaches to debt ratings, some of which are designed to provide very sensitive short-term indicators and others, like the agency ratings, which are designed to evaluate inherent creditworthiness over the longer term.

The agencies are not uniformly transparent in the details of their ratings processes but appear to follow broadly similar approaches. For example, S&P explains that in rating an industrial bond it focuses on the following areas:

- Business risk
- Industry characteristics
- Competitive positioning
- Management

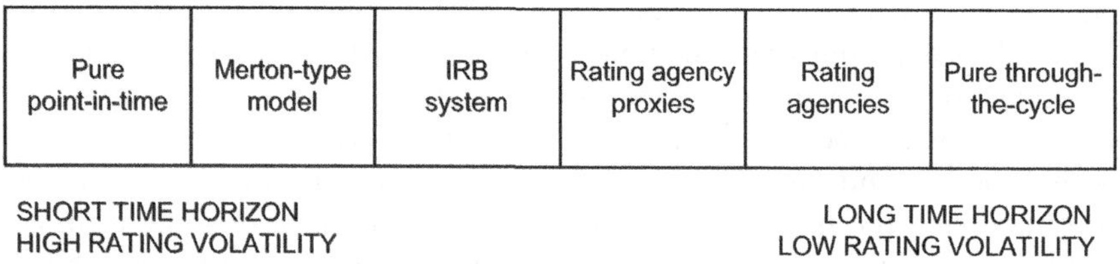

Pure point-in-time	Merton-type model	IRB system	Rating agency proxies	Rating agencies	Pure through-the-cycle

SHORT TIME HORIZON   LONG TIME HORIZON
HIGH RATING VOLATILITY   LOW RATING VOLATILITY

FIGURE 6.2 Point-in-time versus through-the-cycle credit assessments
Source: Gonzalez, et al. 2004, 17.

- Financial risk
- Financial characteristics
- Financial policies
- Profitability
- Capitalization
- Cash flow protection
- Financial flexibility

Of these characteristics, S&P claims that the industry risk—their analysis of the strength and stability of the industry in which the firm operates—probably receives the highest weight in the rating decision. Moody's has refined its approach to an industry by industry basis. At both S&P and Moody's, the industry risk analysis often sets an upper limit on the rating attainable by any firm in that industry. Similarly, internationally, ratings are normally limited to the sovereign rating ceiling of the nation in which the issuer is domiciled.

In analyzing an issuer's financial strength, Moody's and S&P computes a number of financial ratios and tracks them over time. These include measures of debt coverage, leverage, and cash flow. They both emphasize the qualitative such that, while quantification is integral to their rating analysis, it is only a part of their overall approach. While split ratings do occur between the two agencies, in the great majority of cases they agree with each other, at least to the equivalent letter if not to the notch. As shown in Table 15.5 long-term cumulative default rates between these two agencies are likewise quite similar.

With respect to sovereign ratings issued by the agencies, ratings are similar in the investment grade categories, but less so in the below investment-grade area. A comparison of differences is shown in Table 6.4. While agencies need only consider relatively finite factors in the case of corporate ratings, with sovereigns there are a host of other qualitative factors to consider such as the stability of political institutions, social and economic coherence, and integration into the world's economic system. These factors lead to the greater dispersion around quantitative estimates in sovereign ratings.

The internal rating process at the agencies is rigorous. Ratings are produced by teams of analysts, with relevant expertise, led by a senior experienced analyst who coordinates with the issuer. They review public and nonpublic documentation that can be of a varied nature—financial, contractual, technical as well the documentation relating to a specific debt issue involved.

Accounting practices and differences are reviewed and stripped away. The team meets with an issuer's management to review in depth key factors affecting the rating, including operating and financial plans and management

TABLE 6.4   Comparison of Sovereign Foreign Currency Ratings

	Share of Total		Rated Same by Moody's and Standard & Poor's
	Sovereigns Moody's (%)	Sovereigns S&P (%)	Sovereigns (%)
Broad rating categories			
AA/Aa or above	36	34	83
Other investment grade	33	32	79
Below investment grade	31	33	76

Note: The table was obtained by selecting sovereign ratings for 87 countries that are rated by both Moody's and Standard and Poor's.
Source: Credit Suisse (2007) and author compilation.

policies. The purpose of the analysis is to focus on the level and predictability of underlying cash flows. The greater the predictability and the more generous the cushion these cash flows provide, the higher the rating will be, even when exposed to testing against reasonably adverse scenarios. Once this is complete the lead analyst presents the proposed rating to the ratings committee consisting of other senior analysts in the agency. One of the purposes of these cross-group agency reviews is to ensure to the greatest extent possible that each rating category has the same meaning across the entire universe of rated entities and issuers. In other words, that an AA or Aa are of the same credit quality. Once the rating is issued, the agency establishes a surveillance procedure, one part of which is a formal annual meeting with management—who are expected to notify the agency at this meeting and, on an ongoing basis, of any material developments. Agencies reserve the right to change ratings at any time. Normally, however, prospective changes are well signaled to the issuer and to the market through each agency's publications.

The subjective elements in the rating process are desirable and necessary but they do introduce a level of unpredictability into the ratings. For the most part, the agencies have performed their roles well, although in the last 10 years there have been some headline misses with several large U.S. corporate issuers, most notably Enron Corporation and WorldCom Inc., and some Asian countries in the regional crisis of 1998–1999. They take seriously the proposition that all that glitters in an issuer's view of the future is not gold and are parsimonious in their assignment of ratings. All three agencies publish historical data comparing their ratings to the actual occurrence of defaults to allow back testing of their performance.

RATINGS PERFORMANCE

Ratings are used to communicate opinions about the creditworthiness of issuers and obligations. The rating itself contains a lot of pieces of information, including information about the probability of default and the loss severity in the event of default. The track record has been good. As Figure 6.3 demonstrates for corporate bonds, default rates are indeed consistently inversely related to credit ratings over both short and long periods of time. From 1970–2005, the one year default rate of Aaa bonds was zero but it was more than 5 percent for B-rated bonds. Likewise, for each of the given time horizons, the most abrupt increase in default probability occurred between Baa and Ba ratings—the dividing line between investment grade and noninvestment grade bonds. This distinction, in other words, makes good statistical sense.

The market place tends to corroborate the accuracy of the agencies' work. The riskier a fixed income security, the higher the yield investors will require before they buy it. As Figure 6.4 shows, bond yields are indeed closely correlated to with ratings. (Table 6.5 lists the data for this figure.) Although the actual yield differential between triple-A- and double-A-rated

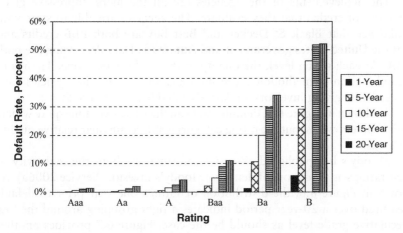

FIGURE 6.3 Corporate Default Rates Based on 1970–2005 Experience
Source: Moody's Investors Service (2005).

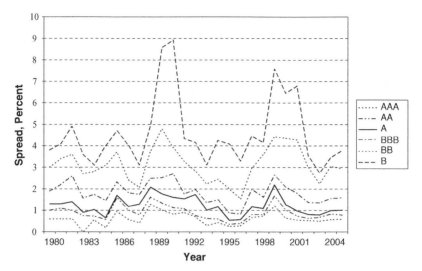

FIGURE 6.4 Bond Yield Spreads over 30-Year Treasury Bonds
Source: Bloomberg and author compilation.

bonds may vary widely over time the relationship remains constant: Investors consistently believe that triple-A-rated bonds are more secure than double-A-rated bonds.

The achievements of the agencies are all the more impressive given the types of credits that they evaluate. The agencies are able to state with confidence that Black & Decker and Best Buy are both BBB credits and that the United States government and Automatic Data Processing are both AAA. At each rating level, the quality of the credit is the same. Thanks to a combination of methodology, technology, and culture the agencies have succeeded in giving investors a relatively reliable guide to credit risk.

As shown in Figure 6.5, default rates can fluctuate over time quite widely with business cycles, but the rating categories still retain their relative quality rankings.

Moody's has published extensive information about the sensitivity of their ratings as predictors of default. (Moody's Investors Service 2006a). As shown in Figure 6.6, the distribution of ratings one year prior to default measured over a 20-year period indicates a tight grouping around the low speculative grade level as should be the case. Figure 6.7 provides another perspective on how well ratings discriminate between defaulters and nondefaulters over a similar time frame. Over 90 percent of all rated companies that have defaulted since 1983 were rated Ba3 or worse at the beginning of

TABLE 6.5 Data for Figure 6.4

Year	AAA	AA	A	BBB	BB	B
1980	0.60	1.00	1.30	1.90	3.00	3.80
1981	0.60	1.10	1.30	2.20	3.40	4.10
1982	0.60	1.00	1.40	2.60	3.60	4.90
1983	0.00	0.75	0.90	1.57	2.70	3.60
1984	0.55	0.73	1.04	1.75	2.80	3.10
1985	0.20	0.58	0.65	1.46	3.10	4.00
1986	0.95	1.59	1.70	2.33	3.70	4.70
1987	0.58	1.02	1.18	1.82	2.43	4.03
1988	0.42	0.79	1.29	1.75	2.07	3.12
1989	1.28	1.61	2.08	2.49	3.76	4.95
1990	1.02	1.34	1.77	2.52	4.78	8.57
1991	0.82	1.13	1.61	2.71	3.92	8.93
1992	0.90	1.08	1.54	1.77	3.29	4.34
1993	0.70	0.76	1.74	1.96	2.82	4.15
1994	0.29	0.62	1.01	1.37	2.23	3.12
1995	0.43	0.60	1.17	1.49	2.45	4.25
1996	0.25	0.35	0.54	0.88	2.00	4.08
1997	0.28	0.39	0.57	0.83	1.53	3.30
1998	0.67	0.81	1.17	1.99	2.97	4.46
1999	0.74	0.81	1.09	1.62	3.59	4.15
2000	1.20	1.67	2.19	2.64	4.42	7.57
2001	0.65	1.03	1.27	2.10	4.36	6.45
2002	0.55	0.75	0.98	1.81	4.28	6.79
2003	0.53	0.63	0.81	1.37	2.99	3.53
2004	0.50	0.68	0.79	1.36	2.25	2.75
2005	0.57	0.83	0.99	1.56	3.05	3.45
2006	0.59	0.78	1.01	1.59	2.94	3.79

Source: Bloomberg and author compilation.

the year in which they defaulted, and almost 80 percent of them were rated Ba3 or worse at the beginning of the fifth year before they defaulted.

Another important consideration with ratings is the extent to which they actually change within relatively short periods of time. Investors expect some movement but if the ratings are indeed long-term in nature the extent of these changes should be relatively modest. Table 6.6 shows the one year average rating transition matrix over an extended period of time. Higher ratings have generally been less likely to be revised than lower ratings over a one-year period. For example the ratings of 89 percent of the Aaa-rated issuers did not change within one year. By contrast, in the B category, only

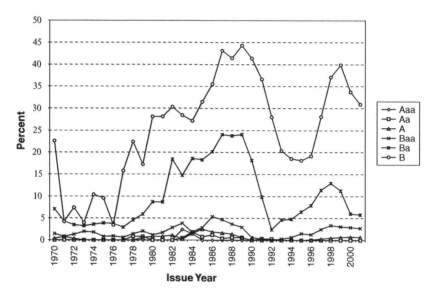

FIGURE 6.5 Trends in Five-Year Default Rates by Original Credit Rating
Source: Moody's Investors Service (2005).

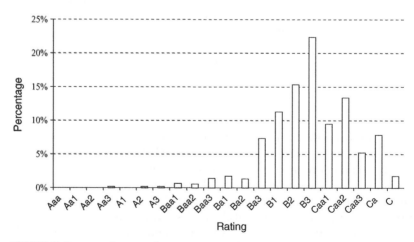

FIGURE 6.6 Distribution of Ratings One Year Prior to Default, 1983–2005
Source: Moody's Investors Service (2006).

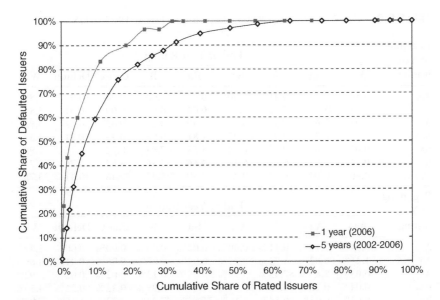

FIGURE 6.7 Cumulative Accuracy Profile: One Year vs. Five Years
Source: Moody's Investors Service (2002).

78 percent of those issuers ended the year in the same category. Also, for issuers in the middle of the ratings scale, Ba and Baa, they are almost equally as likely to move up or down a grade within a one-year time period (Moody's Investors Service 2006).

RATINGS AND REGULATORS

The relationship between regulators and ratings agencies is deep and often ambiguous. The regulators are attracted to the high quality, the independence, and very widespread acceptance of the rating agency opinions on credit quality. On the other hand, they are concerned about putting so much reliance on the agencies over whose activities they have no control. For the agencies, the use of their opinions by the regulators is an important validation of their work. Also, because the regulators only accept the ratings of a few of the agencies (the NRSROs in the United States and the so-called ECAIs under the Basel II Capital Requirements Directive), this creates an important competitive advantage.

TABLE 6.6   One-Year Average Rating Transition Matrix, 1983–2005

Beginning of Year Rating	End of Year Rating								
	Aaa	Aa	A	Baa	Ba	B	Caa-C	Default	WR
Aaa	89.54	7.14	0.41	0.00	0.02	0.00	0.00	0.00	2.89
Aa	1.25	88.82	5.72	0.25	0.04	0.02	0.00	0.01	3.89
A	0.05	2.63	87.35	5.29	0.59	0.13	0.02	0.02	3.92
Baa	0.04	0.22	4.92	83.95	4.81	0.99	0.32	0.21	4.53
Ba	0.01	0.06	0.54	6.10	75.53	7.93	0.72	1.15	7.98
B	0.01	0.05	0.16	0.41	4.66	73.56	6.63	5.76	8.75
Caa-C	0.00	0.04	0.03	0.22	0.60	5.47	59.46	10.41	23.78

Beginning of Year Rating	End of Year Rating								
	Aaa	Aa	A	Baa	Ba	B	Caa-C	Default	WR
Aaa	89.54%	7.14%	0.41%	0.00%	0.02%	0.00%	0.00%	0.00%	2.89%
Aa	1.25%	88.82%	5.72%	0.25%	0.04%	0.02%	0.00%	0.01%	3.89%
A	0.05%	2.63%	87.35%	5.29%	0.59%	0.13%	0.02%	0.02%	3.92%
Baa	0.04%	0.22%	4.92%	83.95%	4.81%	0.99%	0.32%	0.21%	4.53%
Ba	0.01%	0.06%	0.54%	6.10%	75.53%	7.93%	0.72%	1.15%	7.98%
B	0.01%	0.05%	0.16%	0.41%	4.66%	73.56%	6.63%	5.76%	8.75%
Caa-C	0.00%	0.04%	0.03%	0.22%	0.60%	5.47%	59.46%	10.41%	23.78%

Source: Moody's Investors Service (2006).

Congress passed the Credit Rating Agency Reform Act of 2006 to establish a new registration process setting a clear path to being designated an NSRO, and amending the Securities Exchange Act of 1934. The legislation also provides SEC oversight to ensure that registered rating agencies continue to issue credible and reliable ratings and to protect against conflicts of interest and misuse of nonpublic information.

As the Committee of European Banking Supervisors (CEBS) noted, "ECAI recognition for capital purposes does not in any way constitute a form of regulation of ECAIs or a form of licensing of rating agencies to do business in Europe" (CEBS 2005). The regulators do apply certain criteria as shown in Table 6.7.

In general, there are undoubted benefits from this close relationship that has been developed by the regulators with the rating agencies for the financial markets, which is really an extension of the benefits that ratings bring to the markets themselves—namely improving efficiency through providing information reliably, conveniently, and at low cost. The trust placed in the agencies is generally warranted and the agencies are acutely aware of the value of their reputation for quality and objectivity. It is far preferable

TABLE 6.7   Basel II ECAI Eligibility Criteria

Objectivity	The methodology for assigning credit assessments must be rigorous, systematic, and subject to some form of validation based on historical experience. Moreover, assessments must be subject to ongoing review and responsive to changes in financial condition. Before being recognized by supervisors, an assessment methodology for each market segment, including rigorous back testing, must have been established for at least one year and preferably three years.
Independence	An ECAI should be independent and should not be subject to political or economic pressures that may influence the rating. The assessment process should be as free as possible from any constraints that could arise in situations where the composition of the board of directors or the shareholder structure of the assessment institution may be seen as creating a conflict of interest.
International access and transparency	The individual assessments should be available to both domestic and foreign institutions with legitimate interests and at equivalent terms. In addition, the general methodology used by the ECAI should be publicly available.
Disclosure	An ECAI should disclose the following information: its assessment methodologies, including the definition of default, the time horizon, and the meaning of each rating; the actual default rates experienced in each assessment category; and the transitions of the assessments (e.g., the likelihood of AA ratings becoming A over time).
Resources	An ECAI should have sufficient resources to carry out high quality credit assessments. These resources should allow for substantial ongoing contact with senior and operational levels within the entities assessed in order to add value to the credit assessments. Such assessments should be based on methodologies combining qualitative and quantitative approaches.
Credibility	To some extent, credibility is derived from the criteria above. In addition, the reliance on an ECAI's external credit assessments by independent parties (investors, insurers, trading partners) is evidence of the credibility of the assessments of an ECAI. The credibility of an ECAI is also underpinned by the existence of internal procedures to prevent the misuse of confidential information. In order to be eligible for recognition, an ECAI does not have to assess firms in more than one country.

Source: Bank for International Settlements (2004).

that the agencies, however oligopolistic they may be, perform this role of providing creditworthiness opinions than having a government regulator try to do it. There are many complexities, however, in the rating process and by tying regulations closely into ratings there is a danger of magnifying some of these complexities. For example, even though the doors in the United States and Europe have been opened to allow further competition the top three agencies are still dominant and will remain so for the foreseeable future. Also, in the process of adopting rating levels in regulations, especially in Basel II, there is a danger of oversimplifying the ratings process and not sufficiently recognizing the magnitude of the difference between the various rating grades for purposes of capital adequacy. The treatment of split ratings (where agencies' opinions on the same issuer) differ is another similar technicality to consider. Finally, there is a tension between the Basel II assumption of essentially a cardinal scale, and the ordinal scales actually employed by the agencies. Basel II's assumption of specific percentage default rates will eventually conflict with the agencies' won assignment of ordinally ranked ratings whose actual default frequency varies widely over the cycle. Agencies with such heavy reliance on their ratings will begin to make them considerably shorter term in outlook and thereby make them much more procyclical. This could have the effect of increasing the volatility of ratings movements and hence the volatility of capital requirements at the most critical parts of the credit cycle.

EMERGING TRENDS

The more power and influence the rating agencies have acquired the more controversial they have become. By and large market participants, both issuers and investors, are satisfied with the products produced by the agencies. They understand clearly that agency opinions are not intended to be the sole source of information to be used in making credit decisions. They expect there will be transparency in the process so that it will be clear how ratings are derived and what considerations might lead to their being changed. They also expect greater forensic activity from the agencies, to dig into nonpublic information and be more active in questioning key aspects of an issuer's performance. Market participants themselves use financial data and securities prices to track issuer performance but they expect that the agencies will base their views on fundamental credit measures to give a more stable view of intrinsic financial capacity.

We can expect the regulators and lawmakers to be increasingly involved in rating agency activities, and we saw the beginnings of this trend with the Congressional hearings after the collapse of Enron. When other corporate collapses or credit crises occur we can expect there will be more enquiries of the same kind. Oftentimes these hearings are enlivened with criticisms from other rating agencies who are outside those officially recognized by regulators.

The academic community faces many obstacle in generating valuable research on ratings. The ultimate test of a rating—default—is an extremely low frequency event. The rated universes of all three agencies, while adequate for capital markets users, are extremely small in statistical terms. Even a modestly sized commercial bank will likely have more statistically robust data pools for both default frequency and loss severity. Topics for study by both academics and regulators have nonetheless included: Whether widely available market-sensitive data does as good or better a job as the agencies in predicting financial distress, the conflict of interest inherent in having issuers pay the agencies for ratings. Cases, especially in emerging markets, where financial crises were not preceded by ratings downgrades. The question remains, given the unsuitability of agency ratings to capture all elements of credit performance, bank regulators and supervisors should remain cautious about excessive reliance on these ratings for regulatory purposes.

At this writing, the U.S. credit markets are in turmoil caused by concerns over defaults and credit losses arising from lending to subprime borrowers in the housing market. Several substantial U.S. mortgage originators have filed for bankruptcy and the largest full-service mortgage lender, Countrywide, has seen its market value significantly reduced. These concerns have spread into other markets, principally Europe, and into other borrower and product areas causing severe contractions in liquidity and abrupt and significant increases in credit spreads. Structured finance portfolios have been particularly affected because subprime loans have been securitized to an unusually high degree and because subprime loans have also been mixed in with other debt types in CDOs to obtain more beneficial rating outcomes.

The rating agencies are once again in the spotlight and facing heavy criticism for the enabling role they have played in the growth of the structured finance market (Lagard 2007). As a result of the current problems, the agencies have been actively recalibrating the default and loss assumptions in their rating models as well as their correlation assumptions for different asset classes in CDOs.

The agencies are defending themselves by insisting that they have provided transparency in their rating approaches; that they have given plenty of early notice of problems; and have defended the independence of their ratings. They acknowledge issues however, particularly with the quality of the information they were using and the fact that they probably needed to heed other factors than just "pure ability to pay," most importantly liquidity (Clarkson 2007).

It is too early to say what the effects of this credit crunch will be on the agencies, but we expect it will subject them to more intensive review and criticism than either the Asian crisis or Enron and Worldcom. IOSCO announced the formation of a task force in November 2007 to examine the role of the ratings agencies in the subprime crisis and to review the adequacy of their Credit Rating Agency Code of Conduct, referred to earlier in this chapter. Its report will be published in May 2008.

Credit rating agencies are going to remain a major influence in the capital markets and, if anything, their domination will grow stronger. Even though their performance has not been without blemish it is clear that global financial markets need their essential information services. In its October 2007 Financial Stability Report, the Bank of England produced a balanced assessment of the role of the agencies. It noted their vital contributions to investors in the credit markets, principally transparency, independence, and affordability. It summarized the lessons learned so far from the market turmoil and provided the agencies with suggestions to improve the information content of their ratings. These ideas are being evaluated by the agencies and may well provide the basis for the next phase of their evolution.

REFERENCES

Bank for International Settlements (BIS). 2004, June. *Basel II: International Convergence of Capital Measurement and Capital Standards, Part 2: The First Pillar—Minimum Capital Requirements*. Basel.

Bank of England. 2007, October. Financial Stability Report Number 22. London.

Committee of European Banking Supervisors (CEBS). 2005. Consultation Paper on the recognition of External Credit Assessment Institutions, 29 June.

Clarkson, B. 2007. "Market Insight: Transparency and Trust." *Financial Times*, 17 September.

Credit Suisse. 2007. *Country Ratings*. entry.credit-suisse.ch/csfs/p/cb/en/tradefinance/landinfo/lio_laenderratings.jsp (27 December).

Gonzalez, F., F. Haas, R. Johannes, M. Persson, L. Toledo, R. Violi, M. Wieland, and C. Zins. 2004. *Market Dynamics Associated with Credit Ratings: A Literature Review*. Occasional Paper Series, No. 16. Frankfurt am Main: European Central Bank.

Klein, A. 2004. "Credit Rate's Power Leads to Abuses, Some Borrowers Say." *Washington Post*, 24 November.

Lagard, C. 2007. "Securitisation Must Lose the Excesses of Youth." *Financial Times*, 8 October.

Levich, R. M., G. Majnoni, and C. M. Reinhart, eds. 2002. *Ratings, Rating Agencies and the Global Financial System*. Norwell Mass.: Kluwer.

Moody's Investors Service. 2002, May. *Special Comment: Understanding Moody's Corporate Bond Ratings and Rating Process*. New York.

———. 2003, April. *Measuring the Performance of Corporate Bond Ratings,* New York.

———. 2006 *Exhibit taken from Moody's Default and Recovery Rates of Corporate Bond Issuers 1920–2005.* New York.

———. 2006a. *Default and Recovery Rates of Corporate Bond Issuers 1920–2005.* New York.

———. 2006b, January. *Special Comment: Default and Recovery Rates of Corporate Bond Issuers, 1920–2005.* New York.

———. 2006c. *Annual Report 2006.* New York.

———. 2007. Investor Day presentation, 5 June.

U.S. Senate. 2002. Committee on Government Affairs. *Rating the Raters: Enron and the Credit Rating Agencies,* 20 March.

Further Reading

Sandage, S. A. 2005. Chapters 4 through 6 in *Born Losers: A History of Failure in America.* Cambridge, Mass.: Harvard University Press.

CHAPTER 7

Classic Credit Analysis

*From a drop of water a logician could infer the possibility of an
Atlantic or a Niagara without having seen or heard of one or the
other. So all life is a great chain, the nature of which is known
whenever we are shown a single link of it. Like all other arts, the
Science of Deduction and Analysis is one which can only be
acquired by long and patient study; nor is life long enough to
allow any mortal to attain the highest perfection in it.*

—Sir Arthur Conan Doyle, *A Study in Scarlet*

The taking of credit risk is a fundamental function of banks. Over time
it has been the willingness of banks to take credit risk that laid the
foundations of many companies that became the great engines of American
industry. Today the role of the banks has changed and their primacy in
certain areas has diminished. For example, from the early 1990s to 2005,
U.S. banks have lost significant market share to other institutions and to
the capital markets where credit requirements are routine and borrowers
can be easily categorized (IMF 2006, 609). However, the banks remain
leaders and major participants in two general categories of lending. First,
they still uniquely provide essential liquidity facilities to large corporates,
financial institutions, financial intermediaries, and structured transactions.
Second, they are still the largest provider of credit in situations where the
capital markets are inaccessible such as small- and medium-sized business
segments, certain specialized industries (especially real estate), and project
finance. Also their role is usually critical in the resolution of difficult credit
situations, either when companies are in financial trouble or when they are
involved in bankruptcy proceedings. These are all areas where banks can
benefit from the credit expertise that they have developed over many years
and have developed into a formal approach to lending, which we call *classic*

credit analysis. Money managers and institutions that lack core credit skills and training turn to banks to supply the missing expertise. This chapter describes the salient features of the classic credit analysis methodology. Its value lies in the detailed insights that it can reveal. Its flaws are that it is expensive and can be myopic.

CREDIT ANALYSIS AS AN EXPERT SYSTEM

According to Roger Hale's *Credit Analysis: A Complete Guide,* "Credit decisions are the reflection of personal judgment about a borrower's ability to repay" (1983, vii). Classic credit analysis is an expert system that relies above all on the subjective judgment of trained professionals. Individuals are turned into experts over the course of their careers, gaining additional authority as they acquire experience and demonstrate skill. Within the hierarchy of a bank, the more senior an officer, the greater his or her decision-making delegation. Like umpires in baseball, credit officers are authorized to call them as they see them. "It is your decision, and you must feel comfortable with it according to your own judgment," Hale (1983, 215) stresses. "Credit decisions are personal. They cannot be made solely on the basis of guidelines or analytic techniques. Each lending officer must exercise common sense and good judgment."

In this system banks establish their desired target markets (consisting of industries and customers) and their underwriting criteria for lending. Analytic processing screens, which give an indication of the strength of the borrower's financial position, are preestablished based on the accumulated wisdom of the banks' experts. Similarly the types of lending products that the banks wish to provide are based on the banks' own business plans and on their risk appetites. The role of the experienced senior lender is to:

- Set up the screens regarding industries, customers, products, and the underwriting process. The senior lender understands the boundaries of what is possible and what is not in the institution's tradition.
- Focus on the most important issues in each transaction, particularly if there are exceptions to any of the screens that have been established. Typically one the most contentious issues concerns the risk rating of the borrower and of the transaction since these ratings set the parameters for the facility.
- Determine the size, terms and conditions, and pricing of the resulting credit offering. The senior lender is expected to evaluate the proposed transaction in the context of current business conditions, industry trends, and the bank's own portfolio position.

SHIFTING EMPHASIS FROM THE BALANCE SHEET TO CASH FLOW

Classic credit analysis evolved in response to fundamental changes in the banking business. Historically, the primary mission of a bank was to finance working capital and trade, and bankers generally made loans that were secured by assets or other forms of acceptable collateral. These working capital loans were frequently self-liquidating loans (through the seasonal fluctuation in the levels of inventories and receivables) and were typically made against the borrower's current assets. The pledge of these assets provided the bank with a "second way out" and protection from possible loss if the company were to run into financial difficulty. Deciding whether or not to make a loan was largely a matter of deciding whether the collateral was sufficiently valuable.

In addition, banks traditionally made loans with a term of one year or less—typically to enable their commercial customers to meet their seasonal needs. Balance sheets were carefully reviewed but income statements were largely ignored.

Over the past 50 years, there have been many changes. Banks moved beyond short-term lending to financing their customers' acquisition of fixed assets. This shift made collateralization much less relevant to the credit decision since there were generally no liquid markets into which many of these assets, such as plant and machinery, could be sold. This led the banks to focus, above all, on the cash flow from operations generated by their customers.[1] Cash flow lending replaced secured lending as the principal lending style of commercial banks. The value of a firm and its creditworthiness were estimated from the amount of cash that it generated in its business. Today, against the general backdrop of cash flow lending, we see the banks engaged in three broad types of financings. One type, asset-based lending, requires that the lender rely on the borrower's cash flow for some servicing of the debt; but full collection of principal will require liquidation of some or all of the borrower's assets. Understanding the liquidation value of these assets is the critical skill for the lender (see Chapter 8). The second type of lending, used with the financing of projects or highly leveraged companies, requires an almost total reliance by the bank on the borrower's cash flow so that the loans themselves are described as being a multiple of the annual cash flow being leveraged. For example, senior bank loans typically leverage cash flow at multiples of between two and three times. The third type of financing, unsecured general corporate lending, requires that the borrower be an investment-grade company and that the lending facility be either short term (maturity of one year or less) or medium term (three to five years) but with covenants to protect the lender.

Of course, future cash flows cannot be predicted with certainty. The greater the bank's confidence in a company's future cash flow, the more it will be willing to lend against it. A critical part of a credit officer's expertise is to make judgments about the relative risks to a company's cash flow posed by unforeseen events, both external to the company (changes in the economy, competition, suppliers, government regulations) and internal (such as production, labor, marketing or financing).

CREDIT ANALYSIS: GOD IS IN THE DETAILS

Analyzing a credit is a structured and time-intensive process. The ready availability of vast electronic data bases and desktop computer tools has made the process more streamlined and efficient; but it is the skill and experience of the analyst that determines its value. The objective of the analysis is to look at both the borrower and the lending facility being proposed and to assign a *risk rating*. The risk rating is derived by estimating the probability of default by the borrower at a given confidence level over the life of the facility, and by estimating the amount of loss that the lender would suffer in the event of default (see Chapter 9). The process consists of the following steps:

1. A banker begins by finding out why the company needs the facility.[2] Using this preliminary knowledge of the company, the banker tests this need against the bank's current policy and appetite. When the purpose of the loan is in the normal course of business this is straightforward. Greater scrutiny is required for more complex purposes, such as an acquisition or a recapitalization. If there is a tacit green signal from a senior lending officer, the analyst proceeds through the next steps.
2. The company's balance sheet and profit and loss statements are reviewed to highlight period-to-period trends and any volatility in its business. A company's business segment level operating results, budgets, and business plans are also helpful in gaining a perspective on its profit dynamics both in terms of historical results and on a pro forma basis over the life of the proposed facility. The analyst needs a clear understanding of how a company adds value in deriving its profits. Many companies have a portfolio of activities which are in different stages of their life cycles and have different cash flow profiles.
3. Accounting conventions used by the borrower are adjusted to bring them into conformity with the standard format used by the lender. Accounting principles are analyzed to ensure they are consistent. In larger corporate groups it is often helpful to review both the consolidated and consolidating statements.

4. Once the historical performance of the borrower is well understood, the projected profit and loss, balance sheet, and cash flow statements are evaluated. The assumptions underlying these are tested to produce best case and worst case estimates. These estimates are compared against the financial requirements to service the additional debt.

5. For publicly traded companies, there are frequently extensive equity analyst reports available as well as price histories giving the historical market capitalization of the firm. For private firms, estimates should be made of the enterprise value of the company that provides a guide of both the value drivers of the business and the value cushion that may be available to the lender.

6. In addition to the microeconomic analysis of the firm, the analyst needs to review the competitive position of the borrower within its industry and the macroeconomic forces that affect the performance of the industry as a whole. This will improve the testing of the assumptions made by the borrower and provide insight into where the industry is in the business cycle.

7. The capabilities and integrity of the company's executive management need to be evaluated together with their strategy. Do they have the managerial, financial, human and physical resources to achieve their plans? In this context visiting the company's facilities, reviewing the company's reputation with suppliers and customers and understanding the underlying physical flows in the business are all valuable.

8. Once the basic financial analysis is complete the banker needs to prepare and negotiate the documentation for the facility including all terms and conditions, the pricing, the security, the covenants, the conditions precedent to drawdown, the triggers for default and other credit enhancements as available such as guarantees or negative pledges. These are important. Relatively few loans are made which are uncollectible at the outset. Most borrowers who get into trouble do so over a period of time and if the bank has structured its facility tightly it will be much better able to protect itself.

A flow chart is presented in Figure 7.1.

One universal assumption in the traditional credit process is that credit officers should examine the evidence as if they were a detective, questioning the information the borrower has supplied, looking for possible weaknesses or inaccuracies in the story, and trying to anticipate problems that might occur in the future. Sherlock Holmes would have made a good lending officer.

In reaching their subjective judgments, credit officers are assisted by a number of standard analytic techniques for evaluating the likelihood that a borrower will meet a given debt obligation. The classic three Cs of

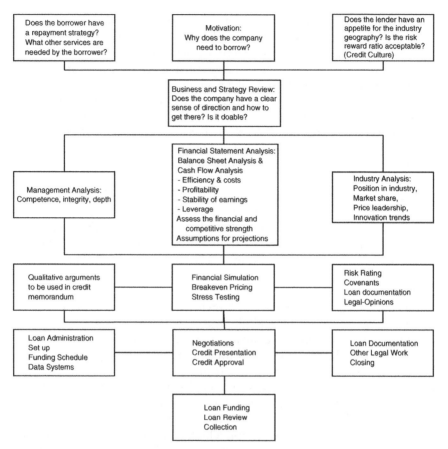

FIGURE 7.1 Credit Analysis Process Flow

credit—*character, cash flow,* and *collateral*—were and are the three essential elements of the credit decision.

FINANCIAL RATIOS: FOOTPRINTS IN THE SAND

Bankers are trained in the details of cash flow and ratio analysis that are basic tools of the trade, required not just for lending but for investing decisions of all kinds. Ratio analysis of some kind dates back to the beginnings of early business dealing. In modern times, in the United States, one of the early pioneers was Robert Morris Associates (now the Risk Management Association or RMA) whose Alexander Wall and Raymond Duning, in

1928, published *Ratio Analysis of Financial Statements*. RMA still produces an annual study of corporate and industry ratios that are widely used by U.S. banks. For publicly traded U.S. corporations, there are other publicly available sources with extensive ratio analysis already prepared.

One of the best known and useful ratios is the Du Pont formula using *return on investment* (ROE), expressed as

$$\text{ROE} = \text{Net profit after taxes} / \text{Total assets}$$

$$= \text{Net profit after taxes} / \text{Sales} \times \text{Sales} / \text{Total assets}$$

In Table 7.1 there is a small sampling of other basic ratios typically reviewed by lenders.

TABLE 7.1 Commonly Used Financial Ratios

Category	Ratio
Operating performance	EBITDA/Sales
	Net income/sales
	Effective tax rate
	Net income/Net worth
	Net income/Total assets
	Sales/Fixed assets
Debt service coverage	EBITDA/Interest
	Free cash flow – Capital expenditure/Interest
	Free cash flow – Capital expenditure – Dividends/Interest
Financial leverage	Long-term debt/Capitalization
	Long-term debt/Tangible net worth
	Total liabilities/Tangible net worth (Total liabilities – Long-term capital)/(Long-term capital)
	Long-term capital = Total net worth + Preferred + Subordinated debt
	Current liabilities/Tangible net worth
Liquidity	Current ratio
	Quick ratio
	Inventory to net sales
	Inventory to net working capital
	Current debt to inventory
	Raw material, work in process and finished goods as percentages of total inventory
Receivables	Aging of receivables: 30, 60, 90, 90+ days
	Average collection period

Ratios for each firm are used to review operating performance and profitability, cash flow, leverage, and liquidity. Each ratio imparts information on both an absolute and comparative basis. A company's return on sales and return on equity, for example, provides information about different dimensions of its profitability. Its debt service coverage is a measure of its ability to pay the interest cost on its borrowed funds. Its current ratio is a measure of its liquidity. Companies can be compared to each other and to industry averages. Most industries have specific ratios that provide particular insight to drivers of performance such as passenger load factors for airlines, or purchased power to revenues for utilities.

In addition to the ratios that can be calculated from the financial statements of publicly traded companies, there is a wealth of information available to analysts from the prices of publicly traded debt and equity instruments from which ratios can also be calculated. This market-derived data is much more sensitive than accounting data, fresher, and often more revealing.

Few analytical terms are more widely used and at the same time more widely misunderstood than the term *cash flow*. Properly speaking, this refers to cash flows from operations that include cash receipts and cash disbursements as well as changes in balance sheet items. A simplified and commonly used indicator of cash flow for a company is to look at EBITDA (earnings before interest, taxes, depreciation and amortization). Bankers use these numbers cautiously because they do not fully capture all the cash flow from operations. Pamela M. Stumpp (2000), Senior Vice President of the Corporate Finance Group at Moody's Investors Service, warned about 10 critical failings in using EBITDA. Among the points she made were the following:

- EBITDA ignores changes in working capital.
- EBITDA can be a misleading measure of liquidity.
- EBITDA does not consider the amount of required reinvestment—especially for companies with short-lived assets.
- EBITDA says nothing about the quality of earnings.
- EBITDA is an inadequate standalone measure for comparing acquisition multiples, and because it fails to distinguish revenues from cash it ignores distinctions in the quality of cash flow resulting from different accounting policies.

INDUSTRY ANALYSIS FOR TERM LENDING

In addition to the particular information available from the firm's financial ratios and historical performance, credit analysis relies heavily on a comparative view of the industry in which the company competes. Undertaking a *strategic analysis,* as it is sometimes called, goes beyond the balance sheet and ratios and cash flow analysis. According to Joseph Rizzi (1984, 4):

> *Strategic analysis concerns the assessment of a firm's long-term prospects within its industrial environment. The analysis is based on three premises. First that a firm must achieve a competitive advantage to remain profitable. Second, the ways and means of achieving a competitive advantage vary by industry. Finally, as industries evolve, the ways of achieving competitive advantage change. The analysis involves three steps: environmental assessment, firm assessment and strategy evaluation.*

Each industry has its own unique structure and dynamics. A firm's position is affected by the relative position of the industry in its life cycle. A mature industry, for example, is characterized by market saturation, lack of technological opportunity and a trend toward a competitive floor rate of return.

A firm attempting to prosper within any industry has to contend with the five forces of potential entrants, existing rivals, suppliers, buyers, and substitute products. Its competitive weapons may include barriers to entry, cost control through economies of scale, control of distribution channels, favorable government policies, retaliatory pricing (actual or threatened), product differentiation, and product innovation.[3] In evaluating a company's current and evolving position the analyst must understand how it intends to make use of its competitive tools in the context of its industry, bearing in mind that "the first fundamental determinant of a firm's profitability is industry attractiveness" (Porter 1985, 4). He or she must make judgments about whether their strategies will succeed, to what extent the strategy should be supported, which variables should be monitored and what the fall back position should be. These are personal decisions and the banker is expected to be able to articulate and defend them.

It is important to the banker to be able to meet with and hear directly from the senior management of the borrowers. When the exposures become large and complex these meetings take place at very senior levels in the bank.

In large regional and national banking companies, it is common for the teams of bankers to be organized first of all by the size of the customers, usually described in terms of sales volumes. These large companies are then subdivided into industry groupings and provided with the full range of financial services offered by that bank. Separately specialized industries are identified which are usually capital intensive (for example utilities, transportation and real estate groups) where the bankers can offer more tailored services. Companies in these groupings are each analyzed in the context of their industries so that unique factors relating to regulations, accounting conventions, or competitive issues can be fully taken into account. From a top-down industry perspective, it is much easier to spot the key trends, the competitive issues, and likely winners and losers than it is from the bottom up using only a firm by firm approach.

CLASSIC CREDIT FOUNDATIONS REMAIN BUT BANKING PRACTICES HAVE MOVED AHEAD

The principles of the classic credit analysis approach remain in place in lending institutions. Banks still actively employ both the principles and practices in their small- and middle-market business banking segments. Elsewhere, in the large customer segments, the practices have been irrevocably altered. The forces of change have been driven by economics and by effectiveness. Economically, the banks have been dramatically affected by disintermediation. Competitor organizations, principally through accessing the capital markets, have been able to provide debt capital at much lower prices and have commoditized the lending product. These competitors have innovated with analytical techniques, documentation and sales and trading and this has broadened and deepened the investor base for loans beyond the banks themselves. Squeezed by pricing reductions the banks have had to respond by abbreviating the intensity of their underwriting activities and reducing their costs to match the reduced revenues. In the process, the quality of the bankers has declined along with their training and their numbers. The second issue with classic credit analysis is in its effectiveness. No matter how skilled the experts and the range of their skills some misjudgments will be made. This means inevitably that some risks will be misjudged and mispriced, and that excessively large exposures may be permitted. Compounding the effectiveness problem are factors relating to the quality of the financial information used, which is often outdated, and the quality of the customers available. All other factors being equal borrowers will tend not to deal with the banks because cheaper fund raising alternatives are available. Portfolio concentrations are hard to avoid. These issues are not apparent during much of the business cycle, but under stress they can cause very severe problems. Concentration risks are generally addressed by limiting the size of the exposure to individual borrowers, although banks occasionally continue to set these limits too high. A more difficult risk to manage is where the financial health of groups of borrowers are positively correlated. U.S.

banking history from the 1970s, 1980s, and 1990s is filled with the collapse of large successful banks that were fatally affected by credit problems caused by these correlations in severe economic downturns. The correlation categories cover specific industries (real estate, shipping, oil and gas), specific regions (New England, Texas), or whole countries as with those affecting LDCs.

As we will see, banking practices have moved ahead such that in the most recent U.S. economic slowdown from 2002–2004 despite severe stresses in a number of major industries the banking industry suffered a noticeable increase in nonperforming loans and losses, but well within its capacity to absorb these from its earnings and reserves.

YOU CAN HAVE YOUR CAKE BUT ONLY A SLICE OF IT

Not surprisingly, many commercial banks have adapted their business lending models and initiated their own intermediation activities. In breaking down the value chain of the services provided, they focus on the origination and packaging of credit offerings and earning arrangement fees and not just interest income from carrying these assets. Instead of booking loans, they create exclusively on their own balance sheets, they widely syndicate, securitize, hedge and trade credit exposures all of which provide their own revenue streams. The creation of an open marketplace for bank loans has benefits for all the participants, be they the original borrower or the new population of nonbank investors. The information conveyed in the price of loan assets in the secondary market is a valuable new addition to the traditional financial data available.

Classic credit analysis is an essential skill for these fundamental activities of originating and trading credit. The expert system developed by banks, adapted to borrow from the new technologies available, is a very good one for selecting risks. The standards that must be applied in originating assets for a third party are as high or higher than those that the bank applied when they intended to retain the assets themselves. Any bank that hopes to engage in selling assets they originate in any volume must develop a reputation as a skillful lender. Federal Reserve Governor Susan Phillips (1996, 13) points out:

That banks can originate and securitize enables them to more fully exploit their special expertise in analyzing the creditworthiness of borrowers. Credit analysis, the intermediation function that banks have traditionally performed so well, can sometimes be difficult for the capital markets. By eliminating the need to provide the financing for all of its loans, securitization enables banks to apply their credit analysis expertise on many more loans. This can boost earnings and lower the cost of accumulating capital.

The ultimate suppliers of debt capital will insist that credit analysis, whether classic or any other kind, take place *somewhere*. The key for banks is to perform this function well and to be adequately paid for it. Thus far we have described the institutional settings in which credit risk is analyzed. In recent decades innovations have altered the classic credit process in two fundamental ways. With respect to transactions, the development of asset-based lending has paved the way for the emergence of structured finance and securitizations. With respect to the process of credit management, a series of advances have been made in the quantification of credit risk as we discuss in later chapters. These range all the way from the credit scoring models used in consumer lending to the sophisticated market value based credit risk models and portfolio models that are used in the corporate lending segment.

It was long believed that credit risk management was an *art*. New techniques have more the look and feel of *science*. As we shall see they still lack the precision and certainty that this term implies. Perhaps at this stage in its development, credit risk management can best be described as a form of *engineering,* where models and structures are created that either prevent financial failure or else provide safeguards against it.

REFERENCES

Boyadjian, H. J., and J. F. Warren. 1987. *Risks: Reading Corporate Signals.* New York: John Wiley & Sons.

Hale, R. 1983. *Credit Analysis: A Complete Guide.* New York: John Wiley & Sons.

International Monetary Fund (IMF). 2006. *IMF International Financial Statistics Yearbook 2006.* Washington, D.C.

Mayer, M. 1974. *The Bankers.* New York: Weybright and Talley.

Phillips, S. M. 1996. "The Place of Securitization in the Financial System: Implications for Banking and Monetary Policy." In *A Primer on Securitization*, edited by L. T. Kendall and M. J. Fishman. Cambridge, Mass.: MIT Press.

Porter, M. E. 1985. *Competitive Advantage: Creating and Sustaining Superior Performance.* New York: Free Press.

Rizzi, J. 1984. "Strategic Analysis; The Neglected Element in the Term Credit Decision." *Journal of Commercial Lending* 66, no. 11 .

Stummp, P. M. 2000, June. *Putting EBITDA in Perspective*. New York: Moody's Investors Service.
Wall, A., and R. Duning. 1928. *Ratio Analysis of Financial Statements*. New York: Harper.

Further Reading

Ganguin, B. 2005. *Standard & Poor's Fundamentals of Corporate Credit Analysis*. New York: Standard & Poor's.
deSevigny, A., and O. Renault. 2005. *Standard & Poor's Guide Measuring Credit Risk*. New York: Standard & Poor's.

CHAPTER 8

Asset-Based Lending and Lease Finance

Simply put, asset-based lending may be looked at as no more than account receivable, inventory or equipment lending but with a much more due-diligence approach on the bank's part to set up proper lending and monitoring programs depending on the collateral. Therefore, I feel such loan secured by most balance sheet assets should fall into the generic category of asset-based lending. But many lenders have broadened or strictly used the asset-based term to include a more exotic and high-risk type of loan such as those perhaps involving higher-leveraged borrowers or borrowers who may have assumed ownership of a company by way of a leveraged buyout by putting little or no equity in the deal.

—Peter S. Clarke (1996, 6)

Lending against collateral is hardly a new phenomenon. British moneylenders introduced the concept of a mortgage in the seventeeth century to better secure debts by conveying the land in *fee simple* to the lender subject to a *subsequent condition*. A significant innovation over the *pledge,* by which the lender took possession of the land, the mortgage permitted the borrower the continued use of the asset; the fee simple was reconveyed upon the redemption of debt. Over the centuries, bankers have advanced money to farmers against the collateral of their land, livestock, and equipment; to railroads against the collateral of their rolling stock; and to oil companies against the collateral of their petroleum reserves. Indeed, bankers have long debated whether they should focus more attention on the value of a borrower's collateral or on the strength of its business enterprise as a whole.

Over the past five decades, however, the rapid spread of asset-based lending has given new life to the concept of collateral. Modern asset-based lending is founded on the notion that a company's assets (e.g., its receivables, equipment, lease revenues, or inventory) can have a substantial life of their own independent of the company itself. The technology of asset-based lending is important in its own right, but it is also significant because of its critical contribution to the success of asset-securitization and structured finance.

Asset-based borrowing has exploded in response to fundamental shifts in the U.S. economy. Earlier in this century, a considerable number of small and midsized business enterprises could still be financed within the scope of the wealth their founders had amassed—sometimes with assistance from family and friends. Leverage was unnecessary. In today's much larger economy, however, businesses must achieve much greater critical mass in order to succeed. Firms have grown so large that their financing needs can be met only through a pooling of resources. Relatively few individuals are wealthy enough to finance an enterprise of any size entirely on their own. According to one estimate, only 11.7 percent of U.S. firms with external capital needs exceeding $1 billion could be funded, without pooling, with the wealth of single U.S. families (Sirri and Tufano 1995, 91). Today, credit is as critical to the growth of a business as water is to the growth of a garden. Many companies, however, do not qualify for unsecured loans.

Starting in the 1950s, commercial finance companies became an increasingly important source of funding for American businesses. In the early days, these companies invented the concept of warehouse financing. Before the creation of the Uniform Commercial Code in 1952, there was no standardized way to place a lien on a company's inventory, equipment, or finished goods. Physical possession of an asset was therefore the key to controlling it. To obtain warehouse financing, a manufacturer would physically move an asset into the lender's warehouse and then receive a receipt. Once the receipt was presented to the finance company, the latter would make a loan collateralized by the asset. The establishment of the Uniform Commercial Code made it possible to put a lien on any kind of property. As a result, warehouse financing of this kind became less necessary. (Of course, filing a lien does not give the lender as much control over the collateral as physical possession, as some companies learned at great cost.)

The Uniform Commercial Code is a common set of regulations that were passed by Pennsylvania in 1953 and subsequently enacted by all the other states (with the exception of Louisiana). Its aim was to simplify, clarify, and modernize the law governing commercial transactions. Making the law uniform among various jurisdictions facilitated the continued expansion of commercial practices through custom, usage and the agreement of parties. The security agreement, perfection of security interest, priorities of proceeds, rights of lien creditors, including trustee in bankruptcy, are some of the important elements of the code that are applicable to all secured commercial transactions (Henson 1979).

Despite the waning of warehouse financing, commercial finance companies continued to grow because they provided a vital service to small- and midsized enterprises—especially those that were growing rapidly. These borrowers were able to finance themselves in return for a pledge of their receivables or inventory. Finance companies would determine how much the assets were worth and then lend at some loan-to-value ratio. They paid less attention to the quality of the enterprise than to the quality of the assets. Typically, these lenders focused on higher-risk customers who may have had few, if any, alternative sources of financing. They were able to charge these customers substantially more than the banks were charging.

In the 1970s and 1980s, many banks discovered that the commercial finance companies had invented an attractive business. The loans on their books performed as well as or better than the banks' own loan portfolios, and they also paid higher spreads. Many commercial banks therefore decided to enter the asset-based lending business—either by acquiring existing players or by establishing their own organizations. Since asset-based lending was a more bare-knuckled business than the typical work of a banker, it was normally housed in a separate subsidiary rather than in the bank proper.

Competition heated up as more and more regional and money-center banks were drawn to asset-based lending. As spreads began to decline, lenders were forced to improve their risk-management techniques in order to remain profitable.

MANAGING THE RISKS

Asset-based loans include additional risk considerations when compared to unsecured loans. Asset-based lending exposes a lender to at least four different types of risks:

A secured loan, like an unsecured one, subjects the lender to credit risk. As Clarke (1996, 15) notes:

> *The nature of the collateral being offered does not alleviate the need for a thorough investigation of the integrity, moral character, debt-paying habits, and ability of the proposed borrower. Next to unsecured credit lending, which does not involve collateral, no other type of loan is as dependent on the honesty and integrity of the borrower. Just having an assignment of the collateral is not a substitute for the absence of any of the above factors.*

The second type of risk is collateral risk. Should the firm prove unable to generate cash to repay the loan, quality collateral will be of the utmost importance. Asset-based lenders investigate whether receivables are collectible, inventory is obsolete, inventory controls are adequate, and so forth.

Collateral illiquidity is the third type of risk. If the lender must liquidate or foreclose on collateral, the necessary time and costs may detract from the ultimate returns. The longer it takes to liquidate assets, the more expensive the process is likely to become because of the increased administrative costs and the difficulties associated with consummating a distressed sale.

The fourth type of risk is legal risk. Asset-based financing requires complex documentation, public filings, strict compliance with the Uniform Commercial Code, and certain borrower impositions. As a result, costly legal mistakes are easy to make. There are hundreds of cases in which secured lenders attempted to liquidate collateral and collect the proceeds only to be enjoined by courts of law, particularly bankruptcy courts, owing to inadequate legal documentation, or mismanagement of the loan facility (Stock 1988, 17).

To manage these risks, asset-based lenders have developed a great deal of expertise in the valuation of collateral. When a loan is backed by trade receivables, for example, they must deal with the issue of dilution. Not every receivable a company books is ultimately paid. Some losses occur because the buyer is unable to pay. Dilution also occurs when the buyer is no longer required to pay because the goods have been returned or because they have spoiled. Department stores, for example, know what proportion of goods is likely to be returned at different seasons of the year. Asset-based lenders take this into account by adjusting their loan-to-value ratios. A lender who would ordinarily be willing to finance receivables at 80 cents on the dollar at most times of the year might drop down to 60 cents on the dollar in the period just after Christmas, when returns are especially high.

A company that makes cookies can anticipate a certain level of returns from supermarkets because of spoilage. This is a mature business with a long history, and asset-based lenders can readily establish an appropriate loan-to-value ratio. A company that makes cigarettes, on the other hand, would probably be accorded a higher loan-to-value ratio because cigarettes are less perishable and are sold through small distributors who are required to pay their bills promptly. Receivables are more valuable when they turn over rapidly and when the company can exercise a high level of control over them.

Because asset-based lenders normally deduct expected dilution and losses, they almost always lend at a discount to the actual amount of receivables being financed. A loan-to-value ratio of 80 percent to 85 percent is considered normal.

When assets are illiquid or hard to value, it is more difficult to finance against them. A company's inventory, for example, is generally more difficult to value, monitor, and liquidate than its accounts receivable, which are fungible. Automobiles or other commodity-like inventories may be relatively easy to deal with. But suppose—that a company is manufactures speedometers under contract to an automaker. If the company itself cannot sell its inventory, then how can a lender expect to do so? Lending against inventory requires a substantial amount of industry-specific knowledge.

Exposure on inventory is approached by gaining knowledge of the following (Iannuccilli 1988, 63–64):

- Product and industry
- Stability and perishability of the product
- Supply and demand considerations
- Obsolescence and style considerations
- Trade creditor's posture to acceptance of an inventory lien
- Priority liens
- Secret liens
- Effect of private label merchandise
- Whether or not the product is bought or manufactured for shelf (speculation) or against firm orders

Lending against a company's plant and equipment likewise requires a considerable amount of additional analysis. Typically, such loans are structured as term loans based on the liquidation value the assets would have in a forced sale. An objective professional appraisal by a reliable firm is normally a key element in the decision to lend. Methods have been developed to determine, for example, what an aircraft with a 20-year life might be worth 15 years hence. Residual value insurance companies, which specialize in making such predictions, may help to facilitate an equipment financing. In valuing receivables, by contrast, a lender simply needs to know how they develop and what dilution to anticipate.

Over time, asset-based lenders have accumulated an enormous body of knowledge about seasonal buildups, trading and cash cycles, working capital and inventory ratios, cyclical production patterns, and the development of losses and dilution in various industries. At the same time, borrowers have learned how to organize their affairs so that they can borrow more money against their collateral. The better their record keeping and administration is, the more comfortable a banker will feel about accepting their assumptions. Lending on a revolving basis against collateral requires constant policing and monitoring of collateral by the lender: loan documentation, collateral reports, accounting, cash flow reports, warehouse reports, and UCC filings are required to control and manage the credit risk.

GROWING RESPECTABILITY

In its early days, asset-based lending was clearly regarded by the mainstream financial world as something that took place on the other side of the tracks. Asset-based borrowers were assumed to be desperate companies not terribly far from bankruptcy court, and asset-based lenders were viewed as little better than loan sharks. All this has changed. As long ago as 1982, John B. Logan (1988, 45), a senior vice president at Barnett Bank in Florida, asserted:

> *First, let's talk about what asset-based lending is not. It is not lending of last resort. I am sure that from time to time we have all heard that if a company has pledged its accounts receivable or inventories for loan purposes, the company must be in serious financial difficulty of some form or another and is using a last ditch effort to raise quick cash. As one who has been involved in the asset-based lending business for the last 11 years, I can assure you this is just not so.*

In the years since 1982, the respectability of asset-based lending has only increased. A company that finances its receivables is no longer stigmatized for doing so. As the costs of asset-based lending have come down, many financial professionals have come to view it as a perfectly acceptable financing alternative that may make good sense for their company under the right circumstances. Two decades ago, a company with a choice between secured and unsecured borrowing would invariable choose the latter because it was less expensive and less complicated. Today, the choice may not be so obvious. An asset-based financing is still more complicated, but it may in fact be cheaper than an unsecured loan. Furthermore, banks today are less interested in making unsecured loans at low spreads to companies that have other alternatives. In deciding between a secured and unsecured loan, a borrower today must make a cost/benefit judgment. And outside observers can no longer assume that a company that finances its receivables is either a first-time borrower or a fallen angel. Rather, they may conclude that such a borrower is a savvy player that knows how to make good use of its assets.

ALTERNATIVES TO ASSET-BASED LENDING

Factoring and credit insurance are two alternative approaches that are closely related to asset-based lending. Factors, which are generally finance companies or bank subsidiaries, are in the business of purchasing receivables rather than of lending against them. In essence, factoring is asset-based lending plus administration. A factor values receivables by subtracting expected losses and the cost of carry from their face value. Historically, factoring has been most important in the apparel industry, where business is highly seasonal, and where fashion-oriented executives in smaller companies have been eager to let someone else take over the hassles and risks of collecting receivables. As companies grow larger, however, they often become less satisfied with factoring because it effectively gives an outside party the power to decide who their customers should be. For this reason, at a certain point in their development, many companies decide to bring the collection of their accounts receivable in house.

A conservative company that wants to monetize its receivables can also purchase credit insurance, which provides protection against the risk that a customer will become bankrupt. While credit insurance is gradually gaining acceptance in the United States, it plays a very important role in Europe, where companies do a great deal of cross-border business with customers they do not know well. In an environment where banks may have little knowledge of companies beyond their own locality and where credit bureaus do not exist, credit insurers provide a very valuable service. They maintain huge databases on companies in many different countries, and they greatly facilitate cross-border trade. Some credit insurers also rely on credit bureaus such as Dun & Bradstreet, which has common-format databases in many countries and alliances with local data providers.

LEASE FINANCE

Lease financing is another vehicle used by companies that have relatively limited access to capital and need, in effect, to borrow on a secured basis. There are two types of leases: capital and operating. Capital (or financial) leases are used by companies to finance long-lived assets instead of resorting to long-term borrowing for acquiring these assets. Operating leases, on the other hand, are shorter-term leases, where the life of the asset being leased is much longer than the lease term (as for example, in the case of aircraft leases). In the case of operating leases, the lessee does not assume the risk of ownership, and the lease expense is treated as an operating expense in the income statement. The operating lease does not affect the balance sheet. In a capital lease, the lessee assumes some of the risks of ownership and enjoys some of the benefits such as depreciation. Companies prefer to treat all leases as operating leases so that their effect is shown in expenses. Capital leases, as the name implies, have to be capitalized on the balance sheet thus revealing the true (and magnified) leverage of the company. For this reason there are strict accounting rules for the classification of a lease as either an operating or a capital lease.

For the lessor, the credit risk involved in the transaction, just as in asset-backed lending, is dependent on the type of business, the lease type and collateral. The essentiality of the equipment being leased for the lessees' operation is a critical element. If the equipment is essential it is a good risk because, even in a bankruptcy, the court may permit the payments to be made on the lease since that is vital to the reorganization and emergence from bankruptcy. Other considerations are the risk of obsolescence/salvage value if the equipment has to be repossessed and re-leased, the costs of repossession, storage and marketing to a new customer. The credit exposure to the lessee is the "replacement cost" of the lease: If the market interest rates, and equipment demand have moved such that the lease rate on new leases is lower than the original lease rate, then if the equipment is repossessed and re-leased, the lessor would get a lower rent than before for the remaining term of the lease. The difference between the initial and current lease rates and repossession/remarketing costs constitute the credit exposure to the lessor.

Leasing companies exist for a wide range of industrial equipment, rolling stock and aircraft and provide an important source of financing in the credit markets.

THE ROOTS OF SECURITIZATION AND LBOs

Asset-backed securities are simply the capital-markets version of asset-based finance, and the same techniques developed by asset-based lenders for evaluating assets and companies have been appropriated by securitization teams. The capital markets require greater precision in the application of these techniques than do the banks because the securities created must be analyzed by the rating agencies and then distributed to investors. Nonetheless, the same fundamental concepts are applied in both markets. In addition, there are times when specific transactions move to the capital markets from asset-based lenders because they are very large or because securitization leads to a lower cost structure. The overlap between these two markets remains very strong.

Asset-based lending methodology also spawned the LBO (leveraged buy-out) market. During the 1980s, financial professionals recognized that a technique developed for growing companies could also be applied to companies that had deliberately been leveraged. And if a small company could borrow on the basis of its assets, then why not a large one?

A company such as CIT Equipment Finance might be able to borrow billions of dollars on an unsecured basis, but it could borrow even more on the strength of its assets. By pledging a company's assets as collateral, acquirers were able to borrow a major share of the money needed to purchase it. Asset-based finance techniques—whether executed in the capital markets or through the syndicated bank market—accessed the untapped borrowing power inherent in the target company's receivables and other assets.

FAVORABLE RESULTS

Asset-based lenders have tended to view their business as a risky one, and they have managed it accordingly—underwriting their loans carefully and monitoring them closely. They have also been quite aggressive in realizing the value of their collateral. They focus on the assets rather than on their relationship with the borrower. They may be willing to negotiate with a borrower because they prefer not to own the collateral, but they are less likely than typical bankers to show much forbearance. As a result, their performance has generally been good.

REFERENCES

Clarke, P. S. 1996. *Asset-Based Lending: The Complete Guide to Originating, Evaluating, and Managing Asset-based Loans, Leasing and Factoring.* Chicago: Irwin Professional Publishing.

Henson, R. D. 1979. *Secured Transactions*, 2nd ed. St. Paul, Minn.: West.

Logan, J. B. 1988. "Clearing Up the Confusion About Asset-Based Lending." In *Asset-Based Lending: A Special Collection from the Journal of Commercial Bank Lending*, edited by C. Weisman. Philadelphia: Robert Morris Associates.

Iannuccilli, J. 1988. "Asset-Based Lending: An Overview." In *Asset-Based Lending: A Special Collection from the Journal of Commercial Bank Lending*, edited by C. Weisman. Philadelphia: Robert Morris Associates.

Stock, K. 1988. "Asset-Based Financing: Borrower and Lender Perspectives." In *Asset-Based Lending: A Special Collection from the Journal of Commercial Bank Lending*, edited by C. Weisman. Philadelphia: Robert Morris Associates.

Sirri, E. R., and P. Tufano, 1995. "The Economics of Pooling." In *The Global Financial System*. Boston: Harvard University Press.

Weisman, C. (ed.). 1988. *Asset-Based Lending: A Special Collection from the Journal of Commercial Bank Lending*. Philadelphia: Robert Morris Associates.

CHAPTER 9

Introduction to Credit Risk Models

The grand aim of all science is to cover the greatest number of empirical facts by logical deduction from the smallest number of hypotheses or axioms.

—Albert Einstein

The previous chapters were concerned with the institutions that manage credit risk and the techniques that they have traditionally employed. We now turn our attention to techniques that have evolved over the last 20 years. These innovations were prompted by a number of secular forces (see also McKinsey 1993), including:

- Deregulation, which has stimulated financial innovation and enabled new entrants to provide services.
- The broadening of the credit markets to encompass new borrowing sectors, both domestically and internationally.
- A continuing shift from balance sheet lending to cash flow lending.
- An increase in off-balance-sheet risks.
- Shrinking margins on loans, which have forced banks to explore less costly ways of measuring and managing credit risk.
- Securitization, which has prompted the development of more efficient (and standardized) credit risk tools.
- Advances in finance theory, which have provided new ways of looking at credit risk.
- Development of over-the-counter credit derivative markets
- Regulatory reform including Basel II for banks and Solvency II for insurance companies.

Tools from statistics and operations research—such as survival analysis, neural networks, mathematical programming, deterministic and probabilistic simulation, stochastic calculus, and game theory—have all contributed to the progress in credit risk measurement. So, too, have advances in our understanding of financial markets, such as arbitrage pricing theory, option pricing theory, and the capital asset pricing model (CAPM). The new tools for measuring credit risk have been applied to a wide range of financial products—consumer loans, residential real estate loans, commercial real estate loans, and commercial loans, as well as swaps, credit derivatives, and other off-balance-sheet products. Notwithstanding all this progress, we should point out that these models are more in the nature of "pioneering" efforts seeking better solutions and not the culmination of the search. Some of the results of these efforts may fall away completely, but most will continue on as pieces of models yet to be constructed. All of these are bridges to the future. In this chapter, we provide an overview of credit models and their areas of application.

MODELS—WHO NEEDS THEM?

Classical economists characterize capital as the *produced means of production,* by which they mean that capital represents the accumulation of wealth generated from the use of labor and land—the two other factors of production. Financial models represent mental labor and capital, and they may be regarded as the *produced means of problem solving.* They represent, in other words, an accumulation of human insight, experience and experiment that can be applied to explaining the way that people behave or that things work. Representing a phenomenon by a model greatly facilitates understanding it and, eventually, exploiting it. Models for measuring credit risk are no exception. The question that a credit model seeks to answer, directly or indirectly, is this: Given our past experience and our assumptions about the future, what is the value of a given loan or fixed income security? Equivalently, what is the (quantifiable) risk that the promised cash flows will not be forthcoming?

Models are often constructed on the basis of theories. The theory of options, for example, might suggest an approach to measuring credit risk. It might be possible to assess the riskiness of a home loan by assuming that the borrower will exercise the *option to default* if there is no longer any equity in the home. A simple model of default may then be built that uses the loan-to-value ratio as a predictor of default. The higher the loan-to-value ratio, the less equity the owner has in the home and the higher the probability of default. Today, this simple model provides a foundation for home mortgage lending.

To generate a more accurate prediction of the probability of default, additional variables could be added to this model. The second variable might be the size of the debt service relative to the borrower's cash flow or disposable income. This is known as the *income ratio*. The higher this ratio, the greater is the likelihood that the individual will default. Adverse life events such as divorce, illness, or death are additional factors affecting the probability of default. A model that could anticipate these life events would assess credit risk with even greater precision.

A variety of tools are used in building financial models. They may be based on econometrics, simulation, optimization or a combination of all three. Neural networks, for example, can be viewed as a simulation technique that includes an element of optimization (finding the lowest error rate or the highest accuracy).

VARIETY IN MODELS

Ratios, option theory, econometrics, expert systems—these are all attempts to isolate a problem in a construct that can be studied, refined, tested, and, if effective, profitably implemented. Many separate elements go into the construction of a credit risk model. First, relationships must be postulated among the variables that seem to affect the risk of default; this is where theory enters in. Then, to derive a formal model, a set of tools must be employed to estimate or simulate outcomes. A body of data is crucial at this point, because a model cannot be created in a vacuum. Lastly, a series of tests must be applied to establish that the model does, indeed, perform as expected. There are also times when the only way to unearth new relationships is to *mine* data without having any particular theory in mind.

In the measurement of credit risk, models may be classified along three different dimensions: the techniques employed, the domain of applications in the credit process, and the products to which they are applied.

Techniques

The more commonly used techniques are:

1. *Econometric techniques.* Linear and multiple discriminant analysis, multiple regression, logit analysis, and probit analysis all model the probability of default, or the default premium, as a *dependent* variable whose variance is explained by a set of *independent* variables. The

independent variables include financial ratios and other indicators as well as external variables used to measure economic conditions. Survival analysis refers to a set of techniques used to measure the time to response, failure, death, or the development of an event.

2. *Neural networks.* Computer-based systems that try to mimic the functioning of the human brain by emulating a network of interconnected neurons—the smallest decision making units in the brain. They use the same data employed in the econometric techniques but arrive at the decision model using alternative implementations of a trial and error method.

3. *Optimization models.* These mathematical programming techniques discover the optimum weights for borrower and loan attributes that minimize lender error and maximize profits.

4. *Rule-based or expert systems.* These mimic in a structured way the process used by an experienced analyst to arrive at the credit decision. As the name indicates, such a system tries to clone the process used by a successful analyst so that this expertise is available to the rest of the organization. Rule-based systems are characterized by a set of decision rules, a knowledge-base consisting of data such as industry financial ratios, and a structured inquiry process to be used by the analyst in obtaining data on a particular borrower.

5. *Hybrid systems using direct computation, estimation and simulation.* These are partly driven by a direct causal relationship, the parameters of which are determined through estimation techniques. An example of this is the KMV model, which uses an option theoretic formulation to explain default and then derives the form of the relationship through estimation. Migration probability matrices are data summaries that help to predict the tendency of a credit to migrate to lower or higher credit quality based on historically observed migration patterns. These matrices are derived by using the *cohort component analysis,* i.e. observing a group of bonds or companies through time from inception to end.

Domain of Application

Financial models are applied in a variety of domains:

1. *Credit approval.* These models are used by themselves or in conjunction with a judgmental override system in approving credit in the consumer lending business. The use of such models has expanded to include small business lending and first mortgage loan approvals. They are generally not used in approving large corporate loans, but they may be one of the inputs to a decision.

2. *Credit rating determination.* Quantitative models are used in deriving "shadow" bond ratings for unrated securities and for commercial loans. These ratings in turn influence portfolio limits and other lending limits used by the institution. In some instances, the credit rating predicted by the model is used within an institution to challenge the rating assigned by the traditional credit analysis process.

3. *Credit pricing.* Credit risk models may be used to suggest the risk premiums that should be charged in view of the probability of loss and the size of the loss given default. Using a *mark to market* model, an institution may evaluate the costs and benefits of holding a financial asset. Unexpected losses implied by a credit model may be used to set the capital charge in pricing.

4. *Financial early warning.* Credit models are used to flag potential problems in the portfolio to facilitate early corrective action.

5. *Common credit language.* Credit models may be used to select assets from a pool to construct a portfolio acceptable to investors or to achieve the minimum credit quality needed to obtain the desired credit rating. Underwriters may use such models for due diligence on the portfolio (such as a collateralized pool of commercial loans). Triggers for reserve levels may be tied to model performance.

6. *Collection strategies.* Credit models may be used in deciding on the best collection/workout strategy to pursue. If, for example, a credit model indicates that a borrower is experiencing short-term liquidity problems rather than a decline in credit fundamentals, then an appropriate workout may be devised.

RELEVANCE OF CREDIT MODELS TO THE DECISION MAKER

Credit models are important today because they provide the decision maker with insight or knowledge that would not be otherwise readily apparent or that could be marshaled only at prohibitive cost. In a marketplace where margins are fast disappearing and the pressure to lower costs is unrelenting, models give the user a competitive edge. In any large financial institution that has a wide variety of exposures, operates in many geographic regions, and has a large and varied workforce, quantitative models help inject a useful degree of objectivity and consistency.

Increasingly, credit risk models are also used to assist in releasing the value of financial assets that would otherwise be hidden from equity investors. For example, structured finance products reallocate credit risk in such a way that the subordinated pieces offer a combination of equity risk and equity return. Credit risk models may be used in the stratification/ construction of such portfolios.

Credit risk models have been built for large corporate commercial and industrial loans (Fortune 500 companies), commercial real estate loans, small business loans (up to $500,000), residential first mortgages (up to $1 million), home equity and consumer loans, loans to financial institutions, and loans to sovereign governments.

Experience shows that the "market penetration" of credit models varies with the size of the borrower as shown in Table 9.1. Consumer sector was the first to use credit risk models in decision making. The use of these models has spread to large corporate, upper middle market and residential real estate lending. In these sectors, these models provide key inputs in credit approval and review. Commercial real estate lending is perhaps the only sector with the smallest use (or potential for use) of credit models today.

PORTFOLIO MANAGEMENT MODELS

Closely related to credit risk models are portfolio models. Historically, lenders have viewed a loan portfolio as an accumulation of individual credit decisions. Portfolio management refers to a controlled process of both acquiring and retaining assets. Using criteria that take into account the impact of adding an asset to the risk-return profile of the overall portfolio, an institution can control the composition of its portfolio. Once an asset has been added, portfolio management tools may be used to identify assets that are no longer desirable because of changing economic or industry conditions. One simple measure of portfolio impact is concentration.

An optimization model may be used to construct a portfolio of loans or securities from a large universe based on the relative profitability and credit risk of the assets. Optimization refers to a set of tools available from operations research that express the relevant trade-offs and constraints as an objective mathematical function to be *maximized* or *minimized.* An optimization problem is characterized by a set of *decision variables:* These are unknowns that the algorithm seeks to find. The decision variables for the construction of an optimum portfolio are the *weights* or the percentages of the individual assets it will include. The decision variables are used to define an *objective function,* which is the sum of the value added by the decision variables to the overall benefit to be derived. The objective function of a portfolio may be expressed as a combination of the portfolio return, which is made up of the returns from the individual assets multiplied by their portfolio weights. The optimization problem always involves constraints. For

TABLE 9.1   Range of Possible Application of Quantitative Credit Risk Model

Large Corporate Borrowers

Publicly traded. Extensive disclosure. Many institutional investors with research capabilities.	Low monitoring. (Annual cycle.)	Potential for higher use of credit scoring models because of better data.

Middle Market Borrowers

Publicly traded. Moderate disclosure. Little or no publicly traded debt.	Low use of credit scoring models. Greater emphasis on management.

Middle Market and Private Borrowers

Stock not publicly traded. No public debt. More information problems.	Reliance on financial statements. Close monitoring. Reliance on Collateral and Covenants.	Limited use of credit scoring models.

Small Business

No stock. Even financial statements are unaudited. Information problems.	Reliance on individuals. Close monitoring. Collateral. Covenants.	Moderate use of credit scoring models.

Commercial Real Estate

No publicly traded stock. Approval based on cash flow projections and collateral value.	Moderate monitoring. More reliance on collateral. Less reliance on covenants.

Residential and Real Estate

Reliance on collateral value.	Greater use of financial data.	Increasing use of credit scoring models.

Consumer

No financial statements. Less information problems because of credit bureaus.	Reliance on demographic variables. Collateral only for consumer durables. No covenants.	Heavy use of credit scoring models.

example, the investment in any single asset may not exceed the institution's lending limit.

Once an optimization problem has been specified, generalized computational techniques such as the *simplex method* from Operations Research are used to arrive at the optimal solution. Computer software packages are readily available to solve optimization problems. The composition of the "optimal" portfolio is derived from a set of assumptions about the risk and returns from a universe of securities. Harry Markowitz's portfolio approach (as described in Chapter 17) is an implementation of an optimization problem.

When the interrelationships among variables are so complex that they preclude a direct mathematical or statistical solution, a simulation may be employed to derive the statistical distribution of the outcomes from a set of decisions. An example of this approach is the preparation of earnings projections for a company based on assumptions about sales and cost of sales. Stress testing the structure of an asset-based security to assess whether the structure can withstand an economic downturn (e.g., there will be claims on the financial guarantee) is another case where simulation is used to understand risk. To produce results that genuinely add value to the decision process, the economic scenarios developed should be internally consistent. For example, if a product price increase is modeled, it should typically be accompanied by a drop in unit sales. Unless care is exercised, simulations may simply generate the results the decision-maker wants to see.

One of the difficulties with simulations is that that it is very difficult to incorporate uncertainty in these calculations. In ordinary simulation models, the probabilities of the independent variables and the joint-probabilities among them (sometimes expressed as the correlations) may be modeled only in a qualitative fashion. A *Monte Carlo* simulation, by contrast, is a procedure in which the input variables are not single values but are drawn from a prespecified statistical distribution. Rather than specifying, for example, a short-term interest rate of 6 percent, a Monte Carlo simulation may use an input specifying that the interest is normally distributed, with a mean of 6 percent and a standard deviation of 3. In selecting this input, an analyst is saying that while he or she believes that the mean of the interest rate is still 6 percent, there is a 34 percent probability that it will be less than or equal to 6 + 3 = 9 percent, and an equal probability that it will be greater than or equal to 6 − 3 = 3 percent.[1] In an ordinary simulation, the entire calculation is performed only once, so for a given set of initial assumptions there is only one result. In a Monte Carlo simulation, the computer will run the calculation many times—in some cases, millions of times. Each time, a sample (a value of the variable) will be "drawn" from the specified distribution. Thus the result from the simulation is not a single value, but a *distribution* of outcome values.

As a Monte Carlo simulation is run more and more times, the resulting output distribution may gradually *converge,* that is, change less and less with additional iterations. Of course, if the model has only one independent variable, the simulation will, by definition, converge on a simplistic outcome: a distribution value that has a one-to-one correspondence with the independent variable's distribution. But the power of this technique comes into play when the problem has more variables and interactions—specifically, when more independent variables are added, and uncertainty is to be modeled in the time dimension as well. When more variables are added, each is assigned its own distribution function. In addition, the interrelationships among the variables are specified in the form of pairwise correlation coefficients. A drift term is added to the variable to model a random variation along with a trend over time. This is typically how the interest rate path is represented.

The first step in constructing a Monte Carlo simulation is to develop an ordinary simulation model employing the same variables. When this simulation is run, the important variables having an effect on the outcomes will become clearer. The next step is to examine each variable and make a hypothesis about how it is distributed. The shape of the distribution is obtained by talking to the people most knowledgeable about the variable, and by consulting the published literature. For example, stock prices are believed to have a log-normal distribution.[2] The parameters of the distribution functions are set by fitting one of the many available distribution functions to the hand-drawn representation of the distribution. The next step is to input the correlation coefficients among the variables. These coefficients are based on experience and offline statistical analysis of relationships among the independent variables.

Once the distributions of the independent variables and their correlations are established, the Monte Carlo simulation may begin. The end result of the simulation is a probability distribution of outcomes. An advantage of Monte Carlo simulation is that it is possible to model complex relationships without having a mathematical solution. You need not be a mathematician to analyze a risk problem. A simulation may be used to test the validity of direct solutions because in a simulation it is necessary to spell out all the variables being used and their distributions, all of which may have been hidden or assumed away in the direct solutions. Monte Carlo simulations are used in CreditMetrics™ (see Chapter 19).

A disadvantage of the Monte Carlo approach is that it may not be able to handle optionality that may be present in the financial structures being evaluated. For example, if an asset may be sold advantageously in any one of several periods, the system will sell it in the first logically permitted period without trying to optimize the timing of the sale. Simulation, by definition, is forward looking, and the algorithms cannot go back and change a decision made in a prior period based on a realization in the subsequent period.

Optimization and simulation models are useful in understanding the risk-return dynamics of an institution. Although they may or may not provide a precise answer to the question, the mere process of going through the exercise will contribute to developing a better understanding of the profit dynamics. These models will become even more useful in pooling assets to stratify, shift or hedge risk because, as Marc Intrater (1997), Director at Oliver, Wyman, Inc. points out, investors are typically more interested in assuming systemic risk (buying a consumer portfolio whose risk is driven by macro factors) than an idiosyncratic risk (buying exposure to a single name).

COMING ATTRACTIONS

In the following chapter we introduce credit risk models starting with Altman's Z-Score model and Altman, Haldeman, and Narayanan's (1977) ZETA® model, both of which are applied to the default risk of corporations. These models use accounting *and* market value measures in deriving the likelihood of financial distress. Next, we describe neural networks, which are computer-based adaptive learning systems that *train* themselves to measure credit quality and are then implemented in various parts of the credit management process. In Chapter 11, we discuss models that employ the volatility of equity prices to predict default probability in debt instruments. In Chapter 12, we describe the use of credit risk models in consumer lending. Default prediction models for other applications such as small business, financial institution risk and real estate lending are reviewed in Chapter 13.

Considerable details accompany these models. While not every reader may need to understand all of the intricacies, most will want to grasp the essential ideas that underlie each model. To make it easier for readers to choose an appropriate level of detail, we open each of the chapters with an overview of its contents before proceeding to present the models in greater depth.

Chapter 14 concludes the section on credit risk evaluation models with a discussion of model implementation and unresolved issues. Chapters 15 and 16 provide some important tools and data on default and credit risk migration that are useful in the pricing and management of credit products. Chapters 17 through 22 consider portfolio management tools and techniques that make use of optimization and simulation.

REFERENCES

Hillier, F. S., and G. J. Lieberman, 1973. *Introduction to Operations Research*, San Francisco: Holden-Day, Inc.

Interater, Mark. 1997. Interview.

Mallios, W. 1989. *Statistical Modeling: Applications in Contemporary Issues*, Ames, Iowa: Iowa State University Press.

McKinsey. 1993. Special Report on "The New World of Financial Services." *The McKinsey Quarterly*, no. 2.

Palisades Corporation. 1996. *@RISK—Advanced Risk Analysis for Spreadsheets*. Newfield, New York.

Trigeorgis, L. 1996. *Real Options: Managerial Flexibility and Strategy in Resource Allocation*. Cambridge, Mass.: MIT Press.

CHAPTER 10

Credit Risk Models Based upon Accounting Data and Market Values

[John Stuart] Mill's Methods of Inquiry are useful only if we have rival hypotheses and must choose between them. The hypotheses come first. This point is made more concisely by some dialogue from a Sherlock Holmes story:

    Colonel Ross: Is there any other point to which you wish to draw my attention?

    Holmes: To the curious incident of the dog in the night-time.

    Colonel Ross: The dog did nothing in the night-time.

    Holmes: That was the curious incident.

    The circumstance noted by Holmes was to Colonel Ross not a circumstance at all, yet this nonfact was the key to the solution: the crime was committed by someone known to the dog.

    —Martin Goldstein and Inge F. Goldstein, *How We Know: An Exploration of the Scientific Process* (1978)

Other than the U.S. government, the corporate sector is one of the largest borrower of funds in the capital market. In 2006, the volume of debt outstanding of the nonfinancial business stood at $9 trillion and $45.1 trillion for all sectors—that is, households, business, state and local governments, the Federal government, and the rest of the world combined. Figure 10.1 shows the growth in volume of bank loans and corporate and foreign bonds respectively in the period 1952–2007. Clearly, the corporate debt market is enormous.

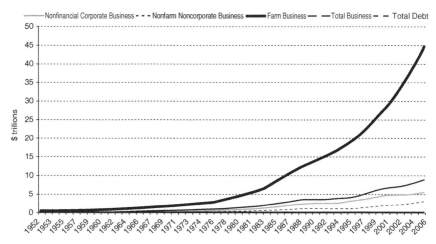

FIGURE 10.1 U.S. Credit Market Debt
Source: Board of Governors of the Federal Reserve System, Flow of Funds
Accounts, 1952–2006, Table L.1.

HUMAN EXPERT SYSTEMS AND SUBJECTIVE ANALYSIS

Fifty years ago, most banks relied exclusively on subjective judgment—classic credit analysis of the kind described in Chapter 7—to assess the credit risk of a corporate borrower. Essentially, bankers used information on various borrower characteristics—such as character (reputation), capital (leverage), capacity (volatility of earnings), and collateral—in deciding whether or not to make a given loan. Developing this type of expert system is time-consuming and expensive. That is why, from time to time, banks have tried to clone their decision-making process. Even so, in the granting of credit to corporate customers, many banks continue to rely primarily on their traditional expert system for evaluating potential borrowers.

ACCOUNTING-BASED CREDIT SCORING SYSTEMS

In recent decades, however, a number of objective, quantitative systems for scoring credits have been developed. In univariate (i.e., one variable) accounting-based credit-scoring systems, the credit analyst compares various key accounting ratios of potential borrowers with industry or group norms and trends in these variables. Today, Standard & Poor's, Moody's,

Fitch, and Risk Management Association can all provide banks with industry ratios. The univariate approach enables an analyst starting an inquiry to determine whether a particular ratio for a potential borrower differs markedly from the norm for its industry. In reality, however, the unsatisfactory level of one ratio is frequently mitigated by the strength of some other measure. A firm, for example, may have a poor profitability ratio but an above-average liquidity ratio. One limitation of the univariate approach is the difficulty of making trade-offs between such weak and strong ratios. Of course, a good credit analyst can make these adjustments. However, some univariate measures—such as the specific industry group, public versus private company, and region—are categorical rather than ratio-level values. It is more difficult to make judgments about variables of this type.

FROM UNIVARIATE TO MULTIVARIATE METHODS

Although univariate models are still in use today in many banks, most academicians and an increasing number of practitioners seem to disapprove of ratio analysis as a means of assessing the performance of a business enterprise. Many respected theorists downgrade the arbitrary rules of thumb (such as company ratio comparisons) that are widely used by practitioners and favor instead the application of more rigorous statistical techniques. In some respects, however, these latter techniques should be viewed as a refinement of traditional ratio analysis rather than as a radical departure from it.

One of the classic studies of ratio analysis and bankruptcy was performed by Beaver (1967). Beaver found that a number of indicators could discriminate between matched samples of failed and nonfailed firms for as long as five years prior to failure. In a subsequent study, Deakin (1972) utilized the same 14 variables that Beaver analyzed but applied them within a series of multivariate discriminant models. Although Deakin achieved a high classification accuracy in the development sample (more than 95 percent for the first three years prior to failure) there was substantial deterioration in the classification accuracy in the hold out sample one year prior, a result that Deakin noted "cannot be explained by the presence of any unusual events peculiar to the sample used." The significance of this finding is that it is premature to conclude from test results from a development sample that valid empirical relationship has been detected.

In general, ratios measuring profitability, liquidity, and solvency appeared to be the most significant indicators in univariate studies. The order of their importance was unclear, however, because almost every study cited a different ratio as the most effective indicator of impending problems. An appropriate extension of the univariate studies therefore was to build upon their findings by combining several measures into a meaningful predictive model. In constructing a multivariate system, the key questions are:

1. Which ratios are most important in detecting bankruptcy potential?
2. What weights should be attached to these selected ratios?
3. How should the weights be objectively established?

We begin this discussion by presenting Altman's (1968, 1995, and 2005) Z-Score models and Atman et al.'s ZETA, which is an update and improvement of the original Z-Score model, is presented next. We will describe commercially available models called RiskCalc, which is a financial ratio based model from Moody's in the spirit of the Z-Score model, CreditModel and Credit Risk Tracker from S&P, and BondScore, which is a product of CreditSights, Inc. This is followed by a description of other developments, including neural networks, artificial intelligence, market-premium based models, and mortality models. Models based on capital market measures are discussed in the following chapter of this book.

ALTMAN'S Z-SCORE MODEL (1968)

Altman's Z-Score models are based on a multivariate approach built on the values of both ratio-level and categorical univariate measures. These values are combined and weighted to produce a measure (a credit risk score) that best discriminates between firms that fail and those that do not. Such a measure is possible because failing firms exhibit ratios and financial trends very different from those of companies that are financially sound. In a bank utilizing such a model, loan applicants would either be rejected or subjected to increased scrutiny if their scores fell below a critical benchmark. Altman based his multivariate model on the financial ratios shown in Table 10.1. The basic Z-Score model has endured to this day, and has also been applied to private companies, nonmanufacturing firms, and emerging market companies. (See Altman 1995 and 2005 for details of these models.)

The resulting discriminant function in the Z-Score model is

$$Z = 1.2X_1 + 1.4X_2 + 2.3X_3 + 0.6X_4 + 0.999X_5$$

Altman found that a lower bound value of 1.81 (failed), and an upper bound of 2.99 (nonfail) to be optimal. Any score in the 1.81–2.99 range was treated as being in the zone of ignorance; that is, where errors were found in the original sample.

TABLE 10.1   Z-Score Model Variable Group Means and F-ratios

Variable	Bankrupt Group Mean[a]	Nonbankrupt Group Mean[a]	F-ratio[b]
$X_1 = \dfrac{\text{Working capital}}{\text{Total assets}}$	−6.1%	41.4%	32.60
$X_2 = \dfrac{\text{Retained earnings}}{\text{Total assets}}$	−62.6%	35.5%	58.86
$X_3 = \dfrac{\text{EBIT}}{\text{Total assets}}$	−31.8%	15.4%	26.56
$X_4 = \dfrac{\text{Market value of equity}}{\text{Book value of liabilities}}$	40.1%	247.7%	33.26
$X_5 = \dfrac{\text{Sales}}{\text{Total assets}}$	1.5 times	1.9 times	2.84

[a] Sample size = 33.
[b] The F-ratio is significant at the 0.001 level for all variables except Sales/Total assets. This ratio tests for the statistical difference between the means of the two groups.
Source: Altman (1968).

As seen in Table 10.1, the means for the two groups for four of the five variables (with the exception of X_5) differed sharply. For a model to predict effectively, the within-group standard deviations should be relatively small.[1] In Altman's sample, the failed group consisted of 33 bankrupt manufacturing firms, and the nonfailed group was a paired sample of manufacturing firms chosen on a stratified random basis.[2] Firms in the nonfailed group were still in existence at the time of the analysis.

The Z-Score model was constructed using multiple discriminant analysis, a multivariate technique that analyzes a set of variables to maximize the between-group variance while minimizing the within-group variance. This is typically a sequential process in which the analyst includes or excludes variables based on various statistical criteria. It should be noted that if the groups were not very different at the univariate level, a multivariate model would not be able to add much discriminatory power.

In order to arrive at a final profile of variables, the following procedures were utilized: (1) observation of the statistical significance of various alternative functions, including determination of the relative contributions of each independent variable; (2) evaluation of correlations among the relevant variables; (3) observation of the predictive accuracy of the various profiles; and (4) judgment of the analyst. From the original list of 22 variables, the final Z-Score model chosen was the following five-variable model (Note that this equation is equivalent to the one shown in Table 10.1. When expressed in this form the ratios X_1 through X_4 are expressed as decimals and not percentages. The fifth ratio is measured in number of times and its coefficient is unchanged from the equation shown in Table 10.1):

$$Z = 1.2X_1 + 1.4X_2 + 3.3X_3 + 0.6X_4 + 0.999X_5$$

1. *X_1, Working Capital/Total Assets (WC/TA).* The working capital/total assets ratio, frequently found in studies of corporate problems, is a measure of a firm's net liquid assets relative to its total capitalization. Working capital is defined as the difference between current assets and current liabilities. Liquidity and size characteristics are explicitly considered. Ordinarily, a firm experiencing consistent operating losses will have shrinking current assets in relation to total assets.
2. *X_2, Retained Earnings/Total Assets (RE/TA).* Retained earnings (also known as *earned surplus*) is the account which reports the total amount of reinvested earnings and/or losses of a firm over its entire life. The retained earnings account is subject to manipulation via corporate quasi-reorganizations and stock dividend declarations. While these occurrences are not evident in this study, it is conceivable that a bias would be created by a substantial reorganization or stock dividend. Appropriate readjustments would then have to be made to the accounts. The age of a firm is implicitly considered in this ratio: a relatively young firm, for example, will probably show a low RE/TA ratio because it has not had time to build up its cumulative profits. It may therefore be argued that this analysis discriminates against the young firm. In reality, however, this bias is perfectly reasonable because the incidence of failure is much higher in younger firms. In 1996, for example, approximately 45 percent of all firms that failed did so in the first five years of their existence (Dun & Bradstreet, 1997—the series has since been discontinued).
3. *X_3, Earnings before Interest and Taxes/Total Assets (EBIT/TA).* This ratio is a measure of the productivity of the firm's assets, independent of any tax or leverage factors. Since a firm's ultimate existence is based on the earning power of its assets, this ratio appears to be particularly appropriate for studies dealing with corporate failure. Furthermore, insolvency occurs when a firm's total liabilities exceed a fair valuation of its assets, as determined by the earning power of those assets.
4. *X_4, Market Value of Equity/Book Value of Total Liabilities (MVE/TL)* Equity is measured by the combined market value of all shares of stock, preferred and common, while liabilities include both current and long-term items. This ratio shows how much a firm's assets can decline in value (as measured by market value of equity plus debt) before

its liabilities exceed its assets and it becomes insolvent. For example, a company with $1,000 of equity market value and debt of $500 could experience a two-thirds drop in asset value (which is $1,000 + $500 = $1,500, thus 2/3 of the assets is $500) before insolvency. However, the same firm with $250 in equity value will be insolvent if assets drop only one-third in value. This ratio adds a market value dimension which other failure studies did not consider. Since the model's inception in 1968, Altman suggested adding capitalized leases, both operating and financial, to the firm's total liabilities.

5. X_5, *Sales/Total Assets (S/TA)*. The capital-turnover ratio is a standard financial ratio illustrating the sales generating ability of the firm's assets. It is one measure of management's capacity to deal with competitive conditions. Based on the univariate statistical significance measure, it would not have appeared at all in the model. However, because of its unique relationship to other variables in the model, the sales/total assets ratio ranks second in its contribution to the overall discriminating ability of the model. Still, there is a wide variation among industries in asset turnover. An alternative model without this ratio was constructed and is described later in this chapter.

The Z-Score model's classification accuracy is as shown in Tables 10.2 and 10.3. The model's overall classification accuracy was 95 percent one year before bankruptcy on the development sample, and 82 percent two years before. Classification accuracy is one of the outputs examined in ascertaining whether a model will perform well in practice. This accuracy is expressed as Type I accuracy (the accuracy with which the model identified failed firms as weak) and Type II accuracy (the accuracy with which the model identified healthy firms as such). Overall accuracy is a combination of Type I and II

TABLE 10.2 Classification Results—Development Sample: One Year Prior to Bankruptcy

Actual Group	No. of Cases	Predicted Group Membership	
		Group 1	Group 2
Group 1 (bankrupt)	33	31	2
		94.0%	6.0%
Group 2 (nonbankrupt)	33	1	32
		3.0%	97.0%

Note: Overall classification accuracy: 95.0 percent.
Source: Altman (1968) and Altman and Hotchkiss (2005).

TABLE 10.3   Classification Results—Development Samples: Two Years Prior to Bankruptcy

Actual Group	No. of Cases	Predicted Group Membership	
		Group 1	Group 2
Group 1 (bankrupt)	33	23	9
		72.0%	28.0%
Group 2 (nonbankrupt)	33	2	31
		6.0%	94.0%

Note: Overall classification accuracy: 82.0 percent.
Source: Altman (1968) and Altman and Hotchkiss (2005).

accuracy. Generally, Type I accuracy is viewed as more important than Type II because the inability to identify a failing company (Type I error) will cost the lender far more than the opportunity cost of rejecting a healthy company as a potential failure (Type II error).

Because the results based on the development sample suffer from sample bias, secondary sample testing is extremely important. One type of testing is to estimate parameters for the model using only a subset of the original sample and then to classify the remainder of the sample based on the parameters established. A simple *t*-test is then applied to test the significance of the results.

Five different replications of the suggested method of choosing subsets (16 firms) of the original sample were tested. The five replications include (1) random sampling; (2) choosing every other firm starting with firm number one; (3) the same test only starting with firm number two; (4) choosing firms 1 through 16; and (5) choosing firms 17 through 32. All the results showed that the discrimination function was statistically significant. Additional tests using secondary samples (completely independent of the development sample) were performed. Type II errors (classifying healthy firms as bankrupt) ranged from 15 to 20 percent in the secondary samples.

Z-SCORES AND BOND RATINGS

One of the primary uses of credit scoring models is to assign a bond rating equivalent to each score. This enables the analyst to assess the default probability of an applicant by observing the historical experience

TABLE 10.4   Average Z-Score by S&P Bond Rating: S&P 500, 1992–2005

Rating	2004–2005	1996–2001	1992–1995
AAA	5.31	5.60	4.80
AA	4.99	4.73	4.15
A	4.22	3.74	3.87
BBB	3.37	2.81	2.75
BB	2.27	2.38	2.25
B	1.79	1.80	1.87
CCC	0.45	.33	0.40
D	−0.19	−0.20	0.05

Source: Compustat Database (see Altman and Hotchkiss 2005).

of each bond rating. These default probabilities are discussed in detail in Chapter 15.

Table 10.4 shows the average Z-Score for bonds of different bond rating classes. Note that the average Z-Score in 2004–2005 ranged from 5.31 for triple-A bonds down to 0.45 for CCC bonds. The average score for B-rated firms is actually in Z-Score's "distress" zone. Indeed, the firms issuing single-B bonds do have distressed firm characteristics. For example, the average B-rated interest coverage (EBIT/Interest expense) for industrial companies is just 1.2 (see Standard & Poor's 2006). In addition, Table 10.4 lists the average Z-Scores at the time of default (D rating). For more detailed and updated data on Altman Z-Scores and rating equivalents, see Altman and Hotchkiss (2005).

It should be noted that the calculation of Z-Scores is readily available on many software packages and is almost instantly accessible on Bloomberg terminals (just enter the ticker symbol or company name and click on "a-z-s" (for Altman Z-Score) and press enter). With respect to the Z- and the Z''-score models (Z'' model is described later in this chapter), we suggest the following procedure to derive the default probabilities:

1. Calculate the Z- or Z''-Score.
2. Match the score with the bond rating equivalent.
3. Utilizing Altman's mortality tables (chapters 15 and 20) observe the marginal and cumulative probabilities.

PRIVATE FIRM Z'-SCORE MODEL

In order to score privately held manufacturing companies, Altman revised the original Z-Score model by substituting book value for market value in calculating the ratio X_4. He arrived at the following Z'-Score model:

$$Z' = 0.717X_1 + 0.847X_2 + 3.107X_3 + 0.420X_4 + 0.998X_5$$

The univariate F-test for the book value of X_4 (25.8), although still very significant, is lower than the 33.3 level for the market value, but the scaled vector results show that the revised book value measure is still the third most important contributor. Indeed, the order of importance (i.e., X_3, X_2, X_4, X_5 and X_1) was retained in the private firm model.

Table 10.5 lists the classification accuracy, group means, and revised cutoff scores for the Z'-Score model. The Type I accuracy (correct identification of bankrupt companies) is only slightly less impressive than that of the Z-Score model (91 percent versus 94 percent), and the Type II accuracy (correct identification of nonbankrupt companies) is identical (97 percent). The nonbankrupt group's mean Z'-Score is lower than that of the original model (4.14 versus 5.02). The distribution of scores is therefore tighter, with greater group overlap. The gray area (or ignorance zone) is wider, however,

TABLE 10.5 Revised Z'-Score Model: Classification Results, Group Means, and Cutoff Boundaries

Actual Group	No. of Cases	Predicted Group Membership	
		Group 1	Group 2
Group 1 (bankrupt)	33	30	3
		90.9%	9.1%
Group 2 (nonbankrupt)	32	1	32
		3.0%	97.0%

Note: Mean of the Bankrupt group = 0.15; Mean of the Nonbankrupt group = 4.14.

$Z' < 1.23$ = Zone I (no errors in bankruptcy classification);

$Z'' > 2.90$ = Zone II (no errors in nonbankruptcy classification);

Gray area = 1.23 to 2.90.

Sources: Altman (1968) and Altman and Hotchkiss (2005).

since the lower boundary is now 1.23 versus 1.81 and the upper boundary is 2.90 versus 2.99 for the original Z-Score model, respectively.

NONMANUFACTURERS Z″-SCORE MODEL

The next modification of the Z-Score model analyzed the characteristics and accuracy of a model without X_5—Sales/Total assets. This was done to minimize the potential industry effect, which is more likely to occur when an industry-sensitive variable such as asset turnover is included. The book value of equity was used for X_4 in this case.

The classification results are identical to the revised five-variable model (Z′-Score). The new Z″-Score model is

$$Z'' = 6.56(X_1) + 3.26(X_2) + 6.72(X_3) + 1.05(X_4)$$

The coefficients for variables X_1 to X_4 are changed, as are the group means and cutoff scores. This particular model is useful in industries where firms finance their assets in very different ways and where adjustments such as lease capitalization are not made. A good example of this is the retailing sector. In the emerging market model discussed below, a constant term of +3.25 was added so as to standardize the scores with a score of zero (0) equivalent to a D-(default) rated bond. This model has been used to assess the financial health of non-U.S. corporates. In particular, Altman, Hartzell and Peck (1997) and Altman (2006) have applied this enhanced Z″-Score model to emerging markets corporates—specifically Mexican firms that had issued Eurobonds denominated in U.S. dollars. A number of researchers and practitioners have developed Z-score type models in many countries outside the United States (see Altman and Narayanan 1997).

EMERGING MARKET SCORING MODEL AND PROCESS

Emerging markets credits may initially be analyzed in a manner similar to traditional analysis of U.S. corporates. Once a quantitative risk assessment has emerged, an analyst can then use a qualitative assessment to modify it for such factors as currency risk, industry characteristics, and the firm's competitive position in that industry. It is not often possible to build a model specific to an emerging country based on a sample from that country because of a lack of credit experience there. To deal with this problem, Altman, et al. (1995) have modified the original Altman Z-Score model to create the EMS (Emerging Market Scoring) model.

Z″-Score		Rating	Z″-Score		Rating	
8.15	>8.15	AAA	5.65	5.85	BBB–	
7.60	8.15	AA+	5.25	5.65	BB+	
7.30	7.60	AA	4.95	5.25	BB	Grey zone
7.00	7.30	AA–	4.75	4.95	BB–	
6.85	7.00	A+	4.50	4.75	B+	
6.65	6.85	A	4.15	4.50	B	
6.40	6.65	A–	3.75	4.15	B–	
6.25	6.40	BBB+	3.20	3.75	CCC+	Distress zone
5.85	6.25	BBB	2.50	3.20	CCC	
			1.75	2.50	CCC–	
			<1.75	1.75	D	

Safe zone — first group. Grey zone and Distress zone — second group.

FIGURE 10.2 Z''-Score and Equivalent Bond Rating
Source: In-Depth Data Corp. Average based on over 750 corporates with rated debt outstanding; 1995 data.

The process of deriving the rating for a Mexican corporate credit is as follows:

1. EMS score is calculated and the equivalent rating is obtained based on the matching of the EMS scores with U.S. bond rating equivalents as shown in Figure 10.2.
2. The company's bond is then analyzed for the issuing firm's vulnerability to servicing its foreign currency-denominated debt. This is based on the relationship between the nonlocal currency revenues minus costs compared to nonlocal currency expense. Then the level of nonlocal currency cash flow is compared with the debt coming due in the next year. The analyst adjusts the rating downward depending upon the degree of vulnerability seen.
3. The rating is further adjusted downward (upward) if the company is in an industry considered to be relatively riskier (less risky) than the bond rating equivalent from the first EMS result.
4. The rating is further adjusted up or down depending upon the dominance of the firm's position in its industry.
5. If the debt has special features such as collateral or a bona fide guarantor, the rating is adjusted accordingly.
6. Finally, the market value of equity is substituted for the best value in variable X_4 and the resulting bond rating equivalents are compared. If there are significant differences in the bond rating equivalents the final rating is modified, up or down.

For relative value analysis, the corresponding U.S. corporates' credit spread is added to the sovereign bond's option-adjusted spread. Only a handful of the Mexican companies are rated by the rating agencies. Thus, risk assessments such as those provided by EMS are often the only reliable indicators of credit risk to overseas investors in Mexico. The author reports that the modified ratings have proven accurate in anticipating both downgrades and defaults (Grupo Synkro in May 1995, 1996) and upgrades (Aeromexico in July 1995).

ZETA® CREDIT RISK MODEL

In 1977, Altman, Haldeman, and Narayanan (1977) presented a second-generation model with several enhancements to the original Z-Score approach. Their purpose was to construct a measure that explicitly reflected recent developments involving business failure and accounting reporting changes such as lease capitalization. Because the average size of bankrupt firms had increased dramatically, the new study focused on larger firms with an average of $100 million in assets two years prior to failure (the original Z-Score model's sample was limited to asset levels below $25 million). The data employed was timely: 50 of the 53 bankrupt firms in the sample had failed within the last seven years. Appropriate analytical adjustments were made so that it became possible to analyze retailing companies—a particularly vulnerable group—on an equal basis with manufacturers. In addition, the new study reflected the most recent changes in financial reporting standards and accepted accounting practices. It also incorporated refinements in discriminant statistical techniques. Due to the proprietary nature of the model we cannot provide the coefficients for the ZETA model.

Principal Findings

The new model, which was named ZETA, was effective in classifying bankrupt companies up to five years prior to failure—with over 90 percent accuracy one year prior and over 70 percent accuracy up to five years prior to failure. The inclusion of retailing firms in the same model as manufacturers did not appear to affect the results negatively.

Variables Analyzed

Twenty-seven variables were selected for inclusion in the analysis based on their widespread use in credit analysis. The variables were classified as measures of profitability, coverage and other variables related to leverage, liquidity, capitalization ratios, and earnings variability.

Reporting Adjustments

The capitalization of leases was the single most important and pervasive adjustment made to the firms' reported data. A capitalized lease amount was added to the firms' assets and liabilities, and an interest cost was imputed to this "new" liability. Other adjustments were made regarding reserves, minority interests on the balance sheet, nonconsolidated subsidiaries, goodwill and intangibles, and capitalized research and development costs.

The 7-Variable Model

The model selected not only classified the test sample well but also proved the most reliable in various validation procedures. Its seven variables are:

1. *Return on assets, X_1.* Measured by earnings before interest and taxes/ total assets. This variable had proved to be extremely helpful in assessing firm performance in several prior multivariate studies.
2. *Stability of earnings, X_2.* Indicated by a normalized measure of the standard error of estimate around a 5- to 10-year trend in X_1. Business risk is often expressed in terms of earnings fluctuations, and this measure proved to be particularly effective.
3. *Debt service, X_3.* Measured by the familiar interest coverage ratio, that is, earnings before interest and Taxes/Total interest payments. This is one of the primary variables used by fixed income security analysts and bond rating agencies.
4. *Cumulative profitability, X_4.* Measured by the firm's retained earnings (Balance sheet/Total assets). This ratio, which imputes such factors as the age of the firm and dividend policy as well as its profitability record over time, was found to be quite helpful in the Z-Score model. Without a doubt, this was the most important variable—whether measured univariately or multivariately.
5. *Liquidity, X_5.* Measured by the familiar current ratio.
6. *Capitalization, X_6.* Measured by Common equity/Total capital. In both the numerator and the denominator, the common equity is measured by a five-year average of the total market value, rather than book value. This five-year average was used to smooth out possible severe, temporary market fluctuations and to add a trend component (along with X_2 above) to the model.
7. *Size, X_7.* Measured by the logarithm of the firms' total assets. This variable was also adjusted for financial reporting changes.

CLASSIFICATION ACCURACY

Table 10.6 compares the classification accuracy of ZETA to that of the Z-Score model. Not surprisingly—in view of the improvements made in developing the model—ZETA is more accurate than Z-Score, especially in the more distant years preceding bankruptcy.

GROUP PRIOR PROBABILITIES, ERROR COSTS, AND MODEL EFFICIENCY

If the model is used as part of a credit approval process, the setting of the cutoff value will necessitate certain trade-offs. If the cutoff score is set too high, then weaker credits will be excluded (increased Type I accuracy), but some good credits will be turned away (lower Type II accuracy). If the cutoff is set too low, then the reverse will occur. Intuitively, the cutoff score should be a function of the cost of a Type I error (loan loss sustained by accepting a bad credit) and the cost of a Type II error (income lost by not lending to a good credit risk due to model error). In addition, the cutoff will be influenced by the prior probability that a credit will be a bad one. If the odds are equal that an incoming credit will be good or bad and if the Type I and Type II costs are equal, then the prior probability is 0.5 and the cutoff score is 0.

But only a small proportion of the borrower population will actually default. Thus, the prior probability will be lower than 0.5. Of course, bad credits are not just those that result in charge-offs. Nonjudicial arrangements, extreme liquidity problems which require the firm's creditors to take over the business or agree to a distressed restructuring, and bond defaults may also be viewed as equivalent to bankruptcy. In the final analysis, the prior probability of bankruptcy cannot be known with precision. In the development of this model, the prior probability estimate was assumed to be in the 1 percent to 5 percent range.

The optimal cutoff score ZETA_c is then equal to

$$\text{ZETA}_c = \ln\frac{q_1 C_1}{q_2 C_2}$$

where q_1, q_2 = prior probability of bankrupt (q_1) or nonbankrupt (q_2), and C_1, C_2 = costs of Type I and Type II errors, respectively. Based on the first study of the recovery experience of commercial banks and opportunity cost of foregone income, Altman, Haldeman, and Narayanan (1977) estimated the cost of a Type I error C_1 to be \$62 per \$100 in loans and that of a Type

TABLE 10.6 Classification Accuracy and Comparison of ZETA with the Z-Score Model

Years Prior to Bankruptcy	ZETA Model		Altman 1968 Model		Altman's 1968 Model with ZETA's Sample		Altman's 1968 Variables, Estimated Using ZETA Sample	
	Bankrupt	Nonbankrupt	Bankrupt	Nonbankrupt	Bankrupt	Nonbankrupt	Bankrupt	Nonbankrupt
1	96.2%	89.7%	93.9%	97.0%	86.8%	82.4%	92.5%	84.5%
2	84.9	93.1	71.9	93.9	83.0	89.3	83.0	86.2
3	74.5	91.4	48.3	n.a.	70.6	91.4	72.7	89.7
4	68.1	89.5	28.6	n.a.	61.7	86.0	57.5	83.0
5	69.8	82.1	36.0	n.a.	55.8	86.2	44.2	82.1

Source: Altman, Haldeman, and Narayanan (1977).

II error C_2 to be \$2 per \$100 in loans per year. The latter amount assumes a spread of 2 percent and a one year maturity. With these assumptions, the critical or cutoff score $ZETA_c$ was found to be

$$ZETA_c = \ln\frac{q_1 C_1}{q_2 C_2} = \ln\frac{0.02*62}{0.98*2} = \ln(0.63) = -0.458$$

With this cutoff score of -0.458, the number of Type I errors increased from two (3.8 percent) to four (7.6 percent) while the Type II errors decreased from 6(10.3 percent) to 4(7.0 percent).

ADJUSTMENTS TO THE CUTOFF SCORE AND PRACTICAL APPLICATIONS

In addition to their use in assessing comparative model efficiency, the prior probability of bankruptcy or default and cost estimates of classification errors could prove valuable in practice. For instance, a bank lending officer or loan-review analyst might want to adjust the critical cutoff score in the light of his or her own estimates of group priors and error costs and/or to reflect current economic conditions. One could imagine the cutoff score falling (thereby lowering the acceptance criterion) as business conditions improve and the banker's prior probability of bankruptcy estimate falls from say 0.02 to 0.015. Or a rise in cutoff scores could result from a change (rise) in the estimate of the Type I error cost vis-à-vis the Type II error cost.

STABILITY OF THE RATIOS IN ZETA®

When ZETA was developed, the ratios that were included in the model were carefully chosen as ones that would not be expected to change over time. With respect to their ability to identify distressed companies, Table 10.7 shows the means and F-ratios of the model variables in the development sample compared with the same ratios for 480 bankruptcies over the period 1981–1993 with randomly paired companies that did not fail. It is seen that the ratios continue to demonstrate consistency and contrast between failed firms and nonfailed firms. The ratio means are in the same order of magnitude, and the F-ratio continues to be statistically significant at .001 level for all of the variables. F-ratios in this period are much higher than in the model developmental sample period reflecting the much greater sample size (480 versus 53 in 1977).

TABLE 10.7 ZETA® Ratio Statistics, 1977 Development Sample and 1981–1993 Sample

Variable	Bankrupt Group Mean	Nonbankrupt Group Mean	F-ratio
		1977 Data	
Return on assets	−0.0055	0.1117	54.3
Stability of earnings	1.6870	5.784	33.8
Debt service	0.9625	1.1620	26.1
Cumulative profitability	−0.0006	0.2935	114.6
Liquidity	1.5757	2.6040	38.2
Capitalization	0.4063	0.6210	31.0
Size	1.9854	2.2220	5.5
		1981–1993 Data	
Return on assets	−.08223	0.09253	316.36
Stability of earnings	0.88471	3.83302	247.28
Debt service	0.87261	1.09928	156.72
Cumulative profitability	−0.21484	0.21139	559.55
Liquidity	1.13783	2.20532	190.48
Capitalization	0.47803	0.58802	44.69
Size	1.63024	2.01598	40.07
		1993–2005 Data	
Return on assets	−0.09	0.02	172.13
Stability of earnings	0.56	3.58	208.98
Debt service	0.81	0.97	98.30
Cumulative profitability	−0.24	−0.01	345.96
Liquidity	1.73	2.21	71.97
Capitalization	0.10	0.41	324.75
Size	1.93	2.06	14.22

Source: ZETA Services, Inc.

REESTIMATION OF COEFFICIENTS

A criticism that may be leveled against ZETA and the Z-Score model is that they may have lost their ability to discriminate between good and bad credits because the coefficients have not continuously been reestimated. However, models that progressively drop older data points and pick up more recent data points may suffer from a serious shortcoming: a model may become more sensitive through the addition of newer observations; but it may lose its ability to predict long-term changes because experience from the distant past has been erased.

Lovie and Lovie (1986) provide insight into why Z and ZETA have continued to be as effective as they have been. For building sturdy models, they offer the following suggestions:

1. Choose the dominant predictor variable/s—usually those with the largest weights as estimated from learning set data. This will at least guarantee that the system produces an above-chance level of discrimination, whatever the weighting scheme used subsequently.
2. Choose the minimum, optimal subset of remaining predictor variables, that is one which produce the largest R^2.
3. Align all predictor variables in the same direction, preferably positively, with respect to the criterion variable to avoid the effects of 'suppresser' variables...
4. Choose a dichotic or dichotomizable criterion variable in order to maximize the discrimination power of the model.

If all the above are satisfied, then "it don't make no nevermind" which weighting scheme is chosen when the models are used in prediction.

When the Z-Score and ZETA models were developed, a great deal of attention was given to choosing the ratios to be used. This may account for the continued stability of their predictive power and to the models' robustness.

ALTMAN AND SABATO SME MODEL

Altman and Sabato (2005) have built a Z-Score-type model for SME (*small- and medium-sized enterprises*, defined as firms with $1 to $65 million in annual sales and $1 to $100 million in total assets). This model employs five financial ratios and uses data on 120 defaults and 1,890 nondefaults through the period 1994–2002 from the Compustat WRDS database. The ratios are as follows (the accounting category of these ratios appears in the parentheses):

- Short-term debt/Book value of equity (leverage)
- Cash/Total assets (liquidity)
- EBITDA/Total assets (profitability)
- Retained earnings/Total assets (coverage)
- EBITDA/Interest expenses (account)

Two versions of the model were built using logistic regression: The first one used the variables as they were and in the second the logarithmic transformation was applied to the variables. The validation results were on a hold-out sample using the two models along with the comparative results on the sample using Altman's Z″-Score model described earlier in this chapter. These are shown in Table 10.8.

The model with the highest prediction accuracy was the one using logged predictors, and produces the p (the probability of a firm being bankrupt) using the following equation:

$$\text{Log}(p/1 - p) = + 53.48$$
$$+ 4.09 - LN(1 - \text{EBITDA/Total assets})$$
$$- 1.13 \ LN(\text{Short-term debt/Equity book value})$$
$$+ 4.32 - LN(1 - \text{Retained earnings/Total assets})$$
$$+ 1.84 \ LN(\text{Cash/Total assets})$$
$$+ 1.97 \ LN(\text{EBITDA/Interest expenses})$$

The model was also reestimated using *multiple discriminant analysis* (MDA) and it was found that MDA validation results were somewhat inferior to the results from logistic regression (accuracy ratio of 59.87 percent

TABLE 10.8 Comparative Results of the Logistic Models and Altman's Z″-Score Model

Risk Factors	Weight
Leverage	26%
Liabilities less cash to assets	
Retained earnings to total liabilities	
Debt Coverage	22%
EBITDA to interest expense	
Activity	13%
Inventory to net sales	
Trade Receivables to net sales	
Liquidity	16%
Cash to total assets	
Profitability	12%
Gross profit to total assets	
Previous Year's net income to sales	
Growth	8%
Net sales growth	
Size	3%
Net sales	

Source: Altman and Sabato (2005).

versus 87.22 percent for the logged predictors). Basel II allows banks the possibility to choose whether to classify SME firms (sales less than €50 million) as *corporate* or *retail*. If the firms are treated as retail, then capital requirements would be based on the retail formula (pooled basis). It is shown that for both approaches the use of a specific the credit scoring model for SMEs will result in lower capital requirements. It is also conclusively shown that a model built specifically for SMEs outperformed the generic corporate model (Z''-Score model). In addition, the capital requirements are higher using whichever model if the SMEs are treated as *corporate*.

RISKCALC® MODEL BY MOODY'S KMV

Moody's KMV RiskCalc is a widely used tool in the credit risk industry to tackle credit risk in private firms across a number of industries and in many countries (e.g., Japan, Germany, Australia). RiskCalc is a model based on financial ratios like the Z-Score and ZETA models. However, it differs somewhat in the modeling methodology. For example, the dependent variable in the RiskCalc model is the proportion of firms that defaulted, whereas for the Z-Score model it is the a priori group membership. RiskCalc draws on "good" and "failed" firm data samples that are significantly larger than those used in the Z-Score models. As of May 2004, the database contained data on over 1.5 million unique private firms and close to 100,000 default events worldwide. The way the ratios are presented to the model is also different: rather than raw values, transformed values of the variable indicative of the ranking within the population are used. The original RiskCalc model, first introduced in 2000 has since undergone improvements in its development.

In building a credit model, it is not only necessary for the development samples to be sufficiently large, it should also be representative of firm characteristics (such as size and industry) in which it will eventually be deployed. For the U.S. model, RiskCalc's access to Moody's Credit Research database enables it have a data sample that spans eight major industry groups and has a balanced representation of various firm sizes. Default in RiskCalc is defined as any of the following conditions: 90 days past due, bankruptcy, placement in nonaccrual status, or write-down. The model is calibrated to a central default tendency to ensure that the average probability of default produced by the model reflects the underlying population.

The RiskCalc model contains three components: the *FSO model* (financial statements only), *industry adjustment*, and lastly, the *credit cycle adjustment* (CCA). It is an econometric model as opposed to a structural model such as Moody's KMV Credit Monitor. RiskCalc is applicable to industrial private firms; that is, it excludes finance, insurance and real estate firms. Typically this model would be used for firms with assets above $100,000. Smaller firms usually do not report financial statements.

There are two reasons why a structural model used to estimate default probabilities from public firms is not used in the case of private firms:

1. The first is that stock market prices of private firms do not exist by definition, and structural models rely on a firm's value of assets, that is derived from the firm's market equity.
2. The second is that the mechanism for default may differ between private and public firms. A private firm may fail where a public firm may not, because the private firm runs out of cash whereas the public firm has access to other sources of financing. Such differences in financing are reflected in private firms having more liquidity and retained earnings and less debt than their public counterparts.

A structural model based on stock price called the *KMV model* (renamed *MKMV Credit Monitor*) is described in Chapter 11. An extension of the public firm applicable to private firms was developed by KMV which is also described in Chapter 11 but this was subsequently largely abandoned. The first RiskCalc model was developed by Moody's Risk Management Services which would later be merged with Moody's KMV. Following the integration of the two entities, elements of the KMV private firm model were incorporated into the new version of RiskCalc, which is now called RiskCalc 3.1 (Dwyer, Kocagil, Stein, 2004 and Dwyer 2007).

RiskCalc® Model Derivation

The RiskCalc model is based on a nonlinear relationship between a number of financial ratios and default probabilities. The challenge, therefore, of building a model consists in choosing from a number of relevant financial ratios (derived from the firm's financial statements) showing the nonlinear relationship with default probability as in other models (e.g. Altman's Z-Score). In its implementation, ratios that have an intuitive relationship with default that is robust across different subsets of the data are favored.

The ratios belong mainly in seven different categories: profitability, leverage, debt coverage, growth variables, liquidity, activity ratios, and size. These factors are the main drivers of a firm's financial performance, and hence of a firm's likelihood of default. While a majority of the ratios chosen correspond to "level" variables, that is, the value of the ratio at one point in time, some of the variables are trend variables. A trend variable could be growth in revenue or growth in profitability, whereas a level variable would be profitability, debt coverage or leverage. The builders of RiskCalc found that level variables are more important than trend variables in predicting default. As a result, trend variables have less weight in the model, and provide less predictive power on a standalone basis.

Once the ratios have been identified, they are individually transformed and mapped to the *expected default frequency* (EDF). That is, each ratio is converted to a percentile score within the sample and is mapped against the rate of defaults observed in that percentile. In this way, the relationship—whether linear or nonlinear—of the ratio to default probability is observed. The weights are derived using a method such that the variable that has the highest marginal impact on the EDF will receive the largest weight; the variable that has the smallest impact will have the lowest weight. By construction, the weights will sum to 100 percent.

As an example, relative weights of the variables for the RiskCalc Japan (2004) model are shown in Table 10.9. RiskCalc models have been developed for individual countries based on local country data and optimized for local country practices.

The EDF from the FSO (financial statement only) model is modified to take industry effects into account. According to RiskCalc, this is because

TABLE 10.9 Risk Factors in RiskCalc v3.1, Japan Model

Risk Factors	Weight
Leverage Liabilities less cash to assets Retained earnings to total liabilities	26%
Debt Coverage EBITDA to interest expense	22%
Activity Inventory to net sales Trade receivables to net sales	13%
Liquidity Cash to total assets	16%
Profitability Gross profit to total assets Previous year's net income to sales	12%
Growth Net sales growth	8%
Size Net sales	3%

the firms with the similar financial ratios but in different industries tend to differ in their creditworthiness.

The *credit cycle adjustment* (CCA) is a further modification to the RiskCalc model's EDF based on an assessment of the current stage of the credit cycle. This is done by using *distance to default* (DD) statistics for the public firms in the respective industry (see Chapter 11 for the definition of distance to default). For our purposes here, we can simply define DD as the distance between the value of the firm's assets and the debt coming due at various points in time in the future. DD has an inverse relationship with EDF: the higher the DD, the lower is the EDF. The RiskCalc model compares the current average of the DD with the historical average for the industry. Depending on whether this variable is increasing or decreasing, the EDF for the private firms is increased or decreased. The presumption here is that the public and private firms within an industry exhibit similar trends in default rates. The extent to which this is true is an empirical question and probably varies across industries and countries.

RiskCalc® Model Performance

The RiskCalc model performance is reported through the *accuracy ratio* (also called the *Gini coefficient*). Accuracy ratio is the ratio of performance of the model relative to the performance of a naïve model. A naïve model is one in which model scores are assigned randomly. The accuracy ratio ranges from 0 (worst) to 1 (best). Graphically, the accuracy ratio is best understood through the cumulative accuracy profile (Moody's Investors Service 2000) as shown in Figure 10.3. The *cumulative accuracy profile* (CAP) is a plot of the percent of the "bads" correctly identified by the model versus the percentage of the total population that is credit approved. Accuracy ratios in the 54 percent to 57 percent range are reported for the RiskCalc 3.1 for the U.S. model. Other country models are reported to have comparable accuracy ratios.

RiskCalc models for individual countries are based on local country data and optimized for local country practices.

STANDARD & POOR'S CREDITMODEL® (2003)

CreditModel is a suite of models offered by Standard and Poor's that uses financial ratios to generate implied ratings. The output of the model is thus a quantitatively derived rating which may be obtained for both private and public companies. The model is not applicable to financial institutions, nor does take into account the benefits/burdens of the parent company. It does

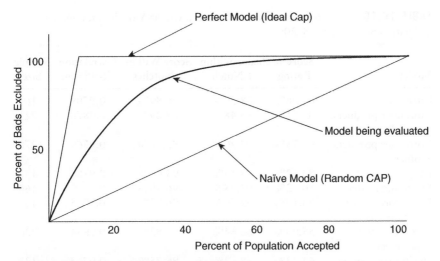

FIGURE 10.3 Cumulative Accuracy Profile
Source: Moody's Investors Service (2000).

not also apply to government-owned businesses. It is not recommended for companies below $50 million in revenues. Submodels within the Credit-Model are specific to region and industry, and use ratios that are considered important within that segment.

CreditModel is also a multivariate model like Altman's Z-Score. It uses a set of financial variables (market value is *not* one of the inputs), but it uses a different technique and target variable. The technique used is the support vector is similar a neural network models which arrive at the optimal weights by minimizing the prediction error. The support vector technique is believed to eliminate pitfalls encountered in other estimation techniques. For example, parametric regression models do not allow for nonlinear, nonmonotonic relationships among the various input and output variables.

To quote S&P (2004):

Support vector machines reduce the task to an optimisation problem, as neural network models do. However, support vector model optimisation problems are strictly convex and tractable. There is one, and only one, global optimum that can reliably be found numerically. These models will not get stuck in a local (false) optimum. Consequently, solutions are stable with respect to small changes in the data. A small change in an input will not result in a large score change. Support vector models have successfully solved problems that have stumped neural network models.

TABLE 10.10 Performance of North American Credit Models, Training and Validation Samples, 1998–2001

Model	Score = Rating	Score Within 1 Notch	Score Within 2 Notches	Correlation Coefficient	Sample Size
Chemicals	67.08%	88.20%	96.89%	0.9709	161
Consumer products, branded	82.81%	95.48%	97.29%	0.9876	221
Consumer products, other	67.78%	93.70%	97.78%	0.9760	270
Drugs	80.32%	88.15%	93.43%	0.9788	137
Electronic media	80.12%	93.98%	96.39%	0.9649	166
Food stores & restaurants	78.10%	92.70%	96.35%	0.9795	137
Forest & building products	55.00%	88.64%	96.82%	0.9634	220
Healthcare services	64.23%	88.62%	96.75%	0.9763	123
Metals	78.80%	86.96%	96.20%	0.9744	184
Retail	53.72%	84.83%	92.45%	0.9308	294
Total	69.37%	90.10%	95.97%	0.9679	1,913

Source: Standard & Poor's (2003).

The target variable for the model is the actual S&P rating. The development sample size ranges from 85 to 400 companies with three to five years of financial data. Twenty percent of the sample is held back to perform out of sample testing. The performance of the model is based on how well the model can predict the (notched) rating of the companies in the sample. The results for the U.S. model are shown in Table 10.10. Additional performance measures such as Ratings correlation coefficient and the Kolmogorow-Smirnow statistics are available from S&P (2003).

The performance of the sub-models on the validation sample in other countries is summarized in Table 10.11.

Standard & Poor's Credit Risk Tracker (2006)

Credit Risk Tracker (CRT) helps facilitate the credit valuation process for middle market, private firms in North America. CRT models exist also for France, Germany, Italy, United Kingdom, and Spain. CRT produces forward-looking, one-year probability of default estimates based on relevant macroeconomic, financial and industry variables for privately held firms with assets over US $100,000. It is a multivariate model using the financial statements, industry data and macroeconomic data. Table 10.12

TABLE 10.11 Performance of CreditModel® in Europe, Training and Validation[a]

Country	Sample Size	Exact	Within 1 Notch	Within 2 Notches
Austria	1	0.0%	0.0%	100.0%
Belgium	8	75.0%	75.0%	87.5%
Denmark	7	42.9%	42.9%	85.7%
Finland	13	7.7%	30.8%	92.3%
France	103	54.4%	81.6%	93.2%
Germany	49	59.2%	81.6%	93.9%
Greece	5	60.0%	80.0%	100.0%
Ireland	10	70.0%	90.0%	100.0%
Italy	8	100.0%	100.0%	100.0%
Luxemburg	7	57.1%	85.7%	100.0%
Netherlands	43	69.8%	90.7%	97.7%
Norway	4	75.0%	100.0%	100.0%
Portugal	6	83.3%	100.0%	100.0%
Spain	8	100.0%	100.0%	100.0%
Switzerland	37	67.6%	81.1%	91.9%
Sweden	37	59.5%	81.1%	94.6%
United Kingdom	182	62.6%	84.6%	95.6%

[a]Excludes model for utilities.
Source: Standard & Poor's (2003).

TABLE 10.12 Variables in the Credit Risk Tracker

Type of Data	Number of Variables
Financial variables	43
Industry-specific variables	7
Macroeconomic variables	30

Category	Number of Financial Ratios
Leverage	7
Liquidity	6
Profitability	11
Size	7
Structure	3
Efficiency	6
Growth	3
Total	43

shows the distribution of the candidate variables used in the model, and more specifically the financial statement based variables. Details of the ratios are available from S&P (2006).

The database used in the development of CRT includes detailed financial information on 17,065 Canadian and United States companies operating in a majority of economic sectors. Most companies within the CRT North America (NA) Database have between three and five years of sequential historical data, with some companies having up to eight years of information. The size of the companies included in the CRT NA database ranges from those with revenues of less than $1 million to over $1 billion.

The development of the model follows a two step approach. The first is the selection of the key variables, and the second step is associating weights to the selected variables. The statistical variable selection approach starts with a step-forward procedure applied to a linear logit model. In this procedure, all possible single-variable models are trained and the best performing one is selected, where the performance is measured in terms of the *expected wealth growth rate pickup* (EWGRP). EWGRP is the pickup in expected wealth growth rate experienced by an investor who bases his investment decisions on the model in comparison to an uninformed investor. It is proportional to the expected utility gain for the investor and to the likelihood ratio between the model and a uniform probability distribution. To arrive at the final variable set, variables are progressively added until marginal gain in performance is negligible.

To derive the weights to be associated with the selected ratios, an optimization process is used with five different methodologies:

- Enhanced linear logit model
- Enhanced quadratic logit model
- MEU modeling methodology
- MEU modeling methodology with Gaussian regularization
- MEU modeling methodology with L1-regularization

The MEU modeling methodology with L1-regularization feature selection is found to delivers the best "out of sample" performance for the CRT NA model.

The *maximum expected utility* (MEU) methodology is a technique based on statistical learning theory. In the MEU approach, the real world probabilities of default are modeled over a fixed time horizon for a given set of explanatory variables. The MEU approach allows the models to incorporate nonlinearities, nonmonotonicities, and interactions present in the data, without overfitting. The performance of the model is summarized in Table 10.13.

TABLE 10.13   Performance of the CRT Model for North America

	EWGRP		Gini Coefficient	
	In Sample	Out of Sample	In Sample	Out of Sample
Linear Logit	78.30	75.35	71.10%	70.23%
MEU	95.32	81.51	76.38%	72.44%

Source: Standard & Poor's (2006).

The Credit Risk Tracker for the United States and Europe has been used in loan securitization as well as in credit decision making.

BONDSCORE® MODEL

This model, developed by CreditSights, Inc. (www.creditsights.com), is similar to the Z-Score model in that it uses key financial ratios (EBITDA/Sales, asset turnover, leverage, size, liquidity, volatility of stock returns, and volatility of cash flow) to model the credit profile of a company. The model is logistic-regression-based and is applicable to nonfinancial, public debt-issuing companies. The way in which outliers are handled by the modeling approach is interesting: the variable values are transformed into percentiles before being used in model estimation. The bond score results in a *credit risk estimate* (CRE, the probability of default in the following year) which is then calibrated to an implied rating by calibrating the CRE to the public rating agency ratings. This scale is then applied to unrated companies. BondScore ratings are tracked over time. In addition, CreditSights publishes narrative credit analysis of public companies.

DEPLOYMENT OF Z-SCORE, ZETA®, RISCCALC®, CREDITMODEL®, CREDIT RISK TRACKER® AND BONDSCORE® MODELS

Z-Score, ZETA, RiskCalc, CreditModel, Credit Risk Tracker, and Bond-Score models have been applied in a variety of situations:

- *Credit policy.* An institution lacking an internal risk rating system may use the rating system developed by relating the model's score range or rating to actual default experience. This model-predicted rating provides an objective and consistent way of dealing with variations in region, size, and ownership. If the model rating is compared to the institution's own rating, any anomalies can be analyzed to validate the assigned rating. For Basel II implementation models, such models are viable and sometimes superior alternatives to internally developed models because of the availability of model validation data.

▪ *Credit review.* As the credit quality of borrowers improves or declines in a fundamental way, these models provide an early warning system to the institution.

▪ *Lending.* These models provide a low-cost and quick assessment of risk for prospecting. Target credit spreads and unexpected losses may be factored into the pricing equation by taking advantage of the consistent relationship between the score and the default rate.

▪ *Validation.* These models may be used to validate internal credit scoring model by providing a score benchmark and generating a rating discrepancy report that may be further analyzed.

▪ *Securitization.* By providing a credible and consistent credit language, these models can facilitate the stratification and structuring of commercial loans for securitization. Indeed such models are a cost-efficient way to underwrite assets to be securitized that provide transparency to the investor on the credit standards being followed by the originator. Securitizations of both consumer and commercial assets are now quite common using such models.

LIMITATIONS OF MULTIVARIATE MODELS

Despite their excellent performance and worldwide acceptance, multivariate models presented here are sometime criticized for being "fitted" or "associative"—that is, they are empirical models lacking a theory. In reality, the theory behind most failure-prediction models is the same as the options theoretic framework for corporate failure: namely, *an overly leveraged firm will fail if unable to generate sufficient earnings.* Scott (1981), however, compared a number of these empirical models with a theoretically sound approach using a bankruptcy construct. He concluded that the ZETA model most closely approximates his theoretical model. MKMV claims to be careful not to overfit the data when building RiskCalc models. Dwyer (2005) presents two examples of fitting the "data collection process" rather than underlying economic relationships that were encountered when building RiskCalc models. His paper describes how the issues were identified through diagnostic techniques and removed from the final model.

While in many cases, multivariate accounting-based credit scoring models have been shown to perform quite well over many different time periods and across many different countries (see Altman and Narayanan 1997), they have also been criticized for a number of other reasons. Because they are based primarily on book-value accounting data (which is measured at discrete intervals), these models may fail to pick up more subtle and fast-moving changes in borrower conditions—that is, those that would be reflected in capital market data and values. In addition, the world is inherently nonlinear. As a result, linear discriminant analysis and linear probability models may fail to forecast as accurately as models that relax the underlying assumption of linearity among explanatory variables. This problem has been addressed in some of the latter models such as RiskCalc and CreditModel.

Insofar as accounting data gives an incomplete picture of a firm's true condition and prospects, any model based on this data must, inevitably, suffer from certain limitations. Since the accounting profession has yet to come up with a good way to report on off-balance-sheet risk, such models cannot handle these risks well. Furthermore, for reasons having to do with asset valuation, balance sheet structure, or regulation, these models are unable to measure the risk of utilities, financial companies, new companies, and companies in extraction industries such as oil and mining.

NEURAL NETWORKS

A relatively new approach to the problem of credit risk classification is the application of neural network analysis. *Neural network* (NN) analysis is similar to nonlinear discriminant analysis, in that it drops the assumption that variables entering into the distress prediction function are linearly and independently related. Neural network models of credit-risk explore potentially "hidden" correlations among the predictive variables which are then entered as additional explanatory variables in the nonlinear distress prediction function. Applications of neural networks to distress prediction analysis include Coats and Fant's (1993) application to corporate distress prediction in the United States and Altman, Marco, and Varetto's (1994) application to corporate distress prediction in Italy; Trippi and Turban (1996) discuss other applications of neural networks to credit risk, including consumer loans, home mortgages, banks, and thrifts. The Altman et al. models are particularly relevant in that they compare NN results with multiple discriminant analysis framework on the same samples.[3]

A neural network is a collection of simple computational elements that are interconnected. The human brain is a collection of interconnected neurons. In the brain, electric signals passed between neurons are either inhibited or enhanced depending upon what the neural network has learned in the past. In a similar fashion, artificial neurons may be constructed using either hardware or software to behave in a manner similar to the biological neuron. The network's behavior derives from the collective behavior of the interconnected units. The links between the units (neurons) are not rigid, but can be modified through the learning processes generated by the network's interaction with the outside world. A simple implementation of a neural network is shown in Figure 10.4.[4]

Each unit i receives an input (X_i) from the outside. The input may be a financial ratio, a market trend, or any other input variable. The input may also be the output signal from another neuron to which this unit is linked. Each input X_i is associated with a weight W_{ij}, indicating that there are j different inputs coming to the unit, where $j = 1 \ldots n$. In addition to the X_i inputs, the unit receives S_i, a constant input value termed the *excitation threshold value* or *bias*. The overall input to neuron i is termed potential P_i, which is equal to

$$P_i = \sum_{j=1}^{j=n} n W_{ji}^* X_i - S_i$$

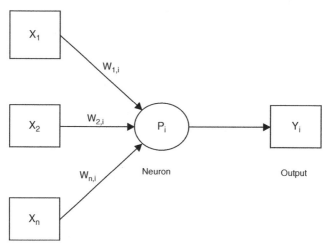

FIGURE 10.4 General Scheme of Neural Unit
Source: Altman, Marco and Varetto (1994).

The purpose of S_i is to limit the neuron's degree of response to the stimuli X_i received. For example, S_i may be set such that the neuron gives a response signal only if the total input exceeds the value of S_i. To eliminate S_i from the above equation, set a dummy input X_0 equal to 1, and set $W_{0i} = -S_i$, thereby obtaining the general expression

$$P_i = \sum_{j=0}^{j=n} n W_{ji} {}^* X_i$$

Notice that P_i is simply a linear combination of weights for the inputs X_i to the neuron.[5] The next aspect of the network is the use of a transfer function by the neuron which converts the potential P_i to an output Y_i. One such function is the logistic or the sigmoid function according to which,

$$Y_i = \frac{1}{1 + e^{-P_i}}$$

Y_i is a value between 0 and 1, and may either be a final output or an input to further neuron units. The transfer function gives the capacity to respond nonlinearly to an impulse. For example, it is believed that if a financial ratio such as the coverage ratio exceeds a certain minimum level (say for an AAA rating), the incremental value beyond this threshold does not to add to credit quality. Linear regressions cannot limit the response in this manner, but the transfer function in a neural network can.

The network may learn either in a *supervised* mode (where the outcomes are known; this is the equivalent of the a priori groups in discriminant analysis) or in an *unsupervised* mode (this is equivalent to factor analysis, where the prior groupings are not known). The network is given a set of inputs and generates a response, which is then compared with the required (or correct) response. If the error rate exceeds a certain tolerance level, revisions are introduced to the weightings and the learning starts again. After a large number of cycles, the error is reduced to an acceptable level. Once the hold-out accuracy level is attained, the learning ends and the weightings are locked. Thus, the process is not dissimilar to the traditional models, with the only difference being that the weights are arrived at by *trial and error or a search mechanism* rather than through a closed-form solution.

One implementation of a neural networks is a *multilayer perceptron* (see Figure 10.5). In this model, there are three layers of neurons, an input layer, a hidden layer and an output layer. Each of the neurons in the input

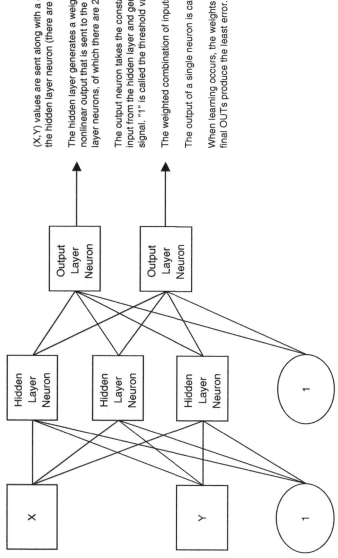

(X,Y) values are sent along with a constant value of 1 to the hidden layer neuron (there are 3 in the illustration).

The hidden layer generates a weight and generates a nonlinear output that is sent to the next layer (the output layer neurons, of which there are 2 shown here).

The output neuron takes the constant value of 1 with input from the hidden layer and generates the output signal. "1" is called the threshold value.

The weighted combination of inputs is called NET.

The output of a single neuron is called OUT.

When learning occurs, the weights are adjusted so that the final OUTs produce the least error.

FIGURE 10.5 Multilayer Perceptron
Source: Berry and Trigueiros (1993).

layers is connected to the each neuron in the hidden layer. The input layer provides the external input to the network. The hidden layer receives inputs from the input layer or another hidden layer, and provides the input to the output layer. The output layer receives the inputs from the hidden layer and then produces the output. The output in the case of a credit model is a "good credit" or a "bad credit" determination. Depending upon the correctness of the prediction, the weights are adjusted.

The input layer neuron sends a signal to the hidden layer that represents the value of the input variable associated with itself. The input variable value may be a ratio-level value or a categorical value and may be any of several input variables. A weight is assigned to the connection from the input neuron to the hidden layer neuron. The hidden layer neuron applies weight on the input value, using a nonlinear transformation to generate a signal Y_i, such that $0 \leq Y_i \leq 1$. This transformation is called a transfer function.

Each output layer neuron receives its input from each hidden layer neuron in the same fashion, that is, using a combination of weights and transfer function. The ovals in the illustration are not neurons. They are signal generators that send a constant value of 1 along the weighted connections to the hidden layer and to the output layer neurons. This signal becomes a part of the P_i representing a threshold value for each receiving neuron. Beyond the threshold value, Y_i rises rapidly. The outputs from the output layer in the case of a two-group problem will be 0 for one neuron and 1 for the other. The network learns to generate these values by adjusting the interconnection weights W_{ji} during the training process, using a feedback loop containing the error which is the output value minus the (expected) target value. The training takes place repeatedly until a preset performance level, expressed as the maximum percent of prediction errors, is reached.

If the network is unable to reach the target accuracy rate, the number of hidden layers may be increased. In some instances, the hidden layer is also changed dynamically by the solution algorithm used to adjust the interconnection weights. Once the training phase is completed, the network may be used for predictive purposes.

The learning mechanism involves a number of problems:

- The learning stage may be very prolonged and require a huge number of cycles.
- The system might lock into a *local* minimum error without ever attaining the *global* (or the best attainable) error rate.
- The system may start oscillating between one or two minimum error points.
- The system may not work well if the actual conditions differ significantly from the test conditions.

■ The analysis of the weightings is complex and difficult to interpret. It is also difficult to know beforehand if the system is robust—that is, insensitive to small variations in input values. This may happen if the neural network suffers from overfitting.

CASA has developed a neural network-based default prediction model.[6] Compustat data for the timeframe 1985–1995 was used in the development sample. Traditional financial ratios, equity prices, and BARRA factors were some of the inputs presented to the network.[7] The validation of the neural net model was performed using a *k-group cross-validation* approach, whereby the sample was divided into *k* groups, with $(k - 1)$ groups providing the training data and the *k*th group the test data. The sample consisted of nonfinancial firms with annual sales exceeding $600 million. Predictions were based on the period preceding the date of financial failure, variously defined. A backward propagation algorithm was used to develop the models.

In a 1997 interview, Camilo Gomez, Director of CASA's Investment Analytics group, discussed his observations that, when compared against a benchmark model based on linear discriminant analysis, the *mean classification error* (MCE) performance of the neural network model was superior. "One of the advantages of neural nets is that they can model nonlinearity through the use of the transfer functions," noted Jose Hernandez, an analyst at CASA in an interview with author Paul Naryanan. He found that the final models exhibited a "weakly nonlinear" tendency. Although it is possible to combine a set of linear models together (one model for each of *k* groups), it is more difficult to integrate a set of nonlinear models constructed this way. "Preparing the data properly to present it to the networks and using robust statistics to handle outliers are important elements of building a neural network model," adds Hernandez.

Cost of misclassification was incorporated in the implementation segment yielding interesting results. Industry groupings, the BARRA factors, and equity prices did not add significantly to the predictive ability of the model. According to Camilo Gomez (1997) the results indicate that accounting statement financial ratios have information about corporate failure.

The neural network approach may be criticized for its ad hoc theoretical foundation and its use of data mining to identify hidden correlations among the explanatory variables rather than having an a priori theory. In a comparison test, Altman, et al. (1994) concluded that the neural network approach did not materially improve upon the linear discriminant structure in predicting bank failure. Notwithstanding this finding, neural networks have a profound potential to improve upon past results and are already being used in credit risk assessment and fraud detection.

EXPERT SYSTEMS

Expert systems also sometimes known as AI (artificial intelligence) are computer-based decision-support systems. Expert systems make inferential and deductive judgment about a credit based on three components:

1. A consultation module that interacts with the user by asking questions, providing intermediate answers and hypotheses, and asking further questions until enough evidence has been collected to support a final recommendation.
2. A knowledge base containing static data; algorithms for financial simulation, optimization and statistical forecasting; and a set of "production rules" telling the system "what to do if."
3. A knowledge-acquisition and learning module that generally consists of two components. The first creates production rules based on inputs provided off-line by an expert. For example, the system will extract from the lending officer the importance of customer background information relative to the business potential. The second component generates additional rules on its own.

Although AI systems appear to hold promise in the credit evaluation area (see Chorafas and Steinmann 1991), there growth in this areas has been gradual—apart from a few specialized applications in selected instances.[8] One reason for the slow market penetration by AI is that the nature of credit risk itself is changing in the global financial system. Even human experts become obsolete quickly, and an automated expert runs the same risk! AI models may need frequent retooling and redesign. New technology has made a stronger contribution to progress in other aspects of the banking business, making it possible for institutions to increase their vigilance on credit exposure[9] and to be more flexible in extending credit because of better information systems.[10] We anticipate further innovations in this area as loan products and risk rating criteria become more standardized and quantitative. In particular there has been a development of rules engines such as Blaze (offered by Fair Isaac) that facilitate the rapid definition and deployment of credit decision processes by financial institutions.

MODELS BASED ON MARKET RISK PREMIUMS

Models of this type seek to impute implied probabilities of default from the term structure of yield spreads between default free and risky corporate securities. An early version of this approach can be found in Jonkhart (1979) and a more elaborate version in Iben and Litterman (1989). These models derive implied forward rates on risk-free and risky bonds and use these rates to extract the market's expectation of default at different times in the future. This approach is based on the assumptions that (1) the expectations theory of interest rates holds; (2) transaction costs are small; (3) calls, sinking fund, and other option features are absent; and (4) discount bond yield curves exist or can be extracted from coupon-bearing yield curves. Other models for defaultable loans include the effect of default risk, term structure risk, and market risk (see for example, Grenadier and Hall 1995; Longstaff and Schwartz 1993; and Das and Tufano 1996). The Jarrow-Chava Model (2004) is a statistical hazard model that relates the probability of firm default to several explanatory variables. The explanatory variables include firm financial ratios, other firm attributes, industry classification, interest rates and information about firm and market equity price levels and behavior. In this model, firm default can occur randomly at any time with an intensity determined by the explanatory variables.

MORTALITY MODELS

The mortality rate model of Altman (1989) and the aging approach of Asquith, Mullins, and Wolff (1989) are both based on the capital markets. These mortality-default rate models seek to derive actuarial-type probabilities of default from past data on bond defaults by credit grade (Moody's, Standard & Poor's) and years to maturity. All of the rating agencies have adopted and modified the mortality approach (e.g., Moody's Investors Service 1990 and Standard & Poor's 1991) and now routinely utilize it in their analysis of structured financial instruments (e.g., Duff & Phelps, McElravey, and Shah 1996). Mortality and default rate models are discussed in greater detail in Chapter 15.

Mortality models have been extended from bonds to loans (e.g. Altman and Suggitt 1998) but to our knowledge have not been adopted by banks perhaps due to lack of sufficient databases. McAllister and Mingo (1994) estimate that to develop stable estimates of default probabilities, an institution would need some 20,000 to 30,000 "names" in its database. With one or two exceptions, very few institutions worldwide come even remotely close to approaching this number of potential defaulted borrowers.

Having presented models based on accounting and market data, we now turn to models that rely exclusively on market data to derive the credit risk of a borrower. This is the topic of the next chapter.

REFERENCES

Altman, E. I. 1968. "Financial Ratios, Discriminant Analysis and the Prediction of Corporate Bankruptcy." *Journal of Finance* 23, no. 4:589–609.
———. 1970. "Corporate Bankruptcy Prediction and its Implications for Commercial Loan Evaluation." *Journal of Commercial Bank Lending* 53, no. 12: 9–19.
———. 1973. "Predicting Railroad Bankruptcies in America." *Bell Journal of Economics and Management Science* 4, no. 1:184–211.
———. 1983. *Corporate Financial Distress*, New York: John Wiley & Sons.
———. 1989. "Measuring Corporate Bond Mortality and Performance." *Journal of Finance* 44, no. 4:909–922.
———. 1993. "Valuation, Loss Reserves and the Pricing of Corporate Loans." *Journal of Commercial Bank Lending* 75, no. 12:56–62.
———. 2000. "Predicting Financial Distress of Companies: Revisiting the Z-Score And ZETA® Models." New York University Salomon Center Working Paper Series.
———. 2002. "Corporate Distress Prediction Models In A Turbulent Economic and Basel II Environment." In *Credit Rating: Methodologies, Rationale and Default Risk*, edited by M. Ong. London: Risk Books.
———. 2005. "An Emerging Market Credit Scoring Model for Corporate Bonds." *Emerging Markets Review* 6, no. 4:311–323.
Altman, E. I., R. G. Haldeman, and P. Narayanan. 1977. "ZETA Analysis: A New Model to Identify Bankruptcy Risk of Corporations." *Journal of Banking and Finance* 1, no. 1:29–54.
Altman, E. I., J. Hartzell, and M. Peck. 1997. "Emerging Markets Corporate Bonds: A Scoring System." In *Emerging Market Capital Flows*, edited by R. Levich. Amsterdam: Kluwer.
Altman, E. I., and E. Hotchkiss. 2005. *Corporate Financial Distress and Bankruptcy*, 3rd ed. New York: John Wiley & Sons.
Altman, E. I., G. Marco, and F. Varetto. 1994. "Corporate Distress Diagnosis: Comparisons Using Linear Discriminant Analysis and Neural Networks." *Journal of Banking & Finance* 18, no. 3:505–529.
Altman, E. I., and P. Narayanan. 1997. "An International Survey of Business Failure Classification Models." *Financial Markets, Institutions and Instruments* 6, no. 2:1–57.
Altman, E. I., and G. Sabato. 2007. Modeling Credit Risk for SMEs: Evidence from the U.S. Market." *Abacus* 19, no. 6:716–723.
Altman, E. I., and H. J. Suggitt. 2000. "Default Rates in the Syndicated Bank Loan Market: A Mortality Analysis." *Journal of Banking & Finance* 24, no. 1–2:229–253.
Asquith, P., D. W. Mullins Jr., and E. D. Wolff. 1989. "Original Issue High Yield Bonds: Aging Analysis of Defaults, Exchanges and Calls." *Journal of Finance* 44, no. 4:923–952.

Beaver, W. 1966. "Financial Ratios as Predictors of Failures." In *Empirical Research in Accounting*, selected studies, supplement to *Journal of Accounting Research* 4, no. 3:71–111.

———. 1968. "Alternative Accounting Measures as Predictors of Failure." *Accounting Review* 43, no. 1:113–122.

Bennett, P. 1984. "Applying Portfolio Theory to Global Bank Lending." *Journal of Banking & Finance* 8, no. 2:153–169.

Chava, S., and R. A. Jarrow. 2004. "Bankruptcy Prediction with Industry Effects." *Review of Finance* 8, no. 4:537–569.

Chirinko, R., and G. Guill. 1991. "A Framework for Assessing Credit Risk in Depository Institutions: Toward Regulatory Reform." *Journal of Banking & Finance* 15, no. 4–5:785–804.

Coats, P., and K. Fant. 1993. "Recognizing Financial Distress Patterns Using a Neural Network Tool." *Financial Management* 22, no. 3:142–155.

Das, S. R., and P. Tufano, 1996. "Pricing Credit-Sensitive Debt When Interest Rates, Credit Ratings and Credit Spreads Are Stochastic." *Journal of Financial Engineering* 5, no. 2:161–198.

Dawes, R. M., and B. Corrigan. 1974. "Linear Models in Decision-making." *Psychological Bulletin* 81:95–106.

Deakin, E. B. 1972. "A Discriminant Analysis of Predictors of Business Failure." *Journal of Accounting Research* 10, no. 1:169–179.

Dun & Bradstreet. 1997. *The U.S. Business Failure Record.* New York.

Dwyer, D. W. 2005. "Examples of Overfitting Encountered When Building Private Firm Default Prediction Models." Moody's KMV, New York.

Dwyer, D. W., A. E. Kocagil, and R. M. Stein. 2004. *Moody's KMV RiskCalc*™ *V3.1 Model.* San Francisco: Moody's KMV Corporation.

Fisher, L. 1959. "Determinants of Risk Premiums on Corporate Bonds." *Journal of Political Economy* 67, no. 3:217–237.

Frydman, H., E. I. Altman, and D. L. Kao. 1985. "Introducing Recursive Partitioning Analysis for Financial Classification: The Case of Financial Distress." *Journal of Finance*, 40, no. 1:269–291.

Goldstein, M., and I. F. Goldstein. 1978. *How We Know: An Exploration of the Scientific Process.* New York: Plenum Press.

Grenadier, S. R., and B. J. Hall. 1996. "Risk-based Capital Standards and the Riskiness of Bank Portfolios: Credit and Factor Risks." *Regional Science and Urban Economics* 26, no. 3–4:433–464.

Iben, T., and R. Litterman. 1991. "Corporate Bond Valuation and the Term Structure of Credit Spreads." *Journal of Portfolio Management* 17, no. 3:52–64.

Jonkhart, M. 1979. "On the Term Structure of Interest Rates and the Risk of Default." *Journal of Banking & Finance* 3, no. 3:253–262.

Kao, D. L., and J. Kallberg. 1994. "Strategies for Measuring and Managing Risk Concentration in Loan Portfolios." *Journal of Commercial Bank Lending* 76, no. 5:18–27.

Lachenbruch, P. A. 1967. "An Almost Unbiased Method of Obtaining Confidence Intervals for the Probability of Misclassification in Discriminant Analysis." *Biometrics* 23, no. 4:639–645.

Lane, W. R., S. W. Looney, and J. W. Wansley. 1989. "An Application of the Cox Proportional Hazards Model to Bank Failure." *Journal of Banking & Finance* 10, no. 4:511–531.

Lee, E. T. 1980. *Statistical Methods for Survival Data Analysis*, Belmont, Ca: Lifetime Learning Publications.

Longstaff, F. A., and E. S. Schwartz. 1995. "A Simple Approach to Valuing Risky Fixed and Floating Rate Debt." *Journal of Finance* 50, no. 3:789–819.

Lovie, A. D., and P. Lovie,. 1986. "The Flat Maximum Effect and Linear Scoring Models for Prediction." *Journal of Forecasting* 5, no. 3:159–168.

McAllister, P., and J. J. Mingo. 1994. "Commercial Loan Risk Management, Credit-Scoring and Pricing: The Need for a New Shared Data Base." *Journal of Commercial Bank Lending* 76, no. 9:6–20.

McKinsey & Co. 1993. "Special Report on The New World of Financial Services." *The McKinsey Quarterly*, no. 2:59-106.

Merton, R. C. 1973. "An Intertemporal Capital Asset Pricing Model." *Econometica* 41, no. 5:867–887.

Moody's Investors Service. 1995, January. *Corporate Bond Defaults and Default Rates*. New York.

———. 2000, May. *Rating Methodology: Benchmarking Quantitative Default Risk Models*. New York.

———. 2000, May. *RiscCalc*™ *Private Model: Moody's Default Model for Private Firms*. New York.

Moody's KMV Corporation. 2004, May 25. *EDF RiskCalc V3.1 Japan*. New York.

Mueller, P. H. 1994. "Credit Policy: The Anchor of the Credit Culture." *Journal of Commercial Bank Lending* 76, no. 7:1–5.

Ohlson, J. 1980. "Financial Ratios and the Probabilistic Prediction of Bankruptcy." *Journal of Accounting Research* 8, no. 1:109–113.

Orgler, Y. 1980. "A Credit Scoring Model for Commercial Loans." *Journal of Money, Credit and Banking* 2, no. 4:435–445.

Scott, J. 1981. "The Probability of Bankruptcy: A Comparison of Empirical Predictions and Theoretical Models." *Journal of Banking and Finance* 5, no. 3:317–344.

Sharpe, W. 1972. "Simple Strategies for Portfolio Diversification: Comment." *Journal of Finance* 27, no. 1:127–129.

Society of Actuaries. 1996. *1986–1992 Credit Risk Loss Experience Study: Private Placement Bonds*. Schlaumburg, Ill.

Standard & Poor's. 1995. "Corporate Defaults Level Off in 1994." *Creditweek*, 1 May, 45–59.

———. 2003, December 8. *CreditModel Performance Statistics*. New York.

———. 2004, January 12. *About CreditModel*. New York.

———. 2006. September 9. *Credit Risk Tracker North America: Technical Documentation*. New York.

Trippi, R. R., and E. Turban (eds). 1996. *Neural Networks in Finance and Investing*, Chicago: Irwin Professional Publishing.

Wuffli, P., and D. Hunt. 1993. "Fixing the Credit Problem." *The McKinsey Quarterly*, no. 2:93–106.

Wyss, D., C. Probyn, and R. de Angelis. 1989. *The Impact of Recession on High Yield Bonds, Alliance for Capital Access*, Washington, D.C.

Zavgren, C. V. 1983. "Corporate Failure Predictors: The State of the Art." *Journal of Accounting Literature* 2:1–38.

Zmijewski, M. E. 1984. "Methodological Issues Related To the Estimation of Financial Distress Prediction Models." *Journal of Accounting Research* 22 supplement:59–82.

CHAPTER 11

Corporate Credit Risk Models Based on Stock Price

The manifest function of financial markets is to allow individuals and businesses to trade financial assets. An additional latent function of the capital markets is to provide information useful for decision-making. As the diversity of financial markets has increased during the past two decades, so too have opportunities to extract useful information from the prices of financial instruments.
—Robert Merton and Zvie Bodie (1995, 15)

The stock market can be viewed as a vast mechanism for valuing companies that are publicly owned. Information about economies, industries, and companies travels at high speed to investment analysts and investors both large and small. As a result, stock prices fluctuate throughout the business day. To the extent that variations in a company's stock price provide reliable evidence of changes in its creditworthiness, lenders have an opportunity to tap into a readymade credit risk management tool of immense scope and power.

A leading example of stock market based credit measures is the EDF model of Moody's KMV (MKMV).[1,2] KMV initially began with the measurement of expected default frequency and has now extended into portfolio management (see Chapter 19).

To understand the KMV model, we begin with the developments in modern finance that led to options pricing methods. For a more detailed description of these developments, we refer the reader to standard texts on finance theory (see, for example, Haugen 1997). The notion that options pricing methods can be used to assess credit risk may at first seem improbable, but the logic of this approach becomes clearer as we trace the evolution of corporate finance theory. After describing and critiquing the KMV model, we contrast it with ZETA, since these are the models for measuring of credit risk that are best known today.

PREDECESSORS OF OPTIONS THEORY

In the 1950s, Franco Modigliani and Merton Miller (1958) began an exploration of the determinants of a corporation's capital structure that ultimately led to a radical revision in corporate finance. A firm's capital structure is the particular mixture of debt, equity, and other liabilities that the firm uses to finance its assets. Until Modigliani and Miller, the prevailing view was that the market place required more return on a firm's debt as its leverage increased, with the natural result that at some level of leverage, the additional required return would make the use of more debt undesirable. In part, this view was based upon the notion that the firm's investment policy was related to capital structure. The required yield on a debt issue would depend on how the firm intended to use the proceeds. As the firm tried to invest more, its return on investment would fall. The overall implication was that there existed a certain level of leverage that would minimize the firm's overall cost of capital. What Modigliani and Miller showed was that, under certain simple conditions, the overall cost of capital was independent of the particular mixture of debt and equity. They also showed that this was the case, even though increasing leverage led to higher required returns on both the debt and equity of the firm.

This was a startling result because it meant that there had to be an additional factor or factors, in addition to leverage alone, to explain a firm's capital structure. The search for the additional factors continues today, with some consensus but much disagreement still on the relative importance of various factors, which include the income tax effects on interest expense and dividends

Equally important to their specific results was Modigliani and Miller's mode of analysis. Their approach was to consider the investment decision and the financing decision separately. A given investment plan implied a stream of expected cash flows for the firm, and that implied a market value for the firm today. This made the market value of the firm into the underlying firm characteristic. The market value of the firm's debt, equity, and other liabilities derived from the overall value of the firm and these, taken together, added up to the firm value.

In essence, the expected operating cash flows of the firm determined its overall value; the capital structure merely represented the division of those cash flows to providers of capital. For instance, more debt meant that debt holders provided more capital and received more of the firm's cash flows. However, it did not intrinsically raise or lower the value of the firm because it was considered separately from the investment program.

Unfortunately, at the time that Modigliani and Miller wrote, there was no known way to separately determine the debt and equity values. By the rules of debt, debt holders are paid before equity holders; debt has seniority. No method existed for determining the value of the debt as a senior claim on the firm's cash flows, nor equity as a junior claim. The world had to wait for the development of options pricing theory.

OPTION PRICING

There are three basic types of financial contracts: spot transactions, forwards, and options. A spot transaction is one that occurs "on the spot," namely, where an asset is sold for the current price and is paid for immediately in cash. A forward transaction is where the price is agreed today, but the delivery of the asset and the payment actually occur at an agreed future date. An exchange traded futures contract is a type of forward transaction.

An option contract is like a forward except that the buyer of the option does not have to carry out the transaction. They can choose whether or not to go through with the transaction on the agreed terms. The option can be either an option to buy (call option) or an option to sell (put option). The option usually has a maturity, and sometimes can be exercised before maturity. The buyer of a call option has an asymmetrical payoff function in that her upside potential is unlimited if the price of the underlying stock goes up, and the downside risk is limited to the price she paid for the option. The seller of this option has exactly the opposite payoff function. She has an unlimited downside as the stock price goes up, but the upside is limited to the price she received when initially selling the call option. The discerning reader can immediately start seeing the similarities between a call option to and the equity itself. Both forward and option contracts are considered derivatives because their values can be derived from the value of the spot transaction. Perhaps the major development in finance in the last 30 years is options pricing theory. This work is due to Fisher Black, Myron Scholes and Robert Merton, and it shows how to derive options prices, including formulas for special cases. The fundamental idea behind options pricing is a generalization of how forward contracts are priced (Black and Scholes 1973, and Merton 1973).

A forward purchase contract involves specifying the terms of transaction that takes place at a later date. The same result as buying an asset forward can be achieved by borrowing money to buy the asset today, and repaying the borrowing at the maturity date. This results in ownership of the asset at maturity by making a payment specified today. Since this yields the same payoff as the forward purchase contract, it must have the same value. Thus, the forward price today must be the cost of buying the good today times one plus the rate of interest one must pay on the borrowing at maturity. In essence, the payoff to the forward contract can be mimicked by buying the asset today and borrowing. Thus these two alternatives must have the same value today.

The payoff to a call option can also be mimicked by buying the asset and borrowing. However, instead of making a single transaction, as in the case of the forward transaction, it is necessary to make an initial transaction and then adjust it as the spot price of the asset changes through time and the maturity decreases. Black and Scholes derived a method for constructing the initial transaction and subsequent adjusting transactions so that the option payoff is mimicked and no additional cash is required or produced. This means that the value of the option must be the same as the cost of the initial transaction.

In order to make their derivation, however, they needed to know one additional piece of information: the volatility of the underlying asset. The volatility measures the likely percentage range of variation of the spot price of the underlying asset. Generally, greater volatility implies a larger purchase transaction and thus a larger value for the call option. The end result of the work of Black, Scholes, and Merton was to derive the "fair value" of an option on the stock of a company in terms of the strike price, the current price, time to expiration, the volatility of the stock price and the riskless rate of interest. As will be explained next, many financial claims such as stocks and bonds, as well as other complex financial instruments lend themselves to be modeled using the option pricing framework.

EQUITY IS A CALL OPTION

The option pricing work of Black, Scholes (1973), and Merton (1973) neatly dovetailed with the capital structure theory of Modigliani and Miller. Junior and senior capital structure claims can be understood as options. Thus, one can determine the value of a firm's equity by reference to the underlying market value of the firm. Options pricing supplied the valuation technique that was missing a decade earlier when Modigliani and Miller realized that equity and debt were derivatives.

How does this work? Consider a very simple holding company, whose only asset consisted of shares in a publicly traded company, say, IBM. Let us assume that the holding company has debt and equity, and the debt consists of a single discount note due in one year. Let D be the face value of the note.

This means that the firm must make a single payment in one year of D, or it must default. If it defaults, it will turn over its assets to the lender, and its equity will be worthless.

Under what circumstances will the firm default? If the value of its asset, the IBM stock, is worth more than D in one year, then the firm will not want to default, and will not have to. By selling enough IBM stock, it can repay the debt, and still retain the difference between the value of the stock and D. On the other hand, if the IBM stock is worth less than D, then the firm will want to default, since it would rather give the lenders the stock than have to come up with additional money to pay off the debt. If it did come up with the additional money, it would get nothing for it, since it would just go to repay the debt. On the other hand, if it defaulted, then it could use the additional money to capitalize a new firm. In short, the firm will default and the equity will be worthless if the assets are worth less than D in one year; and the firm will not default and the equity will be worth the difference between the asset value and D, if the assets are worth more than D in one year.

The equity of the holding company in this example has exactly the same payoff as a call option on the same amount of IBM stock as held by the firm, with an aggregate exercise price of D. In that case, the option would be exercised when the IBM stock was worth more than D, and the payoff would be the difference between the IBM stock value and D; and otherwise the option would be worthless. In other words, the equity of the firm is a call option on the assets of the firm, where the exercise price and maturity are given by the face value and maturity of the debt.

We could explicitly value the equity of this firm if we knew the face value and the maturity of the debt, the value of the assets today and the volatility of the assets. For this simple example, we could actually use the Black-Scholes option pricing formula. For more complicated cases, we could not use the Black-Scholes formula, but we could use their general approach to obtain a value for the equity of the firm.

From the standpoint of credit analysis, the interesting point is that default can be thought of as the failure of exercise an option. Equity holders "optionally" own the firm, but if the firm does poorly enough, they do not exercise their option, but rather allow the firm's ownership to pass to the debt holders in lieu of paying the debt service.

DEBT IS LIKE SELLING A PUT OPTION

This circumstance can also be recast using the so-called "put-call" parity theorem. This says that purchasing a call option with an exercise price of D is equivalent to owning the underlying asset, borrowing with a required repayment of D, and holding a put option with an exercise value of D. At maturity, if the asset is worth less than D, one sells the asset for D using the put option and uses that to pay off the debt, with nothing left over. On the other hand, if the asset is worth more than D, one sells it and uses the proceeds to pay the debt, and does not use the put option. These are both the same payoffs as the call option, thus the equivalence.

Using this result, since the equity is a call option, we have the following interpretation: The equity holders own the asset, have borrowed D, but own a put that enables them to sell the assets for D. In essence, the debt holders of the firm, at the same time that they lent to the firm, by recognizing the possibility of default, have also "sold" a put option to the equity holders. The put enables the equity holders to "put" them the assets in lieu of paying off the debt. Thus the firm's debt is like a default risk-free loan of amount D less a put option. In this case, the event of default is identical to the exercise of the put option by the equity holders.

The firm's debt is always worth less than default risk-free debt because it is "short" a put option. The greater is the default risk of the firm, the more valuable is the put option, and the less valuable is the debt since it is short the put option. Debt subject to default risk can be decomposed into default risk-free debt and a put option. In doing credit analysis, the focus is on understating the value of the put option and the probability of it being exercised.

THE EDF MODEL

Moody's KMV Corporation (1995) has created an approach for estimating the default probability of a firm that is based conceptually on Merton's approach. It determines an *expected default frequency* (EDF) for a company using three steps. In the first step, the market value and volatility of the firm are estimated from the market value of its stock, the volatility of its stock and the book value of its liabilities. In the second step, the firm's default point is calculated from the firm's liabilities. Also an expected firm value is determined from the current firm value. Using these two values, plus the firm's volatility, a measure is constructed that represents the number of standard deviations from the expected firm value to the default point (the *distance to default*). Finally, an empirical mapping is constructed between the distance to default and the default rate, based upon the historical default experience of companies with different distance-to-default values.

In the case of private companies, where stock price and default data are generally unavailable, KMV uses essentially the same approach by estimating the value and volatility of the private firm directly from its observed

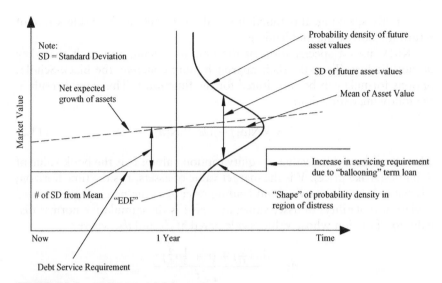

FIGURE 11.1   KMV Model Schematic
Source: Moody's KMV Corporation (1995).

characteristics and accounting data. These estimates, however, are based upon public company data.

The starting point of the KMV model is the proposition that when the market value of a firm drops below a certain level, the firm will default on its obligations (see Figure 11.1).

In Figure 11.1, the value of the firm, projected to a given future date, has a probability distribution, characterized by it expected value and standard deviation (volatility). The area under the distribution below the line representing the book liabilities of the firm, is the probability of default. As may be seen, this probability value depends on the shape of the distribution. The following is a detailed description of the methods used to implement the steps described above to obtain an empirical estimate of this default probability.

For a firm with publicly traded shares, the market value of equity may be observed. Using the previously described option approach, the market value of equity may be expressed as the value of a call option, as follows:

Market value of equity[3]

$= f$ (book value of liabilities, market value of assets,

volatility of assets, time horizon)   (11.1)

Strictly speaking, this function should also include the riskless rate of return for borrowing and lending.

KMV uses a special form of the options pricing approach that they do not disclose. To make their approach more concrete, the Black-Scholes options formula can be substituted for the function f. This would result in the following expression:

$$E = VN(d_1) - De^{-r\tau}N(d_2) \qquad (11.2)$$

where E is the market value of equity (option value); D is the book value of liabilities(strike price); V is the market value of assets; τ is the time horizon; r is the risk free borrowing and lending rate; σ_a is the percentage standard deviation (volatility) of asset value; and $N(\cdot)$ is the cumulative normal distribution function whose value is calculated at d_1 and d_2, where

$$d_1 = \frac{\ln\left(\frac{V}{D}\right) + \left(r + \frac{1}{2}\sigma_a^2\right)\tau}{\sigma_a\sqrt{\tau}}$$
$$d_2 = d_1 - \sigma_a\sqrt{\tau}$$

In equations (11.1) or (11.2), there are two unknowns: the market value of assets (V) and volatility of asset value (σ_a). However, it is also possible to derive another equation from equations (11.1) or (11.2), by taking the mathematical expectation of the total derivative.

Volatility of equity
= g (book value of liabilities, market value of assets,
volatility of assets, time horizon) \qquad (11.3)

Again, this equation can be understood by using the Black-Scholes formula as an example. By taking the first derivative on both sides of (11.2), and applying the *expectation* operator, one obtains the following expression[4] :

$$\text{Volatility of equity} = \sigma_e = \frac{N(d_1)V\sigma_a}{E} \qquad (11.4)$$

In equations (11.2) and (11.4), the known variables are the market value of equity (E), volatility of equity σ_e (estimated from historic data), book value of liabilities (D) and the time horizon τ). The two unknowns are the market value of the assets (V) and the volatility of the assets (σ). Since there are two equations with two unknowns, a solution can be found. This completes the first step.

Next, the expected asset value at the horizon and the default point are determined. An investor holding the asset would expect to get a payout plus a capital gain equal to the expected return. The expected return is related to the systematic risk of the asset. Using a measure of the asset's systematic risk, KMV determines an expected return based upon historic asset market returns. This is reduced by the payout rate determined from the firm's interest and dividend payments. The result is the expected appreciation rate which, applied to the current asset value, gives the expected future value of the asset.

In the previous analysis, it was assumed that the firm would default when its total market value reaches the book value of its liabilities. At that point, its value would just be sufficient to pay off its obligations. Based upon empirical analysis of defaults, KMV has found that the most frequent default point is at a firm value approximately equal to current liabilities plus 50 percent of long term liabilities.

Given the firm's expected value at the horizon, and its default point at the horizon, KMV determines the percentage drop in the firm value that would bring it to the default point. For instance, if the firm's expected value in one year was 100, and its default point was 25, then a 75 percent drop in the asset value would bring it to the default point. The likelihood of a 75 percent drop depends upon the volatility of the firm. By dividing the percentage drop by the volatility, KMV controls for the effect of different volatilities. Thus, if the firm's volatility were 15 percent per year, then a 75 percent drop would correspond to a five standard deviation event.

The number of standard deviations that the asset value must drop in order to reach the default point is called the *distance to default*. Mathematically, this can be expressed as:

$$\text{Distance to default} = \frac{(\text{expected market value of assets} - \text{default point})}{(\text{expected market value of assets})(\text{volatility of assets})}$$

The distance-from-default metric is a normalized measure and thus may be used for comparing one company with another. A key assumption of the KMV approach is that all the relevant information for determining relative default risk is contained the expected market value of assets, the default point and the asset volatility. Differences due to industry, national location, size, etc. are assumed to be subsumed in these measures, notably the asset volatility.

Distance from default is an ordinal measure, akin to a bond rating: it still does not tell you what the default probability is. In order to extend this risk measure to a cardinal or a probability measure, KMV uses historical default experience to determine an expected default frequency as a function of distance from default. It does this by comparing the calculated distances from default and the observed actual default rate for the same group of firms. A smooth curve fitted to those data yields the EDF as a function of the distance from default. The associative relationship between the derived distance to default using stock price data and debt outstanding on the one hand and the observed default frequency on the other constitutes the empirical component of this model.

PRIVATE COMPANY KMV MODEL

Since the EDF relies on market prices to predict default, it cannot be applied directly to private companies. For these, KMV uses data from public firms to develop an estimation model for the market value of assets and the asset volatility. It updates the parameters for these models frequently, as a way of connecting current market information to private firms. However, these models must rely upon the private firm's reported characteristics and accounting data, which may not be as timely or accurate as would be ideal.

The market value of the firm is modeled as shuttling between two values, the operating value and the liquidating value. The operating value is calculated as *earnings before taxes, interest, depreciation, and amortization* (EBITDA) times a multiplier. The multiplier is estimated by stratifying the public companies by country and industry. The liquidating value is based upon the firm's book liabilities. When EBITDA is high, the market value approaches the operating value; when it is low, it approaches the liquidating value. The effect of this formulation is to estimate a larger value than if the operating value were used alone. The liquidating value serves to "hold up" the value of the firm when its cash flow performance is bad.

The asset volatility of the firm is modeled as a function of sales size, industry and asset size. Since the asset volatility has already been estimated for publicly traded firms, the contribution made by sales size, industry group, and asset size are determined by a multivariate statistical technique. This relationship is then applied to a private firm's characteristics to obtain an estimate of its asset volatility.

Using the market value and volatility thus estimated, the EDF is estimated for the distance-from-default ratios on the basis of the public firm default experience in a similar manner to that described above.[5] However, the mapping between distance to default and EDF is slightly different between the public and private models, due to the information lost in using estimated rather than actual market data.

In all cases it is worth noting that the model for firms with nontraded equity is derived from the data for firms with publicly traded equity. Nontraded firms are assumed to behave identically to traded firms, once one takes into account the effects of size, industry and country.[6] Moody's KMV has replaced the private company KMV model by RiskCalc which uses financial ratios in a manner similar to Altman's Z-Score model.

KMV AND OTHER APPROACHES

The EDF model has two fundamental differences with other approaches. First, it relies on the information in equity prices. Two, it does not try explicitly to be predictive. Whereas agency debt ratings are based upon trying to forecast future events, there are no real future forecasts in the EDF model. It simply looks at the current value of the firm relative to its default point and historical volatility. Thus, if it has predictive power, it is because the current value of the firm is a good prediction of future values. Since this value is derived from the firm's equity market value, the EDF model is totally dependent on stock prices for its information content.

The starting point for all models is observation and human reasoning. EDF model comes from a conceptual model of firm value and its relation to debt and equity values, using options theory. The conceptual approach tells us which variables should be important, and mathematically how they should be combined. Statistical approaches identify important factors based on experience and consider structural assumptions and alternative relationships before settling on the most robust one. More general statistical approaches, such as neural nets, make few structural assumptions, but at the expense of requiring large amounts of data to be fit appropriately. All methods, KMV included, have an element of fitting. The difference is at what point the process of fitting to empirical experience is introduced.

There are costs and benefits with either approach. No conceptual approach provides a true ex ante specification of which variables to include and exclude, and historical testing of different alternatives is conceptually the same as statistically fitting a model. By narrowing the range of possible variables and the types of interactions, there is less likelihood of overfitting bias with the conceptual approach. But there is a possibility of underfitting (excluding what may be an important variable). Both overfitting and underfitting can result in less than satisfactory performance.

The stability of the conceptual approach relies upon the concept being correct, being correctly applied, and upon the stability of the estimates going into the model. The stability of the statistical approach relies on having correctly identified the important variables, the structural specification of the relationship, transformations to satisfy distributional assumptions and rigorous testing on independent samples. Both approaches leave open the possibility of refinement over time as better understanding develops of the fundamental forces at work.

Ultimately, however, the real issue is how well the models work and to what extent their use contributes to improved financial performance of the institution. A conceptual model that does not perform has no advantage over a statistical model that does. Unfortunately, there are no published comparisons of the different approaches, and until such time as such studies are made, the jury must remain out on the advantages or disadvantages of the different approaches.

However, rather than emphasizing the differences, it is also interesting to note the similarities. To assess similarities, the Spearman coefficient[7] was calculated for the 1995 EDF and the ZETA score based on book value of equity on a sample of 865 firms. The value of the coefficient came out to be 0.7031 and was significant at the 0.001 level. This indicates a fairly strong association between the two systems. Approximately half the variance in EDF ranks can be explained by ZETA score ranks, and vice versa.

The distance-to-default value contains two primary types of information: leverage and volatility. The relationship between the market value of the firm and the firm's liabilities is a leverage relationship, albeit based upon market rather than book values. This leverage is judged against the volatility of the firm, based again upon market rather than book values. Looking at ZETA, there is also extensive leverage information conveyed by book leverage and coverage ratios, as well as volatility information conveyed by earnings stability and size. It should not be surprising that there is a significant correlation between the two measures.

As noted, the most distinguishing feature of the EDF measure is that it imposes such a direct connection between market values and default probabilities. Historically, there is a close connection between changes in EDF values for a given firm and changes in the equity value of the firm, a much closer connection than exists for any extant statistical models. In KMV view, this is a desirable feature, because it represents a translation of the information in equity prices into credit information. The KMV approach, to a considerable extent, represents a change in paradigm from accounting based approaches to market value based approaches.

PREDICTIVE ABILITY OF DEFAULT MODELS

Most predictive models draw attention to their effectiveness by pointing to recent corporate defaults or bankruptcies that they correctly anticipated.

While this is impressive and necessary, it is rare to see instances publicized where the model predicted financial difficulties but nothing adverse subsequently happened. In looking at predictive models, one therefore must look beyond examples and anecdotal evidence to stronger statistical tests of effectiveness. The discussion that follows, while concerned with aspects of the KMV model, is applicable to other models as well.

The simplest test of the predictive accuracy of a model is to compare a specific prediction with the actual outcome. For example, if a model were to say that the unconditional probability[8] of default is 0.25 for a group of firms over a period of one year, and 25 percent of the firms in that group *actually defaulted* in the ensuing one year period, then the model would be 100 percent accurate and have 0 percent forecast error. The forecast error calculated from ex ante value (estimate) and ex post value (realization) is the best test of performance. If the predicted value of default probability were 25 percent and the realization 35 percent, then the model error would be 40 percent (35 minus 25 divided by 25). If the predicted probability were 25 percent and the realized default was 15 percent, then the error would still be 40 percent (25 minus 15 divided by 25). However, an error of the first kind (not anticipating failure) would cost many, many times more than that of the second kind (overanticipating failure). It should be noted that the forecast error is calculated not by applying it to a single firm, but to a group of firms with similar values of default probability.

The best test of predictive power begins by assembling data on the largest possible set of firms, including firms that subsequently defaulted and firms that did not default. For each firm, the model value is calculated at preset times prior to the event of default (for subsequent defaulters, or contemporaneously to the defaulters for the nondefaulters). For each possible level of model value, one can pretend that firms falling below that level are predicted to default, and firms above that value are predicted not to default. These predictions can then be compared with subsequent outcomes.

As noted thus far, there are two possible types of error: predicting default when it did not occur, and failing to predict default when it did occur. One can determine the error type for each level of model value. The resulting relationships provide a complete characterization of the default predictive power of the model.

The absolute results of such tests are dependent upon the particular samples used. In general, it is not appropriate to compare results from one population with results on a different population. To compare two different models, it is important to use exactly the same sample population, and only include firms on which both model values were simultaneously available.

The limitation of such tests is that they concentrate solely on default prediction. For higher quality segments of the population where defaults are rare, it is difficult to draw conclusions strictly from default prediction power. It is particularly the higher quality ranges where one often wants to use a model to rank firms' risks for purposes of pricing or portfolio management. Models may exhibit similar default prediction power for higher quality firms, but provide surprisingly different rankings of default risk simply because the predicted default rates are small and there are few subsequent defaults to validate one approach versus the other.

In an ideal world, one could test rankings on higher quality firms by looking at the agreement of the default risk rankings with the market pricing of the firm's debt instruments. In practice, this is rendered difficult because the price differences in credit risky assets are not entirely due to risk of default alone: Other factors such as supply and demand conditions, differences in investor risk premium over expected loss, liquidity risk, and state taxes play a role in the asset pricing.

As a final point, it can be argued that comparisons of alternative models are meaningful only in the context of portfolio risk *and* reward. There is a natural distribution of credits in the world (there are far fewer AAA credits than BBB credits, for example), and there is a market-determined risk premium for each of these credits. Rather than comparing prediction error rates among models, a more direct evaluation could be carried out by means of a trading simulation based on consistent decision rules and constraints. The resulting profit and loss numbers could then be compared. Innovations in fixed income portfolio management increasingly use this approach. For example, Diversified Credit Investments, Inc. a money management firm founded by two of the founders of KMV employs an asset valuation approach using the EDF which guides the asset selection process. Implied default probabilities and implied recovery rates feature prominently in the models used to value credit swap spreads today in the credit derivatives markets.

DEFAULT PREDICTION RESULTS FOR THE KMV MODEL

Moody's KMV's published results indicate that it is a more powerful default predictor than S&P's ratings. For example, using an EDF hurdle, which excludes 72 percent of the subsequent defaulters, only eliminates 20 percent of the nondefaulting population. Using an S&P hurdle, which excludes the same 72 percent of the defaulters, excludes almost 30 percent of the nondefaulters. Although agency debt ratings provide a convenient benchmark for judging performance, it should be noted that the markets do not view bond rating changes as conveying timely information (Wakeman 1990). Outperforming the rating agency is thus a necessary but by no means a sufficient condition because bond yields appear to lead the rating agency changes as

TABLE 11.1 Performance of the Helix Model in Anticipating S&P's Rating Changes

	Total	Led	Instances Where Helix Coincided	Followed	Disagreed
Upgrades	203	157	5	5	36
Downgrades	217	144	7	12	54
Total	420	301	12	17	90
Upgrades	100 %	77.3%	2.5%	2.5%	17.7%
Downgrades	100%	66.4%	3.2%	5.5%	24.9%
Total	100%	71.7%	2.9%	4.0%	21.4%

Source: Helix Investment Partners, L.P (1997).

well. For an updated assessment of the EDF model see Bharath and Shumway (2005).

The performance of the Helix model, another market value based approach, in anticipating rating changes by S&P illustrates this point (see Table 11.1). It reinforces the proposition that it *is* possible to anticipate rating changes. Even if the bond rating is not the ultimate arbiter of credit risk, the publication of comparative tables by KMV, Zeta and others will be helpful to the users of these models.

The question then becomes to what extent an EDF model is able to anticipate yield changes of publicly traded bonds. Promising results have been reported to this question, but a definitive study has yet to be published.[9]

APPLICATIONS

Historically, banks have ignored stock market prices in their lending decisions. To the extent that models such as those of KMV or Helix bring market capitalization into the lending equation, they should certainly add to the quality of the decisions made by banks. The actual uses to which financial institutions (mostly commercial banks) put KMV vary widely. At one end of the spectrum, some banks use a company's EDF as one more piece of information among the general sources it consults. Other institutions have formally added EDF values as supplemental information to the traditional credit analysis. Still others use the EDF as way of assigning internal risk ratings to their credits.[10] Some use EDF as an early warning tool in the portfolio review group to alert loan officers about changes in a company's risk profile. And at least one institution uses EDFs as the sole indicator of credit risk in loan pricing as well as in valuation related to the trading of bank debt.

KMV usually recommends that banks use the model in the manner most suited to their circumstances. For some, the EDF may serve as a tool to prioritize credit decisions. It may also help to minimize the time spent in assessing default risk so that greater resources can be focused on structuring a deal to maximize recovery in the event of default. In nearly all cases, the EDF model tends to act as a change agent in stimulating management thinking on credit risk.

In conclusion, the EDF model represents an innovative approach to utilizing stock market information in the valuation of debt. Banks can no longer ignore equity market information. They need to monitor equity market valuations constantly and to interpret the implications for credit risk. If a model is able to do so objectively and consistently, it is, as Brian Ranson of Bank of Montreal puts it in an interview with Paul Narayanan and John Caouette, "another arrow in your quiver." Clearly, as he goes on to point out, an institution cannot rely exclusively on the signals from one model—nor can it ignore them. John Hopper, Director of Structured Finance at Barclays Capital, in an interview with Paul Narayanan, agrees that KMV type models are very useful but points out that their conclusions have to be used along with other information and sometimes modified to suit the unique structure of a particular financing, as for example, funded subparticipations.

USE OF EDF IN ASSET VALUATION: STRUCTURAL MODELS AND REDUCED FORM MODELS

The development of the *credit default swap* (CDS) market in the last decade has led to an unprecedented ability to see how the market is pricing credit risk. Although the CDS spread for a company may be quite different due to various technical and financial factors, from the credit spread paid by it for its borrowed funds, the ability to trade credit risk has given rise to pure credit risk as an asset class, and a new class of investors who buy and sell credit risk. The "Long Short" fund for credit risk is an example. The use of KMV EDF–type tools to value credit risk, as exemplified by MKMV's CreditEdge and RiskMetrics Group's CreditGrades is now on the increase. The derivation of asset value, which has always been at the core of KMV EDF has come out into the open, and models that value credit-risky assets using Merton's construct of Debt as option are called "structural" models. This approach is implemented in KMV's portfolio manager with some modifications to reduce the valuation error from using the simple framework proposed by Merton.

While structural models develop asset values using a causal relationship between asset value and debt value, in the other class of competing models called "reduced form" models the approach used is to value risky assets taking the default process (or default intensity) as "given"; that is, as exogenous. In this approach, the model considers an idealized world where investors behave in a risk neutral fashion: In this world, the default probabilities take on values such that when the probability-weighted future cash flows from a bond are discounted by the risk-free rate, the resulting present value exactly equals the observed price. As mentioned previously structural and reduced form models are finding use in valuations in the CDS market. Turnbull (2005) provides a good summary of the unresolved problems with both types of models.

REFINEMENTS TO THE KMV EDF MODEL (1995–2006)

The KMV EDF originally introduced in 1985 with the modeling of asset volatility model has undergone refinements since its original inception, although the original formulation is believed to be unchanged. Recent refinements include updating the distance to default to a one-year EDF relationship through the use of MKMV's larger, updated default database, the recalibration of the one-year EDF floor from 2 basis points to 1 basis point and the cap from 25 percent to 35 percent, and remapping of the EDF term structure (i.e., two- to five-year EDFs) to be more in line with future "realized" EDF.

Another important change made in the KMV model is to use a slightly different approach for modeling financial institutions in recognition of the finding that the original KMV model tended to overstate the EDFs of financial firms. The unique business nature of a number of financial firms is that they behave as a combination of a portfolio and a number of franchise businesses and have a very real option to expand and shrink their franchise businesses. This makes them different from traditional industrial firms. For these firms the asset value asset volatility is derived from the interaction of these components as they individually pertain to the financial asset portfolio on the one hand and to the franchise or service business on the other. Using this dual-business approach is believed increase the accuracy of the estimated EDF for these firms.

CONCLUDING REMARKS

Innovative approaches such as KMV and ZETA provide decision makers with additional tools to be used in addressing credit risk management in a changing world. In conclusion, it is well to note Jules Henri Poincaré's

(1914) admonition, "To doubt everything or to believe everything are two equally convenient solutions; both dispense with the necessity of reflection." It is probably prudent neither to accept nor to reject these approaches in toto, but to subject them to objective examination and to use them in combination with other sources of information in making credit risk decisions.

REFERENCES

Arditti, F. D. 1996. *Derivatives: A Comprehensive Resource for Options, Futures, Interest Rate Swaps, and Mortgage Securities.* Boston: Harvard Business School Press.

Bharath, S.T., and T. Shumway. 2005. "Forecasting Default with the KMV-Merton Model." University of Michigan Working Paper.

Black, F. 1986. "Noise." *Journal of Finance* 41, no. 3:529–543.

Bohn, J. R., and N. Arora. 2006. EDF Credit Measures: Advancements and Evidence,- presented at Moody's KMV Credit Practitioner Conference, September 18–21, 2005, Key Biscayne, Florida.

Black, F., and M. Scholes. 1973. "The Pricing of Options and Corporate Liabilities." *Journal of Political Economy* 81, no. 2:637–654.

Bodie, Z., and R. C. Merton. 1995. "The Informational Role of Asset Prices: The Case of Implied Volatility." In *The Global Financial System,* by D. B. Crane et al. Boston: Harvard Business School Press.

Fridson, M. S., and J. G. Jónsson. 1997. "Contingent Claims Analysis Does not Cover All Contingencies." *Journal of Portfolio Management* 3, no. 2:30–43.

Galai, D. 1982. "A Survey of Empirical Tests of Option Pricing Models." In *Option Pricing: Theory and Applications,* edited by M. Brenner, Lexington, MA: Lexington Books.

Haugen, R. A. 1997. *Modern Investment Theory,* 4th ed. Upper Saddle River, N.J.: Prentice Hall.

Helix Investment Partners, L.P. 1997. *The Credit Ranker, December 1996/January 1997.* Los Angeles.

———. 1997 *Credit Rankings, October 1997.* Los Angeles.

Jarrow, R. A., and A. Rudd. 1983. *Option Pricing.* Homewood, Ill.: Dow-Jones Irwin.

Kliger, D., and S. Oded, "The Information Value of Bond Ratings." forthcoming.

Kealhofer, S. 1996. *Managing Default Risk in Portfolios of Derivatives,* mimeo. Moody's KMV Corporation.

Lehmann, E. 1975. *Nonparametrics: Statistical Methods Based on Ranks.* San Francisco: Holden-Day, Inc.

Markowitz, H. 1952. "Portfolio Selection." *Journal of Finance* 7, no. 1:77–91.

McQuown J. A. 1995. *A Comment on Market vs. Accounting Based Measures of Default Risk.* San Francisco: Moody's KMV Corporation.

Merton, R. C. 1973. "Theory of Rational Option Pricing." *Bell Journal of Economics and Management Science* 4, no. 1:141–183.

————. 1974. "On The Pricing of Corporate Debt: The Risk Structure of Interest Rates." *Journal of Finance* 29, no. 2:449–470.

Merton, R. C., and Z. Bodie. 1992. "The Management of Financial Guarantees." *Financial Management.* 21, no. 4:87–109.

Moody's KMV Corporation. Undated. Empirical Analysis of EDF as a Predictor of Default, unpublished memorandum.

————. 1992. *Credit Monitor II Overview.* San Francisco.

————. 1995. *Introducing Credit Monitor Version 4.* San Francisco.

————. 2005. *Structural Models of Credit Risk: A Case Study of Three Models.* San Francisco.

Newton, B. 1993. Modeling Credit Risk, presented at Bank Loan Portfolio Management Conference, IMI, New York, New York, October 27–28. Barra Associates, Berkeley, Ca.

Poincaré, H. 1914. *Science and Method*, preface by Bertrand Russell. New York: Dover Publications.

Roll, R. 1994. What Every CFO Should Know about Scientific Progress in Financial Economics: What Is Known and What Remains to be Resolved." *Financial Management* 23, no. 2: 69–75.

Sellers M., and N. Arora. 2004. *Financial EDF Measures: A New Model of Dual Business Lines—Modelling Methodology.* San Francisco: Moody's KMV Corporation.

Sharpe, W. F. 1964. "Capital Asset Prices: A Theory of Market Equilibrium under Conditions of Risk." *Journal of Finance* 19, no. 3:425–442.

Turnbull, S. M. 2005. "Unresolved Issues in Modeling Credit-Risky Assets." *Journal of Fixed Income* 15, no. 1:68–87.

Vasicek, O. A. 1995. *EDF and Corporate Bond Pricing.* San Francisco: Moody's KMV Corporation.

Wakeman, L. M. 1990. "The Real Function of Bond Rating Agencies." In *The Modern Theory of Corporate Finance*, edited by C. W. Smith. New York: McGraw-Hill.

CHAPTER 12

Consumer Finance Models

When you have eliminated the impossible, whatever remains,
however improbable, must be the truth.

— Sir Arthur Conan Doyle,
The Sign of Four

The consumer credit industry is a very large part of the financial markets in the United States and the impact of consumer debt on the economy is substantial and closely watched by policy makers and analysts. Change in the growth of consumer credit is frequently a leading indicator of economic upturns or slowdowns. Deterioration in the consumer debt service ratio, which measures the relationship of personal disposable income to interest and principal payments, is frequently a coincident indicator of recessions. The total size of the industry exceeds $12 trillion in loans. In mid-2006, consumer borrowing for residential real estate exceeded $10 trillion and there was an additional $2.3 trillion in consumer debt borrowed for other purposes according to the Federal Reserve Bank.

Most of us are broadly familiar with the residential mortgage market, whether for single-family homes or multifamily complexes, but less aware of the plethora of other personal borrowings. These range from secured nonrevolving products such as home equity loans or automobile and boat loans to unsecured revolving products, principally credit cards. Table 12.1 provides more details on the principal providers of consumer debt for non-real estate, including commercial banks, savings institutions, credit unions, finance companies, the federal government, and its agencies and nonfinancial companies. Securitizations provide almost 40 percent of the financing of general consumer debt and play an even larger role in the consumer real estate markets where they provide almost 60 percent. General consumer financing products have grown steadily in popularity since the end of World War II as shown in Figure 12.1. Demand for them was inherently high with

TABLE 12.1   Revolving vs. Nonrevolving Debt ($ millions)

	Revolving	Nonrevolving
Commercial banks	$ 300,068	$ 411,189
Finance companies	$ 70,688	$ 448,264
Credit unions	$ 25,575	$ 208,484
Federal government and Sallie Mae	$ —	$ 102,394
Savings institutions	$ 39,876	$ 60,485
Nonfinancial business	$ 11,677	$ 45,400
Securitized pools	$ 397,335	$ 228,114
Total	$ 845,218	$ 1,504,330

Source: FDIC (2006).

many consumers willing to prudently borrow to meet their immediate needs for more consumer durables and services against the promise in the future to repay. The problems were with the lenders, especially the banks, who were hampered for many years, first by restrictive regulations on their ability to raise new deposits paying market rates and to lend at market rates, and second by the slow development of mass consumer-lending technology and skills. These conditions changed in the early 1980s when usury rate ceilings were raised in many states and when banking regulations were changed

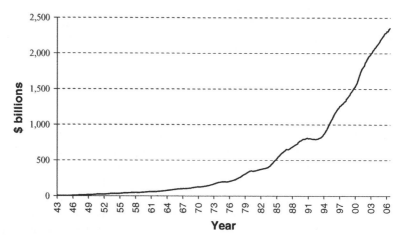

FIGURE 12.1   Consumer Credit, 1946–2006
Note: Series are seasonally adjusted.
Source: Board of Governors of the Federal Reserve System (2006).

to allow money market deposit accounts to be introduced. These changes had the effect of permitting lenders to raise more deposits, to charge higher rates, and to be much more aggressive with their lending policies. Consumer lending became a highly profitable, attractive line of business and the credit infrastructure changed quickly to enable its further growth. Securitizations of mortgage-backed securities were introduced in the mid-1970s and have grown quickly. This technology spread into the general consumer finance products and the first automobile securitizations were done in 1982 and the first credit card securitizations were completed in 1986. Mass-market consumer lending is a scale business requiring heavy up-front investment in systems, processes, and infrastructure that together represent significant barriers to entry.

Consumer credit risk management systems are applied across this whole range of retail products, from installment credit to home equity loans to credit cards and timeshares. These systems employ a whole range of techniques and rely on a deep supporting cast of businesses who supply essential services, from the credit bureaus to the collection agencies. This is where the concept and process of data mining originated.

As consumer debt has soared in recent years, so too have consumer bankruptcies and delinquencies where new records are being set almost annually, as shown in Figure 12.2. Table 12.2 shows clearly that while the number of businesses filing for bankruptcy has fluctuated within a fairly narrow band, the consumer filings have almost invariably increased year to

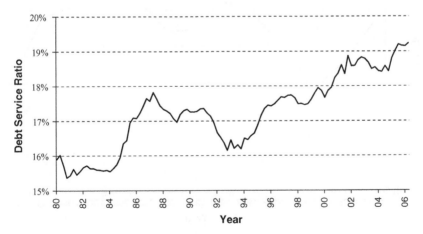

FIGURE 12.2   Debt Service Payments Ratio
Source: Board of Governors of the Federal Reserve System (2006).

TABLE 12.2 Credit Screening Criteria

Maximum debt to salary ratio of 60 percent
Must be 25 or older
Length of time on current job 2 years
Type of industry in which employed, for example,
No show-business people
No taxi drivers

year. This is the case despite the fluctuations in delinquency rates that we have seen over the last 25 years, shown in Figure 12.3.

CREDIT SCREENING MODELS

None of this huge growth in consumer credit would have been possible had it not been for the development of consumer credit scoring models. These were initially based on a judgmental analysis of an applicant's creditworthiness. The criteria shown in Table 12.3 were typical. For secured borrowings,

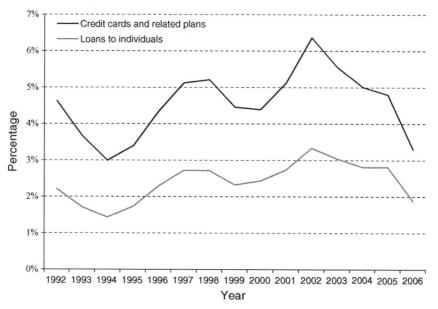

FIGURE 12.3 Delinquency Rates
Source: FDIC (2006).

TABLE 12.3 Judgmental Approval Credit Criteria

At least one year at current residence; phone number required; proof of residence required.
Three years of verifiable residence history on borderline cases.
At least one year in the current job.
Three years of verifiable employment history on borderline cases.
Length of employment requirement waived for recent college graduates.
Minimum $1,500 per month income with proof of income.
Self-employed must provide copies of 1040.
Debt ratio of 50 percent based on auto payment, mortgage, insurance, current loans, and other fixed obligations.
Clean credit bureau rating.

in particular for home mortgages, many lenders still rely primarily on the underlying security and a simple judgmental scorecard.

As loan volumes grew, the velocity of transactions increased many times, the size of transactions diminished, from mortgages to small personal loans, and credit scoring models became purely statistical, based on algorithms, which calculated a consumer's creditworthiness.

These statistical models fall into two categories: *application scoring models* and *behavioral scoring models*. Application models are static models and include a limited number of criteria (see Table 12.4). Behavioral scoring models contain significantly more information, which is dynamic and constantly updated. Many large U.S. banks derive behavioral scoring data from their transactional customers' accounts to better understand their spending and saving patterns and their cash flows.

The largest developers of consumer credit models and providers of credit scores are the credit reporting agencies, also called *credit bureaus*. Three agencies dominate the U.S. market, Experian, Equifax and TransUnion. Experian, for example, in 2006 had more than 215 million consumers and 110 million households in their data base. The models these agencies use are subject to federal regulation, particularly Regulation B of the Federal Reserve, which expressly prohibits the use in any models of race, gender, religion, national origin or marital status, and which requires that the models be statistically sound and empirically based.

Each of these agencies has their own proprietary scores either developed in-house or by outside vendors and the scores on the same individual almost certainly will differ between the agencies since their models, their definitions and their data bases are all independent and slightly different. The largest and most influential of the outside vendors is Fair Isaac Corporation whose products are known as *FICO scores*. These range from 300 to 850. The

TABLE 12.4   Credit Scoring Variables and Impact on Score

Variable	Impact
Rent or own	Own = +
Years at current address	High = +
Income per dependent	High = +
Marital status (single, married, divorced, separated)	Married = +
Occupation	Varies
Credit bureau inquiries[a]	Fewer = +
Other credit cards	Yes = +
Oil company credit cards owned	Yes = +
Number of adverse remarks on credit history	Fewer = +
Number of serious derogatory entries	Fewer = +
Number of inquiries in past 6 months	Fewer = +
Telephone number (yes or no)	Yes = +
Years on current job[b]	Higher = +

[a]Credit bureau reports have been shown to have considerable predictive value. See Chandler and Parker (1989, 47–54)
[b]This is becoming less valuable because creditors now believe that income stability is more important than job stability

median FICO score in the United States is 725 and generally a score of below 660 is regarded as subprime. Although the exact formulas for calculating the scores are not disclosed by any of these companies, Fair Isaac uses 10 distinct scorecards and has identified the following components and their approximate weighting:

- −35 percent based on the punctuality of payments.
- −30 percent based on the amount of revolving debt outstanding to revolving debt limits.
- −15 percent based on the length of credit history.
- −10 percent based on the mix of credit used.
- −10 percent based on any recent enquiries or credit recent successful applications.

In 2005, a new joint venture was formed between the three agencies called VantageScore LLC. In spring 2006, VantageScore rolled out a new scoring system which was developed from 15 million consumer samples, five million from each of the agencies, using information on the same individuals, using consistent definitions all as of the same date. The scores range from 501 to 990 divided into five bands from the A band at 901 to 990 being very low risk to the F band at 501 to 600 being very high risk. These scores could turn out to be very powerful since a new series of multiple scorecards are being used in the same algorithms across the agencies. If there are differences in scores between the agencies, consumers and lenders will know that it will be due to data differences, not scoring model differences. VantageScore has disclosed the outline of the components of their models as follows:

- 32 percent based on payment history.
- 23 percent based on limit utilization.
- 15 percent based on balances outstanding
- 13 percent based on depth of credit history.
- 10 percent based on recent credit enquiries or applications.
- 7 percent based on total credit available.

VantageScore claims that their systems will provide superior risk prediction, better segmentation and will better evaluate "thin" files for consumers with limited credit histories.

Given the importance of these reports, U.S. consumers by law have the ability to request a copy of their own report annually without charge from each of the agencies.

DESIGN OF CREDIT SCORING MODELS

The basic process for the design and implementation of consumer credit scoring models is presented in Table 12.5 below.

The presumption underlying consumer credit scoring models is that there exists a metric that can divide good credits and bad credits into two

TABLE 12.5 Design Process of Scoring Models

Step 1: Business Problem Definition
Step 2: Data Selection, Cleansing, Sampling
Step 3: Selection of Modeling Approach
Step 4: Model Development
Step 5: Interpretation of Results
Step 6: Approve After Independent Review
Step 7: Deploy Into Business
Step 8: Maintenance and Monitoring

Source: Cathcart (2004).

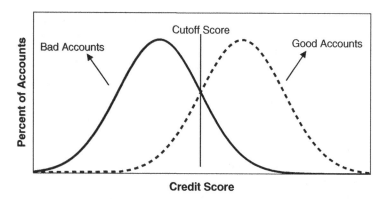

FIGURE 12.4   Distribution of Credit Scores of Good and Bad
Accounts in a Credit Scoring Model

distinct distributions as shown in Figure 12.4. There will be some overlap
between the two populations such that for every 100 applicants accepted
some will cause loss and for every 100 applicants rejected some will not
default. The objective is to set the cutoff point between the two populations
at a point that the income earned from the applicant pool is optimized after
credit losses. This is why defining the initial business problem is the critical
starting point because the population and the financial product have to be
fully understood.

Frequently, when a lender is starting to offer a new product or deal
with a new customer segment they have little data with which to work. In
these cases, they will have to use an outside vendor to provide statistical
samples until they have the opportunity to build their own database. Even
if they have their own data they will need to carefully select and cleanse the
data used. This step requires attention to detail and is often the most time
consuming step in the model building process. However errors at this point
can prove fatal to the final model. Data gathered is divided into a training
set of data, used to build the model, and a test data set used for validating
the model results. Both sets of data have to be statistically comparable.

The development of a credit scoring system typically proceeds as follows.
A representative sample of good and bad credits is developed based on the
lender's own experience.[1] Consistent definitions need too be used for bad
accounts, usually based on three payment delinquencies. Good accounts are
those that have not experienced arrears at that level. Note that at this stage
and in this model there is no consideration of profitability.[2]

A metric or scaling system is developed for each attribute captured in
the credit application form. Each attribute is captured in a way that makes

the application process less burdensome and which has significance in the differentiation process. Univariate statistics such as t, F, and R-squared statistics are employed to identify the important variables. Some analysts recommend the use of principal component analysis to eliminate highly correlated variables. The latter produce multicollinearity, which results in estimation problems.

The account performance information (good vs. bad) is available only for the population that was accepted by the lender. This leaves out the rejected population that was turned away. Lenders understand the critical importance of all data for modeling purposes and will keep records on this rejected population. However, if the lender does not track this population a model is sometimes constructed that distinguishes between the accepted and rejected populations. Using this model, the probability of acceptance, P_a, may be derived for any accepted account. By definition, this implies that for every accepted account fitting this profile there were $(1 - P_a)$ accounts that were rejected. This is weighted by the quantity $1/P_a$ to make the sample resemble the population that originally sought credit. This weighting is done for every account in the sample of accepted credits, both good and bad. For example if the probability of acceptance into the sample originally was .5 it means that one out of two who applied was accepted. Key assumptions are that (1) the rejected population does not contain subgroups that would not qualify for credit under any circumstances (perhaps bankrupts); (2) the accepted population does not contain subgroups that would have been accepted under any circumstances (perhaps employees of the lender); and (3) that sets of data were used for each population in making the original accept/reject decision.

A multivariate technique is used to select the best variables and weights to separate out the two groups with the greatest efficiency. The techniques may be optimization, discriminant analysis, logit analysis, probit analysis, or survival analysis.[3] The equations developed should be able to separate out the good accounts from the bad accounts so that the less overlap there is between the score distributions the better the model.

At this point, the modeler needs to interpret the results and question them intuitively. Do they capture the nuances of the line of business and do they compare reasonably with other results using different methodologies such as vintage analysis or roll rates.

TESTS FOR MODEL ADEQUACY

When a model is tested for statistical validity the weighting of the variables in the scoring model should make intuitive sense—for example, the income

TABLE 12.6   Raw Data

Bads	2.1	2.9	1.2	2.9	0.6	2.8	1.6	1.7	3.2	1.7
Goods	3.2	3.8	2.1	7.2	2.3	3.5	3.0	3.1	4.6	3.2

variable would be expected to have a positive sign. Furthermore, the variables should not run afoul of laws against discrimination in lending. For example, age may be used as a variable as long as it does not award negative points to the score. One commonly used test compares the score distribution of the good and the bad samples. If the tests of significance show that score distributions are statistically different, then the model can be further analyzed for acceptability.[4] Nonetheless, it is important to bear in mind that a model that behaves well diagnostically may not necessarily be the best predictive model.

This may be demonstrated by an example of the Kolmogorow-Smirnow (K-S) test, which is often employed in evaluating credit scoring models. The K-S statistic is the greatest observed ordinate difference between two empirical distribution functions. With equal class limits applied to both samples, the cumulative frequencies F_1 and F_2 are divided by the corresponding sample sizes n_1 and n_2. The K-S statistic D is given by

$$D = \max \left| \left(\frac{F_1}{n_1} - \frac{F_2}{n_2} \right) \right|$$

In the example here, a sample of 10 each yielded the scores as shown in Table 12.6.

To calculate the statistics, these scores are sorted in ascending order as shown in Table 12.7.

As shown in Table 12.8, the frequencies of the score values are then placed in class intervals. There are, for example, four scores in the range 2 to 2.9 for bads and 2 for goods.

The highest value of the absolute difference is $\frac{7}{10}$, which is the critical value for the given sample size.[5] Thus, the score distributions are significantly

TABLE 12.7   Data Arranged in Ascending Order

Bads	0.6	1.2	1.6	1.7	1.7	2.1	2.8	2.9	2.9	3.2
Goods	2.1	2.3	3.0	3.1	3.2	3.2	3.5	3.8	4.6	7.2

TABLE 12.8 Calculation of the K-S Statistics

Region	0.0–0.9	1.0–1.9	2.0–2.9	3.0–3.9	4.0–4.9	5.0–5.9	6.0–6.9	7.0–7.9
f_1	1	4	4	1	0	0	0	0
f_2	0	0	2	6	1	0	0	1
F_1/n_1	$\frac{1}{10}$	$\frac{5}{10}$	$\frac{9}{10}$	$\frac{10}{10}$	$\frac{10}{10}$	$\frac{10}{10}$	$\frac{10}{10}$	$\frac{10}{10}$
F_2/n_2	$\frac{0}{10}$	$\frac{0}{10}$	$\frac{2}{10}$	$\frac{8}{10}$	$\frac{9}{10}$	$\frac{9}{10}$	$\frac{9}{10}$	$\frac{10}{10}$
$F_1/n_1 - F_2/n_2$	$\frac{1}{10}$	$\frac{5}{10}$	$\frac{7}{10}$	$\frac{2}{10}$	$\frac{1}{10}$	$\frac{1}{10}$	$\frac{1}{10}$	0

different. But consider how sensitive this statistic is: If just *one* of the scores happened to be *slightly* different, the statistic would no longer be significant. In the example given, if one observation in the bads group had a score of 2.9 instead of 3.0, then the test statistic would become $\frac{6}{10}$, indicating that the homogeneity hypothesis cannot be rejected. Thus a change of 0.1 in value in 1 out of 20 observations can swing the model from *statistically significance* to *statistical insignificance*.

This model performs more effectively if the score cutoff is set at 3.9: at any score of 3.9 or higher, all bads are excluded. However, if the applicant population is heavily in the 2.0 range and the cutoff has to be reduced to say 2.0, then five bads will be accepted for 10 goods. Clearly, this is not a particularly good outcome. A statistically significant model can thus result in unacceptable results. Although this is a very simplified example using a very small sample, it does illustrate the pitfalls of relying exclusively on statistical tests of significance.

Another measure used to test the quality of the model is the Gini coefficient, which is also called the *cumulative accuracy profile* (see Chapter 10). Here the predictive accuracy of a model across the entire range of scores is compared with the predictive accuracy of a naïve model (i.e., which treats any credit is being equally likely to be good or bad).

OUT-OF-SAMPLE TESTING

Classification results on the development sample will almost always be good because of the sample bias of the model—that is, the model, by definition, was constructed to maximize in-sample discrimination. A more valid test of the model is carried out on an *independent* sample. The test consists of classifying good and bad credits based on the calculated probability of group membership and then looking at the error rate. Type I accuracy is the percent of the bad credits correctly identified: this is indicative of the ability of the model to minimize credit losses. Type II accuracy is the percent of the good credits correctly identified: this is indicative of the model's ability not to deny credit to truly creditworthy customers.[6] Type II accuracy is essential in making sure that the profit side of the equation is not sacrificed in the process of controlling the loss side. To prevent *data mining,* this sample should not be mixed with the development sample and its population characteristics should *not* be analyzed.

While the credit score is normally used only for a go/no-go decision, it is also used by some institutions to set the size of the credit. Others use the scoring model for credit approval, but set the line on the basis of income or some other measure of size. The current trend seems to be to let the market set the line. That is why, on any given day, many Americans may receive two or three unsolicited offers in the mail for a preapproved $10,000 line of credit.

ADVANTAGES AND DISADVANTAGES

Credit scoring models offer many advantages. They are objective and consistent, which are desirable characteristics for any institution, and especially so for those lacking a strong credit culture. If properly designed, they can eliminate discriminatory practices in lending. They tend to be relatively inexpensive, fairly simple and easy to interpret. Installation of such models is relatively straightforward. The methodologies used to build these models are common and well-understood, as are the approaches used to evaluate them. Regulators approve of well-designed, statistics-based models. An institution is able to render better customer service by its ability to approve or deny a loan request speedily. This is an important factor in today's fast-paced world.

However, these models do suffer from some drawbacks. In most cases, they simply automate the prevalent credit practices of the bank. They do little, in other words, to eliminate an institution's historical screening biases. Furthermore, if the variables do not satisfy underlying assumptions such as a multivariate normal distribution, the statistical validity of the models may be questionable. The statistical tests commonly used to whet these models are weak and may mislead the user into overestimating their efficacy. Models are typically tested against a static criterion. For example, the *approval rate* for various cutoff scores is weighed against the corresponding *bad rate*. The problem with this approach is that approval is a *one-time* event, whereas

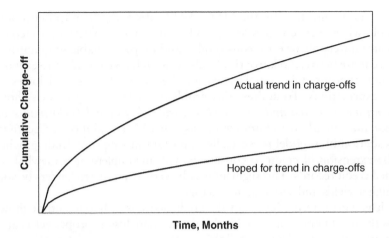

FIGURE 12.5   Charge-off Rate Over Time

charge-offs accumulate over a long period. Charge-offs do not all occur early in the credit cycle; on the contrary, experience suggests that the charge rate tends to hold steady over time as shown in Figure 12.5. The "expected charge" line in the chart below peaks early and flattens as time passes; the "actual charge" does not flatten, which means that losses continue to occur as the portfolio ages. It has been found that even with more stringent acceptance criteria, the slope of the curve does not change; it simply shifts downward. For this reason, any credit screening model should be evaluated in conjunction with the account balances and the cumulative charge rate over the life of the portfolio. With so much consumer finance being securitized, the charge-offs over time are now tracked by issuers and rating agencies. Standard & Poor's (1997), for example, uses ex post information (called *loss curve*) as the foundation for the amount of credit support needed for a given rating category: Both magnitude and timing of losses are important in sizing the credit support.

A credit scoring model may degrade over time if the population against which it is applied diverges from the original population used to build the model. Degradation in portfolio performance may occur if there manual overrides of the model-driven credit recommendations. For this reason, periodically the approval rate and the charge off rate within each score interval should be calculated and compared against the baseline approval rate and charge off rates estimated at the time of model development. If approval rate differs from the benchmark it may be due to a population shift or the presence of manual overrides.

A communication by the FDIC (1997) observes, "Lenders encounter trouble when their credit scoring models or other loan selection methods produce unreliable or erroneous results, and they are unable to quantify or differentiate between relative risk levels accurately. As a result, these lenders are not appropriately compensated for the assumed risks, and losses exceed expectations. To address this problem, credit scoring models should be *continually tested and evaluated to ensure that actual performance approximates initial projections* (emphasis added)." The ability to discern the degradation of a model is especially important in subprime lending, which is the extension of credit to consumers with incomplete or somewhat tarnished credit records. This segment may be very attractive to lenders because of higher yields and servicing fee income.

It is worth noting here that the credit score is only one, although perhaps the most important variable driving ultimate losses: proper verification of applicant data, adequate collection practices, economic forces (interest rates, personal income, unemployment rate, housing prices) and the legal environment (e.g. the bankruptcy laws) also affect the business losses.

DYNAMIC CREDIT RISK MANAGEMENT SYSTEMS

There are many who believe that the act of accepting or rejecting an applicant pretty much determines whether an account will ultimately perform as agreed or will become a charge-off. There are others who maintain that a lender can alter the odds of incurring a credit loss by changing the way it treats an individual borrower after studying his or her behavior. This latter philosophy underlies dynamic systems for credit risk management. Such systems are usually developed from a data warehouse which includes monthly billing history for every account—either at the transaction level or at a summary level. Behavioral models generally fall into the following four categories:

- Line increase/reissue models
- Collection models
- Account cancellation models
- Fraud detection models

Line increase models recognize the fact that the level of line utilization is inversely related to the quality of the credit. In order to encourage better quality credits to use their credit lines, lenders approve line increases with additional inducements, such as tiered pricing. Line increase models are constructed by incorporating line usage and timeliness of payments into the credit score—thereby identifying customers who may be targeted for a line increase without significantly increasing the probability of delinquency.

Collection models deal with the other end of the credit spectrum. When there is high risk that an account may migrate to a charge-off, accelerated collection action may be taken. Experience shows that early intervention helps to minimize delinquencies and also reduces the loss in those accounts that do, indeed, become charge-offs. Collection models are used for frequent monitoring of charge and payment activity in order to identify emerging patterns. Variables used in collection models include the credit score, account source (or the mailing list source), the pattern of line utilization, monthly payment as a percent of balance, and delinquency history. While institutions generally do not obtain periodic credit bureau reports on such borrowers, they are known to do so in selected situations. Some customers must ultimately be classified as *skips,* which means that they have skipped town and cannot be found. The ability to predict future problems is predicated on warning signs such as slow payments and low payments.

According to one report (*Philadelphia Inquirer* 1997), bankers are losing the ability to predict problem loans because "more and more, borrowers are simply stopping problems and declaring bankruptcy."[8] If this is true—and there is no reason to believe otherwise—new strategies have to be devised for managing credit losses. Frequent requalification of borrowers and a more thought-out approach to setting credit limits may be the answer. Some experts believe that there has been a paradigm shift in the way people view credit and that social mores have diluted the stigma attached to declaring bankruptcy. In some areas of the country today, lawyers actively advertise the benefits of declaring bankruptcy and walking away from one's debt obligations.

Stephen Coggeshall, Director, Consumer Analytics Division at CASA, Inc., believes that one key to developing insights into a consumer's behavior is to analyze the credit transactions and all available auxiliary data. He believes that lenders have tended to view the entire process of credit approval, credit monitoring, and collection management in a highly compartmentalized fashion. In order to be more effective, he favors developing strategies that integrate customer selection, product pricing, and credit management in a holistic way. In his view, account activity is just one element in an integrated model of financial product usage that is based on an individual's broad economic and life-cycle profile. An additional challenge is to discover logical relationships without running afoul of the consumer laws and the individual's right to privacy.

Cancellation models are used to limit further draws on an account or even to cancel an account if, barring such action, the customer will borrow more and more and eventually become a charge-off. Cancellation models resemble collection models, but are generally brought into play after a new portfolio has been acquired and has been found to contain less than stellar credits. If there are no legal barriers, cancellation can be a viable way to cap and front-load losses in order to obtain relief under a portfolio repurchase clause.

Fraud detection models attempt to identify fraudulent charges by looking for patterns in previous frauds experienced. For example, if account charges just slightly below the line limit come up for approval, this may be a sign that a card has been stolen. Indictors of fraud are not well publicized by lenders for obvious reasons. Intuitively, fraud may be traced to specific geographic areas, to certain store and merchandise categories, and to unusual charging patterns involving successive big ticket purchases at unusual times. A neural network model may profile the charging pattern of a normal account and send an alert if there is a significant deviation from this pattern—especially if the deviation is associated with a sale category with high fraud potential such as jewelry or a major consumer purchase. Consumer fraud may also be a prelude to a bankruptcy filing. Concealment and/or transfer of assets prior to bankruptcy filing is a common abuse in fraudulent bankruptcies. Computerized records of the applicant's credit history—including the loan application itself—may be helpful in anticipating and analyzing fraudulent bankruptcies.

DECISION TREE MODELS

The statistically developed credit scoring model has a counterpart in operations research. In the decision tree approach, an applicant's attributes are partitioned off successively from most important to least important. An applicant population may be divided into two main branches—say, those who own their residence and those who rent. The owners may then be subdivided into different income levels, and each income level may be subdivided according to the number of years at the current address. The entire population is thus divided into mutually exclusive "buckets". The credit decision can then be made based on the probability of delinquency in each of the stages or buckets. This is graphically illustrated in Figure 12.6 for a two variable system (*own/rent* and *income level*). In the example, as the tree branches are created, the probability of selecting a bad (or a good) account is moved away from 0.5 (a 50–50 chance) to a number closer to 0 or 1, thus increasing the likelihood of being correct.

The proponents of the decision tree approach claim that it deals more effectively with the interaction of variables than do credit scoring models. Decision tree models can also generate a credit score even when some of the

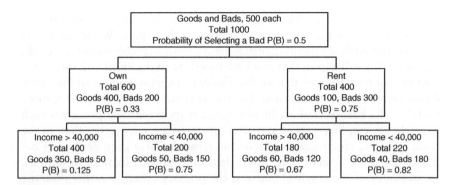

FIGURE 12.6   Credit Screening Decision Tree

variables are missing. However, there are some drawbacks, as well. Some of the lower level cells, for example, may have too few entries to provide credit managers with the level of comfort they get from the more common statistical models.

NEURAL NETWORK MODELS

Neural network (NN) technology has recently been applied to credit scoring models with classification accuracy ranged from 76 to 82 percent in work by Jensen (1996) and Richeson, Zimmermann, and Barnett (1996). Neural networks are artificial intelligence systems that are designed to crudely mimic human thought processes and methods of learning. NN algorithms are a set of inputs (in this case the variables used in the credit application) that are mathematically transformed through a transfer function to generate an output (in this case a prediction of whether an applicant will be a performing credit or a charge-off). During the learning or training phase, the weights are modified to reduce the difference between the desired output (correct prediction) and the actual output (generated prediction). The specifications for a neural model generally include: type of model (feedforward or feedbackward), number of hidden layers, number of processing elements in each hidden layer, number of variables in the input layer, transfer function, and learning rule for modifying the weights. A more detailed description of this technique was presented in Chapter 10.

Richeson, et al. (1996) report classification accuracy of 78 percent for performing accounts and 70 percent for nonperforming accounts. While the results are encouraging, it is by no means clear that models based on neural networks will be acceptable from a regulatory standpoint because it is very difficult to explain the predictions in terms of the inputs. While regulators view a credit analyst's qualitative judgment as an acceptable basis for a credit decision, they still expect that machine-based credit decisions will satisfy the standard of *tractability*—that is, the ability to explain which variables produced an adverse credit decision. For this reason, neural networks are more useful in the back-end of credit management (postapproval processes such as credit review, line increases, collection strategies, etc.) rather than in the front end (i.e., credit-granting). Neural networks have been applied in behavioral scoring systems and fraud detection models. In these situations, the accuracy of the result obtained is the primary criterion rather than the "theory" behind the method. It is more important to detect fraud with acceptable accuracy than to be able to explain what variables were considered and how they were used.

CREDIT SCORING MODELS FOR BUILDING MARKET SHARE

Today, lenders are competing intensely for credit customers. Some institutions have taken an aggressive approach that combines credit risk savvy with marketing in what has come to be called *mass customization*. For example, by targeting the middle and lower ends of the markets, where credit needs are more pressing and pricing the loans to cover the expected higher charge off levels. Often, secondary variables such as the dealer code for indirect originations or the school code for student loans will give indications about the credit quality of the underlying loan. While these may not directly influence the primary credit decision, they are nevertheless extremely important for measuring portfolio risk. As in most credit risk models, data quality lags behind technique. With the current emphasis on data warehousing and data mining, we can expect to see even more innovative approaches to consumer credit management.

When new entrants to the business decide on new loans to build up volume, they are increasingly inclined to rely on credit bureau scores rather than on their own independent application data. One of the risks in this approach is that the lender is, in effect, substituting the credit bureaus' systems for its own credit culture and judgment. The explosive growth in consumer installment credit, the fact that an individual may have multiple lines of credit totaling far more than his/her debt-carrying capacity, and the record number of personal bankruptcies in the United States should be enough to alert any prudent banker or investor. According to one study (Johnson 1989), potentially recoverable debt amounts to just one-fourth of the total debts listed in the average personal bankruptcy filing. Put differently, even if a repayment plan is put in place, lenders will recover *at most 25 percent of the amount owed*. Thus, regardless of the leniency or lack thereof of bankruptcy law, it is the credit granting decision that appears to be responsible for mushrooming credit losses.

When portfolio growth declines and can no longer subsidize losses from credit decisions, credit risk models may be the first (and perhaps the only) line of defense against substantial credit losses. Consumer credit models are also making inroads into small business lending (Johnson 1989).[7] A credit risk manager can therefore no longer simply regard credit risk models as black boxes but should instead become familiar with their design philosophy and with their strengths and weaknesses.

One question that is frequently asked is why are credit scoring models so effective in consumer lending and not as effective in commercial lending. This question has three explanations: institutional, analytical, and economic. Institutionally, corporate lenders have adamantly maintained that corporate lending is a highly complex, multidimensional process requiring expert judgment and this simply cannot be handled by quantitative models. Consumer lenders, on the other hand, have generally been more receptive to modeling approaches—perhaps because they have viewed their product in merchandising terms rather than in lending terms. Analytically, it is somewhat easier to build consumer models because a fixed amount of information is provided on the credit application and a large statistical base of credit experience is available to test and refine credit models. The third reason is economic: losses in a consumer portfolio tend to be relatively large in number but small in size. Losses from a corporate portfolio are infrequent but much more severe in size. Many believe that corporate defaults are less predictable and that reliance on a model may therefore be imprudent. Whatever the reasons, it is certainly true that quantitative credit risk models have not been accepted as widely in corporate lending as they have in consumer lending. But the trend toward greater acceptance has accelerated in recent years.

THE NEXT STEPS

What we have discussed in this chapter is the process of building consumer credit scoring models designed to predict the probability that an individual account will become delinquent and perhaps ultimately default. No matter how sophisticated models become, there will always be issues with the fact that the data used to build the models is dated (often 12 to 18 months have passed by before the model is implemented); that sometimes the causality connections can break down quickly, and lastly that it is hard to eliminate extraneous economic factors from the modeling. That is why a disciplined process of reviewing model validity at introduction and on an ongoing basis is so important. It is also why the "champion-challenger" approach discussed is so important to a healthy process.

The spotlight for consumer modeling is now on two other related issues. First, there is a focus on loss forecasting which looks at portfolios or subportfolios rather than individual accounts. Usually these models include cumulative loss rate models which rely on vintage curve analysis and Markov models which rely on delinquency bucket analysis and roll rates. Driving this is the pending implementation of the Bank for International Settlement Basel II Accord which encourages banks to use their own internal ratings models to assess the creditworthiness of their loans. Under the accord, loans are divided into five categories, one of which is for consumer loans. Banking regulators will require lending institutions to establish adequate reserves for expected losses and to maintain a level of equity capital sufficient to cover unexpected losses from these consumer loans at confidence levels that fluctuate within a band up to 99.9 percent depending on the correlations between loans in the modeled portfolios. In order to use their own models, which are necessary to have the most favorable capital treatment, the banks need to have available three years of data and to have validated their approaches to default and loss estimations. These requirements have required even the most sophisticated banks to drive ahead very rapidly in these new areas.

Second, a continuing focus for consumer credit modeling is on the customization of products and the development of risk based pricing. These are actually two complimentary and parallel developments. In order to appropriately tailor a product to a customer, the lender has to have a relationship perspective which includes all the connections between the two. At the same time the pricing of products in the relationship needs to be on a risk-adjusted basis, so that stronger credits can be encouraged to borrow larger amounts at more advantageous rates and on better terms than weaker credits.

It is clear from looking at the next steps in the evolution of consumer credit modeling that the next ten years will be busier than ever.

REFERENCES

Altman, E. I., R. B. Avery, R. A. Eisenbeis, and J.F. Sinkey, Jr. 1981. *Application of Classification Techniques in Business, Banking and Finance.* Greenwich, Conn.: JAI Press.

Cathcart, R. 2004. EVP CIBC Forum on Validation of Consumer Credit Risk Models, Wharton School Financial Institutions Center, November 19.

Chandler, G. G., and L. E. Parker. 1989. "Predictive Value of Credit Bureau Reports." *Journal of Retail Banking* 11, no. 4:47–54.

Cole, R., and L. Mishler. 1995. *Consumer and Business Credit Management*, 10th ed. Chicago: Richard D. Irwin, Inc.

Federal Deposit Insurance Corporation (FDIC). 1997. "Risks Associated with Subprime Lending." *Financial Institution Letter* FIL-44–97, 2 May.

Hansell, S. 1995. "Loans Granted By The Megabyte: Computer Models Change Small-Business Lending." *New York Times*, 18 April.

———. 1995. "Merchants of Debt." *New York Times*, 2 July.

Jensen, H. 1996. "Using Neural Networks for Credit Scoring." In *Neural Networks In Finance and Investing*, edited by R. R. Trippi and E. Turban. Chicago: Irwin Professional Publishing.

Johnson, R. W. 1989. "The Consumer Banking Problem: Causes and Cures." *Journal of Retail Banking* 11, no. 4:39–44.

McCarthy, J. 1997. "Debt, Delinquencies and Consumer Spending." *Federal Reserve Bank of New York Current Issues in Economics and Finance* 3, no. 3.

Philadelphia Inquirer. 1997. "Debt—and Bad Loans—in National Credit Card Bender." 11 May.

Richeson, L., R. A. Zimmermann, and K. G. Barnett. 1996. "Predicting Consumer Credit Performance: Can Neural Networks Outperform Traditional Statistical Methods?" In *Neural Networks In Finance and Investing*, edited by R. R. Trippi and E. Turban. Chicago: Irwin Professional Publishing.

Sachs, L. 1984. *Applied Statistics*, 2nd ed. New York: Springer.

SAS, Inc. 1997. "Multivariate Statistical Analysis." In *Statistical Manual*. Cray, N.C.

SPSS, Inc. 1997. "Advanced Statistics." In *Statistical Manual*. Chicago.

Standard & Poor's. 1997, May. *Structured Finance*. New York.

CHAPTER 13

Credit Models for Small Business, Real Estate, and Financial Institutions

Prediction is very difficult, especially of the future.

—Niels Bohr

In the preceding three chapters, we considered credit risks models that have been developed for corporations and consumers. This chapter deals with credit risk models created for other classes of borrowers. Those applied to small business and residential mortgage lending are very similar to the consumer risk models that we have described. Those developed for commercial real estate lending tend to be closer to expert systems. The credit (or solvency) risk of financial institutions themselves is another important area of concern. Regulators, correspondent banks, and even nonbank institution use such models to assess the risk of banks because any bank, as a depository institution, is a borrower. It may also be a counterparty in a derivative transaction and pose a risk of default.

SMALL BUSINESS MODELS

Public companies generally provide structured and timely disclosures about their operations through earnings reports and SEC filings. In addition, continuous monitoring of their stock prices provides a mechanism—perhaps too volatile for some—for observing their condition. As we have seen, credit risk models have been built to take advantage of both these sources of information. In the case of small private companies, however, one clearly has

TABLE 13.1   Variables Used in Commercial Credit Scoring Model

	Points for Worst Value	Points for Best Value
Credit characteristic and points	0	10
Number of years in business	Less than 1 year	More than 5 years
Current ratio	Less than 1	More than 1.80
Total debt/net worth	Over 2.0	Under 1.2
Profitability	Loss in most recent year	Profitable for 3 consecutive years
Loan/accounts receivable	1.25	< 0.5
Acceptable financial data	Interim financial statement	Latest 3 annual
Accounts payable	More than 20 percent over 60 days	20 percent credit; rest cash/discount

to look at other means for making a credit risk assessment. Carey, Prowse, Rea, and Udell (1993) suggest that small firms are *information problematic* to lenders because they enter into fewer externally visible contracts with employees, customers, and suppliers. Such firms also tend to be younger. Incentives to engage in behavior that expropriates wealth from lenders are more acute in such observably riskier firms. For this reason, lenders typically employ tight financial covenants, more frequent monitoring and relatively short maturities with these clients.

Table 13.1 lists the variables used in a typical commercial credit scoring model for loans up to $250,000.

In the case of some small businesses, especially proprietorships, it may be difficult to use financial ratios because personal and business activities are combined. This is also true of businesses that operate on a cash flow basis. Small service businesses that are people—rather than equipment—intensive may also be less suited to ratio-based scoring.

In general, small business models use a combination of personal installment credit and financial statement items. For example, as shown above, the model may use financial ratios such as debt service coverage, leverage ratio, and negative or excessive growth in revenues for the business side of the risk. At the same time, credit bureau data is used to generate a personal credit score for the principal owner(s) of the business. The RMA/Fair Isaacs model (Asch 1995) is an example of this approach. According to Paul Ross, a consultant with Oliver Wyman, Inc., New York who was interviewed by the authors in 1997, lenders increasingly are applying the approaches developed in consumer lending to small businesses for several reasons. First, many of the scoring variables applied to consumer lending are effective in differentiating risk in small business lending, where the credit standing of the principal is key. Second, the economics of small business lending require an efficient, inexpensive process for data collection and credit evaluation, which is better met by consumer credit scoring processes. Finally, in many cases, borrowing that is used to finance small businesses is actually accomplished through a consumer vehicle, such as the credit card of the principal. Some of the recent innovations in this market are standardized loan products and documentation. "Preapproved" solicitation by mail as is done for consumer loans is also becoming more common.

Franchise loans are small business loans ranging from $500,000 to $700,000. Loan approvals are based on the analysis of qualitative and quantitative factors about the franchise. Lending is cash-flow-based, with fixed charge coverage being the most important criterion. This ratio varies around 1.5. Credit data vendors such as Dun & Bradstreet, Experian, and Equifax maintain varying levels of data on self-reported financial statement data as well as payment experience collected from reporting financial institutions, other creditors and utilities. Credit bureaus offer models that predict *the ability to timely payment to creditors* (e.g., D&B's Commercial Credit Score and Experian's Intelliscore) or the *likelihood of financial distress that can potentially cause a loss to creditor* (example, D&B's Financial Stress Score). Most of these models place more reliance on credit utilization, suits, lines and judgments, and payment patterns, and less so on financial statement variables per se.[1] Among the financial statement variables current ratio, quick ratio, and the ratio of liabilities to tangible net worth are the most commonly used variables. Other variables found in these models are age of the firm, industry delinquency rate, and number of trade creditors to the firm.

RESIDENTIAL REAL ESTATE MODELS

The residential real estate loan market is a significant user of funds in the U.S. financial markets. As shown in Figure 13.1, the balance outstanding was $9.12 trillion in 2005. It is an innovative market in which originators such as mortgage bankers deliver loans to investors who may, in turn, securitize them. FNMA and FHMLC are two entities that securitize huge volumes of residential mortgage loans.

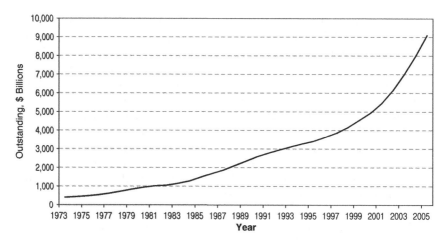

FIGURE 13.1 Residential Mortgages Outstanding 1973–2005
Source: Board of Governors of the Federal Reserve System, Flow of Funds
Accounts, 1973–2006.

As applied to mortgage analysis, credit scoring is a relatively recent
phenomenon. Firms use credit scoring in a variety of ways (Moody's Investor
Service 1996).

- As an underwriting tool to accept or reject applications.
- As a way to determine documentation requirements.
- As a means of assessing the need for property appraisals.
- As support for servicing operations such as collection.

Historically, residential mortgage loans were underwritten in much the
same way that commercial loans were. Classic credit analysis included
a detailed analysis of the borrower's financial ability, combined with an
appraisal of the property. More and more, however, quantitative credit
models are being used—partly because data and computing technology are
more readily available and partly because these models help to cut origination costs.

A mortgage default model based on options theory has long identified
the size of a borrower's equity in a home has long been identified as a
fundamental determinant of default. The borrower's equity is expressed as
the difference between the current value of the home (after adjusting for
sales costs) and the current market value of the debt. The model is modified by two other groups of variables. The first measures the borrower's

ability to pay—for example, the size of the income cushion represented by the debt ratios and savings, and the borrower's earnings stability as evidenced by his or her credit bureau history. The second group is a set of triggering events such as divorce, unemployment, illness, or business failure that will stress the borrower financially. Even under these conditions, however, a borrower is likely to sell the property and repay the loan rather than to default and potentially lose all equity. This is precisely why the borrower's equity in the home is an extremely important variable in the decision to default.

In home mortgages, as in commercial lending, many institutions used to rely exclusively on judgmental credit screening. The following factors were used as important indicators of credit quality:

- Borrower's sources of income
- Debt ratios with and without nonmortgage debt obligations
- Asset holdings
- Employment history
- Credit bureau reports
- Economic conditions in the area

As shown in Table 13.2, comparisons of key underwriting ratios in a sample of mortgages held by a large Pennsylvania bank lend support to such underwriting practices.

In Table 13.2, mortgages were classified as delinquent if they were at least 90 days past due, were in foreclosure, or were closed out through deed in lieu of foreclosure. The performing loans were those that were never more than 30 days delinquent. Both groups were seasoned, with age in the seven-year range. Van Order and Zorn (1995) has confirmed

TABLE 13.2 Group Means of Key Ratios: Residential Mortgage Loans

Variable	Delinquent Mortgages	Performing Mortgages	F-ratio
Loan to Value	.87	.77	33.77
Debt Ratio #1	.24	.19	17.08
Debt Ratio #2	.33	.28	11.90
Total No of Derogatory Remarks in Credit Report	1.94	0	37.52
State	3.45	2.28	56.99

TABLE 13.3   Proportion of Selected Mortgages that Defaulted by Year-end 1993 and Resulting in Loss, Selected Loan-to-Value Ratio Ranges

	Loan-to-Value Ratio (percent)				
Performance measure	10–70	71–80	81–90	91–95	ALL
Proportion defaulted	0.24	1.11	2.74	6.20	2.16
Average loss severity	22.3	29.2	34.4	47.9	39.2

Source: Van Order and Zorn (1995).

that the severity of the loss is also higher at higher loan-to-value ratios (Table 13.3).

In one of the earliest studies to identify the determinants of default in residential mortgages, Campbell and Dietrich (1983) used an optimization model of consumer choice. The borrower choice set consisted of (1) default, (2) delay payment, (3) prepay the mortgage, and (4) continue to service the mortgage.[2] The explanatory variables used were current loan-to-value ratio, current payment-to-income ratio, rate of unemployment in the area of the residence, ratio of mortgage interest rate to prevailing mortgage rate, age of the mortgage at the beginning of the year, age of the mortgage squared, New/Not-New Home dummy.[3] A logit function was used to model the probability of choice i available in each year to the borrower as a function of the explanatory variable vector X in the beginning of the year. This equation is written as an odds ratio:

$$\log \frac{P_i}{P_4} = -\beta_i X$$

P_4 is the probability of continuing to make mortgage payments and P_i is the probability of making one of three choices i, and β_i is the vector of estimated coefficients. The data used consisted of 2.5 million first mortgages insured between 1960–1980. Three regression equations were estimated for the three P_i. The results were found to be consistent with the inverse relationship between initial loan-to-value ratio and default rate. Because the age variables were found to be highly correlated, equations were estimated both with and without these variables. The authors found the regression results to be generally consistent with their hypothesis for prepayment and default decisions. However, the decision to delay payments could not be explained in a satisfactory manner.

FNMA and FHMLC, which are key players in the mortgage market, have encouraged thousands of lenders from whom they purchase loans to consider indexes from credit bureaus and credit history scores in their loan underwriting. The credit bureaus base their credit history scoring systems on an applicant's record of bankruptcy, current credit lines, and history of account delinquency. Lenders combine this score with traditional underwriting factors such as the loan-to-value ratio, the debt ratios, and employment stability. They use credit screening models to identify applicants for streamlined underwriting and to verify the reported information and the evaluation of the collateral. Those that cannot pass the model screen are processed in the conventional manner. Private mortgage insurers are also using such models to determine if a loan is insurable.

Extensive analysis to test the predictive ability of such models was performed by Avery et al. (1994) on a large sample of loans for which proprietary data was provided by Equifax Credit Information Services. The credit score was found to be a good predictor of loan performance across all score levels, both for prospective mortgage borrowers and for those with existing mortgages. The proportion of problem loans increased as credit scores decreased. While the industry is slowly catching on to these systems, it appears that the trend is towards greater use. It is common these days to hear of prime, Alt-A, and subprime mortgages where the distinction is primarily through the credit scores, with FICO (Fair Isaac Co.) being the dominant score being used. These scoring models share the same limitations as commercial and consumer models, the most important of which is the relative inability to be forward-looking. They are not very good, for example, at anticipating an economic downturn characterized by falling home pirces and/or rising unemployment. FICO score projections of delinquency were exceeded in the subprime mortgage sector in 2007. There were many factors that contributed to the woes in this sector, the most notable of them being lax underwriting practices, including the use of stated income (rather than verfied income), failure to apply the fully indexed interest rate to qualify the borrower of adjustable rate mortgages, and failure to consider the possible impact of housing price declines on borrower delinquency.

COMMERCIAL REAL ESTATE MODELS

Judgmental methods—especially *appraisal* of the collateral—continue to dominate in commercial real estate lending. Prevailing market indexes for commercial property and simulations to project cash flow are used to estimate collateral value. Quantitative credit risk models are used rarely, if at all, in this market. The following variables, taken from an expert system that identifies potential problem borrowers, seem to impact the ongoing credit risk of commercial real estate projects:

- Debt coverage ratio below 1.2 and dropping
- Prospective criteria (e.g. major tenant not renewing lease)
- Real estate tax delinquency
- Revenue growth that is flat or worse
- Expense growth that is high relative to revenue
- Recent change in ownership
- Presence of secondary financing
- Refinancing
- Complicated financing structure
- Signs that property is neglected
- Financial statements that are late or not credible (not prepared by a CPA or signed by a senior representative of the owner)
- Property that is not near a strong economic center

These variables have proved to be surprisingly accurate in anticipating borrower problems.

BANK MODELS

Because banks perform an important public function by operating the payment system and acting as the vehicle for the exercise of monetary policy, they are highly regulated. Consequently, they are required to submit detailed financial reports to the regulatory agencies. Over the course of years, these reporting requirements have become more sophisticated and streamlined. Large banks are now required, for example, to disclose extensive information about their interest rate risk exposure, derivative risk, and loan portfolio quality. Bank solvency is of interest not only to regulators but also to other financial institutions and to borrowers. A borrower with a liquidity line, for example, will want to make sure that funds will be available to draw when needed.

The following elements are used in assessing a bank's solvency:

- Asset quality
- Management
- Exception via critical ratios—outlier/peer group comparison
- Multivariate or composite measurements
- Market value based measurements

Asset Quality

Asset quality is the primary focus for both regulators and investors. Indeed, risk-based capital standards for banks are expressed in terms of asset quality (i.e., the credit quality of various asset classes). A bank's risk assets are examined and classified into several categories of risk (i.e., loss, doubtful, and substandard). These categories are assigned equal weights and the bank's capital is reduced to the extent that losses will be experienced. The ratio of the available capital cushion to risk assets, or the net capital ratio, is a measure of a bank's risk of insolvency. Another measure of risk, the adjusted capital ratio, is somewhat more lenient in that it applies a weight of .5 to doubtful loans and of 0 to substandard loans in calculating the numerator. Both of these ratios assess the degree to which a bank will be able to withstand earnings stresses after losses from the nonperforming, substandard, doubtful and loss categories have been taken into account.

Banks face risks because of both internal and external factors. Quality of management personnel, cost controls, and risk appetite are internal factors over which a bank's management can exercise some control. The state of the economy and the actions of competitors are external factors over which a bank has no control. While the above ratios do not appear to take any note of the external conditions faced by a bank, examiners tacitly do take external factors into account when they classify loans. This is most noticeable in recessionary periods. When the economy is fragile, examiners tend to be overzealous in labeling institutions as problem banks. They prefer erring on the side of caution to missing a problem bank by being too liberal.

Management

A different perspective on bank risk is provided by Graham and Horner (1989) of the Office of the Comptroller of the Currency. They put responsibility for bank risk and, by implication, bank failure entirely on internal management factors. While the economy plays an important role in bank failure, many banks in economically distressed areas are able to withstand the adverse economic conditions. OCC studied 171 failed banks, most of them small (under $50 million in assets), 51 rehabilitated banks, and a control group of 38 healthy banks. The study agreed with others that poor-asset quality is the major cause of a bank's decline, but it also attempted to trace the factors that *led* to poor-asset quality. It identified the following the factors.

Uninformed or inattentive board of directors, evidenced by:

- Nonexistent or poorly followed loan policies
- Inadequate systems to ensure compliance

- Inadequate control or supervision of key officers
- Inadequate systems to identify problem loans
- Decisions by one dominant individual

Overly aggressive activity by board or management as evidenced by:

- Inappropriate lending policies
- Excessive loan growth in relation to the abilities of management
- Undue reliance on volatile liabilities
- Inadequate liquid assets for secondary liquidity
- Insider abuse or fraud
- Economic environment

Based on organizational theory, this model of risk assessment examines an institution's processes and systems for early signs of deterioration.

EXCEPTION VIA CRITICAL RATIOS: OUTLIER/PEER GROUP

This approach is based on establishing critical values for important financial ratios, then using these values to identify outliers. If a bank exhibits financial ratios that fail the critical test, it becomes a candidate for the exception list. Clearly, the success of this approach depends on identifying the right ratio and assigning the correct critical value. The tendency with this approaches to set critical values at relatively tolerant levels so that only pathological cases are selected, but they are sometimes selected too late to do any good. The risk in peer group analysis is that exceptions may mask systemic deterioration.

MULTIVARIATE OR COMPOSITE MEASUREMENTS

Multivariate financial ratio models draw upon the extensive information that banks periodically disclose about their financial condition. However, many analysts believe that present accounting policies give a distorted picture of important aspects of a bank's balance sheet and income statement, and provide a picture of risk that is, at best incomplete. Accounting principles are indeed unable to capture many dimensions of risk, both embedded and evolving: interest rate risk, off-balance sheet items such as letters of credit and interest rate swaps, differing standards for classifying performing assets. In spite of these deficiencies, there is enough accumulated evidence to indicate that, when properly analyzed, accounting information can indeed be used for prediction.

Of the best-known multivariate models, the CAMEL system, is used by three Federal regulatory agencies. CAMEL stands for *capital adequacy, asset quality, management, earnings stability,* and *liquidity.* Weights are applied to the ratios in each of the categories to arrive at a final score, and thereby a rating. The weights are not statistically developed, however. The CAMEL rating for a bank ranges from 1 = best to 5 = worst. The agencies do not appear to use this system for bank holding companies nor have they agreed on a uniform system to be used in the surveillance process (Putnam, 1983). The Federal Reserve and the OCC use a composite score; that is, an aggregation of financial ratios in the surveillance process while others use critical ratios.

Regardless of methodology, defining the a priori groups of failed and nonfailed banks must be the first step in the construction of a multivariate model. Since it is theoretically possible for the regulators to keep a bank from failing for an indefinite period of time, some arbitrary definitions must be made. It is customary to define failed banks as those that required out-lays from the Deposit Insurance Fund, including closed banks as well as all assistance cases. Other definitions may rely on examiner determinations such as the *potential payoff, serious problem,* and *other problem categories.* Sometimes the euphemism "vulnerability potential" is substituted for various stages of a bank's demise.

Failed banks are then matched with healthy banks in a random fashion and models are constructed using methods similar to those described in Chapter 10. Important models on bank soundness have been developed by Meyer and Pifer (1970); Martin (1977); Bovenzi, Marino, and McFadden (1983); Lane, Looney, and Wansley (1989); Pantalone and Platt (1987); and Spahr (1989). Sinkey (1977) gives a good summary of the prior work done in this area. Trippi and Turban (1996) study three examples of neural network techniques applied to the prediction of failures in banks, thrifts, and credit unions.

MARKET VALUE-BASED MEASUREMENTS

According to the efficient market hypothesis, the intrinsic value of a firm is represented in its stock price, which quickly and accurately reflects any new information regarding its condition. If investors perceive that a bank's risk has increased, they will require a higher rate of return. To compensate the investor for the increased risk, the stock price will drop to a lower level. A decline in the price of a bank's common stock may therefore precede regulatory awareness that its financial condition has deteriorated significantly.

This hypothesis has been tested. Since the decline in the bank's stock may coincide with a general decline in the stock market, the bank-specific changes must be assessed by means of the capital asset pricing model, using a parameter called *beta*, which is a measure of the relative risk of the bank stock (see Chapter 11 for more details). If the actual return differs from the expected return indicated by the bank's beta, which is measured by a quantity called cumulative average residuals, then it may be concluded that the market has signaled an increase in the bank's risk. Shick and Sherman (1980) found support for this hypothesis. A negative residual pattern could be used to anticipate an adverse examination rating change by at least 15 months.

The survey of quantitative models that we have presented is by no means exhaustive. It is intended merely as an overview of the types of tools currently available. The next chapter takes up questions that typically must be answered in the process of selecting and implementing a credit risk model.

REFERENCES

Altman, E. I., J. Hartzell, and M. Peck. 1995. *Emerging Markets Corporate Bonds: A Scoring System.* New York: Salomon Brothers, Inc.

Altman, E. I, R. B. Avery, R.A. Eisenbeis, and J. F. Sinkey, Jr. 1981. *Application of Classification Techniques in Business, Banking and Finance.* Greenwich, Conn.: JAI Press.

Altman, E. I., and P. Narayanan. 1997. "An International Survey of Business Failure Classification Models." *Financial Markets, Institutions & Instruments* 6, no. 2:1–57.

Asch, L. 1995. "How RMA/Fair, Isaac Credit-Scoring Model Was Built." Journal of Commercial Lending 77 no. 10:10–16.

Bovenzi, J.F., J.A. Marino, F. E. McFadden. 1983. "Commercial Bank Failure Prediction Models." *Federal Reserve Bank of Atlanta Economic Review* 68, no. 11:14–26.

Campbell, T.S. and K. J. Dietrich. 1983. "The Determinants of Default on Insured Conventional Residential Mortgage Loans." *Journal of Finance* 38, no. 5:1569–1581.

Carey, M., S. Prowse, J. Rea, and G. Udell. 1993. *The Economics of the Private Placement Market.—Staff Study 166.* Washington, D.C.: Board of Governors of the Federal Reserve System.

Cates, D. C. 1985. "Bank Risk and Predicting Bank Failure." *Issues in Bank Regulation* 9, no. 2:16–20.

Eisenbeis, R. A., and G. G. Gilbert. 1985. "Market Discipline and the Prevention of Bank problems and Failures." *Issues in Bank Regulation* 8, no. 3–4:16–20.

Graham, F. C., and J. E. Horner. 1988. "Bank Failure: An Evaluation of the Factors Contributing the Failure of National Banks. *The Financial Services Industry in the Year 2000*, Chicago: Federal Reserve Bank of Chicago, 406–435.

Lane, W. R., S. W. Looney, and J. W. Wansley. 1986. "An Application of the Cox Proportional Hazards Model to Bank Failure." *Journal of Banking and Finance* 10, no. 4:511–531.

Martin, D. 1977. "Early Warning of Bank Failure: A Logit Regression Approach." *Journal of Banking and Finance* 1, no. 3:249–276

Meyer, P. A., and H. W. Pifer. 1970. "Prediction of Bank Failures." *Journal of Finance* 25, no. 4:853–868.

Moody's Investors Service. 1996. "A Guide to Credit Scoring of Mortgage Loans." *Moody's Special Report*, May.

Nelson, R. W. 1988. "Management vs. Economic Conditions as Contributors to the Recent Increase in Bank Failures: Commentary." In *Financial Risk: Theory, Evidence and Implications*, edited by Courtney C. Stone. Dordrecht: Kluwer Academic.

Trippi, R. R., and E. Turban (eds.). 1996. *Neural Networks in Finance and Investing.* Chicago: Irwin.

Pantalone, C. C., and Platt, M. B. 1987. "Predicting Commercial Bank Failure Since Deregulation." New England Economic Review *13*, (July–August):37–47.

Pettway, R. H., and J. F. Sinkey, Jr. 1980. "Establishing On-site Bank Examination Priorities: An Early Warning System Using Accounting and Market Information." *Journal of Finance* 35, no. 1:137–150.

Shick, R. A., and Sherman, L. F. "Bank Stock Prices as an Early Warning System for Changes in Condition." *Journal of Bank Research* 11, no. 3:136–146.

Sinkey, J, F., Jr. 1979 *Problem and Failed Institutions in the Commercial Banking Industry*, Greenwich, CT: JAI Press.

———. 1977. "Problem and Failed Banks, Bank Examinations, and Early Warning Systems: A Summary." In *Financial Crises*, edited by E. I. Altman and A. W. Sametz. New York: John Wiley & Sons.

Spahr, R. W. 1989. "Predicting Bank Failures and Intertemporal Assessment of Bank Risk." *Journal of Business Research* 19, no. 3:179–185.

Van Order, R., and P. Zorn. 2000. "Income, Location and Default: Some Implications for Community Lending," *Real Estate Economics* 28, no. 3:385–404.

CHAPTER **14**

Testing and Implementation of Credit Risk Models

Begin at the beginning ... and go on till you come to the end:
then stop.
—Lewis Carroll, *Alice's Adventures in Wonderland*

We are now at the end of the discussion on credit risk models. The question left to be answered is: What should we know about successfully implementing these models? Banks and other financial institutions clearly need tools that can:

- Reinforce a strong credit culture.
- Reduce the high fixed costs associated with credit analytics.
- Establish consistency in assessing and pricing credit risk.
- Assist in active portfolio management and in the efficient allocation of economic capital.
- Help arrive at a level of capital mutually acceptable to the institution and its regulators.

Most financial institutions have now developed credit rating systems for various business segments. Many of these credit systems are quantitative/statistical and have been adapted out of the need to securitize the assets instead of holding them on the balance sheet. Some examples are consumer loans, home equity loans, and corporate loans. In these cases, the use of a statistically valid credit rating system is one of the key requirements for obtaining agency ratings to facilitate securitization. But in other instances, the credit system is homegrown, often subject to overrides. As a consequence, these systems do not yield objective, reproducible results. Indeed, many reflect the subjective preferences of account officers and their superiors rather than the underlying credit risks that are actually associated with each customer. Often, different branches of the same bank apply the systems selectively. It is therefore not unusual for credit officers within a single bank to assign different credit ratings to the very same customer. Even the definitions of ratings tend to be couched in vague generalities that leave substantial room for interpretation.

Bank credit rating systems produce a fuzzy, ordinal risk ranking of customers. A rating of 2 in a typical nine-grade rating system is obviously superior to a 3 and worse than a 1; but it usually conveys little that would help account officers, central credit departments, or senior credit executives to assess expected losses or to price their loans. In the case of a company that also has public debt outstanding, a bank's internal rating for the company does tend to correspond to the public bond rating, which give banks an external point of reference. However, the risk gradings of private companies and companies without public debt ratings are subject to very wide and sometimes arbitrary variations. In some instances, credit professionals are uncertain whether a given risk rating applies to a company as a whole or simply to one among many of its business units. Having a coarse grading system also causes difficulties in setting limits linked to the rating, in pricing and capital allocation because there may be a significant variation in true quality among borrowers within the same rating category. There can be a weak 4 or a strong, and often banks consider adding notches to the 1-to-10 numerical scale.

Subjective systems make it difficult for a lender to recognize the deterioration of its borrowers. Of course, banks have good reason to avoid false alarms in ratings: Bankers know that if they lower their rating on a given borrower, their relationship with this customer will probably suffer. Banks prefer to give customers the benefit of the doubt—waiting to see if they can work things out on their own. Unfortunately, if real deterioration takes place, this reluctance to recognize the truth about a borrower can lead to a loss.

AN INTRINSIC VALUE APPROACH

The first tool that banks require is a standardized way of measuring the inherent risk of each borrower. Grounded in history and unaffected by fads, this tool would measure the risk of default and generate consistent ratings across time for a wide range of borrowers. Such a system could serve as the anchor for a bank's credit policy—providing a common credit language and a feedback mechanism for quality control. Borrowers that did not measure up to this yardstick would be investigated with care. Whenever the system produced a warning that could not be explained by other information, the bank would act on this signal. Such a tool would not supplant the human element in managing risk, but it would—by providing an objective measure of risk—challenge subjectively held beliefs.

Intrinsic value credit models estimate the similarity of any individual company to the hundreds of other companies that have compromised their creditors. Such models focus on a borrower's financial statements. Concepts such as profitability, liquidity and capital structure are important components of the system. These various indicators are combined into a single measure of corporate vulnerability. This approach provides the benchmarks and feedback needed for rational credit grading and loan pricing.

The intrinsic value approach provides a sound foundation for stabilizing a bank's credit culture because it is rooted in accounting fundamentals and in time-tested principles of credit analysis. It is one of the best ways to measure a borrower's intrinsic risk. If enough data exists for empirical validation, this risk can be quantified in the form of an estimate of the probability of default. However, as we have noted in Chapter 10, accounting statements fail to capture many aspects of an enterprise that contribute to its credit risk. They are neither timely nor forward-looking. In view of these limitations, an approach based on accounting standards can prove its worth only by demonstrating an outstanding ability to predict declines in credit quality and/or defaults, it should take into account contemporaneous risk assessments by the capital market when this information is available.

Unfortunately, many published firm-intrinsic models appear to be constructed on the same principle that cooks use in making a stew. Variables or ratios are thrown into a pot and stirred about until they seem to predict something in a test sample. Few of the existing models have been subjected by their creators to rigorous testing. This is a serious shortcoming. If it is truly to anchor a bank's credit process, a scoring system must be both objective and well tested—*objective* in the sense that it follow a statistical or mechanical process to arrive at a rating that is independent of human opinion; and *well tested* in the sense that it has been carefully evaluated not only during the design phase, but also after it has been put into operation. Building a robust model is akin to engineering. Among other things, it requires that pragmatic decisions be made about drawing up the control samples and model evaluation criteria, about handling outliers and missing data, and about making replicable adjustments to the raw data to make it consistent across the sample. These are the actions of an engineer rather than of a scientist who seeks theoretical purity.

INGREDIENTS OF AN EFFECTIVE SYSTEM

A satisfactory credit evaluation system for corporate borrowers should have five key attributes:

1. Sensitivity of ratings to real changes in credit quality.
2. Lead time with respect to recognized real changes in quality.
3. Stability of ratings where no fundamental change has occurred.
4. Graduated tiering of risk assessment that facilitates rationality in the pricing of credit and the setting of loan terms.
5. Consistency of ratings across industries, company sizes, and locations.

Let us examine the different dimensions of the credit evaluation models. These observations are relevant not only to firm-intrinsic models, but also to other market-value or econometric models. They apply to models developed for individuals, small businesses and financial institutions, as well as to those tailored to corporate borrowers.

Definition of the Risk Event

The first step in evaluating a model is discovering what it actually measures. To achieve sensitivity to real changes in credit quality, most models use conditions such as bankrupt/nonbankrupt or default/nondefault as their criterion. Less useful—but still relevant—are models, which are designed to classify companies into bond rating grades or bank loan grades. A criterion such as bankruptcy/nonbankruptcy is preferable because this classification is less subjective than a rating or grade. Bankruptcy is a fact whereas a bond rating or loan grade is a subjective opinion. We know that leading rating agencies disagree with each other in a surprisingly large number of cases and that bankers often disagree with one another on loan grades. Models that are designed to duplicate expert opinion (such as the judgments of rating agencies) must inevitably accept their highly subjective decision criteria.

If a model will be used in prediction, it is also important to define the time frame. To say that a company will default sometime in the indefinite future really tells us nothing. The prediction should be made over some time horizon, such as one, two, or three years before the event, and the prediction error should be tracked.

Target Population

Credit scoring models are generally built for different segments of the borrowing population—rightly so because risk parameters are not the same everywhere. Credit scoring models use different variables for manufacturing and nonmanufacturing corporations, for financial institutions and for individuals borrowing to purchase a home or car. It is important to map out the scope of the market covered by the model, including geography, company size, and industry. The model's market should be compatible with the institution's market coverage. Even within the same borrowing universe, some models function better in one segment (e.g., large corporates) than in another (e.g., middle market). When looking at test results, it is important to look at the size distributions and industry composition of the test population.

Quality of Model Development

The process of developing a credit-scoring model generally involves statistical testing. Many statistical techniques are available, but the actual technique chosen is less important than the definition of risk selected and the care with which the explanatory variables are defined, the data is collected, and the model is tested. The dependent variable may the *a priori* group membership (*good* or *bad*) or default frequency—the percent of the bads within a segment with the same covariates.

In the case of models based on the criterion of bankruptcy/nonbankruptcy, performance is usually measured in terms of two error rates. Type I errors occur when the model classifies bankrupt companies as nonbankrupt. Type II errors occur when the model classifies nonbankrupt companies as bankrupt. Error rate measurement is generally intended to evaluate the sensitivity of ratings to real credit quality changes. Instead of using the raw Type I and Type II error rates, the model performance can also viewed in terms of the total cost of misclassification when information is available about the cost of each type. Typically, Type I error cost (classifying a bad borrower as good) is much larger than the Type II error cost (classifying a good borrower as bad, thereby denying credit to a good borrower).

For testing purposes, a second group of companies is held out of the development sample for use in testing the model. The errors reported on the hold-out or *out-of-sample* test are much more representative of a model's expected performance than are errors in the development sample. *Out-of-time* tests may be carried out to look the performance of the model over time on the same group of customers. In addition to the Type I and Type II error, additional measures of the ability of a model to discriminate are the Kolmogorow-Smirnow statistic and the Gini coefficient. Power curves and the information ratio are other measures similar to the Gini coefficient.

While most credit scoring model work on binary choices (e.g., default vs. no default), the real world of credit seldom presents a clear accept/reject situation. Typically, a borrower is assigned to one of several credit grades. A bank with a nine-level grading system, for example, might decide to accept borrowers graded 1–5 and reject those graded 6–9. At each grade, there will be a different set of Type I and Type II errors. To calculate the different error rates, enough information must be accumulated about nonbankrupt and eventually bankrupt companies in each credit grade for a number of years before bankruptcy. Although it is important to evaluate the success of a credit model over the full range of the credit scale, few models have accumulated enough data to make this possible.

When an institution relies on a vendor to provide statistics of this kind, it is very important to insist on and understand the representations made about the quality, accuracy and completeness of the data employed in constructing the accuracy tests. Vendors may not necessarily be dishonest in omitting unwelcome results; but they can certainly be expected to put their best foot forward in promoting their model. It is up to the consumer to ask the right questions about the comparability of the model's development sample to the institution's market and the performance of the model "out of sample" and "out of time." The worst thing an institution can do—other than doing nothing—is to accept a third party model on faith.

Model Stability

A legitimate concern about mechanical, objective rating systems is that they may be *too* volatile. Will a score change when, in fact, no fundamental change has occurred in the company? Sometimes it will. Short-term, dramatic fluctuations in credit ratings when no fundamental change has occurred result in *noise*. Noise is a subjective quantity. In trading, for example, individual traders may have a time horizon ranging from a day to a week to many months. What looks like a trend to one class of trader may just be noise to another. Random fluctuations undermine the credibility of the pricing and credit approval process and play no productive part in ongoing credit relationships. The ideal model changes only when the underlying facts about the company also change. It is critically important either to minimize noise or to recognize the level at which a message from the model is truly a signal rather than noise. Testing for noise should play a central part in the process of selecting a credit scoring model.

Noise may be a particular concern in models based on stock prices. Some would argue that the volatility exhibited by these models reflects the fact that the credit profile has actually changed. While there is no question that the stock market valuation of a company tends to be accurate over the long term and market value should be incorporated in the lending thought-process, linking credit pricing to short-term market fluctuations may put a bank at a competitive disadvantage. Unless every other bank plays by the same (current market volatility based) criterion for assessing credit risk reacting to short term fluctuations in perceived credit risk may be to the detriment of a bank's relationships.

Predictive Ability of Default Models

Most predictive models draw attention to their purported effectiveness by pointing to recent corporate defaults or bankruptcies that they correctly anticipated. While this is impressive and necessary, it is rare to see instances publicized where the model predicted financial difficulties but nothing adverse subsequently happened. In looking at predictive models, one must therefore look beyond apparent indications of effectiveness.

The simplest test of the predictive accuracy of a model is to compare a specific prediction with the actual outcome. For example, if a model were to say that the unconditional probability[1] of default is 0.25 for a group of firms over a period of one year, and 25 percent of the firms in that group *actually defaulted* in the ensuing one year period, then the model would be 100 percent accurate and have 0 percent forecast error. The forecast error calculated from an ex ante value (estimate) and an ex post value (realization) is the best test of performance. If the predicted value of default probability were 25 percent and the realization 35 percent, then the model error would be 40 percent (35 minus 25 divided by 25). If the predicted probability were 25 percent and the realized default was 15 percent, then the error would still be 40 percent (25 minus 15 divided by 25). However, an error of the first kind (not anticipating failure) would cost many, many times more than that of the second kind (overanticipating failure). It should be noted that the forecast error is calculated not by applying it to a single firm, but to a group of firms with similar values of default probability.

Of course, the error rate is difficult to establish because the world does not stand still after a prediction is made: Both the explainer, in this case, the *expected default frequency* (EDF) and the explained, *the default rate*, are constantly changing. From a practical point of view, the main issues with respect to any predictive model are comparatively less crisp: its ability to *differentiate gradations of risk* and its *early warning properties*. The two criteria are not synonymous. A model may lack the ability to grade risk, but may be a good predictor of default. For example, a model may have only two gradations of risk (good versus bad credits), but may be very good at predicting defaults by downgrading a good credit to bad credit status long before default happens. On the other hand, a model may be very good at *grading* risk, that is, progressively moving a credit from grade 1 to grade 2 to grade 3 and the like, but may not necessarily predict default early. Indeed, a model may have downgraded a risk to a grade 5 (one step before a reaching the classified loan category in a bank, for example) just a month before default. This would suggest that it does not have good early warning properties. Most subjective credit rating systems used in banks fall into the second category. A good system, then, should be capable of properly *grading* riskiness; that is, changes in credit quality, in addition to *predicting* default sufficiently before it happens. *The change in gradations of risk are not always observable. Only its economic consequences are. The consequences may be the event of default/bankruptcy or, if the asset is traded, changes in market value.*

The ability to differentiate gradations of risk may be assessed in absolute terms, such as by looking at Type I accuracy (predicting the failure of companies that did fail) for different levels of Type II accuracy (predicting the continued viability of companies that did not fail) for a certain homogeneous credit grouping such as a score interval or an EDF range. Ideally, this test should be based on an independent sample; that is, a sample of companies that were not utilized in building the model. It should also have a reasonable amount of lead-time in which the outcome is measured. One-year lead-time is usually used, although some might argue that most models, including fairly naive ones, can predict the failure of large companies in this time frame.

A model's ability to differentiate risk may be compared for concordance with other similar models to establish its usefulness. For example, one can compare the way the model grades companies to the way the rating agencies do. This is done by constructing a misclassification matrix, where the rows are actual ratings (from 1 to 10), and the columns are model predicted ratings (also from 1 to 10). Each cell (i, j) in the matrix contains the number companies whose actual rating was i, and the predicted rating was j. The diagonal cells (i, j) where $i = j$ contain the correct classifications. Using this matrix, the accuracy of the model in exactly "predicting" the actual rating, prediction error within ± one notch, and so on may be calculated. However, some model builders may disagree with this approach, arguing that his or her model is a better differentiator of risk than the bond rating and therefore *should* diverge from bond ratings. Even so, using this approach one can take just the companies where there was disagreement and subject them to an ex post analysis.

Comparisons of alternative models are more meaningful if portfolio risk *and* reward analysis is made using simulation with actual price data. Since there is a market-determined risk premium for the bonds and bank loans, rather than comparing prediction error rates among models, a more direct evaluation could be carried out by means of a trading simulation. The resulting profit and loss numbers can then be compared with a benchmark index (efficient portfolio) over a holding period long enough to reflect the maturity of the loan. Since the bid-ask prices for loans and bonds are now more readily available, this test may be performed for at least the large corporate borrowers.

Track Record

Every creator of a new model is understandably excited about it. However, even if the statistical work has been thorough, the model has only made its "predictions" based on hindsight. A good credit model must perform well over time, in good business climates as well as in bad. It must continue to perform well through changes in accounting rules, macroeconomics, stock market P/E ratios, inflation and other conditions affecting it. It should make risk assessments with enough lead-time for action to be taken.

A model's performance should be verified and validated on a continuous basis. Validation tests take advantage of predictions the model has made subsequent to its initial development. The kinds of tests required are similar to model development tests in that they are intended to measure changes in credit quality and the lead-time within which real changes are recognized. There should be a rigorous program to keep track of bankrupt and defaulting borrowers and to monitor a model's success rate.

A considerable amount of data and testing is required to analyze error rates, develop probability of bankruptcy (or loss) functions and instill confidence in the model. Once a model has been seasoned through exposure to new companies and new economic scenarios, it can be tested with greater validity than is possible in the laboratory.

To be worthy of consideration, a credit model should have been tested with at least several hundred companies over a 10-year test period encompassing more than one credit cycle. Particularly if the model is applicable to privately-held entities, it can make predictions for many thousands of companies over the course of 10 to 15 years. Predictions can then be compared with reality, and this performance can be compared with other credit measures (such as bank rankings or bond ratings). The data eventually become rich enough to permit the estimation of loss functions and even of the timing of the loss. Such experience allows bankers to develop much more confidence in the meaning of credit ratings.

Ultimately, the proof of the pudding is in the eating—in the model's performance—not in its construction or in the elegance of its mathematics. Here again, the burden is on the financial institution to sift through the representations of outstanding model performance made by a vendor. Type I and Type II accuracy, forecast horizon, missing companies and missing data, performance in the private company universe, relationship of the risk rating with market yields, "in sample," "out of sample," and "out of time" validations—these are all legitimate issues to examine.

Applicability to Private Companies

Due to practical considerations, most model builders limit their efforts to public companies because data on them is easily accessible. Databases for public companies are usually more reliable and more extensive than those developed for private companies. This allows for more rigorous initial testing. The public/private test is necessary to assure that classification or predictive results for private and public companies are comparable if the same model is to be used for both. Because of information and moral hazard problems, risk assessments are more difficult to make with respect to private companies.

Model Recognition

A good indicator of a model's potential is whether its ratings have credibility in the financial community. Building a model is not difficult; regulators, banks, insurance companies, students, and academics have developed hundreds of them. Only a few have been able to stand up to public scrutiny, and fewer still have been *used*—and not abandoned—by regulators and financial institutions.

Basel II and Model Validation

If a bank uses an *internal ratings based* (IRB) or the advanced approach to derive the regulatory capital, in Basel II it also has to comply with regulatory validation requirements. To quote from the Basel II "Framework" (BIS 2004):

> *Banks must have a robust system in place to validate the accuracy and consistency of their internal models and modeling processes. A bank must demonstrate to its supervisor that the internal validation process enables it to assess the performance of its internal model and processes consistently and meaningfully.*
>
> *Banks must regularly compare actual return performance (computed using realized and unrealized gains and losses) with modeled estimates and be able to demonstrate that such returns are within the expected range for the portfolio and individual holdings. Such comparisons must make use of historical data that are over as long*

a period as possible. The methods and data used in such comparisons must be clearly documented by the bank. This analysis and documentation should be updated at least annually.

Banks should make use of other quantitative validation tools and comparisons with external data sources. The analysis must be based on data that are appropriate to the portfolio, are updated regularly, and cover a relevant observation period. Banks' internal assessments of the performance of their own model must be based on long data histories, covering a range of economic conditions, and ideally one or more complete business cycles.

Banks must demonstrate that quantitative validation methods and data are consistent through time. Changes in estimation methods and data (both data sources and periods covered) must be clearly and thoroughly documented.

Thus, unless a bank decides to forego the use of the internal ratings based system to derive regulatory capital (i.e., chooses to employ the so-called "simplified" approach), the need for rigorous testing and validation is not only a business necessity, but also a regulatory requirement.

Implementation

Whether it has been developed internally or purchased from a vendor, a credit scoring model should be treated as a major system. Installation involves integration with a bank's loan accounting systems, data base spreadsheets and report writing software. It also involves establishing procedures, designing systems and training bank personnel so that the institution can act on warnings and avoid defaults. A good system should be flexible enough to adapt to changes in the type of information it captures.

Implementing a model requires a strong support staff with a variety of skills:

- *Credit and finance.* The basis of a model is the underlying experience of its builders in credit and financial analysis. Those who understand the variables should build the model from the ground up.
- *Statistics.* Objectivity is assured by strict application of statistical principles. Continuing application of those principles amounts to quality control.
- *Actuarial.* Actuarial methods provide the tools to translate credit information into risk-based pricing and portfolio management information.

■ *Systems and programming.* Professionals who have had experience with installation problems can save endless frustration when a credit system is implemented.

Pilot Testing

The pilot test should be the litmus test for accepting a model. It should be performed on a bank's own data covering a period of 5 to 10 years. It should be designed to measure the three key aspects of risk measurement: sensitivity to real change, lead time in recognizing change, and stability in the absence of real change.[2] It must also compare model performance with the institution's performance in each area. Test samples must be carefully selected so that results can be compared for large companies and small, for public companies and private ones. Sufficient defaulted loans should be included, and the full range of the institution's credit grades should be covered. Even the largest banks may not have sufficient data on defaults by large corporate borrowers to attain a reasonable sample size. However, a bank does not need to depend on its own experience for financial information on large companies. Moreover, with the help of proxies such as rating changes and yield changes, tests may be carried out not merely on defaults but also on shifts in credit quality.

Of course, good models should anticipate credit problems that are either unrecognized by the lender or not sufficiently recognized to warrant closer scrutiny. If a model is really effective, it will motivate a reassessment of the loan and perhaps trigger a change in the credit grade assigned by the bank. And it will do so early enough to avoid a loss.

WORK-IN-PROGRESS ISSUES IN CREDIT RISK MODELING

There are still issues in credit risk measurement that are work in progress. Absence of good data with the required level of detail and over time is an issue of continuing concern. While banks and other institutions have been gathering historic data on corporate financial statements, defaults, and recoveries, they have not, for the most part, kept good cross-sectional and time-series data. Let us take the case of industry correlations. SIC groupings at the one-digit level are too coarse to provide meaningful correlations. However, at the two-digit level, the number of data points for calculating correlation coefficients tends to be very small.[3] This problem of data scarcity can be resolved only over time. Indeed, companies that have accumulated reliable data on default and recoveries will find themselves able to put them to good competitive use. Thanks to increasing volumes of securitization, it has now been possible to build credit risk models with much larger data samples. RiskCalc suite of models now being offered by Moody's KMV (MKMV) for assessing nonfinancial companies is a good example of this welcome trend.

Recovery data continues to be limited. While market value based recovery data (based on market prices observed after default) is now available for large corporate borrowers, the data on ultimate recoveries; that is, the actual present value of recovery after reorganization or asset liquidation are not readily available. In addition, the recovery data is scarce for other asset types such as municipal borrowers, sovereigns, and various types of structured securities. The rating agencies Moody's (in 1992) and Standard and Poor's (in 1995) and the Society of Actuaries (in 1997, 2002, and 2006) have started publishing recovery data. S&P documents recoveries at default and also upon emergence from Chapter 11 bankruptcy. These public bond market studies observe recoveries stratified by bond seniority. For commercial loans, the most likely equivalents to the public bond market are the straight (nonconvertible) senior secured and senior unsecured classes. Using bond data, Altman & Eberhart (1994) and Altman and Kishore (1996) provide statistics on this important variable by seniority and industry group. Recent efforts on modeling recoveries are summarized in Chapter 15.

Another key issue regarding credit risk models remains to be resolved: to date, there has more emphasis on predicting default than on predicting value. To predict value, one must have a better understanding of the effects of such variables as correlations, covenants, embedded options, and bankruptcy and tax laws on the value of an asset. Thus far, nobody has developed an effective and efficient model to measure and price credit risk including all aspects of the counterparty credit risk and the credit risk mitigants. The Credit Edge model by MKMV and the Credit Grades model by the Risk Metrics Group are recent innovations where these models derive the risk neutral value of the credit spread based on the expected default frequency implied by the stock price behavior. Nevertheless, classic credit analysis involving fundamental analysis, simulation, stress tests and offline forecasts will continue to be part of the tool set employed in measuring and managing credit risk.

Credit risk models have not evolved to a point where risk at the microlevel of the firm or individual has been linked to factors at the macrolevel of the economy. Most models that have been built rest on historic data and cannot take advantage of macroeconomic forecasts such as those for inflation, GDP growth, or unemployment. In other words, the insights into business failure of economists and financial analysts have yet to be integrated. While some attempts have been made to link the micro- and macrovariables, these are still in the laboratory stage and have not found practical application in the valuation of fixed income assets.

Lastly, while proper ways to evaluate credit risk models are available, presentations of model results often omit important details regarding methodology, data, test statistics, Type I and Type II errors, and holdout results. Until universally accepted standards are developed, decision makers must perform careful due diligence before accepting a model for use in-house. To the extent that every single credit risk model is a prediction (of what the value of an asset should be or what the likelihood of default is), it is useful for an organization to track the prediction-realization on a continuing basis. This may be done by plotting actual outcomes versus predictions over time, or by plotting the directional error and percent error over time.[4] It is useful to obtain the confidence band around the forecast rather than use a point-value. Frequent reestimation of the model may be advisable if it can be shown that this will improve its performance.

The instruments on the control panel of an aircraft provide measurements of its motion and the space in which it is traveling. They make flying safer and facilitate air travel at high speeds and in adverse weather conditions. But whatever they do, they do not replace the skill and judgment of the pilot. Credit risk models may be viewed in a similar fashion. Pilots, however, are urged to attend to the readings of their instruments, which have been placed in the cockpit because of their demonstrated value and reliability. Credit risk models have not yet achieved the same level of respect—or, for that matter, of reliability. The judgment of the analyst therefore remains critically important in the evaluation and pricing of credit.

REFERENCES

Bank for International Settlements (BIS). 2004. *Basel II: International Convergence of Capital Measurement and Capital Standards: A Revised Framework*. Basel.

Moody's KMV Corporation. 2002. *Benchmarking Default Prediction Models: Pitfalls and Remedies in Model Validation, Technical Report #020305, Revised: 6/13/02*. San Francisco.

CHAPTER 15

About Corporate Default Rates

Facts are to mind what food is to body. On the due diligence of the former depend the strength and wisdom of the one...
—E. Burke from *Forbes Scrapbook of Thoughts on Business and Life* (1976).

In the new Basel II framework, and for managing credit risk in general, perhaps the most important element to specify and analyze is the *probability of default* (PD) of a credit-counterparty. Whether debt instruments are considered on a standalone basis or within a portfolio context, default probabilities and adjustments for recoveries (which is discussed in the next chapter) play a critical role in risk assessment and valuation. Indeed, the two main requirements for a financial institution's acceptance as a Basel II "advanced bank" is its implementation of an *internal-rate-based* (IRB) approach, involving a specification of PD and RR (recovery rate) for each counterparty in all asset classes in order to specify the expected and unexpected *loss given default* (LGD).

The most comprehensive and almost universally referred to corporate default statistics available today are stratified by company or facility bond ratings and by some aging period from a base point in time. These data are updated annually by the leading ratings agencies and the latest data through 2006 can be found in Fitch (2007), Moody's (2007) and Standard & Poor's (2007). In addition, Altman and Ramayanam (2007) report updated defaults measured both in a "traditional" and "cumulative mortality" format. We present and discuss each of these statistical methodologies and results carefully as it is very important for the user to understand the subtleties, as well as the magnitudes, of these risk measures when applying them to their own portfolios as well as when determining risk-capital requirements under Basel II. In addition, the *PD* of a corporate counterparty is fundamental to the pricing and evaluation of a *credit default swap* (CDS) or a CDO on a bundle of CDSs.

In this chapter, we focus on corporate bonds and corporate loans in the United States, with some reference to other areas and asset classes, for example, structured products such as asset-backed securities (ABS). In particular, we concentrate on corporate high-yield (or junk bonds) and their loan counterpart, leveraged loans. The reason is that these asset classes are almost always the risk class designation of a corporate credit asset just prior to a default.

HIGH-YIELD BOND DEFAULT RATES

As noted thus far, a relevant metric for assessing default risk in the corporate sector is the high-yield, or junk bond, market default rate over various periods of time. This market has grown from a nearly all fallen-angel market—that is, investment grade that does not age well and gets downgraded to noninvestment grade or junk status—in 1998 of about $7 billion to about $1 trillion in 2006 (see Figure 15.1). In a sense, these high-yield, high-risk bonds are the raw material for possible defaults.

FIGURE 15.1 Size of the U.S. High-Yield Bond Market 1978–2006
Note: Defaults are defined as bond issues that have missed a payment of interest and this delinquency is not cured within the grace-period (usually 30 days), or the firm has filed for bankruptcy under reorganization (Chapter 11) or liquidation (Chapter 7), or there is an announcement of a distressed-restructuring. The latter typically involves a tender for an equity-for-debt swap, where the creditors accept a lower-priority security in lieu of the bond (usually common equity), or a lower coupon rate payment or an extension to repay the bond is proposed.
Source: Authors' compilations.

Default rates can either be calculated in dollar (e.g., by Altman and Fitch Ratings) or issuer-denominated rates (e.g., by Moody's and S&P). Moody's also now reports default rates denominated in dollars. The dollar-denominated rate versus issuer-denominated rate has a very high correlation over time but can be quite different at a particular point in time. For example, Moody's speculative grade issuer-denominated rate in 2006 was 1.57 percent and its dollar-denominated rate was 1.07 percent. In 2002, when default rates were very high, the dollar rate was significantly greater than the issuer rate. In general, dollar-denominated rates are more volatile than issuer-denominated rates. As to which rates are more relevant to investors, the correct answer is that both are relevant, depending on the investment strategy followed. For example, most institutional investors in high-yield bonds or leverage loans do not invest an equal dollar amount in each issue. So for them a dollar-weighted rate would seem to be most relevant. For equal-weighted investors, such as CDOs (collateralized debt obligations), the issuer-rate makes more sense since the collateral in the "pool" is usually equally weighted as to the amount purchased.

Table 15.1, from Altman and Ramayanam (2007), shows the high-yield, dollar-denominated rate for corporate bonds in the United States and Canada, from 1971 to 2006. Since relatively few managers invest in the total spectrum of bond rating classes (from AAA to CCC), the high-yield, speculative-grade rate of default is relevant for analysts and investors in this asset class. We will see, however, that default rates can be broken down by the full spectrum of ratings and are also reported by Altman, the rating agencies and some investment banks. The weighted average (by dollar amount outstanding) annual default rate for the 36-year period 1971–2006 is 4.24 percent per year and the arithmetic-average is 3.17 percent per year, with a standard deviation of 3.07 percent.

We can observe that the annual default rate has varied from as low as 0.158 percent in 1981 to as high as 12.80 percent in 2002. The median rate is 1.80 percent per year and the difference between the averages and median rate can be explained by the truncated distribution of zero (0) as the minimum. In some years, like 1990, 1991, and 2002, the rate can exceed 10.0 percent. Indeed, we can observe that the rate has been about 10 percent or more (including 2001's 9.8 percent) in four out of the 36 years that we have calculated this rate. Since 10 percent or greater is about two standard deviations above the mean, four observations with this amount is more than what one might expect in a 36-year time period if we assumed a normal distribution (i.e., 2.5 percent of the 36 years, or about one observation).

TABLE 15.1 Historical Default Rates: Straight Bonds Only Excluding Defaulted Issues From Par Value Outstanding, 1971–2006 ($ millions)

Year	Par Value Outstanding ($)	Par Value Defaults ($)	Default Rates (%)
2006	993,600	7,559	0.761
2005	1,073,000	36,209	3.375
2004	933,100	11,657	1.249
2003	825,000	38,451	4.661
2002	757,000	96,858	12.795
2001	649,000	63,609	9.801
2000	597,200	30,295	5.073
1999	567,400	23,532	4.147
1998	465,500	7,464	1.603
1997	335,400	4,200	1.252
1996	271,000	3,336	1.231
1995	240,000	4,551	1.896
1994	235,000	3,418	1.454
1993	206,907	2,287	1.105
1992	163,000	5,545	3.402
1991	183,600	18,862	10.273
1990	181,000	18,354	10.140
1989	189,258	8,110	4.285
1988	148,187	3,944	2.662
1987	129,557	7,486	5.778
1986	90,243	3,156	3.497
1985	58,088	992	1.708
1984	40,939	344	0.840
1983	27,492	301	1.095
1982	18,109	577	3.186
1981	17,115	27	0.158
1980	14,935	224	1.500
1979	10,356	20	0.193
1978	8,946	119	1.330
1977	8,157	381	4.671
1976	7,735	30	0.388
1975	7,471	204	2.731
1974	10,894	123	1.129
1973	7,824	49	0.626
1972	6,928	193	2.786
1971	6,602	82	1.242

TABLE 15.1 (*Continued*)

		Standard Deviation (%)	
Arithmetic Average Default Rate	1971 to 2006	3.167	3.072
	1978 to 2006	3.464	3.283
	1985 to 2006	4.189	3.428
Weighted Average Default Rate[b]	1971 to 2006	4.244	
	1978 to 2006	4.258	
	1985 to 2006	4.303	
Median Annual Default Rate	1971 to 2006	1.802	

[a] As of midyear.
[b] Weighted by par value of amount outstanding for each year.
Source: Authors' compilations.

In 2006, the default rate was a miniscule 0.76 percent, the lowest rate in 25 years (since 1981 when the high-yield bond market was only $17 billion). The Moody's issuer-denominated rate was somewhat higher at about 1.57 percent, but it too was at a very low rate compared to its historical average of close to 5 percent per year. Both of these rates are consistent with an extremely benign credit environment. Indeed, from Figure 15.2, we can observe a very low quarterly and annual default rate from 2003 to 2006, with the exception of an upward blip in late 2005 when several very large defaults took place (e.g., Delta and Northwest Airlines, Delphi Corp., Calpine Corp.). Much has been written and discussed, of late (e.g., see Altman, 2006 and 2007), about the unusually low default rate period and whether conditions will revert back to the average rate or whether the extreme, massive liquidity picture will remain with us for a long time to come. As expected, we observed in fall 2007 that liquidity conditions had indeed changed dramatically, although defaults were still very low. The default rate for all of 2007 was a miniscule 0.51 percent. We do observe another benign period from 1993 to 1998, so while it is possible that the current period will persist, we are of the opinion that there will be a reversion to the mean and, indeed, this is perhaps overdue.

MORTALITY AND CUMULATIVE DEFAULT RATES

While the traditional approach to measuring default rates is appropriate for gauging average annual rates for a broad cross-section of high-yield

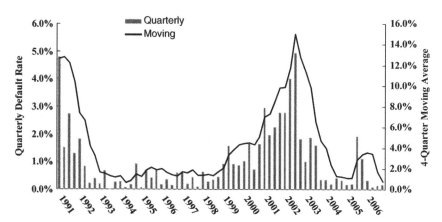

FIGURE 15.2 Quarterly Default Rate and Four-Quarter Moving Average, 1991–2006
Source: Authors' compilations.

bonds, or any asset class that is relevant to the investor/analyst, it is not adequate for a number of reference benchmarks. For one thing, it does not reference specific bond ratings within the high-yield space (e.g., BB, B, or CCC) and, indeed, it does not address, at all, the investment grade classes. In addition, it does not address the timing of the default from some reference date. In order to be more precise about expected default rates for a given credit rating, Altman (1989), Moody's (1990), and S&P (1991 and 1992), all identified the relevant cohort group for measurement as the bond rating at some point in time. As will be shown, however, Altman's mortality measure examines bonds with a certain *original* rating for a period of up to 10 years after issuance. Moody's and Standard & Poor's assess default rates of all bonds of a given bond rating, *regardless of their age*. Moody's was of the view that macroeconomic phenomena are more important than vintage effects for long period averages. It should also be noted that Moody's uses the issuer as the basic unit of account. And recent papers (Hamilton and Cantor 2006 and 2007) discussed Moody's more refined measure that now does specifically incorporate an aging factor in their cumulative default rate calculations as well as the pros and cons of calculating default rates that are adjusted for rating withdrawals. Their method does not, however, analyze default rates from the date of original issuance.

Altman (1989) retains the notion that default rates for individual periods—yearly, for example—are measured on the basis of defaults in the period relative to some base population in that same period. The calculation, however, becomes more complex when we begin with a specific cohort group, such as a bond rating category, and track that group's performance for multiple time periods. Because the original population can change over time as a result of a number of different events, Altman considers mortalities in relation to a survival population and then inputs the defaults to calculate mortality rates. Bonds can exit from the original population because of at least five different kinds of events: defaults, calls, sinking funds, merger-takeouts, and maturities.

The individual mortality rate of bonds in a specific rating class for each year (*marginal mortality rate* or MMR) is calculated using the equation

$$MMR_{(t)} = \frac{\text{Total value of defaulting debt in the year}(t)}{\text{Total value of the population of bonds at the start of the year}(t)}$$

The *cumulative mortality rate* (CMR) is measured over a specific time period $(1, 2, \ldots, T$ years) by subtracting the product of the surviving population of each of the previous years from one (1.0); that is,

$$CMR_{(T)} = 1 - \prod_{t=1}^{T} SR_{(t)}$$

where $CMR_{(T)} =$ cumulative mortality rate in (T) $SR_{(t)} =$ survival rate in (t); $1 - MMR(t)$.

The individual years' marginal mortality rates for each bond rating are based on a compilation of that year's mortality measured from issuance over the entire sample period 1971–2006. For example, all of the one-year mortalities (36 weighted compilations) are combined for the sample period to arrive at the one-year rate; all (35) of the second-year mortalities are combined to compute the two-year rate, and so on.

The mortality rate is a value-weighted rate for the particular year after issuance rather than an unweighted average. If we were simply to average each of the year-one rates, year-two rates, and so on, our results would be susceptible to significant specific-year bias. If, for example, few new bonds were issued in a given year and the defaults emanating from that year were high in relation to the amount issued, the unweighted average could be improperly affected. Altman's (1989) weighted-average technique correctly biases the results towards the larger-issuance years, especially the more recent years. It should be noted that default rates adjusted for survivorship are the most relevant for pricing purposes.

Using data going back to 1971, Altman has measured and updated corporate bond default rates from each of the major S&P rating categories (similar results could be expected if Moody's ratings were used). The most recent estimate of marginal and cumulative mortality rates for up to 10 years after issuance are for the period 1971–2006 and are shown in Table 15.2.

The expected hierarchy of cumulative default rates can be observed; that is, higher rates for comparable years after issuance for lower credit rating cohorts, except for two anomalies. One is the higher AA-cumulative rates than the single A. The other is the second-year marginal rates for BBB bonds compared to BB bonds or compared to year-three BBBs. The former is caused by the large Texaco Corporation's Chapter 11 bankruptcy filing in 1987, which involved over $3.0 billion of originally AA-rated bonds. The latter was due to an even larger amount of WorldCom bonds that were originally rated BBB and issued in 2000 and defaulted two years later in 2002. These anomalies would not manifest if the issuer denominated rates were observed.

The *loss* rates for AA bonds show the expected hierarchy, however, as Texaco's bonds recovered over 80 percent of their face value just after default-far above the average recovery of about 40 percent for all bonds. Table 15.3 shows the mortality-loss rates for the same period 1971–2006. Note that the loss rates are based on the mortality default rates found in Table 15.2, adjusted for recoveries at default. (For an in-depth discussion of recovery rates, see Chapter 16.)

There are several noteworthy aspects to the mortality rate table. First, we can observe that the marginal rates for high-yield bonds in the first three or four years of a bond's life rise each year and then tend to level off for several years thereafter. Hence, we do note an aging effect, which can be observed only by tracking default rates from original issuance. The aging effect is intuitively sound, since most companies have a great deal of cash just after they issue a bond. Even if their operating cash flow is negative, they are usually able to meet several periods of interest payments.

It should be noted that the lower-rated categories, such as single B, have default rates that appear to be very high. Cumulative defaults are nearly 28 percent by the fifth year and 37 percent by the tenth year. But these rates are not so high when viewed in relation to promised yield spreads, which averaged nearly 5 percent per year over the sample period. Factoring in average recovery rates of at least 40 percent (and higher of late), a 28 percent five-year default rate results in an 18 percent cumulative loss rate, or a loss of about 2.5 percent per year. Indeed, the high-yield bonds, of which single B's have been the dominant category, returned 2.56 percent

TABLE 15.2 Mortality Rates by Original Rating: All Rated Corporate Bonds, 1971–2006[a]

| | | Years After Issuance | | | | | | | | | |
		1	2	3	4	5	6	7	8	9	10
AAA	Marginal	0.00%	0.00%	0.00%	0.00%	0.05%	0.03%	0.01%	0.00%	0.00%	0.00%
	Cumulative	0.00%	0.00%	0.00%	0.00%	0.05%	0.08%	0.09%	0.09%	0.09%	0.09%
AA	Marginal	0.00%	0.00%	0.30%	0.14%	0.02%	0.02%	0.00%	0.00%	0.05%	0.01%
	Cumulative	0.00%	0.00%	0.30%	0.44%	0.46%	0.48%	0.48%	0.48%	0.53%	0.54%
A	Marginal	0.01%	0.08%	0.02%	0.06%	0.06%	0.09%	0.05%	0.20%	0.09%	0.05%
	Cumulative	0.01%	0.09%	0.11%	0.17%	0.23%	0.32%	0.37%	0.57%	0.66%	0.71%
BBB	Marginal	0.33%	3.13%	1.34%	1.24%	0.74%	0.31%	0.25%	0.19%	0.14%	0.40%
	Cumulative	0.33%	3.45%	4.74%	5.92%	6.62%	7.10%	7.33%	7.51%	7.63%	8.00%
BB	Marginal	1.15%	2.42%	4.32%	2.26%	2.53%	1.27%	1.61%	1.11%	1.71%	3.47%
	Cumulative	1.15%	3.54%	7.72%	9.88%	12.10%	13.20%	14.60%	15.56%	17.00%	19.88%
B	Marginal	2.84%	6.78%	7.35%	8.49%	6.01%	4.32%	3.95%	2.40%	1.96%	0.83%
	Cumulative	2.84%	9.43%	16.08%	23.21%	27.82%	30.94%	35.67%	35.26%	36.53%	37.06%
CCC	Marginal	8.12%	15.42%	18.75%	11.76%	4.14%	9.33%	5.79%	5.70%	0.85%	4.70%
	Cumulative	8.12%	22.30%	36.86%	44.30%	46.60%	51.57%	54.38%	56.98%	57.34%	59.36%

[a]Rated by S&P at issuance based on 1,955 issues.
Source: Standard & Poor's and authors' compilation.

TABLE 15.3 Mortality Losses by Original Rating: All Rated Corporate Bonds, 1971–2006[a]

		Years After Issuance									
		1	2	3	4	5	6	7	8	9	10
AAA	Marginal	0.00%	0.00%	0.00%	0.00%	0.01%	0.01%	0.01%	0.00%	0.00%	0.00%
	Cumulative	0.00%	0.00%	0.00%	0.00%	0.01%	0.02%	0.03%	0.03%	0.03%	0.03%
AA	Marginal	0.00%	0.00%	0.05%	0.04%	0.01%	0.01%	0.00%	0.00%	0.02%	0.00%
	Cumulative	0.00%	0.00%	0.05%	0.09%	0.10%	0.11%	0.11%	0.11%	0.13%	0.14%
A	Marginal	0.00%	0.03%	0.01%	0.04%	0.03%	0.04%	0.02%	0.03%	0.06%	0.00%
	Cumulative	0.00%	0.03%	0.04%	0.08%	0.11%	0.15%	0.17%	0.20%	0.26%	0.26%
BBB	Marginal	0.23%	2.19%	1.06%	0.45%	0.44%	0.21%	0.10%	0.11%	0.07%	0.23%
	Cumulative	0.23%	2.41%	3.45%	3.88%	4.31%	4.54%	4.63%	4.74%	4.80%	5.02%
BB	Marginal	0.67%	1.41%	2.50%	1.27%	1.47%	0.65%	0.90%	0.48%	0.85%	1.25%
	Cumulative	0.67%	2.07%	4.52%	5.73%	7.12%	7.72%	8.55%	8.99%	9.76%	10.89%
B	Marginal	1.83%	4.74%	4.92%	5.49%	3.90%	2.37%	2.56%	1.34%	1.03%	0.61%
	Cumulative	1.83%	6.48%	11.08%	15.97%	18.37%	19.24%	21.31%	22.36%	23.16%	23.63%
CCC	Marginal	5.44%	11.10%	13.50%	8.46%	2.90%	7.00%	4.34%	4.41%	0.51%	3.01%
	Cumulative	5.44%	15.94%	27.38%	33.44%	35.37%	39.89%	42.50%	45.04%	45.32%	46.96%

[a] Rated by S&P at issuance based on 1,777 issues.
Source: Standard & Poor's and authors' compilation.

per year above the risk-free rate in the 1978–2006 period (Altman and Ramayanam 2007). The investor should also factor in the volatility of returns as well as the average spread.

COMPARING CUMULATIVE DEFAULT RATES

We have mentioned the major differences between the rating agencies' reported default rates and Altman's. These different methodologies, which are summarized in Table 15.4, include (1) face-value-dollar amount (Altman) versus issuer basis; (2) actual ratings (Altman) versus implied senior-unsecured rating; (3) domestic straight debt only (Altman) versus domestic (including convertibles) and foreign; (4) original issuance (Altman) versus cohort grouping, regardless of age; (5) mortality rates (Altman) versus default rates; and (6) different sample periods. Of particular relevance is point (4). In contrast to Altman's original issue rating approach, Moody's and the other rating agencies "cohort method" is based on pools of issuers holding a given rating on the cohort date regardless of original rating or time since issuance.

TABLE 15.4 Comparing Cumulative Default Rate Methodologies

Altman	Moody's/S&P
1. Face-value-weighted basis.	1. Issuer, unweighted basis.
2. Domestic, straight bonds.	2. Domestic straight and convertible and foreign bonds—considered at the issuer level.
3. Based on actual rating from original issuance up to 10 years.	3. Based on implied senior unsecured rating from cohort or static pool groups, combining bonds of all ages up to 20 years (Moody's) and 15 years (S&P).
4. Mortality default calculation adjusting for calls, maturities, and defaults.	4. Default rate based on percentage of original cohort group. Adjusts for withdrawn ratings in marginal default rate calculations.
5. Based on full rating class categories, AAA to CCC (no subgrades).	5. Based on full rating class categories and also subgrades, Aaa to Caa/AAA/CCC.
6. Sample period 1971–2006.	6. Moody's sample period 1970 for full grade and 1983–2006 for subgrades; S&P 1981–2006.

Table 15.5 shows the 1- to 10-year cumulative rates from the three primary sources of data. The primary empirical difference between the mortality/original issuance approach, the *static pool* method used by Standard & Poor's, and the *dynamic cohort* method used by Moody's, is the observed default rates in the first several years—particularly in the lower-grade classes. For example, Altman's first-year rate for single-B bonds is 2.84 percent, while Moody's and Standard & Poor's are 5.24 percent and 4.99 percent, respectively. These relative differences persist until the third year, after which the results are quite similar. For example, the fifth-year Moody's rate is 26.79 percent versus 27.82 percent for Altman. Standard & Poor's rate is actually lower (22.55 percent) than Altman's in the fifth year due to lower marginal rates in some years. This difference is difficult to explain, although S&P does not adjust for rating withdrawals. As noted earlier, the main reason for these differentials is the aging effect. Indeed, Moody's has calculated vintage issuer-weighted defaults rates but they have not reported it as yet.

Which method is best to use probably depends upon the age distribution of the relevant portfolio of individual bonds. For new issuance analysis, which is often the perspective for investors in corporate bonds, the mortality rate approach would seem to be more relevant. For portfolios of seasoned bonds, the rating agency approach would perhaps be more relevant. All of the methods include sample periods that cover many business cycles.

Altman's marginal rates could also be used, but only for assessing the one-year marginal default rates for bonds which have survived up to that point. A portfolio manager's strategy regarding the weighting of bonds could also influence the choice of approach. Altman weights the larger issues more than smaller ones, while the rating agencies weight each issuer equally.

AGE OF DEFAULTS

Table 15.6 shows the age distribution of defaults for the period 1989–2006. Note that the traditional pattern of low defaults in the first year after issuance followed by increased levels for years two and three are found in 2006 as well as for the entire sample period. All of these years, however, had lower proportions in 2006 compared to historical averages. Also, the distribution is rather flat in 2006 in the periods two to nine years after issuance, with a slight spike in the sixth year (by number of issues). However, 2006 follows a trend seen over the last several years in which defaults are occurring later (years 6–9), than are observed from the historical averages.

TABLE 15.5 Cumulative Default Rate Comparison (in % for up o 10 years)

	1	2	3	4	5	6	7	8	9	10
AAA/Aaa										
Altman	0.00	0.00	0.00	0.00	0.05	0.08	0.09	0.09	0.09	0.09
Moody's	0.00	0.00	0.00	0.03	0.10	0.17	0.25	0.34	0.42	0.52
S&P	0.00	0.00	0.09	0.19	0.29	0.43	0.50	0.62	0.66	0.70
AA/Aa										
Altman	0.00	0.00	0.30	0.44	0.46	0.48	0.48	0.48	0.53	0.54
Moody's	0.01	0.02	0.04	0.11	0.18	0.26	0.34	0.42	0.46	0.52
S&P	0.01	0.05	0.10	0.20	0.32	0.43	0.56	0.68	0.78	0.89
A/A										
Altman	0.01	0.09	0.11	0.17	0.23	0.32	0.37	0.57	0.66	0.71
Moody's	0.02	0.10	0.22	0.34	0.47	0.61	0.76	0.93	1.11	1.29
S&P	0.06	0.17	0.31	0.47	0.68	0.91	1.19	1.41	1.64	1.90
BBB/Baa										
Altman	0.33	3.45	4.74	5.92	6.62	7.10	7.33	7.51	7.63	8.00
Moody's	0.18	0.51	0.93	1.43	1.94	2.45	2.96	3.45	4.02	4.64
S&P	0.24	0.71	1.23	1.92	2.61	3.28	3.82	4.38	4.89	5.42
BB/Ba										
Altman	1.15	3.54	7.72	9.88	12.10	13.20	14.60	15.56	17.00	19.88
Moody's	1.21	3.22	5.57	7.96	10.22	12.24	14.01	15.71	17.39	19.12
S&P	1.07	3.14	5.61	7.97	10.10	12.12	13.73	15.15	16.47	17.49
B/B										
Altman	2.84	9.43	16.08	23.21	27.82	30.94	35.67	35.26	36.53	37.06
Moody's	5.24	11.30	17.04	22.05	26.79	30.98	34.77	37.98	40.92	43.34
S&P	4.99	10.92	15.90	19.76	22.55	24.72	26.54	28.00	29.20	30.42
CCC/Caa										
Altman	8.12	22.30	36.86	44.30	46.60	51.57	54.38	56.98	57.34	59.36
Moody's	19.48	30.49	39.72	46.90	52.62	56.81	59.94	63.27	66.28	69.18
S&P	26.29	34.73	39.96	43.19	46.22	47.49	48.61	49.23	50.95	51.83

Source: Altman: market value weights, by number of years from original Standard & Poor's issuance, 1971–2006, based on actual ratings (Altman and Ramayanam 2007); Moody's: issuer-weighted, cohort analysis, 1971–2006, based on actual or implied senior unsecured ratings (Moody's Investors Service 2007); and S&P: issuer-weighted, static pool analysis, 1981–2006, based on actual or implied senior unsecured ratings (Standard & Poor's 2007).

TABLE 15.6 Distribution of Years to Default From Original Issuance Date by Year of Default, 1989–2006

Years to Default	1989 No. of Issues	1989 Total (%)	1990 No. of Issues	1990 Total (%)	1991 No. of Issues	1991 Total (%)	1992 No. of Issues	1992 Total (%)	1993/1994 No. of Issues	1993/1994 Total (%)	1995 No. of Issues	1995 Total (%)	1996 No. of Issues	1996 Total (%)	1997 No. of Issues	1997 Total (%)	1998 No. of Issues	1998 Total (%)
1	4	6	3	3	0	0	0	0	175	9	1	3	2	8	5	20	2	6
2	12	18	25	23	18	13	0	0	333	17	9	28	3	13	4	16	5	15
3	15	23	23	21	26	19	7	13	362	19	7	22	3	13	4	16	10	30
4	13	20	18	17	29	21	10	19	291	15	3	9	8	33	9	36	3	9
5	1	2	23	21	35	26	8	15	239	12	1	3	1	4	3	12	10	30
6	7	11	5	5	10	7	12	22	151	8	2	6	5	21	0	0	2	6
7	7	11	5	5	4	3	5	9	124	6	2	6	0	0	0	0	1	3
8	2	3	4	4	10	7	4	7	56	3	4	13	0	0	0	0	0	0
9	1	2	1	1	3	2	0	0	38	2	1	3	0	0	0	0	0	0
10	3	5	1	1	2	1	8	15	164	8	2	6	2	8	0	0	0	0
Total	65	100	108	100	137	100	54	100	1,933	100	32	100	24	100	25	100	33	100

Years to Default	1999 No. of Issues	1999 Total (%)	2000 No. of Issues	2000 Total (%)	2001 No. of Issues	2001 Total (%)	2002 No. of Issues	2002 Total (%)	2003 No. of Issues	2003 Total (%)	2004 No. of Issues	2004 Total (%)	2005 No. of Issues	2005 Total (%)	2006 No. of Issues	2006 Total (%)	1989–2006 No. of Issues	1989–2006 Total (%)
1	32	26	19	10	40	12	29	8	18	9	8	10	16	9	2	4	184	9
2	37	30	51	28	69	21	51	15	30	15	7	9	13	7	4	8	344	17
3	15	12	56	31	87	26	61	18	26	13	8	10	9	6	6	12	368	18
4	14	11	14	8	65	19	56	16	23	11	6	8	22	12	5	10	300	15
5	7	6	13	7	27	8	45	13	40	20	10	13	14	8	4	8	246	12
6	8	6	5	3	14	4	21	6	20	10	16	21	17	9	9	17	161	8
7	10	8	12	7	21	6	8	2	25	12	9	12	13	7	6	12	135	7
8	2	2	4	2	5	1	7	2	3	1	6	8	11	6	7	13	67	3
9	0	0	3	2	4	1	12	3	5	2	1	1	5	3	6	12	45	2
10	0	0	6	3	3	1	54	16	13	6	6	8	64	34	3	6	168	8
Total	125	100	183	100	335	100	344	100	203	100	77	100	184	100	52	100	2018	100

Source: Authors' compilations.

FALLEN ANGEL DEFAULTS

One factor that can impact the aging of defaults is whether the defaulting issues were at any point in time investment grade and then downgraded (*fallen angels*). Table 15.7 shows a time series of the proportion of

TABLE 15.7 Defaults by Original Ratings: Investment Grade vs. NonInvestment Grade by Year, 1977–2006

	Total Defaulted Issues[a]	Originally Rated Investment Grade (%)	Originally Rated Noninvestment Grade (%)
2006	52	13	87
2005	184	49	51
2004	79	19	81
2003	203	33	67
2002	322	39	61
2001	258	14	86
2000	142	16	84
1999	87	13	87
1998	39	31	69
1997	20	0	100
1996	24	13	88
1995	29	10	90
1994	16	0	100
1993	24	0	100
1992	59	25	75
1991	163	27	73
1990	117	16	84
1989	66	18	82
1988	64	42	58
1987	31	39	61
1986	55	15	85
1985	26	4	96
1984	14	21	79
1983	7	43	57
1982	20	55	45
1981	1	0	100
1980	4	25	75
1979	1	0	100
1978	1	100	0
1977	2	100	0
Total	2,110	26%	74%

[a]Where we could find an original rating from either S&P or Moody's.
Source: Authors' compilations from Standard & Poor's and Moody's records.

defaulting issues that were fallen angels. Table 15.8 shows that comparison between the fallen angel default rate (measured as a percent of issuers) and original issue high-yield bonds. Although fallen angels have a lower average annual rate, the difference (about 1.0 percent) is not statistically significant.

TABLE 15.8   Fallen Angels vs. Original Issue and All U.S. High-Yield Default Rates

Year	Fallen Angel Average 12-Month Default Rate	Original Issue Speculative Gradew Default Rates[a]	All Speculative Grade Bond Default Rates
2006	1.40%	1.23%	1.26%
2005	2.74%	3.70%	2.48%
2004	0.83%	2.65%	2.23%
2003	5.88%	5.46%	5.53%
2002	6.59%	8.55%	8.32%
2001	8.46%	10.14%	10.99%
2000	7.01%	7.10%	7.03%
1999	4.01%	5.10%	4.62%
1998	3.31%	2.75%	2.23%
1997	2.04%	2.10%	1.71%
1996	1.38%	2.00%	1.71%
1995	0.25%	3.90%	3.07%
1994	0.00%	2.31%	1.70%
1993	1.72%	1.99%	1.79%
1992	4.50%	5.48%	5.45%
1991	7.53%	10.86%	11.66%
1990	5.77%	8.30%	8.20%
1989	3.74%	4.93%	5.33%
1988	4.25%	3.39%	3.95%
1987	4.36%	2.92%	2.41%
1986	2.46%	6.29%	4.78%
1985	6.77%	4.06%	3.24%
Arithmetic Average	3.86%	4.78%	4.69%
Weighted Average (by number of issuers)	4.22%	5.15%	5.10%
Standard Deviation	2.43%	2.67%	2.96%

[a]S&P did not calculate this rate in 2006.

Source: Authors' compilation from Standard & Poor's Credit Pro database except in 2006.

INDUSTRY DEFAULTS

Tables 15.9 and 15.10 show the number of defaults from the large industrial sectors over the period 1970–2006 and by dollar amount per year from 1990–2006. We can observe that the largest "contributor" has been the communications sector, with more than $100 billion of defaults, the bulk in the four-year period 2000–2003, led by telecoms. One firm, WorldCom, contributed about $30 billion! More recently, the sector with the most financial distress has been the automotive industry, primarily auto parts suppliers.

FORECASTING DEFAULT RATES

When discussing the forecast of annual default rates, we again differentiate between dollar-denominated and issuer-denominated rates. In either case, the fact that default risk is a critical measure in determining required rates of return on investing in any debt class makes this estimation important. So, in a benign default risk environment, a seemingly small yield spread available may be acceptable if default rates are expected to continue at a very low rate.

ISSUER-BASED DEFAULT RATE FORECASTS

A very fine summary of issuer-based default rate forecasting is provided in Keenan, Shtogrin, and Sobehart (1999). Probably the first study on the topic was Fons (1991), where he found that about half of the variation in historical default rates could be explained by credit quality and the overall state of the economy. The former was proxied by the historical one-year default rates by rating category and the distribution of issuers at the point in time that the forecast was being made. It was found that the distribution of current ratings plus the expected variation based on the state of the economy did a very good job in terms of forecasting accuracy. A consensus forecast of GNP growth was used as a proxy for the expected state of the economy and a two-factor regression model fit the data very well.

Helwege and Kleiman (1997), building upon the Fons framework, explained the annual fluctuation in high-yield bond default rates with an adjusted R^2 of as much as 81 percent. They added an aging factor, discussed earlier in the Altman models, as well as an adjusted nonsymmetrical group of macroeconomic factors. They found that an economic growth threshold of 1.5 percent (dummy variable) was important in determining if default

TABLE 15.9 Corporate Bond Defaults by Industry (number of companies)

Industry	1970–1982	1983	1984	1985	1986	1987	1988	1989	1990	1991	1992	1993	1994	1995	1996	1997	1998	1999	2000	2001	2002	2003	2004	2005	2006	Total
Auto/motor carrier	3							3	3					1				1						4	3	19
Conglomerates								1	1	3	3	3									1	1	1	1		15
Energy	3	3	5	7	12	2				4	3	3		1	1	1		13	1		8	9			2	78
Financial services	4	1	1					11	7	14	6	2	3	2	1	2	6		6	4	5	6	2	3	3	88
Leisure/ entertainment	4					2	4	4	8	2	4	3	4	3		5	5	8	9	6	5	6				81
General manufacturing	9	1	1	2	6	3	3	1	5	8	8	7	3	8	6	7	6	16	23	43	22	13	17	12	6	236
Health care			2	6	3		2		2	1	1	1							6		4	3	6	2		39
Miscellaneous industries	3	1				1	2		4	4	3	1	1	1		3	3	16	34	38	25	16	6	1	4	176
Real estate/ construction	7					1	1	3	7	5	1			2		2	1	4	6	4	3		2	1		53
REIT	11					1									1			1								14
Retailing	6	1	2	1			1	2	6	15	6	4	5	6	3	6	6	12	7	12	5	5	3	2	2	115
Communications	7	2		1	1		1		3	4	1	1	3	2	2	1	6	11	8	39	26	21	6	3	2	156
Transportation (nonauto)	4	2		1	1			1	1	2			2					8	5	7	7	6	2	5	1	58
Utilities						1	1				1				1	1			1		0	0				6
Total	57	12	12	19	23	15	24	26	47	62	34	22	19	28	15	29	37	98	107	156	112	86	39	34	23	1,134

Source: Authors' compilations.

TABLE 15.10 Corporate Bond Defaults by Industry (amounts in $ millions)

Industry	1990	1991	1992	1993	1994	1995	1996	1997	1998	1999	2000	2001	2002	2003	2004	2005	2006	Total
Auto/motor carrier	468	90				215		300	100	430	120	3,737	285		280	3,573	2,692	12,290
Conglomerates													100	690	275			1,065
Energy		60	103	600		75	100			3,812	217	4,200	4,085	11,857		8,895		34,004
Financial services	928	696	536		78	687	700	66	689	375	1,968	5,062	3,803	1,079	110	541	156	17,474
Leisure/entertainment	498	1,191	159		138	435	293		245	1,100	2,891	3,437	21,242	633	1,286	6,861	715	41,124
General manufacturing	2,675	3,695	488	118		616	641	123	247	2,092	2,507	3,138	2,455	2,108	225	1,396	1,486	24,010
Health care	18	1,120				75			125	2,214	1,715	692	115	3,843		360		10,277
Miscellaneous industries	1,968	4,911	1,378	1,056	317	1,286	832	461	1,290	7,615	8,352	9,715	5,594	4,494	1,977	569	409	52,224
Real estate/construction	2,605	417	113	49	75	190		258	383	385	252	1,110	1,088	77	1,783	174		8,959
Retailing	4,443	2,937	1,489	18	2,814	395	164	2,504	1,241	2,052	3,081	1,586	4,092	877	749	1,059	332	29,833
Communications							460	286	1,549	2,980	5,983	34,827	47,953	7,603	2,551	150	1,496	105,838
Transportation (nonauto)	1,028	1,452			301	562			1,125	310	2,890	1,430	4,711	2,086	2,421	12,376	272	30,964
Utilities		1,452	617	85			275	202		75			1,150	1,417				5,273
Total	14,631	18,021	4,883	1,926	3,723	4,536	3,465	4,200	6,994	23,440	29,976	68,934	96,673	36,764	11,657	35,954	7,559	373,336

Source: Authors' compilations.

rates were going to spike up for the bottom-tier of speculative grade credits (e.g., B3 or lower), while higher-tier speculative grade credits would not be as vulnerable. An arbitrarily determined GDP growth threshold was also used in explaining default recovery rates (see Chapter 16), but with very little added explanatory power to their supply/demand based model.

Jonsson and Fridson (1996) and Jonsson, Fridson, and Zhong (1998), using a different set of issuer-based default rate macroeconomic indicators, were able to explain 86.5 percent of the variation in historical speculative-grade default rates. Their models also included a variable that measured the aging factor of existing issuers and the existing credit profile of issuers. The latter was based on the proportion of existing issuers with a B3 or lower rating—again the concentration on the "bad-cohort." The macroeconomic factors included corporate profits as a percentage of GNP, the size of current liabilities of business failures, the Nasdaq and S&P 500 Index P/E ratios and the gross proceeds of IPOs. These measures were used to assess the degree of optimism/pessimism of the economy, as well as the cost of equity capital and access to equity capital for firms in the economy. The expected inverse correlation between macroeconomic performance and optimism with default rates were shown to be evident.

Finally, with respect to a global, speculative grade issuer-based default rate forecasting model, Keenan et al. (1999) provided an approach that as of this writing is still being used by Moody's Investors Service. They used a revised measure of possible defaulting issuers which subtracted out those issuers which had their rating "withdrawn" over the past 12 months. So a forecast of market size reflecting the expected withdrawal rate was necessary. The authors argued that the withdrawals were fairly stable over time averaging about 4 percent for speculative grade issuers and 2 percent for all-corporate categories. A simple autoregressive model was used to extrapolate this withdrawal rate. Withdrawals play an important role in Moody's published cumulative default rates—discussed earlier—and also in Altman's mortality rate estimates discussed earlier and also to come in his default rate forecasting model.

The Moody's model then proceeds to forecast the next 12-month default rate based on a Poisson regression model postulated to be appropriate when the variable to be estimated is a nonnegative integer value, which is a function of a set of explanatory variables. They argue that the Poisson-based model was appropriate for the Duffie and Singleton (1997) aggregated default activity model as well as CSFB's CreditRisk$^+$ portfolio model (1997). An important assumption of this modeling process is the assumption that the defaults within each monthly observation can be assumed to be uncorrelated. The authors state that they find little evidence of clustering, whether across industries or within an industry, even in high default months.

Moody's predictors of default included (1) changes in credit quality; (2) the aging effect of existing issuers; and (3) a number of variables that reflect macroeconomic conditions in the economy. The latter include the index of total industrial production in the United States, adjusted by the producer price index, and the 10-year U.S. Treasury bond yield. The authors found that they could explain up to 85 percent of the variation in the all-corporate global-trailing 12-month default rate and about 80 percent of the variation in the 12-month trailing speculative-grade default rate.

THE MORTALITY DOLLAR-BASED RATE APPROACH

Using the mortality rate approach to calculating default rates, discussed earlier in this chapter, Altman has for a number of years, been forecasting future one-year default rates (Altman and Ramayanam 2007). This dollar-denominated rate yields both a dollar estimate as well as a percentage of the high-yield market that can be expected to default. The approach is extremely simple and does not utilize any forecasts of macroeconomic factors to arrive at its forecast. He simply observes the past 10 years' new issuance of bonds of all ratings, from AAA to CCC, and applies the latest, updated mortality rate matrix (see Table 15.2) to estimate the marginal mortality rates and dollars expected to default in the next calendar year. So, for example, the single-B new issuance in 2006 multiplied by the one year's marginal mortality rate 2.84 percent will give us the B-rated first year's contribution to 2007's defaulted bonds' dollar amount; the second year's marginal rate (6.78 percent) multiplied by 2005's new issuance of single-B bonds will give us that year's contribution, and so on. One can then simply aggregate each year's contribution by rating class for all rating classes to determine the total amount of defaults one year ahead. Since Altman's default rate method (see Table 15.1), uses the midyear convention for determining the denominator in its calculation, the total forecasted default rate calculation requires an estimate of the size of the high-yield bond population as of midyear of the year the forecast is for.

A FINAL NOTE ON FORECASTED DEFAULT RATES

Both of the forecasting methods described in this chapter, were forecasting at the start of the year, approximately a 2.5 percent high-yield bond default rate for 2007. While these techniques were quite accurate in their forecasts in the past, they all over-estimated the 2006 rate by a considerable margin.

The extreme low rate in 2006 was consistent with the recent benign credit markets and if these conditions continue in 2007 (the time of the writing of this chapter), then we can expect that forecasting techniques that rely on estimates based on a long history of observations (e.g., over 35 years in the case of the Moody's and Altman's methods) will again overestimate the default rate. At some point, however, we expect a reversion to the mean default rate and a more accurate set of forecasts.

LEVERAGE LOAN DEFAULT RATES

The loan analog to the high-yield bond market is known as the *leverage loan market*. These are mostly term-loans provided to noninvestment grade companies or loans which yield at least 150 basis points over LIBOR. Most of these loans are held by nonbank, institutional investors and are typically three- to seven-year maturities with similar covenants to their public bond "cousins." This market has grown tremendously of late and was estimated to be about $1.4 trillion in 2006 (Figure 15.3), about 40 percent larger than the high-yield bond market in the United States. Indeed, in 2006, the new issuance was a record $480 billion compared to a near record $140 billion of newly issued high-yield bonds. These loans are the main provider of debt financing in the recent binge of *highly leveraged transactions* (HLTs), *primarily leverage buyouts* (LBOs).

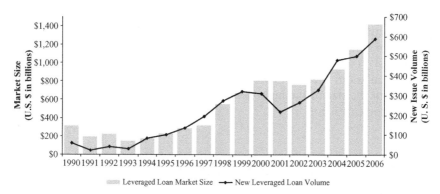

FIGURE 15.3   Leveraged Loan Market: U.S. Distressed Market Update, 1990–2006[a]
[a]Defined as speculative grade with a LIBOR spread of a 150 basis points or better.
Source: Credit Suisse, from Avenue Capital (2006) presentation.

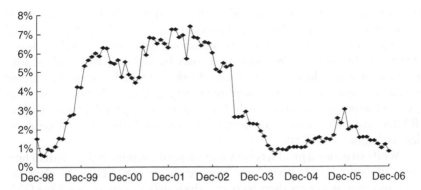

FIGURE 15.4 S&P Leveraged Loan Index: 12-Month Moving Average
Default Rate, 1998–2006
Source: Standard & Poor's/LCD compilation.

Similar to the unusually low default rates in the high-yield bond market
in 2006, we can observe a very low default rate in the leverage loan market
(see Figure 15.4). Indeed, the last 12- month, dollar-denominated default rate
(from S&P/LCD) fell from about 3.0 percent in 2005 to 1.1 percent in 2006
and fell even further to 0.40 percent in September 2007. The comparable
issue-denominated rate was about 0.80 percent of the pool of 2006, down
from 2.0 percent one year earlier and also fell to a miniscule 0.46 percent
in February. These statistics are consistent with our observation that the
risky debt markets were enjoying an unusually high liquidity, low-default
risk environment in 2006 and the remarkable thing was that lenders were
requiring an almost all-time low yield spread over risk-free Treasuries. Some
observers (e.g., Altman 2006) felt that the risk fundamentals of the market
were far greater than the yield spreads, default rates, and credit default
swap premiums were implying and that a reversion-to-the-mean was likely
to manifest in the next few years. Still, others were arguing that a type of
new paradigm had taken place and that the 2006 scenario of credit risk
management was likely to continue for the foreseeable future. We guess the
old adage, "time will tell," is relevant here! And, indeed it did as the credit
market's bubble burst in mid-2007.

STRUCTURED FINANCE DEFAULT RATES

The focus of this chapter has been on default rates in the corporate bond
sector, but we would be remiss not to comment on the structured finance

product sectors, given the turmoil in that market in 2007 (also discussed in Chapters 24 and 25). Structured products started with mortgage-backed securities in the 1970s, followed by nonmortgage securities such as leases (1985), credit cards (1986), and many asset-backed securities such as auto loans, boat loans, home equity loans, bank-originated student loans, and the current asset of concern, subprime mortgages. In addition, major categories of structured products include residential mortgage-backed securities (RMBS), commercial mortgage-backed securities (CMBS), and collateralized debt obligations (CDOs).

While structured products have experienced phenomenal growth of late, especially since 2002, there have been relatively few studies on their default and even fewer on their recovery-given default experience. One fairly comprehensive default study on structured finance was by Fitch Ratings in 2006 (Mah and Verde 2006). This study covered the period 1991–2005 and included the ABS, RMBS, CMBS, and CDO markets. Throughout most of this 15-year period, upgrades exceeded downgrades of ratings, except in the 2000–2002 period and again since early in 2007. Over the period 1991–2005, Fitch recorded 1,027 structured defaults with 90 percent having occurred since 2001. When their data will be updated for 2006/2007, the number of defaults, especially in the ABS and RMBS markets, will increase dramatically.

The major findings of the 2006 Fitch study were:

- The average annual default rate across investment grade bonds was 0.13 percent, while the speculative grade annual default rate was 3.4 percent.
- These structured finance default rates were found to be comparable to corporate bond default rates (0.11 percent [investment grade] and 3.27 percent [speculative grade] respectively). See Table 15.11.
- In general, default rates were consistent with ratings prior to default— the lower the rating, the higher the default rate in subsequent periods.

Defaults in the structured finance market are defined by Fitch as a securities that suffer unrecoverable losses whether in the form of an interest or principal shortfall or write-down. Public, private, and 144a issues were included. Default rates are based on the number of issues, not issuers or dollar amounts. The latter is also published by Fitch for corporate issues only.

Over the period 1991–2005, the vast majority of the defaults in structured products were in the ABS sector (55 percent), with 18 percent of the total in each of the CDO and RMBS markets; and the MBS sector experienced the fewest. Over 97 percent of all global structured defaults were from the United States. (This will be even higher when data through 2007

TABLE 15.11   Global Structured Finance and Corporate Average Cumulative Default Rates (%), 1991–2005

	Average One Year		Average Three Year		Average Five Year	
	Structured	Corporate	Structured	Corporate	Structured	Corporate
AAA	0.02	0.00	0.10	0.00	0.14	0.00
AA	0.07	0.00	0.36	0.00	0.58	0.07
A	0.11	0.04	0.95	0.34	1.95	0.71
BBB	0.41	0.28	3.11	1.79	5.75	3.65
BB	1.13	1.39	4.97	6.26	7.01	9.80
B	3.11	1.63	9.79	6.40	12.00	7.58
CCC	24.87	23.87	49.40	37.04	50.21	33.09
Investment Grade	0.13	0.11	0.95	0.68	1.75	1.31
High Yield	3.40	3.37	8.78	8.83	10.24	11.30
All Structured Finance or All Corporate Finance	0.70	0.65	2.37	1.97	3.30	2.77

Source: Fitch; Mah and Verde (2006).

is included). The bulk of ABS defaults were attributed to the *manufactured housing* (MH) and *home equity loan* (HEL), and franchise loan sectors. When subprime ABS structures will be included, the ABS market will be even more dominant.

While the corporate and structured products sectors showed comparable one-, three-, and five-year cumulative default rate results through 2005 (Table 15.11), this comparison may change when 2006/2007 are recorded. In these years, the number of subprime related structured product defaults soared while corporate defaults remained at near record low levels. Finally, we await more definitive results on the recovery rates of structured finance defaults.

REFERENCES

Altman, E. 1989. "Measuring Corporate Bond Mortality and Performance." *Journal of Finance* 54, no. 4:909–922.
———. 2006. Are Historically Based Default and Recovery Models in the High Yield and Distressed Debt Markets Still Relevant for Investment Funds in Today's Credit Environment? Working Paper, NYU Salomon Center, November.

————. 2007. "Global Debt Markets in 2007: New Paradigm or the Great Credit Bubble?." *Journal of Applied Corporate Finance* 19, no. 3:17–31.

Altman, E., and S. Ramayanam. 2007. Defaults and Returns in the High-Yield Bond Market: 2006 in Review and Outlook. NYU Salomon Center, February.

Avenue Capital. 2006. 2006 Investor Conference, New York, October.

Credit Suisse Financial Products. 1997. *CreditRisk$^+$: A Credit Risk Management Framework*. London.

Duffie, D., and K. Singleton. 1997. "Modeling Term Structures of Defaultable Bonds." *Review of Financial Studies* 12, no. 4:687–729.

Fitch Ratings. 2007. "The Shrinking Default Rate and the Credit Cycle – New Twists, New Risks." *Credit Market Research*, February 20.

Fons, J. S. 1991. "An Approach to Forecasting Default Rates." *Moody's Special Reports*, August.

Hamilton, D., and R. Cantor. 2006. *Special Comment: Measuring Corporate Default Rates*, November. New York: Moody's Investors Service.

————. 2007. "Adjusting Corporate Default Rates for Rating Withdrawals." *Journal of Credit Risk* 3, no. 2:3–26.

Helwege, J., and P. Kleinman. 1997. "Understanding Aggregate Default Rates of High Yield Bonds." *Journal of Fixed Income* 7, no. 1:55–61.

Jonsson, J. G., and M. S. Fridson. 1996. "Forecasting Default Rates on High Yield Bonds." *The* Journal of Fixed Income 6, no. 2:66–77.

Jonsson, J. G., M. S. Fridson, and H. Zhong. 1998. Advances in Default Rate Forecasting. Merrill Lynch's Global Securities Research & Economics Group, May.

Keenan, S. C., I. Shtogrin, and J. Sobehart. 1999. "Historical Default Rates of Corporate Bond Issuers, 1920–1999." *Moody's Special Reports*, January.

Mah, S. and M. Verde. 2006. "Fitch Global Structured Finance 1991–2005 Default Study," *Fitch ratings*, November 28.

Moody's Investors Service. 1990. "Corporate Bond Default and Default Rates." *Moody's Special Reports*, February.

————. 1999. "Predicting Default Rates: A Forecasting Model for Moody's Issuer-Based Default Rates." *Moody's Global Credit Research*, August.

————. 2007. "Corporate Default and Recovery Rates: 1920–2006." *Moody's Special Report*, February.

Standard & Poor's. 1991. "Corporate Bond Defaults Study," parts 1–3. *Credit Week*, 15 and 16 September; and 21 December.

————. 2007, February. *Ratings Performance 2006: Stability and Transition*. New York.

CHAPTER 16

Default Recovery Rates and LGD in Credit Risk Modeling and Practice

"Data! data! data!" he cried impatiently. "I can't make bricks without clay."

—Sir Arthur Conan Doyle, *The Adventures of the Copper Beeches*

INTRODUCTION

Three main variables affect the credit risk of a financial asset: (1) the *probability of default* (PD); (2) the *loss given default* (LGD), which is equal to PD times one minus the *recovery rate* (RR) in the event of default; and (3) the *exposure at default* (EAD). While significant attention has been devoted by the credit risk literature on the estimation of the first component, PD, much less attention has been dedicated to the estimation of RR and to the relationship between PD and RR. This is mainly the consequence of two related factors. First, credit pricing models and risk management applications tend to focus on the systematic risk components of credit risk, as these are the only ones that attract risk premia. Second, credit risk models traditionally assumed RR to be *dependent* on individual features (e.g., collateral or seniority) that do not respond to systematic factors and, therefore, to be *independent* of PD.

This traditional focus on default analysis has been partly reversed by the recent increase in the number of studies dedicated to the subject of RR estimation and the relationship between the PD and RR (Fridson, Garman, and Okashima 2000; Gupton, Gates, and Carty 2000; Altman, Resti, and

Sironi 2001; Altman, Brady, Resti, and Sironi 2005; Frye 2000a, 2000b, and 2000c; Hu and Perraudin 2002; Hamilton, Gupton, and Berthault 2001; Jarrow 2001; Jokivuolle and Peura 2003; and a number of contributors to Altman, Resti, and Sironi 2005). This is partly the consequence of the parallel increase in default rates and decrease of recovery rates registered during the 1999–2002 period. More generally, evidence from many countries in recent years suggests that collateral values and recovery rates can be volatile and, moreover, they tend to go down just when the number of defaults goes up in economic downturns.

This chapter presents a detailed review of the way credit risk models, developed during the last 30 years, have treated the recovery rate, and, more specifically, its relationship with the probability of default of an obligor. In addition, we provide timely empirical data on recovery rates on bonds and loans. These models can be divided into two main categories: (1) credit pricing models and (2) portfolio credit *value-at-risk* (VaR) models. Credit pricing models can in turn be divided into three main approaches: (1) first-generation structural-form models; (2) second generation structural-form models; and (3) reduced-form models. These three different approaches together with their basic assumptions, advantages, drawbacks, and empirical performance are reviewed in the next three sections. Credit VaR models are then examined in the subsequent section. The more recent studies explicitly modeling and empirically investigating the relationship between PD and RR are then reviewed. In the next section, we discuss the Bank for International Settlement's (BIS) efforts to motivate banks to consider "downturn LGD" in the specification of capital requirements under Basel II. Then the very recent efforts by the major rating agencies are reviewed to provide explicit estimates of recovery given default. The final sections revisit the issue of procyclicality and present some recent empirical evidence on recovery rates on both defaulted bonds and loans and also on the relationship between default and recovery rates.

FIRST GENERATION STRUCTURAL-FORM MODELS: THE MERTON APPROACH

The first category of credit risk models are the ones based on the original framework developed by Merton (1974) using the principles of option pricing (Black and Scholes 1973). In such a framework, the default process of a company is driven by the value of the company's assets relative to its liabilities and the risk of a firm's default is therefore explicitly linked to the variability of the firm's asset value. The basic intuition behind the Merton model is relatively simple: default occurs when the value of a firm's assets (the market value of the firm) is lower than that of its liabilities. The payment to the debtholders at the maturity of the debt is therefore the smaller of two quantities: the face value of the debt or the market value of the firm's assets. Assuming that the company's debt is entirely represented by a zero-coupon bond, if the value of the firm at maturity is greater than the face value of the bond, then the bondholder gets back the face value of the bond. However, if the value of the firm is less than the face value of the bond, the shareholders get nothing and the bondholder gets back the market value of the firm. The payoff at maturity to the bondholder is therefore equivalent to the face value of the bond minus a put option on the value of the firm, with a strike price equal to the face value of the bond and a maturity equal to the maturity of the bond. Following this basic intuition, Merton derived an explicit formula for risky bonds which can be used both to estimate the PD of a firm and to estimate the yield differential between a risky bond and a default-free bond.

In addition to Merton (1974), first generation structural-form models include Black and Cox (1976), Geske (1977), and Vasicek (1984), among others. Each of these models tries to refine the original Merton framework by removing one or more of the unrealistic assumptions. Black and Cox (1976) introduce the possibility of more complex capital structures, with subordinated debt; Geske (1977) introduces interest-paying debt; Vasicek (1984) introduces the distinction between short and long term liabilities which now represents a distinctive feature of the most successful of the practitioner versions of Merton's approach, the Moody's KMV model.[1] We have discussed the KMV model earlier in Chapter 11.

Under these conceptual models, all the relevant credit risk elements, including default and recovery at default, are a function of the structural characteristics of the firm: asset levels, asset volatility (business risk) and leverage (financial risk). The RR is therefore an endogenous variable, as the creditors' payoff is a function of the residual value of the defaulted company's assets. More precisely, under Merton's theoretical framework, PD and RR are inversely related. If, for example, the firm's value increases, then its PD tends to decrease while the expected RR at default increases (*ceteris paribus*). On the other side, if the firm's debt increases, its PD increases while the expected RR at default decreases. Finally, if the firm's asset volatility increases, its PD increases while the expected RR at default decreases, since the possible asset values can be quite low relative to liability levels.

Although the line of research that followed the Merton approach has proven very useful in addressing the qualitatively important aspects of pricing credit risks, it has been less successful in practical applications.[2] This lack of success has been attributed to different reasons. First, under Merton's model the firm defaults only at maturity of the debt, a scenario that is at odds with reality. Second, for the model to be used in valuing default-risky debts of a firm with more than one class of debt in its capital structure (complex capital structures), the priority/seniority structures of various debts have to be specified. Also, this framework assumes that the absolute priority rules are actually adhered to upon default in that debts are paid off in the order of their seniority. However, empirical evidence, such as in Franks and Torous (1994), indicates that the absolute-priority rules are often violated. Moreover, the use of a lognormal distribution in the basic Merton model (instead of a more fat tailed distribution) tends to overstate recovery rates in the event of default.

SECOND GENERATION STRUCTURAL-FORM MODELS

In response to such difficulties, an alternative approach has been developed which still adopts the original Merton framework as far as the default process is concerned but, at the same time, removes one of the unrealistic assumptions of the Merton model; namely, that default can occur only at maturity of the debt when the firm's assets are no longer sufficient to cover debt obligations. Instead, it is assumed that default may occur anytime between the issuance and maturity of the debt and that default is triggered when the value of the firm's assets reaches a lower threshold level.[3] These models include Kim, Ramaswamy, and Sundaresan (1993); Hull and White (1995); Nielsen, Saà-Requejo, and Santa Clara (1993); Longstaff and Schwartz (1995); and others.

Under these models, the RR in the event of default is exogenous and independent from the firm's asset value. It is generally defined as a fixed ratio of the outstanding debt value and is therefore independent from the PD. For example, Longstaff and Schwartz (1995) argue that, by looking at the history of defaults and the recovery rates for various classes of debt of comparable firms, one can form a reliable estimate of the RR. In their model, they allow for a stochastic term structure of interest rates and for some correlation between defaults and interest rates. They find that this correlation between default risk and the interest rate has a significant effect on the properties of the credit spread.[4] This approach simplifies the first class of models by both exogenously specifying the cash flows to risky debt in the event of bankruptcy and simplifying the bankruptcy process. The latter occurs when the value of the firm's underlying assets hits some exogenously specified boundary.

Despite these improvements with respect to the original Merton's framework, second generation structural-form models still suffer from three main drawbacks, which represent the main reasons behind their relatively poor empirical performance.[5] First, they still require estimates for the parameters of the firm's asset value, which is nonobservable. Indeed, unlike the stock price in the Black and Scholes formula for valuing equity options, the current market value of a firm is not easily observable. Second, structural-form models cannot incorporate credit rating changes that occur quite frequently for default-risky corporate debts. Most corporate bonds undergo credit downgrades before they actually default. As a consequence, any credit risk model should take into account the uncertainty associated with credit rating changes as well as the uncertainty concerning default. Finally, most structural-form models assume that the value of the firm is continuous in time. As a result, the time of default can be predicted just before it happens and hence, as argued by Duffie and Lando (2000), there are no sudden surprises. In other words, without recurring to a "jump process," the PD of a firm is known with certainty.

REDUCED-FORM MODELS

The attempt to overcome the above mentioned shortcomings of structural-form models gave rise to reduced-form models. These include Litterman and Iben (1991); Madan and Unal (1995); Jarrow and Turnbull (1995); Jarrow, Lando, and Turnbull (1997); Lando (1998), Duffie (1998); and Duffie and Singleton (1999). Unlike structural-form models, reduced-form models do not condition default on the value of the firm, and parameters related to the firm's value need not be estimated to implement them. In addition, reduced-form models introduce separate explicit assumptions on the dynamic of both PD and RR. These variables are modeled independently from the structural features of the firm, its asset volatility and leverage. Generally speaking, reduced-form models assume an exogenous RR that is independent from the PD and take as basics the behavior of default-free interest rates, the RR of defaultable bonds at default, as well as a stochastic process for default intensity. At each instant, there is some probability that a firm defaults on its obligations. Both this probability and the RR in the event of default may vary stochastically through time. Those stochastic processes determine the price of credit risk. Although these processes are not formally linked to the firm's asset value, there is presumably some underlying relation. Thus Duffie and Singleton (1999) describe these alternative approaches as reduced-form models.

Reduced-form models fundamentally differ from typical structural-form models in the degree of predictability of the default as they can accommodate defaults that are sudden surprises. A typical reduced-form model assumes that an exogenous random variable drives default and that the probability of default over any time interval is nonzero. Default occurs when the random variable undergoes a discrete shift in its level. These models treat defaults as unpredictable Poisson events. The time at which the discrete shift will occur cannot be foretold on the basis of information available today.

Reduced-form models somewhat differ from each other by the manner in which the RR is parameterized. For example, Jarrow and Turnbull (1995) assumed that, at default, a bond would have a market value equal to an exogenously specified fraction of an otherwise equivalent default-free bond. Duffie and Singleton (1999) followed with a model that, when market value at default (i.e., RR) is exogenously specified, allows for closed-form solutions for the term-structure of credit spreads. Their model also allows for a random RR that depends on the predefault value of the bond. While this model assumes an exogenous process for the expected loss at default, meaning that the RR does not depend on the value of the defaultable claim, it allows for correlation between the default hazard rate process and RR. Indeed, in this model, the behavior of both PD and RR may be allowed to depend on firm-specific or macroeconomic variables and therefore to be correlated.

Other models assume that bonds of the same issuer, seniority, and face value have the same RR at default, regardless of the remaining maturity. For example, Duffie (1998) assumes that, at default, the holder of a bond of given face value receives a fixed payment, irrespective of the coupon level or maturity, and the same fraction of face value as any other bond of the same seniority. This allows him to use recovery parameters based on statistics provided by rating agencies such as Moody's. Jarrow, Lando, and Turnbull (1997) also allow for different debt seniorities to translate into different RRs for a given firm. Both Lando (1998) and Jarrow, Lando, and Turnbull (1997) use transition matrices (historical probabilities of credit rating changes) to price defaultable bonds.

Empirical evidence concerning reduced-form models is rather limited. Using the Duffie and Singleton (1999) framework, Duffee (1999) finds that these models have difficulty in explaining the observed term structure of credit spreads across firms of different credit risk qualities. In particular, such models have difficulty generating both relatively flat yield spreads when firms have low credit risk and steeper yield spreads when firms have higher credit risk.

A recent attempt to combine the advantages of structural-form models—a clear economic mechanism behind the default process—and the ones of reduced-form models—unpredictability of default—can be found in Zhou (2001). This is done by modeling the evolution of firm value as a jump-diffusion process. This model links RRs to the firm value at default so that the variation in RRs is endogenously generated and the correlation between RRs and credit ratings, reported first in Altman (1989) and Gupton, Gates, and Carty (2000), is justified.

CREDIT VALUE-AT-RISK MODELS

During the second half of the 1990s, banks and consultants started developing credit risk models aimed at measuring the potential loss, with a predetermined confidence level, that a portfolio of credit exposures could suffer within a specified time horizon (generally one year). These were motivated by the growing importance of credit risk management especially since the now complete Basel II was anticipated to be proposed by the BIS. These VaR models include JPMorgan's CreditMetrics (Gupton, Finger, and Bhatia 1997), Credit Suisse Financial Products' CreditRisk+ (1997), McKinsey's CreditPortfolioView (Wilson 1998), KMV's CreditPortfolioManager, and Kamakura's *Risk Manager* (see Moody's/KMV's and Kamakura Inc.'s web sites).

Credit VaR models can be gathered in two main categories: (1) *default mode* (DM) models and (2) *mark-to-market* (MTM) models. In the former, credit risk is identified with default risk and a binomial approach is adopted. Therefore, only two possible events are taken into account: default and survival. The latter includes all possible changes of the borrower creditworthiness, technically called *credit migrations*. In DM models, credit losses only arise when a default occurs. On the other hand, MTM models are multinomial, in that losses arise also when negative credit migrations occur. The two approaches basically differ for the amount of data necessary to feed them: limited in the case of default mode models, much wider in the case of mark-to-market ones.

The main output of a credit risk model is the *probability density function* (PDF) of the future losses on a credit portfolio. From the analysis of such a loss distribution, a financial institution can estimate both the expected loss and the unexpected loss on its credit portfolio. The expected loss equals the (unconditional) mean of the loss distribution; it represents the amount the investor can expect to lose within a specific period of time (usually one year). On the other side, the unexpected loss represents the deviation from expected loss and measures the actual portfolio risk. This can in turn be measured as the standard deviation of the loss distribution. Such a measure is relevant only in the case of a normal distribution and is therefore hardly useful for credit risk measurement: indeed, the distribution of credit losses is usually highly asymmetrical and fat-tailed. This implies that the probability of large losses is higher than the one associated with a normal distribution. Financial institutions typically apply credit risk models to evaluate the economic capital necessary to face the risk associated with their credit portfolios. In such a framework, provisions for credit losses should cover expected losses,[6] while economic capital is seen as a cushion for unexpected losses. Indeed, Basel II in its final iteration (BIS 2004) separated these two types of losses.

Credit VaR models can largely be seen as reduced-form models, where the RR is typically taken as an exogenous constant parameter or a stochastic variable independent from PD. Some of these models, such as CreditMetrics, treat the RR in the event of default as a stochastic variable – generally modelled through a beta distribution—independent from the PD. Others, such as CreditRisk+, treat it as a constant parameter that must be specified as an input for each single credit exposure. While a comprehensive analysis of these models goes beyond the aim of this review,[7] it is important to highlight that all credit VaR models treat RR and PD as two independent variables.

RECENT CONTRIBUTIONS ON THE PD-RR RELATIONSHIP AND THEIR IMPACT

During the last several years, new approaches explicitly modeling and empirically investigating the relationship between PD and RR have been developed. These models include Bakshi, et al. (2001); Jokivuolle and Peura (2003); Frye (2000a and 2000b); Jarrow (2001); Hu and Perraudin (2002); Carey and Gordy (2003); Altman, Brady, Resti, and Sironi (2001, 2005, and 2005) and Acharya, Bharath, and Srinivasan (2003 and 2007).

Bakshi et al. (2001) enhanced the reduced-form models (presented in the previous section) to allow for a flexible correlation between the risk-free rate, the default probability, and the recovery rate. Based on some evidence published by rating agencies, they force recovery rates to be negatively associated with default probability. They find some strong support for this hypothesis through the analysis of a sample of BBB-rated corporate bonds: more precisely, their empirical results show that, on average, a 4 percent worsening in the (risk-neutral) hazard rate is associated with a 1 percent decline in (risk-neutral) recovery rates.

A rather different approach is the one proposed by Jokivuolle and Peura (2003). The authors present a model for bank loans in which collateral value is correlated with the PD. They use the option pricing framework for modeling risky debt: the borrowing firm's total asset value triggers the event of default. However, the firm's asset value does not determine the RR. Rather, the collateral value is in turn assumed to be the only stochastic element determining recovery.[8] Because of this assumption, the model can be implemented using an exogenous PD so that the firm's asset value parameters need not be estimated. In this respect, the model combines features of both structural-form and reduced-form models. Assuming a positive correlation between a firm's asset value and collateral value, the authors obtain a similar result as Frye (2000a and 2000b), that realized default rates and recovery rates have an inverse relationship.

The model proposed by Frye draws from the conditional approach suggested by Finger (1999) and Gordy (2000). In these models, defaults are driven by a single systematic factor—the state of the economy—rather than by a multitude of correlation parameters. These models are based on the assumption that the same economic conditions that cause defaults to rise might cause RRs to decline; that is, that the distribution of recovery is different in high-default periods from low-default ones. In Frye's model, both PD and RR depend on the state of the systematic factor. The correlation between these two variables therefore derives from their mutual dependence on the systematic factor.

The intuition behind Frye's theoretical model is relatively simple: If a borrower defaults on a loan, a bank's recovery may depend on the value of the loan collateral. The value of the collateral, like the value of other assets, depends on economic conditions. If the economy experiences a recession, RRs may decrease just as default rates tend to increase. This gives rise to a negative correlation between default rates and RRs.

While the model originally developed by Frye (2000a) implied recovery to be taken from an equation that determines collateral, he (2000b) subsequently modeled recovery directly. This allowed him to empirically test his model using data on defaults and recoveries from U.S. corporate bond data. More precisely, data from Moody's Default Risk Service database for the 1982–1997 period were used for the empirical analysis.[9] Results show a strong negative correlation between default rates and RRs for corporate bonds. This evidence is consistent with U.S. bond market data, indicating a simultaneous increase in default rates and LGDs for the 1999–2002 period.[10] Frye's (2000b and 2000c) empirical analysis allows him to conclude that in a severe economic downturn, bond recoveries might decline 20 to 25 percentage points from their normal year average. Loan recoveries may decline by a similar amount, but from a higher level. In all cases, Frye and others compare defaults and recoveries just after default, not the ultimate recovery after the restructuring, or recovery period.

Jarrow (2001) presents a new methodology for estimating RRs and PDs implicit in both debt and equity prices. As in Frye, RRs and PDs are correlated and depend on the state of the macroeconomy. However, Jarrow's methodology explicitly incorporates equity prices in the estimation procedure, allowing the separate identification of RRs and PDs and the use of an expanded and relevant dataset. In addition to that, the methodology explicitly incorporates a liquidity premium in the estimation procedure, which is considered essential in light of the high variability in the yield spreads between risky debt and U.S. Treasury securities.

Using four different datasets (Moody's Default Risk Service database of bond defaults and LGDs, Society of Actuaries database of private placement defaults and LGDs, Standard & Poor's database of bond defaults and LGDs, and Portfolio Management Data's database of LGDs) ranging from 1970 to 1999, Carey and Gordy (2003) analyze LGD measures and their correlation with default rates. Their preliminary results contrast with the findings of Frye (2000b): Estimates of simple default rate LGD correlation are close to zero. They find, however, that limiting the sample period to 1988–1998 gives estimated correlations more in line with Frye's results (0.45 for senior debt and 0.8 for subordinated debt). The authors postulate that during this short period the correlation rises not so much because LGDs are low during the low-default years 1993–1996, but rather because LGDs are relatively high during the high-default years 1990 and 1991. They therefore conclude that the basic intuition behind Frye's model may not adequately characterize the relationship between default rates and LGDs. Indeed, a weak or asymmetric relationship suggests that default rates and LGDs may be influenced by different components of the economic cycle.

Using defaulted bonds' data for the sample period 1982–2002, which includes the relatively high-default years of 2000–2002, Altman, Brady, Resti, and Sironi (2005), following Altman, Resti, and Sironi (2001), find empirical results that appear consistent with Frye's intuition: a negative correlation between default rates and RRs. However, they find that the single systematic risk factor (i.e., the performance of the economy) is less predictive than Frye's model would suggest. Their econometric univariate and multivariate models assign a key role to the supply of defaulted bonds (the default rate) and show that this variable, together with variables that proxy the size of the high-yield bond market and the economic cycle, explain a substantial proportion (close to 90 percent) of the variance in bond recovery rates aggregated across all seniority and collateral levels. They conclude that a simple market mechanism based on supply and demand for the defaulted securities drives aggregate recovery rates more than a macroeconomic model based on the common dependence of default and recovery on the state of the cycle. In high default years, the supply of defaulted securities tends to exceed demand,[11] thereby driving secondary market prices down. This in turn negatively affects RR estimates, as these are generally measured using bond prices shortly after default. During periods of low defaults, as we have observed in the 2004–2006 cycle, recoveries increase.

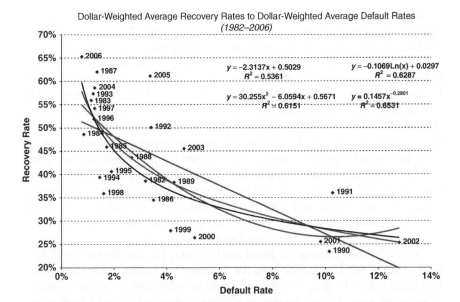

FIGURE 16.1 Recovery Rate/Default Rate Association
Source: Altman Defaulted Bond Database, NYU Salomon Center, Stern School of Business.

The coincident relationship between high-yield bond default rates and recovery rates is shown in Figure 16.1. This graph shows the association of weighted average default rates and recovery rates over the period 1982–2006, using four bivariate regression specifications. The actual regressions are based on data from 1982–2003 and the subsequent three years (2004–2006) are inserted to show the regressions estimate compared to the actual. Note that the degree of explanatory power is excellent with as much as 65 percent of the variation in aggregate bond recovery rates explained by just one variable—the aggregate default rate. These regressions include linear (53.6 percent), quadratic (61.5 percent), log-linear (62.9 percent) and power function (65.3 percent) structures. The clear negative relationship between default and recovery rates is striking with periods of excess supply of defaults relative to demand resulting in unusually low recoveries in such years as 1990, 1991, 2001, and 2002.

One can also observe, however, that the most recent years, 2005 and 2006, which are part of an extremely low default cycle, show estimates which are far below the actual results. For example, our model would have predicted an above average recovery rate of about 56 percent in 2006. Instead, the actual rate was 65.3 percent (Altman and Ramayanam 2007). And the 2005 estimate of about 45 percent compares to the actual recovery rate of over 61 percent. Either the model has performed poorly or the default market has been influenced by an unusual amount of excess credit liquidity, and perhaps other factors, which have changed, perhaps only temporarily, the dynamics in the credit markets. A recent paper by one of the authors (Altman 2007) argues that there was a type of credit bubble that causes seemingly highly distressed firms to remain nonbankrupt when, in more "normal" periods, many of these firms would have defaulted. This, in turn, produced an abnormally low default rate and the huge liquidity from distressed debt investors bid up the prices of both existing and newly defaulted issues. Time will tell if we will observe a regression to the long-term mean; that is, lower recoveries, or a "new paradigm," has evolved and the high recoveries will remain (see Figure 16.1).

Using Moody's historical bond market data, Hu and Perraudin (2002) also examine the dependence between recovery rates and default rates. They first standardize the quarterly recovery data in order to filter out the volatility of recovery rates due to changes over time in the pool of rated borrowers. They find that correlations between quarterly recovery rates and default rates for bonds issued by U.S.-domiciled obligors are 0.22 for post-1982 data (1983–2000) and 0.19 for the 1971–2000 periods. Using extreme value theory and other nonparametric techniques, they also examine the impact of this negative correlation on credit VaR measures and find that the increase is statistically significant when confidence levels exceed 99 percent.

CORRELATION RESULTS' IMPACT AND DOWNTURN LGD

The impact of Altman et al. (2001 and 2005), as well as Hu and Perraudin (2002) and Frye (2000a, 2000b, and 2000c), was almost immediate, resulting in suggested changes in Basel II's "Pillar I" guidelines. Specifically, the final BIS Accord (2004) suggested, via its paragraph 468 declaration, a "downturn," or "stressed" LGD for banks. According to this document, *internal rate-based* (IRB) banks are required to use estimates of LGD parameters, where necessary, to capture the relevant risks. The guidelines were in general terms only and left specific details of the quantification process to supervisors to develop in collaboration with the banking industry. The underlying theory was that recovery rates on defaulted exposures may be lower during economic downturns than during more normal conditions and that a capital rule be realized to guarantee sufficient capital to cover losses during these adverse circumstances. Paragraph 468 also stated that loss severities may not exhibit such cyclical variability, especially if based on ultimate recoveries, and, therefore, LGD estimates of downturn LGD may not differ materially from the long-run weighted average.

Many banks reacted negatively to this conservative approach and proposed more modest adjustments. Indeed, Araten et al. (2004) suggested that correlations are not usually material. All of this discussion and debate resulted in a set of more explicit guidelines and principles in *Guidance on Paragraph 468 of the Framework Document* (BIS 2005). In this report, the BIS found (1) that there is a potential for realized recovery rates to be lower than average during times of high default rates and failing to account for this could result in an understatement of the capital required to cover unexpected losses; (2) that data limitations pose a difficult challenge to the estimation of LGD in general and particularly in downturns; and (3) there is little consensus with respect to appropriate methods for incorporating downturn conditions in LGD estimates. The BIS was careful to state that any principles be flexible enough to allow for a range of sound practices and to encourage continued refinements. In other words, while requiring analysis and reports about "downturn LGD" amongst its members, banks appear to be free to specify if there should be any penalty or not to their average assessments of LGD parameters.

The principles (BIS 2005) were that banks must have a rigorous and well-documented process for assessing, if any, economic downturn's impact on recovery rates and that this process must consist of (1) the identification of appropriate downturn conditions for each asset class; (2) identification of adverse dependencies, if any, between default and recovery rates; and (3) incorporating them to produce LGD estimates. The recovery cash flows should utilize a discount rate that reflects the costs of holding defaulted assets over the workout period, including an appropriate risk premium. These costs should be consistent with the concept of economic loss, not an accounting concept of economic loss (e.g., not the interest rate on the old loan). This can be accomplished either with a discount rate based on the risk-free rate plus a spread appropriate for the risk of recovery and cost of cash flows or by converting the cash flows to certainty equivalents (described in footnote 3 in BIS 2005) and discounting these by the risk-free rate, or, by a combination of these adjustments to the discount rate.

By specifically referring to the stream of cash flows over the restructuring period, the BIS and other banks are embracing the use of ultimate recoveries and not recoveries at the time of default. As such, the correlation between default and recovery rates observed in the bond markets by several researchers, discussed earlier, may not imply a negative correlation between default and ultimate recovery rates. Indeed, there is a timing disconnect that may be important, especially if the distressed loan market is not efficient and the discounted values of ultimate recoveries are materially different from the recovery values at the time of default. Finally, the BIS principles refer to the possibility that stress tests performed under normal expected values of recoveries will not produce different results than downturn LGD estimates under paragraph 468. It remains to be seen how bank regulators will respond to efforts by banks to assess downturn LGD estimates.

One regulator in the United States, the Federal Reserve System, has suggested that IRB banks in the United States use a simple formula to specify downturn LGD, of the form[12]

$$LGD \text{ in downturn} = .08 + .92\ LGD$$

where LGD = long-term LGD average. So, where the long-term LGD equals, for example, 0.3 (i.e., recovery rates of 0.7), the downturn LGD would increase modestly to 0.356 (about 19 percent). If this modification were applied to Foundation Basel II banks, not possible in the United States, then the downturn $LGD = 0.494$ on unsecured exposures, $(.08 + .92\ (.45) = .494)$, an increase of about 10 percent of the normal conditions' expected recovery. For secured loans, the analysis requires a stress test on the collateral itself.

Miu and Ozdemir (2006) analyze this downturn LGD requirement and suggest that the original LGD assessment by banks, without considering PD and RR correlation, can be appropriately adjusted by incorporating a certain degree of conservatism in cyclical LGD estimates within a point-in-time modeling framework. They find even greater impacts on economic capital than even Altman, Resti, and Sironi (2001) did—with as much as an increase of 35 percent to 45 percent in corporate loan portfolios and 16 percent for a middle-market portfolio to compensate for the lack of correlations. Altman et al. (2001) had found, through simulations of loan portfolios that about 30 percent needed to be added. Both studies, however, suggest that banks determine these penalties, if any, without abandoning the point-in-time, one-year perspective as to estimating LGD.

SOME FINAL REFERENCES

A number of related studies on LGD can be found in Altman, Resti and Sironi's (2005) anthology. These studies, found in this volume, include Chabane, Laurent, and Salomon's credit risk assessment of stochastic LGD and correlation effects; Friedman and Sandow's conditional probability distribution analysis of recovery rates; Laurent and Schmit's estimation of distressed

LGD on leasing contracts; DeLaurentis and Riani's further analysis of LGD in the leasing industry; Citron and Wright's investigation of recovery rates on distressed management buyouts; and Neto de Carvalho and Dermine's (2003) empirical investigation of recoveries' impact on bank provisions. Schuermann (2006) provides an overview on what we know and do not know about LGD, as well, in the volume.

Gupton and Stein (2002) analyze the recovery rate on over 1,800 corporate bond, loan and preferred stock defaults, from 900 companies, in order to specify and test Moody's *LossCalc* model for predicting LGD. Their model estimates LGD at two points in time—immediately and in one year—adding a holding period dimension to the analysis. The authors find that their multifactor model, incorporating microvariables (e.g., debt type, seniority), industry and some macroeconomics factors (e.g., default rates, changes in leading indicators) outperforms traditional historic average methods in predicting LGD.

Using data on observed prices of defaulted securities in the United States over the period 1982–1999, Acharya, Bharath, and Srinivasan (2003, 2007) find that seniority and security are important determinants of recovery rates. While this result is not surprising and in line with previous empirical studies on recoveries, their second main result is rather striking and concerns the effect of industry-specific and macroeconomic conditions in the default year. Indeed, industry conditions at the time of default are found to be robust and important determinants of recovery rates. They show that creditors of defaulted firms recover significantly lower amounts in present-value terms when the industry of defaulted firms is in distress and also when nondefaulted firms are rather illiquid and if their debt is collateralized by specific assets that are not easily redeployable into other sectors. Also, they find that there is little effect of macroeconomic conditions over and above the industry conditions and the latter is robust even with the inclusion of macroeconomic factors. Acharya, et al.suggest that the linkage, again highlighted by Altman, Brady, Resti, and Sironi (2005), between bond market aggregate variables and recoveries arises due to supply-side effects in segmented bond markets, and that this may be a manifestation of Shleifer and Vishny's (1992) industry equilibrium effect. That is, macroeconomic variables and bond market conditions may be picking up the effect of omitted industry conditions. The importance of the "industry" factor in determining LGD has been recently highlighted by Schuermann (2006) in a survey of the academic and practitioner literature.

Frye (2000a), Pykhtin (2003), and Dullmann and Trapp (2004) all propose a model that accounts for the dependence of recoveries on systematic risk. They extend the single factor model proposed by Gordy (2000), by assuming that the recovery rate follows a log-normal (Pykhtin 2003) or a logit-normal (Dullmann and Trapp 2004) one. Dullmann and Trapp empirically compare the results obtained using the two alternative models (Frye 2000a; Pykhtin 2003). They use time series of default rates and recovery rates from Standard and Poor's *CreditPro* database, (now included in S&P's RatingsExpress database) including bond and loan default information in the time period from 1982 to 1999. They find that estimates of recovery rates based on market prices at default are significantly higher than the ones obtained using recovery rates at emergence from restructuring. The findings of this study are in line with previous ones: systematic risk is an important factor that influences recovery rates. The authors show that ignoring this risk component may lead to downward biased estimates of economic capital.

RECOVERY RATINGS

There has been a debate in the practitioner literature about how recovery rates impact bond ratings ascribed to default risk estimates from the various major rating agencies. One agency, Moody's, has always maintained that it explicitly considered recoveries in the bond rating of a particular corporate issue. Others, such as S&P and Fitch typically adjusted, through "notching," the senior unsecured issuer rating based on whether the particular issue was investment grade or speculative grade given a certain seniority priority. For example, a subordinated issue of an investment grade company was typically "down-notched" by one notch and a speculative grade issue was penalized by two notches if subordinated. The Moody's assertion was questionable since prior to the 1990s there simply was no reliable database on recoveries available.

Regardless of the "ancient" approaches used, all three rating agencies have recently recognized the heightened importance of recoveries for a number of applications including Basel II, structured products, the credit default swap market, as well as traditional default analysis, and have introduced *recovery ratings* as a complementary risk rating indicator.

Table 16.1 reviews these recovery ratings, first introduced by S&P on U.S. senior bank loans in December 2003 and discussed in Chew and Kerr (2005) published Altman et al., (2005). Fitch then introduced, in late 2005, their recovery analysis on all highly speculative grade issues rated B or below. Finally, Moody's, in September 2006, introduced their rating of U.S. nonfinancial speculative grade issues and expected to do the same in Europe in 2007. We expect that all of the rating agencies will expand their coverage if the market deems this information valuable.

As shown in Table 16.1, each of the recovery rating classes, six in each case, has a quantitative estimate of the proportion of the issue that can be

TABLE 16.1   Recovery Ratings from the Rating Agencies

Recovery Ratings from the Rating Agencies			
Agency	Moody's	Standard & Poor's	Fitch
Ratings type	Loss given default ratings	Recovery ratings	Recovery ratings
Ratings scale	LGD1 0–9% LGD2 10–29% LGD3 30–49% LGD4 50–69% LGD5 70–89% LGD6 90–100%	1+ 100% 1 100% 2 80–100% 3 50–80% 4 25–50% 5 0–25%	RR1 91–100% RR2 71–90% RR3 51–70% RR4 31–50% RR5 11–30% RR6 0–10%
Assets rated	Nonfinancial corporate speculative-grade issuers in the United States.	U.S. and Canadian secured bank loans to which it assigns bank loan ratings, to senior secured loans in Europe, and to any secured bonds issued along with rated bank loans.	All corporate, financial institutions and sovereign issuers rated in the single-B category and below.
Methodology	1. Establish priority of claim. a. Jr. bonds are subordinated to Sr bonds, but may or may not be subordinated to other unsecured obligations. b. Prioritize claims across affiliates.	1. Review transaction structure. 2. Review borrower's projections. 3. Establish simulated path to default.	1. Estimate the *enterprise value* (EV). a. Establish the level of cash flow upon which it is most appropriate to base the valuation. b. Apply a multiple reflecting a company's relative position within a sector based on actual or expected market and/or distressed multiples.

(Continued)

TABLE 16.1 (*Continued*)

	Recovery Ratings from the Rating Agencies		
Agency	Moody's	Standard & Poor's	Fitch
	2. Assume a beta probability distribution for potential *enterprise value* (EV) outcomes.	4. Forecast borrower's free cash flow at default based on our simulated default scenario and default proxy.	2. Estimate the creditor mass, ie identify existing claims.
	a. For most issuers, assume a beta distribution of EV relative to total liabilities.	5. Determine valuation.	a. Claims taken on as a company's fortunes deteriorate.
	b. Corporate LGD distribution will have 50% mean and 26% standard deviation.	6. Identify priority debt claims and value.	b. Claims necessary to the reorganization process.
	3. For each EV outcome, calculate LGDs for each security class implied by absolute priority.	7. Determine collateral value available to lenders.	c. Claims that have priority in the relevant bankruptcy code.
	4. Expected LGD equals the probability-weighted averages of LGDs across EV outcomes.	8. Assign recovery rating.	3. Distributing the EV.
		9. Convey the recovery analytics to the issuer and investment community.	a. The resulting value is allocated to creditors according to jurisdictional practice.

Note: In all cases, the recovery ratings are available in addition to the traditional default ratings. It remains to be seen as to the market's acceptance of this second set of ratings and whether they will form a material part of their investment decisions.
Source: Moodys.com, RatingsDirect.com, and Fitchratings.com.

expected to be recovered given a default. These range from as high as 100 percent down to estimates of 0 percent to 10 percent. In addition to the recovery percentage estimates, Table 16.1 reviews each rating agency's methodology for arriving at their estimate. Fundamental valuation techniques are employed followed by priority analysis of each issue under consideration.

RECOVERY RATES AND PROCYCLICALITY

Altman et al. (2005) also highlight the implications of their results for credit risk modelling and for the issue of procyclicality[13] of capital requirements. In order to assess the impact of a negative correlation between default rates and recovery rates on credit risk models, they run Monte Carlo simulations on a sample portfolio of bank loans and compare the key risk measures (expected and unexpected losses). They show that both the expected loss and the unexpected loss are vastly understated if one assumes that PDs and RRs are uncorrelated.[14] Therefore, credit models that do not carefully factor in the negative correlation between PDs and RRs might lead to insufficient bank reserves and cause unnecessary shocks to financial markets.

As far as procyclicality is concerned, they show that this effect tends to be exacerbated by the correlation between PDs and RRs: low recovery rates when defaults are high would amplify cyclical effects. This would especially be true under the so-called "advanced" IRB approach, where banks are free to estimate their own recovery rates and might tend to revise them downwards when defaults increase and ratings worsen. The impact of such a mechanism was also assessed by Resti (2002), based on simulations over a 20-year period, using a standard portfolio of bank loans (the composition of which is adjusted through time according to S&P transition matrices). Two main results emerged from this simulation exercise: (1) the procyclicality effect is driven more by up- and downgrades, rather than by default rates; in other words, adjustments in credit supply needed to comply with capital requirements respond mainly to changes in the structure of weighted assets, and only to a lesser extent to actual credit losses (except in extremely high default years); and (2) when RRs are permitted to fluctuate with default rates, the procyclicality effect increases significantly.

FURTHER EMPIRICAL EVIDENCE

This section focuses on different measurements and empirical evidence of default recovery rates. Most credit risk models utilize historical average empirical estimates, combined with their primary analytical specification of the probability of default, to arrive at the all-important LGD input. Since very few financial institutions have ample data on recovery rates by asset-type and by type of collateral, model builders and analysts responsible for Basel II inputs into their IRB models begin with estimates from public bond and private bank loan markets. Of course, many banks will research their own internal databases in order to conform to the requirements of Basel II's advanced IRB approach in Pillar I.

Early Empirical Evidence

Published data on default recovery rates generally, but not always, use secondary market bond or bank loan prices. The first empirical study, that we are aware of, to estimate default recovery rates is in Altman, Haldeman, and Narayanan's (1977) ZETA model's adjustment of the optimal cutoff score in their second generation, which follows Altman's (1968) first generation Z-Score model (discussed in Chapter 10). Interestingly, these bank loan recovery estimates did not come from the secondary loan trading market—they did not exist then—but from a survey of bank workout-department experience (1971–1975). The general conclusion from the early experience of these departments was a recovery rate on nonperforming, unsecured loans of only about 30 percent of the loan amount plus accrued interest. The cash inflows for three years postdefault was not discounted back to default date. We will refer to this experience as the "ultimate nominal recovery" since it utilizes post-default recoveries, usually from the end of the restructuring period. More recent estimates on ultimate rates are considerably higher (see our review of these estimates shortly).

In later studies, ultimate recovery rates refer to the nominal or discounted value of bonds or loans based on either the price of the security at the end of the reorganization period (usually Chapter 11) or the value of the package of cash or securities upon emergence from restructuring. For example, Altman and Eberhart (1994) observed the price performance of defaulted bonds, stratified by seniority, at the time of the restructuring emergence as well as the discounted value of these prices. They concluded that the most senior bonds in the capital structure (senior secured and senior unsecured) did very well in the postdefault period (20 percent to 30 percent per annum returns) but the more junior bonds (senior subordinated and subordinated) did poorly, barely breaking even on a nominal basis and losing money on a discounted basis. Similar, but less extreme, results were found by Fridson et al. 2001) when they updated, for the period 1994–2000, Altman and Eberhart's earlier study that covered the period 1981–1993.

Other studies that analyzed bank loans recovery rates were by Asarnow and Edwards (1995) and Eales and Bosworth (1998). The first study presents the results of an analysis of losses on bank loan defaults based on 24 years of data compiled by Citibank; its database comprises 831 *commercial and industrial* (C&I) loans, as well as 89 structured loans (highly collateralized loans that contain many restrictive covenants). Eales and Bosworth's results (based on "ultimate" recoveries) indicate a LGD of about 35 percent for C&I loans (with larger loans, above $10 million, showing a somewhat lower loss rate of 29 percent); unsurprisingly, the LGD for structured loans is considerably lower (13 percent), due to the role played by collateral and covenants in supporting the early default-detection and recovery processes. In the second study, the authors report the empirical results on recovery rates from a foreign bank operating in the United States, Westpac Banking Corporation. The study focuses on small business loans and larger consumer loans, such as home loans and investment property loans.

Neto de Carvalho and Dermine (2003) analyze the determinants of loss given default rates using a portfolio of credits given by the largest private Portuguese bank, Banco Comercial Portugues. Their study is based on a sample of 371 defaulted loans to small- and medium-size companies, originally granted during the period June 1985 to December 2000. The estimates of recovery rates are based on the discounted cash flows recovered after the default event. The authors report three main empirical results which are consistent with previous empirical evidence: (1) the frequency distribution of loan losses given default is bimodal, with many cases presenting a 0 percent recovery and other cases presenting a 100 percent recovery; (2) the size of the loan has a statistically significant negative impact on the recovery rate; while (3) the type of collateral is statistically significant in determining the recovery, this is not the case for the age of the bank-company relationship.

More Recent Evidence

In Table 16.2, we present recent empirical evidence on ultimate bank loan recoveries from Moody's (Emery et al. 2007) and S&P (Vazza et al. 2007) and on corporate bonds by seniority in Altman and Ramayanam (2007). The latter is based on the average prices of these securities just after the date of default. Not surprisingly, the highest median recovery rates at the time of default were on senior secured bank loans (73.0 percent) followed by senior secured bonds (59.1 percent).[15] Although the data from Moody's and Altman and Ramayanam were from different periods and samples, it is interesting to note that the recovery on senior unsecured bonds (45.4 percent) was similar, but lower than senior unsecured bank loans (49.3 percent), with similar standard deviations. The estimates of median recoveries on the senior-subordinated and subordinated bonds were very similar. Similar recoveries on defaulted bonds can be found from Moody's in Varma et al.

TABLE 16.2 Recovery at Default on Public Corporate Bonds, 1978–2006 and Bank Loans 1989–2006, 2Q[a]

Loan/Bond Seniority	Number of Issues	Median (%)	Mean (%)	Standard Deviation (%)
Senior secured loans	260	73.00	69.20	24.60
Senior unsecured loans	48	49.20	51.10	25.20
Senior secured bonds	332	59.08	59.65	27.00
Senior unsecured bonds	1017	45.40	36.85	24.40
Senior subordinated bonds	414	32.79	30.60	24.00
Subordinated bonds	249	31.00	31.17	25.70
Discount bonds	156	19.80	25.90	20.20
Total sample bonds	2168	41.77	37.68	25.56

[a]Based on prices just after default on bonds and 30 days after default onloans.
Source: Bank loans: Moody's (Emery et al., 2007); and bonds: Altman and Ramayanam (2007).

(2003). For example, Altman and Ramayanam's value-weighted mean recovery rate on over 2,000 bond default issues was 37.7 percent compared to Moody's value weighted mean of 33.8 percent and issuer-weighted mean of 35.4 percent on 1,239 issues.

Altman and Ramayanam (2007) further break down bond recoveries just after the default date by analyzing recoveries based on the original rating (fallen angels versus. original rating noninvestment grade, or (junk,) bonds) of different seniorities. For example, in Table 16.3, we observe that senior secured bonds that were originally rated investment grade recovered a median rate of 50.5 percent versus just 38.0 percent for the same seniority bonds that were noninvestment grade when issued. These are statistically significant differences for similar seniority securities. Since fallen angel defaults are much more prominent in some years in the United States (e.g., close to 50 percent in dollar amount of defaults in 2001 and 2002 were fallen angels prior to default), these statistics are quite meaningful. The median differential was just as great (43.5 percent versus. 31.2 percent) for senior unsecured bonds. Note that for senior subordinated and subordinated bonds, however, the rating at issuance is of little consequence, although the sample sizes for investment grade, low seniority bonds were very small. Varma et al. (2003) also conclude that the higher the rating prior to default, including the rating at issuance, the higher the average recovery rate at default. Apparently, the quality of assets and the structure of the defaulting company's balance sheets favor higher recoveries for higher quality original issue bonds.

TABLE 16.3 Investment Grade vs. Noninvestment Grade (original rating)

Investment Grade vs. Noninvestment Grade (original rating)
Prices at Default on Public Bonds (1978, 3Q 2006)

Bond Seniority	Number of Issues	Median Price (%)	Average Price (%)	Weighted Price (%)	Standard Deviation (%)
Senior secured					
Investment grade	134	50.50	54.91	59.63	25.62
Noninvestment grade	263	38.00	41.58	42.02	27.39
Senior unsecured					
Investment grade	320	43.50	47.47[a]	46.38[a]	25.47
Noninvestment grade	566	31.15	35.52	33.88	22.92
Senior subordinated					
Investment grade	15	28.00	38.91	36.36	27.44
Noninvestment grade	396	27.50	32.4	29.14	23.81
Subordinated					
Investment grade	10	35.69	37.67	25.29	32.99
Noninvestment grade	214	29.00	32.03	28.77	22.30
Discount					
Investment grade	1	13.63	13.63	13.63	—
Noninvestment grade	116	17.67	23.88	26.43	20.34
Total sample	2035	33	37.46	34.82	25.17

[a]Including WorldCom, the Average and Weighted Average were 44.96% and 34.34%.

Note: Nonrated issues were considered noninvestment grade.

Source: Altman and Ramayanam (2007).

In Table 16.4, we again return to the data on ultimate recoveries, only this time the results are from Standard & Poor's (2006) assessment of bank loan and bond recoveries. These results show the nominal and discounted (by the loan's predefault interest rate) ultimate recovery at the end of the restructuring period for well over 3,000 defaulted loans and bonds over the period 1988 to 2006. Several items are of interest. First, the recovery on senior bank debt, which is mainly secured, was quite high at 87.3 percent and 77.2 percent for nominal and discounted values respectively. The comparable discounted ultimate recovery rate on all bank loans from Moody's is 81.67 percent. Senior secured and senior unsecured notes, which include loans and bonds, had lower recoveries and the more junior notes (almost all bonds) had, not surprisingly, the lowest recoveries. Note the differential between the nominal and discounted recovery rates diminish somewhat at the lower seniority levels.

TABLE 16.4   Ultimate Rates on Bank Loan and Bond Defaults

Ultimate Recovery Rates on Bank Loan and Bond Defaults
(nominal and discounted values, 1988–2006)

	Observations	Ultimate Discounted Recovery	Standard Deviation	Ultimate Nominal Recovery[a]
All bank debt (S&P Data)	1320	77.20%	31.10%	87.32%
Secured Bank Debt	1205	78.50%	30.00%	n. a.
Unsecured Bank Debt	119	64.20%	38.20%	n. a.
All bank debt (Moody's Data)	668	81.67%	30.37%	90.61%
Secured loans	609	84.58%	27.59%	93.46%
Unsecured loans	59	52.67%	39.96%	62.63%
Senior secured bonds	320	62.00%	32.90%	76.03%
Senior unsecured bonds	863	43.80%	35.10%	59.29%
Senior subordinated bonds	489	30.50%	34.10%	38.41%
Subordinated bonds	399	28.80%	34.00%	34.81%

[a]1998–2006.
Source: Standard & Poor's LossStats Database, 3,395 defaulted loans and bond issues that defaulted between 1987–2006, 3Q (recoveries are discounted at each instruments' predefault interest rate); and Moody's Ultimate Recovery Database (Emery et al. 2007) for the period 1987–2006 (both nominal and discounted rates).

Keisman (2004) also finds, not shown in any table, that during the most recent "extreme stress" default years of 1998 to 2002, the recovery rates on all seniorities declined compared to their longer 1988–2002 sample period. Since 1998 and 1999 were not really high default years, the results of S&P for 2000–2002 are consistent with Altman, Brady, Resti, and Sironi's (2001, 2005) predictions of an inverse relationship between default and recovery rates. Indeed, recovery rates were a relatively low 25 percent in the corporate bond market for both 2001 and 2002 when default rates were in the double digits but increased to over 70 percent in 2006 when default rates tumbled to well below average annual levels (Altman and Ramayanam 2007).

In the Moody's study (Emery et al. 2007), a number of interesting results were revealed on a sample of about 3,500 loans and bonds from over 720 U.S. nonfinancial corporate default events over the period 1987 to 2006. These include:

- The average discounted ultimate recovery rate on loans was 81.7 percent (100 percent median recovery), but the average and median on bonds was 32.0 percent and 24.0 percent respectively—not surprisingly with these statistics, loan recoveries had a noticeable right-side skew and bond recoveries a left-side skew.

- Corporate family (loans and bonds) recovery rates were widely dispersed and exhibit considerable cyclicality as measured by their correlation with the U.S. speculative-grade default rate, confirming what Altman et al. (2005) found. Loan recovery rates, on the other hand, exhibit considerable less cyclicality.

- There existed a close association (about 50 percent explanatory power) between discounted ultimate recovery rates and postdefault debt trading prices.

- The timing difference between the number of defaults in a particular year and the number of resolutions of past defaults (usually emergence from Chapter 11) in that same year was quite different (see Figure 16.2). This shows the relatively high number of defaults to resolutions in the early years of a high-default credit period and the reverse in the early years of a low-default period.

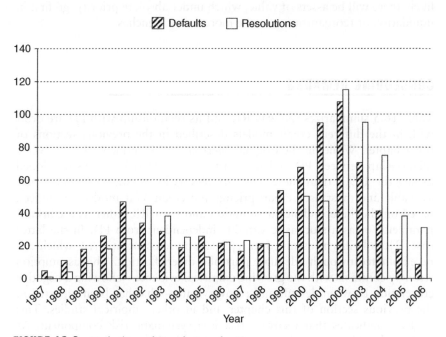

FIGURE 16.2 Defaults and Resolutions by Year
Source: Emery et al. (2007).

Some recovery studies have concentrated on rates across different industries. Altman and Kishore (1996) and Verde (2003) report a fairly high range across industrial sectors although the statistical variance was not that high. For example, Verde, (2003) reports that recovery rates in 2001 versus 2002 varied dramatically from one year to the next (e.g., gaming, lodging, and restaurants recovered 16 percent in 2001 and 77 percent in 2002, Retail recovered 7 percent in 2001 and 48 percent in 2002, while transportation recovered 31 percent in 2001 and 19 percent in 2002), but returned to more normal levels in 2003. Emery et al. (2007) showed industry nominal ultimate recoveries varying from as low as 27.5 percent and 37.5 percent on environmental and telecom sectors, respectively, to as high as 88.0 percent and 72.0 percent on aircraft companies—these were "family recoveries" on both loans and bonds combined. Most industry recoveries fell between.

Another issue highlighted in some studies, especially those from S&P (Van de Castle and Keisman 1999; Keisman 2004; and Emery et al. 2007), is that an important determinant of ultimate recovery rates is the amount that a given seniority has junior liabilities below its level; the greater the proportion of junior securities, the higher the recovery rate on the senior trenches. The theory being that the greater the equity cushion, the more likely there will be assets of value, which under absolute priority, go first in liquidation or reorganization to the more senior trenches.

CONCLUDING REMARKS

Table 16.5 summarizes the way RR and its relationship with PD are dealt with in the different credit models described in the previous sections of this Chapter. While, in the original Merton (1974) framework, an inverse relationship between PD and RR exists, the credit risk models developed during the 1990s treat these two variables as independent. The currently available and most used credit pricing and credit VaR models are indeed based on this independence assumption and treat RR either as a constant parameter or as a stochastic variable independent from PD. In the latter case, RR volatility is assumed to represent an idiosyncratic risk which can be eliminated through adequate portfolio diversification. This assumption strongly contrasts with the growing empirical evidence—showing a negative correlation between default and recovery rates—that has been reported in the previous section of this chapter and in other empirical studies. This evidence indicates that recovery risk is a systematic risk component. As such, it should attract risk premia and should adequately be considered in credit risk management applications.

TABLE 16.5 The Treatment of LGD and Default Rates within Different Credit Risk Models

Main Models and Related Empirical Studies	Treatment of LGD	Relationship Between RR and PD
Credit Pricing Models		
First generation structural-form models	Merton (1974), Black and Cox (1976), Geske (1977), Vasicek (1984), Crouhy and Galai (1994), Mason and Rosenfeld (1984).	PD and RR are a function of the structural characteristics of the firm. RR is therefore an endogenous variable.	PD and RR are inversely related (see Appendix A).
Second generation structural-form models	Kim, Ramaswamy and Sundaresan (1993), Nielsen, Saà-Requejo, Santa Clara (1993), Hull and White (1995), Longstaff and Schwartz (1995).	RR is exogenous and independent from the firm's asset value.	RR is generally defined as a fixed ratio of the outstanding debt value and is therefore independent from PD.
Reduced-form models	Litterman and Iben (1991), Madan and Unal (1995), Jarrow and Turnbull (1995), Jarrow, Lando and Turnbull (1997), Lando (1998), Duffie and Singleton (1999), Duffie (1998) and Duffee (1999).	Reduced-form models assume an exogenous RR that is either a constant or a stochastic variable independent from PD.	Reduced-form models introduce separate assumptions on the dynamic of PD and RR, which are modeled independently from the structural features of the firm.

(Continued)

TABLE 16.5   (*Continued*)

	Main Models and Related Empirical Studies	Treatment of LGD	Relationship Between RR and PD
Latest contributions on the PD-RR relationship	Frye (2000a and 2000b), Jarrow (2001), Carey and Gordy (2003), Altman, Brady, Resti and Sironi (2001, 2003 and 2005), Acharya Bharath and Srinivasan (2003, 2007), Miu and Ozdemir (2006), Emery et al. (2007).	Both PD and RR are stochastic variables which depend on a common systematic risk factor (the state of the economy).	PD and RR are negatively correlated for bonds; less negatively correlated for loans. In the "macroeconomic approach" this derives from the common dependence on one single systematic factor. In the "microeconomic approach" it derives from the supply and demand of defaulted securities. Industry health is also a major factor. Downturn LGD studies.
	Credit Value-at-Risk Models		
CreditMetrics®	Gupton, Finger and Bhatia (1997)	Stochastic variable (beta distribution)	RR independent from PD
CreditPortfolio View®	Wilson (1998)	Stochastic variable	RR independent from PD
CreditRisk+®	Credit Suisse Financial Products (1997)	Constant	RR independent from PD
PortfolioManager®	McQuown (1997), Crosbie (1999)	Stochastic variable	RR independent from PD

Empirical results, especially demonstrated by historical record levels of recovery in the extreme benign credit environment of 2004–2006, show the potential cyclical impact as well as the supply and demand elements of defaults and recoveries on LGD. Finally, we feel that the microeconomic/financial attributes of an individual issuer of bonds or loans combined with the market's aggregate supply and demand conditions can best explain the recovery rate at default on a particular defaulting issue. An even greater challenge is to accurately estimate the ultimate recovery rate on individual issue as well as aggregate recoveries when the firm emerges from its restructuring.

REFERENCES

Acharya, V. V., S. T. Bharath, and A. Srinivasan. 2003. Understanding the Recovery Rates on Defaulted Securities. Working Paper, London Business School.

———. 2007. "Does Industry-wide Distress Affect Defaulted Firms? Evidence from Creditor Recoveries." *Journal of Financial Economics* 85, no. 3:787–821.

Altman, E. I. 1989. "Measuring Corporate Bond Mortality and Performance." *Journal of Finance* 54, no. 4:909–922.

———. 2007. "Global Debt Markets in 2007: New Paradigm or the Great Credit Bubble?" *Journal of Applied Corporate Finance* 19, no. 3:17–31.

Altman, E. I., B. Brady, A. Resti, and A. Sironi. 2005. "The Link Between Default and Recovery Rates: Theory, Empirical Evidence and Implications." *Journal of Business* 78, no. 6:2203–2227.

Altman, E. I., and A. Eberhart. 1994. "Do Seniority Provisions Protect Bondholders' Investments?" *Journal of Portfolio Management* 20, no. 4:67–75.

Altman, E. I., R. Haldeman, and P. Narayanan. 1977. "ZETA Analysis: A New Model to Identify Bankruptcy Risk of Corporations." *Journal of Banking & Finance* 1, no. 1:29–54.

Altman, E. I., and V. M. Kishore. 1996. "Almost Everything You Wanted to Know About Recoveries on Defaulted Bonds." *Financial Analysts Journal* 52, no. 6:57–64.

Altman, E. I., and S. Ramayanam. 2006. The High-Yield Bond Default and Return Report 2006 Review. Special Report, NYU Salomon Center.

Altman, E. I., A. Resti, and A. Sironi. 2001, December. *Analyzing and Explaining Default Recovery Rates.* London: ISDA.

Altman, E. I., A. Resti and A. Sironi. 2005. *Recovery Risk.* London: Risk Books.

Araten, M., M. Jacobs and P. Varshny. 2004. "Measuring LGD on Commercial Loans." *The RMA Journal* 86, no. 3: 24–36.

Asarnow, E., and D. Edwards. 1995. "Measuring Loss on Defaulted Bank Loans: a 24 year Study." *Journal of Commercial Bank Lending* 77, no. 7:11–23.

Bakshi, G., D. Madan, and F. Zhang. 2001. *Understanding the Role of Recovery in Default Risk Models: Empirical Comparisons and Implied Recovery Rates,*

Finance and Economics Discussion Series. 2001–37. Washington D.C.: Federal Reserve Board of Governors.

Bank for International Settlement (BIS), Basel Committee on Banking Supervision. 2003. The New Basel Capital Accord: Consultative Document, Basel, April.

————. 2004. International Convergence on Capital Measurement and Capital Standards, Basel, June.

————. 2005. Guidance on Paragraph 468 of the Framework Document, Basel, July.

Black, F., and J. C. Cox. 1976. "Valuing Corporate Securities: Some Effects of Bond Indenture Provisions." *Journal of Finance* 31, no. 2:351–367.

Black, F., and M. Scholes. 1973. "The Pricing of Options and Corporate Liabilities", *Journal of Political Economy* 81, no. 3:637–659.

Carey, M., and M. Gordy. 2003. Systematic Risk in Recoveries on Defaulted Debt [memo], Federal Reserve Board of Governors, Washington D.C.

Chabane, A., L Jean-Paul, and J. Salomon. 2004. "Double Impact: Credit Risk Assessment and Collateral Value." *Revue Finance* 25, no. 1:157–78.

Chew W. and S. Kerr. 2005. "Recovery Ratings: A Fundamental Approach to Estimating Recovery Risk." In edited by E. Altman, A. Resti and A. Sironi. *Recovery Risk*, London: Risk Books.

Credit Suisse Financial Products. 1997. *CreditRisk+. A Credit Risk Management Framework.* London.

Crosbie, P. J. 1999. Modeling Default Risk [memo], Moody's KMV Corporation, San Francisco.

Crouhy, M., D. Galai, and R. Mark. 2000. "A Comparative Analysis of Current Credit Risk Models." *Journal of Banking and Finance* 24, no. 1:59–117.

Das, S., and P. Hanonna. 2006. Implied Recovery. White Paper, University of Santa Clara, July.

Duffee, G. R. 1999. "Estimating the Price of Default Risk." *Review of Financial Studies* 12, no. 1:197–225.

Duffie, D. 1998. Defaultable Term Structure Models with Fractional Recovery of Par. Working Paper, Graduate School of Business, Stanford University.

Duffie, D., and K. J. Singleton. 1999. "Modeling the Term Structures of Defaultable Bonds", *Review of Financial Studies* 12, no. 2:687–720.

Duffie, D., and D. Lando. 2000. "Term Structure of Credit Spreads With Incomplete Accounting Information." *Econometrica* 69, no.2:633–664 .

Düllmann, K., and Trapp, M. 2004. Systematic Risk in Recovery Rates—An Empirical Analysis of U.S. Corporate Credit Exposures. EFMA 2004 Basel Meetings Paper, June.

Eales, R., and E. Bosworth. 1998. "Severity of Loss in the Event of Default in Small Business and Large Consumer Loans." *Journal of Lending and Credit Risk Management* 12, no. 1:58–65.

Emery, K., R. Cantor, and R. Avner. 2004. "Recovery Rates on North American Syndicated Bank Loans: 1989–2003." *Moody's Special Report*, March.

Emery, K., R. Cantor, D. Keisman, and S. Ou. 2007, April. *Moody's Ultimate Recovery Database.* New York: Moody's Investors Service.

Finger, C. 1999. "Conditional Approaches for CreditMetrics® Portfolio Distributions." *CreditMetrics Monitor*, April.

Franks, J., and W. Torous. 1994. "A Comparison of Financial Recontracting in Distressed Exchanges and Chapter 11 Reorganizations." *Journal of Financial Economics*, 35, no. 2:349–370.

Fridson, M. S., C. M. Garman, and K. Okashima. 2000. "Recovery Rates: The Search for Meaning." In *Merrill Lynch & Co., High Yield Strategy*. New York: Merrill Lynch.

Frye, J. 2000a. "Collateral Damage." *Risk* 4, no. 1:91–94.

———. 2000b. Collateral Damage Detected. Federal Reserve Bank of Chicago Emerging Issues Series, October, 1–14.

———. 2000c. "Depressing Recoveries." *Risk* 4, no. 2:82–86.

Geske, R. 1977. "The Valuation of Corporate Liabilities as Compound Options." *Journal of Financial and Quantitative Analysis* 12, no. 2:541–552.

Gordy, M. 2000. "A Comparative Anatomy of Credit Risk Models." *Journal of Banking and Finance* 24, no. 1:119–149.

Gupton, G. M., C. Finger, M. Bhatia. 1997. *CreditMetrics-Technical Document*. New York: JPMorgan.

Gupton, G. M., D. Gates and L.V. Carty. 2000. "Bank Loan Loss Given Default." *Moody's Special Report*, November.

Gupton, G. M., and R. M. Stein. 2002. *LossCalc: Moody's Model for Predicting Loss Given Default (LGD)*. New York: Moody's Investors Service.

Hamilton, D. T., G. M. Gupton, and A. Berthault. 2001, February. *Default and Recovery Rates of Corporate Bond Issuers: 2000*. New York: Moody's Investors Service.

Hamilton, D. T., S. Ou, F. Kim, and R. Cantor. 2007, February. *Special Comment: Corporate Default and Recovery Rates: 1920–2006*. Moody's Investors Service.

Hu, Y., and W. Perraudin. 2002. The Dependence of Recovery Rates and Defaults. White Paper, BirkBeck College and CEPR Working Chapter, February.

Hull, J. 1997. *Options, Futures and Other Derivative Securities*, Englewood Cliffs, N.J.: Prentice Hall.

Hull, J., and A. White. 1995. "The Impact of Default Risk on the Prices of Options and Other Derivative Securities." *Journal of Banking and Finance* 19, no. 2:299–322.

Jarrow, R. A. 2001. "Default Parameter Estimation Using Market Prices." *Financial Analysts Journal* 57, no. 5:75–92.

Jarrow, R. A., D. Lando, S. M. Turnbull. 1997. "A Markov Model for the Term Structure of Credit Risk Spreads." *Review of Financial Studies* 10, no. 5:481–523.

Jarrow, R. A., and S. M. Turnbull. 1995. "Pricing Derivatives on Financial Securities Subject to Credit Risk." *Journal of Finance* 50, no. 1:53–86.

Jones, E., S. Mason, and E. Rosenfeld. 1984. "Contingent Claims Analysis of Corporate Capital Structures: An Empirical Investigation." *Journal of Finance*, 39, no. 2:611–627.

Jokivuolle, E. and S. Peura. 2003. "A Model for Estimating Recovery Rates and Collateral Haircuts for Bank Loans." *European Financial Management* 6, no. 2:113–131.

Keisman, D. 2004. "Ultimate Recovery Rates on Bank Loan and Bond Defaults." *S&P Loss Stats*. New York: Standard & Poor's.

Kim I.J., K. Ramaswamy, and S. Sundaresan. 1993. "Does Default Risk in Coupons Affect the Valuation of Corporate Bonds? A Contingent Claims Model." *Financial Management* 22, no. 3:117–131.

Lando, D. 1998. "On Cox Processes and Credit Risky Securities." *Review of Derivatives Research* 2, no. 1:99–120.

Litterman, R., and T. Iben. 1991. "Corporate Bond Valuation and the Term Structure of Credit Spreads." *Financial Analysts Journal* 47, no. 1:52–64.

Liu, S., J. C. Lu, D. W. Kolpin, and W. Q. Meeker. 1997. "Analysis of Environmental Data with Censored Observations." *Environmental Science and Technology* 31, no. 12:3358–3362.

Longstaff, F. A., and E. S. Schwartz. 1995. "A Simple Approach to Valuing Risky Fixed and Floating Rate Debt." *Journal of Finance* 50, no. 2:789–819.

Madan, D., and H. Unal. 1995. "Pricing the Risks of Default." *Review of Derivatives Research* 2, no. 1:121–160.

Merton, R. C. 1974. "On the Pricing of Corporate Debt: The Risk Structure of Interest Rates." *Journal of Finance* 29, no. 2:449–471.

Miu, P., and B. Ozdemir. 2006. "Basel Requirements of Downturn Loss-Given- Default: Modeling and Estimating Probability of Default and LGD Correlations." *Journal of Credit Risk* 2, no. 2:43–68.

Neto de Carvalho, C., and Jean Dermine. 2003. Bank Loan Losses-Given-Default— Empirical Evidence. Working Paper, INSEAD.

Nielsen, L. T., J. Saà-Requejo, and P. Santa-Clara. 1993. Default Risk and Interest Rate Risk: The Term Structure of Default Spreads. Working Paper, INSEAD.

New York University Salomon Center Defaulted Debt Database, Stern School of Business, Annual Updates.

Pan, J., and K. Singleton. 2005. Default and Recovery Implicit in the Term Structure of Sovereign CDS Spreads. Working Paper, Stanford University.

Pykhtin, M. 2003. "Unexpected Recovery Risk." *Risk* 16, no. 8:74–78.

Resti, A. 2002. *The New Basel Capital Accord: Structure, Possible Changes, Micro- and Macroeconomic Effects*. Brussels: Centre for European Policy Studies.

Saikat, N. 1998. "Valuation Models for Default-Risky Securities: An Overview." *Federal Reserve Bank of Atlanta, Economic Review*, Fourth Quarter 20, no. 4:2–28.

Schleifer, A., and R. Vishny. 1992. "Liquidation Values and Debt Capacity: A Market Equilibrium Approach." *Journal of Finance*, 47, no. 5:1343–1366.

Schuermann, T. 2006. "What Do We Know About Loss Given Default?" In *Credit Risk Models and Management*, 2nd ed., edited by D. Shimko. London: Risk Books.

Van de Castle, K., and D. Keisman. 2000. "Suddenly Structure Mattered: Insights into Recoveries of Defaulted." *S&P Corporate Ratings*, May 24.

Varma, P., R. Cantor, and D. Hamilton. 2003, December. *Recovery Rates on Defaulted Corporate Bonds and Preferred Stocks*. New York: Moody's Investors Service.

Vasicek, O. A. 1984, March. *Credit Valuation.* San Francisco: Moody's KMV Corporation.

Vazza, D., D. Aurora, and C. Miller. 2007, February. *U.S. Recovery Study: Liquidity Avalanche Propels Recovery Rates into the Stratosphere, Global Fixed Income Research.* New York: Standard & Poor's.

Verde, M. 2003, September. Recovery Rates Return to Historic Norms. New York: Fitch Ratings.

Wilson, T. C. 1998. "Portfolio Credit Risk." *Federal Reserve Board of New York Economic Policy Review* 33, no. 10:71–82.

Zhou, C. 2001. "The Term Structure of Credit Spreads with Jump Risk." *Journal of Banking and Finance* 25, no. 10:2015–2040.

CHAPTER 17

Credit Risk Migration

*The Moving Finger writes; and having writ, Moves on: nor all
your Piety nor Wit Shall lure it back to cancel half a Line Nor all
your Tears wash out a Word of it.*
—The *Rubháiyát* of Omar Khayyam, stanza 71 (translated by
Edward FitzGerald)

As we discussed elsewhere in this book, the rating agencies typically rate public debt when it is issued and then periodically review it in subsequent years. If a company's credit quality has improved or deteriorated significantly over time, such a review usually prompts the agency to raise or lower its rating. Since the market considers bonds and loans with high ratings to be more valuable (less risky) than those with low ratings, an upgrade or downgrade is generally accompanied by a change in the price of an issue. In the majority of cases, however, the bond market has already observed a change in the issuer's credit quality before the rating itself is changed, and the price has already moved accordingly. While there is some debate about how much residual price movement still takes place at the time of the actual rating change, there is no doubt that credit risk migration, or drift, affects value. And we can observe that a bond rating that has drifted down seldom goes up to its original level.

Throughout this chapter, we will be referring to changes in credit quality manifesting in the form of bond and loan rating changes. An alternative metric to use is a model that provides credit scores or default probabilities that can be mapped to bond rating equivalents. The advantage of this metric is that the credit quality and its changes are a continuous measure (e.g., credit scores), while the bond ratings from agencies are relatively infrequent occurrences. For example, Altman's Z-Scores (Chapter 10) or Moody's KMV (MKMV) EDF-credit monitor (Chapter 11) both have rating equivalents. In reality, EDFs are more volatile than Z-Scores and both are far more volatile than rating changes.

Migration in credit quality and ratings can affect fixed income investors in a number of ways. When the price of a bond changes, investors clearly gain or lose. The impact on the overall credit quality of a portfolio may be equally important. Some institutions have explicit policies regarding the quality of the instruments that they may hold, and rating migration may cause them to exceed these established limits. A bank, for example, may have a policy of holding no more than 5 percent of its portfolio in loans with ratings below the equivalent of a BB rating. Likewise, an investment-grade, fixed income mutual fund may have rules that allow it to continue to hold 5 percent of its portfolio in securities that have fallen below investment grade but that require it to sell any security with a rating that has dropped below B. Rules of these kinds may be self-imposed, or they may reflect regulatory constraints.

Certain fixed income investment strategies are predicated on assumptions about credit migration. It is possible, for example, that as yield spreads on corporate debt narrow, some investment-grade investors can adopt a crossover strategy, purchasing some bonds that have split ratings (investment grade from one agency and noninvestment grade from the other) or that are at the high-end of the noninvestment grade spectrum. The first of these possibilities is called a *5-B strategy* because the bonds carry one triple-B and one double-B rating. The second approach is called a *4-B strategy* because the bonds carry two double-B ratings. In addition, some fixed income managers are known to take positions on corporate bonds based on predictions about an upgrade or downgrade.

One argument for crossing over is that these bonds have acceptable credit risk but offer significantly greater yield than those that are 6-B (i.e., have investment grade ratings from both agencies). Should the agency that presently assigns the noninvestment grade rating eventually upgrade the issue just one notch, the spread could narrow considerably and the price will rise significantly. Many of these bonds also have substantial call potential—either from high cash flows available to pay off the existing bondholders or from mergers and acquisitions. Is crossing over a rational investment strategy? Over a relatively short-term horizon, in other words, what are the chances that a 5-B bond will become 6-B or better or 4-B or worse? The question can be answered only with a systematic understanding of credit risk migration and an examination of historical transition patters.

Apart from the specific needs of fixed income investors, the analysis of rating migration plays an integral part in broad-gauge strategies for credit risk management (see Lucas 1995). Indeed, the CreditMetrics methodology utilizes credit migration analysis as one of its centerpieces (Gupton, Finger, and Bhatia 1997). This important seminal study emphasized that upgrades and downgrades cause market-pricing reactions that result in immediate gains and losses in a mark-to-market accounting environment. Failure to recognize the impact of these events on both individual security and portfolio values will miss a significant component of risk. See out discussion of CreditMetrics in Chapter 20. While credit risk migration analysis is not a completely new focus for banks, most institutions that are aware of its importance are struggling to find methods and data sources that will allow them to evaluate rating drift in a sound and comprehensive way.[1] Indeed, rating downgrades of structured financial products, especially where the underlying collateral is comprised of subprime mortgages or derivatives of same, have rattled the global financial world in 2007. Some analysts and commentators have questioned the role of rating agencies in this serious crisis.

METHODS FOR TRACKING RATING MIGRATION

Thus far, at least three sets of studies have been published on the rating migration phenomenon. The first is a series of articles by Altman and Kao (1991a, 1991b, 1992a, and 1992b) that utilized data from Standard & Poor's rating changes over the period 1971 to 1989. The second is a group of special studies from Moody's, first published as a special comment in 1991 and reproduced in Lucas and Lonski 1992, Carty and Fons (1993), and Carty (1997).[2] Finally, Standard & Poor's periodically examines rating migration, and its latest report (2007) covers its rating changes over the period 1981 to 2006. Altman and Kao (1991b) report on migration patterns of industrials, finance companies, and public utilities. They, as well as Carty and Fons (1993), also examine the autocorrelation of the rating changes (Altman and Kao 1992b). Standard & Poor's has released products named CreditPro and Ratings Xpress (via WRDS from Wharton) that make available the default and migration data for over 6,000 obligors for the period 1981–present. While the Altman and Kao studies have not been updated, it is still instructive to observe the difference in their results compared to the rating agencies.

There are some basic differences among these three sets of studies. While all look at the rating migration of credit quality for up to ten years (and more) from some initial level, Altman and Kao assess the changes from the initial bond rating, usually at issuance, for a period of up to 10 years postissuance. Moody's and Standard & Poor's, by contrast, assess rating changes from some initial period, regardless of the age of the bonds constituting the initial rating class. Moody's and Standard & Poor's include newly issued bonds as well as seasoned bonds of all ages in their static pool as of some date (e.g., 1981), and then follow the ratings of the pool for up to 15 years from that date.[3] This distinction is important because an aging effect is observable in the early years after issuance—one that disappears within four or five years. Older bonds appear to have a greater short-term tendency to be upgraded or downgraded than do newly issued bonds. We observed similar differences between the studies of the rating agencies and Altman in Chapter 15 when we discussed default rates.

Altman and Kao differ from the two rating agencies in another aspect, as well. Their method is issue-based, whereas the agencies assess the senior bond equivalent of each issuer, regardless of the size of a particular issue or of the number of issues outstanding from that issuer. In addition, Altman and Kao present several Markov chain models for estimating migration patterns.[4]

Furthermore, it is significant that the various studies cover somewhat different time periods. Moody's now covers the longest period (1938 to 2006), Altman and Kao include the 1970s in their analyses and end at mid-1989 and Standard & Poor's data start in 1981 and end in 2006. In fact, the relative likelihood of upgrades and downgrades has varied over time. For all rating classes, the decade of the 1970s was typified by more upgrades than downgrades, but the period from 1981 to 1998 saw more downgrades than upgrades in every single year. Since 1998, the upgrade/downgrade ratio varied dramatically, with downgrades dominating in the period 1999–2002 and upgrades since the beginning of 2003.

One final difference between the rating agency methodology and that of Altman and Kao is that the two former studies include the category *rating withdrawn*. This usually means that a bond has been called or redeemed for some reason, such as a call or an acquisition of the issuing firm. It may also mean that there was insufficient information to rate the bond. This is quite an important distinction. After one year, anywhere from 2 percent to 3 percent of issuers may fall into the rating withdrawn category, and after five years, as many as 25 percent to 40 percent of the issuers may be placed in this classification. Since most redemptions result in a return of 100 percent (or more) of principal to the bondholders, one might choose to include the withdrawn-rating proportion in the same rating class the issuers initially occupied. In calculations of the impact on returns, the rating withdrawn category might also reflect the average price at call or redemption, which is typically 1 percent to 5 percent above par value for calls and par value for redemption at maturity. We will return to this factor at a later point.

THE TIMELINESS AND ACCURACY OF RATING CHANGES

In a series of studies by Altman and Rijken (2004 and 2006), the role and performance of credit rating agencies are analyzed. These studies were particularly timely since rating agency performance has been debated in recent years. Altman and Rijken leverage off the results from several surveys conducted in the United States, for example, by the Association of Financial Professionals (2002) and Baker and Mansi (2002). Baker and Mansi (2002) found that most investors believe rating agencies are too slow in adjusting their ratings (migration policy) due to their through-the-cycle methodology, and their hesitance to reverse a rating once the change is recorded. Altman and Rijken (2004 and 2006) provide quantitative insights into the question from an investor's point-in-time perspective and try to shed light on the three, somewhat conflicting objectives of rating stability (preferred by issuers), rating timeliness, and performance in predicting defaults (preferred by investors). Among other things, the authors find that rating migrations are triggered when the difference between the actual rating and the model-predicted rating exceeds a certain threshold level. When rating migrations are triggered, however, agencies tend to adjust their ratings only partially, consistent with known serial dependency of rating changes (e.g., downgrades are more frequently followed by subsequent downgrades rather than upgrades) (Altman and Kao 1992a and 1992b).

RATING MIGRATION RESULTS COMPARED

Tables 17.1, 17.2, and 17.3 compare the 1-year, 5-year, and 10-year transition matrices of the three studies noted earlier. The Altman and Kao results are adjusted somewhat for more complete default statistics. Their findings differ strikingly from those of the two rating agencies, primarily because of the aging effect and the impact of the *rating withdrawn* (RW) category. Again, the data from Altman and Kao are for the years 1971 to 1989, except through 2006 for the *default* migration, while the Moody's and S&P data are updated through 2006.

What is the best reference point to use for bonds or loans of different ages? A new or very young loan or bond is likelier to conform to the Altman and Kao results, since their reference point is newly issued bonds. For an existing or seasoned bond, the appropriate reference point is less clear. The more seasoned the issue, the less likely that Altman and Kao will be the relevant reference. While Moody's and Standard & Poor's would probably

TABLE 17.1   Rating Transition Matrix: One-Year Horizon (all numbers are %)

A/K Moody's S&P	Aaa AAA	Aa AA	A A	Baa BBB	Ba BB	B B	Caa CCC-C	Default Default	RW NR
(A/K)	94.32	5.50	0.10	0.00	0.00	0.00	0.00	0.00	—
Aaa (M)	88.82	7.50	0.67	0.00	0.02	0.00	0.00	0.00	2.99
AAA (S&P)	88.20	7.67	0.49	0.09	0.06	0.00	0.00	0.00	3.49
(A/K)	0.70	92.62	6.40	0.20	0.11	0.10	0.00	0.00	—
Aa (M)	0.83	87.84	7.04	0.28	0.06	0.02	0.00	0.01	3.93
AA (S&P)	0.58	87.16	7.63	0.58	0.08	0.11	0.02	0.01	3.85
(A/K)	0.00	2.62	94.14	4.70	0.32	0.20	0.00	0.00	—
A (M)	0.06	2.55	88.10	4.95	0.51	0.10	0.02	0.02	4.70
A (S&P)	0.05	1.90	87.24	5.59	0.42	0.15	0.03	0.04	4.58
(A/K)	0.00	0.00	5.50	90.00	2.82	1.12	0.12	0.32	—
Baa (M)	0.05	0.21	4.93	84.72	4.39	0.80	0.24	0.18	4.28
BBB (S&P)	0.02	0.16	3.85	84.13	4.27	0.76	0.17	0.27	4.37
(A/K)	0.00	0.00	0.00	6.82	86.13	6.30	0.91	0.00	—
Ba (M)	0.01	0.06	0.48	5.67	76.38	7.59	0.58	1.16	8.08
BB (S&P)	0.03	0.04	0.25	5.26	75.74	7.36	0.90	1.12	9.28
(A/K)	0.00	0.00	0.20	1.63	1.72	93.72	1.70	1.10	—
B (M)	0.01	0.04	0.17	0.37	5.69	74.16	5.38	5.00	9.18
B (S&P)	0.00	0.05	0.19	0.31	5.52	72.67	4.21	5.38	11.67
(A/K)	0.00	0.00	0.00	0.00	0.00	2.81	92.52	4.62	—
Caa (M)	0.00	0.04	0.04	0.23	0.70	9.31	62.01	16.38	11.30
CCC (S&P)	0.00	0.00	0.28	0.41	1.24	10.92	47.06	27.02	13.06

Source Key:
A/K = Altman and Kao (1971–1989) and Altman and Ramayanam (2007)
M = Moody's (1970–2006)
S&P = Standard & Poor's (1981–2006)
RW = Rating Withdrawn
NR = Not Rated

be better references for more seasoned bonds, it is not clear which of the two or if either one is superior.

The three sources generate radically different results. In the case of B-rated bonds, Altman and Kao show that 93.7 percent of newly issued bonds are still B-rated after one year, and 53.3 percent are after five years. Moody's and Standard & Poor's, however, show that only 74.2 percent and 72.7 percent (after one year) and 29.6 percent and 20.4 percent (after five years) retain their ratings. While Altman and Kao do not specify a *rating withdrawn* (RW) category, it is not likely that many bonds will be called

TABLE 17.2   Rating Transition Matrix: Five-Year Horizon (all numbers are %)

A/K Moody's S&P	Aaa AAA	Aa AA	A A	Baa BBB	Ba BB	B B	Caa CCC-C	Default Default	RW NR
(A/K)	69.82	28.52	2.91	3.60	0.11	0.00	0.10	0.12	—
Aaa (M)	56.88	23.78	5.58	0.46	0.40	0.04	0.08	0.11	12.67
AAA (S&P)	53.57	23.85	5.01	1.06	0.13	0.13	0.03	0.30	15.92
(A/K)	2.40	67.11	22.54	5.01	1.02	0.32	0.11	1.70	—
Aa (M)	4.16	53.86	23.13	3.58	0.90	0.29	0.02	0.21	13.84
AA (S&P)	1.75	51.00	24.05	4.25	0.66	0.39	0.04	0.34	17.52
(A/K)	0.40	9.21	72.22	15.10	1.92	0.71	0.00	0.71	—
A (M)	0.25	8.15	57.83	14.20	2.95	0.82	0.16	0.43	15.22
A (S&P)	0.13	5.62	53.01	15.49	2.58	1.02	0.18	0.73	21.24
(A/K)	0.40	1.62	19.61	65.42	7.61	1.70	1.90	1.81	—
Baa (M)	0.24	1.51	15.64	47.05	9.58	2.65	0.47	1.72	21.14
BBB (S&P)	0.07	0.81	10.57	46.23	8.75	3.08	0.53	2.97	26.99
(A/K)	0.00	0.00	7.72	20.41	40.81	16.51	7.81	6.82	—
Ba (M)	0.08	0.25	2.98	12.63	32.12	11.10	1.07	8.12	31.76
BB (S&P)	0.03	0.15	1.59	12.32	27.49	10.87	1.63	11.42	34.49
(A/K)	0.11	0.00	2.31	4.10	7.72	53.31	16.81	20.81	—
B (M)	0.05	0.08	0.51	2.82	12.55	29.56	2.31	20.58	31.54
B (S&P)	0.03	0.07	0.58	2.07	10.06	20.41	2.90	25.73	38.14
(A/K)	0.00	0.00	2.61	3.61	2.62	30.71	26.52	34.01	—
Caa-C (M)	0.00	0.00	0.00	3.03	5.62	7.06	15.12	42.85	26.31
CCC (S&P)	0.00	0.00	0.29	1.18	2.95	9.64	3.93	51.13	30.88

Source Key:
A/K = Altman and Kao (1971–1989) and Altman and Ramayanam (2007)
M = Moody's (1970–2006)
S&P = Standard & Poor's (1981–2006)
RW = Rating Withdrawn
NR = Not Rated

within just one year after issuance since most issues have at least a three- or five-year no-call provision. Moody's and Standard & Poor's, on the other hand, indicate that 9.2 percent and 11.7 percent of the issuers, respectively, have their ratings withdrawn after one year, and as many as 31.5 percent and 38.1 percent after five years. It is obvious, in these cases, that the initial baskets included issuers of seasoned bonds. These comparisons are fairly strong evidence of an aging effect with respect to rating drift—similar to the documented aging effect with respect to defaults that we discussed in Chapter 15.

TABLE 17.3 Rating Transition Matrix: 10-Year Horizon (all numbers are %)

A/K Moody's S&P	Aaa AAA	Aa AA	A A	Baa BBB	Ba BB	B B	Caa CCC-C	Default Default	RW NR
(A/K)	52.10	35.62	7.11	4.61	0.00	0.40	0.10	0.20	—
Aaa (M)	32.38	30.47	10.41	2.97	0.76	0.10	0.05	0.60	22.26
AAA (S&P)	30.37	27.08	10.60	3.86	0.13	0.00	0.00	0.88	27.08
(A/K)	3.50	45.73	22.11	19.00	2.41	0.22	0.00	2.11	—
Aa (M)	4.83	30.20	28.25	7.94	2.32	0.58	0.09	0.78	25.01
AA (S&P)	1.65	29.65	27.44	7.54	1.15	0.36	0.02	0.93	31.25
(A/K)	0.82	17.33	60.92	20.01	3.46	0.91	0.62	1.11	—
A (M)	0.36	10.40	38.29	15.66	4.32	1.53	0.24	1.24	27.96
A (S&P)	0.22	5.86	35.54	16.58	3.43	1.16	0.06	1.91	35.25
(A/K)	0.00	2.82	36.11	42.33	8.20	4.62	1.91	4.13	—
Baa (M)	0.21	2.38	17.33	26.84	7.81	3.08	0.38	3.63	38.35
BBB (S&P)	0.06	1.45	11.88	28.47	7.13	2.22	0.22	5.57	43.01
(A/K)	0.00	0.00	10.32	25.54	20.62	12.56	17.22	13.91	—
Ba (M)	0.20	0.81	5.26	11.37	11.30	6.82	0.70	13.67	49.87
BB (S&P)	0.04	0.15	1.59	12.32	27.49	10.87	1.63	11.42	34.49
(A/K)	0.00	0.00	5.72	8.61	6.70	40.10	6.61	31.51	—
B (M)	0.06	0.03	1.62	3.98	8.58	9.41	0.75	27.39	48.18
B (S&P)	0.00	0.04	0.83	3.88	6.76	6.38	0.83	29.75	51.53
(A/K)	—	—	—	—	—	—	—	—	—
Caa-C (M)	0.00	0.00	0.00	4.49	1.92	1.85	2.14	50.42	39.17
CCC (S&P)	0.00	0.00	0.36	0.72	3.23	2.33	0.36	51.17	41.83

Source Key:
A/K = Altman and Kao (1971–1989) and Altman and Ramayanam (2007)
M = Moody's (1970–2006)
S&P = Standard & Poor's (1981–2006)
RW = Rating Withdrawn
NR = Not Rated

The rating withdrawn category deserves further analysis. In their works, Carty (1997) and Cantor & Hamilton (2007) provide important evidence on this phenomenon, first observed by Altman 1997. They show the one-year migration patterns including the rating withdrawn possibility and, in addition, the patterns conditional upon no rating. Analyzing over 35,000 withdrawn debt ratings (Carty 1997) finds that 92 percent were withdrawn because an issue had matured or had been called and that, of the remaining 8 percent of cases, one-half were withdrawn for unspecified reasons. He concludes that as many as 95 percent of the ratings were withdrawn for reasons other than credit deterioration. Hence, their impact should be positive, or neutral at worst, when considering the effect of the Moody's and Standard & Poor's transition matrices on bond valuation.

It is not completely clear why Moody's and Standard & Poor's results diverge so much after five years. More than likely, the different study periods have impacted their results as well as the RW experience. One could also make the case that differences in the rating criteria employed by the two agencies contributed to the differences in their rating changes, but the systematic effects of the differences are not apparent. Altman and Kao diverge from the other two sources for all rating classes, with the difference most pronounced at the lower end of the credit spectrum. In most cases, Altman and Kao find a higher proportion of bonds that retain their ratings, mainly due to the vintage and aging effects.

Most likely, Altman and Kao find a lower migration pattern because of the rating process itself, the rating withdrawn category, and the aging effect. With respect to the latter, rating agencies and bank loan review groups do not begin to review most bonds or loans for at least one year. The change in the credit quality of the issuer would have to be substantial to motivate a change in the early years. On the other hand, a seasoned bond may have deteriorated (or improved) slowly for several years before the agencies decide to change its rating. As we have noted, however, in Chapter 15, Moody's has recently embraced the aging concept in their cumulative default models but this has not shown up as yet in their migration tables (see Tables 17.4 and 17.5).

IMPACT ON RESULTS

When a company's credit quality migrates and its ratings change, the holders of its securities experience an increase or decrease in the value of their investment, either before and/or after the rating change. How large is the shift? There are at least four possible ways to determine the price impact of a rating change.

One possibility is to multiply the change in yield spread between the initial rating and the new rating by the modified duration (the percentage change in price associated with a 100 basis point move in interest rates) of the bond. This methodology utilizes either the average yield-to-maturity or the option (primarily call option) adjusted spread by bond rating class. As an example, Table 17.4 contains this data for the period 1985 to 1996. Table 17.5 presents modified duration data for different bond grades for the same period. For updated information on spreads by duration, see Table 17.6. It should be noted that these spreads have widened significantly in mid-2007

TABLE 17.4 Average Yields and Spread by Rating Class, 1985–1996

	AAA Avg. YTM		AA Avg. YTM		A Avg. YTM		BBB Avg. YTM		BB Avg. YTM		B Avg. YTM		CCC Avg. YTM	
	%	Spread	%	Spread	%	Spread	%	Spread	%	Spread	%	Spread	%	Spread
1985–96														
Average	8.21	54.82	8.73	60.44	8.89	85.31	9.52	139.79	10.91	326.13	13.04	538.73	17.59	1027.91
Std. dev.	1.58	22.22	1.44	18.42	1.53	24.52	1.54	36.81	1.76	76.18	2.20	140.23	5.50	520.48

Note:
YTM, yield-to-maturity (%); average based on 12 (months) observations.
YTW, yield-to-worst (%); average based on 12 (months) observations.
Spread, average option-adjusted spread over U.S. Treasury Bonds (basis points)
1985–96 averages = monthly observations.
Source: Professor Edward I. Altman, New York University Salomon Center.

TABLE 17.5   Average Modified Duration by Rating Class, 1985–1996 (S&P ratings)

1995–1996	AAA	AA	A	BBB	BA	B	CCC
Average	5.32	6.48	6.24	6.22	5.49	4.86	4.30
Standard Deviation	0.84	0.36	0.29	0.28	0.71	0.57	0.94

Note: 1985–1996 averages = monthly observations.
Source: Professor Edward I. Altman, New York University Salomon Center and Moody's Investors Service data.

compared to 2006. An example of how this information may be used is shown in Table 17.7, for the price impact on BBB bonds.

A second method for calculating the impact of rating migration on a bond's value is to estimate the possible rating change for the next period, such as one year, and then discount the remaining cash flows from that period to maturity using the forward zero-coupon curve for bonds in the new rating class. Rather than trying to estimate the forward interest rate curves, the first method (above) assumes no change in rates. If, however, we are simultaneously estimating the impact of all possible rating migration patterns on a portfolio of many securities, then a type of forward-yield-curve simulation analysis would appear to be a reasonable approach.[5]

A third method for analyzing the price impact of a rating change is direct observation of the price changes of a large sample of bonds of different rating

TABLE 17.6   Median Credit Spreads: Bonds over U.S. Treasuries (view by duration), 2006

Duration	Aaa	Aa	A2	B	Ba2	B2	Caa-C
1	40	61	66	71	268	453	865
2	47	70	82	94	277	442	757
3	52	76	92	111	282	436	701
4	55	81	101	125	286	431	663
5	58	85	108	137	289	428	636
6	61	88	114	148	291	425	614
7	63	91	119	158	293	423	596
8	65	94	124	166	295	421	581
9	66	96	129	175	297	419	568
10	68	98	133	182	298	417	557

Note: Spreads in basis points.
Source: Moody's Investors Service (2007).

TABLE 17.7   Example of the Price Impact of Migration for a BBB Bond

	AAA	AA	A	BBB	BB	B	CCC
Average spread (from Table 17.4)	54.8	60.4	85.3	139.8	326.1	538.7	1027.9

Note:
Average modified duration for a BBB bond (from Table 17.5): 6.2 years.
Average expected price change because of upgrade to A = 6.2 × (139.8 − 85.3) = 338 bps.
Probability of migrating from BBB to A (from Table 17.2: *A* and *K* values) = 19.6 percent
Expected impact of the migration = (0.196) (338) = 66 bps.

classes. The main difficulty in this technique is the need to determine the correct date to measure the price change. It is obviously too late to measure the change at the exact time of the rating change since most, if not all, of the change has already occurred by then. An alternative possibility is to use the date when the rating agency first placed the bond on its Watch List and published this event (e.g., in Standard & Poor's *Credit Week*). See Altman and Rijken (2008) for a discussion of the timeliness improvement when we observe Watchlist and Outlook changes compared to the actual rating changes themselves. The price changes over time will not always be the same since market conditions are constantly changing. This type of event-study analysis is an elusive methodology.

A final possibility is to decompose the observed market spreads of bonds in various rating classes so that we can isolate the impact of expected rating drift. Combined with historical rating drift patterns, these observed spreads can reveal the expected economic consequence of a change in rating. Problems in such decomposition are formidable, however.

A complete analysis of the impact of credit risk migration on returns must go beyond the assessment of individual assets to evaluate the probabilities that different fixed income assets in a portfolio will migrate in the same direction over time. This involves calculating migration correlations and their total portfolio effects. In Chapter 20, we discuss the CreditMetrics (Gupton, Finger, and Bhatia 1997) methodology for evaluating migration patterns across all major rating class categories, including the default status. One of the key issues in analyzing these correlations is selecting a basis for determining the correlation matrix. Four candidates have been identified: the historical rating series itself, a model that estimates the rating equivalent of its credit score, equity prices, and models that explain equity prices. We lean toward the second of these approaches, although equity prices and related models are quite popular.

CREDIT RISK MIGRATION AND LOAN LOSSES

A fair amount has been written about estimating both the expected and un-expected losses from bank loan portfolios. With the increased importance of mark-to-market price disclosure, gains and losses due to deteriorating credit risk patterns should now be included. The impact of these changes can now be quantified more precisely by an expected price change methodology for rating levels combined with our expected recovery approach (see Chapter 16) for the default scenario.

FUTURE DIRECTIONS

We have highlighted some rather great differences between the various published reports on rating migration. These differences are based on different sample methodologies, rating systems, and periods of observation. We have also explored a number of direct applications for this data, including expected returns for various types of investors. Organizations buying and selling credit derivatives (see Chapter 21), especially total-return swap derivatives, have an especially great need to understand rating migration. We encourage even more in-depth studies on rating migration patters, covering all relevant time periods. In the previous edition of this book, we also advocated the compilation of migration stats based on rating-notch differentials and this has, indeed, taken place since.

REFERENCES

Altman, E. I. 1997. Rating Migration of Corporate Bonds-Comparative Results and Investor Implications. Working Paper, NYU Salomon Center.

Altman, E. I., and D. L. Kao. 1991a. *Corporate Bond Rating Drift: An Examination of Rating Agency Credit Quality Changes.* Charlottesville, VA: AIMR.

————. 1991b. Appendices to the AIMR Report on "An Examination of Rating Agency Drift over Time. Working Paper no. S-91-40, NYU Salomon Center.

————. 1992a. "Rating Drift of High-Yield Bonds." *Journal of Fixed Income* 2, no. 1:15–20.

————. 1992b. "The Implications of Corporate Bond Rating Drift." *Financial Analysts Journal* 48, no. 1:64–75.

Altman, E. I., and H. Suggitt. 1999. "Default Rates in the Syndicated Bank Loan Markets: A Mortality Analysis." *Journal of Banking and Finance* 24, no. 1–2:229–253.

Altman, E. I., and S. Ramayanam. 2007. Defaults and Returns on High Yields Bonds: Analysis Through 2006. Special Report, NYU Salomon Center, February.

Altman, E.I., and H. Rijken. 2004. "How Rating Agencies Achieve Rating Stability." *Journal of Banking & Finance* 28, no. 10:2679–2714.

———. 2006. "A Point-in-Time Perspective on Through-the-Cycle Ratings." *Financial Analysts Journal* 62, no. 1:54–69.

———. 2008. "The Added Value of Rating Outlooks and Rating Reviews to Corporate Bond Ratings." Working Paper, NYU Salomon Center (New York) and Free University (Amsterdam).

Cantor, R. and D. T. Hamilton. 2007. "Adjusting Corporate Default Rates for Rating Withdrawal." *Journal of Credit Risk* 3, no. 2:3–26.

Carty, L. 1997. "Moody's Rating Migration and Credit Quality Correlation, 1920–1996." *Moody's Special Report*, July.

Carty, L., and J. Fons. 1994. "Measuring Changes in Credit Quality." *Journal of Fixed Income* 4, no. 1:27–41.

Hamilton, D. T. 2007. "Default and Recovery Rates of Corporate Bond Issuers. 1938–2006." *Moody's Special Report*, January.

Gupton, G. M., C. C. Finger, and M. Bhatia. 1997, April. *CreditMetrics: The Benchmark for Understanding Credit Risk*. New York: JPMorgan.

Lucas, D. 1995. "The Effectiveness of Downgrade Provisions in Reducing Counterparty Risk." *Journal of Fixed Income* 5, no. 1:32–41.

Lucas, D., and J. Lonski. 1992. "Changes in Corporate Credit Quality: 1970–1990." *Journal of Fixed Income* 2, no. 1:7–14.

Moody's Investors Service. 2007. *Special Comment: Structured Finance Rating Transitions: 1983–2006*, January. Moody's Investors Service.

Oleksin, I. M. 1997. "Using Risk Migration Analysis for Managing Portfolio Risk: Results of Study." *Journal of Lending and Credit Risk Management* 8, no. 1:49–56.

Standard & Poor's. 2007. *Ratings Performance 2006: Stability and Transition*. New York.

———. 1997b. *CreditPro*. New York

Further Reading

Altman, E. I. 1989. "Measuring Corporate Bond Mortality and Performance." *Journal of Finance* 54, no. 4:909–922.

———. 1998. "The Importance and Subtlety of Credit Risk Migration." *Journal of Banking and Finance* 22, no. 5:1231–1247.

Altman, E.I. and H. Rijken. 2006. "A Point-in-Time Perspective on Through-the-Cycle Ratings," *Financial Analysts Journal* 12, no. 1:54–69.

Austin, D. 1992. "Use Migration Analysis to Refine Estimates of Future Loan Losses." *Commercial Lending Review* 25, no. 1:34–43.

CHAPTER 18

Introduction to Portfolio Approaches

Even though many economic and financial variables fall into distributions that approximate a bell curve, the picture is never perfect. Once again, resemblance to truth is not the same as truth. It is in these outliers and imperfections that the wildness lurks.
—Peter Bernstein (1996, 335)

The chapter introduces portfolio theory as applied to managing the fixed income assets of banks and insurance companies. In the past, these institutions suffered the consequences of having paid insufficient attention to portfolio management. Because they focused on analyzing individual loans with little regard for the portfolio implications, they created excessive concentrations and experienced excessive losses. Recognizing and dealing with concentration by financial institutions is now more the rule than the exception. Development of the secondary loan market, structured finance products, and credit derivatives are all partly because of the desire on the part of banks and insurance companies to address portfolio concentration.[1]

Broadly stated, excessive concentration results when a financial institution has a level of exposure to a single name, product, sovereign or sector such that seriously adverse developments in this exposure could hamper the institution's ability to continue functioning. A Federal Reserve report (1993) sums it up as follows:

> Concentration of credit risk may generally be characterized as inordinately high levels of direct or indirect exposures to a single or related groups of borrowers, credit exposures collateralized by a single security, or securities with common characteristics, or credit exposures to borrowers with common characteristics within an industry or similarly affected group.

One level of protection against concentration is the single obligor limit (legal lending limit) set by regulators and by the financial institution's own credit policy. Other controls that exist are industry, country, and collateral limits,[2] which are generally based on judgment. This chapter and the next deal with the questions of how portfolio concentrations can be measured objectively and how a value or cost can be assigned to them. After introducing the classic portfolio theory, we consider the problems that arise in adapting it to banking and insurance assets. Then we review the alternative approaches that have been taken.

DIVERSIFICATION IS GOOD, OTHER THINGS BEING EQUAL

The very mention of a portfolio approach brings to mind Harry Markowitz and the theory of diversification (Markowitz 1959). The idea behind Markowitz's theory is the notion, that while the *riskiness* of the return from a security may be characterized by its *variance,* the comovement or *covariance* among a group of securities will influence risk and return from a *portfolio* of securities. Using the historical variance-covariance matrix as representative of the future, Markowitz formulated the classic quadratic optimization problem, where the objective function is couched in terms of the resulting portfolio's expected return and the variance of return, subject to the constraint that the weights invested in the securities add up to one. The procedure led to finding the portfolio with the highest return for a given level of risk, or the portfolio with the least risk for a given level of return.

Although this is a highly simplified depiction of the investment model, it is introduced here because insights from portfolio theory have had profound effect on subsequent development in the theory and practice of financial management. Variability in investment returns may be minimized by investing in assets that are *negatively correlated* with one another. One classic pedagogical example is the notion of investing in a company that manufactures skis and in another that manufactures swimsuits. Since the first company prospers when it is snowing and the second when the sun is shining: the combination of these investments will minimize overall earnings variability of a portfolio that is invested in these two companies. As more and more securities are added to a portfolio, even the mere *absence* of positive correlation can be shown to be beneficial in diversifying a portfolio as is described next.

A NUMBER OF SMALL BETS VERSUS A SINGLE LARGE BET

It is better to make a series of small bets than one large bet because as the number of bets is spread out over a fixed amount of capital, the variance of the results is reduced.

This concept may be illustrated with an example involving ship owners (Mason 1995). Imagine a group of risk-averse merchants, each of whom owns one ship with the following risk profile. If the ship returns safely, the merchant will make a profit of $100,000. However, there is a 0.2 probability that the ship will sink, in which case the owner will receive nothing. The expected value of the payoff is $100,000 \times 0.8 - 0 \times 0.2$, which equals $80,000. The "riskiness" of the investment, measured by the standard deviation is

$$\sqrt{[(0.2)(0 - \$80,000)^2 + (0.8)(\$100,000 - \$80,000)^2]} = \$40,000$$

If the probability that one ship will sink is completely independent of the others (for example, if they ply different routes), two owners can make an agreement to exchange one-half of the payoff from one ship for one-half of the payoff from the other. Now, the probabilities of outcome are no longer 0.2 for the ship sinking and 0.8 for not sinking. Instead, there are three possible outcomes: that both ships sink, that neither of them sinks, and that one of them sinks. These are shown in Table 18.1.

The expected value is still the same, that is, $80,000, but the volatility has been reduced from $40,000 to $28,864. The standard deviation is now.

$$\sqrt{[(0.04)(0 - \$80,000)^2 + (0.64)(\$100,000 - \$80,000)^2 + (0.32)(\$50,000 - \$80,000)^2]}$$
$$= \$28,864.$$

The merchant has spread his bet from one ship to two ships. Suppose that more and more ship owners adopt this strategy. It may be shown that if there are 100 ship owners, the standard deviation drops to a mere $4,000.

TABLE 18.1   Three Possible Outcomes

Probability	Payoff
Both sink: $0.2 \times 0.2 = .04$	0
Neither sinks = $0.8 \times 0.8 = 0.64$	100,000
One of them sinks = $1 - .04 - .64 = .32$	50,000

The power of diversification is such that if there are N ship owners, the standard deviation drops to $\$40,000/(N)$. This result is applicable if and only if the outcomes from the trials are independent. Alternatively, if all the ships were on the same voyage, the risk of many of them sinking would be greatly magnified. Moreover, this is *not* the diversification Markowitz was talking about; he was looking at the existence of *negative correlations,* or very low positive correlations. With negative correlations you need fewer investments to achieve the desired result. *Independent trials,* by contrast, are a special case of zero correlations: as you add more assets, the volatility diminishes. When fixed income fund managers talk about diversification, they are primarily referring to finding investments that are uncorrelated or weakly correlated—not ones that are negatively correlated, such as the makers of swimsuits and skis.

One example of creating and measuring diversification in asset-based securities is *Moody's diversity index* for the collateral, where the individual assets are distributed as companies across many industries. Moody's diversity score is based on the concept of low or zero correlation. It assumes that firms in the same industry tend to be correlated and that firms in different industries are less correlated. In other words, industry dispersion is used as a measure of independence. The scoring system for diversity takes account of the number of different risks in the population and their degree of independence based on industry membership. There are 32 industries in Moody's classification system. This index (Moody's Investors Service 1991, 9) is used to measure the degree of diversification of collateral in structured finance transactions. Table 18.2 shows the diversity score for the number of firms in the same industry in a portfolio. The score values appear to be arbitrarily derived because they do not reflect the underlying sources of risk, but conceptually they are based on the same principle illustrated by our story about ship owners.

The diversity index is calculated as the lower (more conservative) of two calculations. The first assumes that the portfolio has the smallest possible number of companies, given the single-company limit. The second assumes that the portfolio has the smallest number of industries, given the single industry limit. Let us assume, for example, that an issuer uses a 2 percent maximum per name and a 5 percent maximum per industry. From the first calculation, this implies that there will be at least $100/2 = 50$ companies in the portfolio, each accounting for 2 percent of it. You can only place two companies from the same industry in the portfolio because if you place three, the industry exposure rises to 6 percent. With two companies per industry, there will be at least 25 industries represented, using the diversity score of 1.5. From Table 18.2, the diversity score in this example works out to 25×1.5, that is, 37.5. The second calculation indicates that the

TABLE 18.2 Diversity Score Calculation Table

Number of Firms in the Portfolio	Diversity Score If the Companies Are in the Same Industry	Diversity Score If Each Company Is in a Different Industry
1	1	1
2	1.5	2
3	2	3
4	2.33	4
5	2.67	5
6	3.00	6
7	3.25	7
8	3.5	8
9	3.75	9
10	4	10
>10	Evaluate on a case-by-case basis	

minimum number of industries is 20. Since there is a limit of 2 percent per name, at least three companies must be included from each industry. If just two are included, they will each be 2.5 percent (half of the 5 percent from the industry), and this will violate the limit. Using the diversity score of 2 from the table, the diversity index is 40. The diversity score selected is the lower of 37.5 and 40, that is, 37.5.

The diversity score is one of the factors Moody's uses in deciding whether a structured finance transaction qualifies for a particular rating. In addition to calibrating its requirements to the score, Moody's puts an absolute limit on concentrations: The percentage one risk represents in a pool of risks; and the percentage of one industry present in the total portfolio. These limits are factored into the actual score. The diversity score is used in association with the Binomial Expansion Technique (BET) to model the portfolio as consisting of identical, uncorrelated assets with the same default probability. The expected loss at various attachment points (1 to N defaults, where N is the diversity score) is used to assign the rating to the corresponding CDO tranche based on the expected losses historically associated with that rating level for corporate bonds.

The diversity score is a simple way to understand the degree of diversification by obligor and industry in any portfolio. It is important to remember, however, that the diversity index makes the assumptions that the correlation *among* (or between) industries is zero and the correlation *within* an industry is high. These assumptions may not be valid in all instances. Nonetheless, in the absence of any good alternative, the same approach may be used to quantify the degree of diversification. Moody's diversity score, however imperfect it may be is widely used in practice in characterizing the diversification of a pool of debt securities used in collateralized debt obligations.

Sometimes, diversification exacts a price. Municipal bond insurers MBIA and Ambac diversified from their core business of municipal bond underwriting into structured finance in the 1990s. This was because, while municipal underwriting was a stable business, there was really no opportunity for growth. The move into the structured finance business, as the securitization market grew, was extremely profitable to the insurers. There was a growing variety of asset classes that were securitized. But as they diversified further into new products in structured finance, the insurers got involved with the subprime mortgage market. This particular diversification effort within structured finance unfortunately turned out to be very costly for them as evidenced by the impact on their stock prices in 2007–2008 and fears that they would lose their coveted triple-A rating.

Seizing the opportunity presented by the troubles faced by these firms, Warren Buffett, chairman of Berkshire Hathaway, Inc. announced plans to start a bond insurer for local governments. According to the *Wall Street Journal* (2007), Buffett's company will not insure structured finance products such as collateralized debt obligations or any asset-backed securities. Apparently, Buffett is not charmed by the benefits of diversification for his bond insurance company. "It makes sense provided it sticks to the knitting of insurance for municipal bond insurance," according to Ed Grebeck, chief executive of Tempus Advisors, quoted in the *Wall Street Journal* (2007).

It would be incorrect to declare at this time that that the bond insurers' entry into the structured finance business was a mistake. At the time of this writing most of the problem has come from mark-to-market losses—not actual losses. While there may well be actual losses to contend with, so far the cumulative municipal losses suffered by the insurers have been much larger than the cumulative structured finance ones. But the main point here is that diversification in and by itself does not guarantee the elimination of risk, systematic or otherwise.

ISSUES IN IMPLEMENTING THE STANDARD PORTFOLIO APPROACH TO CREDIT PORTFOLIOS

Markowitz won the Nobel Prize for his work on portfolio theory and there is no question that this approach is extremely useful. However, there are practical difficulties in applying the standard portfolio model (mean-variance optimization for asset selection) to investments, and to fixed income or loan asset portfolios in particular. We discuss some of these problems and then present the solutions that have been proposed. The problems have to do with the following:

- Correlation estimates
- Distribution of returns
- Multiperiod choices
- Lack of price data
- Lack of fundamental data

Portfolio selection as Markowitz originally envisioned, dealt with choosing among individual securities. The first problem with this is that the number of correlations to be calculated increases very rapidly as the number of securities being considered increases.[3] For example, a covariance matrix of 30 different assets will have 435 different covariances. (For an N-asset portfolio, the number of correlations needed is $N(N − 1)/2$.) Let us say we have time series data for 12 quarters (3 years). We are then estimating 435 unknown values with 12 times $30 = 360$ known values. This is absurd. In statistical terms, the data available would result in a matrix of rank 66. This is equivalent to saying that only 66 out of the 435 entries would contain information whereas the remaining 369 would be noise (Beckers 1995).

The second issue is that while correlations of *equity returns* are used in applying the theory to equity markets, the variable to be used with regard to fixed income assets is not so clear. These could be correlation of total returns, correlation among factors explaining returns, correlation of default probabilities, correlation of cash spreads, correlation of option adjusted spreads, or all of the above. Equity return correlations may be measured, but correlation of the tendency to default is not observable. In the large corporate sector, defaults themselves are infrequent. Sometimes the time series of *forecasted probabilities of default* for different companies are used to calculate *default correlations*. The problem with this approach is that the forecasted probability of default is, as its name implies, merely a forecast. It therefore contains an element of forecast error. A correlation calculated on the basis of a series of forecasts has little or no operational meaning if it turns out that the standard error of the underlying forecast is very high.

Furthermore, every definition of correlation has its own properties and limitations. The correlation coefficient captures only the *linear* relationship between two random variables. If two variables have a nonlinear relationship, the coefficient will be unable to capture the *strength* of this relationship. To understand this, consider the set of X and Y values in Table 18.3.

The correlation coefficient between X and Y comes out 0.88 indicating a less than perfect correlation. In fact, Y is completely defined by X in this example and is exactly equal to x^4.

TABLE 18.3   Linear Correlation Example

X	Y
1	1
2	16
3	81
4	256
5	625
6	1.296
7	2.401
8	4.096
9	6.561
10	10.000

The third difficulty with implementation is that most correlations are *unconditional* in that they are calculated without holding the other structural variables constant. It is difficult to model the change in correlation if the structural variable changes, or if the structure itself changes. A simple example of this problem arises when there is sudden shock to the system (such as the outbreak of hostilities or an oil embargo). In such situations, correlations of risk typically break down, just when they are needed most! When there is shock to the system, typically seemingly uncorrelated variables become correlated in what is commonly referred to as "contagion" or "tail correlation." The problems with default correlations are not academic. A senior banker alludes to the impact of an unstable correlation estimate on the business of lending (Hopper 1997):

> *We were recently told to amend our correlation matrices very substantially. This is the sort of thing that can have a huge impact internally if you are using this matrix. You have been told all along that your sectoral concentration limit is okay and this is your capital. Suddenly, you are told, "Whoops, you have gobbled up your capital! That particular sector is now okay, but this one is not." You cannot get used to some of that stuff.* (Interview by Paul Narayanan, July 1997)

DISTRIBUTION OF RETURNS

The standard portfolio model is not directly applicable to fixed income portfolios because the equations for the portfolio return and variance apply if and only if the individual security return distributions are symmetrical—that is, they may be completely characterized by a mean and a variance. If they are not, then the equations no longer hold. While we do not know the precise shape of the distribution of returns from debt securities, we do know that it is not symmetrical. One possible shape of the returns from fixed income securities is shown in Figure 18.1, but it has not been derived empirically. Intuitively, this distribution says what bankers know only too well: when you make a loan, you get none of the upside and all of the downside. That is because you can lose all or most of your investment, but your upside is limited to the promised yield. In the region of loan loss, probability density is higher than that implied by a normal distribution curve. This is known as the *fat-tail problem.* Note that the X-axis measures the magnitude of the loss. The graph will be laterally transposed if the X-axis is the rate of return. The fat tail will then be to the left of the mean.

HOLDING PERIOD

The standard portfolio approach is usually stated as a single-period problem. Only if the model is constructed as a multiperiod model can transaction costs come into play as the optimal solution swaps from one asset to another. For securities that are innately illiquid, transaction costs may be so large that they will dominate or even preclude a solution. Of course, a liquid market for

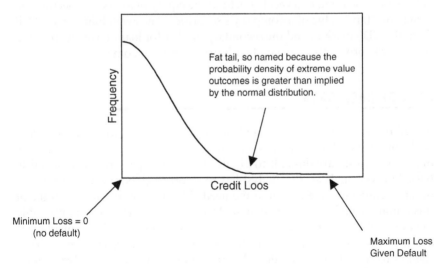

FIGURE 18.1 Possible Shape of the Distribution of Credit Loss

credit derivatives will ameliorate this problem. The single-period limitation of the standard model is often handled by running the model repeatedly; that is, the solution is implemented in period t, and when period $t + 1$ is reached, the model is run again with new inputs. Necessary adjustment can then be made. The drawback of this approach is that while it obviates the need to formulate a multiperiod model, it still does not address completely the issue of transaction costs. Of perhaps greater concern is the fact that there really is no way to know if repeated optimization leads to globally optimum outcomes—that is, whether the results achieved without fully incorporating intertemporal choices in the model are still optimal.[4]

ABSENCE OF PRICE DISCOVERY

Although equities offer the possibility that returns may be modeled in a smooth continuum, at least in the short run, debt securities are less tractable. There are simply too many variables in the instruments themselves that may affect the magnitude of the outcome. Seniority, covenants, and call options all have an impact on value. In the equity markets, analysts come to a collective judgment on these and other value-impacting variables and total return as measured by (sale price minus acquisition cost) plus dividends may be measured. However, with the exception of the bonds of large corporations, and, to some extent, high-yield securities, the markets are quite thin and the bid-ask spreads wider than in the equity market. Even when the value of an instrument can be determined from its characteristics, many observers believe that the bond markets lag behind the equity markets in reflecting the "true" or "fair" value of a company's securities. The availability of TRACE data, the CDS market, and the secondary market for loans have ameliorated some of the problems associated with pricing fixed income assets.

LACK OF GOOD DATA

Added to all the diffculties in modeling is the fact that, with the exception of the public bond market, good data on variables that can impact the value of a debt security are difficult to obtain. Even when performing some fairly basic kinds of analysis, the analyst has to resort to elaborate adjustments in order to transform the data into the needed form. The simplest example of this is bond default and recovery data. Defaults by bond ratings are probably the only publicly available database on corporate defaults.[5] If someone has a homegrown risk rating system and wants to use it to project defaults, he or she has to rely on the bond default data. In other words, to analyze a non-bond portfolio, one must map the homegrown rating system to the implied bond rating and thence to the default probability. If an error is introduced in the scaling process that links the homegrown risk rating to the bond rating, it will be passed on to the estimated probability of default as well. A second problem arises because, despite claims to the contrary by the rating agencies, bond ratings themselves have not been a constant measure of credit risk. An AA-rated company of the 1950s may not be the same as an AA-rated company in the 2000s because the default probabilities have changed over years as have the complexities of the firms. These are important concerns because default probabilities based on bond defaults are the foundation of many of the portfolio approaches currently being proposed/used.[6]

Data problems are also common with regard to geography and industry identification. With the exception of real estate and consumer loans, it is very hard to pin down the "geographic dimension" of a borrower. For one thing, the corporate address may have nothing to do with the location of the company's manufacturing operations—which may span many countries—and even less to do with the location of its customers. Consider the shoe manufacturer Nike, Inc. Nike is based in Beaverton, Oregon. In 1994, it employed 700 people there, out of the 9,600 people in 86 sites worldwide on its payroll. Chances are that lenders' MIS (management information systems) list Nike as being located in Beaverton and very little else. The company's "geographic location" is equated with the address of its corporate office. With regard to SIC (standard industrial classification) codes, most MIS systems do not provide for more than one SIC for a given company. In some instances, several SIC categories share the same concentration risk. Although they are classified as different groups, automobile battery manufacturers and airbag manufacturers, for example, share common industry risk factors; that is, they behave in the same way.

A company may be in more than one SIC, but a bank's data systems are designed only to capture the primary SIC (see Ranson 1993). It is difficult to decide whether to deal with the SIC code at the one-, two-, or three-digit level. As industry detail is increased, it becomes possible to pinpoint the economic activity accurately; but there may not be enough data points to create a meaningful summary of the characteristics of an industry group.

Unless a conscious effort is made to profile all of the possible indirect exposures, it is difficult to identify *latent concentrations*. While the link between the fortunes of industries in Louisiana to oil prices is fairly obvious, the dependency of a group of seemingly unrelated customers in the portfolio to a common cause such as export risk is not so apparent. To give an example, if Boeing company starts to depend less on purchases by U.S. carriers and the U.S. government and more on those by overseas buyers, then this shift will mean that events in the foreign economies will have an impact on Boeing's suppliers. Indeed, the entire state of Washington will exhibit behavior that resonates with foreign aircraft purchase trends. It is this "latent" concentration that is more difficult to grapple with. Unless the analyst tags Boeing and its related companies with export risk classification, concentration will not be apparent from routine portfolio analysis. Portfolio models such as Moody's KMV's Portfolio Manager attempt to capture these not-so-obvious correlations through the use of factors that drive correlated default.

According to one senior banker (Hopper 1997), it is difficult to obtain even a baseline database of assets with their risk characteristics:

The active management portfolio is still in its early days. I suspect you've heard this from others. I don't think we're any different from any other organization. Over the last two or three years, as we've gotten active with portfolio management, the biggest problem of the lot has been getting data of decent integrity. The corporations seem to have management information, but actually getting good quality information in a bank is unbelievably difficult. It's partly because we have some bookkeeping systems that are out of the ark and some that are enormously complicated, altogether different systems that don't talk to each other. We have one portfolio in the States, which has one accounting system. We have another portfolio in the U.K., which has three or four accounting systems—some of them still manual. Then you go to Europe and they've got different accounting systems. So, with all these different accounting systems, we've been trying to develop some systems that can actually go in and pluck out the data.

The problem is that the accounting records are there for a specific purpose, and they were not designed to give all the information and granularity you need to actually undertake all the portfolio management analytics. So, yes, they'll tell us what the drawn balance is. They probably won't tell us what the maturity of the facility is because they don't really need to know that. So we've been trying to develop some records that actually do have the limit, the balance, the product type, all the pricing details, the right maturity, the BIC code the grading, and the developed severity, and have all this readily available. We're in the throes of introducing a totally new bookkeeping system in the next year, a loan administration system that would be a big step forward. At that stage, we'll be able to go into this system and get most of what we need. And this system will probably need to access one or two other systems to have the complete picture. The major focus has been getting some data that we actually thought was robust enough to produce some output that's worthwhile.

The implementation of BIS II capital standards has accelerated the implementation of improved information systems in banks, but perfection is still years away.

SOLUTION FOR THE CORRELATION MATRIX

One approach to handling the large size of the correlation matrix is to solve the problem not with individual companies, but with industry average or aggregates or with a representative company as a proxy for an industry. Econometric solutions, notably factor or principal component analysis, have been used to isolate fundamental macrofactors affecting corporate financial distress. Failure rate is expressed as a function of external variables such as industry, unemployment, and the like. (Chirinko and Guill 1991; and McKinsey 1997). The estimate of the failure rate is then equated to the probability of failure of a single firm that fits the profile indicated by the independent variables. Another approach expresses the *return on equity* as a function of a set of index variables (in the spirit of earlier work on multiindex models (see Elton & Gruber 1981) or the later arbitrage pricing theory (see Ross 1984)) and then uses the calculated returns to derive the implied correlation of return among firms. Such frameworks typically are hybrids of econometrics, optimization, univariate time series predictions of exogenous variables, and simulation. This approach may be adequate for broad asset-allocation or sector decisions, but *in the absence of acceptable validation results,* it is probably less applicable to individual asset decisions. But as the saying goes, getting it broadly right (asset allocation) is clearly better than being precisely wrong (selecting individual assets).

How does one project *future* correlations? Various alternatives have been proposed. Treynor and Black (1973, 66–86) suggested one of them. Their approach is based on the capital asset pricing model, which, in effect, argues for holding a market portfolio instead of attempting "to translate these insights (of security analysts) into the expected returns, variances, and covariances the algorithms require as inputs." Treynor and Black divide a portfolio into three parts: a riskless part, a highly diversified part resembling the market portfolio, and an active part which has both diversifiable risk and market risk. The active portfolio is created to allow the portfolio manager to monetize additional insights that the market lacks. Portfolio performance is then measured in terms of how much market risk is taken over the riskless rate, and how much specific risk (called *appraisal risk* by Treynor and Black) is taken. This approach includes a role for individual risk assessment and, therefore, diverges from the capital asset pricing model, which rules it out altogether. To our knowledge, Treynor and Black's approach has not been used in the management of fixed income portfolios, but it could be applied here because it is able to split market returns from nonmarket returns, and only the beta of the loan return relative to the market needs to be estimated.

Another way of handling differing expectations about the future, given a correlation matrix, is the scenario approach proposed by Markowitz and Perold (1984). In this approach, the returns are linked to future states of the world (scenarios), and a probability distribution is assigned to each scenario. Equity portfolios are often constructed using the scenario approach. In his loan portfolio analysis, Bennett (1984) suggests that this approach be used in setting the rating impact of factors and thereupon combining the effect of multiple factors constituting a scenario. His work is described in greater detail in Chapter 19. This approach is also used by Chirinko and Guill (1991).

CURRENT PORTFOLIO APPROACHES

Portfolio approaches used by financial institutions run the gamut from simple to complex. At the simplest level, institutions apply a "slicing and dicing" approach, whereby they set limits on the various types of concentration and monitor their exposure accordingly. For example, it is common to see banks set limits by state, country (in-country and cross-border), industry, transaction type and collateral. These limits are primarily based on judgment but employ off-line analysis to support the limits derived. The limits are generally developed based on one or more of the following approaches:

- Historical or recent loss experience.
- Standards based on maximum loss tolerance relative to capital.
- Risk-adjusted return on capital, where the risk is evaluated relative to the risk either at the transaction level or at the business unit level.

Some of the recently introduced concepts are the diversity index, expected and unexpected losses, RAROC, RAROC 2020, credit value-at-risk and variants of the Sharpe Ratio.[7] Some overlap exists among the items on this list. For instance, RAROC, CreditMetrics, and CreditRisk+ use the unexpected loss concept, and all these methods may include migration, security, covenants, and so on.

EXPECTED VERSUS UNEXPECTED LOSSES

Beset by the difficulties in trying to adapt the approach based on the return and variance of return on individual assets to illiquid fixed income securities, portfolio analysts have turned to modeling the problem through the notion of unexpected and expected losses. Expected losses are long-run average losses and thus can be reflected in pricing. Unexpected losses are not directly reflected in pricing but require that capital be set aside to absorb the shock so that the organization is not debilitated by their occurrence. *Unexpected loss* sounds like a contradiction in terms. After all, once a loss is quantified, it can no longer be called "unexpected." However, the term really means *maximum potential loss,* or the maximum loss at a given level of confidence—say 95 percent.[8] One rationale behind the concept of unexpected losses is that losses may be incurred because of a joint default that may be attributable to portfolio concentration or because a single obligor has defaulted with great severity. Another rationale is that the expected loss value may be incorrect, and it is therefore important to know the underlying distribution that produced this value. Because unexpected losses are derived based on default probabilities and recovery rates, this approach is driven more by *intrinsic value* (the so-called "model value") than by *market value* (see Figure 18.2).

The concept of expected and unexpected credit losses is shown in the Figure 18.2. The expected loss is that associated with the mean of the loss

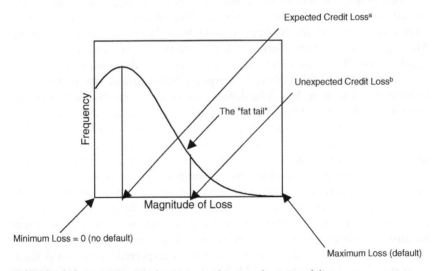

FIGURE 18.2   Expected and Unexpected Losses for a Portfolio
[a] For which reserve should be held, pricing should include this element.
[b] For which capital should be held, pricing should include ROE.
Source: Adapted from Mark (1996).

distribution of a loan or a portfolio. The unexpected loss is that associated with 95 percent (for instance) of the area under the loss curve. The area to the right is expected with such rarity that it would be uneconomical to hold 100 percent capital against that contingency. Note that this is the graph for a single asset. If all the assets are combined, the resulting area to the right of the 95 percent level is the loss level for which capital is needed. Capital may not be dollar for dollar, but it has to have some relationship to the *value at risk*. Although the term unexpected loss is somewhat recent, the underlying rationale for it has existed for a long period. For example, Vojta (1973, 18) termed the "unexpected" loss as the deviation from average historical loss by "a prudent margin, say a factor of two." Indeed, Vojta's model for capital adequacy considered even concentration, but in a heuristic manner.

The expected loss is represented by the equation:

$$\text{Expected Loss} \mid \text{Probability of default} \times \text{Default severity}$$

where default severity is defined as a percent of the loan that is lost. For example, if the probability of default is 30 percent and the default severity is 60 percent (which is the same as a recovery rate of 40 percent), the expected loss is 30 percent times 60 percent, or 18 percent of par.

This concept is widely used. Moody's uses diversity scores and the expected and unexpected losses associated with collateral of a particular rating level to come up with the credit protection desired to achieve a certain rating. The higher the diversity score, the lower are the unexpected loss coverage requirements. Table 18.4 illustrates the degree of credit protection (overcollateralization) Moody's (1991, 12) requires before it will rate a structured finance transaction as Aaa. The degree of credit protection can also be understood as the level of losses that the pool of assets can withstand.

If the probability of default for a risk class (such as rating) is stable, then we can factor credit losses into the expected value calculations for inclusion in pricing. But, as mentioned earlier, the probability of default itself is an estimate and is subject to uncertainty. The concept of unexpected loss *attempts* to takes account of the uncertainty associated with the ex ante probability of default. When actual default rate of different bond grades are examined, it becomes clear that they fluctuate over time—to a great extent because of changing economic conditions.[9] The standard deviation of this default rate may be used as a proxy for the "unexpected" aspect of default. Two standard deviations are added to the mean to derive a "95 percent confidence level" default probability. It is this higher value that is used to derive the unexpected value of the loss to arrive at the capital to be set aside.

TABLE 18.4 Losses Required to be Sustained: Percent of Collateral Rating

Diversity Score	B3	B2	B1	Ba3	Ba2	Ba1	Baa3	Baa2	Baa1	A3	A2	A1	Aa3	Aa2	Aa1
1[a]															
2	100	100	100	100	100	100	85	71	57	52	49	47	45	42	39
3	99	98	97	95	95	92	75	59	43	38	36	35	33	32	30
4	95	92	91	87	84	80	64	50	36	33	31	29	27	25	24
6	90	87	85	83	76	73	58	44	30	27	25	23	22	21	20
7	81	77	73	69	66	60	49	38	27	24	22	20	19	18	17
10	75	69	65	59	58	51	41	33	25	22	20	19	18	17	16
15	66	60	56	51	46	43	36	30	24	21	19	18	17	16	15
20	62	56	51	46	42	38	33	28	23	20	18	17	16	15	14
25	58	53	48	43	38	35	30	26	22	19	17	16	15	14	13
30	56	51	46	40	35	32	28	24	20	17	16	15	14	13	12
35	54	48	44	38	35	30	26	22	19	16	15	14	13	12	11
40	52	47	42	37	33	29	24	20	17	15	14	13	12	11	10

[a]Evaluated case by case.
Source: Moody's (1991)

TABLE 18.5   Average One-Year Default Rate by Bond Rating

Rating	1-Year Default Average 1970–2006 (%)	1-Year Default Std. Deviation 1970–2006 (%)
Aaa	0	0
Aa	0.02	0.10
A	0.02	0.05
Baa	0.17	0.33
Ba	1.14	1.26
B	5.87	4.49
Caa-C	23.34	20.73

Source: Moody's Investors Service (2007).

Table 18.5 shows the one-year default rates experienced by bond rating. Based on this historic experience, the probability of default over a one-year period is 1.14 percent and its standard deviation is 1.26 percent for Ba-rated bonds. In Figure 18.3 the horizontal lines are drawn to show the average and average plus two times the standard deviation. It is worth noting that at least once, the actual default rate crossed over the 95 percent confidence level; that is, exceeded the "unexpected" level.

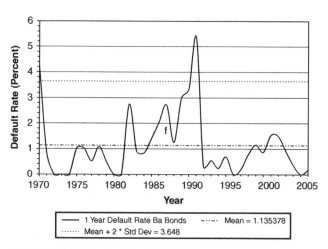

FIGURE 18.3   Ba Defaults 1970–2006
Source: Moody's Investors Service (2007)

OPTIMIZATION OF CAPITAL USAGE

Since economic capital is a scare resource, an optimal portfolio is one that uses it in the most efficient manner. Economic capital is the resource needed to cushion unexpected losses. This reasoning may be used to set up an optimization problem where the objective function is to minimize expected losses in the portfolio, subject to the constraints that:

1. The sum of the unexpected losses is less than or equal to the risk capital.
2. The assets are allocated from among only those available.

Although this approach to portfolio management is on a name by name basis, for *strategic* analysis, the problem may be stated in terms of allocation among asset *classes*.

The portfolio problem may also be restated as follows:

$$\text{Minimize: } -\sum (\text{Unexpected Loss})^i$$

Subject to:

1. $\sum (\text{Portfolio weights})^i = 1$
2. $\sum (\text{Expected interest income} - \text{Expected loss}) \geq \text{target return on equity}$
3. (3) Total assets $\leq 100/\text{Capital ratio}$.

Note that the higher return required to justify higher expected losses is modeled in the second constraint. Given next is an example using a portfolio of bonds. Table 18.6 contains the input data for the portfolio. How much should be invested in AAA, AA, A, BBB, BB, B? Given the information provided, is there an obvious answer for the optimum portfolio?

The objective function is to minimize unexpected losses:

$$\frac{\sum_{i=1}^{i=6} w_i(p_i + 2^*d_i)(1 - r_i)}{C}$$

In this equation, w_i is the fraction invested in bond rating i. This is multiplied by the term $(p_i + 2^*d_i)$, which is default probability plus 2

TABLE 18.6 Input Data for the Optimization Problem

	Portfolio Weights	Overall Capital Ratio (constant): Capital/Total Risk Asset (%)	Spread (%)	Probability of Default (%)	Standard Deviation (%)	Recovery Rate (%)
Symbol	w_i	C	m_i	p_i	d_i	r_I
AAA	?	8.00	0.40	0.00	0.00	78
AA	?	8.00	0.65	0.02	0.12	77
A	?	8.00	1.20	0.01	0.05	57
BBB	?	8.00	1.60	0.15	0.30	53
BB	?	8.00	2.40	1.22	1.35	42
B	?	8.00		6.32	4.78	35

standard deviations. This is multiplied by $(1 - r_i)$, which is the amount of the loan that cannot be recovered. The sum of this quantity taken over all the bond ratings and divided by the capital ratio gives the total value of the unexpected losses from the portfolio, sometimes referred to as the *economic capital*. This value will scale to the true capital that will be needed either dollar for dollar or in some other proportion.

The first constraint is that the portfolio weights add up to 100 percent:

$$\sum_{i=1}^{i=6} w_i = 100$$

The second constraint is that the rate of return on the equity is greater than or equal to a target amount. This constraint captures the leverage, because it is only through leverage that earnings may be magnified.

$$\frac{\sum_{i=1}^{i=6} w_i m_i}{C} \geq \text{Target return on ROE}$$

This is a simple optimization problem that may be solved on a personal computer using commercially available optimization software. The solution calculated using various levels of target ROE is shown in Table 18.7.

The results are what one would expect. To increase the net earnings, you have to go down-market and be prepared for more losses albeit with higher revenues. Note that the losses grow at a very rapid rate. Since probabilities and standard deviations are based on actual bond market experience over

TABLE 18.7 Optimal Solutions

Target ROE	Optimal Solution	Expected Loss	Unexpected Loss	Net Income
5%	100% in AAA	0	0	5.00
10%	49.7% in AAA 50.3% in A	0.027	0.297	10.00
15%	98.7% in A 1.3 % in BBB	0.0644	0.640	15.00
20%	56.7% in BBB 53.3% in BB	4.3278	14.798	20.00

a very long period, it does not appear to make economic sense (on a risk-reward basis) to go below BB or equivalent to achieve 15 percent to 20 percent ROE. The highest ROE attainable in this portfolio was found to be 21.5 with the available risk-return choices. While these conclusions may be obvious for a small number of securities, the problem soon gets more complicated as further gradations of risk are added and limits are imposed on (1) various segments to reflect the limited number of borrowers of a certain credit quality in that segment; and (2) risk-based regulatory capital. This is where an optimization approach will help reveal the trade-offs.

We did not consider any covariances or multiperiod choices. Special risk-based capital constraints were not imposed because the capital required is the same for all bond grades. Since the bond ratings are considered to apply consistently across all industries, it is quite likely that the correlation of defaults among the rating classes is very low; in other words there will be some gain in diversifying across bond ratings. The results of the foregoing example should therefore vary if correlations are incorporated and a longer time dimension (say, five years) is used.[10]

Portfolio approaches for fixed income assets are still in the process of evolution. Most portfolio optimization solutions proposed today share the approach just described but may differ in (1) the design of the objective function; (2) the sources of data for correlation and default probability; and (3) attention to credit migration before an asset reaches one of the final states (maturity of the loan, refinancing or default).

VARYING OBJECTIVES

Managing a portfolio of assets means different things to different people. Pension plan managers may look at portfolio management as an asset allocation problem—how much to invest in various sectors and how to re-balance the portfolio as expectations change. Capital constraints or taxes are not a part of their investment equation. Brinson, Hood, and Beebower (1986) decomposed the way professional money managers view investment returns and found that they identified three basic components—investment policy (asset mix), market timing, and security selection. Their research indicated that market timing and security selection influenced total plan returns far less than asset allocation policy did. Insurance companies and banks, by contrast, have to take into account regulatory capital and the capital charges applied by the rating agencies. They also have a different liability structure, which must be accommodated by the portfolio strategy. Some of the assets available for investment (such as credit card receivables) come *prediversi-fied;* the portfolio model used by an investor should be able to distinguish between these and other single-risk securities such as corporate bonds. For financial guarantee companies, the option feature of the guarantee (there are no claims until the transaction-specific first loss levels in the portfolio are exceeded) should be modeled in assessing the earnings variability to be expected from a portfolio of businesses. At the business unit level, default correlation between one transaction and another or between two portfolios may be difficult to estimate. The next two chapters consider the approaches that are available to address these questions.

REFERENCES

Beckers, S. 1996. "Survey of Risk Measurement Theory and Practice." In *Handbook of Risk Management,* edited by C. Alexander. New York: John Wiley & Sons.

Bennett, P. 1984. "Applying Portfolio Theory to Global Bank Lending." *Journal of Banking and Finance* 153–169.

Bernstein, P. 1996. *Against the Gods: The Remarkable Story of Risk.* New York: John Wiley & Sons.

Brinson, G.P, L.R. Hood, and G.L. Beebower. 1986. "Determinants of Portfolio Performance." *Financial Analysts Journal* 40–48.

Chirinko, R. S., and G. D. Guill. 1991. "A Framework for Assessing Credit Risk in Depository Institutions: Toward Regulatory Reform." *Journal of Banking and Finance* 785–804.

Coopers and Lybrand. 1993. "Growth and Diversification: Are the Benefits Always There?" In *Mortgage Banking,* edited by J. Lederman. Chicago: Probus.

Credit Suisse Group. 1996, December. *CreditRisk+.* New York.

Elton, E., and M. Gruber. 1981. *Modern Portfolio Theory and Investment Analysis,* 1st ed. New York: John Wiley & Sons.

————. 1995. *Modern Portfolio Theory and Investment Analysis,* 5th ed. New York: John Wiley & Sons.

Federal Reserve System, Board of Governors. 1993. Risks of Concentration of Credit and Nontraditional Activities, Washington D.C., March 26.

Gupton, G. M., C. C. Finger, and M. Bhatia. 1997, April. *CreditMetrics: The Benchmark for Understanding Credit Risk.* New York: JPMorgan.

Hopper, J. 1997, July. John Hopper, Barclays Bank, London, interviewed by P. Narayanan.

Klein, R. A., and J. Lederman. 1996. *Derivatives Risk and Responsibility.* Chicago: Irwin Professional Publishing.

Lucas, D. J. 1995. "Default Correlation and Credit Analysis." *Journal of Fixed Income.*

Markowitz, H. 1959. *Portfolio Selection: Efficient Diversification of Investments.* New York: John Wiley & Sons.

Markowitz, H., and A. Perold. 1981. "Portfolio Analysis with Scenarios and Factors." *Journal of Finance* 36:871–877.

McKinsey & Co. 1997. Measuring Credit Portfolio Risk: A New Approach. IAFE Annual Meeting, Zurich, June 10.

McQuown, J. 1994. All That Counts is Diversification: In Bank Asset Portfolio Management. IMI Bank Loan Portfolio Management Conference, May 11, 1994.

Merton, R. C. 1974. "On the Pricing of Corporate Debt." *Journal of Finance* 449–470.

Moody's Investor's Service. 1990. "Corporate Bond Defaults and Default Rates, 1970–1989." *Moody's Special Report,* April.

———. 1991. "Rating Cash Flow Transactions Backed by Corporate Debt." *Moody's Structured Finance,* March.

———. 1996. "The Binomial Expansion Method Applied to CBO/CLU Analysis." *Moody's Special Report,* December.

Ranson, B. 1993. "Rabbit Stew." *Balance Sheet* (Spring):37–40.

Ross, S. A., and R. Roll. 1984. "The Arbitrage Pricing Theory Approach to Strategic Portfolio Planning." *Financial Analysts Journal.*

Sharpe, W. 1994. "The Sharpe Ratio." *Journal of Portfolio Management* 49–58.

Standard & Poor's. 1991. "Corporate Bond Default Study." *Credit Week,* 16 September.

Treynor, J. L., and F. Black. 1973. "How to Use Security Analysis to Improve Portfolio Selection." *Journal of Business* 46, no. 1:66–86.

Vojta, G. J. 1973. *Bank Capital Adequacy.* New York: First National City Bank.

CHAPTER 19

Economic Capital and Capital Allocation

Essential as it is to put aside "unimportant" features and to stress
"important" ones in formulating classes [abstract concepts], the
dangers of this intellectual operation are great. A necessary
generalization can easily evolve into an overgeneralization. And as
a rule we have no opportunity to test in advance whether a
concept we have developed has struck the right degree of
abstraction or is an overgeneralization.

—Dietrich Dörner (1995, 94)[1]

A question that might come to an astute reader at the mention of economic capital is *what does economic capital have to do with managing credit risk?* The term *economic capital* made its appearance in the previous chapter, but no attempt was made to directly relate it to credit risk. When any institution operates a business, it has to deal with a number of risks, sometimes just a handful, and sometimes hundreds of risks. A short list for a major bank would include interest rate risk, currency risk, credit risk, country risk, and operational risk. For an insurer, there will be insurance risk (such as the risks of catastrophic events or mortality risks) as well. With every risk type, there would be concentration and diversification effects in the portfolio from the constituents of the portfolio. In addition, there can be correlation *between* risk types such as between credit and market risk. *Required* economic capital for a firm as a whole is the notional amount of capital to withstand an extreme but rare loss event after taking into account all the interactions of the risks in the portfolio. For example, if we were to construct a loss distribution showing the total loss to the firm at various probability levels after combining all of its individual risks, then we can arbitrarily chose a confidence level of, say, 99 percent and pick the loss at that level and call that the required economic capital.[2] The firm needs to have sufficient *real* capital to withstand this loss and still remain solvent. The solvency criterion is important to not only the owners of the firm, but also its creditors. It is for this reason that the rating agencies look at the economic capital of the institutions for which they issue a rating either for the firm's debt or its claims paying ability (see Standard & Poor's 2007). If the loss distribution is symmetrical, then the multiple of the standard deviation of the distribution is a sufficient measure of the extreme loss (for example for a normal distribution mean plus three times the standard deviation yield the loss at 99.73 percent confidence level). But for other skewed and fat-tailed distributions the use of the standard deviation would not lead to an accurate value of the loss at a specified confidence level.

Once the required economic capital of a firm is estimated, it should be compared with the total capital of the firm. Total capital of the firm is its market capitalization. If firm's equity capital less than the economic capital then firm is in a risk position that cannot be sustained because the available capital is negative. If the total capital of the firm is greater than the required economic capital, then it means that the market views the firm as having additional value that gives it the resilience to absorb shocks and continue in business, and have the elbow room to grow, or the capacity to refund the excess capital if it does not see growth opportunities. Economic capital is thus a useful yardstick both internally and externally. It is inherently a *portfolio* concept in that the total risk taking ability of any firm is increased if it is able to diversify instead of concentrating: concentration can lead to larger than normal losses. However, it is possible to isolate the economic capital impact of an *individual asset* or a *subportfolio* or a *product* if we were to view it in association with the rest of the portfolio. The allocated capital can then become a benchmark against which ex ante decisions (such as pricing) and ex post analysis (such as performance evaluation) may be undertaken. Since economic capital is a measure of the solvency risk to the firm rather than an accounting number such a book value of equity, it provides the management of the firm to assess the performance of business units of varying risk on a common benchmark. Economic capital is concept that applies to all risks, but for banks, it is most pertinent with regard to credit risk because *most banks failures are traceable to credit losses.*

Before we delve into the use of economic capital, let us return to the three basic questions that an institution faces as it takes an incremental credit risk:

1. What kind of "gatekeeping" function is needed such that every incremental asset originated is acceptable from a portfolio perspective? In other words, how should the originator operate?

2. After assets have been acquired, what can be done about the composition of the portfolio? What, in particular, is the right level of diversification? In other words, how should the portfolio manager operate?
3. How much capital was consumed in taking on the incremental risk?

Answers to these approaches depend partly on how well a bank can measure the risk and return attributes of the investment, but even more so on portfolio strategies available to the institution. Quite clearly, the strategy of "originate and retain" will provide a solution different from a strategy of "originate and retain or hedge or sell."

USE OF THE PRICING MECHANISM

Historically, when acquiring an asset, an institution used the pricing mechanism in conjunction with product, geography, industry, or tenor limits. For example, if a bank believes that construction loans for suburban malls are unattractive from a portfolio perspective, it can raise the price of these loans to a level that will act as a disincentive to borrowers. This is an instance of marginal cost pricing—the notion that the price of an asset should compensate the institution for its marginal cost as measured on a risk-adjusted basis. The more a product increases a lender's portfolio concentration, the higher its marginal cost to that lender. Marginal cost pricing may not always work. A bank may have idle capacity—a large cost base and capital that has not been deployed. While such an institution clearly would not want to make a loan at a negative spread, it would probably view even a small positive spread as worthwhile as long as the added risk was acceptable it is able to justify the transaction in the context of overall relationship profitability.

Institutions tend to book unattractively priced loans when they are unable to allocate their cost base with clarity or to make fine differentiations of their risks. If a bank cannot allocate its costs, then it will make no distinction between the cost of lending to borrowers that require little analysis and the cost of lending to borrowers requiring a considerable amount of review and follow up. Similarly, if the spread is tied to a too-coarsely graded risk rating system (one, for example, with just four grades) then it is more difficult to risk differentiate in pricing than if the risk rating is graduated over a larger scale with, say, 15 grades.

A cost-plus-profit pricing strategy works in the short run, but in the long run competition exerts a downward pressure on pricing. Cost-plus-profit pricing will still work so long as a bank has some flexibility to compete on an array of services rather than exclusively on price. The difficulties with pricing are greater in markets where the lender is a price taker rather than a price leader.

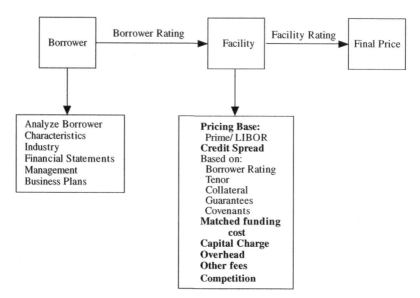

FIGURE 19.1 Traditional Loan Pricing Methodology

Traditional pricing for credit risk has followed the cost-plus-profit approach as shown in Figure 19.1.

An illustrative example using the traditional approach is given below. The pricing is based on the borrower's risk rating, tenor, collateral, guarantees, and covenants. A capital charge is applied based on a hurdle rate and a capital ratio. Table 19.1 shows the historic loss rate used for each of the risk rating categories. This is used to calculate the expected loss allowance to be built into the price.

Based on the yield curve, Table 19.2 shows the cost of funds for various maturities from one to five years.

TABLE 19.1 Historic Loss Rate by Internal Risk Rating

Rating	Historic 5 Year Lost Rate (%)
Aaa	0.034
Aa	0.106
A	0.264
Baa	1.166
Ba	6.371
B	15.737

Source: Moody's Investors Service (2007).

TABLE 19.2 Term Structure of Rates

Maturity	Cost of Funds (%)
1	5
2	5.5
3	6
4	8
5	10
10	12

The two other inputs needed are the capital ratio (8 percent) and the required rate of return on capital (16 percent). Using these assumptions, the rate to be charged for a five-year unsecured loan to a customer rated 5 (equivalent to Ba) comes to 11.75 percent, or a spread of 1.75 over the cost of funds as shown in Table 19.3.

This simple approach to credit pricing works well as long as the assumptions are correct—especially those about the borrower's credit quality.

TABLE 19.3 Price Buildup Based on Cost plus Profit

Item	Calculation	Amount/Value
Borrower's risk rating		5 (Ba)
Loan maturity		5 years
5-year loss rate (mortality)		6.371 percent
Capital ratio		8 percent
Hurdle rate		16 percent
Loan amount		1,000,000
Capital required (8 percent of loan amount)	.08*1,000,000	80,000
Price buildup		
Annual capital charge at 16 percent	0.16*80,000	12,800
Annual funds cost at 10 percent fixed	0.10*920,000	92,000
Annual loan-loss allowance	.01*6.371*1,000,000/5	12,742
Breakeven annual interest income		117,542
Loan interest rate (with no funding risk)	117,542/1,000,000	11.75 percent
Minimum spread	11.75–10.00	175 bp

This method is used in many banks today. Its main drawback is that only "expected" losses are linked to the borrower's credit quality. The capital charge on an 8 percent capital ratio at 16 percent (cost of equity) may not be sufficient if (1) the loan is very risky or (2) very large. Even with same default probability, a loan for $100 million poses a greater risk to the bank than 100 loans for $1 million each: in the former case in case of default, the entire $100 million would be at the risk of nonpayment. In the latter case even with the same default probability is highly unlikely that all 100 loans would default at the same time. A capital charge of 8 percent applied to all loan sizes ignores the effect of severity. Another drawback of this method is that it implicitly assumes only two possible states for a loan—"default" or "no default." It does not model the credit risk premium or discount resulting from improvement or decline in the borrower's financial condition: that is meaningful only if the asset may be repriced or sold at par. This is where the concept of economic capital is helpful. A loan's credit risk may be seen as consisting of two part: an expected loss part which is directly compensated for in pricing (charged to the loan loss reserve) and unexpected loss which is the loan's contribution to the portfolio's extreme loss potential because of the size of the loan, and the degree to which the loan adds to the concentration in the portfolio. The latter is captured by the economic capital measure.

Financial institutions have long grappled with the best ways of allocating capital in a manner consistent with the risks taken. They have found it difficult to come up with a consistent and credible way of allocating capital for such varying sources of revenue as loan commitments, revolving lines of credit (which have no maturity), and secured versus unsecured lending. One approach is to allocate capital to business units based on their asset size. While it is true that a larger portfolio will have larger losses, this approach also means that the business unit is forced to employ all the capital allocated to it. Moreover, this method treats all risks alike. Another approach is to use the regulatory (risk-adjusted) capital as the allocated capital. The problem with this approach is that regulatory capital may or may not reflect the true risk of a business. Yet another approach is to use unexpected losses in a subportfolio (standard deviation of the firm-wide annual losses taken over time) as a proxy for capital to be allocated. The problem with this approach is that it ignores default correlations across subportfolios. The volatility of a subportfolio may in fact dampen the volatility of the institution's portfolio, so pricing decisions based on the volatility of the subportfolio may not be optimal. In practical terms, this means that one line of business within a lending institution may sometimes subsidize another. The resulting synergy makes the institution stronger because the direction of the subsidy may reverse at some future time. Allocated economic capital is a measure that takes into account all these interactions and provides a common framework for assets with differing risk characteristics.

Allocating capital is a goal that can be attained, but in the absence of adequate data and analytics, most banks have largely relied on approximations such as return on assets in the pricing of loans and the measurement of performance. Covenant-specific step-up or step-down pricing, and pricing for migration, or—more generally—for event risk, are rare. It is important for lenders to develop a well-thought out pricing strategy because, in the eyes of shareholders, this is ultimately what drives their performance. In a 1997 interview with the authors, Marc Intrater (1997), Director at Oliver, Wyman & Company observes:

> *Typically "the market" is blamed for pricing inadequacies. It is true that market pricing, on average, is insufficient to meet a risk-adjusted hurdle rate in some markets. However, even as a pure price taker, a bank can select opportunities for participation based upon whether pricing adequately covers risk and/or leads to sufficient relationship profitability. Furthermore, most banks are not pure price takers in all, or even most, lending situations. In price making situations, a well-designed pricing strategy is obviously critical.*

The development of a good pricing strategy is a matter of understanding the loan's component parts: be it the cash flow sources that make up the total revenue, the term of the loan, the impact of the loan on the risk profile of the portfolio, and the rating/pricing that the loan will obtain in the open market, and the value of the embedded options in the loan commitment. Quantification of the value at risk for a portfolio of loans would be a lot easier were there to be readily available market prices corresponding to the credit terms and credit quality. After all, the value at risk for credit factors is simply one component of the portfolio value at risk due to other factors such as interest rate risk, currency risk, and the like. But if the economic capital needed to support an asset were to be available then that would be the amount based on which the capital charge should be applied, not the flat rate of 8 percent used in the example.

INNOVATIONS BY BANKERS TRUST IN CAPITAL ALLOCATION

The first innovation is capital allocation then logically came from the portion of a bank's balance sheet that can be readily marked to market. Bankers Trust led the charge by articulating and implementing the RAROC (risk-adjusted return on capital) concept. Here, according Gene Guill (2007, 4) is how it started:

> *Like most innovations that drive the economic system forward, modern risk management practices were born out of economic opportunity and competitive pressures to survive. But innovations require entrepreneurs, and the key entrepreneur in this story is Charles Sanford. Sanford joined Bankers Trust in 1961 after completing an MBA at the Wharton School and a brief sojourn in academics. He started his banking career as a commercial lending officer, but moved to the bank's Resources Management department in 1969 and subsequently became department head in 1973.*
>
> *Initially, Resources Management was responsible for trading foreign exchange, government bonds, municipal bonds, and other short-term financial instruments, funding the bank, and managing the bank's investment account. Its mandate was later expanded to include trading of corporate bonds, derivatives, and equities. Several months into his position as department head, Sanford ran into a government bond trader as he was leaving for the day. As they walked out of the building, Sanford asked, "How did you do today?" The trader responded, "I brought 'em in and shot 'em out. Didn't make any money."*
>
> *The shallowness of that statement stuck in Sanford's mind. Did this trader have a good day or a bad day? Did he pay/receive a good price or a bad price for the bonds that he bought/sold? How should his performance be evaluated? Should it be evaluated relative to the market or against an absolute benchmark? In general, what is the correct way to think about a trader's performance?*
>
> *In considering these questions, Sanford hit upon three principles well established in modern finance but never integrated and applied to managing a firm:*
>
> 1. *By taking a position—that is, by buying bonds—the trader brought risk into the bank and used the bank's capital.*
> 2. *The only reason to take risk is to earn a return. In taking the position, the trader should have had an expectation of earning a return. Furthermore, the higher the risk, the higher the return the trader should expect.*
> 3. *To justify the use of shareholders' capital, the trader's expectation for return must be consistent with the minimum return for similar risk required by shareholders. Working with these principles, Sanford set out to relate individual transactions to the use of the bank's capital.*

Sanford hypothesized that the value-creating capacity of an asset (or a business), when expressed as ratio of return to the risk taken allows comparisons to be made between assets (or businesses) of varying sizes and risk characteristics. When an institution can observe asset prices directly (and/or infer risk from observable asset prices) then it can determine how much shareholder's capital it needs to hold based on the volatility of the asset. If the capital to be held is excessive relative to the *total return* that would be earned from the asset, then the bank will not acquire it. If the asset is already in the bank's portfolio, it will be sold or hedged. Bankers Trust called the metric that captured the value-creating capacity of an asset or a product is RAROC—*risk-adjusted return on capital.* [3]

As defined by Bankers Trust (1995), RAROC allocates a capital charge to a transaction or a line of business at an amount equal to the maximum expected loss (at 99 percent confidence level) over one year on an after-tax basis. As may be expected, the higher the volatility of returns, the higher the capital allocated. The higher capital allocation means that the transaction has to generate cash flows large enough to offset the volatility of returns, which results from the credit risk, market risk and other risks taken. The RAROC process estimates the asset value that may prevail in the worst-case scenario and then equates the capital cushion to be provided to loss that would be sustained. There are four basic steps in this process:

Step 1. Analyze the activity or product and determine the basic risk categories that it contains such as interest rate (country, directional, basis, yield curve, optionality), foreign exchange, equity, commodity, credit, and operating risk.

Step 2. Quantify the risk in each category by a market proxy.

Step 3. Using the historical price movements of the market proxy over the past three years, compute a market risk factor, given by the equation:

- RAROC risk factor $= 2.33 \times$ Weekly volatility $\times \sqrt{52} \times (1 -$ Tax rate)
- In the above equation, the multiplier 2.33 gives the volatility (expressed as a percent) at the 99 percent confidence level. (It is assumed that the distribution is normal.) The term $\sqrt{52}$ converts the weekly price movement into an annual movement. The term $(1 -$ Tax rate) converts the calculated value to an after-tax basis.

Step 4. Compute the dollar amount of capital required for each risk category by multiplying the risk factor by the size of the position.

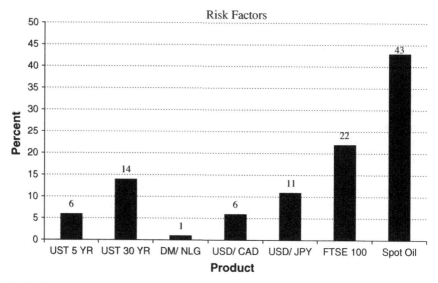

FIGURE 19.2 RAROC Risk Factors

Figure 19.2 gives the risk factors for a sample of seven products: 5- and 30-year Treasuries, Deutsche Mark/Guilder, U.S. dollar/Canadian dollar, U.S. dollar/Yen, FTSE 100, and spot oil.

Establishing the maximum expected loss in each product line and linking the capital to this loss makes it possible to compare products of different risk levels by stating the risk side of the risk-reward equation in a consistent manner. The risk to reward ratios thus becomes comparable. To illustrate, let us compare two traders: one trading U.S. government bonds with a US$100 million position and the other trading Canadian dollars with an average position of US$100 million.

According to Figure 19.2, the government trading unit would require a capital allocation of $14 million and the Canadian dollar trader would require only $6 million. If both units made the same profit of, say, $2 million, then the bond trader's RAROC is 2/14 = 14.3 percent whereas the FX trader's RAROC is 2/6 = 33.3 percent. In an institution that uses RAROC, a business unit does not have a fixed amount of capital. Rather, sufficient capital is allocated to it based on the need to support the desired business volume.

RAROC is an improvement over the traditional approach in that it allows one to compare two businesses with different risk (volatility of returns) profiles. Using a hurdle rate, a lender can also use the RAROC principle to set the target pricing on a relationship or a transaction. Although not all assets have market price distribution, RAROC is a first step toward examining an institution's entire balance sheet on a mark-to-market basis—if only to understand the risk-return trade-offs that have been made.

The astute reader will no doubt have observed that the RAROC for the individual line of business is explicitly neither penalized nor rewarded for concentrations, and the return correlations are basically those that are the consequence of the correlations in the historical time series and are not prospective.

In 1991, Bankers Trust expanded RAROC into what it has termed a *comprehensive risk management system* and named it *RAROC 2020*, signifying that "this platform will serve . . . clients well into the next century." RAROC 2020 includes portfolio concepts, and it assumes that market prices are available for the products in the portfolio. By implication, the market prices include credit risk, so there is little direct emphasis on default as an event that drives asset value. One of the elements of RAROC 2020 is the calculation of *daily price volatility* (DPV). This is a *value-at-risk* measure that shows the maximum potential economic loss of the portfolio overnight.

Table 19.4 summarizes some of the newly coined acronyms and some of the older ones that have appeared in the literature for these ratios. The most important of these, the RAROC, is described next.

VALUE AT RISK

Bankers Trust introduced the notion of daily price volatility. JPMorgan built RiskMetrics on a similar idea: to calculate the market value at risk for a portfolio of liquid assets if varying complexity in terms of interest payment terms, maturity, currency, and optionality.

Many assets in a bank's balance sheet have options embedded in them—some of them deliberate, and others introduced through custom and practice. A floating rate loan, for example, may have a rate cap, and a mortgage has a prepayment option. When options are involved, the value of an asset can change in nonlinear fashion with respect to the underlying variables.[4] When there are nonlinearities, the impact on value of future market conditions may be estimated only through simulations (see Chapter 9).

RiskMetrics is a collection of methodologies and datasets designed to help an institution derive its portfolio value at risk. It provides a set of tools to map its products to standardized risk positions. These positions are fed into a variance-covariance matrix to derive the portfolio return and variance. RiskMetrics estimates this matrix using historic data and a multitude of techniques ranging from simple exponential smoothing, autoregressive moving

TABLE 19.4 Risk-adjusted Performance Measurements

Acronym	Definition	Numerator	Denominator
ROA (return on assets) expressed in basis points	This is the venerable ratio that banks have historically used to measure performance. Unfortunately this measure does not account for risk.	Net income after loan loss provision	Average or end-of-period assets (book value)
ROE (return on equity) expressed as a percentage	This is measure does not take into account risk. It also begs the question of what the denominator should be for a single loan or line of business.	Net income after loan loss provision	Average or end-of-period equity (equity capital and retained earnings)
VaR (value at risk) expressed in Maximum $ loss at 99 percent confidence level	This is a late arrival on the scene, but the quantity it represents is based on the long-held view that capital allocated should serve as the cushion against all unexpected losses. VaR is a measure of maximum expected loss from an asset. Sometimes VaR = Allocated capital. At other times the relationship is governed by the confidence level desired.	Maximum dollar loss expected with probability of 99 percent	Acquisition cost of the asset (Note that this quantity will account for the premium or discount paid when the asset was acquired. For a bank, most of the time it will be the book value of the asset.)
MTM (mark to market) expressed as a percentage of par (book value)	This is the present market value of an asset. The relationship between VaR and MTM is that MTM is a realization of a statistical distribution, whereas VaR is the value associated with the 99 (for example) percent probability in the distribution. MTM is a measure of value as it is; VaR is a measure of the impact of value as it could be under adverse conditions.	Market value of asset	Book value of asset

Measure	Description	Numerator	Denominator
MTM (mark to model) expressed as a percentage of par (or book value)	This is the present market value of an asset. The relationship between VaR and MTM is that MTM is a realization of a statistical distribution, whereas VaR is the value associated with the 99 (for example) percent probability in the distribution. MTM is a measure of value as it is; VaR is a measure of the impact of value as it could be under adverse conditions.	Market value of asset	Book value of asset
RORAA (return on risk-adjusted assets)	This is a refinement of ROA, with the denominator adjusted to account the varying riskiness of the asset classes.	Net income	Assets grossed up or down based on credit risk. For example, U.S. Treasuries may have a risk weighting of 1, whereas C&I loans, a weighting of 1.15.
RAROC (risk-adjusted return on capital)	Return on capital allocated to the business. The allocation is based on unexpected losses.	Net income	Position size multiplied by the risk factor. Risk factor is based on volatility of market value (see details in chapter).

average models, and other sophisticated forecasting techniques. This set of tools provides an institution with an easy way to calculate its risk positions directly, without having to invest in the development of databases and software. It may be noted that the value at risk calculated is the daily value and may be calculated only in a mark-to-market world. Where prices are unavailable, mark-to-model approaches may have to be used. Even in simulations, components using no-arbitrage arguments may prove to be unreliable when there are large price movements and a drop in liquidity.[5]

Analytically, the VaR concept as described before are equally applicable to credit risk. The only difficulty is that unlike market risk, the change in value attributable to credit risk is not readily observable. This has led to innovations that link the value of the credit risky asset to its credit quality change. Moody's KMV Portfolio Manager is a good example.

ECONOMIC CAPITAL AND REGULATORY CAPITAL

Economic capital is management's internal assessment of the capital cushion to be provided to the asset or the line of business. Regulatory capital is what the regulators think is the capital required by an institution in order to operate in a safe and sound manner so that public interest is protected. How regulatory capital is derived varies with the type of financial institution. For banks, it is based on BIS (Bank for International Settlement, Basel) standards commonly referred to as BIS I and II, but would have to be formally accepted by various sovereign jurisdictions.[6] In Europe and other parts of the world, regulation of banks is generally within the purview of a single agency (FSA in the United Kingdom, for example). In the United States, regulatory authority for shared between the Fed (Federal Reserve), OTS (Office of Thrift Supervision), FDIC (Federal Deposit Insurance Corporation), and OCC (Office of the Controller of Currency). Capital adequacy of broker-dealers is regulated by the SEC (Securities and Exchange Commission). For insurers, which are state-regulated, capital requirements are recommended by the NAIC (National Association of Insurance Commissioners) and adopted by the states. In Europe, the regulation for insurers is under Solvency I and II. Rating agencies (Moody's, S&P, Fitch, A.M. Best, etc.), which issue ratings for the insurer's debt and their claims paying ability, also closely monitor insurers' capital adequacy. While all agencies are concerned with solvency the regulations vary widely in complexity.

When regulatory capital is used in the pricing of assets, there is no a priori reason for the total capital needed to equal the regulatory capital. Regulatory capital often does not give credit for diversification. In Basel II, for example, the capital required for one A-rated loan for $10 million is the same as for 10 A-rated loans of $1 million each. Another example, Basel II, regulatory capital does not increase with maturity beyond five years whereas some would argue that the value at risk is greater for longer maturities of say 30 years. While in order to set optimal allocations of capital, therefore, both economic and regulatory constraints have to be taken into account, regulatory capital would be inaccurate for transaction pricing.[7] Regulatory capital requirements are designed to be applicable to a wide range of institutions. They are, of necessity, blunt instruments (Marvin 1996, 2) requiring simplified assumptions, and they achieve consistency at the expense of accuracy.

ESTIMATION AND OPTIMIZATION OF ECONOMIC CAPITAL

Mathematical optimization introduced in Chapter 17 is useful in deciding on the right amount of capital to be allocated among competing assets and products. The regulatory capital ratio, economic capital, and the book value of equity may be modeled as constraints, so that the resulting capital allocated to an asset class satisfies all of them. The assumption made in this approach is that an institution should have no more capital than it needs (because that will result in lower return on stockholders equity) and no less capital than would be dictated by the risk exposure (unexpected losses) it has assumed. In the optimization process, any resulting excess capital is treated as if it were invested at a riskless rate of return, signaling to the objective function that excess capital is economically unattractive. In practical terms, if an institution discovers that it has more capital than it needs, it may either take on more risk or decide to repurchase its stock. The latter sends a signal to the market that the institution is not prepared to alter its chosen tolerance for risk. *Postoptimality analysis* is very helpful in identifying the factors and their marginal cost that constrain the institution from reaching goals superior to those indicated by the optimal solution.

In mathematical optimization, the objective function is set up such that the total profit contribution made by a decision variable increases (or decreases) with the increase or decrease in the value of the variable. For example, if the decision variable is the percent to be invested in BBB bonds, then as this quantity increases, the total income from the investment in BBB's increases. The increase in the profit may be linear or quadratic, or in the opposite direction, but whatever it is, it is always assumed to be *monotonically increasing or decreasing*. But what about an investment in the interest rate cap business or an option? The profit contribution will be positive for some values of interest rates, and zero or even negative for others, depending on interest rates. In the case of options, the payoff is nonlinear in some parts of the profit function and zero or negative in others. Because it is difficult to model such products with the standard optimization techniques, Monte Carlo simulation (introduced in Chapter 9) is perhaps the only way to assess the impact by modeling the behavior of the asset under a variety of stochastic scenarios.[8] Of course, when Monte Carlo simulation is used, we no longer have the benefit of being able to find the optimum strategy directly because the simulations merely sample the world as we describe it to the computer. The degree of detail to be used in formulating the optimization or simulation model depends on the complexity of the institution and on whether the objective is strategic or tactical. As Dörner (1996) notes in the passage quoted at the beginning of this chapter, what may be a generalization to one institution—such as treating all bonds as one category of investments—may be an overgeneralization to another, which would prefer to break them down, for example, by sector, maturity, and risk rating.

Competition, risk-based capital standards, scale economies attained through industry consolidation, capital allocation techniques, lessons from history—whatever may be the driving factors, innovation in pricing and portfolio management is evident in today's financial institutions. New approaches have been developed to estimate the credit value risk for economic capital and techniques for allocating it to individual assets and businesses. These applications are described in the next chapter.

REFERENCES

Altman, E. I, and V. M. Kishore. 1997. Defaults and Returns on High Yield Bonds: Analysis Through 1996. White Paper, NYU Salomon Center.

Bankers Trust New York Corporation. 1995, August. *RAROC*ϑ *& Risk Management: Quantifying the Risks of Business*. New York.

Beckers, S. 1996. "A Survey of Risk Measurement Theory and Practice." In *Handbook of Risk Management and Analysis*, edited by C. Alexander. New York: John Wiley & Sons.

Dörner, D. 1996. *The Logic of Failure*. New York: Holt.

Guill, G. D. 2007. Bankers Trust and the Birth of Modern Risk Management. White Paper, Wharton Financial Institutions Center, University of Pennsylvania.

Intrater, M. 1997. Marc Intrater, Director, Oliver, Wymon & Company, interviewed by authors.

Jorian, P. 1997. *Value at Risk: The New Benchmark for Controlling Derivatives Risk*. Chicago: Irwin.

JPMorgan, Inc., 1997. *RiskMetrics*®, 4th ed. New York.

Marvin, S. G. 1996. Capital Allocation: A Study of Current and Evolving Practices in Selected Banks. OCC Staff Study 96–1, December.

Matten, C. 1996. *Managing Bank Capital: Capital Allocation and Performance Measurement.* New York: John Wiley & Sons.

Moody's Investors Service. 2007. *Special Comment: Corporate Bond Defaults and Default Rates, 1920–2006.* New York.

Robert Morris Associates, Inc., First Manhattan Consulting Group. 1997. Credit Portfolio Measurement and Management Survey Findings. Philadelphia, August 21.

Standard & Poors. 2007. Request for Comment: Economic Capital Review Process for Insurers, Standard and Poor's Corporation, Standard & Poor's Rating Service, February 5, 2007.

Wilson, T. C. 1996. "Calculating Risk Capital." In *Handbook of Risk Management and Analysis*, edited by C. Alexander. New York: John Wiley & Sons.

CHAPTER 20

Application of Portfolio Approaches

If I have seen further it is by standing on the shoulders of Giants.
—Sir Isaac Newton (1675)

The assessed probability of default on the part of the borrower is an important input in the credit decision. At portfolio level, other factors come into play: the actual exposure at default (the extent to which a credit line has been utilized); how the probability of default evolves over time; how underlying factors can affect the probability of default of many credits simultaneously; and lastly, the prospects of recovery once default has occurred. These other considerations lie at the heart of new approaches to portfolio analysis and for deriving the capital requirements—both internally and externally.

Innovations in financial modeling have led to the development of *credit value at risk* in a manner similar to market *value at risk* (VaR). Financial regulators have also kept up with these innovations as evident in the refinements made in BIS II relative to BIS I. In BIS I, capital requirement was primarily driven by the probability of default.[1] While it is hard to pinpoint a single reason as the cause for these financial innovations, it is fair to say that concentration risk and the lack of discrimination in BIS I in assigning the same capital charge for corporate credits regardless of default risk were two primary drivers of change, which gave rise to improved portfolio modeling, asset securitization for capital relief, and the development of credit derivative markets.

In a 1997 interview with the authors, Stephen Thieke, Retired Chairman, Risk Management Committee of JPMorgan, Inc., stated:

Previously, banks had only two options with regard to loans: go long or go longer. The current changes in the market allow a bank to go short. This greatly changes the flexibility banks have in managing portfolio concentration.

Marking to market, or valuing assets and liabilities at market prices, has been adopted by major banking institutions—not only for purposes of selling assets, but also for help in deciding which risks to retain in the portfolio and which markets to emphasize. Valuation is applied to both liquid and illiquid assets. According to Thieke, JPMorgan marks its portfolio to market for internal management purposes:

> *Management sees the portfolio on a total return basis, adjusted for changes in rating and credit/market spreads. The nature of the valuation is more by way of mark-to-model than mark-to-market because correlations of credit risk cannot be observed, and there is a large judgmental element in credit assessment. The system is driven by the internal risk rating, which is assigned by a disciplined analytic process to reflect all the expectations of the key factors. The default probabilities and recovery assumptions are not changed frequently, but the results are a lot better than those obtained by taking the view that a loss is not a loss until it is written off. The old way meant not coming to grips with the asset value until it was too late.*

Deciding what constitutes an acceptable or unacceptable risk profile has both quantitative and qualitative aspects. Quantitatively, an institution can approximate the spreads desired for components of risk. The key components of risk are market risk and credit risk, but there are other risks too, such as operational and settlement risk. Market risk is the risk that the value of the asset will drop due to changes in interest rates, as happens when you are using short-term money to finance a long-term fixed rate mortgage and the funding rate goes up. Credit risk is the risk that a borrower's ability to pay will diminish or disappear altogether (see our discussion of credit migration in Chapter 16). In Steve Thieke's words:

> *It means moving away from a two-state model to a multistate model. If you hypothesize in taking credit risk that there are a lot of states between life and death, then you come to a different conclusion. When you made that 5-year loan to a AA-rated credit, you may have been right about its credit quality. Five years later that credit has turned into a BB+. You got your money back, but you sure have wasted the shareholders' resources in mispricing it as an AA.*

Marking to market for *market risk* is more straightforward because the market prices are available every day. Marking to market for *credit risk* is more difficult because it is very subjective: it is much harder to detect changes is credit quality and even harder to incorporate default correlations. Linking the factors driving credit quality change, modeling correlated credit quality and the estimating the value of a credit asset in its changed credit state are answers to the credit VaR puzzle that was solved by the solutions described in this chapter. JPMorgan was among the first to develop credit value at risk in a manner similar to market risk with the release of CreditMetrics with its market risk counterpart, RiskMetrics. Around the same time somewhat alternative approaches were proposed by McKinsey's Credit Portfolio View and Credit Suisse's CreditRisk$^+$. The ideas developed in these approaches have become well accepted and are contained, for example, in Algorithmics' Portfolio Credit Risk Engine Standard and Poor's CDO Evaluator and in Fitch's Vector model for the analysis of collateralized debt obligations. In this chapter we summarize the recently developed models and also some of the earlier efforts. The survey is not exhaustive, but represents the more popular and interesting solutions that have been developed. We conclude this chapter with a discussion of BIS II, which embodies many of these recent innovations.

The studies described in this chapter are summarized in Table 20.1.

MKMV'S PORTFOLIO MANAGER

Moody's KMV (MKMV) Portfolio Manager deals with a portfolio's credit migration, concentration and diversification. To understand how it does this, it would be helpful to start with concepts that have preceded the development of ideas dealing with credit correlation. These ideas were first developed in investment finance (as opposed to banking) and are found to have strong parallels in credit portfolio risk.

OPTIMAL PORTFOLIO AND THE EFFICIENT FRONTIER

The first concept of interest is the idea proposed by Harry Markowitz (1959) on diversification. Markowitz's ideas were related to equities, which have potential for both upside and downside, whereas fixed income assets such as bank loans and bonds have limited upside potential and much greater downside risk. Markowitz showed that, because of low or negative correlation between the returns of individual assets, it is possible to derive optimum weights (proportions of holding) such that, for a given level of return, the optimum portfolio has the lowest level of risk expressed in terms of portfolio standard deviation. Indeed, we can construct an efficient frontier, which is the set of efficient portfolios for different levels of risk and return. Once an investor has derived an efficient frontier, he or she can choose the

TABLE 20.1 Alternative Portfolio Approaches

Technique	Author	Scope	Key Assumption	Ouput
Optimization	Altman (1996)	Individual high yield bonds.	Historic correlations will prevail in the future.	Optimum portfolio weights.
Monte Carlo Simulation	MKMV Corporation (1995)	All assets sensitive to credit risk and for which market prices may be observed or inferred. Includes derivatives. Does not include real estate loans, exotic assets. The next release of MKMV called *Risk Frontier* (2007) handles CDOs, Credit Default Swaps, Equity, and Credit products with embedded options.	Asset value correlations approximate credit quality correlations.	Expected loss, unexpected loss, and portfolio value distribution.
Monte Carlo Simulation	RAROC 2020 (1995)	All assets for which market prices may be observed. Includes derivatives. Does not include real estate loans, consumer loans, exotic assets.	Normal distribution of prices. Historical correlations will hold. Credit risk changes are reflected through the changes in credit spread. Credit migration and default are not explicitly modeled.	Risk-adjusted return on capital, daily price volatility, and limit usage.

Analytical approximation	CreditRisk+	Loans, derivatives, and bonds.	Volatility of default probabilities incorporates the effect of default correlations.	Expected loss, risk contribution, and 99th percentile loss.
Monte Carlo simulation	CreditMetrics (1997)	All assets for which market prices may be observed. Includes derivatives. Does not include real estate loans, consumer loans, exotic assets.	Econometric estimates of parameters will continue to prevail in the future. Equity correlations approximate asset value correlations, which approximate credit quality correlations	Portfolio value, standard deviation of value, and 1% value, marginal risk.
Monte Carlo simulation	McKinsey & Co./Wilson (1997)	Applies to all assets, including real estate and consumer loans.	Econometric estimates of relationships will continue to prevail in the future. The number of firms in a segment is a proxy for portfolio diversification.	Portfolio value distribution.
Optimization	Altman (1996)	Individual high-yield bonds.	Historic correlations will prevail in the future.	Optimum portfolio weights.

optimum portfolio based on his or her risk appetite expressed as the volatility of returns from the portfolio.

Markowitz's pioneering work found application in the domain of market risk; that is, in the analytical space of volatility and correlation of lognormally distributed prices and normally distributed returns. At a basic level, (1) the idea of looking at a collection of holdings as a "portfolio" and the considering investment consequence not in the sense of a single holding, but as it affects the other holdings; and (2) the notion of value at risk; that is, expressing risk as portfolio volatility (standard deviation or unexpected loss) or as tail risk, have their origins in Markowitz's work.

The capital asset pricing model, and the models that followed Markowitz's work, have attempted to simplify and extend these ideas by linking a security's return to market return through the notion of beta. Beta defines an asset's covariance with the market and is used to describe co-movement in security returns. This simplifies the problem so that it is not necessary to keep track of the entire variance-covariance matrix of assets returns. It is pertinent here to note that Markowitz's ideas in portfolio optimization have generally *not* been applied in the fixed income securities mainly because of the asymmetric and fat-tailed nature of fixed income security returns. However, following the publication of the Black-Scholes model for equity options, Robert Merton pointed out that equity and debt, in and by themselves, may be modeled as options and pointed the way to analyzing debt using techniques commonly used in equity analysis. This made it possible use equity portfolio concepts to model correlation of credit quality through "asset" correlation, which is the primary idea behind MKMV's Portfolio Manager.[2] Before showing how this is done, it is useful to touch on the definition of MKMV's EDF (expected default frequency).

From a company's point of view, equity can be described as selling a call option to equity holders on the firm's assets. The equity holders' position is a long call on the firm's asset value—their downside is limited to the invested capital, but their upside is unlimited. From the company's point of view, the debt obligation is equivalent to a long position in a put option. If the value of the company's assets drops below the debt then the put will be exercised by putting the assets to the debt holders. If the company asset value is above the debt obligation then the put will not get exercised. In MKMV's EDF, the model derives the asset volatility of a firm from its equity volatility and total assets. The equity volatility to equity options is what asset volatility is to debt as an option. In other words, the Black-Scholes model of the firm's debt is represented as a put option with debt due as the strike price and the asset volatility, risk-free rate and the time to maturity as the other components of the option. The relationship between the asset value distribution and debt indicates the likelihood that the firm would default. This relationship is measured through the "distance to default," which is empirically calibrated to the failure rates of firms with similar distances to default to arrive at the EDF.

The existence of the asset value distribution (as distinct from the distribution of credit losses) can thus *indirectly* model credit quality changes or default on the risky debt of two firms. Correlation of default can be modeled through the correlation of the more symmetrically (i.e., normally) distributed asset returns between two firms. MKMV's Portfolio Manager models default correlation through asset return correlations. It should be noted that the term *asset return correlation* refers to the period to period return; that is, growth rate on the total assets of the firm (which may be equated with the sum of the market values of the firm's equity and debt). In its literature, MKMV uses the term *asset* to refer to the total assets of the firm and not to a liability of the firm, which would be its debt—typically these are referred to as an asset from the investor's perspective). This can lead to some confusion.

RISK-NEUTRAL PRICING FOR CREDIT VALUATION

The second important idea from market risk that has been applied to credit risk is the principle of risk-neutral pricing using the default probability of the firm. The principle of risk-neutral pricing arises from the idea of arbitrage-free pricing of contingent claims, which is based on the law of one price. The law of one price states that two securities with exactly the same cash flows must sell for the same price. This is because, if there are differences in price then that implies the existence of profitable and risk-less investment opportunity called an arbitrage opportunity. Since traders can jump in and make limitless profits without taking any risk this opportunity cannot exist except briefly.

Given a security, the value of a contingent claim on the security (such as a call option) may be derived by constructing a replicating portfolio of the security and risk-less borrowing or lending so that the payoffs from the two are identical. This finding was a breakthrough in finance because it made financial engineering possible by allowing for a straightforward way for pricing contingent assets that allowed an entity to take on the risk that it wanted, and to lay off the rest that it did not want by creating a hedging vehicle.

Risk-neutral pricing is a shortcut for the computation of arbitrage-free contingent claim pricing. Instead of going through the trouble of constructing a replicating portfolio, it uses the principle that for any asset there exists a set of pseudo-probabilities such that the expected rate of return from the cash flows obtained by applying these probabilities is equal to the risk-free rate of return. Stated differently, we can generate from a security whose price is known, a set of pseudoprobabilities such that the discounted (by the risk-free rate) expected value of the cash flows equals its current price. Then we would apply these same probabilities to a security or a portfolio whose payoffs are known but whose price is unknown, to solve for the price. In this hypothetical risk-neutral world, the investors are indifferent between two investments that have the *same expected value*. The risk-neutral setting does not actually exist, since investors are actually risk averse, but this risk-neutral definition gives us a technique to value an asset or a contingent claim (whose price is unknown) based on one or more assets whose price is known by constructing payoffs that replicate the cash flow behavior of assets whose prices are known.

For a risk-neutral investor, the price of a contingent asset—whose value depends on the value of the underlying asset of known price—would simply be the expected value of the asset based on the risk-neutral probabilities and the risk-free rate of return. In the case of credit risk, the same idea of risk-neutral pricing is used for valuing risky debt when credit risk is considered *not* in the context of *a buy and hold strategy* but in terms of *mark to market* (and by implication, total return, in much the same way as we would consider equities). By the way, risk-neutral pricing is a technique not to be confused with market-neutral investment—the latter refers to investing in such a way that returns are supposedly independent of the direction of the market.

In the credit risk domain, the risk-neutral probabilities are obtained by assuming that risk-neutral investors would demand *only* the risk-free rate plus expected loss based on the "true probability" of default. Risk-averse investors, on the other hand, would require an additional premium because they prefer certain outcomes to uncertain outcomes and expected loss from a loan may not necessarily be the actual loss incurred if the loan defaults. Thus, the risk-neutral probability of default would always be *higher* than the true probability of default. The price of a credit-risky asset is established by discounting at the risk free rate the cash flows that are devoid of market risk (i.e., for any asset we would first generate the option-free cash flows net of amortization) and are subject only to credit risk; that is, with a payoff of $1 - LGD$ (loss given default) with a default probability p and payoff of 100 with a probability of $1 - p$, where the p is the pseudo-default probability; that is, the risk-neutral default probability, which, as mentioned before would always be more than the "true" default probability or the EDF. When the probability of default changes, then the *expected loss* would change and so would the risk-neutral default probability. A risk-neutral pricing approach is thus used to separate the effect of expected loss and the risk premium for unexpected loss—loss in excess of the probabilistically expected loss for example—in arriving at the market value of any credit-risky asset which has a particular EDF.

The risk-neutral pricing for credit is relevant in the calculation of value at risk when there is credit quality migration. The possible gain or loss of value of an asset due to credit quality change is derived by certainty-equivalence-adjusting the cash flows at risk using the risk-neutral probabilities and then discounting them at the appropriate risk-free rate. In *CreditMetrics,* which is described later in this chapter, credit quality migration is handled through a ratings transition matrix; that is, the future credit states are *discrete* but in MKMV PM the credit states are in a *continuum.* EDF itself is in a continuum of 0 through 100 percent and the change in EDF is arrived at by deriving the changed distance to default resulting from the changed asset value distribution at the horizon. Similar to the difference between EDFs and ratings, MKMV's Empirical Credit Migration Model is believed to provide a more accurate and dynamic assessment of the distribution of credit states than ratings transition matrices.

When building up the portfolio value distribution, each obligor's asset return is simulated to horizon. The change in asset value for each obligor is calculated where the value change is based on the value of the factors driving asset value: asset value correlations are mirrored from the factor correlations. Focusing on a particular borrower, an asset return realization can fall below or above the default threshold. If the borrower defaults, a recovery value is realized. In nondefault, the borrower can migrate in credit quality. The probability of realizing any particular nondefault credit state is determined by MKMV's Empirical Credit Migration Model. Once the borrower's horizon credit state (i.e., horizon EDF) is realized, the market value of the loan is calculated using the risk-neutral pricing methodology described above.

FACTORS DRIVING ASSET VALUE

The first two parallels between market risk and credit risk were that a credit-risky portfolios may be able use the "technology" of correlations and optimizations though asset return volatility and asset return correlations (here the term asset is used refer to the total assets of the firm that issued the debt). The third analogy between market risk and credit risk is the use of factors in quantifying risk.

Market risk is the potential downside deviation of the market value of the transactions in a (trading) portfolio. Market risk is measured by portfolio volatility and value at risk. At the heart of market risk are standalone risk and portfolio risk. Looking at standalone risk, to derive risk-neutral pricing, it is popular to use factor models. The *one-factor* model assumes that each state of the world is completely determined by that factor (e.g. six-month LIBOR). Using this assumption, the evolution of this rate through future time steps (up and down for each step) is the starting point for deriving the risk-neutral probabilities, which in turn may be used to value other cash flows to arrive at the risk-neutral price. For example, in the Ho-Lee (1986) model the future interest rate is the previous interest plus a drift term—a constant term added to both up and down states, and a random shock term. The risk-neutral probabilities of up and down are set equal to 0.5 and the value of the drift and the volatility (random shock) are estimated by looking at the current price. Using this framework, the price of any other security can be derived from its future cash flows.

Once the model parameters are calibrated from the current price the realization of the discount factor in the Monte Carlo simulation is used to discount the cash flows to arrive at the value of the asset. Because the factors for some of the instruments can be many and the evolution of the factor into the tree structure can grow to be huge (for example, a one-factor model for a 10-year security with semiannual steps will have 500,000 nodes in the last period), many shortcuts are used to simplify the process of revaluing the assets in VaR calculations. One way is to map each of the asset (returns) to a small set of market-risk drivers. The sensitivities of the returns to the market risk drivers are measured. The risk driver scenarios are then generated and the assets are revalued using the sensitivities. Alternatively, a full valuation is done. Correlation of returns among various securities is captured through imposing the correlation structure for the factors in the simulation. Once the pricing models are in place, the value of the portfolio (and thereby the value at risk) is calculated. Similar to credit risk there can be "migration" in the sense that a risk driver may migrate to a lower or higher state, resulting in increase or decrease in asset value.

While considerable understanding exists about the risk drivers for market risk, the same cannot be said for drivers of credit risk. Both the migration of credit quality (expressed for example though rating downgrades) and credit quality correlation (both comovement in credit quality and coincidence of default) are difficult to estimate and model.

In MKMV Portfolio Manager, the firm's asset return is modeled as a function of three components: (1) global, country and industry factors; (2) an R-squared term; and (3) a random term. The "weights" of the asset return—the relationship between the asset return and factor returns—are econometrically derived. Factor returns are constructed using information on the cross-section of individual firm asset returns. The process involves many steps including aggregating/averaging the cross-section of individual assets and techniques similar to principal components analysis to produce a set of orthogonal factors. Recall that the asset return is the rate at which the total assets of the obligor who has issued the debt security will have grown/changed at the horizon.

The R-squared is a measure of the extent to which the firm's asset return is influenced by the factors. An additional random term is used to represent the part of the return that is idiosyncratic (i.e., uninfluenced by the factors). Taken together, these three drivers (weights, R^2, and random term) determine the asset return for the obligor. The asset return leads to the distance to default or the horizon EDF. The realization on the Monte Carlo trial may either lead to a default state (in which case the value would be based on a random LGD) or to a nondefaulted state. The credit quality in the nondefaulted state may be an "upgrade," "downgrade," or "no change" from the initial state based on the EDF. For the nondefaulted state the asset's value is derived using the risk-neutral framework for credit risk described before. For the defaulted state the value is based on the assumed LGD. The values for all the assets in the portfolio so derived are summed to arrive at the portfolio value. The outcome of all the trials then leads to the value distribution of the portfolio. The value distribution minus the initial portfolio value is the *loss distribution*. MKMV defines capital as the amount needed to set aside at the analysis date to absorb losses $x\%$ of the time where χ is the confidence level desired. As such, it measures a point on the horizon loss distribution discounted back to the analysis date. MKMV allows users to measure capital in excess of expected loss or total spread. When in excess of expected loss, the loss reference point is the expected value of the value distribution. When in excess of total spread, the loss reference point is the portfolio value at the analysis date brought forward to horizon at the risk free rate (alternatively, the reference point for capital is the portfolio value at the analysis date). The standard deviation of the loss distribution is the unexpected loss.

Correlation of default/credit quality in MKMV is thus captured through the correlation structure of the underlying factors and the factor weights for the firms, which in turn operate on the asset returns of the firm leading to the credit state at the horizon. Thus credit quality migration and its effect of value is handled through factors in a way similar to what is done in market risk.

MKMV Portfolio Manager simulation results include the credit value at risk (which is equivalent to the required economic capital at a particular confidence level), an estimate of the portfolio expected loss, and the capital allocated to each asset in the portfolio. The capital allocated to each asset is a function of the contribution of the asset to the unexpected loss (standard deviation) of the portfolio. Portfolio Manager also outputs optimal portfolio weights, risk contribution, and tail risk contribution.

While MKMV Portfolio Manager's main purpose was to assist in the measurement and management of portfolio Credit Risk, it is now increasingly used in the estimation of economic capital.

CREDITMETRICS (1997)

CreditMetrics is a set of analytical methods and databases to measure portfolio value and risk released by JPMorgan in April 1997. This product is now offered by Risk Metrics Group. The objective of CreditMetrics is to provide a process for estimating the *value distribution* of any portfolio of assets subject to changes in credit quality (including default).

The centerpiece of CreditMetrics is the notion that asset or portfolio value should be viewed not just in terms of the likelihood of default but also in terms of changes in credit quality over time, of which default is just a special case.[3] This approach is not new. As early as in the 1960s Cyert, Davidson, and Thompson (1962 and 1968) considered using transition probabilities in looking at a portfolio's credit profile as expressed in delinquency levels. Altman and Kao (1991) and Altman (1996) examined ratings migration over time. What is new, however, is that CreditMetrics is the first attempt to consider the problem of credit quality drift, default, recovery, and default/rating correlation in a consistent and comprehensive framework. Of particular note is CreditMetrics' approach for handling correlation of credit quality. It derives probabilities of the "next" period rating of an asset derived by using *equity index correlations*.

The input specifications and the calculation methodology are presented in reverse order to help the reader follow the analytical process. A schematic of CreditMetrics appears in Figure 20.1.

The initial portfolio is defined in terms of individual assets with the necessary information to project future contractual cash flows. One needs to know, for example, the loan balance, its amortization schedule and the

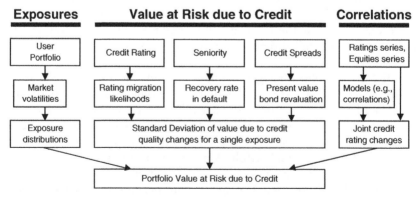

FIGURE 20.1 CreditMetrics Schematic
Source: CreditMetrics (1997).

TABLE 20.2   One-Year Transition Matrix

Initial Rating	Rating at Year-End (%)							
	AAA	AA	A	BBB	BB	B	CCC	Default
AAA	90.81	8.33	0.68	0.06	0.12	0.00	0.00	0.00
AA	0.70	90.65	7.79	0.64	0.06	0.24	0.02	0.00
A	0.09	2.27	91.05	5.52	0.74	0.26	0.01	0.06
BBB	0.02	0.33	5.95	86.93	5.30	1.17	0.12	0.18
BB	0.03	0.14	0.67	7.73	80.53	8.84	1.00	1.06
B	0.00	0.11	0.24	0.43	6.48	83.46	4.07	5.20
CCC	0.22	0.00	0.22	1.30	2.38	11.24	64.86	19.79

Source: CreditMetrics (1997, 25).

coupon rate. Each asset is identified by bond rating. If there is no rating, some other grouping may be used as long as the user has the analytics and data to express the probability of default and the probability of migration to other "ratings" in the time interval over which the analysis is performed. In nearly all cases, CreditMetrics uses the bond rating as the grouping criterion. A "shadow" rating may be used when no explicit bond rating is available.

An asset may be in one of eight future states, each state representing a bond rating to which it may migrate (the number of credit states may be increased if the associated transition matrix is also available). The state to which an asset can migrate is characterized by a transition probability. A sample transition matrix for the seven bond rating grades is shown in Table 20.2.

To explain this table, consider a BBB bond. It has a 0.02 percent probability of being upgraded to a AAA bond, 0.33 percent probability to be upgraded to AA, and so on. The probability of being of continuing to be rated BBB is 86.93 percent. Each of the future "states" has a different credit spread, as represented by a zero-coupon forward yield curve, which is used to discount the promised cash flows to a present value. The discount rate to be used is based on the rating that the bond/loan has migrated to. Table 20.3 shows the forward zero-coupon rates for various rating grades.[4] As it stands today, these spreads are fixed in the model; the risk due to their volatility is not incorporated.

If the bond defaults, there is no longer any "promised" cash flow. Instead there are recoveries, which may vary by the seniority of the asset. Since the recoveries are a range rather than point-estimates, an adjustment is made using the *standard deviation* of the recovery to the value of the asset. The *expected value* of the asset is unchanged by the fact that recoveries are random.[5] The

TABLE 20.3   Example One-Year Forward Zero Curves by Credit Rating Category

Category	Year 1	Year 2	Year 3	Year 4
AAA	3.60	4.17	4.73	5.12
AA	3.65	4.22	4.78	5.17
A	3.72	4.32	4.93	5.32
BBB	4.10	4.67	5.25	5.63
BB	5.55	6.02	6.78	7.27
B	6.05	7.02	8.03	8.52
CCC	15.05	15.02	14.03	13.52

Source: CreditMetrics (1997, 27).

recovery estimates used to project cash flows upon default are shown in Table 20.4.

Given the present value of the asset in the future "states" and the probabilities of attaining these states, CreditMetrics calculates the expected value of the asset. To describe the volatility of the value, CreditMetrics uses two alternative measurements. The first is the standard deviation. This measure is sometimes unsatisfactory when the variable is asymmetrically distributed, which is the case for debt securities. An alternative measure of volatility that captures its essence is the "1 percent value"—the value of the distribution corresponding to a state with a transition probability of 1 percent.[6] Table 20.5 shows the derivation of future value of a BBB-rated bond. The expected value of the bond is $107.09 and its standard deviation is $2.99. For example, looking at the second data column, at the 1 percent probability level the value of the bond corresponds to a B and is 98.10 (see column 3). The 1 percentile value (a measure of credit value at risk) is the Mean Value minus 98.10; that is, $107.09 − $98.10 = $8.99.

TABLE 20.4   Recovery Rates by Seniority Class (% of face value, i.e., par)

Seniority Class	Mean (%)	Standard Deviation (%)
Senior secured	53.80	26.86
Senior unsecured	51.13	25.45
Senior subordinated	38.52	23.81
Subordinated	32.74	20.18
Junior subordinated	17.09	10.90

Source: CreditMetrics (1997, 26).

TABLE 20.5 Calculating Volatility in Value Due to Credit Quality Changes

Year-end Rating	Probability Weighted of State (%)	New Bond Value Plus Coupon ($)	Probability Weighted Value ($)	Difference of Value from Mean ($)	Probability Weighted Difference Squared
AAA	0.02	109.37	0.02	2.28	0.0010
AA	0.33	109.19	0.36	2.10	0.0146
A	5.95	108.66	6.47	1.57	0.1474
BBB	86.93	107.55	93.49	0.46	0.1853
BB	5.30	102.02	5.41	(5.06)	1.3592
B	1.17	98.10	1.15	(8.99)	0.9446
CCC	0.12	83.64	1.10	(23.45)	0.6598
Default	0.18	51.13	0.09	(55.96)	5.6358
		Mean = $107.09		Variance = 8.9477	
				Standard deviation = $2.99	

Source: CreditMetrics (1997, 28).

To recap, CreditMetrics derives the future value on the basis of the promised cash flows and recovery rate and derives its distribution on the basis of seniority, the probability distribution of the future states, and the new-rating-specific forward zero curve. The value of the asset pursuant to credit migration is summarized by the transition probability-weighted expected value and either its standard deviation or its 1 percent value. Note that so far, no assumptions have been made about credit quality correlations. The analysis is on a standalone basis.

TREATMENT OF DEFAULT CORRELATION

The next question is how to incorporate the effect of the correlation between the credit quality of the assets in the portfolio. The approach taken by CreditMetrics is similar to that by MKMV, which is that credit quality transitions are best captured through asset value returns and asset correlations and the credit migration model.

Give an initial rating level, the transition probabilities to other "states" are based on the distribution of the *asset value return* (change in the value of the firm's assets from one period to next, expressed as a rate of return percent). In Figure 20.2, the asset value return for a BB-rated bond is graphed. Depending on the distribution of the return, the rating will remain at its initial level or migrate to a higher or lower (including default) level.

It is assumed that this asset return is normally distributed with a mean μ and a standard deviation σ. The *rating change thresholds* are points in

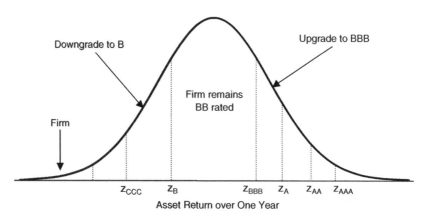

FIGURE 20.2 Distribution of Asset Returns with Rating Change Thresholds
Source: CreditMetrics (1997, 88).

TABLE 20.6   Transition Probabilities and Asset Return Thresholds for A Rating

Rating	Probability	Threshold	Value
AAA	0.09%		
AA	2.27%	Z'_{AA}	$3.12\sigma'$
A	91.05%	Z'_A	$1.98\sigma'$
BBB	5.52%	Z'_{BBB}	$-1.51\sigma'$
BB	0.74%	Z'_{BB}	$-2.30\sigma'$
B	0.26%	Z'_B	$-2.72\sigma'$
CCC	0.01%	Z'_{CCC}	$-3.19\sigma'$
Default	0.06%	Z'_{Def}	$-3.24\sigma'$

Source: CreditMetrics (1997, 89).

the firm asset value return distribution. Assuming a normal distribution, the probability from the transition matrix is mapped to the distribution to derive *rating change thresholds expressed as a multiple of the standard deviation.* The threshold values of an A-rated bond, given transition probabilities, are as shown in Table 20.6.

The probability of transition from A to one of the eight other states is taken from actual historical data. The threshold probability according to the asset value model is in the third column. Here is how the values are interpreted. Given the return (μ and σ) for an A-rated obligor, a return value greater than 1.98 σ will cause an upgrade from an A to an AA. A firm asset value return of less than -1.51σ will cause a downgrade from A to BBB.

Thus, the rating probabilities have been mapped to the firm's asset value returns. If we now know the *correlation* of the asset returns between two bonds, then we can determine the joint effect on the rating by integrating the bivariate normal distribution function encompassing the two sets of thresholds and the firm asset value correlation coefficient. Assuming a correlation coefficient of 20 percent, the transition matrix in Table 20.7 is derived for a pair of obligors, BB- and A-rated. The correlation coefficient of firm asset value return drives the calculations.

This brings up the key question: how does one derive the asset correlations for two or more firms? CreditMetrics uses the correlation between equity returns as a proxy for the correlation of asset returns. It uses industry indexes in particular countries to construct a matrix of correlations between the industries. The individual obligors in the portfolio are mapped by industry and country participation. Using these weights and the index correlations, the equity correlation between obligors is obtained. The equity correlation is then used as a proxy for the asset value correlation.

TABLE 20.7 Joint Rating Change Probabilities for BB- and A-rated Obligors (%)

Rating of First Company	Rating of Second Company								
	AAA	AA	A	BBB	BB	B	CCC	Def	Total
AAA	0.00	0.00	0.03	0.00	0.00	0.00	0.00	0.00	0.03
AA	0.00	0.01	0.13	0.00	0.00	0.00	0.00	0.00	0.14
A	0.00	0.04	0.61	0.01	0.00	0.00	0.00	0.00	0.67
BBB	0.02	0.35	7.10	0.20	0.02	0.01	0.00	0.00	7.69
BB	0.07	1.79	73.65	4.24	0.56	0.18	0.01	0.04	80.53
B	0.00	0.08	7.80	0.79	0.13	0.05	0.00	0.01	8.87
CCC	0.00	0.01	0.85	0.11	0.02	0.01	0.00	0.00	1.00
Def	0.00	0.01	0.90	0.13	0.02	0.01	0.00	0.00	1.07
Total	0.09	2.29	91.06	5.48	0.75	0.26	0.01	0.06	100.00

Source: CreditMetrics (1997, 90).

To recap, the probability distribution of credit quality migration is obtained by considering the correlation of the firm's asset value returns. Assuming equity returns as a proxy for asset value returns, the equity return correlations are estimated based on industry return correlations, country and company size. CreditMetrics provides users with a spreadsheet of industry returns and correlations.

CREDITMETRICS IMPLEMENTATION—CREDITMANAGER

The methodology in CreditMetrics is implemented in a Microsoft XP or Vista-based software product named CreditManager by Risk Metrics Group.

The software produces reports that quantify the credit value at risk broken down by country, industry, maturity, and rating. The asset types modeled by CreditManager are bonds, commitments to lend, standby letters of credit, loans, market-driven instruments (swaps, caps, etc.), and trade receivables. The user constructs exposure profile of the portfolio by specifying the following components for every asset in it:

- Asset type
- Currency
- Maturity
- Spread curve
- Rate terms

- Seniority
- Recovery rate
- Recovery rate standard deviation
- Exposure amount

The input items vary slightly for individual asset type. For example, for loan commitments, the total draw-down, current draw-down, and expected draw-down are specified.

Credit Manager computes each asset's volatility caused by possible upgrades, downgrades, and defaults. The asset's expected value and volatility of value are estimated using a transition matrix. The transition matrix selected should correspond to the risk rating system used for the assets (Moody's 8-state, Standard & Poor's 8-state, Moody's 18-state, or custom). The yield curve by currency and the spread curve by rating is maintained and updated by the system. The system uses a horizon of one year. Default recovery rates may be user-specified or based on one of four recovery studies (e.g., Altman and Kishore 1996). Foreign Exchange rates are user-specified to convert all calculated values to the base currency used for reporting.

Obligor-specific volatility (as a percent) is specified by the user, which defines the extent to which a company's volatility is correlated with the market. The total asset size decides how much it is related to the index and is provided by the Credit Manager as default value. The weights of country and industry are specified by the user. These weights will be used along with the respective equity indexes to derive the distribution of asset value. For each obligor, the degree to which its asset value is related to equity market indexes is specified through weights in up to three countries and three industries. Suggested weights are provided by fitting the historic stock returns to the returns of equity indexed. Alternatively, the user may purchase data from Dow Jones which produces weights for a firm based on a fundamental analysis of its financial statements. RMG provides a time series that is used to derive the correlations between different market indexes used in estimating asset value correlations.

The correlation between each of the events (upgrade, downgrade, or default) is assessed using a equity returns and is used to combine the individual volatilities to arrive at the aggregate volatility of value for the portfolio. Either a constant correlation may be used, or one based on the proprietary method developed by RMG. The obligor correlation matrix is created by generating an asset value profile based on simulation and calculating the pairwise correlations based on the resulting sets of firm values.

The results of the Monte Carlo simulation are current value by industry and country, 95th percentile loss amount, and the marginal risk by risk category for the portfolio.

COMMENTS ON CREDITMETRICS

CreditMetrics is an important attempt by a key industry participant to address some of the long-standing problems in pricing and unbundling credit risk. By shifting the focus from default to changes in credit quality and the consequent changes in value as the basis for action, CreditMetrics has led the way for the practical management of asset concentration. The growth in the credit derivatives market has provided opportunities for active balance sheet management. As the liquidity in the credit market increases, market participants will have the ability to track *market-determined* as opposed to *model-determined* credit pricing.

Because so much of the methodology revolves around publicly rated bonds, fixed income portfolio managers are likely to find immediate application for this tool. Wholesale institutions whose assets are largely denominated in publicly traded names—may be able to use the concepts readily. Institutions that face capital allocation choices to support unexpected credit losses will also find the approach useful. But for multiproduct banks and middle-market lenders, more work has to be done before the analytics can be applied to a number of important product types. For example, how do you reliably derive the firm asset value of a privately held firm, municipal bonds, sovereign bonds, and various types of structured finance assets such as ABS, RMBS, CDOs, and so on?

One thing is clear: if the initial rating assigned to the asset is wrong and does not accurately represent its credit identity, then the remaining analytics are not terribly useful. This is especially true at the noninvestment grade level, where a misclassification of as little as one or two notches can result in the assignment of a default probability that is several percentage points above or below its intrinsic level. Another subtle but critical element is taking into account the age of an asset in assessing its migration patterns. As we have seen in Chapter 16, doing so can dramatically alter the resulting probabilities. Two bonds with the same rating but of different vintages may have widely differing paths to default. There have been studies linking the overall default rates to recoveries: The relationship is that when the default rates are elevated, the recoveries tend to be lower. This is termed the PD-LGD (loss given default) link (Altman 2005). While the variation in the LGD is taken into account in CreditMetrics, the PD-LGD link is not.

If the equity and debt values are assumed to be correlated to specific factors, then their patterns and inputs need to be estimated from past relationships. Typically, debt and equity values move together; that is, are positively correlated, and this will be implicit in the model. But in response to certain critical events—such as a leveraged restructuring or a spinoff of assets—debt and equity values can move in opposite directions. We believe that value-at-risk models need to be sufficiently robust to handle these abnormalities.

CREDITRISK⁺ (1996)

The CreditRisk⁺ framework, introduced by Credit Suisse Financial Products (CSFP) is a statistical model of credit default risk employing the default rate as a continuous random variable, and incorporates the volatility of default rates in order to capture the uncertainty in the level of default rates. This approach is conceptually similar to the term structure models of the yield curve used in modeling market risk. Pairwise correlation of defaults is handled through dividing the portfolio into homogenous sectors within which a collection of obligors is presumed share the same systematic risk factor. Each obligor may be apportioned to more than one sector. Country of domicile is cited as one example of a sector

The number of default events over a specified time horizon is approximated by a Poisson distribution.[7] The volatility of default rate is incorporated into the Poisson model (whose standard deviation is equal to the square root of the average number of defaults) by dividing the exposure into sectors each of which is independent of other sectors. The basic premise in CreditRisk⁺ is that it is possible to obtain a portfolio's risk exposure from the following input data:

- Exposure from individual assets.
- Mean default rate.
- Standard deviation of the default rate.
- Sectors and the respective loss percentiles over which each exposure is distributed.

The technical document provides a theoretical derivation of the relationships that lead from the default probability and recoveries to the loss distribution estimates.

MCKINSEY & CO./WILSON MODEL (1997)

Wilson (1997) has described a recent attempt to analyze portfolio risk and return through econometrics and Monte Carlo simulation. He recognizes many of the realities faced by financial institutions that are often omitted in portfolio solutions. The following are among the refinements his approach offers:

- It explicitly models actual, discrete loss distribution dependent upon the number and size of credits in a subportfolio.
- Rather than being based passively and unconditionally on historic averages, the loss distributions are conditional on the state of the economy.
- The losses are measured on a mark-to-market basis both for exposures that may be liquidated and for those that cannot be.
- The approach is applicable to single obligors as well as to collections of obligors such as retail portfolios.
- The approach captures the uncertainty regarding recovery rates as well as losses arising from country risk.

On the basis of historic macroeconomic variables and an average default rate time series, this approach builds a multifactor model for different country and industry segments. Sample default rate relationship estimates for certain countries are as shown in Table 20.8.

This is a top-down approach in that the model starts with a probabilistic assumption about the state of the world, which is then passed on to a segment model that calculates the conditional probability of default for each customer segment (subportfolio). In predicting defaults and default correlations, the model assumes no further information other than country, industry, rating and state of the economy. Portfolio diversification within a segment is characterized by the number of companies in the segment. The larger the number of companies, the lower are the implied losses for the segment index. Retail portfolios are handled as diversified index portfolios. Default losses are projected based on marginal default probabilities over time and discounted to the present. Liquid positions are marked to market. The output of the simulation is the portfolio loss/gain distribution—a plot of the gain or loss against the probability.

Wilson (1997) notes in conclusion that a strong analytic foundation should precede any portfolio management strategy. Portfolio management begins when senior management asks some basic and intuitive questions about an institution's mix of assets and the economic prognosis. "The sign of a successful credit portfolio risk management process is therefore not the number of Greek letters used; but rather whether or not your management asks, and answers these questions" (Wilson 1997). He points out that any portfolio strategy should be tailored to the specific needs of the institution.

TABLE 20.8 Default Rate Prediction Equation Coefficients

Country	Constant	Unemployment	GDP Growth	Government Disbursements	Long-Term Interest Rates	Exchange Rates	Gross Savings	R-Squared
Germany	8.41[a] (30.66)	−0.074[a] (4.87)	−0.063[a] (7.74)	0.025[a] (2.15)	—	—	—	95.7
France	5.37[a] (29.92)	−0.148[a] (5.41)	—	—	−0.047[a] (2.36)	0.080[a] (2.26)	—	89.7
Spain	3.87[a] (35.43)	−0.065[a] (17.23)	—	0.027[a] (9.47)	−0.013[a] (3.25)	—	—	77.5
UK	−0.11[b] (0.12)	−0.12[a] (4.35)	—	0.08[a] (3.80)	—	—	0.15[a] (5.38)	65.5
US	5.48[a] (32.2)	−0.001[b] (0.04)	0.03[b] (1.84)	—	−0.165[a] (11.28)	—	—	82.6

[a]Significant at the 99% level.
[b]Significant at the 95% level.
Source: Wilson (1997).

KAMAKURA CORPORATION'S DEFAULT AND PROBABILITY MODELS

Kamakura offers three default probability models in its KRIS default probability service: a reduced form model developed by Professor Robert Jarrow who is a researcher associated with this firm, an advanced version of the Merton model of risky debt, and a hybrid model. Kamakura has derived the macroeconomic factors that best drive defaults through the credit cycle and has embedded these macroeconomic factors in its default probability models. These macrofactors are explicitly linked to default probabilities in the estimation process.

In addition, Kamakura provides default probability correlations for all companies currently covered by default probability service. Default probability correlations are provided for all pairs of companies in user-defined portfolios like those represented by first to default swap baskets or the underlying reference names in a collateralized debt obligation structure. In total, 32 million correlations are maintained in the default probability service. The exact methodology for deriving the default correlations and the validation results of the correlations are not publicly available, but may be obtained directly from the firm (www.kamakuraco.com).

ALTMAN'S (1997) OPTIMIZATION APPROACH

Altman's approach is noteworthy because it is an attempt to apply the portfolio optimization techniques to fixed income securities. Instead of minimizing variance, a variant of the Sharpe Ratio is used in creating an optimum portfolio of bonds if market prices of the bonds are available. The measurement of expected portfolio return is actually quite straightforward for fixed income bond and loan assets. The investor is promised a fixed return (yield-to-maturity) over time and should subtract from this promised yield the expected losses from a default of the issuer. For certain measurement periods, the return will also be influenced by changes in interest rates, but it is assumed, for purposes of exposition, that these changes are random with an expected capital gain of zero.[8]

The expected annual return is therefore

$$EAR = YTM - EAL \qquad (20.1)$$

where

EAR = Expected annual return
YTM = Yield-to-maturity (or Yield-to-worst)
EAL = Expected annual loss

The EAL is derived from Altman's prior work on bond mortality rates and losses (Altman 1988 and 1989). Each bond in the portfolio is analyzed based on its initial (or existing)[9] rating, which implies an expected rate of default for up to 10 years after issuance. Table 20.9 and Table 20.10 list cumulative mortality rates and cumulative mortality losses, respectively, covering the period 1971–1994.[10] Table 20.11 annualizes these mortality rates and losses. So, for example, a 10-year BB (Standard & Poor's rated) bond has an expected *annual loss* of 91 basis points per year. If the newly issued BB-rated bond has a promised yield of 9.0 percent with a spread of 2.0 percent over 7.0 percent risk-free U.S. Treasury bonds, then the *expected* return is 8.09 percent per year, or a risk premium of 109 basis points over the risk-free rate. If the measurement period were quarterly returns instead of annual, then the expected return would be about 2.025 percent per quarter. The expected return measure is focused primarily on credit risk changes and not on the yield curve.

The problem of measuring expected returns for commercial loans is a bit more complex. Because commercial loans usually do not have an explicit risk rating attached to them by the rating agencies,[11] the loan portfolio analyst must utilize a proxy measure. Altman advocates using the bank's own internal systems or commercially available systems[12] as long as each of the ratings is linked with the public bond ratings such as those used by Altman, Moody's, or Standard & Poor's in their cumulative default studies. Only by linking with the public rating systems can a bank utilize the credit migration, default, and recovery experience from a large database of debt securities. These statistics are more reliable because they are based on a large sample extending over three decades. Data integrity is also not a concern because these securities are tracked by the rating agencies from origination or from a specific pool of bonds at a point in time (*static pool* approach).

The expected portfolio return (R_p) is therefore based on each asset's expected annual return, weighted by the proportion (X_i) of each loan/bond relative to the total portfolio;

$$R_p = \sum_{i=l}^{N} X_i EAR \tag{20.2}$$

The classic portfolio variance framework given in Equation 20.3 is appropriate when a short holding period, (e.g., monthly or quarterly) is used, and historical data exists for the requisite period to calculate correlation of returns among the loans/bonds.

$$Vp = \sum_{i=l}^{N} \sum_{j=l}^{N} X_i X_j \sigma_i \sigma_j \rho_{ij} \tag{20.3}$$

TABLE 20.9 Mortality Rates by Original Rating: All Rated Corporate Bonds, 1971–2003[a]

		1	2	3	4	5	6	7	8	9	10
AAA	Marginal	0.00%	0.00%	0.00%	0.00%	0.05%	0.03%	0.01%	0.00%	0.00%	0.00%
	Cumulative	0.00%	0.00%	0.00%	0.00%	0.05%	0.08%	0.09%	0.09%	0.09%	0.09%
AA	Marginal	0.00%	0.00%	0.30%	0.14%	0.02%	0.02%	0.00%	0.00%	0.05%	0.01%
	Cumulative	0.00%	0.00%	0.30%	0.44%	0.46%	0.48%	0.48%	0.48%	0.53%	0.54%
A	Marginal	0.01%	0.08%	0.02%	0.06%	0.06%	0.09%	0.05%	0.20%	0.09%	0.05%
	Cumulative	0.01%	0.09%	0.11%	0.17%	0.23%	0.32%	0.37%	0.57%	0.66%	0.71%
BBB	Marginal	0.33%	3.13%	1.34%	1.24%	0.74%	0.31%	0.25%	0.19%	0.14%	0.40%
	Cumulative	0.33%	3.45%	4.74%	5.92%	6.62%	7.10%	7.33%	7.51%	7.63%	8.00%
BB	Marginal	1.15%	2.42%	4.32%	2.26%	2.53%	1.27%	1.61%	1.11%	1.71%	3.47%
	Cumulative	1.15%	3.54%	7.72%	9.88%	12.10%	13.20%	14.60%	15.56%	17.00%	19.88%
B	Marginal	2.84%	6.78%	7.35%	8.49%	6.01%	4.32%	3.95%	2.40%	1.96%	0.83%
	Cumulative	2.84%	9.43%	16.08%	23.21%	27.82%	30.94%	35.67%	35.26%	36.53%	37.06%
CCC	Marginal	8.12%	15.42%	18.75%	11.76%	4.14%	9.33%	5.79%	5.70%	0.85%	4.70%
	Cumulative	8.12%	22.30%	36.86%	44.30%	46.60%	51.57%	54.38%	56.98%	57.34%	59.36%

[a]Rated by S&P issuances based on 1,955 bonds.
Source: Standard & Poor's and authors' compilations.

TABLE 20.10 Mortality Losses by Original Rating: All Rated Corporate Bonds, 1971–2003[a]

		1	2	3	4	5	6	7	8	9	10
AAA	Marginal	0.00%	0.00%	0.00%	0.00%	0.01%	0.01%	0.01%	0.00%	0.00%	0.00%
	Cumulative	0.00%	0.00%	0.00%	0.00%	0.01%	0.02%	0.03%	0.03%	0.03%	0.03%
AA	Marginal	0.00%	0.00%	0.05%	0.04%	0.01%	0.01%	0.00%	0.00%	0.02%	0.00%
	Cumulative	0.00%	0.00%	0.05%	0.09%	0.10%	0.11%	0.11%	0.11%	0.13%	0.14%
A	Marginal	0.00%	0.03%	0.01%	0.04%	0.03%	0.04%	0.02%	0.03%	0.06%	0.00%
	Cumulative	0.00%	0.03%	0.04%	0.08%	0.11%	0.15%	0.17%	0.20%	0.26%	0.26%
BBB	Marginal	0.23%	2.19%	1.06%	0.45%	0.44%	0.21%	0.10%	0.11%	0.07%	0.23%
	Cumulative	0.23%	2.41%	3.45%	3.88%	4.31%	4.54%	4.63%	4.74%	4.80%	5.02%
BB	Marginal	0.67%	1.41%	2.50%	1.27%	1.47%	0.65%	0.90%	0.48%	0.85%	1.25%
	Cumulative	0.67%	2.07%	4.52%	5.73%	7.12%	7.72%	8.55%	8.99%	9.76%	10.89%
B	Marginal	1.83%	4.74%	4.92%	5.49%	3.90%	2.37%	2.56%	1.34%	1.03%	0.61%
	Cumulative	1.83%	6.48%	11.08%	15.97%	18.37%	19.24%	21.31%	22.36%	23.16%	23.63%
CCC	Marginal	5.44%	11.10%	13.50%	8.46%	2.90%	7.00%	4.34%	4.41%	0.51%	3.01%
	Cumulative	5.44%	15.94%	27.38%	33.44%	35.37%	39.89%	42.50%	45.04%	45.32%	46.96%

[a]Rated by S&P issuances based on 1,777 bonds.
Source: Standard & Poor's and authors' compilations.

TABLE 20.11 Annualized Cumulative Default Rates and Annualized Cumulative Mortality Loss Rates, 1971–2006

Original Rating/Year	Annualized Cumulative Default Rates (%)									
	1	2	3	4	5	6	7	8	9	10
AAA	0	0	0	0	0.01	0.01	0.01	0.01	0.01	0.01
AA	0	0	0.1	0.11	0.09	0.08	0.07	0.06	0.06	0.05
A	0.01	0.05	0.04	0.04	0.05	0.05	0.05	0.07	0.07	0.07
BBB	0.33	1.74	1.61	1.51	1.36	1.22	1.08	0.97	0.88	0.83
BB	1.15	1.79	2.64	2.57	2.55	2.33	2.23	2.09	2.05	2.19
B	2.84	4.83	5.68	6.39	6.31	5.98	6.11	5.29	4.93	4.52
CCC	8.12	11.85	14.21	13.61	11.79	11.38	10.61	10.01	9.03	8.61

Original Rating/Year	Annualized Cumulative Mortality Loss Rates									
	1	2	3	4	5	6	7	8	9	10
AAA	0	0	0	0	0	0	0	0	0	0
AA	0	0	0.02	0.02	0.02	0.02	0.02	0.01	0.01	0.01
A	0	0.02	0.01	0.02	0.02	0.03	0.02	0.03	0.03	0.03
BBB	0.23	1.21	1.16	0.98	0.88	0.77	0.67	0.61	0.55	0.51
BB	0.67	1.04	1.53	1.46	1.47	1.33	1.27	1.17	1.13	1.15
B	1.83	3.29	3.84	4.26	3.98	3.5	3.37	3.11	2.88	2.66
CCC	5.44	8.32	10.12	9.68	8.36	8.13	7.6	7.21	6.49	6.14

Source: Calculation from data from Tables 20.9 and 20.10.

where

V_r = Variance (risk) of the portfolio

i = The proportion of the portfolio invested in bond issue i

s_i = Standard Deviation of the return for the sample period for bond issue i

r_{ij} = Correlation coefficient of the returns for bonds i and j

The portfolio ratio η is a variation on the so-called Sharpe Ratio, first introduced as a reward-to-variability ratio by Sharpe (1966), later popularized as the Sharpe Index or Sharpe Ratio by many such as Reilly (1989), Morningstar (1993), and finally generalized and expanded to cover a broader range of applications by Sharpe (1994). Most often applied to measuring the performance of equity mutual funds, this ratio captures the average differential return between a fund and an appropriate benchmark and the standard deviation of the differences over the period. It therefore captures the average differential return per unit of risk (standard deviation), assuming the appropriate risk measure is the variance of returns.

Other applications of a version of the Sharpe Ratio to fixed income asset portfolios and derivatives were proposed in unpublished manuscripts by McQuown (1994) and Kealhofer (1995 and 1996). They utilize a risk of default model developed by KMV (see Chapter 11), which itself is based (indirectly) on the level, variability and correlations of the stock price of the existing and potential companies in the portfolio. Altman's fixed income asset portfolio model has many similarities to that of McQuown but uses a different measure of default risk (see our discussion in Chapters 10 and 11 of the Z and ZETA risk measures and the KMV expected default frequency approach). The objective function may be written formally as

$$\eta = \frac{R_p}{\sqrt{V_p}}$$

Maximize

$$\sum_{i=1}^{N} X_i = 1$$

subject to

$R_p \geq$ Target return

$X_i \leq$ Individual bond investment limit

If returns on all assets exist for a significant period of time—say, 20 quarters—then the correlations may be considered meaningful and the classic efficient frontier can be calculated. Figure 20.3 shows an efficient

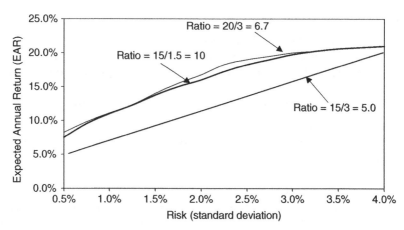

FIGURE 20.3   Portfolio Ratio Approach for Risk Return Assessment

frontier; that is, maximization of expected return for given levels of risk or minimization of risk (variance of returns) for given levels of return, for a hypothetical high-yield bond portfolio. Note that an existing portfolio with a η of 5.0 can be improved to 6.67 holding risk constant or to 10.0 holding return constant.

Figure 20.4 shows an efficient frontier for a potential portfolio of 10 high-yield corporate bonds that is based on actual quarterly returns from the five-year period 1991–1995. The return-risk trade-off of the efficient portfolio is considerably better than that of the equally weighted portfolio. For example, the η goes from about 0.67 (2.0/3.0) to 1.14 (2.0/1.75) for the

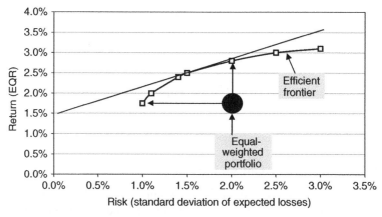

FIGURE 20.4   Efficient Bond Portfolio Using Returns (10 issues)

same expected return and to 1.0 (3.0/3.0) for the same variance of return. Note also the link between the risk-free rate at about 1.4% per quarter and the tangent line to the efficient frontier, indicating various proportions of risky versus risk-free fixed income assets. The efficient frontier, calculated without any constraint as to the number of issues in the portfolio, involved investment in eight of the possible 10 high-yield bonds. When we constrain the model so that no issue can be greater than 15 percent of the portfolio, the actual number of issues is either seven or eight, depending upon the different expected returns, (see Table 20.9).

PORTFOLIO RISK AND EFFICIENT FRONTIERS USING UNEXPECTED LOSS

The reality of the bond and loan markets is that even if one were comfortable with the distribution qualities of returns, the need to analyze a reasonably large number of potential assets precludes the use of the classic mean-variance of return framework. Specifically, there simply is insufficient historical high-yield bond return and loan returns data to compute correlations. The same problem would be true if, instead of using return correlations, which can vary due to maturity differences between bonds, we utilized the correlation of the duration of each bond with other bonds and with the overall index of bonds to calculate the correlation between bonds and variance of the portfolio. Other sample selection problems include the change in maturities of individual bonds over the measurement period and the exclusion of bonds that defaulted in the past.

Altman analyzed the potential to use returns or durations in the high-yield corporate debt market. Out of almost 600 bond issues that existed as of year-end 1995, fewer than 40 had 20 quarters of historical data. He concluded that if this scenario is added to the other conceptual concerns, as indicated previously, it is simply not appropriate (theoretically or empirically) to utilize the variance of return as the measure of risk for either the individual assets or the portfolio.

One possible approach for determining unexpected losses is to utilize a variation of the Z-Score model, called the Z''-*Score* model (Altman 1993) to assign a bond rating equivalent to each of the loans/bonds that could possibly enter the portfolio (see Table 20.12).[13] As noted earlier, these scores and rating equivalents can then be used to estimate expected losses over time. If we then observe the variation (e.g., standard deviation) around the expected losses, we have a procedure to estimate unexpected losses. For example, the expected loss on a BB-rated equivalent 10-year bond is 91 basis points per year (Table 20.11). The standard deviation around this expected

TABLE 20.12   U.S. Bond Rating Equivalent, Based on Z''-Score

Average U.S. Equivalent Rating[a]	Sample Z''-Score	Sample Size
AAA	8.15	8
AA+	7.60	—
AA	7.30	18
AA−	7.00	15
A+	6.85	24
A	6.65	42
A−	6.40	38
BBB+	6.25	38
BBB	5.85	59
BBB−	5.65	52
BB+	5.25	34
BB	4.95	25
BB−	4.75	65
B+	4.50	78
B	4.15	115
B−	3.75	95
CCC+	3.20	23
CCC	2.50	10
CCC−	1.75	6
D	0.00	14

[a]Average is based on over 750 U.S. industrial corporates with rated debt outstanding; 1994 data. An updated table for the Z'' model appears in Chapter 10.
Source: Salomon Brothers, Inc., May 15, 1995 and In-depth Data Corporation.

value is computed to be 2.65 percent, or 265 basis points per year. The standard deviation is computed from the individual issuance years' results, which are independent observations that were used to calculate the cumulative mortality losses. For example, there are 24 one-year default losses for bonds issued in a certain rating class over the 1971–1995 period—that is, bonds issued in 1971 that defaulted in 1972, bond issued in 1972 that defaulted in 1973, and so on. In the same way, there are 23 two-year cumulative loss data points, 22 three-year loss observations, and so on., up to 15 10-year observations.

As noted above, the model used here is the Z''-Score, risk rating model, indicated in Equation 20.4 with the bond rating equivalents shown in Table 20.12. Other bond rating models such as ZETA, KMV, or Finance

FX could also have been used:

$$Z''\text{-Score} = 6.56(X_1) + 3.26(X_2) + 6.72(X_3) + 1.05(X_4) + 3.25$$

$$(20.4)$$

where

X_1 = Working capital/Total assets
X_2 = Retained earnings/Total assets
X_3 = EBIT/Total assets
X_4 = Equity (book value)/Total liabilities

PORTFOLIO RISK USING UNEXPECTED LOSSES

The formula for Altman's (1997) portfolio risk measure is given in equation (20.5).

$$UAL_p = \sum_{i-1}^{N} \sum_{j-1}^{N} X_i X_j \sigma_i \sigma_j \rho_{ij} 1 \qquad (20.5)$$

The measure UAL_p is the unexpected loss on the portfolio consisting of measures of individual asset unexpected losses (σ_i, σ_j) and the correlation ($\rho_{i,j}$) of unexpected losses over the sample measurement period. Again, these unexpected losses are based on the standard deviation of annual expected losses for the bond rating equivalents calculated at each quarterly interval.[14] All that is necessary is that the issuing firm (or borrower) was operating for the entire sample period (e.g., five years, and had quarterly financial statements). The actual bonds/loans did not have to be outstanding in the period as is necessary when returns and variance of returns are used. Since the actual bond/loan may not have been outstanding during the entire measurement period, leverage measures will likely also vary over time. Still, it is expected that most of the covariance of default risk between firms will be captured.

EMPIRICAL RESULTS OF ALTMAN'S ALTERNATIVE APPROACH

A portfolio optimizer program[15] on the same 10 bond portfolio analyzed earlier was used, this time using the Z''-Score bond rating equivalents and their associated expected and unexpected losses instead of returns.

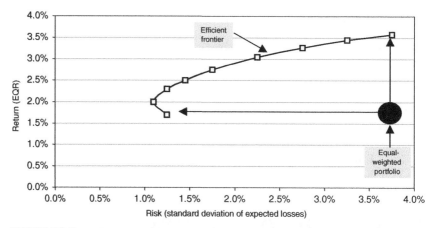

FIGURE 20.5 Efficient Bond Portfolio, Using Z″-Score (10 issues)

Figure 20.5 shows the efficient frontier compared to an equal-weighted portfolio. As observed earlier, the efficient frontier indicates considerably improved values of η. For example, the return/risk ratio of just above 0.50 for the equal-weighted 10-bond portfolio can be improved to 1.60 (2.00/1.25) at the 2.00 percent quarterly return level and to about 1.00 for the same risk (3.75-percent) level.

Table 20.13 shows the portfolio weights for the efficient frontier portfolio using both returns and risk (unexpected losses) when the individual

TABLE 20.13 Relative Weightings of Optimal Portfolios[a]

Company Ticker	Weights Using ZETA Scores	Weights Using Quarterly Returns
AS	0.0000	0.1065
BOR	0.0776	0.0000
CGP	0.1500	0.1500
CQB	0.1500	0.1500
FA	0.0000	0.0000
IMD	0.1500	0.1351
RHR	0.1500	0.1209
STO	0.1500	0.1500
USG	0.1500	0.1500
WS	0.0224	0.0376

[a]For a return of 1.75 per quarter and a 15 percent maximum weighting constraint.

weights are constrained at a maximum of 15 percent of the portfolio. This is for the 1.75 percent quarterly expected return. Note that both portfolios utilize eight of the 10 bonds and very similar weightings. Indeed, seven of the eight bonds appear in both portfolios. These results are comforting in that the unexpected loss derived from the Z''-Score model as an alternative risk measure appears to be consistent with the approach based on actual ratings. Test results from this small sample are encouraging and indicate that this type of portfolio approach is potentially quite feasible for fixed income assets. It should be noted that these are preliminary findings. Subsequent conceptual refinements and empirical tests with larger samples are necessary to gain experience and confidence with this portfolio technique for fixed income assets (including loans).

BANK REGULATIONS (BIS II) AND PORTFOLIO MODELING

Since regulators are concerned about the risk of unexpected losses and would like to set capital requirements to cover this contingency, it s not surprising that that they have followed the developments in the banking industry to measure credit portfolio risk and the regulations have evolved to take advantage of the innovations by the industry. This is evident in both BIS II (for banks) and Solvency II (insurance companies).

BIS II was formulated with the help of many of the concepts that had been developed during that time such as KMV's Portfolio Manager and CreditMetrics—that correlation of credit state could be inferred by looking at underlying factors such as equity indexes or multifactor models for asset returns. In 1988 BIS I was introduced wherein, for the first time capital requirements were standardized for banks throughout the world. While assets that were presumed to have no credit risk (government and agency securities for instance) attracted no capital charge, corporate loans were assessed 8 percent regardless of loan quality. Capital relief for hedging/shedding of credit risk was provided with several restrictions. For example, credit support by a third-party institution resulted in a lower capital charge only if the guarantor was an OECD bank.

BIS II has attempted to rectify some of the shortcomings in BIS I. These were:

- *Risk differences between obligors.* BIS II allows for an internal ratings based approach which can stratify the borrowers in terms of credit quality. It is no longer the case that 8 percent capital ratio is needed for all corporate borrowers regardless of credit quality.

- *Credit migration versus default/no default.* BIS II recognized that credit migration can occur. This is reflected in the rules through additional capital requirement based on maturity since the longer the maturity, the greater is the possibility of credit migration
- *Correlation effects on the portfolio.* This is done through the use of a correlation factor. The correlation factor is the degree to which the asset values in the portfolio are correlated with each other.
- *Basing the capital needed on unexpected loss.* BIS II capital is based on the assumption that the loss distribution is normal the capital requirement is based on the 99th percentile of the loss distribution. This is called the *conditional expected loss* based on the conditional default probability and the "downturn" loss given default. The conditional default probability is the average default probability adjusted upward for stressed conditions and correlation.
- BIS II assumes that the portfolio is infinitely granular; that is, it is already highly diversified and the only risk it is subject to is the systematic risk. The systematic risk is captured through the relationship of portfolio defaults to the individual default probability as well as the correlation of asset values to a single factor that drives the systematic risk.
- BIS II offers banks the option to use the advanced approach wherein it can use its own models for deriving the capital requirements so long as it is found satisfactory by the regulators.

BIS II consists of three pillars. The first pillar deals with minimum capital requirements and sets the three alternative methods for a bank to calculate its minimum capital. The second pillar deals with the supervisory process that is intended to ensure that the bank has a sound process for assessing its capital position using one of the three methods set forth in the first pillar, and the bank's strategy/ability to maintain the regulatory capital levels. In this pillar, the robustness of the models and data used by the bank would be assessed as well as stress test on the capital calculations. The third pillar emphasizes market discipline by requiring appropriate public disclosure of material and significant information about the institution's financial condition.

BIS II Pillar I defines that minimum capital requirements will equal the sum of the capital required for credit risk, market risk, and operational risk. This statement implies that that credit risk, market risk, and operational risks are perfectly correlated. In deriving the minimum capital requirement for credit, a bank can use one of three approaches:

1. The basic standardized model.
2. The internal ratings model foundation approach.
3. The advanced internal-ratings-based (IRB) model.

The basic standardized model is for the banks that do not have an internal ratings system, and for these the external ratings assigned by independent ratings agencies are to be used. The weights assigned for the ratings range from 20 percent for AAA- to AA-rated credits, 50 percent for A+ to A, 100 percent for 100 percent for BBB+ to BB−, and 150 percent for credits rated below BB−. Curiously, the risk weight is 100 percent for unrated credits. A capital ratio of 8 percent is applied to the weighted exposures. The risk weights for claims on sovereigns and their central banks are also graduated in a similar manner although they are somewhat lower. For example, sovereigns with rating of A+ to A− have a risk weight of 20 percent versus 50 percent for corporations with a similar rating. This approach, while an improvement over BIS I, shows insufficient sensitivity to credit losses in various risk grades. For example, the risks in BBB+ through B− are known to encompass a wide range both in default probability and loss given default and yet they are placed in a single risk bucket.

In the foundation and advanced IRB approach, an institution should use a statistically valid risk rating system that can assign a risk rating (and probability of default) for each of its transactions. Additional required inputs are *exposure at default* (EAD) with LGD provided by BIS II (for example, 50 percent for senior claims and 75 percent for subordinated claims). For the advanced foundation approach the bank should provide its LGD figures and *maturity* (M). The model assumes correlation set by BIS at 10 to 20 percent as decreasing function of default probability. The model used in BIS II is based the Merton model, which is also at the core of CreditMetrics and MKMV Portfolio Manager.

The credit risk capital required is the excess of the unexpected loss in stressed conditions over the expected loss. The expected loss is presumed be covered by loan loss reserves. The maximum loss in excess of expected loss (which is equal to $EAD \times LGD \times PD$) in the portfolio of principal amount EAD and loss given default LGD at the chosen confidence level CL is given by

$$CVaR(CL) = EAD \bullet LGD \bullet \left(\Phi \left(\frac{\sqrt{\rho}\Phi^{-1}(CL) + \Phi^{-1}(PD)}{\sqrt{1-\rho}} \right) - PD \right)$$
$$\times \frac{1 + (M - 2.5) \bullet b(PD)}{1 - 1.5b(PD)}$$

where

    $CVar$ = Credit value at risk at the confidence level CL
    EAD = Exposure at default
    LGD = Loss given default
      M = Maturity
      b = Maturity adjustment given by $b = (0.11852 - 0.05478 \times ln(PD))^2$

Correlation $(\rho) = 0.12 \times (1 - EXP(-50 \times PD))/(1 - EXP(-50)) + 0.24$

$\times [1 - (1 - EXP(-50 \times PD))/(1 - EXP(-50))]$

The first part of the expression

$$\left(\Phi \left(\frac{\sqrt{\rho}\Phi^{-1}(CL) + \Phi^{-1}(PD)}{\sqrt{1 - \rho}} \right) - PD \right)$$

measures the stressed default probability at the confidence level CL, usually set 99.9 percent with the assumption that default probability is standard normally distributed in the portfolio that is infinitely granular with an asset correlation of ρ. The term to the right is the maturity adjustment, basically increasing the maximum loss for increasing maturities. Φ is the value of the standard normal distribution evaluated at a particular point and Φ^{-1} is the inverse of the normal distribution function at a particular point. Thus this expression derives the value of the stressed PD minus the normal PD, given the normal PD, and correlation ρ.

A detailed analysis of all aspects of BIS II is outside the scope of this book. However the reader may refer to BIS's web site (http://www.bis.org) on the extensive amount of analyses that have been performed on these regulations. Several books have appeared on the subject as well (see Saunders and Allen 2002).

BIS II has gained acceptance in Europe, and has been slowly adopted in the developing countries. In the United States, the implementation time frame for BIS II has not been firmly established due a number of regulatory and banking industry factors. Some of the stumbling blocks are the significant expenditures it takes to establish risk systems, calibration and validation of the models, and a possible concern on the part of some regulatory agencies that the capital requirement based entirely on the model results may not be adequate.[16]

THE FUTURE OF CREDIT PORTFOLIO TECHNIQUES

Since the credit portfolio modeling framework embodies a number of assumptions about the future that may or may not have been tested, validation of the models to actual experience is therefore critical in minimizing model risk (see Chapter 14 on this point). One approach to dealing with model is risk to perform stress tests to assess the range of possible outcomes that deviate significantly from the baseline estimates of expected losses and credit value at risk.

The risk emphasis in portfolio management differs from one player to the next. A financial guarantor will perhaps be more interested in understanding the structural aspects of the credit risk (covenant triggers, first loss level, issuer financial strength, etc.) and the *current* rating distribution of the insured assets rather than in understanding rating migration—even though the latter may be important to the issuer who uses the services of the guarantor. In looking at a portfolio, a consumer bank, on the other hand, would be less concerned about concentration risk and more concerned about systemic risks, such as a nationwide recession or changes in the bankruptcy laws. An insurance company will want to model its strategy to take advantage of regulatory arbitrage opportunities (e.g., differing capital charges for rated versus unrated securities), and the pricing, term, seniority, first-loss protection, diversification features implicit in asset-backed securities such as credit card receivables, CLOs, and CBOs.

Some institutions have found it necessary to combine the oversight of credit and market risk. Banks have moved more and more into an *origination and distribution* strategy rather than *origination and retention*, there is a convergence of credit and market risk measurement methodologies. As Allen (1996) points out, integration of the two functions is desirable for three reasons. First, there is a lot of transactional interaction between credit and market risk; second, there is a need for comparability between returns on credit and market risk (example: emerging market debt); and third, the emergence of hybrid credit and market risk product structures, as well as credit derivatives, makes this necessary.

Value at risk has been criticized because it is just a single number: It does not tell management where the risks are or what it should do. In the case of portfolio solutions, management should likewise be wary of single indexes that purport to signify everything. Management should understand the assumptions behind the numbers and be familiar with the analytics so that it is aware of a model's strengths and weaknesses. Although this is a tedious and difficult process, it is a simple fact that management, not the model, must ultimately take responsibility for the organization's operating results.

Even before portfolio analytics may be applied, an institution should invest in an information system that makes such analysis possible. Deal structure, product data, industry membership, geography, loss/claim history, borrower's sources of revenue, key borrower-specific indicators, ratings where available, and stock price where available, are some of the obvious variables that should be scrubbed and maintained. Reliance on third-party data is acceptable, but management should ensure that the data is of acceptable quality and is applicable to its own environment. For example, bond default recovery data may not apply to bank loans or derivative exposures unless properly adjusted for differences in collateral, seniority, call provisions, industry segment, and the like. In an interview with Paul Narayanan and Jack Caouette, Brian Ranson, formerly Senior Vice President at Bank of Montreal and currently a managing Director at Moody's MKMV, likens the implementation process to making rabbit stew according to an old recipe. He says that before getting into the details of the ingredients and the way to make the soup, the recipe directs you to go out and catch a rabbit. "Ironically, it is much more difficult to get a rabbit in your own backyard than one in the forest. For many institutions, the external market provides far better data on credit risk than do their own systems."

Portfolio management raises organizational as well as analytical issues. An asset originator in a bank is part of a profit center, but a portfolio analyst tend to occupy a staff position—often in a cost center with power and influence that is more imagined than real. While an asset originator is perceived to be creating value, a portfolio manager's recommendations may be viewed as negative to neutral—advising the bank to do nothing, to stop a deal or to sell an asset. Because these roles are in such innate conflict, the portfolio manager may be reduced to a passive role.

The burden often falls on the CEO to prevent organizational dysfunction, maintain consistency, foster participative management and provide the necessary empowerment through fiat, compensation, and rational transfer-pricing mechanisms. The compensation system should focus on the value, quality and quantity of what is originated and less on its endowment impact. In a 1993 interview with the authors, Brian Ranson (1993) explains that at Bank of Montreal, the portfolio manager occupies an influential position:

> *The job of relationship management is one of asset origination. They go out and find assets, and negotiate an appropriate price and structure. We (in portfolio management) decide how much we will invest, and the rest of it is disposed of by loan sales and trading. The head of the portfolio has the position of asset manager and in many ways has the same responsibility as the manager of a large albeit relatively illiquid mutual fund.*

Communication—both formal and informal—is an excellent aid to refocus attitudes about the portfolio. Clearly, the more the asset originator acts as a portfolio manager, and vice versa, the more the organization benefits. Lastly, success in managing the portfolio can come only if an appropriate risk culture is established and maintained.

REFERENCES

Adamidou, E., Y. Ben-Dov, L. Pendergast, and V. Pica. 1995. "The Optimal Portfolio System: Targeting Horizon Total Returns under Varying Interest-rate Scenarios." In *Financial Optimization*, edited by S. A. Zenios. Cambridge: Cambridge University Press.

Allen, R. A. 1996. "Integrating Credit and Market Risk Management." *Journal of Lending and Credit Risk Management* 78, no. 6.

Altman, E. I. 1988. "Default Risk, Mortality Rates, and the Performance of Corporate Bonds. Research Foundation, Institute of Chartered Financial Analysts, Charlottesville, VA.

———. 1989. "Measuring Corporate Bond Mortality and Performance." *Journal of Finance* 44, no. 4:909–922.

———. 1992. "Revisiting the High Yield Debt Market." *Financial Management* 78–92.

———. 1993. *Corporate Financial Distress and Bankruptcy*: 2nd ed. New York: John Wiley & Sons.

———. 1997. Corporate Bond and Commercial Loan Portfolio Analysis. Working Paper S-97–12, NYU Salomon Brothers Center.

Altman, E. I., A. Resti, and A. Sironi. "The PD/LGD Link: Implications for Credit Risk Modeling." In *Recovery Risk*, edited by E. I. Altman, A. Resti, and A. Sironi. London: Risk Books, 2005.

Altman, E. I., and A. Saunders. 1997. "Credit Risk Measurement over the Last 20 Years." *Journal of Banking and Finance* 21, no. 11:1721–1742.

Altman, E. I., and D. L. Kao. 1992. "The Implications of Corporate Bond Rating Drift." *Financial Analysts Journal* 64–75.

Altman, E. I., and P. Narayanan. 1997. "Business Failure Classification Models: An International Survey." In *International Accounting and Finance Handbook*, 2nd ed., edited by Frederick Choi. New York: John Wiley & Sons.

Altman, E. I., and V. M. Kishore. 1996. *Default and Returns in the High Yield Debt Market, 1991–1995*. White Paper, NYU Salomon Center.

Altman, E. I., G. Marco, and F. Varetto. 1994. "Corporate Distress Diagnosis: Comparisons using Linear Discriminant Analysis and Neural Networks (The Italian Experience)." *Journal of Banking and Finance* 505–529.

Altman, E. I., J. Hartzell, and M. Peck. 1995, May 15. *A Scoring System for Emerging Market Corporate Debt*. New York: Salomon Brothers.

Altman, E. I., R. Haldeman, and P. Narayanan. 1977. "Zeta Analysis: A New Model To Identify Bankruptcy Risk Of Corporations" *Journal of Banking and Finance* 29–54.

Asquith, P., D. W. Mullins Jr., and E. D. Wolff. 1989. "Original Issue High Yield Bonds: Aging Analysis of Defaults, Exchanges and Calls" *Journal of Finance* 923–953.

Bankers Trust New York Corporation. 1995, August. *RAROC & Risk Management: Quantifying the Risks of Business*. New York.

Bennett, P. 1984. "Applying Portfolio Theory to Global Bank Lending." *Journal of Banking & Finance* 8, 153–169.

Bessis, J. 2004. *Risk Management in Banking*. New York: John Wiley & Sons.

Black, F., and M. Scholes. 1973. "The Pricing Of Options And Corporate Liabilities." *Journal of Political Economy* 8, 637–659.

Bluhm, C., L. Overbeck, and C. Wagner. 2003. *Introduction to Credit Risk Modeling*. London: Chapman & Hall /CRC.

Brewer, E., and G. D. Koppenhaver. 1992. "The Impact of Standby Letters of Credit on Bank Risk: A Note." *Journal of Banking and Finance* 1616, 1037–1046.

Chava, S., and R. A. Jarrow. 2004. "Bankruptcy Prediction with Industry Effects." *Review of Finance* 8, no. 4:537–569.

Chirinko, R. S., and G. D. Guill. 1991. "A Framework for Assessing Credit Risk in Depository Institutions: Toward Regulatory Reform." *Journal of Banking and Finance* 15, no. 4:785–804.

Dev, A. 2004. Editor, *Economic Capital*. London: Risk Books.

Duffie, D., and Singleton, K. J. 2003. *Credit Risk*. Princeton, N.J.: Princeton University Press.

Coats, P., and L. Fant. 1993. "Recognizing Financial Distress Patterns Using a Neural Network Tool." *Financial Management* 142–155.

Cyert, R. M., H. J. Davidson and G. L. Thompson. 1962. "Estimation of the Allowance for Doubtful Accounts by Markov Chains." *Management Science* 287–303.

Cyert R. M and G. L. Thompson. 1968. "Selecting a Portfolio of Credit Risks by Markov Chains." *Journal of Business* 1, 39–46.

Elton, E., and M. Gruber. 1995. *Modern Portfolio Theory and Investment Analysis*, 5th ed. New York: John Wiley & Sons.

Freedman, D., R. Pisani, and R. Purves. 1997. *Statistics*, 3rd ed. New York: W.W. Norton.

Gupton, G. M., C. C. Finger, and M. Bhatia. 1997, April 3. *CreditMetrics+: The Benchmark for Understanding Credit Risk*. New York: JPMorgan.

Ho T. S. Y., and S. B. Lee. 1986. "Term structure movements and pricing interest rate contingent claims." *Journal of Finance* 41 no. 5:1011–29.

Hull, J., and A. White. 1995. "The Impact of Default Risk on the Prices of Options and other Derivative Securities." *Journal of Banking and Finance* 299–322.

Iben, T., and R. Litterman. 1989. "Corporate Bond Valuation and the Term Structure of Credit Spreads." *Journal of Portfolio Management* 52–64.

Izan, H. Y. 1984. "Corporate Distress in Australia." *Journal of Banking and Finance*, 303–320.

JPMorgan. 1997. *RiskMetrics+—Technical Document*, 4 ed. New York.

Jagtiani, J., A. Saunders, and G. Udell. 1995. "The Effect of Bank Capital Requirements on Bank Off-Balance Sheet Financing." *Journal of Banking and Finance* 647–658.

Jonkhart, M. 1979. "On the Term Structure of Interest Rates and the Risk of Default." *Journal of Banking and Finance* 253–262.

Journal of Banking and Finance. 1984. Special Issue on "Company and Country Risk Models." *Journal of Banking and Finance* 151–387.

Kealhofer, S. 1995. "Portfolio Management of Default Risk." White Paper, Moody's KMV Corporation.

Kealhofer, S. 1996. Measuring Default Risk in Portfolios of Derivatives, White Paper, Moody's KMV Corporation.

Lawrence, E., L. D. Smith, and M. Rhoades. 1992. "An Analysis of Default Risk in Mobile Home Credit." *Journal of Banking and Finance* 299–312.

Markowitz, H. M. 1959. *Portfolio Selection: Efficient Diversification of Investments*, John Wiley & Sons, New York.

Markowitz, H. M., and Perold, Andre F. 1981. "Portfolio Analysis with Factors and Scenarios." *Journal of Finance.*

Martin, D. 1977. "Early Warning of Bank Failure: A Logit Regression Approach." *Journal of Banking and Finance* 249–276.

McAllister, P., and J. J. Mingo. 1994. "Commercial Loan Risk Management, Credit-Scoring and Pricing: The Need for a New Shared Data Base." *Journal of Commercial Bank Lending* 6–20.

McElravey, J. N., and V. Shah. 1996, September. "Rating Cash Flow Collateralized Bond Obligations." In *Special Report, Asset Backed Securities.* Chicago: Duff & Phelps Credit Rating Co.

McKinsey & Co. 1993. "Special Report on The New World of Financial Services." *The McKinsey Quarterly* 59–106.

McQuown, J. 1994. All That Counts is Diversification: In Bank Asset Portfolio Management. IMI Bank Loan Portfolio Management Conference, May 11, 1994.

Merton, R. C. 1974. "On the Pricing of Corporate Debt." *Journal of Finance* 449–470.

Moody's Investors Service. 1990. "Corporate Bond Defaults and Default Rates, 1970–1989." *Moody's Special Report*, April.

Moody's KMV Corporation. 1993. *Credit Monitor Overview.* San Francisco.

Morgan, J. B. 1989. "Managing a Loan Portfolio Like an Equity Fund." *Bankers Magazine*, January–February.

Morgan, J. B., and T. L. Gollinger. 1993. "Calculation of an Efficient Frontier for a Commercial Loan Portfolio." *Journal of Portfolio Management.*

Morningstar, Inc. 1993. *Morningstar Mutual Funds User's Guide.* Chicago.

Platt, H. D., and M. B. Platt. 1991a. "A Note On The Use Of Industry-Relative Ratios In Bankruptcy Prediction." *Journal of Banking and Finance* 1183–1194.

———. 1991b. "A Linear Programming Approach to Bond Portfolio Selection." *Economic Financial Computing* 71–84.

Ranson, B. J. 1993. "Rabbit Stew." *Balance Sheet* 37–40.

———. 2005. *Credit Risk Management.* Austin, TX: Sheshunoff/Alex eSolutions Inc.

Santomero, A., and J. Vinso. 1977. "Estimating the Probability of Failure for Firms in the Banking System." *Journal of Banking and Finance* 185–206.

Saunders, A. 1997. *Financial Institutions Management: A Modern Perspective*, 2nd ed. Burr Ridge, Ill.: Irwin.

Saunders, A., and L. Allen. 2002. *Credit Risk Measurement*, 2nd ed. New York, John Wiley & Sons.

Scott, J. 1981. "The Probability of Bankruptcy: A Comparison of Empirical Predictions and Theoretical Models." *Journal of Banking & Finance* 317–344

Sharpe, W. 1966. "Mutual Fund Performance." *Journal of Business* 111–138.

———. 1994. "The Sharpe Ratio." *Journal of Portfolio Management* 49–58.

Smith, L. D., and E. Lawrence. 1995. "Forecasting Losses on a Liquidating Long-Term Loan Portfolio." *Journal of Banking and Finance* 959–985.

Sommerville, R. A., and R. J. Taffler. 1995. "Banker Judgment versus Formal Forecasting Models: The Case of Country Risk Assessment." *Journal of Banking and Finance* 281–297.

Standard & Poor's. 1991. "Corporate Bond Default Study." *Credit Week*, September 16.

Thieke, S. 1997. Stephen Thieke interview with Paul Narayanan and Jack Caouette.

Trippi, R., and E. Turban. 1996. *Neural Networks in Finance and Investing*, rev. ed. Chicago: Irwin.

Vanderhoof, I. T. 1997. "Variance of a Fixed-Income Portfolio." *Contingencies*, September/October.

West, R. C. 1985. "A Factor-Analytic Approach to Bank Condition." *Journal of Banking and Finance* 253–266.

Wilcox, J. W. 1973. "A Prediction of Business Failure Using Accounting Data." *Journal of Accounting Research* 11, Supplement: Empirical Research in Accounting: Selected Studies 1973:163–179.

Wilson, T. 1997. Measuring Credit Portfolio Risk: A New Approach. IAFE Annual Meeting, Zurich, June 10.

CHAPTER 21

Credit Derivatives

Ah, take the Cash, and let the Credit go,
  Nor heed the rumble or a distant Drum!
  —*The Rubhaiyat of Omar Khayayam,* stanza 13 (translated by
                                        Edward FitzGerald)

Credit derivatives are financial instruments whose payoffs are linked in some way to a change in credit quality of an issuer or group of issuers. Banks introduced them in the early 1990s to help them deal with their paradoxical desire to enjoy the benefits of asset concentration[1] without having to face the attendant risks. Implausible as this may seem at first sight, it has proven possible for banks to resolve this paradox to the benefit of all concerned. The solution required the banks to find counterparties that are willing to assume the credit risk in exchange for a fee, while the bank itself retained the asset on its books. A credit derivative is so named because it is *derived* from the existence of an underlying asset, for example, a loan. Just as a bank is able to swap the fixed rate on an asset for a floating rate, it can now, by paying a premium, swap the *default risk* on an asset for *the promise of a full or partial payout* if the asset defaults. Credit derivatives can be tailored to lay off any part of the credit risk exposure, amount, recovery rate, and maturity. They can even be constructed for events such as a rating downgrade that do not involve default.

The credit derivative market has exploded in the past 10 years. Its development and continuing innovation has transformed both the banking and fixed income markets irrevocably and some feel we are still in the early stages of the growth in this market.

Table 21.1 and Figure 21.1 below tell the story of how the market has grown and attracted new participants.

TABLE 21.1 Institutions Using Credit Derivatives to Buy and Sell Protection

Type	Buyers of Credit Protection				Sellers of Credit Protection			
	2000	2002	2004	2006	2000	2002	2004	2006
Banks—Trading activities	81%	73%	67%	39%	63%	55%	54%	36%
Banks—Loan portfolio	81%	73%	67%	20%	63%	55%	54%	9%
Hedge funds	3%	12%	6%	28%	5%	5%	15%	32%
Pension funds	1%	1%	3%	2%	3%	2%	4%	4%
Corporates	6%	4%	3%	2%	3%	2%	2%	1%
Monoline insurers	7%	3%	2%	2%	23%	21%	10%	8%
Re-insurers	7%	3%	3%	2%	23%	21%	7%	4%
Other insurance companies	7%	3%	2%	2%	23%	12%	3%	5%
Mutual funds	1%	2%	3%	2%	2%	3%	4%	3%
Other	1%	2%	1%	1%	1%	0%	1%	1%

Source: Bear Stearns (2006).

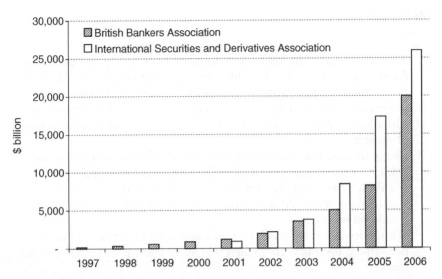

FIGURE 21.1   Credit Derivative Notional Outstanding
Source: Bear Stearns (2006).

Even though credit derivatives developed after the introduction of interest rate derivatives, they are actually the less exotic of these instruments. Apart from the newness of the name, credit derivatives resemble credit insurance products such as monoline guarantees or standby letters of credit. Indeed, the resemblance is close enough that banking regulators see credit swaps as analogous to letters of credit, and total return swaps as equivalent to equity swaps.[2] Lloyd's of London offered reinsurance on trade credit as early as 1893 (Cockerell 1984). It was the development of standardized terms and products in the late 1990s that gave the market the impetus to move beyond the bank and insurance markets. Today, in addition to the banks who were the market pioneers, insurance companies and hedge funds have become big players. A recent report by Bear Stearns indicates the market is constantly evolving (see Table 21.2).

CREDIT DERIVATIVES: AN EXAMPLE

Broadly stated, a *credit derivative* is a bilateral financial contract that derives its value from a change in credit quality of an issuer or group of issuers. The most common form of credit derivatives is an arrangement between two parties by which they agree to exchange predetermined or

TABLE 21.2   Evolution of Structured Credit: An Update on Market Participants in 2006

- The structured credit market has developed a diverse participant base.
- As managers of credit risk, banks are significant buyers and sellers of protection, but their relative dominance has decreased as the market has grown. As would be expected, they are net buyers of protection.
- Monoline insurers continue to play a large role and remain net sellers of protection.
- Hedge fund activity will continue to increase due to their ability to:
  - Capture arbitrage opportunities in this adolescent market.
  - Take advantage of the opportunity to cross the debt and equity markets in the credit derivative arena.Create unique positions and tailored investment.
- With more favorable regulatory and accounting treatment of credit derivatives, insurance companies will likely become more active in the market.

Source: Bear Stearns (2006).

formula-determined cash flows, contingent on the occurrence of a credit event over the course of a preset future time period. The event must be observable and is generally, but not always, associated with an adverse development such as default, bankruptcy filing, rating downgrade, or a significant drop in market price. The intent of the derivative is to provide default protection to the risk seller and compensation for taking risk to the risk buyer. In credit derivative parlance, the *derivative seller* is the *protection seller*—the party that sells the put (*the right to put the asset back in exchange for cash for par, for example*). Consider the following example.

Let us say that Bank A has an exposure of $10 million with Corporation X for five years and wants to reduce it without actually selling all or part of it to another institution. This is a common dilemma for banks in their lending relationships because borrowers often are unwilling to have their debt sold. Banks fear that if they sell a loan, they may lose the opportunity for future business with the borrower.

Faced with exposure that it wants to minimize, Bank A can enter into an agreement with Bank B whereby, in exchange for a fixed periodic fee of 50 basis points, Bank A obtains protection for all or part of its exposure. If Corporation X defaults on its obligation, Bank B will pay Bank A a sum representing the loss that Bank A incurred in the credit event. Bank B may have several different reasons for entering into this transaction. It may wish to gain exposure where, because of barriers to entry, it had none before. It may wish to diversify its portfolio. Finally, it may have better information than Bank A about the creditworthiness of Corporation X, and it may therefore value the risk differently.

Bank B's contingent obligation may be defined in a variety of ways, such as:

- Cash settlement for the loss in value of the loan.
- A fixed amount (binary).
- Par value of the loan, with the loan delivered to Bank B and so on.

The period for which this arrangement may be in effect also varies. Bank A may obtain protection for just the first two years, on the theory that Corporation X faces the greatest uncertainty during this period; it may, for example be a pharmaceutical company awaiting regulatory approval of a new drug. The credit event need not be default on the underlying obligation per se.

Credit derivatives are not currently traded on exchanges, but are arranged on an over-the-counter basis, in much the same way as reinsurance is arranged. Banks do not like to use the "I" word (insurance) for fear that this product will be legally termed insurance, thereby setting off alarms in the insurance industry and in the offices of insurance regulators.[3]

In the first edition of *Managing Credit Risk,* we interviewed Blythe Masters (1997) who was at the time heading up JPMorgan's efforts to develop the market for credit derivatives. JPMorgan had a huge lead in what was then the very early stage of the market. At the time in late 1997, according to Masters, the notional principal outstanding was somewhere around $200 billion versus the loan market size of size of $1.2 trillion. Masters proselytized this new market and tried to move it beyond the early adopting banks that made up most of the market. Much of that 1997 interview focused on the regulatory treatment of credit derivatives. Banking regulators were clearly biased against protection sellers other than from banks domiciled in countries within the Organization for Economic Development and Co-Operation (OECD). The banks were trying to move this market beyond what then amounted to spreading the risk amongst them, to include new investors and risk takers who were not banks. Masters could see that the market's future depended upon making changes in the regulatory treatment.

We contacted Masters to get an update for the revision. She had moved on within JPMorgan and directed us to a colleague Tom Benson, Managing Director in its Credit Derivatives Division. Benson had joined the

JPMorgan effort early in its development, so he has seen tremendous change in the market over the past 10 years. "I remember when we were doing 15 trades a week," he recalled. "Now we do that in a few minutes. Early on, the market was mostly small volume in single name swaps. Most deals were pretty good sized, but there was certainly no flow" (1993). In our interview, Benson talked a lot about the effort that had been made to standardize documentation, terms, and ways of settling trades. The major dealers working through their trade group, The International Swap Dealers Association (ISDA) has made significant progress on these issues and this was a major part of the reason the market had taken off. He explained how a lot of effort had gone into solving the problem of how to deliver a portion of an issue that was in an index trade. As we listened to Benson, we could see that the market was maturing; the effort now was mostly directed at trying to facilitate electronic trading and processing. The question was no longer whether the market was going to be big and important, but rather how to handle the volume and cut down on problems and issues. As he explained, the liquidity in credit derivatives "is bringing more liquidity and better pricing discipline to the bond market. The involvement of the hedge funds has really changed the market. Now we have nonbank players who are prepared to go both directions—both sell and buy protection, depending upon what they see in the opportunity. It has changed the market forever (Benson 1993)."

STRUCTURAL FORMS OF CREDIT DERIVATIVES

Looking at the market from a high level, there are two types of credit derivatives. A *credit default swap* (CDS) is a contract where buyers and sellers can bet on a corporate or sovereign risk either in single name form or in groups of names in an index. The second type is the CDO, where a pool of credits is created synthetically, creating debt instruments independent of the underlying cash market. The credit derivative market has been the focus of significant financial innovation in recent years and there are many variations within these categories. The rating agencies actively report on developments in the market and want to create broad buckets that they can monitor over time.

Figure 21.2 outlines how the credit derivative market currently breaks down according to a recent report by Fitch. The list is a mixture of types of risk—single-name risk or groups of companies such as you would find in an index or CDO——and other categories that mostly represent the way the deals are constructed. The credit derivatives market has seen substantial

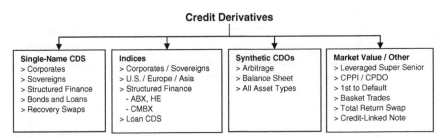

FIGURE 21.2 Overview of Credit Derivatives
Source: Fitch Ratings (2007).

innovation in recent years, so the categories are constantly changing and vary somewhat depending upon which agency list you use.

The creativity and innovations of financial engineers who focus on credit derivatives make it difficult to cover all the variations in this chapter. For some types of the credit derivatives, such as single-name CDS seems likely to remain fairly staple in terms of construction. Others are definitely the objects of innovative thinking and "tweaks" are constantly reshaping the transactions they represent. The following subsections illustrate the structures of some of the most popular forms of credit derivatives.

Credit Default Swap (CDS)

The plain vanilla version of a credit derivative is a credit swap where the protection buyer pays a fixed recurring amount in exchange for a payment contingent upon a future credit event. If this event occurs, then the protection seller pays the agreed amount to the protection buyer to cover the credit loss pursuant to default. The credit swap structure is illustrated in the Figure 21.3. There may also be an intermediary who arranges this structure (not shown).

Credit swaps often contain a *materiality* clause that ensures that the credit default is not triggered by minor, nonmaterial, or staged events. Materiality is usually defined as significant price deterioration based on a dealer poll in a preset period following an apparent credit default event. If there is truly a default event, the reasoning is that its economic effect will be reflected in a change in the price of the reference security. The credit swap resembles a loan guarantee and may in fact be priced using the same methodology.

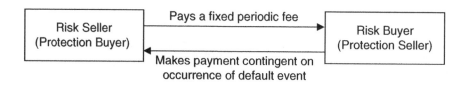

Default: Based on the default of a reference security by a reference credit.

Alternative Settlement Forms:
(1) Fall in market value of the reference security at x-number of months from default date.
(2) Physical Delivery of Notional Principle in exchange for defaulted security.
(3) Binary: Payment of a predetermined fixed amount.

Materially:
There should be a significant deterioration in the price of the reference security before settlement is triggered.

FIGURE 21.3   Single Name Credit Default Swap

An alternative way of analyzing this transaction is to treat it as an asset swap. Because of its simplicity, a credit swap is easy to arrange as long as the parties can agree on the definition of the credit event.

Synthetic CDO

In a synthetic CDO, the manager does not purchase actual bonds, but instead typically enters into several credit default swaps with a third party, to create synthetic exposure to the outstanding debt issued by a range of companies. The *special purpose company* formed to hold these exposures then issues financial instruments, which are backed by credit default swaps rather than any actual bonds. The development of synthetic CDOs has transformed the market as this has allowed this segment of the market to grow without regard to the availability of bonds or other cash debt instruments. Figure 21.4 features a basic schematic for a synthetic CDO.

Total Rate of Return Swap

The *total rate of return* (TROR or TR swap is a bilateral financial contract in which the total return of an asset during the holding period is exchanged

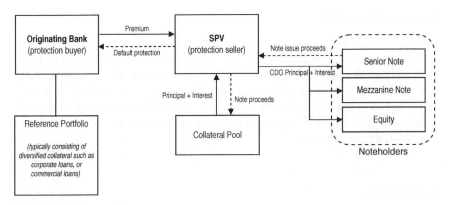

FIGURE 21.4   Synthetic CDO
Source: Author's compilation.

for another cash flow. It differs from the credit swap in that the credit swap is credit event-specific, whereas the TROR exchanges the cash flows whether there is a default or not. The schematic diagram for a TR swap is shown in Figure 21.5. The TR swap has the effect of completely removing the economic risk of an asset without the actual sale of the asset.

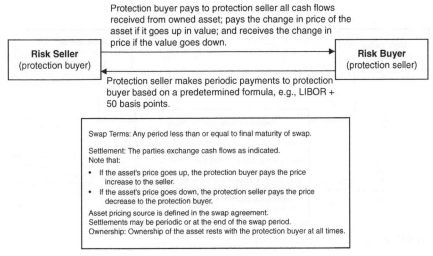

FIGURE 21.5   Total Return (TR) Swap

Credit-Linked Note

A credit-linked note is described in Figure 21.6. A special purpose vehicle is set up to issue notes and/or certificates. The proceeds are invested to acquire cash collateral equal to the amount of protection sought by the protection buyer. The yield from the collateral plus the fees paid the protection buyer is passed through to the investor. If there is a default, the cash collateral is liquidated to satisfy the protection buyer and the remaining proceeds are distributed to the investor.

Index Swap

An index swap is a combination of a bond and a credit option. The bond coupon payments and/or the principal payments are recalculated based on the provisions of the credit option. Suppose, for example, that a finance company has issued a fixed rate bond to finance its operations. The credit option may provide that the applicable interest rate will decrease by x basis points for every y percent increase in past due loans nationally. Thus, the company is protected from having to continue making high loan repayments if consumer delinquencies increase; it has bought insurance in the form of a credit option. In the context of credit derivatives an index swap will typically be considered a swap that references a pool of credits. Figure 21.7 summarizes what an index swap is about.

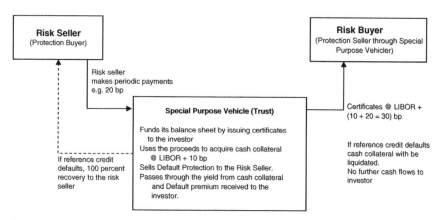

FIGURE 21.6   Credit-Linked Note

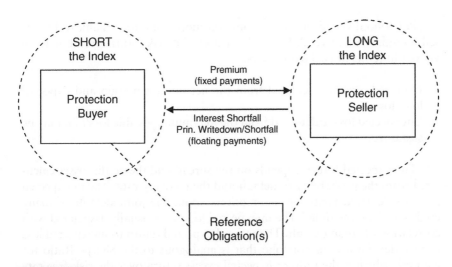

FIGURE 21.7   Index Swap
Source: Wachovia Capital Markets LLC (2007).

FEATURES OF CREDIT DERIVATIVES USEFUL TO A RISK SELLER

Banks make their profits by making loans and selling other complementary credit market services. This inevitably places them in a long position vis-à-vis credit risk. As Blythe Masters (1993) observes:

> *Lending, loan syndication, derivatives intermediation, underwriting, market making, credit enhancement are credit functions which generate systematic credit exposures for banks and financial institutions. In the past, it was not possible to actively manage credit portfolios: you cannot short a loan; there was no repo market for loans. Similarly you could not sell your business concentration risk without getting out of the business. Now, portfolio managers have a set of tailored credit risk management tools. With increasing liquidity we can completely reverse or change or optimize our credit risk profile, which—keeping the future in perspective—is extremely valuable to us at this point of the credit cycle.*

Portfolio diversification is a common motivation for a bank to buy or sell a credit derivative. A bank's loan portfolio risk-return profile may be viewed in terms of two parameters:

1. Expected return, calculated from the net interest margin and expected loan losses.
2. Unexpected loss, calculated from the maximum possible loss that may be sustained.

The expected return depends on the spread and the credit losses calculated from the probability of default and the recovery rate. The unexpected loss is calculated based on assumptions about the joint default of many credits at the same time.[4] The unexpected losses are usually associated with correlation of credit default. The ratio of expected return to unexpected loss is an index for a loan portfolio that is analogous to the Sharpe Ratio for equities (which is the ratio of expected excess return over the risk-free rate divided by the standard deviation). The expected portfolio performance is improved by improving the Sharpe Ratio. This is accomplished by either or both of two strategies.

1. Reducing the assets currently in the portfolio that have relatively lower returns for higher unexpected losses.
2. Adding other assets that will make a positive contribution to the Sharpe Ratio.

Until now, a bank could implement either of these strategies only through buying or selling loans. Although a loan sales market now exists, it is still better suited for investors with a long-term investment orientation, than for traders who wish to speculate on credit movements or for portfolio managers who want to shape their portfolios. With credit derivatives, however, these strategies may easily be implemented. A bank no longer needs a relationship building/loan organization infrastructure to acquire exposure. Furthermore, some risk mitigation strategies such as the hedging of commitment risk and the selective hedging of tenor risk cannot be accomplished through the sale or purchase of loans.[5]

A credit derivative allows a bank to take advantage of arbitrage opportunities such as pricing discrepancies across classes, geographic locations, maturity ranges, and investor classes. In short-term assets, for example, there are discrepancies in pricing past the 13-month maturity. Likewise, differing philosophies exhibited by rating agencies present arbitrage opportunities: in assigning a rating Moody's appears to consider both default probability and expected recovery rate, whereas S&P is said to be biased more toward the default probability. According to Blythe Masters (1993), in the past these discrepancies were either interesting or frustrating, but there was nothing that a bank could do because it had no way to execute the short leg of the transaction. Credit derivatives open these possibilities for banks.

Since credit derivatives enable banks to lend at lower risk, they tend to increase liquidity in the banking industry. Banks are willing to make more loans to their customers when they know that they can sell interests in those loans. In some cases, banks are now willing to consider lending in some industries and to some customers that they would not have considered prior to having a dependable place to distribute the risk. Thinking about it from the perspective of the corporate customers of the banks, credit default swaps have significantly increased the possibilities for borrowing from banks.

Credit derivatives are transforming the market in a number of ways. One advantage of credit derivatives is confidentiality. An investor that owns a risk asset can obtain credit protection against its defaulting without the obligor even knowing about it. If the bank decides to use a third-party *reference credit,* the protection seller also need not know the identity of the obligor. A bank, for example, that has lent to ABC Corporation in South Korea may obtain a credit derivative whose default provisions are based on South Korea's sovereign debt rather than on ABC Corporation. This will make sense only if the *basis risk* (the relationship between the basis, South Korea, and the underlying risk) is acceptable. At the same time, as the market develops and prices are published, additional information about companies are now available to market participants. At a time when the credibility of the credit rating agencies is being questioned by many observers, the price of credit swap transactions can provide a valuable credit signaling function to market participants.

A bank can choose from a wide variety of coverage's depending on its tolerance for risk and the price at which credit risk may be laid off. A credit derivative can be customized, for example, to cover a portion of the notional principal, a fraction of the period exposed, or a recovery rate ranging from 0 percent to 100 percent in the event of default.

Documentation has tended to be quite simple because the more complex it is, the greater the likelihood for disputes in the case of a claim. According to Blythe Masters (1993), it takes just a few hours to set up a credit derivative—in contrast to a loan syndication, which requires substantial time to negotiate and close. Because this was a new market, there was an opportunity to standardize documentation. This has facilitated deal doing, but it has also reduced the cost of transacting and made credit derivates a very cost-effective way of transferring risk between institutions.

FEATURES OF CREDIT DERIVATIVES USEFUL TO A RISK BUYER

A buyer of exposure can take on credit risk without having to fund a loan or having to develop any origination capability. This is the credit equivalent of buying a future or an option. Some entities have unique credit-monitoring resources in certain industries or countries that other players may lack. They can use this information advantage to become protection sellers.

Credit derivatives are a special class of *event derivatives* because they contract for a cash flow that is contingent on some event that may or may not occur. Even nonfinancial companies that are concerned about the solvency of their suppliers and customers may find them helpful. Using a credit derivative, a company can also profit from pricing discrepancies in its own capital structure. If, for example, a company's senior unsecured debt is priced more thinly than its secured debt, it can buy its senior unsecured exposure and short its secured exposure.

Synthetic CDOs generate investment opportunities that otherwise would not be available. Because investments in CDO's often have credit ratings that are higher than the ratings of the underlying bonds, they provide a new opportunity for investors. Also, many investors, because of regulation or investment criteria, have limitations on their investment alternatives. Some investors might not be able to buy the underlying bonds in a CDO, given the low credit rating of the bonds. However, they can buy the more highly rated CDO constructed from the pool of bonds. Similarly, some regulated investors—banks and insurance companies—could purchase the underlying bonds, but would have to pay high capital charges due to regulations that depend on credit ratings. The higher rated CDO would produce a lower capital charge and make this purchase more attractive for them.

The speed with which credit derivatives have grown in the past decade is indicative of their versatility.

POSSIBLE APPLICATIONS OF CREDIT DERIVATIVES

Credit derivatives are another development in the steady march of the financial markets toward products that are identified less by the institutions that sell them than by the economic function they perform. Banks were traditionally—and still are—regarded as the evaluators of credit risk: They not only *assess* credit risk, they also *assume* it.

In the residential mortgage market, GNMA, FNMA, and FHMLC have created uniform underwriting and documentation standards. These have made it possible for separate entities to serve as originators of mortgage assets and as investors in mortgage assets. The same has not happened in the commercial and international loan markets, where loan standardization is more the exception than the rule. Banks custom tailors their loans. They worry that selling loans to free up capacity will endanger their relationships with customers. Credit derivatives offer an unobtrusive way to reduce or increase their credit exposure.

Of course, credit derivatives presuppose the existence of willing buyers and sellers, and of *market clearing*; that is, bid-ask spreads at which such transactions may be consummated. The market can have very wide bid-ask spreads, and it often takes time to find counterparties and to come to an agreement. But the market is now much deeper and has increased the liquidity.

Credit derivatives thus have the potential to help banks balance their conflicting goals—the goal of focus (achieving comparative advantage[6] in credit evaluation administration by concentrating in selected areas) and the goal of diversification.

For perhaps the first time in history, the investment banker selling this product has something to offer the corporate lending officer or the bank portfolio manager. Since credit derivatives can eliminate all or part of the credit risk of a transaction, both banks and their regulators have begun to learn to look at credit risk not only at the individual transaction level but also at the portfolio level. Regulators now may permit a bank to use an internal model to derive the value at risk due to credit risk that can be used in computing its regulatory capital.

Banks can buy or sell protection or act as intermediaries. They may employ credit derivatives to increase their income by using their unique ability to assess risk without going on to fund the loan. Banks may also benefit from the chance to spread the fixed costs of their credit analysis infrastructure. Ultimately, banks may divide themselves into pure *credit risk takers* and pure *loan funders*.

Good credit is a valuable and scarce commodity. Obligors are always trying to borrow money at the lowest possible cost with the least impact on their creditworthiness. Special purpose subsidiaries and captive finance companies are two examples of corporate structures aimed at managing credit risk from the obligor's side. The first category insulates the parent from liability by providing a corporate veil; the second category minimizes borrowing costs by putting only high-quality financial assets on the borrowing company's balance sheet—thus making it possible for the subsidiary to access the (lower cost) commercial paper market. It may be recalled that Chrysler Financial enjoyed access to the commercial paper market because of the high quality of its assets even when its parent, Chrysler Corporation, was undergoing financial difficulties in the 1980s. Ford and General Motors are more recent examples as their financing arms continued to have high-grade access to the capital markets while their parent's debt ratings sunk precipitously in recent years.

There is always an unspoken tug-of-war between lenders who want to obtain the greatest amount of protection for a given set of loan terms and borrowers who want to obtain funds with the least encumbrance on their resources. The availability of credit derivatives greatly facilitates the achievement of both of these goals. Even after the loan has been consummated, both borrower and lender can shop credit more easily. Corporate borrowers may fine-tune their debt structure without acquiring or retiring debt, and they may also be able to hedge the credit risk premium for future borrowing costs.

NOT EVERYTHING IS GOOD ABOUT CREDIT DERIVATIVES

There is no doubt that the credit derivative market has delivered many upsides to the capital markets. However, the same technology that has offered so many benefits has some unintended consequences that are not necessarily positive and will need to be managed. One of the issues attracting attention in the current market turmoil is the distance between the borrower and the ultimate lender. This has been cited as an issue creating problems in the structured finance markets[7] and is an issue for credit derivatives as well. The traditional role for the banker included being corporate governance "activist" when things went array. It is not unusual to see banks insist that a CFO be changed or to require a restructuring specialist be added as a condition of a refinancing. When companies go into bankruptcy, banks are often central to the decision making process that follows. In today's markets, however, the fact that a group of banks has exposure to a troubled company doesn't necessarily mean that they have much "skin in the game" (Lubben 2007). If they don't, and these days it is reasonable to assume that is the case, then there may be a moral hazard regarding their role in the mix.

Enron's bankruptcy seems to be an illustration of this phenomenon. Major banks such as JPMorgan Chase, Citigroup, and others had lent billions to Enron; but there was little evidence that they exercised much oversight, either before or after Enron's credit started to decline. While Enron was not any easy company to understand, let alone coral, it does seem like the banks were willing to lend more to them and to stand back when they started to deteriorate because they had sold off much of their exposure using credit derivatives.

Another issue emerging as an issue is the different perspectives of some of the major players in the credit markets. Hedge funds, in particular, are very different from the banks that they are purchasing the loans from using credit derivatives. Hedge funds are not relationship lenders, so they seldom are sympathetic to the complexities or nuances of a company's economic condition. Also, they typically engage in a wide variety of trading strategies and could be shorting the company's equity while buying their credit risk using credit derivatives. They also could be playing with options and warrants on the credit. In some circumstances, this means that they have an incentive to affirmatively destroy corporate value because of a trading position that benefits from a decline in credit worthiness. How often this happens is difficult to determine, particularly since most hedge funds do not disclose their trading positions or strategies.

One recent example that received some notoriety involved Tower Automotive, which supplies truck frames to the auto industry. In 2004, Tower borrowed roughly $580 million under a pair of loans arranged by JPMorgan Chase and Morgan Stanley (Sender 2005). After its financial condition deteriorated, Tower tried to arrange additional loans from the same group of lenders. The new loan would have required Tower's existing lenders to free up a portion of their collateral and to lower their interest rate. Apparently, JPMorgan and the bank syndicate it led were willing to make the concessions to keep Tower alive; but the hedge fund participants would not agree and no new loan was made. Two months later, Tower filed for bankruptcy. According the *Wall Street Journal,* "Some bankers believe hedge funds triggered the filing to make their short positions (in the equity) worth more" (Sender 2005).

Credit default swaps are structured as over-the-counter derivatives and they are unregulated. This means that it is very difficult to know about the details of any individual transaction. Exacerbating the problem is that swaps are heavily traded among players. It is very difficult for a borrower to know whether the banker who they arranged the loan with is still a principal or just the "front man" for his loan. There is no way to know who may have an interest in the loan until something bad happens. This is changing the whole nature of the lending business.

Credit derivatives also raise systemic concerns. More players, different perspectives, and the frequent use of leveraged positions, particularly by hedge funds, means that the market probably is operating with hair triggers that can be set off by relatively minor events. The rush to unwind a vast array of interconnected contracts, as we saw in summer 2007, was no doubt a result of these factors.

Finally, while credit derivatives have had an overall positive influence on the pricing of credit risk, there are a number of pricing issues that arise from this market. The market for credit default swaps, except for a handful of major credits, is not particularly deep and can be moved relatively easily by players who may wish to do so. So the pricing of CDS frequently are outside the ranges of the underlying cash instruments. Over time this should diminish; but it represents an opportunity for some aggressive behavior for hedge funds and other players who may be looking to arbitrage the market. Even more troubling is the pricing associated with synthetic cash flow CDOs. The fact that a CDO manager can create a CDO and price it such that it can acquire each piece of the CDO "at a market rate," and then pay themselves, their legal advisors, the rating agencies, and credit market spread required to finance the CDO and still have something left over for profits, suggests that there is something going on which suspends normal economic theory. The fact that this has been one of the fastest growing activities in recent years would lead to the conclusion that there is some form of "structural arbitrage" at work in these markets. Some of this can be explained by the regulatory restrictions many investors operate under and also by the fact that most investors operate within "investment silos," which restrict their ability to move between investment types. However, some observers believe that the investment bankers who do most of the analysis have created a complex system that only they understand and benefit from.

THE REGULATORY VIEW OF CREDIT DERIVATIVES

Credit derivatives provide new insights into credit risk and its management. Just as the futures and options markets help in price discovery, credit derivatives help to develop efficient credit pricing, providing the benefits that a free competitive market affords. They make it possible, for example, to understand the term structure of credit premiums.

It is thus not surprising to expect that regulators view the development in the credit derivative market with interest. At the same time, because credit derivatives are noncash off-balance-sheet instruments, they have the potential for increasing the system risk. It should be no surprise that regulators can see both bad and good in the development of the market.[8] The current regulatory view on credit derivatives may be summarized as follows:

1. The bank providing the guarantee should treat it as a direct credit-substitute (i.e., put it on the balance sheet) and the notional equivalent should be converted at 100 percent. The regulators view the provision of a loan guarantee by a bank as equivalent to having the loan on its book.
2. For the protection buyer, the underlying asset will be considered guaranteed for capital purposes as long as the underlying assets and the reference assets are obligations of the same legal entity, have the same level of seniority in bankruptcy, and are subject to mutual cross-default provision. Basis risk, the relationship between the underlying asset and the

reference asset, is of concern to the regulators. Although it is a real risk, basis poses no major problems to a bank. In most cases, the reference asset is a publicly traded security whose process can readily be obtained. But there is a risk that the reference asset will not track the real risk being hedged against.

3. If the guarantor is an OECD bank, or if it is provided by a highly rated counterparty, (AAA, AA), then the underlying asset should be assigned to the 20 percent risk category. If the guarantor is an institution other than an OECD bank, as a lower-rated entity it is to be treated at the 100 percent risk category for the purposes of risk-based capital. The implication is that regulators view regulated banks, regardless of their creditworthiness, as excellent credit counterparties. Basel II regulatory changes have made nonbank protection sellers attractive to banks and have fueled the rapid development of the credit derivatives market. In reality, many AAA-rated insurance companies would be stronger counterparties then, say, a highly leveraged bank.

Although the examiners take note of credit derivative-based guarantees designed to mitigate asset concentrations, for reporting purposes, the existence of such guarantees is not deemed to reduce asset concentration. If, for example, a bank that has loan concentration in China purchases a credit derivative to protect it, the regulators would note this fact but continue to view the bank as having loan concentration in China.

CREDIT RISK OF CREDIT DERIVATIVES

Counterparty Risk

When an institution has sold exposure to another institution, it has exchanged the risk of default of the underlying asset for the joint risk of defaults by the counterparty and the underlying asset. Clearly if only *one* of the two defaults, then there is no credit risk. The probability of default by *both* depends on the marginal probability of default of either and the *correlation* between the two default probabilities. This may be expressed by the equation:[9]

$$P(A \text{ and } B) = \text{Corr}(A, B) \times [P(A)(1 - P(A))]^{1/2} \times [P(BI)(1 - P(B))]^{1/2}$$
$$+ P(A) \times P(B)$$

where

$A = $ Default by the underlying obligor
$B = $ Default by guarantor or protection seller

TABLE 21.3   Five-year Default Correlations

	Aaa	Aa	A	Baa	Ba	B
Aaa	0					
Aa	0	0.00				
A	0	0.01	0.01			
Baa	0	0.01	0.01	0.00		
Ba	0	0.03	0.04	0.03	0.15	
B	0	0.04	0.06	0.07	0.25	0.29

Source: Reprinted from *Journal of Fixed Income,* Lucas, "Default Correlation and Credit Analysis," p. 81, March 1995, with permission of Institutional Investor, Inc.

$P(A \text{ and } B)$ = Probability that both default together
$P(A)$ = Probability of default of underlying obligor (assuming a binomial distribution)
$P(B)$ = Probability of default of guarantor (assuming a binomial distribution)
$\text{Corr}(A, B)$ = Correlation between the two events, A and B

Although this equation is straightforward, it must be borne in mind that it is difficult to obtain dependable estimates for *P(A)* and *P(B),* and even more so for the correlation of *A* and *B* (which, being a product of two quantities, is the equivalent of squaring one's uncertainty). If the two default events are independent, then the correlation is 0, in which case purchasing the credit protection would have brought the probability of loss from *P(A)* down to *P(A)* × *P(B)*. Generally, however, there will be some degree of correlation between the guarantor and the underlying credit—for example, because they both participate in the same national economy.

Five-year default correlations for various bond ratings were reported by Lucas (1997) as shown in Table 21.3. This table is provided only for the purpose of illustration. The correlation to use would consider not only the rating class of the two names but also other variables such as geography, industry, and size that may impact its value.

Model Risk

Major financial institutions use internal models for measuring market risk such as value-at-risk (VaR). Typically, these models project a term structure of interest rates and make some assumptions about a statistical process for the movement of security prices. VaR includes credit risk as reflected in the security prices. VaR itself may be criticized because volatility, which drives this measurement, is difficult to forecast. When it is a matter of modeling default *events* rather than *rates*, the VaR model will not be satisfactory. Unlike interest rate or stock price movements, the occurrence of a default significantly changes the value of a debt security. CreditMetrics is a step in the direction of recognizing that it is perhaps more reasonable to model the volatility of returns from credit-risky assets through rating migration, and thence rating-specific values. In spite of the altered view of the value at risk, CreditMetrics, in its current state of development, can provide only an approximate view of risk exposure—we stress the term approximate because the assumptions built into it make it necessary to constantly review the output. Moreover, it will not give prescriptions for dealing with risk exposure. However, tools like CreditMetrics may yield insights in managing the portfolio through credit derivative products.

VALUATION OF CREDIT DERIVATIVES

In general, the variables that have impact on the *intrinsic value* of a credit derivative are the same variables used to value a credit risk asset. The following is a partial list of the variables that may enter the calculation for intrinsic value:

- Likely probability of default of the underlying credit and the protection seller.
- Pessimistic probability of default.
- Joint probability of default of the underlying credit and the protection seller.
- Timing of default.
- Recovery rate distribution.
- Workout cost distribution.
- Asset's seniority.
- Timing of recovery.
- Interest rate.
- Prepayment probability distribution.
- Pricing basis—fixed versus floating.
- Amortization structure.
- First loss level ("deductible" in insurance parlance).
- Correlation structure for the default, prepayment, recovery interest rates.

A probabilistic cash flow approach may be taken to calculate value based on assumptions on these variables. The value so calculated may be compared with the current market spreads to estimate the cost of the protection. Approaches taken to calculate the outcomes may be deterministic (e.g., scenario analysis) or stochastic (Monte Carlo simulation). The limitation of scenario analysis is that the calculations follow a limited number of paths that the analyst has defined. With Monte Carlo simulation, because the variable values are not preset and are drawn from a distribution, calculations may be performed over a larger number of paths, presumably resulting in a range of likely outcomes instead of point estimates (see Trigeorgis (1996) for a summary of standard numerical procedures for solving such problems).

CURRENT PRICING PRACTICE

Although credit derivatives have existed in alternative forms for a long time, their current form is relatively new, and pricing methodologies are still evolving.[10] Here we will describe a practitioner's approach based on information gathered in 1997. Today, the pricing of credit derivatives is based on that of asset swaps. That is because an asset swap is a close substitute for a credit derivative. Let us consider why.

An asset swap is a package consisting of a fixed income security and an interest rate or a currency swap. It is constructed by using the price discovery of the swap and options markets to strip out the effect of the noncredit components of the security. Once a fixed-income security is bundled with a swap to remove the interest rate and currency risk, for example, it is turned into a pure credit-based opportunity. A relative value comparison can then be made between this and an existing investment choice.

For example, an investor whose current investment choices are U.S. dollar, LIBOR-based may consider a package whose ultimate cash flows are also LIBOR-based: a euro sterling noncallable bond (a fixed rate sterling security) on XYZ company combined with a currency swap of fixed GBP (British pounds) at 8.875 in exchange for U.S.$ LIBOR + 20 basis points. The resulting cash flows have no currency or interest rate risk because both are removed by the currency swap.

Let us see how the transaction works. Initially, the proceeds from the currency swap are used to purchase the XYZ bonds. The exchange rate for the purchase of the XYZ bond is the same as that used for the principal exchange on the currency swap at maturity. The risk assumed is the credit risk of XYZ and the counterparty credit risk for the swap. By buying this package the investor has purchased XYZ exposure. This has the same effect as selling a put: assuming the risk of default in exchange for the credit spread.

The only differences are (1) that the buyer of the asset swap *already owns* the XYZ bond, whereas the derivative seller does not; and (2) that the asset swap buyer has credit contingent interest and foreign exchange rate, since if the bond defaults the swap buyer will typically need to terminate the swap hedge, costing the buyer money. In both instances, there is no interest rate or currency risk.

Let us say Little Bank wants to buy a put; that is, buy credit protection from Big Bank. The pricing of a credit derivative can start from the pricing of an asset swap. The buyer of the put (say, Little Bank) wants to shed XYZ Corporate exposure, which is now assumed by Big Bank. Big Bank could have taken on this exposure simply by buying a synthetic XYZ security, a fixed rate bond bundled with an interest rate swap to convert the asset into a LIBOR-based floating rate instrument (thereby taking on pure credit risk and no market risk). Let us say that the spread over LIBOR for this asset swap for XYZ is 50 basis points. Note that this spread is compensation for pure credit risk of XYZ as priced by the market. Intrinsic value does not enter into the calculation because the institution is taking market pricing as the basis for deriving the arbitrage-free price. Arbitrage-free pricing (also known as the law of one price) would dictate that the put and the asset swap are equivalent, all other things being equal. Thus the put should also be priced at 50 basis points.

However, a credit derivative will pay more than an asset swap because of a risk, however slight, about the settlement in case of a default event and greater uncertainty in case Big Bank wants to make a clean exit and close its position. If Little Bank's price for terminating the contract is unattractive, Big Bank has to find some other way of covering its exposure. For this reason, Big Bank, the seller of the put, adds a premium, of say, 25 percent of the risk spread. Thus the derivative will be priced at $50 + 0.25 \times 50 = 62.5$ basis points.

This practice will apply when the risk of the counterparty selling protection is not an issue. But what if the seller of the put—say, a bank named NoHopeBank—is perceived to be more risky? In this case, Little Bank may not want to buy the put because of the possibility that NoHopeBank may not be able to perform when default occurs. To mitigate this risk, Little Bank will want cash collateral. This is where the credit-linked note comes in. With this instrument, NoHope puts up cash collateral with Little Bank, receiving in exchange an additional premium representing the risk of Little Bank—say, 10 basis points. The net result of this transaction is that NoHope will receive a return of $50 + 12.5 + 10 = 72.5$ basis points over LIBOR from Little Bank. NoHope bank has taken on XYZ risk and also Little Bank risk with respect to return of cash collateral when the put expires unexercised.

In applying this approach, we should distinguish between investment-grade and noninvestment-grade credits. For investment-grade credits, because the pure credit spread is already quite small, compensation for illiquidity and structure uses a greater multiplier, say 50 percent as used in the above example. The term structure of credit spreads in the market may be observed in the marketplace (see Table 21.4), which helps to validate the pricing.

For noninvestment-grade names, since the credit spread is already much larger, the illiquidity and structural premiums do not add so much proportionally. A name with a spread of 250 basis points may have a default swap spread of 300 (20 percent markup). The increment is greater as the maturity increases. Illiquidity is not as significant an issue in the short term (e.g., one year) as it is for the longer term. These credits are difficult to price because there is not a term structure to observe; it has to be guessed. Noninvestment-grade default swaps tend to be in the one- to three-year range, whereas investment-grade default swaps may be for longer maturities, as much as 10 years. Generally speaking, CDS spreads are usually tighter than cash. As a result, the basis is driven by supply and demand between cash and derivative market rather than any fundamental value. The next layer of innovation is the *first-to-default swap*. Let us say the basket has four credits, A, B, C, and D, with swap spreads of 30, 35, 40, and 50 basis points, respectively. The asset swap spreads are added up, giving a total of 155 basis points. If the credits are highly correlated, then a lower percentage is applied to the total to arrive at the pricing. The investor may apply, say, 15 percent, and arrive at $155 \times 0.15 = 23$ basis points. If the credits are uncorrelated, then a higher percentage is applied—perhaps 75 percent—to arrive at a price of 116 basis points. The reasoning behind this appears to be that if the risks are correlated, the investor expects the hit to come from a single underlying cause, whereas if they are poorly correlated, the hit may come from any of four different causes; therefore the risk is greater. In this exceptional case, correlation is good for the structure.

As the observant reader will have noted, credit derivative pricing depends on the availability of market-based credit spreads. If all assets were

TABLE 21.4 Term Structure of Credit Spreads, December 2006

Category	1 Year	2 Years	3 Years	5 Years	7 Years	10 Years
A1 Industrials	38	36	51	67	57	70
A2 Industrials	40	37	53	69	59	73
A3 Industrials	52	50	66	80	72	84
BBB1 Industrials	62	59	73	88	83	103

Source: Bloomberg.

marked to market, it is almost a certainty that credit derivatives would gain wide usage. Today, most credit risky assets are not marked to market, but indexing (such as linking delinquencies on a consumer portfolio to regional unemployment rate) makes it possible to use credit derivatives nonetheless.

Thus far, there have been far more theoretical studies on the pricing of debt subject to interest rate risk than on the pricing of assets when credit ratings and spreads are stochastic. Studies of the latter type have just begun. A paper by Das and Tufano (1996) provides a good review of the theoretical work and proposes a model for the pricing of credit-sensitive debt when interest rates, credit ratings, and credit spreads are stochastic. As credit derivatives gain wider acceptance, the pricing methodology will also evolve to handle defaults and credit quality migration.

An institution that wants to reduce its credit risk exposure using derivatives should attempt to answer the following basic questions:

- Will the transaction really reduce the credit risk that is to be reduced? Are the credit event and the time frame linked to the underlying credit in a reasonable way? Does the transaction make sense for the overall portfolio?
- Do the numbers add up? Are the assumptions made about the future states of the world consistent with historic experience, and is there solid reasoning to support the assumptions? Has the analysis dealt correctly with the credit risk and market risk of the asset? Is the price right?
- Is the counterparty risk tolerable? Is there liquidity for the transaction so that it can be closed out during its life?

Credit derivative transactions should be subjected to the same kind of evaluation as other derivatives. It is important that the institution exercise its own independent judgment rather than simply accepting the recommendation of an intermediary. After all, credit data on default, recovery, and correlation of default are generally among the weakest of all financial market data. With regard to pricing, the applicability of these data to the instruments owned by the institution should be carefully examined. The pricing model should be calibrated with live data and thoroughly stress-tested to reveal the financial implications of the transactions.

REFERENCES

Benson, T. 2007. Tom Benson, JPMorgan Chase, interviewed by authors.

Board of Governors of the Federal Reserve System, 1996. Supervisory Guidance for Credit Derivatives SR 96–17 (GE). Washington, D.C.

Cockerell, H. 1984. *Lloyd's of London: A Portrait.* Homewood, IL: Dow-Jones Irwin.

Das, S. R., and P. Tufano. 1996. Pricing Credit-Sensitive Debt When Interest Rates, Credit Ratings and Credit Spreads Are Stochastic. *Journal of Financial Engineering* 5, no. 2:161–198.

Greenspan, A. 2002. *Remarks by Chairman Alan Greenspan at Lancaster House,* London, U.K., September 25.

Irving, R. 1996. "Credit Derivatives Come Good," *Risk* 9, no. 7:23–27.

Lubben, S. J. 2007. Credit Derivatives & the Future of Chapter 11. Seton Hall Public Law Research Paper No. 906613, July 17.

Lucas, D.J. 1995. Default Correlation and Credit Analysis. *Journal of Fixed Income* 4, no. 4:76–87.

Masters, B. 1997. Blythe Masters, JPMorgan, interviewed by authors.

Minton, B., R. Stulz, and R. Williamson. 2006. "How much do banks use credit derivatives to reduce risk?", Ohio State University Fischer College of Business Working Paper Series, June.

Sender, H. 2005. "Hedge Funds Shake Up Lending Area," *Wall Street Journal,* 18 July.

Trigeorgis, L. 1996, *Real Options: Managerial Flexibility and Strategy in Resource Allocation.* Cambridge, Mass.: MIT Press.

Usman, P. 2001. New Applications for Credit Derivatives. Working Paper, University of Queensland, June.

CHAPTER 22

Counterparty Risk

Credit risk is the risk that a loss will be incurred if counterparty defaults on a derivatives contract. The loss due to a default is the cost of replacing the contract, less any recovery. The replacement cost represents the present value, at the time of default, of expected future cash flows. It is important to emphasize that a credit loss will occur only if the counterparty defaults and the derivative contract has a positive mark to market value to the nondefaulting party. Both conditions have to be satisfied simultaneously for a loss to be incurred.
—Global Derivatives Study Group, Group of Thirty

Most derivative transactions are by nature highly leveraged. In the futures market, it is possible to speculate on the entire value of a U.S. government bond just a fraction of the money needed to purchase the bond in the cash market. Leverage is a financial technique frequently used by hedge funds and others. It is a powerful tool that can increase risk if not used appropriately.[1] Counterparty risk can be substantial—indeed, so large that the marketplace imposes strict credit quality requirements on participants. Although defaults figure prominently in the assessment of credit risk in the G-30 definition, a mere change in the credit quality of the obligor can signal a change in the credit risk of a transaction. In this chapter, we consider the approaches that can be used to analyze counterparty credit risk as it related to *over-the-counter* (OTC) derivatives. For a discussion of clearinghouses and margining in relation to derivatives, please see Chapter 5.

Derivative volume, both on organized exchanges and in OTC markets has grown tremendously in the last 25 years. Table 22.1 shows the volume over a five-year period for U.S. commercial banks. The volume has tripled from 2001 to 2006, reaching over $122 trillion in notional value.

TABLE 22.1 Commercial Bank Derivatives

	Dec-01	Dec-02	Dec-03	Dec-04	Dec-05	Dec-06
Total Derivatives (notional amounts, in billions of dollars)	44,905	55,567	70,098	85,526	95,615	122,480
Futures and Forward Contracts	9,335	11,376	11,400	11,365	12,056	14,877
Interest rate contracts	5,330	7,380	7,213	6,520	7,060	8,535
Foreign exchange rate contracts	3,864	3,866	4,079	4,717	4,828	6,143
Other futures and forwards[a]	142	130	109	128	168	199
Option Contracts	9,924	11,574	14,613	17,750	18,856	26,275
Interest rate options	8,487	9,898	12,542	14,950	15,160	20,515
Foreign currency options	746	911	1,300	1,734	2,360	3,273
Other option contracts[b]	693	766	771	1,065	1,336	2,487
Swaps	25,646	32,617	44,085	56,412	64,704	81,328
Interest rate swaps	24,402	31,195	42,107	54,048	62,299	78,366
Foreign exchange rate swaps	1,129	1,304	1,805	2,155	2,101	2,484
Other swaps[c]	115	118	172	208	303	478
Memoranda						
Spot foreign exchange contracts	111	196	273	419	431	664
Credit derivatives	421	642	1,001	2,347	5,822	9,019
Number of banks reporting derivatives	369	447	580	684	838	917
Replacement cost of interest rate and foreign exchange rate contracts	598	1,118	1,118	1,268	1,129	1,019

[a]Does not include foreign exchange rate contracts with an original maturity of 14 days or less or futures contracts.
[b]Not reported by banks with less than $300 million in assets.
[c]Reflects replacement cost of interest rate and foreign exchange contracts covered by risk-based-capital requirements.
Source: FDIC (2007).

Although figures based on notional principal outstanding make derivative volume seem very large, the replacement value (shown in the last line of the table) gives a more accurate sense of the overall size of the exposure. On the basis of this measure, the swaps of U.S. banks had a replacement value of 2.33 percent in 2001 (598/25,646) and 1.25 percent in 2006 (1,019/81,328). Chew (1996) estimates the replacement values to be in the range 0.6 to 2.4 percent for interest rate derivatives and 1.1 to 3.8 percent for foreign exchange derivatives.

DERIVATIVE LOSSES

Concern about derivatives has recently been magnified by a series of derivatives-related disasters occurring over the last 15 years. Japan's Kahima Oil, America's Procter & Gamble, Gibson Greetings, Germany's Metallgesellschaft, Great Britain's Barings Securities, and the collapse of Long-Term Capital Management in 1998 to name a few, all suffered spectacular losses in which derivatives figured prominently in the 1990s. More recently[2] the financial markets have seen Enron go bankrupt (2001), AIB losing $750 million (2002), China Aviation losing $550 million in speculative trade (2004), Refco suspending trading (2005), Amaranth losing $6 billion (2006), and Bear Stearns closing down two hedge funds and seeing its stock value decline sharply (2007).

The reasons typically given to justify the losses related to derivatives trading are among the following:

- Insufficient management oversight
- Mark-to-model risk
- Improper hedging techniques
- Unexpected market moves
- Too much risk relative to capital
- Fraud
- Improper input assumptions in model
- Lack of diversification
- Reliance on a single trading strategy

Losses here mean that the derivative transaction failed to produce the intended result, not that one party lost in a zero-sum game. Credit losses on derivatives are just beginning to emerge. Because of the decline in the overall credit quality of the banking system, the credit quality of derivative transactions entered into with financial institutions cannot be taken for granted. To undertake derivative-based transactions, counterparties have had to establish AAA-rated special purpose derivative vehicles. After many years of financial innovation, it is fair to say that the critical issue facing the global players today is the control of credit exposure both at the individual deal level and at the portfolio level.

When reference is made to derivative risk it usually pertains to *all* risk associated with using derivatives. Banks (1997) mentions the following risks in the capital markets: operational risk, legal/documentary risk, liquidity risk of the asset or collateral, hedging risk, sovereign risk, counterparty default risk, market risk, delivery risk, position risk, and provisional risk (additional risk exposure due to a weakening credit). All these risks apply to derivatives as well. Here, however, we are concerned with the *counterparty credit risk of derivatives*—the amount of current and future exposure to a counterparty as a consequence of a derivative transaction; the likelihood; that the counterparty will default on the financial obligation coming due; and the magnitude of the recovery upon default.

THE ROLE OF COUNTERPARTY CREDIT RISK

The measurement of credit risk is important to the derivatives market for a variety of reasons, of which pricing is the most important. It is only through sensible pricing that a firm can ensure that it is adequately compensated for assuming current and future counterparty credit risk. There are many subtle issues in pricing. For example, the credit risk of a five-year, pay-fixed swap is *not* identical to the credit risk of a five-year, fixed rate loan. In the case of a loan, the borrower does not need to go to the market for five years, but in the case of the swap, the borrower needs to roll over the principal every three to six months because the underlying financing will be three to six months floating. Second, both principal and interest are at risk in a loan, whereas an interest swap involves interest alone. Moreover, because the periodic cash flows are based on the difference between two interest rates in the swap, they are smaller in magnitude to those on a comparable loan.[3] Third, a default in a swap requires two events to occur jointly: that the party to the swap is in distress *and* the value of the contract to the party is negative (i.e., money is owed). Fourth, a swapper can more easily put collateral and credit triggers onto a swap. These variables, taken together, can influence the credit spread to be applied, which may generally be lower for a swap than for a loan.

Once counterparty risk is understood, it can be mitigated through deal structure or hedging. Banks have a unique advantage here over the exchange-traded derivatives markets, where standardization prevails. Banks, by contrast, can be more flexible in meeting the needs of the borrower.

An understanding of counterparty risk is also necessary for purposes of setting aside an appropriate level of capital to weather adverse outcomes. This, in turn, makes it possible to evaluate the profitability of a derivatives operation on a rational basis

In some circumstances the need of independent third-party agencies capable of assessing a counterparty's credit risk may be necessary. The rating agencies often play this role and their ratings are taken as an estimation of the exposure to the counterparty's credit risk. Ratings are helpful when dealing with private firms that do not report financial statements, or to unregulated entities such as hedge funds.[4]

DERIVATIVE EXPOSURE

In the case of a derivative, the amount at risk is not the notional principal and will vary based on what assumptions are made about the financial variables. Generally, the exposure is expressed as the *current exposure*—the current cost of finding a replacement for the existing counterparty; the *potential exposure*—based on what might happen to interest rates in the future; and the *peak exposure*—the replacement cost in a worst-case scenario, sometimes called a *stress scenario*. Why replacement cost? In the case of an interest rate swap, the contract calls for exchanging cash flows in every reset period. The amount of the cash flow represents the difference between the fixed and floating interest rates multiplied by the notional principal. Suppose the counterparty defaults and files for bankruptcy. This has a financial impact only if money was owed by the counterparty because the interest rate difference was against it for the remainder of the contract. The counterparty will no longer be available to hold up its end of the bargain, so a replacement must be found. If rates have moved, replacement will be based on the current interest rate differential and on expectations about rates. The important point to remember is that the estimate of this exposure is influenced by a number of exogenous variables that themselves cannot be determined in advance.

Another key feature of derivative credit risk is that it may be nonlinear. For example, if you have purchased an interest rate cap, your counterpaty credit risk increases as interest rates increase beyond the cap. However, if rates are below the cap, the counterparty risk is zero.[5] In the case of the holder of an over-the-counter call option, the current exposure is equal to the current payoff, but only if te option is in the money. If the option is out of the money, the current exposure is zero.

INTEREST RATE SWAPS

The intermediary in an interest rate swap between two counterparties faces exposure because if either party defaults, the intermediary will have to step in and fulfill the terms of the contract with the nondefaulting counterparty. As summarized in Table 22.2, the impact of default on the intermediary is determined by the direction of the rate change and by which party defaults. The intermediary's exposure is equal to the replacement cost[6] of the swap, or the loss sustained by selling the remainder of the unmatched swap in the secondary market. The replacement cost if found by simulating a scenario of rates and projecting the period net cash flows to the party at risk. This notion of replacement cost is applicable not only to interest rate swaps but also to currency swaps, forward rate agreements, caps, and floors. The size and direction of the interest rate move is based upon historical data on interest rates, their mean values, and standard deviation, considering an interest rate model (presented later in the chapter) and a certain confidence interval coupled with a time horizon.

An example may clarify the concept of potential loss. Let us assume that a bank enters into a $100 million, five-year swap with a company. The bank will receive a fixed rate of 10 percent against six-month LIBOR. Initially, the

TABLE 22.2   Interest Rates and Exposure in Interest Rate Swaps

	Effect on the Intermediary	
Interest Rate Environment	If the Fixed Payer (floating receiver) Defaults	If the Fixed Receiver (floating payer) Defaults
Interest rate unchanged	None	None
Interest rates increase	Intermediary gains because the replacement cost of finding a new fixed payer is lower.	Intermediary incurs loss because the nondefaulting unmatched fixed pay swap is now worth less in the marketplace.
Interest rates decline	Intermediary incurs a lost. Loss corresponds to the increase in price of lower fixed rate for remainder of swap.	Intermediary gains. Gain corresponds to increase in price of the nondefaulting, unmatched fixed pay swap.

Source: Das (1994). Reprinted with permission.

TABLE 22.3 Example Showing Increasing *Potential* Credit Exposure in a Swap

Beginning of Year	Volatility Effect (rate increase from year 1, basis points)	Amortization Effect (time remaining, years)	Exposure ($ millions)
1	0	5	0
2	100	4	$4
3	200	3	$6
4	300	2	$6
5	400	1	$4
6	NA	0	$0

exposure is zero. Let us assume that the swap rate then declines to 9 percent. At the end of the first year the market value of the receive-fixed swap will go up by an amount equal to the *present value* (PV) of an annuity of $1 million for four years (1 percent of $100 million). This is the replacement cost of the swap at the end of the first year under this scenario. At the end of the second year, if the rates go up by another 100 basis points, the replacement cost will be the PV of an annuity of $2 million for three years, and so on, returning to zero at the end of the fifth year. The nominal (undiscounted) value of the exposure for the expected interest rate scenario is shown in Table 22.3. It is seen that the exposure is subject to two effects: changes because of the amortization (passage of time) and volatility (changes in interest rates).

In any year, the current exposure will equal the potential exposure estimated for that year to maturity. The peak exposure in the preceding example is $6 million, which corresponds to the value of an annuity of $2 million multiplied by three years remaining to maturity of the contract. Note that the credit exposure on the swap can vary dramatically, depending on the divergence in interest rates and the time to maturity. The changing exposure results in the familiar inverted-cup graph associated with the modeling of interest rate scenarios adverse to the party at risk (Figure 22.1). The exposure in future time periods may also be expressed in present-value terms by discounting at the prevailing interest rate.

The potential exposure for other derivatives such as futures and options may be similarly derived by postulating a future financial scenario and projecting cash flows, which then may be translated into a replacement cost. If the counterparty has a bilateral netting arrangement, then the exposures should be netted out before arriving at the exposure at the institution level. If there is no netting, only the positive (in the money) exposures should be added up. For futures, the exposure will increase linearly. For some options,

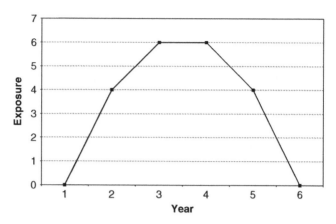

FIGURE 22.1 Potential Swap Exposure

the presence of an exchange will eliminate the need to calculate counterparty exposures, but some institutions may want to do it for tracking purposes.

CALCULATION OF EXPOSURE AND EXPECTED LOSS

Although most people agree on the constituents of credit risk, the actual calculation of it is subject to wide variation. At the rudimentary level, as we have just seen, exposure is calculated by using worst case senarios to derive a value to use in conjunction with the credit limits. At a more-advanced level, yield curve and default probability models may be used in a Monte Carlo simulation to develop a distribution of exposure and losses. A Monte Carlo simulation models a future distribution of asset returns at a given date, based on current asset prices, volatilities and correlation structure, taking into account as an input assumption that asset returns are normally distributed and that the expected asset return is the risk-free rate.

The detailed method for calculating the future credit exposure in an interest rate swap may be summarized in two steps: the calculation of exposure and the calculation of losses.[7]

Calculation of Exposure

Distributions of future credit exposure are estimated at many discrete points over the life of the instrument or portfolio. A standard Monte Carlo simulation involves setting the future dates where the value of the exposure is to be calculated. A number of discrete exposures aggregated together will conform a distribution. These distributions are conditioned on the current state of the financial variables (such as the prevailing yield curve and credit spreads), but not on the probability of counterparty default. The future state of the financial variables is specified through a Monte Carlo employing an interest rate term structure model that has been calibrated with historical data, namely mean interest rates and their standard deviation. The interest rate model will, at the minimum, contain a volatility component to model the random behavior of interest rates. The replacement value of the contract (mark to market) is calculated at each point along each time path. The replacement value assumes riskless replacement. The resulting exposures are used to calculate the average and maximum exposures.

Calculation of Losses

After the exposure is measured, other elements affecting credit risk must be evaluated, including the counterparty's financial condition, which will influence the probability of default, and the seniority structure of the borrower's liabilities, which will influence the recovery. The probability of default and expected recovery rate are then applied to the replacement value of the contract to obtain the average loss and the maximum loss given default. Having opened up this line of reasoning, we can also apply the concepts of expected and unexpected losses and correlation of defaults (see Chapters 17 and 18). In particular, the transition probability from one risk category to the next may be applied in deciding on the correct pricing to be used or in recouponing should there be a downgrade or upgrade during the life of the contract.

Let us illustrate the calculations by a simple example. Bank X enters into an interest rate swap with company Y. It receives semiannual payments at an interest rate of 8 percent against payment of six month LIBOR for a period of three years. Assuming a notional principal amount of $1,000,000, we can calculate X's exposure for two scenarios: (1) the swap rate goes down to 6 percent; and (2) the swap rate goes up to 10 percent. Figure 22.2 depicts the flow of payments between the two counterparties in an interest rate swap.

There is exposure to bank X when the swap rate falls (if Y defaults) because X now must replace the existing swap at (and receive thereafter) *lower rates.* The exposure is the present value of the remaining payment differential in the swap discounted at the new (replacement) swap rate. For a swap rate of 6 percent, the replacement cost is $45,797 (see Table 22.4) at the end of the first interest payment and gradually drops to zero, reflecting the reduction in the number of interest payments for the remaining life of the swap (the exposure is shown as negative values). There is no exposure to Y for X when the swap rate goes to 10 percent, because X will now make an additional profit if it has to replace the swap at a higher prevailing rate.

TABLE 22.4 Calculation of Swap Exposure

Interest period	Fixed rate payment at 8 percent	Fixed rate payment at 6 percent	Fixed rate payment at 10 percent	Cash flow differential at 6 percent to X	Cash flow differential at 10 percent to X	PV of remaining cash flows discounted at 6 percent	PV of remaining cash flows discounted at 10 percent
1	40,000	30,000	50,000	(10,000)	10,000	(45,797)	43,295
2	40,000	30,000	50,000	(10,000)	10,000	(37,171)	35,460
3	40,000	30,000	50,000	(10,000)	10,000	(28,286)	27,232
4	40,000	30,000	50,000	(10,000)	10,000	(19,135)	18,594
5	40,000	30,000	50,000	(10,000)	10,000	(9,709)	9,524
6	40,000	30,000	50,000	(10,000)	10,000	0	0

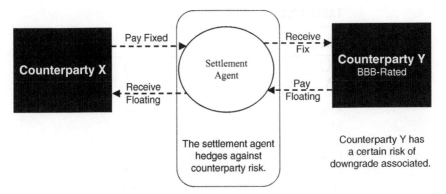

FIGURE 22.2 Interest Rate Swap between Two Counterparties

If company Y is rated BBB, then the bank's implied credit spread in the swap would be equivalent of 78 basis points on the exposure (based on the credit spreads shown in Table 22.5). Put differently, entering into this swap transaction is the equivalent of making an amortizing loan of $45,797 to Y at a 78 basis point credit spread, and this is built into the percent fixed rate on the swap. The implied credit margin for the swap, spread over the notional principal amount of $1,000,000 is then .08 × 45,797/1,000,000 = 37 basis points.

This analysis assumes that company Y remains a BBB throughout the life of the swap. But what if it gets downgraded or defaults sometime along the way? And what is the likelihood that it may happen? Table 22.6[8] gives one-year transition probabilities for a BBB-rated company. Based on this table, the probability that Y will be downgraded to BB or B, 4.55, 0.77, and 0.13 percent, respectively. Corresponding to these ratings, the incremental

TABLE 22.5 Credit Spreads

Rating	1 year	2 years	3 years
AAA	50	100	150
AA	65	105	155
A	75	110	170
BBB	100	150	200
BB	250	280	350
B	300	380	480
CCC	1200	1200	110

TABLE 22.6   Transition Probabilities

Rating	Probability
AAA	0.02
AA	0.17
A	3.76
BBB	84.09
BB	4.55
B	0.77
CCC	0.13
D	0.28
N.R.	6.23

Source: S&P Annual 2005 Global Corporate
Default Study and Rating Transitions.

credit spread, taken from Table 22.5, is 56 (that is, 134 – 78), and 135 (that is, 213 – 78) basis points. This equates to a fixed rate basis of 8.56, and 9.35 percent, from the base of 8 percent for the company. In a worst case scenario, a number of consecutive downgrades would drive counterparty Y to bankruptcy.

Using this amount, the downgrade premium applicable to this credit may be calculated by the expected value of the incremental interest based on the transition probability for the exposure amount (in this case $45,797). In Table 22.7, this comes out to $435, which translated to 4 basis points on the notional principal. Thus, in this arrangement, the credit spread for the swap is 37 basis points along with an additional 4 basis points to protect bank X against the downgrading risk of Y.

Another example of incorporating migration and default likelihoods is provided in Gupton, Finger, and Bhatia (1997, 47). Bond market default and migratioin data (discussed in Chapter 15 and 16) are useful to the analyst in extracting alternative market value-based credit spreads.

TABLE 22.7   Effect of Rating Migration on Spreads

Downgrade from BBB	Incremental Credit Spread (basis points)	Transition Probability (%)	Incremental Expected Value of Loss (on exposure of $45,797)
BB	56	4.55	254
B	135	0.77	181
			Total = 435

Although we utilized a single value for the swap rate in the example, in practice, institutions use stochastic models[9] to generate the trajectory of the interest rates, and Monte Carlo simulations are employed to derive the swap exposures.

CURRENCY SWAPS

From the point of view of exposure, currency swaps resemble interest rate swaps, but with two exceptions. First, the cash flow projections are affected not only by the two interest rate but also by the currency exchange rate. Second, at maturity there is an exchange of principal between the two parties. The general impact on an intermediary for a default in a fixed A$ (i.e., Australian dollar) to fixed US$ currency swap is summarized in Table 22.8. A fixed A$-floating US$ swap may be analyzed by splitting it into two swaps: Fixed A$-fixed US$ and fixed US$-floating US$.

MANAGEMENT OF DERIVATIVE CREDIT RISK

Derivatives are executed either on an exchange or in the OTC market. In the exchanges, the process of margining (see Chapter 5) provides credit risk management. By serving as a hub, an exchange is able to add up and net

TABLE 22.8   Effect of Counterparty Default on Intermediary

	Effect on Intermediary	
Interest Rate Environment	Default by Fixed A$ Payer	Default by Fixed US$ Payer
Rate same as contract rate	No effect	No effect
A$ rate higher than contract rate	Intermediary gains	Intermediary loses
A$ rate lower than contract rate	Intermediary loses	Intermediary gains
US$ rate higher than contract rate	Intermediary loses	Intermediary gains
US$ rate lower than contract rate	Intermediary gains	Intermediary loses
Currency Rate Environment		
Rate same as contract rate	No effect	No effect
A$ appreciates against US$	Intermediary loses	Intermediary gains
A$ depreciates against US$	Intermediary gains	Intermediary loses

Source: Das (1994). Reprinted with permission.

out all of a member firm's exposures. It thus makes it possible to manage the exposure on an aggregate single-risk basis. In comparison to the OTC approach, this is not only safer from a credit risk perspective, but also more economical. Currently, no mechanism exists for knowing, on a current basis, the total value a counterpaty has at risk in the OTC market. Most institutions rely on the counterparty's public bond ratings and their own internal "house limits" to manage credit risk exposure. Default prediction models such as ZETA or KMV may also be used to assess a counterpaty's financial condition. Portfolio management methods based on these tools may be applied to portfolios of derivatives. Published and proprietary models also exist for assessing the solvency risk of banks.[10]

MASTER NETTING AGREEMENTS

Adoption of master netting agreements allow a bank to net out all its exposures to a given counterparty rather than having the exposure from each individual transaction stand on its own. The netting includes both payments and balances.[11] When a bilateral "closeout netting" arrangement has been signed, a counterparty that is defaulting on derivative contracts on which it owes money cannot simultaneously demand payment on contracts on which it is owed money.[12]

- *Time puts* in swap agreements give a party the option to get out of all deals after a preset period.
- *Collateral arrangements* require the counterparty to post collateral in support of the transaction. These were quite common with capital poor thrifts that entered into interest rate swaps in the late 1980s. The collateral would be topped up to keep up with changing exposures.
- *Creation of a cash buffer* may be used to mitigate settlement risk with a weaker counterparty by altering the timing of the cash flows between the amount to be received and the amount to be paid out.
- *Rating downgrade triggers* allow a bank the option to presettle outstanding transactions should a counterparty's grade fall below a certain level (Lucas 1995).

STRUCTURED FINANCE SOLUTIONS TO DERIVATIVE CREDIT RISK

Some organizations have set up bankruptcy-remote SPDVs (special purpose derivative vehicles) to gain a AAA rating. Major financial institutions require that nonbank counterparties such as securities firms establish SPDVs to enter into derivatives transactions in the OTC market with them. SPDVs are well-capitalized, stand alone entities that "ring-fence" the transactions and are protected from their parent's (the securities firm's) bankruptcy (Derek 1995). Three types of structures have been set up: joint ventures, *separately capitalized vehicles* (SCVs) with a continuation structure, and SCVs with a termination structure.

In the joint venture structure, a derivatives firm teams up with a stronger partner to enhance its credit rating, presumably in exchange for a share of the profits in the joint venture or some other quid pro quo. Goldman Sachs's joint venture with Mitsui is an example of this structure.

In the SCV with a continuation structure, a contingent manager is appointed to step in to continue the transactions through the maturity of the open deals. The parent posts sufficient collateral to the subsidiary to obtain a top rating. This approach was pioneered by Merrill Lynch and appears to have greater market acceptance than the termination structure.

In the termination structure, which has been pioneered by Salomon Brothers, existing derivative transactions are terminated at agreed-upon termination values. Thereupon the SCV is liquidated.

EVALUATING THE CURRENT METHODS FOR ASSESSING DERIVATIVE CREDIT RISK

Exposure—the amount at risk—is dynamic and subject to variability because of uncertainty about the future of market variables and about their impact on a derivative transaction. Exposure measurements may also be impacted by *model at risk,* that is, how the effects of external variables are modeled. There are, for example, many interest rate models available today, such as the Ho-Lee model (Ho and Lee 1986),[13] the Black-Derman-Toy model (Black, Derman, and Toy 1990),[14] and the Heath, Jarrow, and Morton (Heath et al. 1987) model.[15] Each of these models makes a set of assumptions based on which the output, that is, time path of the interest rates, is generated. Within the yield curve itself, the mathematical methods for deriving the zero-coupon rates for various maturities are subject to variation depending upon which interpolation technique is used.

Duffee (1996) compared calculations of potential exposure by the Monte Carlos method using three progressively sophisticated models: a Cox-Ingersoll-Ross (1985) model for interest rates with fixed parameters; a Cox-Ingersoll-Ross model with probabilistically selected parameters; and a bootstrap method that directly employed actual historic data. The third method is unconditional in that it uses the actual price paths. He found that the Monte Carlo methods using yield curve models tended to underestimate the magnitude of the exposure relative to the unconditional distributions. His research indicates that model risk may lead to mismeasurement of credit risks for typical derivative instruments and third parties.

Duffee found that stochastic models used in projecting future values are accepted at face value, without proper regard for the behavior of the underlying financial variables. A second problem is that the financial variables driving the interest rate paths are not used jointly to determine the firm's credit quality. Third, correlations among derivative instruments are not taken into account either in measuring exposure or in pricing. Specifically, Duffee points out that current derivative credit risk methodologies do not consider adequately the correlations of default and the marginal effect of a derivative instrument on the upper bound of credit losses associated with the portfolio.

COMBINING CREDIT AND MARKET RISK

In traditional credit products, it was relatively simple to separate the credit risk from the market risk. Indeed, the credit function was often functionally separate from the treasury (market risk) function. But as is evident with off-balance-sheet assets, credit risk and market risk are closely interlinked. It is also not uncommon for an on-balance-sheet asset to be bundled with off-balance-sheet assets (a loan combined with a cap, or an asset swap, for example). In such instances, the credit and market functions need to be combined because the credit risk in the transaction depends on market value. Diversification applies both to credit risk and market risk.

If an organization has multiple derivative contracts, the volatility of its portfolio's value will be influenced not only by the volatility of the individual contracts but also by the extent to which the contracts move together in response to changing market conditions. Since domestic and foreign interest rates and exchange rates are closely related, the volatility of the market portfolio is *not* a simple sum of the component volatilities. In some cases, the increase in exposure due to interest rates will be offset by changes in exchange rates. A portfolio that is evenly divided between pay-fixed and pay-floating swaps will exhibit low volatility because when rates rise, the increase in the value of the pay-fixed swaps will be offset by a fall in value of the pay-floating swaps.

Increasingly, large institutions are combining the oversight of market risk and credit risk. According to Steve Thieke (1997), managing director and head of credit and market risk management at JPMorgan in the late 1990s, found that as it moved away from the classic "buy and hold" strategy to a strategy of "originate, package, and distribute," it was increasingly exposed to market risk both because of its need to distribute the loan assets and because of its derivatives transactions. In return for transferring market risk, the bank was also taking on counterparty risk. Moreover, the bank finds business opportunities such as credit derivatives that revolve around the concept of credit intermediation. To manage the portfolio on a total return basis, the bank recognized that it needed to view credit and market risks consistently. In a market populated by a finite number of financial institutions dealing in derivatives, concentration risk (single entity, country, and product type) can reach sufficiently high levels to cause concern. For these reasons, having a view that combines both credit and market risk is considered essential.

Today credit losses are generally projected over the remaining life of the contract assuming that the contract will be retained until maturity. If the market for credit risk becomes more liquid, it will become possible for banks to terminate or assign the contract to other dealers. By means of credit derivatives, a bank may be able to shield itself from the credit risk associated with a derivative contract. Thus, the credit risk of derivatives must be analyzed in the context of an entire portfolio—one that may consist of the combined effect of all the exposures an institution has to a single obligor, currency, country, or product type. This approach may be used to arrive at pricing, selling, or hedging decisions. This is one of the basic goals of tools such as CreditMetrics used to combine default prediction with correlation of default, and correlation of credit quality change.

REFERENCES

Ali, P.U. 2001. New Applications for Credit Derivatives. Working Paper, University of Queensland, T. C. Beirne School of Law.

Banks, E. 1997. *Volatility and Credit Risk in the Capital Markets*. Chicago: Irwin.

Baxter, M., and A. Rennie. 1997. *Financial Calculus*. Cambridge: Cambridge University Press.

Beder, T. S. 1996. Lessons from Derivatives Losses. In *Derivatives Risk and Responsibility*, edited by R. A. Klein and J. Lederman. Chicago: Irwin.

Black, F., E. Derman, and W. Toy. 1990. A One-Factor Model of Interest Rates and Its Application to Treasury Bond Options. *Financial Analysts Journal* 46, 33–39.

Chew, L. 1996. *Managing Derivatives Risks*. New York: John Wiley & Sons.

Cox, J. C., J. E. Ingersoll, Jr., and S. A. Ross. 1985. "A Theory of the Term Structure of Interest Rates." *Econometrica* 53, no. 2:385–407.

Das, S. 1994. *Swaps and Financial Derivatives*. 2d ed. London: IFR.

Derek, R. 1995. "Special Purpose Derivative Vehicles." *Accountancy* 1.

Duffee, D. 1996. "On Measuring Credit Risks of Derivative Instruments". *Journal of Banking and Finance* 20, 805–833.

Fitch Ratings. 2006. *2006 Global Structured Finance Outlook: Economic and Sector-by-Sector Analysis, Credit Policy Special Report.* New York.

Global Derivatives Study Group, Group of Thirty. 1995. *Principles and Practices for Wholesale Financial Market Transactions* 1.1. Washington, DC: Group of Thirty.

Gupton, G. M., C. C. Finger, and M. Bhatia. 1997, April 3. *CreditMetrics: The Benchmarke for Understanding Credit Risk.* New York: JPMorgan.

Heath, D., R. Jarrow, and A. Morton. 1992. "Bond Pricing and the Term Structure of Interest Rates: A New Methodology for Contingent Claims Valuation." *Econometrica* 60, 77–105

Hendricks, D. 1994. "Netting Agreements and the Credit Exposures of OTC Derivatives Products." *Federal Reserve Bank of New York Quarterly Review* 19, no. 1:7–18.

Ho, T., and S. Lee. 1986. "Term Structure Movements and Pricing Interest Contingent Claims." *Journal of Finance* 41, no. 5:1011–1029.

Jobst, A. A. 2002. Collateralised Loan Obligations – A Primer. Center for Financial Studies, Johann Wolfgang Goethe-Universitat, No 2002/13.

Jobst, A. 2005. "What Is Structured Finance?," *ICFAI Journal of Financial Risk Management* 4, no. 2:37–45.

Kabance, G. 2007. *Structured Finance in Latin America's Local Markets: 2006 Year in Review and 2007.* New York: Structured Finance International.

Lucas, D. J. 1995. "The Effectiveness of Downgrade Provisions in Reducing Counterparty Credit Risk." *Journal of Fixed Income.*

Minton, B., R. M. Stulz, and W. Williamson. 2006. How Much do Banks Use Credit Derivatives to Reduce Risk. Fisher College of Business Working Paper Series, The Ohio Sate University.

Thieke, S. 1997. Steve Thieke, JPMorgan, interviewed by the authors.

U.S. General Accounting Office. 1994. *Financial Derivatives: Actions Needed to Protect the Financial System.* Washington, D.C.

U.S. House. 1996. Committee on Banking and Financial Services. Hearings. Congr. Sess. 104.

van Deventer, D. R., and K. Imai. 1997. *Financial Risk Analytics.* Chicago: Irwin.

CHAPTER 23

Country Risk Models

Our task now is not to fix the blame for the past, but to fix the course for the future.

—John F. Kennedy

As discussed in Chapter 7, Classic Credit Analysis, outcomes from credit decisions are not only uncertain based on the borrower or counterparty's position but may also be affected by macrovariables that are outside the control of the borrower. These variables include exogenous factors such as the general economic environment as well as specific issues impacted by government actions such as taxes and regulations in a country. In this chapter, we build on the concept that evaluations of creditworthiness need to be disaggregated and introduce country risk, sovereign risk, and transfer risk as major qualifiers in credit decision making. We provide some historical context, review the important issues in country risk and risk assessment tools, and conclude the chapter with a description of a few country risk models.

First, it is important to clarify the terms we will be using. Country risk is the broadest and most inclusive level of credit risk. It is the risk that the full and timely servicing of obligations may be adversely affected by the normal, ambient country specific economic factors, and also by *transfer risk*. Transfer risk arises when credit and counterparty obligations are extended across national borders and involve different currencies, different legal systems and different sovereign governments. Sovereign risk is the risk that a sovereign entity, usually a country, acting through its authorized intermediary (usually the Ministry of Finance or Central Bank) repudiates, delays, or amends its obligations. Most lending organizations do not separately evaluate country risk or sovereign risk for their—home countries. For example, U.S. banks do not have U.S. country limits, nor do they have restrictive limits for exposure to the U.S. government.

Often, when problems do arise in country lending, all of these risk types tend to operate together. Economic conditions deteriorate. Borrowers, whether commercial or sovereign, become stressed. Central banks act to preserve scarce foreign exchange reserves and impose restrictions on currency convertibility, triggering transfer risk. The consequences are payment defaults and debt restructuring. In practical terms, this means that to arrive at an appropriate risk decision, an analysis needs to be made of all the usual exogenous factors as well as the transfer risk itself, namely that the sovereign can make foreign exchange available to service foreign currency obligations. One unusual added dimension to country credit risk is that of "contagion"—where, rightly or wrongly, concerns about one country can spread rapidly to other similar countries and cause crises.

HISTORICAL CONTEXT

There has been a long history of cross-border lending and of sovereign defaults as shown in Figure 23.1. In this chart, developed by Standard & Poor's (2006)[1] the incidence of default on sovereign bonds was generally high over the entire period 1820–1990, only abating in the 1960s when issuance of these bonds was minimal and the emphasis shifted to bank lending in the 1970s and 1980s. Defaults on these bank loans peaked in the late 1980s and early 1990s. Since that time, defaults have continued to occur

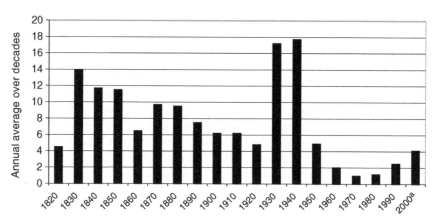

FIGURE 23.1 Sovereigns with Foreign Currency Bond Defaults, 1820–2006
[a]Through 2006.
Source: Suter (1992) and Standard & Poors (2006).

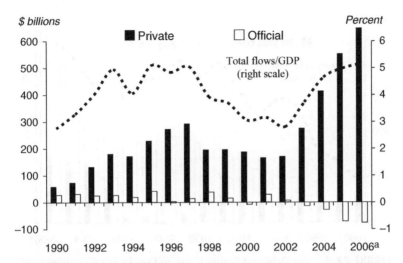

FIGURE 23.2   Net Capital Flows to Developing Countries, 1990–2006
[a]Preliminary estimate for 2006.
Source: World Bank (2007) Debt Reporting System and staff estimates.

sporadically, with several Asian countries and Russia in the late 1990s and Argentina in 2001–2002. In the last five years, however, from 2002 to 2006, there has been a series of positive improvements, focused on the developing countries which is where much of the real country risk lies (see Figure 23.2).

First of all, from 1990 to the present, there has been a substantial increase in net capital flows to these countries (see Figure 23.2) (World Bank 2007). In 1990, net capital flows were approximately US$100 billion, consisting of roughly two-thirds private capital and one-third official capital, representing about 3 percent of developing country GDP. Most of these flows were debt (see Figure 23.3), with the equity flow component estimated at 1 percent of developing country GDP.

In 2006, the World Bank estimates that net capital flows to developing countries were $571 billion, with private debt and equity inflows of $647 billion and net repayments of official capital of $76 billion. Those inflows represented approximately 5 percent of developing country GDP, equal to the level attained prior to the Asian crisis of 1997–1998.

Equity flows, consisting of both foreign direct investment and portfolio equity investment, have outstripped net debt flows every year since 1996, and were in excess of $400 billion in 2006, equal to approximately 3.8 percent of GDP, a new high over the previous peak of 3.35 percent in 1999 (World Bank 2007).

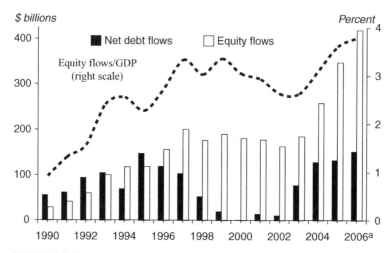

FIGURE 23.3   Net Debt and Equity Flows to Developing Countries,
1990–2006
[a]Preliminary estimate for 2006.
Source: World Bank (2007).

There are several noteworthy points in these charts, in particular that
net private capital flows have been so strong over this period when compared
to net official flows (from 2003 to 2006 there were net repayments of $185
billion to official creditors and net borrowings from private creditors of
$1.9 trillion), and that the equity flows have been so strong even during the
1998–2002 period when net debt flows were very weak because of concerns
about Asia, Russia, and Argentina.

Looking just at net private debt flows from 1994 to 2006 as shown
in Figure 23.4 (World Bank 2007), it is clear how lenders behaved during
the last stress period from 1998–2002. Those with short-term credit were
able to reduce their exposures over this period; the bank lenders were able
to lower their net inflows and eventually reduce their exposures in 1999
and 2000, and the bond underwriters, serving only the strongest developing
country borrowers, continued to write business, but at reduced levels.

In summary, there has been a lot of good news to report in country
credit risk over the past several years. Net capital flows have been increasing
substantially year on year; the costs and terms of borrowing has declined;
availability of credit and access to markets has grown (the World Bank estimates that almost 90 percent of developing countries have accessed syndicated loan markets (122 out of 135 countries) and 40 percent of developing
countries have accessed the bond markets (56 of the 135 countries). For
the developing countries as a whole, their foreign currency earnings (their

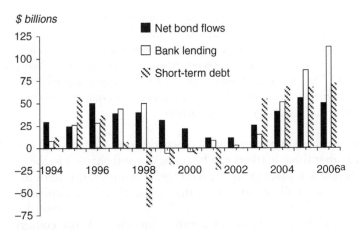

FIGURE 23.4 Net Private Debt Flows to Developing Countries, 1994–2006
[a]Preliminary estimate for 2006.
Source: World Bank (2007).

current account position) have been improving ($348 billion in 2006, or 3.1 percent of GDP, up from a low point in 1998 when their collective current account position was negative). Their liquidity has been improving, with foreign exchange reserves now at approximately 25 percent of GDP, up from less than 10 percent 10 years ago. Sovereigns are increasingly shifting their borrowing to their domestic markets and corporates are assuming a bigger share of external long-term debt (from less than 20 percent in the late 1990s to approximately 50 percent in 2006; and consequently country credit ratings have been improving, with upgrades exceeding downgrades every year since 2001. There are good reasons to believe that debt and equity investments in emerging economies have become well accepted asset classes with investors willing to accept more volatility balanced against higher returns, higher growth (over 7 percent GDP growth for developing economies in 2006 compared to 3 percent for the advanced world) and diversification benefits. Even over the last four years of particularly strong performance there have been turbulent periods which the markets have accommodated well.

Perhaps most reassuring of all, developing countries have taken preemptive action to strengthen themselves financially. According to the World Bank (2007, 1),

Most developing countries have taken advantage of favorable external conditions to implement domestic policies designed to reduce their vulnerability to financial turmoil and reversals in capital flows.

In particular, countries have reduced their external debt burden and lengthened the maturity structure of their debt. Several have bought back large amounts of external debt, using abundant foreign exchange reserves, and refinanced existing debt on more favorable terms. The market for sovereign debt has evolved significantly, as governments have turned from borrowing externally to borrowing domestically, usually in local currency.

Despite these impressive developments, major concerns still exist. First, it is clear that these markets can be turbulent and changes in the economic environment will place great stress on these countries. It is hard to imagine that conditions will get any easier than those they have experienced over the last several years; and if concern develops that some risks have been underpriced, there could be an abrupt adjustment. Many countries have opened up their markets and liberalized their economic policies but their ability to manage these markets under stress is open to question. Also, progress and growth is uneven across these developing countries. The *BRIC* countries (Brazil, Russia, India, and China) are growing their GDP at rates in excess of the developing country average and they account for over half of all developing country foreign currency reserves. Access to debt markets is still dominated by a few developing countries, even for syndicated loans, where the top 10 countries accounted for almost 75 percent of all borrowing. "Many of the factors supporting the expansion in capital flows over the past few years could turn out to have strong cyclical components, which could create strong headwinds for even the most resilient countries." (World Bank 2007, 39,)

In 2007, the issue of managing country risk is as relevant as ever.

FUNDAMENTAL ANALYSIS: KEY RATIOS

There is a wealth of information available to perform detailed fundamental analysis on country risk available from supranational agencies such as the World Bank, IMF, BIS, and OECD. Just as there are key statistics and indicators to follow for other forms of credit analysis, so there well accepted quantitative are for country risk assessment also. The major rating agencies have developed this into a very well defined set of approaches. Moody's Investors Service publishes their *Country Credit Statistical Handbook* semi-annually, which breaks down their analysis into coverage of "advanced industrial" countries and "developing." They have some 53 different ratios that they follow broken down into four categories of *economic structure and performance; government finance; external payments and debt;* as well as *monetary, external vulnerability,* and *liquidity factors*. They focus on certain areas, like indebtedness levels and balance of payments information for developing countries and other areas such as fiscal indicators for the advanced countries. They and the other agencies emphasize that, as with their other rating services the ratios, quantitative analysis and stress testing needs to be heavily supplemented by judgment and qualitative review. "Sovereign analysis is an interdisciplinary activity in which the quantitative skill of the analysts must be combined with sensitivity to historical, political, and cultural factors that do not easily lend themselves to quantification" (Moody's Investors Service 2006).

Standard & Poor's (2006) has developed an analytical framework consisting of nine categories within which they rank countries from one (the best) to six and then go on to assign actual ratings to sovereigns (see Table 23.1). As always they are evaluating both the willingness to pay, which they measure through political risk, and ability to pay which is measured by the economics of the country.

Within the eight of these nine categories that can be quantified (excluding political risk), S&P discloses the median results for some of the key factors for the countries it rates. For example, in terms of income and economic structure, the rankings are apparently well correlated to GDP per capita so that the AAA median is estimated for 2006 at approximately $40,000, the BBB median approximately $7,000, and the B median approximately $1,000. Similarly, when examining the general government debt burden, S&P uses the net general government debt: GDP ratio, so that for 2006 the AAA-country median is estimated at approximately 20 percent compared to the B-country median estimated at approximately 40 percent. Like a number of the other measures used, however, this series of medians is not a consistent progression from AAA countries to B countries because there are anomalies that require use of judgment. For example, Japan and Belgium are AA countries. They are amongst the most indebted of sovereigns rated by S&P and help to bring the AA median for this measure to over 30 percent, which is actually higher than both the A median and the BBB median. However, as S&P notes "these countries have the wealth, level of development, and revenue raising capacity that allow their governments to support such high debt levels."[7]

Interestingly both Moody's and S&P report that they have been able to apply their analytical techniques to ranking sovereign creditworthiness sufficiently well that sovereign default rates and corporate default rates are similar in most cases. They both caution that the number of countries rated is small (S&P now has ratings on 113 sovereigns and Moody's approximately 100) and the number of issues that become defaulted is also small, especially in the very lowest grades. Table 23.2 shows the S&P experience.

TABLE 23.1 Sovereign Ratings Methodology Profile

Political Risk
> Stability and legitimacy of political institutions
> Popular participation in political processes
> Orderliness of leadership succession
> Transparency in economic policy decisions and objectives
> Public security
> Geopolitical risk

Income and Economic Structure
> Prosperity, diversity, and degree to which economy is market oriented
> Income disparities
> Effectiveness of financial sector in intermediating funds; availability of credit
> Competitiveness and profitability of nonfinancial market sector
> Efficiency of public sector
> Protectionism and other nonmarket influences
> Labor flexibility

Economic Growth Prospects
> Size and composition of savings and investment
> Rate and pattern of economic growth

Fiscal Flexibility
> General government revenue, expenditure, and surplus/deficit trends
> Revenue-raising flexibility and efficiency
> Expenditure effectiveness and pressures
> Timeliness, coverage, and transparency in reporting
> Pension obligations

General Government Debt Burden
> General government gross and net (of assets) debt as a percent of GDP
> Share of revenue devoted to interest
> Currencycomposition and maturity profile
> Depth and breadth of local capital markets

Offshore and Contingent Liabilities
> Size and health of NFPEs
> Robustness of financial sector

Monetary Flexibility
> Price behavior in economic cycles
> Money and credit expansion
> Compatibility of exchange-rate regime and monetary goals
> Institutional factors, such as central bank independence
> Range and efficiency of monetary policy tools

TABLE 23.1   (*Continued*)

External Liquidity
> Impact of fiscal and monetary policies on external accounts
> Structure of the current account
> Composition of capital flows
> Reserve adequacy

External Debt Burden
> Gross and net external debt, including deposits and structured debt
> Maturity profile, currency composition, and sensitivity to interest rate changes
> Access to concessional funding
> Debt service burden

Source: Standard & Poor's (2006).

COUNTRY RATING SYSTEMS

Today many organizations have dismantled or significantly reduced the resources they used to dedicate to analyzing country risk. They are focusing
more on management and mitigation techniques relative to their own businesses and exposures and relatively less on having a customized understanding of the macrocountry environments. They have turned to external service
providers for information and analysis, amongst whom are the rating agencies, who, as we have seen, have stepped up their coverage considerably and

TABLE 23.2   Sovereign and Corporate Default Rate Comparison

Percent of Rated Issuers	One-year		Three-year		Five-year	
	Sovereign	Corporate	Sovereign	Corporate	Sovereign	Corporate
AAA	0.0	0.0	0.0	0.1	0.0	0.3
AA	0.0	0.0	0.0	0.1	0.0	0.3
A	0.0	0.1	0.0	0.3	0.0	0.7
BBB	0.0	0.2	2.0	1.2	5.1	2.6
BB	1.0	1.1	5.0	5.6	8.7	10.1
B	1.9	5.0	8.5	15.9	16.8	22.6
CCC/CC	41.2	26.3	58.8	40.0	58.8	46.2

Note: Implied senior debt ratings through 1995; issuer credit ratings thereafter.
Source: Standard & Poor's Risk Solutions CreditPro 7.0 sovereign ratings for
1975–2006 and corporate ratings from 1981–2006.

have established and strengthened their presence in many foreign countries. Among the leading providers of these services are:

- Economist Intelligence Unit
- Euromoney
- Institutional Investor
- Fitch
- Moody's Investors Service
- Standard and Poor's
- Export credit agencies of major OECD countries (U.S. Eximbank; Hermes; ECGD; and others)
- Political Risk Services

In Chapter 6, we discussed the rating agencies, the different types of ratings offered depending on the characteristics of the issuers and instruments, and their methods of ranking creditworthiness. They provide forward-looking opinions about pure sovereign risk, namely the ability and willingness of sovereigns to service their own obligations. Ratings assigned to nonsovereign issuers are influenced by many of the same factors that affect the sovereign rating. The agencies offer both local currency and foreign currency ratings.

The Economist Intelligence Unit (EIU) offers a Country Risk Service covering 120 countries, which include forecasts and risk ratings. The ratings are updated monthly with broader reports provided on a quarterly basis. Their methodology examines two different types of risk: country risk, as determined by political (22 percent weight), economic policy (weight 28 percent), economic structure (27 percent), and liquidity (23 percent); and specific investment risk. The specific investment risk ratings are divided between currency risk, sovereign debt risk, and banking sector risk, and then evaluated using the same factors as used to evaluate overall country risk.

Euromoney publishes semiannual country risk ratings and rankings. Countries are given their respective scores based on nine components and ranked accordingly. The components are political risk (weighted at 2 percent), economic performance (25 percent), debt indicators (1 percent), credit ratings (10 percent), access to bank finance (5 percent), access to short-term finance (5 percent), access to capital markets (5 percent), and trade finance (5 percent).

Institutional Investor (II) provides semiannual country credit surveys which are based on responses provided by leading international banks. Bankers from approximately 100 banks rate 174 countries on a scale of 0 to 100, with 100 representing the lowest risk. Individual responses are weighted by II and then the resulting surveys are published semiannually in the II magazine.

The OECD export credit agencies have formed the OECD ECG forum (export credit agency group) and each individually provide their own ratings and analysis. Some of these agencies are in the public sector, some are private, but operating with a government mandate. Many of these organizations are also members of the Berneunion, the International Union of Credit and Investment Insurers.

Political Risk Services publishes the *International Country Risk Guide* (ICRG), which has been a well-established service for over 25 years. The ICRG system is worth looking at in some detail because it is widely used, very detailed and quite transparent (see the Political Risk Services web site www.prsgroup.com). The system consists of 22 variables representing three major components of country risk, economic, financial, and political. Each of the variables is assigned a range of possible weights, the lower the rating the higher the risk.

The political risk rating which can have a weight of up to 100 points, measures the political stability of a country, which affects the country's willingness and ability to service its debt. The variables and their point ranges are listed in Table 23.3.

The economic risk rating measures a country's current economic strengths and weaknesses. The variables and weightings are listed in Table 23.4.

The financial risk rating measures the ability of a country to service its foreign currency liabilities. The variables and their weightings are shown in Table 23.5.

Using each set of variables, a separate risk rating is created for each of the three components. The five variables for financial risk and the five

TABLE 23.3 ICRG Model: Political Risk Variables

Government stability (0–12)
Socioeconomic conditions (0–12)
Investment profile (0–12)
Internal conflict (0–12)
External conflict (0–12)
Corruption (0–6)
Military in politics (0–6)
Religious tensions (0–6)
Law and order (0–6)
Ethnic tensions (0–6)
Democratic accountability (0–6)
Bureaucratic quality (0–4)

Source: ICRG Political Risk Services (2007).

TABLE 23.4 ICRG Model: Economic Risk Variables

GDP per head of population (0–5)
Real annual GDP growth (0–10)
Annual inflation rate (0–10)
Budget balance as percentage of GDP (0–10)
Current account balance as percentage of GDP (0–15)

Source: ICRG Political Risk Services 2007

variables for economic risk each give a score of up to 50 points. The 12 variables for political risk give a score of up to 100 points. The composite risk rating for the country is simply the combined score of the three variables, meaning that of the total, the political risk accounts for 50 percent and the financial and economic risks for 25 percent each. Countries with very low risk score in the 80 to 100 range and the very high-risk countries score in the 0 to 49.5 range.

The components in the ICRG approach are quite similar to those used by the rating agencies, although weightings may be different and the agencies use qualitative as well as quantitative factors.

A number of academics and service providers have offered more sophisticated quantitative models, which incorporate multiyear trend analysis and which attempt to predict probability of default using analysis on selected variables or through identifying key indicators of default through regression analysis. As discussed by Richard Cantor and Frank Packer (1996) most country risk analysis and modeling tends to centre on a small number of variables which explain most of the predictive power of these models and analytics.

Once a country risk rating approach has been established, often using a combination of rating sources, lenders use this to create a scale to limit their country risk and transfer risk exposures. Typically an overall country

TABLE 23.5 ICRG Model: Financial Risk Variables

Foreign debt as percentage of GDP (0–10)
Foreign debt service as percentage of goods and services exports (0–10)
Current account as percentage of goods and services exports (0–15)
Net liquidity as months of import cover (0–5)
Exchange rate stability (0–10)

Source: ICRG Political Risk Services (2007).

risk limit will be established which consists of a local currency portfolio, if one exists; any equity capital that has been invested; and any foreign currency lending or counterparty portfolio that has been created. The size of the local currency portfolio limit is dependent on the availability of local currency deposits. The size of the overall limits are proportional to the lending institution s risk appetite and to the ratings. Low ratings would permit only small exposures with short tenors. Exposures to both sovereigns and corporates need to be accommodated within these overall country limits, and, of course, some of them will be in local currency and some in foreign currency.

For trade finance, some banks are willing to allocate a lower country and transfer risk weighting when financing exports, particularly of essential commodities such as foodstuffs. Their rationale is the belief that a sovereign or central bank in difficulty will be more likely to default first on foreign currency debt service obligations, and would try and quarantine scarce hard currency reserves to maintain supply of critical imports. The short term, transactional profile of trade finance also provides banks the opportunity to cancel trade lines at short notice, thus quickly and relatively easily reducing country risk exposure.

Another approach to credit evaluation of corporates in developing countries has been proposed by Altman. This approach proposes that a Z-score be developed for the obligor and then adjusted for foreign currency devaluation vulnerability, for industry riskiness, for competitive position, for special debt issue features (if any), and then adjusted by adding the required sovereign spread over the rate that comparable U.S. obligors would pay for equivalent domestic debt. This approach is a useful, pragmatic approach to decision making in a commercial environment but relies on market prices to be the proxy for setting the level of country risk.

CHALLENGES IN ASSESSING COUNTRY RISK

There are a number of difficulties in assessing country risk. First, even though there have been defaults occurring fairly consistently for many years; still the actual number of defaulting countries is relatively small. For a few defaulting countries, there has always been a straightforward issue of simply not having sufficient financial resources to service debt. Although the reasons behind default can be complex, they usually combine both an inability to easily service debt as well as an unwillingness to suffer the economic disruption and sacrifice necessary to create the ability to pay.

Also, the interdependencies of variables in country analysis can be so complex that it is difficult, if not impossible, to model or anticipate outcomes. The notion that traditional macroeconomic analysis that uses national income accounts is sufficient for analyzing the risk and reward for the international lender or investor is open to criticism. Macroeconomists are now accepting microfactors such as the agency problem. (An *agency problem* exists when the principals—owners or shareholders, agents, bank management—have a conflict of interest that can lead to different behavior, which, in turn, can influence the behavior of important foreign and domestic institutions and result in unusual, unexpected outcomes.)

It is unfortunate, but true, that as long as the investment returns are good, no one finds fault with a financial system's vulnerability, corruption, or other inadequacies. Even if these are known, they are noted, but few take the view that the problems are serious enough to withdraw from the market. When there is general prosperity and lack of transparency, then investors and lenders indulge these idiosyncrasies as cultural differences with the saying "that is the way business is done in that country." Indeed, this is true even for domestic obligors—when you are winning, you can do no wrong. Country risk analysts who find themselves swimming against the current usually mute their criticism for fear of sounding alarmist. Only when there is a major downturn does the criticism come out. Haggard and Lee (1995), for example, reveal how sanguine the view was about these economies until recently.

The advent of personal computers and databases has facilitated the construction of country risk models. These models, however, are also prone to failure because the data used in them may often be suspect or stale. Just as any troubled domestic corporate borrower will furnish incomplete or inaccurate data on its conditions or delay it altogether, the same is true of sovereigns and foreign borrowers. According to the *Wall Street Journal* (1998a), most of Indonesia's private foreign debt was hidden until mounting pressures on the rupiah prompted the central bank to order commercial banks to disclose their exposures. When the disclosure came, the rupiah plummeted even further. Even official reserve statistics are known to be reported incorrectly in some instances. According to the *Financial Times* (1998), Thailand's foreign exchange reserves and the central bank's loan volumes had been hidden from the public for months. Similarly, it only became clear after the fact that a significant amount of South Korea s foreign currency reserves were deposited with local commercial banks.

Country-level information is available only after significant delay. Data collected by agencies such as the IMF, the World Bank, OECD, Bank for International Settlements, and the United Nations tend to emphasize the individual needs of the organization, not those of the lenders and investors. Even if the data being fed into the models are of satisfactory quality, model risk—the risk that the structure has shifted away from the model's original premise—can be a problem.

Furthermore, while econometric models may yield nice, neat numerical rankings and default probabilities, political factors can shape the business environments in a dramatic fashion. These are subjective and qualitative variables, less amenable to modeling. Nor are the interactions of these variables self-evident. According to PERC (1996, 1):

> *More than numbers, Asia is about people and the systems in which they live. Just as it is much less important to have access to a balance sheet of a typical Asian company, than it is to know the dynamics of the families who stand behind these companies, macroeconomic statistics often tell little about the quality of the government that put them together. Yet it is the quality of the government (at the national and local levels) and its policies that often make or break the business environment.*

To understand country risk, then, one needs expertise in political risk, macroeconomics, and an understanding of the *structure of the financial system*. Lending decisions made by the financial intermediaries played no small role in the events leading to the Asian collapse. In a portfolio context, it is generally also conceded that data historically failed to reveal the contagion effect—the manner in which events unfolding in Thailand spread to Indonesia, Malaysia, Philippines, and Korea.

IN EVERY CLOUD A SILVER LINING

The last country risk crisis in Asia, although extremely painful to the local economies and international lenders and investors, has proven to be beneficial to the countries concerned over the long term. To restore growth in these countries, investor confidence had to be restored and this has been accomplished by revamping the regulatory system and improving corporate disclosure.

Moody's (2007) produced an interesting retrospective on the Asian crisis that shows that even after 10 years a number of Asian countries still have not regained the rating levels they enjoyed prior to the crisis (see Figure 23.5)

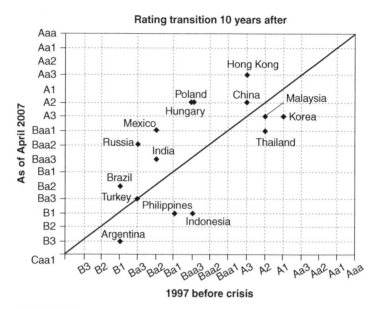

FIGURE 23.5 Rating Transition Since the 1997 Crisis
Source: Moody's Investors Service (2007).

Moody's goes on to make a number of important points including that periods of boisterous financial liberalization often end in tears and that liquidity is a key to sovereigns in successfully managing through a crisis. They also point out that a number of key issues remain unknown including being able to disentangle structural from cyclical factors, anticipating political risk, and deciphering the risk of contagion from one country to the next.

COUNTRY RISK MANAGEMENT

Just as developing countries have learned to improve their own financial profiles and risk management, so too have the lenders and investors become more sophisticated in the ways they manage and mitigate their risk. First of all, they have become more discriminating in their selection of counterparties and borrowers. The loan markets have become more open as noted earlier but the large bulk of transactions are done with customers in relatively few countries. This has had the effect of incentivizing countries to improve their creditworthiness so that they can attract more financing on more favorable terms. Secondly, the lenders have also become much more selective in the types of financing they will provide. In the late 1970s and early 1980s, when bank lenders were extremely aggressive in county financing a lot of financing was done on a general balance of payments basis to assist with current account shortfalls. In the last decade, cross-border financing has been much more targeted to specific projects and corporations for specific purposes that generate adequate foreign currency means of repayment.

Third, where possible foreign financial institutions have created local currency-based businesses in the major developing countries. This has meant that they can work with extensive client lists in these countries, and with the sovereigns themselves, but without transfer risk. This has been extremely beneficial to the countries since sophisticated infrastructures have been established with efficient, competitive products and markets created for the benefit of all the participants.

Fourth, the foreign financial institutions have become capable of providing a wider range of foreign currency services which range from short-term trade finance, correspondent banking and commodity, interest rate and currency dealing; to debt arrangements in the medium-term syndicated loan, private placement and securities markets. This has attracted a much more diverse set of clients to the foreign institutions which has helped in mitigating risk. It has also meant that these institutions can calibrate their reaction to the inevitable dynamic economic cycles more easily than before. Having a $100 million medium unsecured term loan exposure with low amortization is more problematic than having a similar exposure in short-term currency trading exposures or a self-liquidating export bill.

Finally, financial institutions are using the full range of techniques that they and their regulators have developed to measure, manage, and mitigate risk in their domestic markets. This means better pricing of risk, better allocation of risk capital, reducing concentrations of risk, hedging risk through derivatives, avoiding illiquid collateral and instruments, and more informed and active stress testing of exposures to understand potential loss in the event of a downturn.

REFERENCES

Altman, E. I. 2005. "An Emerging Market Credit Scoring System for Corporate Bonds." *Emerging Markets Review* 6.

Altman, E. I., J. Hartzell, and M. Peck. 1995. *Emerging Markets Corporate Bonds: A Scoring System.* New York: Salomon Brothers, Inc.

Altman, E. I., and P. Narayanan. 1997. An International Survey of Business Failure Classification Models. In *International Accounting and Finance Handbook,* edited by F.D.S. Choi, New York: John Wiley & Sons.

Financial Times. 1998. "Asia in Crisis—A 5 Day Series: The Day the Miracle Came to an End." 12 January.

Babbel, D. F., and S. Bertozzi. 1996. Insuring Sovereign Debt Against Default. World Bank Discussion. Paper No. 328, The World Bank. Washington, D.C.

Belcsak, S. 1995. "Country Risk Assessment." In *Handbook of International Credit Management*, edited by B. Clarke. London: Gower.

Clark, E. 1991. "Cross Border Investment Risk:" In *Applications of Modern Portfolio Theory.* London: Euromoney.

Clark, E., and B. Marois. 1996. *Managing Risk in International Business: Techniques and Applications.* London: International Thomson Business Press.

Dym, S. 1997. "Credit Risk Analysis for Developing Country Bond Portfolios." *Journal of Portfolio Management* 23, no. 2:99–103.

The Economist. 1997. "Rating Agencies: Risks beyond Measure."13 December, 68–69.

Erb, C. B., R. H. Campbell, and T. E Viskanta. 1996. "Political Risk, Economic Risk, and Financial Risk." *Financial Analysts Journal* 52, no. 6.

Feder, G., and R. E. Just. 1977. "A Study of Debt Servicing Capacity Applying Logit Analysis." *Journal of Development Economics* 3.

Federal Reserve Bank of New York. 1996. Determinants and Impact of Sovereign Credit Ratios, October.

Fukuyama, F. 1998. "Asian Values and the Asian Crisis." *Commentary* 105, no. 2.

Greider, W. 1997. *One World Ready, or Not.* New York: Simon & Schuster.

Haggard, S., and C. H. Lee (eds.). 1995. *Financial Systems and Economic Policy in Developing Countries.* Ithaca, N.Y.: Cornell University Press

Institutional Investor. 1997. *Institutional Investor's 1997 Country Credit Ratings.* New York.

Krayenbuehl, T. E. 1988. *Country Risk.* Cambridge, England: Woodhead-Faulkner.

Krugman, P. 1998. What Happened to Asia? White Paper for a conference in Japan, January, http://web.mit.edu/krugman/www/DISINTER.html.

Moody's Investors Service. 2006, December. *Rating Methodology: Sources and Uses of Statistical Data in Moody's Sovereign Credit Analysis.* New York.

———. 2007. *International Policy Perspectives.* New York.

Morris, A. 1997. "Quantifying Sovereign Credit Risks: Methods and Issues." *SBC-Prospects* 4–5:8–13.

Political and Economic Risk Consultancy, Ltd. (PERC). 1996. "The Importance of Political Risk." *Asian Intelligence*, Issue 456, March 6.

———. 1997. Transparency Problems in Asia. *Asian Intelligence*, Issue 498, November 19.

Solberg, R. L. (ed.). 1992. *Country Risk Analysis.* London: Routledge.

Sommerville, R. A., and R. J. Taffler. 1995. "Banker Judgment versus Formal Forecasting Models: The Case of Country Risk Assessment." *Journal of Banking and Finance* 19, no. 2:281–297.

Suter, C. 1992. *Debt Cycles in the World-Economy: Foreign Loans, Financial Crises, and Debt Settlements, 1820–1990.* Boulder: Westview Press.

Standard & Poor's. 2006. *Sovereign Credit Ratings: A Primer.* October 19, 2006. New York.

Walt Street Journal. 1998. "Foreign Banks Lent Blindly." 4 February.

World Bank. 2007. "Financial Flows to Developing Countries: Recent Trends and Prospects." *Global Development Finance.* Washington, D.C.

Further Reading

Beers, D. T. 2004, "Credit FAQ: The Future of Sovereign Credit Ratings." *Standard & Poor's Sovereigns*, 23 March.

Beers, D. T., and M. Cavanaugh. 2004. "Sovereign Credit Ratings: A Primer." *Standard & Poor's Sovereigns*, 15 March.

Daly, K., and M. Cavanaugh. 2006. "Sovereign Ratings History Since 1975," *Standard & Poor's research*, 1 December.

Hoti, S., and M. McAleer. 2007. *Modelling the Riskiness in Country Risk Ratings.* Elsevier 2005 IFC Foreign Investment Advisory Service 2007. London: Elsevier.

Kastein, E. B. 1994. *Governing the Global Economy.* Cambridge, Mass.: Harvard University Press.

Kindleberger, C. E. 1996. *World Economic Primacy, 1500–1990.* Oxford and New York: Oxford University Presss.

Kraemer, M., J. Chambers and B. Merino. 2005. "In the Long Run, We Are All Debt: Aging Societies and Sovereign Ratings." *Standard & Poor's Research*, 18 March.

CHAPTER 24

Structured Finance

*But Mr. Paulson, a former banker from Goldman Sachs, defended
the hedge fund industry, the target of frequent political attacks
both in France and Germany. The crisis had been fuelled by bad
lending practices and not the development of new financing
techniques; changes in regulation should be carefully considered.
(Peggy Hollinger from the* Financial Times*).*
  *"We want to get the balance right. The whole world and the
U.S. has benefited from innovative financing techniques and
innovation in terms of securitisation and credit availability, and so
we need to make sure we think this through carefully and don't
rush to judgment and overreact," he said.*
                            —Hank Paulson, U.S. Treasury Secretary, Paris
                                                             (Hollinger 2007)

A sset securitization is a technique for transforming illiquid financial flows
such as home mortgages, credit card receivables, and corporate accounts
receivable into tradable *asset-backed securities* (ABS). In the securitization
process, a company or financial institution typically sells the good assets it
has originated to a special purposed company that then issues high-quality
securities.[1] Interest and principal payments from these securities depend on
cash flows from the underlying assets. The burden of repayment is thus not
on the originator, but on the pool of assets generating future cash flows and,
in the event of a shortfall, on the entity—if there is one—providing credit
support. Securitization; enables issuers of lower credit quality to tap into
the capital markets at more advantageous rates by establishing a structure
whose credit risk is better than—and largely independent of—their own even
though they usually continue to service those assets. Such a structure can be
engineered by means of such techniques as overcollateralization (a form of

self-insurance), third-party credit enhancement, and the creation of credit tiers (tranches) with differentiated pricing and rights to the cash flow "waterfall" under various conditions. Techniques such as these have proved to have applications beyond the securitization of assets. The term *structured finance* encompasses the full range of these applications—asset securitization, mortgage securitization and considerably more as well.[2]

Many financial institutions, including banks, thrifts, and finance companies, have benefited from structured finance. Commercial banks, for example, were able to become very active home mortgage lenders because FNMA, FHMLC, and GNMA could securitize and sell the mortgage loans they had made. Public corporations have also benefited—most dramatically in the case of Chrysler Financial Corporation (CFC). In 1980–1981, Chrysler Corporation was on the brink of collapse and CFC itself had a CCC rating. After the bankruptcy of Penn Central, commercial paper investors abandoned all firms perceived to be weak, and CFC was unable to fund is activities with commercial paper. It could, however, sell its receivables as securities, and it continued to finance itself by doing so. By 1996, CFC had grown into one of the largest issuers of ABS in the United States (Cantwell 1996).

American taxpayers have also benefited from securitization. In the 1990s, this was one of the principal strategies used by the Resolution Trust Corporation to liquidate assets accumulated in the course of closing hundreds of thrifts. By securitizing single family and commercial real estate loans, the RTC raised approximately $43 billion (Jungman 1996). A significant amount of credit enhancement accompanied these commercial transactions—more, perhaps, than will ever be seen in the nongovernmental sector, however, because the RTC was able to move these assets off their balance sheet into the capital markets this was viewed at the time as a great success.

Securitization was first developed in 1970, when Ginnie Mae Pool #1 was issued. Subsequently, the issuance of mortgage-backed and asset-backed securities expanded rapidly in the United States. During 2006, there were more than $2 trillion of mortgage-backed securities issued in the United States compared to only $500 billion issued in 1996 (see Table 24.2). Similarly, the growth in the ABS markets in the United States has been meteoric as well, reaching $1.5 trillion in 2006, compared to $480 billion in 1997, as pointed out in Table 24.1 below. Total ABS volume includes public nonmortgage debt, private debt (Section 144A), and asset-backed commercial paper. Approximately $625 billion of ABS were issued in 2006 in the United States alone, excluding home equity loans and other mortgage-related sectors, compared to $151 billion in 1996 (Thomson Financial 2007) Within Europe, ABS have been issued in the United Kingdom, France, Germany, Spain, Italy, Belgium, the Netherlands, and Sweden. They have also been issued in Japan, Canada, Australia, New Zealand, and other countries in

TABLE 24.1 Total Issuance of Various Asset Classes

Data in $ billions	Municipal	Treasury[a]	Mortgage-Related[b]	Corporate Debt[c]	Federal Agency Securities	Asset-Backed	Total
1996	185.2	612.4	507.8	343.6	277.9	168.4	2,095.3
1997	220.7	540.0	640.1	466.1	323.1	223.1	2,413.2
1998	286.8	438.4	1,167.3	610.7	596.4	286.6	3,386.1
1999	227.5	364.6	1,046.1	629.2	548.0	287.1	3,102.5
2000	200.9	312.4	708.1	587.4	446.6	337.0	2,592.4
2001	387.7	380.7	1,671.4	776.1	941.0	383.3	4,540.2
2002	357.5	571.6	2,219.2	636.7	1,041.5	469.2	5,295.7
2003	282.7	745.2	3,071.0	775.9	1,267.5	600.2	6,742.5
2004	359.7	853.3	1,779.1	780.7	881.8[d]	869.8	4,642.6
2005	408.2	746.2	1,966.3	752.8	669.0	1,172.1	5,714.6
2006	386.8	788.5	2,002.6	1,058.9	747.2	1,251.9	6,235.9
2006							
Q1	68.8	234.9	497.2	248.7	187.9	287.9	1,525.4
Q2	109.4	201.1	510.7	278.8	189.9	316.9	1,606.8
Q3	87.6	163.6	501.5	239.4	169.4	311.7	1,473.2
Q4	120.9	188.9	493.2	292.1	200.0	335.4	1,630.5
2007							
Q1	107.0	188.5	536.7	305.1	265.3	309.8	1,712.4
YTD '06	68.8	234.9	497.2	248.7	187.9	287.9	1,525.4
YTD '07	107.0	188.5	536.7	305.1	265.3	309.8	1,712.4
% Change	55.5%	−19.8%	7.9%	22.7%	41.2%	7.6%	12.3%

[a] Interest bearing marketable coupon public debt.
[b] Includes GNMA, FNMA, and FHLMC mortgage-backed securities and CMOs and private-label MBS/CMOs.
[c] Includes all nonconvertible debt, MTNs, and Yankee bonds, but excludes CDs and federal agency debt.
[d] Beginning with 2004, Sallie Mae has been excluded due to privatization.
Source: SIFMA (2007a).

Asia and Latin America. Another form of securitization that proved to be quite popular internationally was "future flow" ABS, which securitized remittances from citizens living abroad, and other types of dependable future receipts in countries which had limited access to the capital markets. Examples include Turkey, Egypt, Qatar, and even Kazakhstan.

Table 24.1 shows how the U.S. credit markets have grown over the past decade and how securitized debt, mortgage-related and asset-backed, have grown from about one-third of the market in 1996 to over one-half of the market by 2006.

The underlying assets in the ABS market are a mixture of credit cards, auto loans, home equity loans, and manufactured housing loans, as well as securities backed by commercial loans, both large and small. In the early days of the ABS market, it was almost entirely consumer oriented, but in recent years, the market for securities backed by commercial loans (both large and small) has boomed.[3] Table 24.2 shows the composition of the ABS market by collateral type. Credit cards, home equity loans, and auto loans all have major shares of the market.

USES OF SECURITIZATION

Structured finance techniques assist in the delivery of all four core functions of the financial markets. The first of these is a depository function: people need a place to store their money. The second is an investment function: people need ways to grow their capital by investing in assets that match their preference with respect to yield, liquidity, maturity, and so on. The third is a credit function: people need a place where they can borrow money. The fourth is a risk-management function: people need a way to transfer financial risks that they are not comfortable bearing on their own. These core functions have remained quite stable over time; in 1897 as in 2007 people turned to the financial markets for these same fundamental reasons.

Although the functions themselves have changed little, the institutions providing them have changed dramatically. For many years, banks and insurance companies were the dominant suppliers of depository, investment, credit, and risk management services. Today, specialty finance companies, specialty insurance companies, brokerage houses, pension funds, mutual funds, and hedge fund companies all give these traditional providers stiff competition. Burdened with excess capital and high costs, banks and insurance companies have been losing out to the newer and often more efficiently managed entrants.

Structured finance is an important tool for all these parties. Banks and insurance companies use it to improve their efficiency. Instead of holding all loans as they did in the past, most banks now originate certain financial

TABLE 24.2 ABS Outstanding

Data in $ billions	Automobile Loans	Credit Card Receivables	Equipment Leases	Home Equity Loans	Manufactured Housing	Student Loans	Commercial Loans	Total
1996	71.4	180.7	23.7	51.6	14.6	10.1	52.3	404.4
1997	77.0	214.5	35.2	90.2	19.1	18.3	81.5	535.8
1998	86.9	236.7	41.4	124.2	25.0	25.0	192.3	731.5
1999	114.1	257.9	51.4	141.9	33.8	36.4	265.3	900.8
2000	133.1	306.3	58.8	151.5	36.9	41.1	344.1	1,071.8
2001	187.9	361.9	70.2	185.1	42.7	60.2	373.2	1,281.2
2002	221.7	397.9	68.3	286.5	44.5	74.4	449.9	1,543.2
2003	234.5	401.9	70.1	346.0	44.3	99.2	497.7	1,693.7
2004	232.1	390.7	70.7	454.0	42.2	115.2	522.9	1,827.8
2005	219.7	356.7	61.8	551.1	34.5	153.2	578.2	1,955.2
2006	202.4	339.9	53.1	581.2	28.8	183.6	741.4	2,130.4
2006								
Q1	220.3	359.8	60.7	552.6	33.5	162.9	575.7	1,965.5
Q2	215.3	354.4	60.4	564.7	32.4	175.5	583.1	1,985.8
Q3	212.0	352.9	57.6	574.8	29.9	182.0	607.5	2,016.7
Q4	202.4	339.9	53.1	581.2	28.8	183.6	741.4	2,130.4
2007								
Q1	202.6	338.1	50.6	583.4	28.7	199.4	835.3	2,238.1

Source: SIFMA (2007b).

assets with the express intention of selling them off. Banks traditionally worked with other banks in sharing credit risk, but they are now letting other capital market participants (such as guarantee companies, investors, and rating agencies) become involved with their asset origination and sale activities. Meanwhile, specialty finance and specialty insurance companies are using structured finance techniques to fund the clever ideas they are dreaming up and to increase their capabilities. Some specialized companies are applying these same techniques in the capital markets for purposes of risk management, defeasing insurance risk through finite risk products. Because catastrophic risks tend to be uncorrelated to financial markets, CAT bonds which exchange the premium flows for claim payments are favored as a diversification play by investors. Indeed, CAT bonds have become another source of capital to insurers similar to reinsurance. Investors, too, are beginning to use the tools of structured finance to create the investment structures they want and to obtain the assets they need.

In structured finance, the focus often shifts from what the issuer wants to what the investor wants. Rather than generating assets that suit borrowers and then trying to find a home for them, the issuer looks at the available investor classes and structures a security that enough of them will buy. In this way, the issuer tailors the origination strategy to fit the needs of the investor who provides the cash to finance the loan production activities. This change in mindset is subtle but crucial.

Structured finance is expanding rapidly because there is something in it for virtually everybody. The asset supplier is able to raise funds to support more originations and retain a spread. The guarantor earns a fee. The servicer earns a fee for asset management. The rating agency gets a fee for rating the securities. The investor has an earning asset that is tailored to its risk/return preferences. The secondary market maker earns a bid-ask spread by providing liquidity. Most players in the financial markets already benefit in some way, and those that do not benefit today can be expected to do so tomorrow.

Why is this happening now? Information technology is part of the answer. Structured finance demands comprehensive and thorough financial analysis of a kind that would have been impractical before the widespread availability of the computers.

BENEFITS FOR ISSUERS

The following are among the key reasons why issuers choose to securitize assets:

- *Liquidity*. Banks and other issuers can convert their illiquid assets into cash.

- *Reduced borrowing costs.* Independent and captive finance companies have securitized assets to obtain capital at attractive rates.
- *Tax management.* Some jurisdictions charge taxes based on asset size.
- *More efficient use of capital.* Securitization can be used to multiply the assets created without increasing leverage of the originating entity.
- *Regulatory capital arbitrage.* Because of high regulatory capital charges for loans to high-quality borrowers, lenders are unable to earn an attractive return on equity when they hold these loans. Under the Basel accords for banks it is advantageous for them to securitize these assets, taking them off-the-balance sheet and placing them in a nonbank special purpose vehicle. Insurance companies, as well, can use securitization to reconfigure the financial assets on their balance sheets to obtain more favorable treatment under risk-based capital rules, although they do have to be careful to structure the securitization to avoid recourse that might trigger consolidation.
- *Reach more investors.* Insurers wish to expand their borrowing reach to more institutional investors who could play a future roll in other financial needs the issuer may have, on or off balance sheet.

To date, the expansion of structured finance in the United States has been driven largely by the needs of issuers. Banks and insurance companies have had to reduce their costs and gain greater economies of scale by removing assets from their balance sheets—while retaining their franchise. The introduction of risk-based capital standards has been a major factor here. These standards have forever changed the banking and insurance industries. Banks face much higher capital requirements for the loans they hold than for the securities they own.[4] If a bank wants to improve its capital ratio, it can therefore invest in securities—especially when demand for loans is weak and security yields are acceptable. This may explain why the proportion of mortgage-backed securities in bank asset portfolios increased significantly from 2.9 percent in 1988 to 7.6 percent in 1995, to 9.6 percent in 2006 (FDIC 2006).

For insurance companies, too, the regulatory treatment of securities differs from that for whole loans and real assets. Table 24.3[5] gives the National Association of Insurance Commissioners (NAIC) capital guidelines.

Prior to the imposition of risk-based capital standards, relatively few bankers or insurance executives paid much attention to their return on equity relative to the risk taken. But under the terms of the Basel accords (for banks) and the NAIC capital standards (for insurance companies) these institutions must allocate specific amounts of capital to specific asset classes on their balance sheets. This means that they must track their ROE and ROA closely. Banks and insurance companies now manage their balance

TABLE 24.3 Capital Reserve Factor for Different Asset Types

Asset Category	Rating Range	Security Type	Reserve Factor (%)
Securities			
U.S. government	NA	Treasuries, GNMAs	0.0
NAIC1	AAA-A	Agency debentures, corporate bonds, MBS, ABS, CMBS	0.3
NAIC2	BBB	Agency debentures, corporate bonds, MBS, ABS, CMBS	1.0
NAIC3	BB	Agency debentures, corporate bonds, MBS, ABS, CMBS	4.0
NAIC4	B	Agency debentures, corporate bonds, MBS, ABS, CMBS	9.0
NAIC5	CCC	Agency debentures, corporate bonds, MBS, ABS, CMBS	20.0
NAIC6	Default	Agency debentures, corporate bonds, MBS, ABS, CMBS	30.0
Whole Loans			0.5
Single/multifamily residential mortgages			0.1
Guaranteed municipal mortgages			3.0
Other mortgages including commercial real estate			10.0

Source: Jacob and Duncan (1995).

sheets far more actively than they did in the past, using structured finance as their most effective tool for doing so.

SECURITIZING MORTGAGES

The first widespread application of structuring technology occurred in the residential mortgage market. In 1938, the federal government established the Federal National Mortgage Association (FNMA, or Fannie Mae) to ensure that mortgage capital would be readily available to large numbers of American home buyers. Fannie Mae bought qualified mortgages and issued its own securities. In 1968, the Government National Mortgage Association (GNMA, or Ginnie Mae) was split off from Fannie Mae and authorized to guarantee the principal and interest on mortgage securities from other issuers. This guarantee is backed by the full faith and credit of the U.S. government. Figure 24.1 shows how the securitization process for a GNMA works (Kinney and Garrigan 1985).[5]

Mortgage-backed issues may take the form of a *pass-through security,* in which the assets are sold to a trust and investors buy shares of the trust, or of a *pay-through security,* in which the assets are sold to a special purpose vehicle that issues debt to finance their purchase. Both types of security include internally generated credit support in the form of accumulated reserves from excess cash flows and of subordinated interest (first loss absorption) on the part of the asset originator. There may also be external credit support in the form of a letter of credit, loan insurance (e.g., a cash collateral account), a corporate guarantee, a surety bond, or cross-collateralization. A trustee responsible for monitoring collateral value and cash distributions helps hold the structure together.

Mortgage securitization has been a huge success in the United States and in many European countries as well. The proportion of residential mortgages in the United States that are securitized has increased from 1 percent in 1970 to 56.5% in the first quarter of 2007. Knowing that they can raise capital by selling the loans they have originated, many new and different players have been encouraged to enter the mortgage markets. In the real estate section of their local newspapers along with Internet advertisements, Americans can compare offerings from mortgage brokers and mortgage bankers, as well from commercial banks and thrifts—all of whom are competing to lend them money. Often it is hard to tell from the advertisement exactly how and by whom the loan will be made. No matter which lender the homebuyer selects, the mortgage will, in all likelihood, be securitized within a matter of weeks. Securitization has reduced the cost of a residential mortgage in the United States by about one-third (from 0.5 to 1.0 percent over the funding rate). There is no doubt that the availability of credit has made home ownership available to many borrowers that would not have qualified in the past. In many emerging nations where governments are eager to establish vibrant mortgage markets, the U.S. model has enormous appeal.

Residential mortgages are relatively easy to securitize. To begin with, the mortgage market is large enough to make securitization interesting to financial professionals. In addition, this is a consumer financing activity

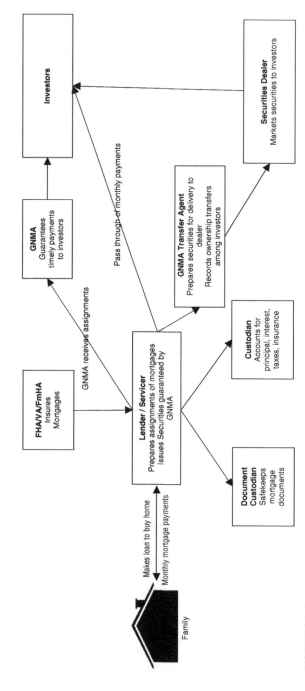

FIGURE 24.1 The GNMA Mortgage-Backed Securities Program
Source: Kinney and Garrigan (1985).

where the law of large numbers can be applied and an actuarial base readily established. Since record keeping has generally been good, abundant data are available for this purpose. Finally, mortgage documentations in the States have been standardized over the last 30 years. Whether Citibank in the Bronx, a mortgage banker in Des Moines, or a broker in San Diego originates a mortgage, the documentation is largely standardized. This makes it easy to collect, maintain, and evaluate data across portfolios and originators. Federal agencies have been the major force behind this standardization.

Securitization has transformed the U.S. mortgage market, mostly in a positive way. The separation of funding from lending has driven the costs down dramatically and created competition for all the separated functions. Consumers have more options than ever and arranging financing for a new home is relatively easy and can be accomplished quickly. However, every market tends to overshoot its boundaries and in the summer of 2007, the U.S. mortgage market is embroiled in a doozy of an overshoot created by practices in the "subprime segment" of the mortgage market. We'll discuss this further in the section Perils of Securitization.

SECURITIZING OTHER ASSETS

After residential mortgages, the first nonmortgage assets to be securitized were computer leases in 1985. Next came auto loans (*certificates of automobile receivables* or CARS). Securitization of other consumer assets, such as credit card receivables, was a natural next step. The first credit card deal was completed in 1986. Here, again, the asset class is sufficiently large to enable structured finance professionals to create mathematical models to predict consumer behavior. Unlike mortgages, however, the documentation for credit cards has yet to be standardized, but consolidation in the U.S. credit card market has made for very little variation between structures.

In the course of the transition from mortgages to credit cards, the definition of an asset shifted to some extent. A mortgage, after all, is a legal right to a home. The underlying real asset is the home. But in the case of a credit card, what is the asset—the sweater that the cardholder bought? The semester of college courses that was charged to the card? Clearly not. The asset in this case is the cash flow from cardholders as they pay their credit card bills. Securitization techniques have evolved to the point where cash flow is the primary source of value. When a transaction involves hard assets that can, in fact, be realized, these represent no more than a secondary element in the deal structure—one that serves to mitigate the risks. Today, the absence of such hard assets presents no serious impediment to the securitization process.

Over time, many types of consumer assets have been securitized, including home equity loans, *recreational vehicle* (RV) loans, boat loans, auto loans, leases, utility payments, and bank-originated student loans.

Corporate assets have been securitized in considerable volume, but the pace here has been somewhat slower. Since corporate assets tend to be "lumpier"—the average loan size is $1 million—than consumer ones—the average loan size is $3,000—they do not lend themselves as readily to the application of actuarial principles. In addition, banks have generally kept less thorough records of their corporate lending experience. When things have gone wrong and a bank has actually experienced a loss, this fact has been recorded. But when things have gone right and a loan has been repaid, banks have generally kept no record of any migration in the borrower's credit quality that may have occurred along the road to this happy outcome. Even if the obligor came perilously close to default at some point, the bank has not normally recorded this fact.[5]

Recently this has all begun to change. Over the past two decades the major credit rating agencies and others have been working to develop default prediction models that make it possible to evaluate corporate credit more effectively. More importantly banks began to make loans with the intention of securitizing them in trade receivables or CLO structures as information has become easier to come by for investors. This has caused the securitization market to broaden and deepen. Two approaches are available for modeling default. The first is to study the historical behavior of pools either as cohorts or as static pools and to use the default experience over time to stress portfolios of rated assets. The second approach, which follows from the first, is to risk rate each asset (by means of either agency ratings or a model) and to link the default likelihood and recovery to the rating and seniority. These methods have been discussed in Chapters 15 through 20.

As in the consumer sector, the easiest corporate assets—trade receivables—were the first to be securitized. Trade receivables are relatively low-risk, short-term assets. Any ongoing commercial enterprise will pay its suppliers so that it can continue to receive the supplies it requires. A wide range of other corporate assets have also been securitized, including rolling stock leases for utilities, worker compensation insurance premium receivables, real estate tax lien receivables, and the future receivables of a major film studio. *Collateralized bond obligations* (CBOs) and *collateralized loan obligations* (CLOs) are additional types of corporate ABS that are discussed in some detail in Chapter 25.

SEGMENTATION OF RISK

The key to a structured financing is segmentation of cash flow into common risk buckets. Assume for a moment that we have a $100 portfolio of assets with an expected loss ratio, based on past experience, of 10 percent. If we have just one asset in the portfolio, then there is very little we can do except to hope that we have chosen it well and priced it correctly. If we have 100 items in the portfolio, each worth $1, then we have reason to expect that 90 of them will be good and 10 bad. We do not know which are which, but we do know that 9 of every 10 payments are likely to be made on time.

If we decided to give the first 90 payments that came in to some other party and to hold the other 10 back in a reserve, then owning the first 90 payments would be an extremely safe activity and owning the 10 others would be very speculative. If, instead, we said that the first 50 payments would go to one party and that we would keep the last 50, then we would have created two new investment alternatives—the first one extremely secure and the second one more risky than the first but less risky than the 90/10 split. Just by altering the priority of payment, we alter the dynamics of the deal, even though the fundamentals of the transaction remain unchanged.

Suppose, instead, that we split the payments into four tranches: 40/20/20/0. The dynamics of each tranche would differ with respect to earnings as well as risk. The first 40 payments would represent the first bite of the apple—a safe deal. The investor in the next tranche would demand somewhat greater earnings than for the first tranche because the risks are somewhat greater. The holder of the third tranche would want even more yield. The last investor would face a fair amount of risk and would therefore expect an equity-like return.

The lowest or equity tranche of an asset-backed transaction is critical to the entire structure. It is only by concentrating risk in this tranche that it becomes possible to create more highly rated senior tranches above it. If a deal makes sense for the equity holder, then it will generally make sense for everybody else. The key is finding the real risk taker who will accept this lowest tranche. Who is this investor? What are his or her motivations?

There are, generally speaking, two possibilities. In many instances, it is the originator of the assets—often a bank—that retains the equity tranche in order to enable the transaction as a whole to be consummated. In other cases, an outside investor purchases the equity tranche. For someone who is knowledgeable and adequately capitalized, this may be a perfectly reasonable investment decision. For an investor who is highly leveraged or unfamiliar with asset-backed structures, this investment may well lead to a loss the next time the economy turns down. Having been burned once, such an investor will probably avoid such investments in the future.

By calculating the risks of the equity tranche accurately and pricing this investment appropriately, structured finance professionals should be able to expand the universe of investors with an appetite for this vital portion of an asset-back issue. Consider how investors assess securities backed by home equity loans. Those who purchase the senior classes look at the least creditworthy collateral because it has the greatest prepayment stability. For the B-pieces (low-rated or junior tranches), however, credit quality concerns dwarf prepayment concerns. The key question about the B-pieces is whether the credit enhancement will hold up under the most severe stress. The rating agencies need to feel confident that the B-piece will not be paid off early, since this would expose the senior classes to credit risk. Although this structure was designed for credit reasons, the B-piece actually has less prepayment sensitivity and relatively higher value per unit of risk than does the senior piece (Wagner and Callahan 1997).

Optimization techniques, such as nonlinear, mixed-integer programming may be used to develop alternative financial structuring strategies. A structured financing is a prediversified portfolio that may be treated as a mathematical programming problem in which constraints of liquidity, rating agency requirements, regulatory limits, and internal capital allocation may be modeled. Once the alternative structures have been developed, the solution may be stress tested in the same optimization scheme using post optimality analysis. If this proves difficult or insufficient, simulation may be used.

If the assets in question are interest bearing (e.g., junk bonds or residential mortgages), then the timing of defaults becomes a critical issue. Suppose that we have a $100 portfolio with a loss expectation of 10 percent and an earnings expectation of 10 percent. If the portfolio of assets lasts for 10 years, then over that period, without losses, we would earn $100 on a simple interest basis. A 10 percent loss coming in the first year would hurt us much more than one coming in the last year. Today, the structured finance markets are devoting substantial attention to formulating assumptions about the level and timing of defaults (see Table 24.4). A security that is very sensitive to timing—that is, the longer the time before problems develop, the better the overall performance—may attract investors who would otherwise turn it down. By the same token, prepayment risk is also a consideration because ABS generally does not have prepayment protection.

Table 24.4 illustrates some of the financial analyses performed in structuring the security. The first section contains the important assumptions made with respect to the cash flows, defaults, and recoveries. Only the results for years 1, 5, and 10 are shown. An important assumption is the cumulative default rate and its timing. The total default rate is assumed to

TABLE 24.4 Example of CLO/CBO Analysis

Assumptions, Collateral Balance, and Coverage Ratios

Assumptions	Base Case			Stress Case		
Cumulative default rate	34%			48%		
Default timing (% of total per annum)	41,24,18,11,6			50,33,8,8		
Recovered amount	32%			15%		
Recovery timing	Immediate			One-year delay		
Asset coverage test	110%			110%		
Interest coverage test	125%			125%		
LIBOR	6%			6%		
Scheduled interest	L + 3%			L + 3%		
Reinvestment period	4 years			4 years		
Year	1	5	10	1	5	10
Collateral Balance						
Beginning balance	490,000,000	409,893,105	398,757,266	490,000,000	259,135,912	259,135,912
Principal payments received	0	0	398,757,266	0	0	259,135,912
Defaults on original collateral	68,600,000	9,800,000	0	117,600,000	0	0
Defaults on reinvested recoveries	0	614,656	0	0	0	0
Defaults on reinvested spread	0	721,184	0	0	0	0
Balance after defaults	421,400,000	398,757,266	0	372,400,000	259,135,912	0
Reinvestment of recoveries	21,952,000	0	0	0	0	0
Reinvestment of excess spread	9,621,432	0	0	5,211,432	0	0
Ending asset balance	452,973,432	398,757,266	0	377,611,432	259,135,912	0
Ratios an Tests						
Asset coverage ratio[a]	133.25	120.79	111.00	111.93	91.49	111.00
Interest coverate ratio[b]	174.03	164.68	126.00	153.79	124.30	126.00
Reinvestment period	Yes	No	No	Yes	No	No
Termination event occurs[c]	No	No	No	No	Yes	No

(Continued)

TABLE 24.4 (*Continued*)

	Sources and Uses of Cash			
Assumptions	Base Case		Stress Case	
Cash Flow from Assets				
Principal payments received	0	398,757,266	0	259,135,912
Cash recoveries	21,952,000	3,136,000	2,940,000	0
Total principal received	21,052,000	3,136,000	2,940,000	0
Scheduled interest on original assets	44,100,000	44,100,000	44,100,000	44,100,000
Scheduled interest not received	6,174,000	14,994,000	10,584,000	21,168,000
Net interest received on original assets	37,296,000	29,106,000	33,516,000	22,932,000
Interest received on reinvested recoveries	0	4,073,288	0	390,232
Interest received on reinvested excess spread	0	2,708,866	0	0
Total interest received	37,926,000	35,888,154	33,516,000	23,322,232
Total Cash Sources	59,878,000	434,645,419	26,262,232	282,458,144
Less Uses				
Interest on senior debt	21,973,203	19,266,393	18,762,142	16,811,633
Interest paid on sub debt	6,511,365	5,744,454	6,511,365	6,510,599
Accrued interest paid	0	0	0	0
Surety bond reimbursement	0	0	0	0
Principal to senior	8,804,985	293,532,714	7,500,090	256,666,154
Principal to mezzanine	1,914,601	63,827,267	0	2,469,758
Reinvestment of recoveries	21,952,000	0	0	0
Reinvestment of excess spread	9,621,432	0	5,211,432	0
Junior subordinated payments	0	52,314,591	0	0
Total Cash Uses	59,878,000	434,645,419	26,262,232	282,458,144

Year	1	5	10	1	5	10
Senior Debt						
Beginning balance	332,720,660	332,720,660	293,532,714	332,720,660	286,444,913	256,666,154
Principal paydown	0	8,804,985	293,532,714	0	7,500,090	256,666,154
From residual account	0	0	0	0	0	0
End balance	332,720,660	323,915,675	0	332,720,660	278,944,823	0
Mezzanine Debt						
Beginning balance	72,348,496	72,348,496	63,827,267	72,348,496	72,348,496	72,348,496
Principal paydown	0	1,914,601	63,827,267	0	0	2,469,758
End balance	72,348,496	70,433,895	0	72,348,496	72,348,496	69,878,739
Accrued and unpaid interest	0	0	0	0	29,777,311	78,274,118
Accrued interest paid at termination	0	0	0	0	0	0
Principal and accrued interest balance	72,348,496	70,433,895	0	72,348,496	102,125,807	148,152,857
Junior Subordinated						
Beginning balance	84,930,844	84,930,844	84,930,844	84,930,844	84,930,844	84,930,844
Principal paydown	0	0	52,314,591	0	0	0
End balance	84,930,844	84,930,844	32,616,253	84,930,844	84,930,844	84,930,844
Surety Bond						
Beginning balance	0	0	0	0	0	0
Draw	0	0	0	0	0	0
Reimbursement	0	0	0	0	0	0
Interest	0	0	0	0	0	0
Ending balance	0	0	0	0	0	0

[a] Asset coverage ratio (ACR) = (Balance after defaults/Beginning senior debt).
[b] Interest coverage ratio (ICR) = (Interest received/Interest on senior debt).
[c] ACR < 110% or ICR < 125%.

be 34 percent in the base case scenario. The structure is stressed for default timings of 41, 24, 18, 11, and 6 percent of this total in successive years. In the stressed case, the total default rate is assumed to be 48 percent, and the default timing is accelerated to 50, 33, and 8 percent in successive years. This structure has three tranches—senior, mezzanine, and junior subordinated.

The asset coverage ratio and the interest coverage ratio are set at the required levels and the structure is tested to see whether termination will be triggered because of failure to meet one or both. The second section of the table shows the projected cash flows and distribution to the three tranches. It may be observed that for the junior subordinated piece, the only principal pay down of $52,314,591 occurs in the tenth year in the base case, but it does not occur at all in the stressed scenario. The pay down for all three tranches is shown in the third section of Table 23.2. In both the base and stressed case the senior and mezzanine tranches are paid down in year 10. The junior subordinated tranche is paid down to $32,616,253 in year 10 in the base case but remains at $84,930,844 in the stressed case.

Of course, a good asset selection process or a good portfolio manager can also stack the deck in the investor's favor. A manager who is reasonably knowledgeable should be able to select assets that will perform well for at least the first few years. Uncertainty will come into play only over time. If the portfolio manager is skilled at anticipating problems and has the power to sell assets, then the value of the portfolio can probably be enhanced—as long as assets can be sold for more than 90 cents on the dollar.

FINANCING RISKY CREDITS

One of the great virtues of structured finance is that it makes it possible to finance risky credits as well as strong ones. If a pool of assets is large enough to be actuarially sound (40 to 50 names or more), then it can include some relatively low-rated assets along with better ones. If we want to make a loan to someone whose credit is questionable, this kind of structure provides an excellent way to do so—as long as we price our loan appropriately. The good assets in the structure will offset the bad. This is the very same process that insurance companies use to manage risk in other business segments. Every day, they insure people who may have short life expectancy by pooling them with people who have long life expectancy. The risks are blended out. Moreover, the senior tranche in a structure may be sized so that even at the highest expected stress, cash flow to this tranche will remain within the risk boundaries set by investors in this class and by the rating agencies.

In the financial markets, structured solutions allow lenders to broaden their customer base—mitigating their credit risk by creating portfolios of loans. That is why Americans today receive so many unsolicited credit card offers in the mail. Once the insurance model has been applied to the financial markets, it becomes possible for lenders to offer credit cards, mortgages, and auto loans to people they would not have been willing to finance in the past.

Bear in mind, however, that portfolios are not immune to systemic risk. The current turmoil in the subprime mortgage market has demonstrated the interdependence of market segments. The subprime market was able to grow dramatically in recent years because the securitization market for mortgages was looking for more product to provide diversification in investment structures as well as additional investment product for yield-hungry investors. Some observers will say that the demand from the capital markets was a catalyst for the development of poor lending practices in the subprime mortgage origination system. Now that those practices have generated substantial losses, the portfolios that have been distributed into CLOs and CDOs are now creating delinquencies and downgrades in those supposedly diversified investments. The first evidence of this was the admission by Bear Stearns in June 2007 that the two funds that they had sponsored had lost about 60 percent and 100 percent respectively of their value because of problems in the subprime market. Other investment vehicles have also reported significant problems from investments in subprime paper including funds run by Goldman, UBS and BNP Paribas. Now the rating agencies are projecting that many investment structures that include subprime mortgages may have delinquencies and losses as high as 19 percent of their value. The subprime market has brought home the challenges of systemic risk in the securitization markets.

THE ANATOMY OF AN ASSET-BACKED SECURITY

Presented next are two examples of ABS. The first, illustrated in Table 24.5, is structured as a revolving trust using closed end loans. During a fixed revolving period, as long as the performance of the portfolio does not deteriorate beyond established loss levels, a portion of the principal payments will be used to purchase new loans. In the second example (Table 24.6), the security is backed by bullet loans with monthly payment of interest (no call prepayment protection). When the loans are paid off, the life of the security ends. Both securities received credit support as described.

TABLE 24.5 Example of Consumer Asset-Backed Security

	AmeriCredit Automobile Receivables Trust 2007-C-M
Class	Class A-2 Notes
Description	Senior principal and interest
Amount	$370 million (aggregate transaction size: $1.5 billion)
Coupon	5.43%
Rating	Aaa
Structure	Surety bond/amortizing trust
Credit support	Unconditional and irrevocable guarantee of MBIA (rated AAA/Aaa) to the noteholder of current interest and ultimate principal payments; initial enhancement totals 9.0% (2.0% reserve fund and 7.0% overcollateralization); the target overcollateralization level is 11.0%, while the 2.0% reserve fund remains at 2.0% of the original pool balance.
Issuer	AmeriCredit Automobiled Receivables Trust 2007-C-M
Seller	AFS SenSub Corp.
Originator/servicer	AmeriCredit Financial Services, Inc.
Trustee	Wells Fargo Bank, N.A.
Underwriter	Credit Suisse
Tax election	Debt for tax
Pool summary type	Fixed rate, fully amortizing subprime automobile loans
Number of loans	80,593
Average loan	$18,324
Maximum loan	$71,396
Seasoning	1 month
WAC	16.56%
WAM	69 months
Coupons	4.4%–29.99%
State concentration	13% TX, 10% FL, 9% CA, 5% OH, 4% PA
Comments	Aaa rating is based primarily on the MBIA financial guaranty policy Underlying credit support is provided by excess spread, a reserve fund, and overcollateralization. After excess spread, the overcollateralization created by the excess of loan balance over the note balance will provide the first loss protection by absorbing loan losses before claims on the MBIA policy. Potential interest shortfalls could occur as a result of declining interest rates and prepayments. The rating addresses credit risk only.

PREPS 2007-1 Mezzanine CLO

Issuer	PREPS 2007-1plc
Amount	EUR 248m
Seller/Servicer	PREPS 2007-1plc
Investment services provider	Capital Efficiency Group AG
Account bank	JPMorgan Chase Bank, NA
Recovery manager	CMP Recovery Management
Placement	Public
Loan characteristics	Subordinate loans to small-and-medium-sized corporates
Interest	Quarterly fixed interest of 7.8% p.a. and profit-related component
Pool summary	52 subordinated loan agreements to SMEs in Europe
Amount summary	EUR 1.5 million to EUR 9.5 million

	Class A1	Class B1	Junior
Rating	AAA	A	NR
ISIN	XS0289620709	XS0289620881	XS0289621343
Placement	Public	Public	Public
Payment frequency	Semiannually	Semiannually	Semiannually
Interest rate	6 month Euribor + 0.32%	7 month Euribor + 0.83%	Junior Coupon Rate[a]
Nominal amount	EUR 186 million	EUR 35 million	EUR 27 million
Legal maturity	Mar/2016	Mar/2016	Mar/2016
Stated average life	6.8 years	7 years	7 years

Credit support: The PREPS 2007-1 transaction features a strong PDL mechanism. Any default of a portfolio company is registered in the PDL, prompting the trapping of excess spread until the ledger is reduced to zero. Principal deficieny events include:

- The liquidation of or the application for insolvency proceedings against the company or, if applicable, the guarantor.
- A failure to pay, i.e. nonpayment of the outstanding interest if overdue for more than 90 days.
- The sale of the issuer's rights and interests in a financing agreement.
- The termination of a financing agreement.

[a] Steps-up from 14.50% to 16.60%.
Source: Fitch (2007). Reprinted with permission.

EVALUATING ASSET-BACKED SECURITIES

When they evaluate an asset-backed issue, structured finance profession-als focus on three key areas: the originator (or seller/servicer), the assets themselves, and the structure of the transaction.

Who made the loans? What process did the originator use? How good is it at selecting and sizing credits? What has been its past experience? Why does it want to sell the assets? These are among the key questions to be asked about the originator.

The assets themselves must also be studied. If they are consumer as-sets, what are the interest rates? What kinds of purchases were they used to finance—homes? Boats? Recreational vehicles? The quality of an asset is often related to the importance of the item being financed. Under acute financial pressure, most individuals will do everything in their power to avoid defaulting on their home mortgage. Relatively few, however, will feel as strong a compulsion to continue meeting lease payments on a sports car. The characteristics of the asset need to be thoroughly understood. Location and industry concentration should be identified. Other features of the as-sets should also be studied. In one instance in the authors' experience, the preapproval criteria used in a solicitation systematically drew a dispropor-tionately large number of inferior credits into a portfolio. Even though it had no geographic concentration, the portfolio had a steep loss curve.

If the assets are corporate receivables, other issues arise. Are there cir-cumstances under which the receivable might be extinguished? A book-seller's unsold inventory, for example, can normally be returned to the pub-lishers. In certain businesses, a high level of returns must be factored into the equation. Are the assets subject to economic cycles? To interest rate shifts? To natural catastrophes? If the originator started to experience financial difficulties, would the nature of the assets change? Once a company realizes that one of its suppliers is about to go out of business, it may delay making payments.

Servicing quality is also critical to the valuation of assets. If a portfolio depends on monthly billing, then collection may deteriorate if the loans are not effectively serviced. The staffing levels of the collection departments and the tools for the management of delinquencies must be analyzed. In the subprime auto sector, for example, where the credit quality of the obligor is low, aggressive servicing may be needed to keep the payments flowing in. From the investor's perspective, the servicer should collect and apply the payments promptly and carry out reporting, remittance, and reconciliation on a timely basis. The servicer should be strong enough that bankruptcy is not an imminent risk.

Assets must be evaluated by people who truly understand them—professionals who have worked at rating agencies or bank credit card operations, or who have studied the business and become experts.

Finally, the legal structure must also be evaluated. The key question here is ownership and control of the assets. Has ownership truly been transferred to a special purpose vehicle? If the originator were to become bankrupt, could a court take the assets away?

On all three counts—the originator, the assets, and the structure—evaluating an asset-backed issue requires the close scrutiny of experienced professionals.

IMPACT ON THE BANKING INDUSTRY

The opportunity to securitize assets is gradually transforming the primary role of a bank. Increasingly, banks are in the business of originating, promoting, and servicing assets rather than warehousing them. To fill this role effectively, bankers must become better at creating and pricing assets properly so that they can later be sold off. In the past, many banks, particularly smaller regional banks, did not price debt rationally. Saddled with excess capacity in a mature business, they faced a Hobson's choice: either to make loans or to go out of business. To preserve their client base, their first response has been to lower prices and continue making loans.

By separating the holder of a loan from its originator, the structured finance process brings pricing discipline to the debt market. If a loan has not been priced correctly, no one will buy it. An investment fund is not a business; it has no borrower base to preserve. Its decisions are based on relative value, not absolute value. A similar pattern is evident in other dealer markets, such as the art and antiques markets. Collectors who fall in love with works of art are liable to pay any price to own them. But dealers are inherently more disciplined in their approach. They are careful to pay a price that will allow them to resell the work with some additional margin for themselves. Unlike principal players, they are in the business of knowing values. They rarely make mistakes.

Structured finance is transforming the banking industry in emerging countries as well as in developed ones. Not long ago, the importance of a nation's banking industry could generally be judged by its stage of economic development: the less developed the country, the more important the banks. As an economy develops, the banking sector generally loses prominence as other institutions, such as pension funds, command a growing share of the investable capital. This pattern would suggest that banking is a mature business in OECD countries but still a growth business in emerging countries.

However, globalization of the financial markets appears to be undermining this truth. In normal markets, a finance company based in Mexico readily can complete a private placement of ABS in the U.S. capital markets. Even in the absence of significant local pension funds or insurance companies, this possibility changes the competitive dynamics for banks in emerging markets. In emerging markets, in other words, banking may prove to be a more mature business than many observers realize.

OTHER APPLICATIONS OF STRUCTURED FINANCE

Although the issuance of ABS remains the single largest application of structured finance technology, other uses are gaining in importance. An insurance company, for example, wanted to increase the yield from its investment portfolio, but was unable to make further high-yield investments because of regulatory constraints. A portion of the company's existing high-yield portfolio was structured as a $500 million collateralized bond obligation and wrapped with a surety bond from CapMAC. The CBO reduced the company's exposure to high-yield investments, enabling it to create additional capacity to purchase high-yield bonds. As a result, the insurer was able to increase the overall effective yield on its investment portfolio. When packaged in this manner, the bonds that originally carried a risk rating of 3 through 6 carry a rating of 1 or 2. The *asset valuation reserve* (AVR) is correspondingly reduced. This strategy has been dubbed "AVR-bitrage" because it is an arbitrage based on the difference in AVR treatment.

In another example, a major film studio in the United States financed the production cost of recently completed, ready-for-release films through the innovative use of structured finance. Traditionally, this cost would be financed largely through equity, with some additional funding from bank loans. Using off-balance-sheet financing, however, the studio was able to diversify its sources of funding—tapping the capital markets rather than the banking industry. By means of limited-recourse debt, it was also able to raise more money. Gross receipts from the films and the film rights themselves provided the security for this medium-term-note financing. In a traditional asset-backed securitization, the performance of the asset is either delinked from the originator or reserved to protect the creditors and guarantors from the originator's credit problems. In this instance, however, the performance of the asset—the films—still depends on the studio's success in distributing the films and in exploiting film rights through various channels of distribution. How did this financing become possible now?

In the past, banks were the only players who were in a position to extend credit for projects of this type. Flotation costs and other institutional considerations would probably have impeded access to the capital markets. Today, however, two more players have entered the picture: the rating agency and the guarantor. By rating the financing as investment grade, the rating agency threw its weight behind the transaction. This opened the door to investment by institutional investors. MBIA, which provided the financial guarantee, acted as a key facilitator for the transaction. It offered its guarantee on the basis of both modern portfolio concepts and classic credit analysis. The financing is backed by an entire portfolio of films. A film that generates above-average revenues can therefore make up for one with below-average performance. Classical credit analysis was used to assess the financial viability of the studio and its management over the life of the transaction. The studio's performance relative to the industry, factors in its distribution strategies, and stress tests of the future outcomes were among the components of this analysis. Optionality is built into the financing as well, in the form of trigger events that will cause the structure to liquidate more rapidly if the studio's financial viability should become impaired.

Structured capital markets' techniques are also be used to finance projects and activities in a number of developed and developing countries. One recent example has been in the U.K. pub industry. The familiar neighborhood pub has been transformed and become the focus of significant financial engineering in recent years. There were two catalysts: the first was a change in regulation aimed at increasing competition in the United Kingdom; and the second was a need to find a method of financing newly formed pub groups in the capital markets. Previously, most pubs were operated as franchises of the beer companies or, if independent, tied themselves to one or another of the beer companies as a way of getting cheap financing or pooling resources or buying. Under the new regulations, the beer companies needed to disinvest. The only problem being that few pub operators had the financial resources to help with this process. Enterprising buyout firms and individuals with knowledge of the industry quickly saw the opportunity, but needed huge financial resources to handle the thousands of pubs which needed to change hands. A series of pub deals were floated into the markets beginning 1994, the first deal being Phoenix Inns with an issuance of £337 million. These deals were built upon a fundamental understanding of the pub business and the cash flows that it creates. Rating agencies and bond insurance companies along with major investors were able to do their homework and float nearly £26.9 billion since 1994.

Structured capital markets' techniques are also being used to finance projects in a number of developed and developing countries. One early example is the refinancing of a power generation company in England. The deregulation of the U.K. electric supply industry has created opportunities for independent power generation companies. The European Investment Bank (EIB), a financing institution of the European Union, can provide long-term loans to assist in economic development. However, EIB is not permitted to vary its spread to borrowers in step with their varying credit risk. To be eligible for the spread that EIB charges, a financing must therefore be wholly or partly guaranteed. This financing was based partly on the power purchase arrangements that were in place, partly on the stable regulatory environment, and partly on the expected profitability of the power generation system. Rating agencies gave a "shadow rating" of investment grade to the financing, and CapMAC provided a surety bond that guarantees timely payment of principal and interest to EIB and the other lender in the transaction. Here, too, structured finance techniques enabled a borrower to tap the capital markets rather than relying on traditional sources such as commercial banks. Over the past decade, European project lending has become a major source of structured finance activity. Privatization initiatives in the United Kingdom created a major financing opportunity and the markets responded. Hospitals, toll roads, water companies, other transportation systems such as airports and rail all were sold off to private investors and most financing was done in the capital markets using techniques known as *private finance initiatives* (PFI). Under these systems, investors accepted some commercial risks, but generally got comfortable with the essentiality of the projects and the indirect backstop of the U.K. government. While not every European country has embraced this type of financing, it has grown in Continental Europe as well. Spain, Portugal, Italy, and France have all financed infrastructure in the capital markets for the first time. All used some form of structured finance techniques. These markets are expected to grow further in the future.

In other parts of the world, there are examples of similarly structured financings in which commercial banks, financial guarantors, and other capital market participants play a role. Examples include several toll road projects in Chile, a Peruvian power plant, gas liquefaction projects in Qatar, and airports in Chile and Australia amongst others. For many of these deals, the object was to gain access to the U.S. 144A market that required, among other things, that the bonds be rated investment grade. Often this was made possible by a surety bond from a financial guarantor.

By means of asset-based financings, securitization, financings based on future revenues, and other innovations, the capital markets have been able to bear credit risk that was hitherto borne mainly by commercial banks and government entities such as states, municipalities, and sovereigns.

PERILS OF SECURITIZATION

Although securitization has helped to transform the capital markets and has done much to restore luster to the banking industry, it has a dark side that has emerged as a major challenge in 2007. Securitization technology is sophisticated and relies on advanced mathematical techniques and modeling skills. However, the technology of securitization is still being proven and frequently relies on a wide variety of assumptions that are "estimates" because the information required for the model or mathematical formula cannot be known or calculated with precision. This means that securitization technology is particularly vulnerable to the limitations of "garbage in, garbage out." This appears to be one of those things that happened to the securitization markets in the subprime crises of 2007. The ensuing crisis has focused us once again on the issues of competence, model risk, liquidity, and integrity. In particular, integrity seems to have broken down as many investment banks, especially Merrill Lynch, were like hogs at the trough. These investment banks controlled originators such a mortgage companies whose loans they packaged and sold into the capital market with a questionable attention to their consequences and possible conflicts of interest embodied in the securities. In addition to the breakdown in common sense on Wall Street, the subprime crisis seems to have involved massive fraud on the part of speculators and some mortgage bankers in this overheated marketplace.

Because of the Federal Government sponsorship that agencies such as Fannie Mae, Freddie Mac, and Ginnie Mae enjoy, those firms set the credit and collateralization standards for the conventional mortgage market. The standards are relatively conservative and were designed to make mortgage lending a relatively low-risk activity. However, many potential homebuyers were left out—particularly those who were buying upper-end homes or those at the bottom of credit worthiness. Armed with a variety of new analytical techniques and a way, via securitization, to spread the risk the mortgage market perfected financing techniques for those who would not qualify for the federally sponsored loans. Funding for these nonconforming loans found their way into the securities markets via securitization and the market has mushroomed in recent years. The market for U.S. *mortgage-backed securities* (MBSs) has more than tripled since 2000; $2.4 trillion of MBSs were issued in 2006 according to the Securities Industry and Financial Markets Association in New York. Last year was the first time that more than half of the securities were backed by subprime and other nonconforming loans, according to the trade group.

It is now clear that the separation of those making the loans from those who are funding them have led to overly aggressive practices and created turmoil in the industry. As we go to press, the full scale and scope of the problem has not yet been determined. However, we can already see that huge losses will be distributed throughout the securities markets and a significant number of specialty mortgage lenders as well as some hedge funds will go perish in this market crisis. To help us understand exactly what happened in these markets we interviewed Jim Jones (2007), CEO of Residential Capital. Jones has had a long career in consumer finance having served in senior positions at Providian, Bank of America and Wells Fargo:

Q: What caused the subprime mess?

A: The subprime market grew from a number of factors:

- Low interest rates that encouraged people to refinance their loans or to buy new homes.
- A robust housing market, particularly in fast growing areas.
- Subprime lending was quite successful for a number of years largely because of home appreciation.
- The availability of capital markets financing for mortgage lenders:
  - Mortgage-backed securities.
  - CDOs.
  - What seemed like an insatiable appetite by investors for new products.

Q: When did it come apparent that there was a problem in the subprime markets?

A: The market had a great ride for several years. Starting in 2002 and continuing into 2005, just about everything turned out positive. Financing was available and it was easy to make profits. Underwriting got easier because the most recent experience demonstrated that it was okay to do that. The problems first surfaced in the second half of 2005. One of the market practices that developed in the early years was the provision of an *early payment default warrant*. This provision allowed investors to "put" loans back to the lender if losses in the early months proved to be higher than warranted. No one paid too much attention to these provisions in the early days. I believe the investment banks created this provision to keep investors out of the businesses of the lenders and were designed to cover the occasional "underwriting mistakes." In the early part of the decade, this warranty was rarely called upon. Beginning in mid-2005, things began to change and many loans started coming back to the lenders. By 2006, this became a flood of contingent obligations for many mortgage originators.

In 2006, some players started to loosen underwriting to keep their machines running. About that time, and continuing into 2007, things just kept getting worse:

- Lower home prices started to show up in the Midwest.
- Delinquencies and defaults started to mount.

- More and more mortgages were "put" back by Wall Street under early payment default warrants.
- Costs of origination increased because of higher interest rates, and higher costs associated with the warrants.
- Attempts to tighten credit standards slowed down originations and put stress on the organizations.
- Reduced volumes stressed the entire market which was built for high transaction levels.
- Slower markets led to more home price reductions and less alternatives for refinancing for highly leveraged borrowers.

What Jones described looked like a "perfect storm" in this segment of the mortgage market. "A whole industry has been wiped out in just a few months. Those finance arms that are sponsored by a major financial institution will survive, otherwise names such as Greenpoint and BNC will be history." We are looking at a much smaller market in the future, with fewer entities dedicated to the nonconforming market, and many fewer specialist lenders. In the end, "subprime lending doesn't scale well in monoline organizations."

Table 24.7 shows a list of subprime lenders that filed for bankruptcy in the last 12 months.

The subprime mess was clearly an unintended consequence of the ability to securitize. But its consequences will be felt well beyond those directly involved in the mortgage business. As we discuss in Chapter 25 and 26, subprime mortgages were used in many CDOs as a method of diversifying across both geography and industry. This diversification strategy depended upon the accuracy of the underlying rating on the subprime loans. When the rating agencies admitted in July 2007 that they may have systematically

TABLE 24.7 Bankruptcies in the Subprime Turmoil

Company	Status	Date
American Home Mortgage Investment Corporation	Bankrupt (Ch. 11)	August 6, 2007
SouthStar Funding	Bankrupt (Ch. 7)	April 11, 2007
New Century Financial	Bankrupt (Ch. 11)	April 2, 2007
People's Choice	Bankrupt (Ch. 11)	March 20, 2007
ResMae Mortgages Corp.	Bankrupt (Ch. 11)	February 12, 2007
Mortgage Lenders Network USA	Bankrupt (Ch. 11)	February 5, 2007
Ownit Mortgage Solutions	Bankrupt (Ch. 11)	December 1, 2006

Source: Author's compilation.

overrated subprime, any CDO manager who used these instruments to hedge other risks realized they had a problem. Many attempted to hedge, causing even more dislocations to the market. As one market observer commented at the time, "If you think having a subprime mortgage portfolio is a problem to manage, try having a subprime mortgage portfolio buried in a CDO with 25 times leverage."

STRUCTURED FINANCE TECHNIQUES AND INVESTMENT MANAGEMENT

The rate of growth in the ABS industry has outpaced our ability to understand those instruments, so as a result, we have had to rely on outside parties such as the rating agencies.
— Ralph Daloiso, Natixis (2007)

When an investment product is new and unfamiliar to investors, efforts are made to make it look and act like more familiar, established products. One of the obvious ways of doing so is to obtain an acceptable rating from an established rating agency. The rating agencies maintain stringent credit standards and provide a common credit language. They can perform an important service in bringing new credits to the market (please see also Chapter 6).

Structured finance techniques such as pooling, senior/subordinated structures, reserves, and guarantees can transform the risk/return profile of a product so that it qualifies as an acceptable investment. Taken one at a time, all auto loans may not be of investment grade, but structured finance techniques can transform a pool of them into a security that insurance companies are able to buy. An asset may even be turned into a close substitute for the investor's current preferred investment. A good example of this is an *asset swap*—typically a combination of a long-term fixed-rate bond with an interest-rate swap that converts it to a floating-rate asset. The combined product, sometimes termed a *synthetic bond,* enables an investor to take on the credit risk of the issuer (and thereby earn a credit spread) without taking any interest-rate risk because the asset return floats with LIBOR. Many features of an asset—including its payment frequency—can limit its acceptance by investors. Lewis Ranieri (1996), who is often credited with the invention of the *collateralized mortgage obligation* (CMO) notes that when John Hancock Insurance initially bought a mortgage pass-through security, it complained because the security paid monthly instead of semiannually like other bonds. In recent years, these issues have become less of a concern, as many investors have developed special portfolios for these types of investments.

Last, transparency in pricing and liquidity are two other issues of concern to investors. The more liquid the market, the easier it is to mark the securities to market instead of relying on models. Until the recent market upheaval brought the structured finance markets to a grinding halt, this might have been described as one of the major improvements of the structured markets in the last 10 years. Unfortunately, the subprime market fiasco has bled into the CLO and CDO markets and has shaken everyone's confidence about what ratings mean in the structured markets. So, in January 2008, it is impossible to finance a new portfolio of structured loans and difficult, if not impossible, to get reliable prices on the old portfolios. This is happening because most of the major players in the market have declared some sort of moratorium on new investments until the market "sorts itself out" Of course that won't happen until most of these investors move back into the market. No one knows right now how long this will take, but there is no doubt that the market is being tested right now.

> *Pricing of credit has gone from too low to too high.*
> —Greg Reiter, UBS (November 2007)

FUTURE OF SECURITIZATION

There is no doubt that the securitization market is facing a major challenge in early 2008. Confidence in structured finance ratings is at an all-time low and it will probably be some time before investors look favorably at any structured involving residential mortgages. Most issuers are holding back new issues and no one is quite sure how, or when, the market will resume at anything near recent volume levels. Still, there are many reasons to think that this market will weather this storm and return to substantial growth in the coming years.

A major driving force for the further development of the securitization markets will be Basel II. For most major banks, the decrease in regulatory capital requirements for off-balance-sheet exposures will be a powerful incentive to securitize. Basel II regulations, in general, will bolster growth in the asset-backed markets because:

- There will be continued demand for conduit structures that minimize the need for bank liquidity and facilitate balance-sheet management. According to rating agency reports, the pipeline for rating of new conduits is very strong (Moody's Investors Service 2007).

- Collateralized debt obligation issuance is likely to increase as more and more corporate and synthetic securitizations are used to optimize regulatory capital requirements.
- Under Basel II, most affected banks will have a strong capital incentive to securitize their credit card receivables instead of keeping those assets on balance sheet, as well as to minimize the amount of the seller's interest in a securitization. Smaller banks will prefer to securitize their high-credit-quality portfolios, while retaining their low-quality portfolios on balance sheet.
- With the onset of Basel II in Europe, most rated funds, which generally are money market and enhanced cash funds that invest in securitized assets of the highest quality, will be put on equal footing with bank deposits, with just a 20 percent risk weighting under the standardized approach. This low-risk weighting should attract sizable investment inflows.
- Even though there is plenty of blame to go around (including investor greed buying on ratings and not knowing what they really purchased), the rating agencies have lost a huge amount of credibility. Accordingly, investors are in the process of revising their criteria for structured product, and will probably not rely as much on ratings in the future.

While the treatment of RMBS under Basel II will not provide the same level of capital arbitrage as for ABS markets, it is reasonable to think that these markets will continue to use securitization as its primary form of long-term financing.

The securitization markets are being tested. Investment bankers will be challenged to provide more information to investors about the performance of structures and types of credits and complexity will not be viewed positively for some time to come. Nevertheless, we expect that this market will eventually return to the levels of issuance that we have seen in recent years.

REFERENCES

Baum, S.P. 1996. "The Securitization of Commercial Property Debt." In *Primer on Securitization*, edited by L. T. Kendall and M. J. Fishman. Cambridge, Mass.: MIT Press.

Board of Governors of the Federal Reserve System. 1997. *Federal Reserve Bulletin.* Washington, D.C.

Cantwell, L. T. 1996. "Securitization: A New Era in American Finance." In *Primer on Securitization*, edited by L. T. Kendall and M. J. Fishman. Cambridge, Mass.: MIT Press.

Daloiso, R. 2007. Speech at the American Securitization Conference, New York City, September 19.

Federal Deposit Insurance Corporation (FDIC). 1988. *Statistics on Banking.* Washington, D.C.

———. 1995. *Statistics on Banking.* Washington, D.C.

Hollinger, P. 2007. "Paulson Seeks to Assuage Subprime Concerns." *Financial Times,* 18 September.

Jacob, D. P., and K. R. Duncan. 1995. Commercial Mortgage-backed Securities. In *Handbook of Mortgage-backed Securities,* 4th ed., edited by F. Fabozzi. Chicago: Probus.

Jones, J. 2007. Jim Jones, Residential Capital, interviewed by authors.

Jungman, M. 1996. "The Contribution of the Resolution Trust Corporation to the Securitization Process." In *Primer on Securitization,* edited by L. T. Kendall and M. J. Fishman. Cambridge, Mass.: MIT Press.

Kinney, J. M., and R. T. Garrigan. 1985 The *Handbook of Mortgage Banking: A Guide to the Secondary Mortgage Market.* Homewood, Ill.: Dow Jones-Irwin.

Moody's Investors Service. 1995. *Moody's Global Credit Analysis.* London: IFR Publishing.

———. 2007. "SIVs: An Oasis of Calm in the Sub-Prime Maelstrom." *Moody's Special Report,* 20 July.

Mortgage Market Statistical Annual. 1997. Washington, D.C.: Inside Mortgage Finance Publications.

Ranieri, L. S. 1996. "The Origins of Securitization, Sources of its Growth, and Its Future Potential." In *Primer on Securitization,* edited by L. T. Kendall and M. J. Fishman. Cambridge, Mass.: MIT Press.

Reiter, G. 2007. Speech at the American Securitization Conference, New York City, September 19.

Samuel, T. 1997. "Customers' Debt Is Catching Up to Credit-Card Firm." *Philadelphia Inquirer.* 18 March.

Santamero, A. M., and D. F. Babbel. 1997. *Financial Markets, Instruments and Institutions.* Chicago: Irwin.

Securities Industry and Financial Markets Association (SIFMA). 2007a. Asset-Backed Securities Outstanding. www.sifma.org/research/pdf/ABS_Outstanding. pdf.

———. 2007b. Issuance in the U.S. Bond Markets. www.sifma.org/research/pdf/ Overall_Issuance.pdf.

Standard & Poor's. 2007. New Risk-Based Insurance Capital Model. Standard & Poor's Research, 24 May.

Wagner, K. and E. Callahan. 1997. B-Pieces on Home-Equity Loan ABS. *Mortgage-backed Securities Letter,* 14 July.

Future Reading

Rosenthal, J. A., and J. M. Ocampo. 1988. *Securitization of Credit: Inside the New Technology of Finance.* New York: John Wiley & Sons.

Schiavetta, J., J. Zelter, R. Hrvatin, M. Koo, S. Bund, and R. Hardee. 2007. "Global Criteria Change for U.S. Structured Finance CDOs Reflects Heightened Subprime Risks." *Derivative Fitch Structured Credit Criteria Report,* 15 August.

Langellier, G., P. Walsh, J. Martin, and K. Brown. 2006. "Time for One Last Smoke: Pub Securitisation Update 2006." *Fitch Ratings Whole Business/UK Special Report*, 10 August.

Global Structured Credit Strategy. 2007. Citi Global Structured Credit Strategy, 26 June.

King, M. 2007. Short Back and Sides: Subprime Haircuts – Too Much Off the Top? *Citi Fixed Income Quantitative Research*, 3 July.

Merrill Lynch Structured Finance Europe. 2006. European Structured Finance Annual Review 2006/2007: Running Fast While Standing Still, 24 November.

Jobst, A. A. 2002. Collateralised Loan Obligations (CLOs) – A Primer Center for Financial Studies Working Paper No. 2002/13, December.

Jobst, A. A. 2005, 2006. What is Structured Finance? *The Securitization Conduit*, Vol 8.

Fitch Ratings Credit Policy Special Report. 2006. Global Structured Finance Outlook: Economic and Sector-by-Sector Analysis. 17 January.

CHAPTER 25

New Markets, New Players, New Ways to Play

Credit risk is moving to the securities market. One of the historic barriers to securitization was that the securities market was reluctant to take real credit risk. Increasingly, the securities market is willing to take real credit risk.

—Lowell Bryan

A growing number of organizations, both old and new, manage credit risk by applying the tenets of portfolio theory. *Portfolio managers* focus closely on diversification. These organizations devote more energy to managing risk than they do in acquiring it, an approach predicated on the existence of a liquid secondary market for loans. Such a market has evolved in recent decades as an outgrowth of the loan syndication of the banks and more recently the *collateralized debt obligation* (CDO) and credit derivative markets. It is this dependency on liquid markets and realistic pricing that has produced the conditions for the "perfect storm" in the structured markets in 2007. At the same time, there is a parallel group of investors who do the opposite. *Specialized lenders* are concentrated and focused on a narrow market segment or approach as a way to exploit opportunities and manage credit and other risks. Both types of players—*portfolio managers* and *specialized lenders* play critical roles in the huge credit markets of the twenty-first century. Market developments and most innovations are either created by them, or directed toward them.

Prior to the 1970s, bank syndication was a kind of club activity. When General Motors wanted to raise a lot of money, it asked its various house banks to arrange a loan. Although one bank would be designated as the agent and lead, in reality, the banks all acted in concert in what was, in effect, an insider's game.

The bank syndication business, which was centered in London and New York, began to expand in the 1970s. After OPEC raised the price of oil from $3 to $20 a barrel, the global financial system had to readjust so that petrodollars could be recycled effectively. When Japan and Korea purchased oil from countries in the Middle East, the latter transferred the money to banks, which could lend it to Japan and Korea. It was a zero-sum game. As this kind of international lending came into vogue, banks needed to spread out their risks. Syndication evolved into a mechanism by which banks could manage their exposures as they originated business.

In the 1980s and 1990s, syndication evolved further, to the point where the buying and selling of loans became a regular practice in the banking industry. By then, most money center banks had established specialized trading desks to buy and sell bank loans, and a secondary market for those loans emerged—particularly for large loans. Trading of "junk" loans—loans to companies of below investment grade credit quality—became particularly active. Please see Figure 25.1.

Typically, U.S. money center banks served as both originators and traders in this market, whereas regional banks and European banks are the end buyers. In recent years, European money center banks have begun to challenge the dominance of the American banks but the early moving U.S. banks continue to lead this business segment.

Money center banks are usually asset long and liquidity short, whereas regional banks in the United States and in Europe are typically liquidity long and asset short. Regional banks have a limited number of assets that they can create themselves and a longer list of what they wish to buy, including

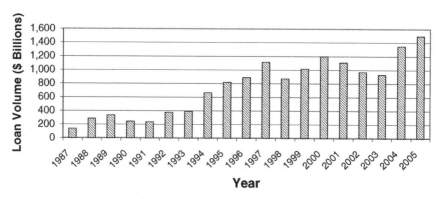

FIGURE 25.1 U.S. Syndicated Loan Volume
Source: Loan Pricing Corporation (1997). Reprinted with permission.

government or near government securities, mortgages, syndicated loans, and other types of securitized debt. The latter are attractive because they offer superior yields. Foreign banks operating in the United States have a similar motivation. Those wanting to book U.S. assets often found it difficult to compete directly with U.S. banks as loan originators. As an alternative, they can buy good loans in the secondary loan markets and add them to their portfolios.

Syndicated loans are typically five to eight years in tenor but can frequently be longer or shorter depending upon the purpose of the financing. They use the London Inter-Bank Offer Rate (LIBOR) as the reference for their pricing. Term loans are generally divided into tranches (A, B, C, D, etc.) with each tranche generally one year longer in maturity than the preceding one. The A tranche is normally of shorter maturity (three to five years) and generally contains a revolving portion. The other tranches (also called *institutional tranches*) have a predetermined principal and a longer maturity (around 7 to 10 years). There is typically a higher spread for each year although this has changed somewhat recently as spreads have become lower as a result of high demand and low loss experience. The ownership interest is conveyed either through an assignment (whereby the investor has a direct debtor-creditor relationship) or through a loan participation agreement. In the latter case, the buyer has an undivided interest in the loan but no direct relationship with the debtor. Early in the development of the market, there was a significant reluctance on the part of many commercial borrowers to have their loans sold into the secondary markets without their permission, in recent years this seems to have become less of an issue and more loans are transferred on assignments or into structured vehicles such as CLOs without the knowledge of the creditor.

At first, the purchasers of bank loans came to the market with a buy-and-hold mentality. As the secondary market expanded, however, new players such as hedge funds with a different orientation began to enter. Investment managers of all types hired experts in bank loans and began to buy these assets for their portfolios. Unlike the regional banks and foreign banks, they were competing against, these early adopters were steeped in portfolio theory, and they were inclined to manage their portfolios actively—selling loans as well as buying them. Investment management companies also developed structures and funds that were specialized in buying bank loans into which the loans could be placed. An early example was when Eaton Vance developed a "prime rate mutual fund" dedicated to these assets in 1989. Just about every major fixed income player has at least one of these types of funds in 2007.

A large number of special-purpose companies have been established to acquire assets, create diversified portfolio, and then sell off tranches

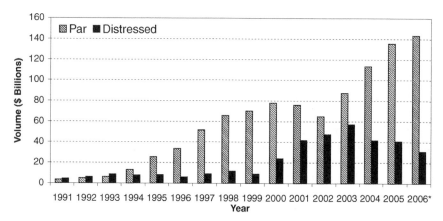

FIGURE 25.2 Secondary Loan Market
Source: Reuters Loan Pricing Corporation (2007). Reprinted with permission.

of these portfolios to different investor types. For example, managers of CDOs are major buyers of bonds and loans. Chapter 21, Credit Derivatives, and Chapter 24, Structured Finance, discussed these various structures and businesses that are based upon these concepts. The growth in the secondary market for loans in Figure 25.2 demonstrates the importance of these activities.

The investors in the senior tranches of these portfolios are those who invest in the highly rated floating rate instruments (AAA and AA) and are often organizations that also use structured finance techniques as a trading strategy. Examples would be *structured investment vehicle* (SIVs) such as *alpha, beta,* or *centauri.* But banks also play in these markets, particularly those banks that are long deposits and short of loans as is the norm for regional banks in Europe. The investors in the lower-rated pieces have traditionally been the place where insurance companies play. More recently, a huge increase in liquidity in the market and declining spreads have been associated with the involvement of the hedge funds. In the early days of the market, these players (to the extent they played at all) limited themselves to what was then described as *equity pieces,* where yields were high enough to get them interested. Nowadays, hedge funds are active in a spectrum of credit starting at less-than-investment grade to single A. Meanwhile, the rating agencies have become increasingly comfortable rating investments of this kind, focusing on the issues of diversification, liquidity, and active asset management. All of this comes together in the development of the market for CDOs.

CDOs: CLOs AND CBOs

Collateralized debt obligations come in two primary flavors: *Collateralized bond obligations* (CBOs) and *collateralized loan obligations* (CLOs) are structured financings backed by bonds (sovereign or corporate) and bank loans, respectively. These structures have the virtue of turning (primarily) below-investment-grade assets into investment-grade securities. Pooling, tranching, diversification, and various forms of credit enhancement combine to work this alchemy. While securities of this kind were issued as early as 1987, the volume of issuance has surged in recent years. A number of factors are driving this growth: the arbitrage opportunity created by the disparity in coupon payments between high-yield and investment-grade assets; the need on the part of many banks and insurance companies to lower their capital requirements by removing assets from their balance sheets; the number of special purpose vehicles set up to own these assets; and investors' appetite for securities offering attractive yields and diversified exposure. Two developments in the late 1990s also contributed to the market growth. The first synthetic CDO was rated by S&P in 1997; and in 2000 came the first ABS CDO. Collateralized loan obligations represent the last frontier in banks' ability to manage their balance sheets. In the mid-2000s, this market has really accelerated and along with the secondary loan market has had an impact on the financial landscape as dramatic as that had by interest rate swaps.

Figure 25.3 shows a typical CDO structure. The issuer establishes a bankruptcy-remote special purpose vehicle, which purchases bonds/loans from the portfolio on the basis of preset criteria approved by the rating agency. The portfolio manager will manage the assets in the special purpose vehicle. The management activities include loan administration, asset replacement, and receipt and distribution of funds. The special purpose vehicle may enter into an interest rate swap to eliminate interest rate risk, thereby providing the debt holders with a LIBOR-plus-spread cash flow augmented by any return of principal from prepayments. The redistribution of risk and return is brought about by tranching. This structure creates senior obligations (which may be rated AAA) that have lower expected returns but a higher rating than the overall portfolio. The subordinated debt also earns an investment-grade rating (such as BBB). The junior subordinated tranche, which represents the true equity piece, may be unrated. The structure may include reserve accounts or a liquidity line of credit, and/or guarantees. As investors have become more comfortable with the structure and quality of CLOs and CBOs, the need for guarantors in these transactions have diminished. The resulting savings flow to the investor or the manager (usually the borrower), depending on supply and demand conditions—in recent years the managers have been the main beneficiaries.

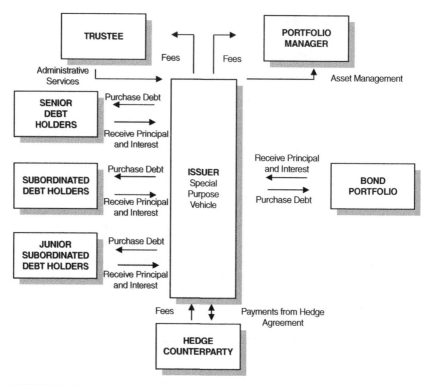

FIGURE 25.3 CLO/CBO Structure

Initially the markets developed two main forms of CBOs. In a *cash flow CBO*, also referred to as an *arbitrage CBO*, the cash flow generated by the underlying assets is used to pay interest and principal to investors. A *market-value CBO*, by contrast, requires that the market value of the assets in the portfolio always be sufficient to pay off the liabilities. Portfolio management is based on the total return concept: Cash flows for payments to investors are derived from trading profits as well as from principal and accrued interest received on the underlying bonds.

In recent years, however, the global CDO/CLO markets have surged in both volume and types of structures. The following summary from Moody's (2007a, 1) U.S. CDO Review for 2006 and Figure 25.4 tell the story:

> *The record breaking year 2006 may go down in the books as the year in which final doubts were swept away and the last skeptics conceded that CDO technology was not restricted to a specialized corner of the capital markets. For the year, Moody's rated 630 U.S.*

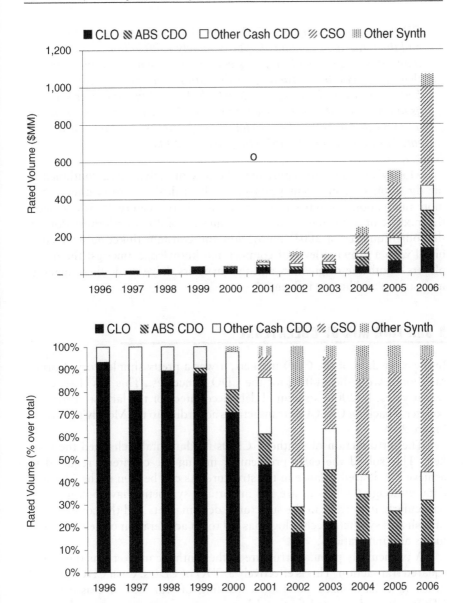

FIGURE 25.4 U.S. CDO Transaction Volume, 1996–2006
Source: Moody's Investors Service (2007a, 2).

CDO transactions, up over 70% from the number rated in 2005, and the total rated volume of approximately $320 billion was more than 90% larger than last year's volume. Phenomenal numbers in their own right, but bordering on aberration when place in context: 2005 was a record setting year in which the final two quarters saw as many deals rated as in the entire year of 2004. That achievement was repeated in 2006 when the final two quarters saw as many deals rated as in the entire record-setting year of 2005.

Moody's goes on to report that the mix of activity had continued in the direction seen in recent years—more loan deals, more synthetics and more innovation. Moody's transaction mix charts (Figure 25.5) compares the mixture of deals done in the fourth quarter of 2006 with those done in the fourth quarter of 2005. Innovation and constant tinkering have combined with a growing level of comfort and knowledge amongst the major players—both the originators and the investors, have made these markets mainstream and hugely influential.

A SHIFTING MIX OF COLLATERAL

In the early days of the CDO markets, it was a pretty simple story. Corporate bonds were the stuffing for the CDO structures., This has changed in recent years. In 2006, structured debt accounted for the largest portion of collateral backing U.S. CDO transactions according to the Moody's charts in Figure 25.6.

The introduction of synthetic CDOs fundamentally changed the markets. This solved the early problem of finding the collateral required to achieve the desired balance in the structure. As can be seen in the Moody's data, although Cash deals are still important, synthetics have become been particularly important in the structured debt markets and the combination of cash and synthetic technology has led to an acceleration of new developments and innovations.

A particularly popular structure in the synthetic market was the CDO-squared transaction. This is effectively a CDO of CDOs. Cash CDO-squared deals, (a collateralized portfolio consisting of tranches of existing cash CDOs), were developed first and became an important part of the market in early 2003–2004. However, this market evolved toward synthetic deals by 2005. Synthetic CDOs-squared involve a portfolio of credit default swaps (CDS) and have a two-layer structure of credit risk. In most synthetic CDOs-squared, the underlying CDOs are created for the sole purpose of being included in the CDOs-squared. Because of its synthetic nature, these

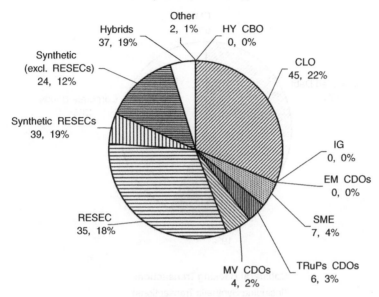

Q4 2005 Number of Rated Deals
(Number, % of Total)

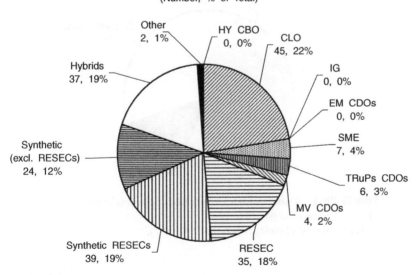

Q4 2006 Number of Rated Deals
(Number, % of Total)

FIGURE 25.5 Number and Percent of Rated Deals, 2005 Q4
Source: Moody's Investors Service (2007a, 5).

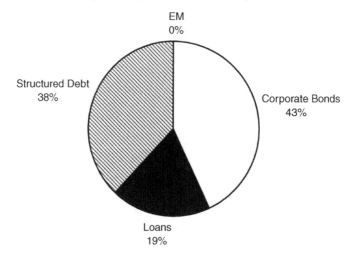

Collateral Backing Transactions
(Excluding Synthetic Transactions)

EM
0%

Structured Debt
38%

Corporate Bonds
43%

Loans
19%

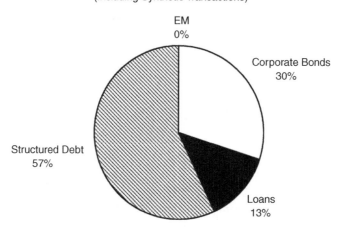

Collateral Backing Transactions
(Including Synthetic Transactions)

EM
0%

Corporate Bonds
30%

Structured Debt
57%

Loans
13%

FIGURE 25.6 Collateral Backing Transactions (excluding synthetic transactions)
Source: Moody's Investors Service (2007a, 7).

underlying CDOs are simply conceptual and used to calculate cash flows in value of the CDOs-squared. Therefore, a synthetic CDO-squared may be viewed as a complex derivative instrument, while its cash counterpart is simply a repackaging of existing CDOs. In this way and without much fanfare or discussion CDOs-squared turned out to be a prime example of excess and greed triumphing over common sense and conservatism. Because of the high levels of leverage used by CDOs-squared, even the use of diversification worked against them as sub prime loans infected the other reference loans and made the whole structure collapse while serving up huge mark to market losses.

The markets became more complex and much riskier in the period 2005–2006. As stated by Richard Bookstaber (2007) in *Wall Street's Summer of Scary Numbers,* "The products are getting an order of magnitude more complex. Things change slightly and get correlated where they weren't correlated before. You can't make it without understanding it, but you can buy it."

DISTRESSED DEBT MARKETS

The distressed debt markets also have their roots in bank lending. Banks learned early on that the informal rescue of a good client could be important and lucrative. Banking history is full of examples where banks bailed out companies viewed to be important to the stability of the financial system, often at the urging of the Central Bank. In nineteenth century Great Britain, Rothschild's bailed out Barings at the behest of the Bank of England. In the United States, Chrysler and much of the airline industry has benefited from this kind of support. Similar examples exist in France, Germany, Japan, and most major economies.

The business of distressed debt grew out of this tradition, but built upon some very different concepts. First, the concept of "too important to fail" has little meaning in this new world. Secondly, while the banks continue to play an important role in funding the market, this market was mainly a creation of U.S. bankruptcy lawyers. During the 1980s and early 1990s, bankruptcy lawyers were enjoying a big increase in work. Chapter 11 bankruptcy gave the restructuring/reorganization business a boost while diminishing the importance of liquidation. Reemphasizing reorganizations, as opposed to cashing in the assets, meant that those involved in bankruptcy had to take a more "entrepreneurial" view of their roles. The crucial players were the lawyers, given that bankruptcy in the United States is driven by lawyers, but the market really took off when their efforts were joined by investors—some banks, some vulture funds and eventually hedge funds who saw the potential, had the funds to invest and were willing to take the risks.

The distressed debt markets can be viewed as a subset of the larger leverage loan market. The growth in U.S. leveraged (defined as *speculative grade debt*) has continued to accelerate behind the notion of *leveraging* introduced in Chapter 1. Good companies with good businesses are frequently loaded up with debt as a way of increasing returns to shareholders. This makes sense if the business is steady and does not suffer some sort of setback; or the economy does not serve up some surprise. If either of these things happens, then those companies move down into the *distressed* or *defaulted categories* listed in Figure 25.7. These are definitely the world of the specialized lender—banks, hedge funds, and other investment companies have teams dedicated to these markets. These teams are stocked with lawyers and bankers who have had substantial experience in the area of bankruptcy and workouts. For the most part, this is not the place for the bright but inexperienced traders or deal doers you see elsewhere in the capital markets. This is a place for those who know what they are doing, and in recent years they have done well.

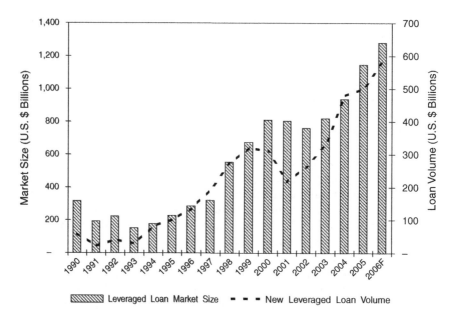

FIGURE 25.7 U.S. Leveraged Loan Market, 1990–2006
Source: Credit Suisse (2007).

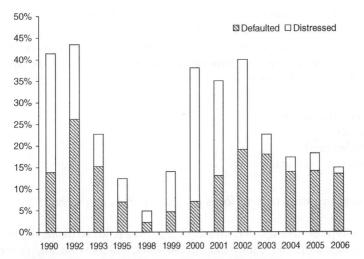

FIGURE 25.8   Distressed and Defaulted Debt as a Percentage of
High-Yield and Defaulted Debt Markets, 1990–2006
Source: Citigroup (2007).

More recently concerns have arisen in these markets. It used to be that a
company's bankruptcy was the end of the story for those who were trying to
prevent it, and the beginning of the story for those who dealt with defaulted
debt. The old market expectation was for the debt to be trading the day after
the bankruptcy at something around 20 cents on the dollar. This gave the
brave defaulted debt buyer some considerable room to operate—particularly
if the company looked like a going concern. In 2006, however, the average
trading value of defaulted debt has risen to over 80 cents on the dollar—a
lot less to work with than the old days of just a few years ago. This is
reflective of several things, including the reality that much of what happens
in bankruptcy these days has been prepackaged. However, there can be no
doubt that too much money is now chasing limited opportunities in these
areas. One of our authors cannot wait for a real downturn in the economy
to create some real demand for distressed lending. See Figure 25.8.

WHO'S BUYING?

The growth in the capital markets in recent years is clearly driven by a
dramatic change in attitudes from investors and lenders. Much of this change
can be seen in the structured finance and credit derivative markets. Ten years

ago these markets were developing markets with limited audiences. Today they are mainstream. While investors everywhere seem to participate in these markets to some degree, there are notable differences between regions and between types of investors. Broadly speaking we can break the investors down into four categories:

- Asset managers
- Banks
- Hedge funds
- Insurance companies

These investors tend to focus on certain areas as Figure 25.9. demonstrates.

The type of investor that invests in segments tends to define the market: Some investors prefer equity-like investments, others want higher returns but some income and they prefer mezzanine investments. Then there are the lower-risk investors who generally want to see only senior tranches. Within each category of investor—banks, insurance, hedge funds, and asset managers—there are investors who fit into each of the risk/reward categories, but generally it is the institutional money managers at the hedge funds and asset management firms who tend to buy the greater percentages of higher

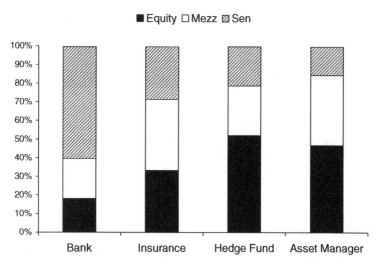

FIGURE 25.9 Who Buys Which Tranche?
Source: Citigroup (2007).

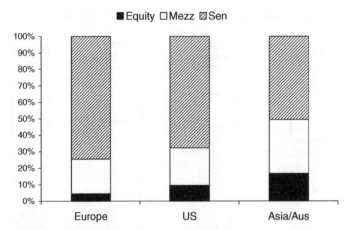

FIGURE 25.10 Tranches Bought by Region
Source: Citigroup (2007).

risk, higher return investments. Figure 25.10 demonstrates how this looks across market segments.

There are also differences amongst investors and lenders domiciled in different geographical regions. Figures 25.11 and 25.12 shows what investments tend to be purchased in these different regions and what kinds of investors are located in the three regions identified in a recent Citibank report (2007).

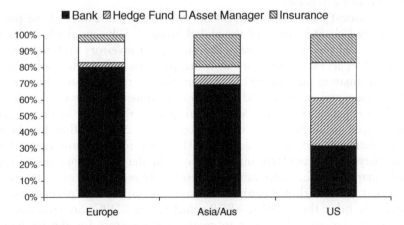

FIGURE 25.11 Investor Types by Region
Source: Citigroup (2007).

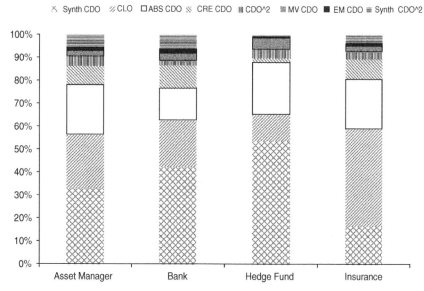

FIGURE 25.12   Product Investments by Investor Type Globally
Source: Citigroup (2007).

Finally, investors can be differentiated according to the type of investments they make. Figure 25.12 illustrates the portfolio preferences of the
four-investor categories.

Investment banks and frequent borrowers are well aware of the preferences and characteristics of the global investor. Substantial efforts have
been directed towards increasing the number of investors and improving
the comfort levels of investors who are participating in the credit markets. Information technologies have been directed towards providing more
information and analysis and innumerable conferences have been dedicated to these markets. The substantial growth the credit markets have
experienced in recent years is evidence of the progress that has been
made. But it is not the whole story. There are four investor types that
have played a particularly important role in the transformation of the
credit markets. One, hedge funds, represents the redirection of an investor
type that was developed with other markets—equities in particular—in
mind. The other three—SIVs, ABCP vehicles, and CDPCs are creatures of
the credit markets. They exist to create new investors for the booming
markets.

FOUR MAJOR PLAYERS THAT HAVE MADE A DIFFERENCE TO THE WAY THE GAME IS PLAYED

Hedge Funds

If you were to ask anyone deeply involved in the credit markets today how they have changed in recent years, they undoubtedly would talk about how hedge funds have influenced the credit market—for both good and bad. Hedge funds are unregulated, private pools of capital. Hedge fund managers can and do invest in a wide variety of assets and pursue many investment strategies that range from high-risk investments to arbitrage. The type of trading strategies and financial instruments they use does not restrict most hedge funds. They make use of short-selling, derivatives and options and frequently use the equity markets as a integral part of their credit risk strategies. Hedge funds also make liberal use of leverage, either directly by borrowing against their portfolios or indirectly through leverages embedded in derivatives and options. The are differentiated from other types of investment managers because of the freedom they enjoy as managers as well as the leverage they employ but also because they are usually careful to exempt themselves from the regulatory umbrella's in the United States and Europe by structuring their portfolios so that they are only available to accredited investors (large sophisticated investors who typically dedicate a small portion of their portfolios to such funds). Their unregulated status allows them to operate with a high degree of opacity. Most hedge funds are black boxes and this market is rife with rumor and legend. Finally, hedge fund managers are typically compensated based on both scale and absolute returns through a dual fee structure whereby managers often retain 2 percent of the net asset value of the fund and 20 percent of returns in excess of some benchmark. This combination of the opacity and high compensation tends to differentiate hedge funds from other investment managers such as mutual funds that operate in open, regulated markets with compensation structures tied to market benchmarks. Opacity and highly convex compensation structures also has the potential to create excess risk-taking, and clearly this has been the result in some cases.

For the most part, however, hedge funds have been very successful in recent years and the amount of funds under management by the industry has grown exponentially in the last decade. Figure 25.13 illustrates the growth of the industry as a whole. Not all of these funds are involved in the credit markets, but there is no doubt that a sizable portion is engaged in credit-risk-taking activities. They tend to dominate certain segments: in 2005, by one estimate, they accounted for 89 percent of U.S. trading volume in convertible bonds, 66 percent of volume in distressed debt, 33 percent

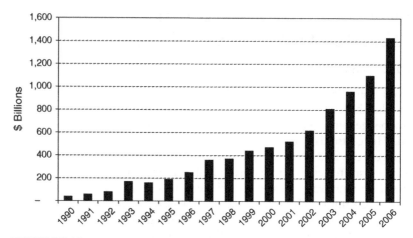

FIGURE 25.13 Total Assets Under Global Management of Hedge Funds
Source: Hedge Fund Research, Inc. (2007).

of volume in emerging market bonds and in leverage loans, 20 percent of speculative-grade-bond volume, and 38 percent of credit derivatives volume (Sender and Raghavan 2006). By early 2006 their estimated share of credit derivatives trading had increased to 58 percent (Greenwich Associates 2007).

The growth in these markets in recent years has to be viewed as evidence of their success during the period, but also is a cause for concern for many market observers, particularly the regulators. These investors can afford to accumulate talent and it seems that they have done so. However, most of the good performance has come during a very benign period in the capital markets—a time when leverage and aggressive trading strategies have clearly paid off. If the current market turmoil reverses some of this fortune, there is likely to be little sympathy for these investors in central banks and other regulators around the globe. However, it may not be so simple. The hedge fund industry has become a major customer base to banks and investment banks that have benefited from the transaction volumes they produce. The banks are frequently the counterparties to many of the hedge fund trades, and also provide liquidity and other credit facilities to the industry. There are significant counterparty risks at banks that serve the industry and banking regulators are encouraging good *counterparty credit risk management practices* (CCRM) (see Schuermann and Stiroh 2007). Even more of a concern to regulators is the systemic risk associated with a large segment of the credit markets operating outside of their review. Leading capital market participants are also concerned with the risks to the financial system from counterparty risk in times of financial upheaval as is evidenced by the work done by the Counterparty Risk Management Policy Groups I and II. The current market turmoil may provide an opportunity for central bankers and other regulators to establish some controls on these activities and players.

Structured Investment Vehicles (SIVs)

SIVs are not new to the capital markets. The first SIV, Alpha Finance Corporation, was first rated by S&P in 1989, with Beta Finance Corporation, following shortly thereafter (Standard & Poor's 1998). Both Alpha and Beta were sponsored by Citibank, which went on to create a third vehicle, Centauri Corp. before the general market figured out what they were doing and began in the 1990s to emulate them with a series of SIVs being created, many by alumni from Citibank. What Citibank did with those early vehicles was to establish an investment vehicle that they could control, but keep off their regulatory and financial balance sheet. This allowed them to implement a *buy-and-hold* investment strategy in high-grade securities that never could be held on the bank's balance sheet given the capital requirements. Mostly the investments were in highly rated securities (AA and AAA), so credit losses are seldom an issue, although their early arrangements with the rating agencies required marking their portfolios to market and liquidation of investments that drop below agreed upon levels (usually single A). The main risks the SIV had to manage were on the liability side of the balance sheet. These investment vehicles operate almost exclusively with debt capital and they must pay close attention to the management of their liabilities. Figure 25.14 illustrate the structure of a typical SIV.

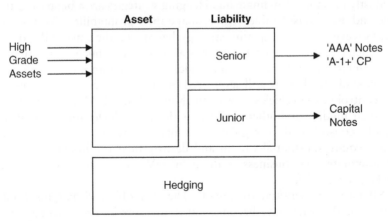

FIGURE 25.14 Simple SIV Balance Sheet
Source: Standard and Poor's (2007).

This typical SIV issues short-term and long-term liabilities and purchases assets with the proceeds. These assets will pay a coupon rate that is higher than the interest rate the SIV needs to pay on its issued liabilities including the junior capital notes. This price differential is the key element that makes the SIV profitable. And, of course, little or no equity capital requirements makes this a high-return activity. Twenty-five years ago, Citibank had pulled off a real feat of financial engineering. It created a profitable controlled vehicle that could purchase loans and other securities originated by Citibank (or others) and finance them off-balance-sheet with little or no capital consequences—all the while achieving at triple-A rating for the vehicle. On top of this, it could do this in size. Citibank sponsored vehicles grew dramatically in the early 1990s. Citibank's fingers were all over the original vehicles. They were created and run by Citibank employees, Citibank provided most of the assets and even some of the liabilities. Citibank clients, mostly correspondent banks and high net worth investors, bought the junior capital notes. Citibank backup lines provided backstop to the commercial paper. It was no surprise that the early SIVs ran fairly low-key operations and attracted little attention. Citibank had developed a *better mousetrap* and they were reluctant to help their competitors join the party.

Eventually their competitors caught on and the last 10 years has seen explosive growth in a number of these vehicles and the amount of assets they have under management. In July 2007, Moody's (2007b) reported there were $370 billion of assets under management across 28 vehicles, 10 of which were launched in the last 18 months. Over the years, SIVs business strategies have become more sophisticated, particularly on the liability side where they run major gaps—taking exposure to long-term assets while relying mostly on short-term financing. Hedging strategies are a big part of their game and, to a considerable degree, shape their profitability. For the most part, however, the asset quality strategy has stayed the same. SIVs do not take much credit risk. This growth has also attracted much more attention from regulators, rating agencies and independent accounting firms. As a result, most of the SIVs are still sponsored by major financial institutions, but their control of the vehicles is now much more limited. Most sponsors also limit their funding and other activities with these vehicles for fear that they might be consolidated for regulatory or financial accounting, an event that would require substantial capital and destroy their profitability. Citibank still dominates the business with eight SIVs under their management (Fleckenstein 2007).

SIVs are very sensitive to spreads. They live off small margins. So it is no surprise that they have become major investors in asset-backed, CDOs and mortgage-backed paper. Anything that comes in volume, has some liquidity and pays a little more spread is made to measure for their investment

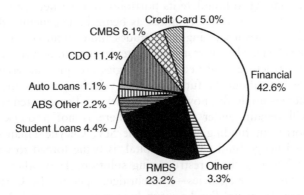

Sector Composition - SIVs

Credit Card 5.0%
CMBS 6.1%
CDO 11.4%
Auto Loans 1.1%
ABS Other 2.2%
Student Loans 4.4%
Financial 42.6%
RMBS 23.2%
Other 3.3%

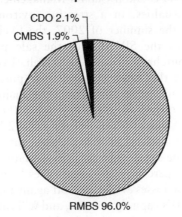

Sector Composition - SIV-lites

CDO 2.1%
CMBS 1.9%
RMBS 96.0%

FIGURE 25.15 Sector Composition
Source: Moody's Investors Service (2007b).

strategies. The figures in Figure 25.15 demonstrate the sector compositions for SIVs—and SIV-*lites*, a derivation of the original SIV that reflects its more limited asset portfolio.

A SIV typically only invests in assets of the highest credit quality following conservative diversification guidelines and obligor limitations. The goal is the reduce credit risk in the portfolio to a minimum. In addition, after some poor experiences with some of the earlier versions that were forced to liquidate significant portions of their portfolios, in recent years their liability structures are tranched in junior and senior debt, sometimes accompanied by a mezzanine position, which allocates any potential credit risk to the debt (from riskiest to less risky in sequence). This is designed to shelter the SIV from having to liquidate its portfolio in a market crisis. Although the SIV market is still seen very much as being homogeneous, the risk of having funding problems, rating downgrades and/or liquidation varies considerably by vehicle. Their investment strategies tend to be very similar, but their liability structures and hedging strategies are quite different, so it is hard to generalize about the future of these vehicles post the market crisis of 2007. There is no doubt, however, that they are being tested right now.

SIVs will remain under pressure if there is not a quick improvement in short-term funding markets. One SIV, Cheyne Finance, run by London-based hedge fund Cheyne Capital, is being forced to wind down operations while it seeks a restructuring solution. Two others have had their rating cut by the agencies—Rhinebridge, operated by German bank IKB, and Axon Financial Funding, run by a manager-owned, New York–based hedge fund TPG-Axon Capital Management. They are not expected to be the last casualties. In a stressful environment, as SIVs have experienced during the summer of 2007, the likelihood that an asset sale leads to a loss to the SIV due to the sale price of the assets being lower than the purchase price is very high. Even though the managers would pick assets that trade around their purchase price, in a market where credit spreads have blown out, the majority of assets will experience a loss. According to a recent Fitch (2007) report, over a 90-day period beginning August 1, 2007, a total of $4.2 billion of assets sold from Fitch-rated SIVs at an average price of 98.4 cents compared to a final mark of 99.4 cents on the same portfolio. This equates to a loss per asset sale of approximately 1.3 percent, with some losses being as high as 13.7 percent (Fitch 2007). These losses are written off against the lowest notes (after any reserving) in the SIVs capital structure, and will eat their way up the liability structure, as more assets have to be sold to meet maturing liabilities. The longer the current crisis continues, the more losses this will create. Forecasting the magnitude of this problem is impossible in September 2007. What can be forecasted, however, is that the SIV investor segment will be shrinking in the coming months. Investors in the commercial paper and senior and junior notes of SIVs are experiencing an outcome they did not expect, and will not like. It is reasonable to expect a major pullback from these vehicles. If that happens, then the SIV market will become far less important for structured finance issuers.

Asset-Backed Commercial Paper (ABCP) Conduits

Commercial paper issuing conduits are another product of Citibank financial engineering. In the early 1980s, Citibank's asset-based lending unit formed its first conduit to purchase and fund trade receivables. The idea was very similar to that of the SIV: create a funding vehicle that can be used by Citibank's customers to finance their businesses, without using the bank's balance sheet. It came at a time when the bank's balance sheet was strained by the weight of its earlier expansion into international lending, so lending activities that did not involve increasing assets—even if they were low risk assets—was highly desirable. Trade receivables were always low credit risk activities for banks, as they turn over frequently and going concerns will always pay their suppliers first. These types of financial assets were perfect for financing in the capital markets, as long as dedicated reserves were in place to cover discounts, returns and limited bad debts and the funding could be flexible to account for seasonal fluctuations in the amount financed. Commercial paper was traditionally used to finance working capital for major corporations, so it was a natural funding market for these first asset-based conduits.

From its early beginnings as a way of financing trade receivables, ABCP Conduits have grown in numbers and importance. Figure 25.16 shows how the market for ABCP has grown.

While the ABCP Conduit market has been in existence since the mid-1980s, the vehicles issuing ABCP today bear little resemblance to those earlier versions. The market has evolved and different structures and purposes have been introduced. Meanwhile most financial institutions, including a majority of banks, many insurance companies, hedge funds, and others,

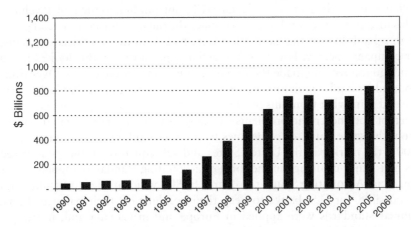

FIGURE 25.16 U.S. ABCP Outstandings [a]

[a] ABCP per U.S. Federal Reserve report includes fully enhanced ABCP conduits.

[b] Projection based on Standard & Poor's econometric model.

Source: Standard & Poor's (2006c).

have sponsored the nearly 200 conduits worldwide that are investing and issuing in this market. Banks are by far the largest operators, accounting for nearly two-thirds of the rated vehicles (Moody's Investors Service 2007c).

Today ABCP Conduits finance a wide array of investments. Trade receivables remain an important segment; however, most conduits are highly diversified. According to a recent report by Moody's (2007c), 113 U.S. bank-sponsored conduits have total ABCP outstanding of $522 billion as of June 30, 2007. Of these, 62 are multiseller programs, with $461 billion outstanding, 22 are securities arbitrage, with $67 billion outstanding and 10 are hybrids with $32 billion outstanding.[1] Moody's (2007c, 5) goes on to note that the multiseller programs they rate are highly diversified.

> *We have 62 programs funding 10 different asset types. The largest asset types by outstanding amounts are credit cards at 15%, trade receivables at 13%, commercial loans at 11%, auto loans at 10% and securities at 9%. Mortgages also make up 9% of the total, mostly in the form of warehousing lines that fund newly originated mortgages for short periods of time. Highly rated CDOs comprise about 3% of the assets. Note that U.S. multiseller programs typically have 8% to 10% program credit enhancement, nearly covering any single one of these asset classes.*

A major factor in the substantial growth of ABCP was the willingness of the bank sponsors to provide committed backup liquidity facilities for the full amount of the *commercial paper* (CP) outstanding to the ABCP vehicle. This meant that the conduit could replace the outstanding commercial paper with a bank loan if the CP market were to evaporate in a crisis—systemic or company specific. For the commercial paper investor, this looked like a bank guarantee and made their credit evaluation relatively easy. Over time, spurred by bank regulators and the major accounting firms, banks have retreated somewhat from this position, so now conditions apply and generally exempt specific credit problems—usually covered by credit enhancement from the same bank, or sometimes by another bank or credit enhancer. In 2003, the market in the United States and subsequently in Europe received its first major challenge in the form of accounting standards applied by the Financial Accounting Standards Board (FASB), which made it difficult, if not impossible, for U.S. banks to keep their conduits off their balance sheets. Similar standards were applied in Europe and in Canada and, in the period 2001–2004, there was little or no growth in the outstanding amounts of *credit derivative product companies* (CDCPs), which are discussed in the next section. However, funding advantages, some clever restructuring and reengineering has restored growth to the market and it seems likely to expand rapidly in the future. The decrease in regulatory capital for off-balance-sheet exposures for banks under Basel II should also be a powerful incentive for banks to continue to develop new conduits and expand those they already have.

The assets in these conduits are generally of very high quality and mostly short term. So far, no asset problems have been reported at conduits in the crisis of 2007. Some ABCP programs have not been able to rollover their commercial paper in the current liquidity squeeze, but their liquidity facilities have operated as expected and bank loans have substituted for the commercial paper. Conduits are not required by the agencies to mark their portfolios to market, so there is no pressure for them to sell off assets. It seems likely that this market will survive the current crisis and is most likely to be the first market to return to normalcy when the crisis has run its course.

Credit Derivative Product Companies

Hedge funds, SIVs, and ABCPs have added significant investment capacity to the markets, but the credit markets still need sophisticated investors who understand credit risk and are prepared to take risks and hold them to maturity. This is particularly true in the credit derivative market where SIVs and ABCP conduits do not operate. As the credit derivative market has matured there are plenty of players who are willing to take and then trade out of those risks (hopefully at a better price). The investment banks, hedge funds and many investors are willing to buy risk—by purchasing cash securities or writing protection on individual corporate credits or pool of risk in some type of structure. But few of them do so with the intension of holding the risk for long. In many cases, they are hedging their position by shorting something else at the same time. Often it is the same security. This is okay to a point. But there is a cost built into this kind of investment trading and so the market really would like to see the development of synthetic investors and counterparties whose natural position is to *buy-and-hold credit risk* in derivative form.

As we have seen in other chapters, in today's credit market, if there is a vacuum in some market segment, it is not long before some enterprising group has developed a way to fill that vacuum. So it is here. The latest innovation in the credit markets in the last couple of years was the development of credit derivative product companies or CDPCs. They are meant to address the shortage of long-term credit investors in the credit derivative market. Not too surprisingly, they tend to be sponsored by some of the major dealers, but some are already public entities[2] and we expect to see these types of vehicles broadening their business mix over the coming years. In early 2007, there were 18 vehicles said to be in formation by the rating agencies. Most of this activity seemed to reflect the challenges felt by the SIVs in funding themselves cheaply enough in the low spread environment. By moving into the derivative markets, risk takers could avoid having the finance their portfolio. Under the rating agency guidelines for this kind of activity, leverage could also be used in the capital structure making these vehicles a very efficient way of taking on credit risk. Unfortunately for many of the planned vehicles, getting investors to participate in structured credit vehicles became a very difficult sell in middle 2007. On the other hand, those companies who were able to get into operation prior to the crisis found that the spreads in the credit markets were suddenly quite attractive.

Calyon (2007) reviewed and summarized the CDPC market as of June 2007 in Table 25.1. A typical CDPC is shown in Figure 25.17.

In September 2007, there were seven CDCPs operating with triple-A ratings from one or more of the rating agencies. Table 25.2 lists those

TABLE 25.1 Review and Rationale behind a CDPC

Review

Buy-and-hold strategy:	A CDPC's main business is selling credit protection.
CDPCs have a triple-A counterparty rating:	The counterparty rating addresses the risk that the protection buyer faces in respect of the nonpayment of amounts owing under the CDS contracts.
Rating methodology:	A CDPC's capital model is a proprietary model used to determine capital adequacy requirements.
Number of CDPCs set to increase:	Out of a total of 24 CDPC transactions as of January 2007, three-quarters were in the United States and the remainder in Europe.

Rationale

The basic premise is to arbitrage the spread implied by CDS spreads and historical defaults.

Although CDPCs are generally long credit risk, a CDPC manager may also be permitted to purchase protection (short credit risk).

A CDPC can sell protection of a variety of segments in the credit markets, but it will be limited to those specified in its operating guidelines.

Credit exposures on which protection is sold include: corporate obligations, sovereign and municipal obligations, asset-backed securities, and CDO tranches and indexes.

Source: Calyon (2007).

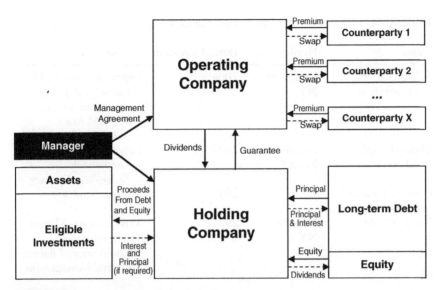

FIGURE 25.17 Typical CDPC Structure
Source: Calyon (2007).

companies. They generally fall into two categories. Primus was the first company established in 2003 and they focus on taking credit risk on single-name corporates. Accordingly, their average transaction is limited to around $20 million. Athilon was the second CDCP formed and their business strategy was to take aggregate risks on portfolios of credits. The five CDCPs formed in 2007 tended to follow the Athilon strategy, however, we expect over time to see a blurring of these distinctions. So far CDCPs are a relatively small participant in the credit derivative market, but substantial growth in the portfolios of the existing companies and eventually in the number of CDCPs makes it likely that these players will be significantly larger in a few years.

A Major Test Arrives in 2007

The new markets we discussed, and most of the new players, are creatures of the rating agencies. The agencies play an absolutely critical role in these markets from design to issuance to trading. The fascinating element is that their control of the market is passive. Someone else has to initiate a new product or type of intermediary before the rating agencies will turn their attention to the area. But once the rating agencies do get comfortable with

TABLE 25.2 CDPCs rated by the Rating Agencies[a]

Name	Headquarters	Date of Creation	Sponsor
Athilon Capital Corporation	New York, NY	2004	Lightyear Capital LLC, Caisse de dépôt et placement du Québec, and GM Asset Management
Channel Capital Advisors	Dublin, Ireland	2007	Calyon, KBC Bank and Landesbank Baden-Wurttemberg
Cournot Financial Products	-	2007	Morgan Stanley
Invicta Credit	New York, NY	2007	Massachusetts Mutual Life Insurance Company and Babson Capital Management LLC
Koch Financial Products	Scottsdale, AZ	2007	Koch Financial Group
Newlands Financial	Ireland, Dublin	2006	Deutsche Bank and Axa Investment Managers
Primus Financial Products	New York, NY	2004	Primus Guaranty

[a] As of September of 2007.
Source: Moody's Investors Service (2007c), Standard & Poor's (2006b), and Fitch Ratings 2007.

the structure, then others quickly copy the idea and begin an iterative process of improving the structure or intermediary.

This process has been the catalyst for a huge amount of innovation in the capital markets and has allowed this market to expand at an exponential rate. The rating agencies have provided a standard and a discipline which allowed new markets, new players, and new ways to play, to become the big story in the financial world of the twenty-first century. At the end of 2007, however, confidence in the ratings has been shaken by the credit crisis and many of these new markets are now in freefall. No one can be sure how or when stability will be restored. Yet the fundamentals are that these markets and players provide a crucial service and that suggests that it will happen. The credit markets need investors and structures that can buy and hold credit risk as a major part of their core business strategies. Those that survive the current crisis will be better for it. And, of course, the history of the credit markets has shown that these markets ebb and flow but never go away. Memories are too short for that.

REFERENCES

Bahar, Reza. 1998. *Structured Investment Vehicles*. New York: Standard & Poor's.

———. 2003. "Structured Investment Vehicle Criteria: New Developments." *Standard & Poor's Credit Ratings – Credit Ratings Criteria*, 4 September.

———. 2006a. "As Structured Investment Vehicles Become More Popular Risk Models Become More Sophisticated." *Standard & Poor's Credit Research*, 11 October.

———. 2006b. "Innovative Structures Are Moving ABPC Beyond the Basics." *Standard & Poor's Ratings Direct*, 16 October.

Fitch Ratings. 2007. "Rating Performance of Structured Investment Vehicles (SIVs) in Times of Diminishing Liquidity for Assets and Liabilities." *Derivative Fitch*, 20 September.

Fleckenstein, B. 2007. "Leveraged Black Boxes lists: Beta Finance, Centauri, Dorada, Five Finance, Sedna Finance, Vetra Finance and Zela Finance." In *SIV: Structured Investment Vehicles*.

Greenwich Associates. 2006.

Kambhu, J, T. Schuermann, and K. J. Stiroh. 2007. "Hedge Funds, Financial Intermediation, and Systemic Risk." *Federal Reserve Bank of New York, Economic Policy Review*, Staff Report No. 291, July.

Moody's Investors Service. 2002. "An Introduction to Structured Investment Vehicles." *Moody's Special Report*, 25 January.

———. 2003. "Structured Investment Vehicles – Recent Developments." *Moody's Special Report*, 21 January.

———. 2007a. "2006 U.S. CDO Review & Outlook 2007: Growth, Redefined." *Moody's Structured Finance Special Report*, 6 February.

———. 2007b. "SIVs: An Oasis of Calm in the Sub-prime Maelstrom: International Structured Finance." *Moody's Special Report*, 20 July.

———. 2007c. "Update on Bank-Sponsored ABCP Programs: A Review of Credit and Liquidity Issues." *Moody's Special Report*, 12 September.

Sender H., and A. Raghavan. 2006. "Private Money: the New Financial Order." *Wall Street Journal*, 27 July 27, A1.

Further Reading

Anderson, R. 2004. "How to Make a Virtue Out of Non-Performing Loans." *Financial Times*, 1 November.

Economist. 2003. "Bad Loans in Japan: Bust and Boom." 23 October.

———. 2005. "German Bad Loans: Augean Stables." 28 July.

———. 2005. "Hedge Funds: The New Money Men." 17 February.

————. 2006. "American Investment Banks: Streets Ahead of the Rest." 19 December.

————. 2006. "Buttonwood: Spread Too Thinly." 29 December.

————. 2006. "Corporate Debt: Barbarians at the Gates of Europe." 16 February.

————. 2007. "Investing in Distress: the Vultures Take Wing." 27 March.

Hughes, C. 2007. "Bankers Warn on Distressed Debt." *Financial Times*, 1 February.

Hughes, C. 2007. "Lombard: Distressed Hedge Funds." *Financial Times*, 11 April.

Ohashi, K. and M. Singh. 2004. Japan's Distressed-Debt Market. IMF Working Paper 04/86, May.

Parhar, H. 2007. "A review of the CDPC Market." Calyon Credit Research, 2 May.

Ratner, J. 2003. "The Distressed Side of Loans." *Financial Times*, 1 August.

Scholtes, S. 2007. "Distressed Investing Takes a Creative Turn." *Financial Times*, 24 May.

Standard & Poor's. 2006. "Distressed Debt Monitor." *Standard & Poor's Global Fixed Income Research*, December.

CHAPTER 26

Market Chaos and a Reversion to the Mean

The Rediscovery of Culture as a Critical Risk Management Tool

The world breaks everyone and afterward many are strong at the broken places. But those that will not break it kills. It kills the very good and the very gentle, and the brave impartially. If you are none of these you can be sure that it will kill you too but there will be no special hurry.

—Ernest Hemingway, *A Farewell to Arms*

Managing credit risk was once considered to be the realm of the artist. With time and experience, a banker could master the art of lending and rise to positions of greater and greater authority. A senior lending officer was an expert who—whatever analytical aids might be applied along the way—ultimately made an individual decision about a particular borrower at a particular moment in time. Banks took pride in the depth of the cadre of lending officers that they developed. But competitive pressures on pricing made it difficult to keep up with the high cost of classic credit analysis. Many banks found corporate lending to be unprofitable relative to the credit analysis cost and capital required. Practically none of the corporate-lending-only banks such as JPMorgan and Bankers Trust remain today. They did not fail, but they did not succeed either. The shifting of credit risk taking from the banks to capital markets accelerated with the development of the high-yield market and now practically all bank-originated assets are being securitized. Banks have concluded that "if you can't beat them, then join them." These trends have taken their toll on the way credit gets analyzed.

In recent years, the number of analytical techniques available for managing credit risk has expanded exponentially. Information technology has made information and analytics readily available to anyone with a computer. Additionally, we have seen a flood of new global players with huge liquidity and a willingness to put risk capital to work in the credit markets. It seems that managing credit risk has become a science. While it is true that credit risk management is more scientific, the market events of 2007 have clearly demonstrated that risk management is not yet a science. The management of credit risk lies somewhere between art and science, the realm we commonly call *engineering*. Financial engineers stand ready to convert a "sow's ear into a silk purse" as it were, by taking assets, sometimes those of less than pristine credit quality, and converting them to tranches whose credit profile matched the preference of its clientele. Triple-A-rated, floating rate tranches went to money market funds and the higher-yield mezzanine prices; or equity pieces were bought by alpha-seeking hedge funds. This slicing and dicing of credit portfolios was extremely successful if the measure was just the ability to create and place such instruments. If we were to look more deeply, however, the difficulty of modeling complex asset-backed transactions is now much clearer in the aftermath of the current market crisis. Collapsing asset values have forced massive write-downs and sent many CEOs packing, and the forced liquidation of some funds and most SIVs. The rating agencies and the sales forces of the securities industry have a big job in front of them to restore confidence in the securitization markets.

Today practitioners are different from previous generations. Anyone who has visited a modern financial trading room or met with hedge fund managers knows that these organizations are chockfull of smart, well-educated young people who are armed with an array of systematic techniques and tools that their predecessors could not imagine. And they have huge resources at their disposal. They are like drivers who have acquired a modern super sports car—a Ferrari with much more horsepower than anything they have driven previously. They have a flood of information about the road conditions ahead and they are getting real-time readings on the performance of the car and changing environment. As impressive as this technology may be, you probably would not argue that the roads would be safer because of it. Similarly, the new credit market technology has facilitated unprecedented growth in the capital markets. The markets are now larger, deeper, and broader than ever before. On the other hand, with all this new talent, loaded with technology but not much experience, is it a surprise that the markets have become more volatile? Nevertheless, who could have predicted the market reaction that we are experiencing in the summer of 2007?

Of course, this is not to say that no one saw it coming. Herb Greenberg (2007) writing in the *Wall Street Journal* has this to say:

> *Now that we know what we should have been looking for, it is easy to spot signs that the mortgage morass was occurring long before it actually happened.*
>
> *Some warnings were more obvious than others, even if they went unheeded. Take, for example, the matter of insurance at NovaStar Financial, once one of the leading independent subprime-mortgage lenders.*
>
> *In its heyday, as its stock was spiraling higher with a dividend yield exceeding 10 percent, insurance was a big part of the NovaStar story. It was so big that whenever I would raise red flags over its business, which I often did, investors would pepper me with emails that said that the company couldn't lose because its loans were insured....*
>
> *As it turns out, as far back as 2003, insurer PMI started refusing to pay on claims on NovaStar loans that had defaulted. That, in retrospect, was the first of three insurance-related matters that should have been a clue that the mortgage industry was starting to spin out of control....*
>
> *Yet PMI didn't let the matter rest. In denying the claims, according to court records, it cited material errors and omissions in loan-origination documents. It went so far as to blame NovaStar's "own unclean hands." Furthermore, PMI said it had been under the impression that the subprime-mortgage lender "would use the income stated on a borrower's loan application to qualify the borrower for a stated income loan."*
>
> *According to PMI, that isn't what happened. And in a deposition, according to court papers, NovaStar President Lance Anderson testified that NovaStar didn't use incomes stated on the applications to qualify borrowers. Instead, according to the deposition, Mr. Anderson said if the income "seems reasonable, then we're comfortable not verifying it and not using it in our underwriting decision."*

This is just one story. There are bound to be many others like it before the crisis is finally behind us.

Many market observers, including our coauthor Ed Altman, have been predicting a credit market correction for some time. Looking at the way the market performance had improved in terms of loss experience and spread reductions during the last four years these skeptics could not help but wonder when some event, most likely an economic downturn, would trigger a reversion to the mean of normal credit loss history and increase spreads to perhaps more rational levels. They could not explain why loss rates have been so low despite the relatively low quality of new issues in the high-yield market—over 42 percent of all new issues were rated B– or lower in the past three years. Yet spreads continued to decline and seemed to be way out of line from what a reasonable credit quality assessment would require in terms of returns on investment.

Spreads reached the lowest ever in the modern high-yield market on June 5, 2007 of 268 basis points. Over the next two months, the market did an about face and spreads are now hovering around 450 basis points. It appears that sanity may have returned, but even at these levels, spreads are still below the historical average of 480 basis points.

While long-suffering doomsayers finally are experiencing their day in the sun, most would admit that they never would have expected a market freefall occurring at a time of strong economic performance in most of the world. Even now the high-yield market has not seen an increase in credit losses to justify the higher spreads. So what has happened? At this writing, events in the financial market bear a striking similarity to the toy recall by Mattel after lead had been discovered in its toys manufactured in China. Toys in China and subprime loans in the United States are similar in that a significant distance exists between the point of production and the point of sale, creating risk in the production chain. All it takes is one link in the chain to fail. In the case of mortgages, the failure had to do with flaws in credit quality (design and execution) in the lending process. In the case of Mattel, the failure had to do with design flaws and poor execution in production in the factory. The outcome was the same, an outcome both unexpected and unacceptable that has "tainted" the markets in which they operate.[1]

The U.S. subprime mortgage market has now collapsed and has revealed that the credit markets are like the naked emperor in the fable of the new clothes. The actual problem, an overheated market for mortgage seekers with poor credit in the United States, has had a huge global impact, one well beyond the relatively modest size of that actual market. The overall U.S. mortgage market is huge and, thus far, is performing well. At the most, subprime borrowers represent no more than 20 percent of the market. And even within the subprime sector 80 to 85 percent of those mortgages are performing as expected. No one could have predicted the turmoil that this relatively small segment of the credit market could have triggered. Actually some investors and market observers did think the market had overshot, particularly in areas such as U.S. subprime mortgages, but the generalized euphoria for these credits prevented concerned investors from getting additional risk premiums from these assets. The only option available if you

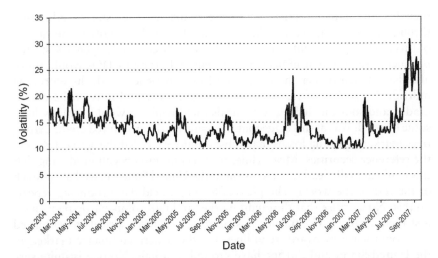

FIGURE 26.1 Chicago Board of Exchange (CBOE) Volatility Index (VIX Close)
Source: CBOE (2007).

were a market skeptic was to abstain from the market. But until the market crisis of summer 2007, the skeptics had little effect on the ability to place a lot of this paper into credit portfolios. As we pointed out in earlier chapters, the credit markets have grown tremendously in the past decade and these markets are now more correlated because of efforts to diversify and apply good portfolio theory. Subprime mortgages were particularly favored as a diversification strategy by investment vehicles focusing on corporate loans as well as those with a European emphasis. Figure 26.1 shows what happens when these markets smell a rat in the mixture.

This chart of equity option volatility shows what has happened. When the news came out that subprime mortgage paper had made it way into the hedge fund industry and, as a kind of stocking stuffer for most CLOs and CDOs, many market participants went from believing they had no exposure to the subprime markets into a full-fledged search into what they actually had. This led to some quick decisions to put any new purchases of any investment that might have subprime exposure on hold. Since this means most structured investments, the securitization markets quickly started to slow and then to grind to a halt by midsummer 2007. As bad as this is for companies who depend on securitization for their funding, it probably would have all blown over by fall 2007 if investors hadn't begun demonstrating increasing concerns about underlying asset qulity. This lack of confidence drove a further pullback and then became a major crisis when the rating agencies started admitting through their rating actions that perhaps they had not gotten the ratings of structures quite right. In July 2007, the three rating agencies started producing reports that indicated that many CLOs and CDOs would probably have much higher than expected loss experiences and, therefore, the individual tranches of many of these structures would have to be downgraded and some, including some deals rated triple-A, would actually have some losses. It was at this stage that the panic hit the structured credit derivatives markets, causing losses that substantially exceeded the actual losses in the reference securities. Meanwhile, some economists began predicting that this could actually lead to a recession in the United States as well as in much of the rest of the world. The press is having a field day producing reports on this. No surprise that the credit market and most of its participants have lost their swagger. Confidence has been lost. Market spreads have busted out from their downward trend lines and the structured finance markets in the United States and Europe have ground to a halt. No one is quite sure when these markets will reopen for business. In the meantime, the loss of confidence in the rating agencies, structured vehicles and most asset-based lenders has dropped to what seems to be irrationally low levels. The market has impacted even the "innocent bystanders" such as high-grade mortgage lenders, and investors in the securities created from prime mortgages. They have also been subject to liquidity pressures. It is almost like guilt by association: If your balance sheet has residential mortgage exposure of any kind, you are suspect.

This has led to an international liquidity crisis. The U.K. government had to come to the rescue of their fifth-largest mortgage producer, Northern Rock PLC, because of a depositor run on that bank after press reports brought public attention to its failure to finance its mostly high-grade mortgage portfolio. Goldman Sachs announced in August 2007 that they were increasing their equity position in one of their investment funds. The German government engineered a bailout of the IKB as a result of investments in U.S. subprime investments. A large number of *structured investment vehicles* (SIVs), which we discussed in Chapter 25, have had failed commercial paper offerings and many are now trying to liquidate their portfolios. The U.S. auction rate preferred market has several failed auctions for *credit derivative product companies* (CDCPs). Everywhere you look there are reports of delayed or cancelled deals and a lot of worried chief financial officers at financial firms. It is tempting to speculate that we are about to see the markets do a complete about face in terms of how economic activity gets funded. That is, will we see the return of the preeminence of relationship banking and the shrinking of the structured finance market? But that is unlikely to happen. Bob Lewis, Chief Risk Officer at AIG, in an interview with the authors stated that there is "no way we are going back to the old ways. Banks have reorganized themselves so their business model is all about creating assets that they can distribute into the capital markets. No way *that* changes. No way do they return as the primary financiers of our economy."

Problems with the old way were the subject of much of what we felt was wrong with the market in the first edition of *Managing Credit Risk*. So going back to a day when banks were the primary source of finance seems impossible. A bank is not constructed to be a long-term supplier of financing and years of consolidation have removed capital from what was once a dominant global industry. The regulators have developed regulatory capital requirements that make buy and hold strategies for banks a distant memory. The commercial banks will undoubtedly be a part of the near-term solution to provide some stability to the markets and to help to restore confidence. But they are not the long-term solution to a stable financial marketplace.

While it might be tempting to lay the blame for the market turmoil of 2007 on the financial engineers, a few obvious points should be noted.

First, the ability to create and sell tranches from the underlying mortgages provides an efficient distribution of risk to according to the risk appetite and risk sophistication. It is unfortunate that the so-called "sophisticated" investors were not sophisticated at all, having accepted the agency ratings at their face value, and not asking the tough questions about loan quality when there were enough doubts about limited documentation, stated income, reliance on credit scores and the use of piggyback loans for the purchase of a home. Many institutional investors trusted the ratings because they simply did not understand the complexity of the structured products, such as CDO-squared, they are investing in. One could ask why these investors accepted the ever-improving statistics regarding home prices, and the performance of subprime portfolios. But as David Tuckett pointed out in the *Financial Times*, "Good and bad practice are always much easier to assess after the fact. Professional investors are usually very thoughtful. What we have to explain, therefore, is how usually thoughtful investors do with certain regularity make judgments which they might not have made if they had attended, so to speak, to the small print of their own thinking."[2]

Second, the subprime market has rendered a valuable public welfare function by making housing finance more easily available. Owning a home is the American dream, and this also leads to lower urban decay and crime because people are now stakeholders in the communities in which they live. Besides most of the new loans are still performing. The growth of the subprime market may have done more good to housing than the government funded programs that excluded this population.

So, the solution for the policy makers and market participants is not to throw the baby out with the bath water, but, as Robert Lewis says, "to recalibrate the credit scales, so the risk being taken is correctly reflected in the rating." Investors will need to do much more homework on the things they invest in, and use the rating agencies as another source of analysis, not the primary source.

LIQUIDITY RISK IS THE NEXT BIG CHALLENGE

When the dust settles on the current market turmoil, it will be clear to those who are looking to understand exactly what happened that the roots of the problem were not really the subprime mortgage market, but rather the degree that interdependent market players were operating on faulty liquidity and value assumptions.

Liquidity refers to the ability of a business or individual to have enough cash resources to meet their financial obligations. A liquidity crisis is a state where there is a short supply of cash to lend to businesses and consumers, and interest rates are generally high. For individual businesses, a liquidity crises occurs whenever the firm is unable to pay its bills on time or lacks sufficient cash to expand inventory and production or violates some term of an agreement by letting some of its financial ratios exceed limits. It is the financial manager's job to see that this never happens. But it does happen, and it now seems that liquidity crises, like hurricanes, are occurring more frequently and with more force. Liquidity for the financial intermediary is the ability to meet the redemption needs of its own creditors and investors.

Liquidity risk is not new. This has always been a risk to manage for any commercial enterprise and also for individuals. The financial markets' main tool for managing this risk is a bank. The core function of the banking industry is to help their customers manage liquidity by taking deposits of their excess liquidity and lending it to other customers who have a short-term need for additional cash. Bankers generally have been very good at this function. Banks pay a lot of attention to their own liquidity needs and rarely have a problem meeting customer requirements—when they do, a "run on the bank" is the outcome and after some early experiences with this risk, independent central banks were created by governments that understood that it was critical for liquidity to be maintained in a modern economy. The Federal Reserve Bank was formed in the United States to solve an earlier liquidity crisis; they stand ready to lend emergency funding to any bank that requires it and pump liquidity into the system by buying Treasury securities in its open-market operations. The Bank of England, the European Central Bank, the Bank of Japan and central banks in other economies have the same job and use the same tool—a discount window where financial assets held by the banks can be used as collateral for loans made to those banks when required. Sometimes, as we have seen in the United Kingdom with the Northern Rock bank, this is not enough. Depositors can get "spooked" by news that they don't understand and begin to queue up to withdraw their savings from that institution. A "run on the bank" can only be solved by government action. Deposit insurance in the United States was designed to give comfort to depositors, but sometimes governments have to intervene if necessary to restore confidence in the banking system. This is exactly what happened during the U.S. savings and loan crisis of the 1990s and more recently in the United Kingdom with Northern Rock.

Generally, this support system to the banking industry has worked very well in recent years. The Northern Rock story is an aberration. "Runs" on banks are mostly historical events. But still we hear liquidity crisis being bantered about as something new and different and not always associated with banking. The reason for this is that something *new* has happened to the financial markets. Central Banks were created at a time when most financial assets (80 percent or more) were held in banks. Over the past two decades, beginning in the United States and more recently in Europe, we have witnessed a disintermediation of the banking industry such that commercial banks hold a relatively small portion of the financial assets of the largest economies. It is worth noting here that when the Fed took the initiative in helping to facilitate a bailout of Long-Term Capital Management (LTCM), it did so not because it was LTCM's regulator but rather out of concern for what might happen to the financial markets if LTCM were allowed to fail. That, the Fed also added liquidity to the system during this period is a matter of public record. As we have remarked earlier in this book, hedge funds, pension funds, mutual funds, insurance companies, and individuals now hold most of their assets outside of the banking system. This disintermediation of the banks means that the central bankers are now one big step away from where liquidity may be required in a crisis. It is a big step removed because the central bank does not have a direct relationship with the borrower and, therefore, little control over them. We have also gone from a relatively centralized system—a limited number of banks—to an almost limitless system of financial market participants who could need liquidity in a crisis. While examples such as LTCM exist where the problem is so large as to cause central banker intervention, in most cases central bankers can only encourage and support the banks that are now on the frontline when it comes to providing needed liquidity to the system.

We are, as of January 2008, in the midst of a liquidity crisis that is unlike any experienced before. Most investors have plenty of cash, but are showing an unwillingness to make it available. It is a crisis primarily affecting nonbank financial institutions. We have seen a plethora of new market players created in the last decade. They make loans, buy and hold securities, and invest in the full range of credit instruments. They represent a very large segment of the capital markets and it is the capital market that provides most of the funding required for their business models. Liquidity risk arises for these players when they go to trade, finance, or sell an asset but nobody in the market wants to trade that asset, or with them. For many new market participants, this is the one contingency that they had not prepared for. Their financial survival depends upon having a market to finance their inventories, or to liquidate assets when required.

Liquidity risk can quickly become life threatening in a crisis. An institution (or structured finance vehicle) might lose liquidity if its credit rating falls, it experiences sudden cash outflows, or some other event causes counterparties to avoid trading with or lending to the institution. Most firms have backup lines in place to deal with these problems if they are of a temporary basis. But few can survive when the problem is prolonged or if the problem is systematic and markets on which they depend are subject to a loss of liquidity. For subprime mortgage lenders in the United States, this is what has happened and in a matter of a few months we have seen the demise of an entire industry. These lenders have experienced the functional equivalent of a run on the bank. Unfortunately, for them, they were not banks and without some third party support they had no place to go but bankruptcy.

Liquidity risk tends to compound other risks. If a trading organization has a position in an illiquid asset, its limited ability to liquidate that position at short notice will compound its market risk. If that organization was attempting to liquidate that asset to meet an obligation to another counterparty and does not have the ability to raise cash from other sources on a timely basis, it will default. Their counterparty now has a liquidity problem that may require them to raise cash to offset the loss of the expected payment from the first counterparty. Should the second counterparty fail, it too will default. Here, liquidity risk is compounding credit risk.

There is little doubt that the easy money markets of the past few years have contributed to an increase in liquidity risk. When a firm has many funding sources it is easy to think they will always be available. Short-term financing is usually cheaper and more readily available than long-term finance. When markets are deep and volumes are high, it is hard to imagine how and when they might close. As sophistication and complexity becomes the norm, it is easy to see why many would think that there would always be a price at which the market would clear. It costs money to be conservative. It is tempting to use free but cancelable lines of credit instead of paying for committed facilities, or not to keep extra cash on hand when it does not seem to be needed. With the growth of the markets and the number of participants, it is not surprising that there has been a dilution of wisdom and conservatism about risks with low probabilities and high severity.

Meanwhile, much of what is described as good market practices for managing credit risk actually may have increased liquidity risks. Here is a partial list:

- Tight loan covenants that provide controls to the lender, but can be deadly for the borrower.
- Collateralization requirements for trading limits that are reduced if collateral cannot be posted in a timely fashion. This can require massive cash resources to meet collateralization demands if the market is particularly volatile.
- Credit derivative markets that require either collateral to be posted or payments to be made by sellers of protection. These requirements can be sudden and substantial.
- Marking-to-market portfolios of loans can trigger loan documents or other contractual obligations that may require cash to correct the situation.
- Keeping loans tenors shorter than the life of the assets. This practice can be good for the lender, but makes the obligor vulnerable to refinancing risks.
- Collateralizing contingents such as guarantees and options is a good practice for those who are dependent upon the contingent payments, but may stress the cash resources of those obligated to make the payment under the current market conditions.

These practices all make sense. If liquidity is not a problem, then credit risks are frequently reduced by their application. However, like so many things in our complex world, it is the unintended consequences that now need to be managed. Liquidity risk has to be managed in addition to credit, market, and other risks.

Managing credit risk in a complex, interdependent capital market will not be easy. Because of its tendency to compound other risks, it is difficult or impossible to isolate liquidity risk. In all but the most simple of circumstances, comprehensive metrics of liquidity risk do not exist. For most players in the market, it will be necessary to pay close attention to the liquidity requirements of the markets in which they participate and the tools and instruments that they use. They need to pay closer attention to the primary and secondary *sources* of liquidity as well as probability, high-severity *uses* of cash reserves. Scenario analysis is likely to become an important tool for market participants to review the full range of possibilities in their business model and then to assess the day-to-day cash requirements under each scenario. Those who do not learn how to manage and limit liquidity risk will be destined to join the long line of failed financial institutions that mismanaged this risk.

As we argued earlier in this chapter, commercial banks are built to handle liquidity risk. Their primary business, deposit taking with an uncertain timing of redemption, has required them to focus on this risk. In addition the development of independent central banks to serve as a lender of last resort for the commercial banking industry of just about every country demonstrates the importance of managing this process. Everyone in the banking industry is aware of, and has developed and implemented risk management strategies to prevent a run on the bank. In addition, the safety net around the banking industry provided by their governments, has been the justification for the capital adequacy standards embedded in the Basel I and Basel II accords that banks everywhere must observe. This is simply not the case with other investors. There are no regulatory requirements for hedge funds or other investors to maintain a certain amount of liquidity resources, or capital for that matter.

The first big mistake in recent years was the assumption that much of what we previously did in the global banking industry could be switched into the capital markets without a commensurate effort at understanding and managing the liquidity risks associated with it. To be sure, some efforts were made in this direction. Backup facilities, collateralization requirements, marking-to-market policies, among others were implemented to help mitigate the risk. However, even these strategies were presenting their own liquidity risk issues. It is fair to say that not enough was done to fully understand these issues in the heady days of the past few years. All that is likely to change now.

THE IMPORTANCE OF A STRONG CREDIT CULTURE

If nothing else, the current market turmoil will be a reminder to some market participants and a lesson to others that, contrary to what they have been led to believe, they do not own a black box that will reliably spit out the right answer to each and every question fed into it. Financial professionals must now also add model risk to the other risks—interest rate risk, credit risk, market risk, operational and liquidity risk—impacting their business. Model risk arises from many sources. One is that a model may not have captured all the relevant risk factors correctly. For example, the subprime mortgage models failed to predict the increased probability of default because the housing price appreciation risk was not a factor in these models. Another source of model risk is that all the participants use the same model to come to the same conclusion (rightly or wrongly) and there is a market stampede and "crowded trades." Yet another source of model risk is sometimes models cannot anticipate the changing behavior.

Very low loss experiences in the subprime mortgage market in the early years of this decade led to changes in model assumptions that resulted in more aggressive portfolios. This had the positive outcome of opening up mortgage credit to a new cohort of borrower. The bad news, which took some time to develop, was that the historical loss assumptions no longer work. Unfortunately, in an experiential model, assumptions are not changed until it is too late for the current portfolio that is now behaving in unintended ways. And, of course, this is not just a story of problems in the mortgage market. Those subprime loans, with their faulty loss assumptions, became an important ingredient in CLOs and CBOs, which developed the same set of problems—their models now longer produced the expected outcome. As we commented earlier in this chapter, the high-yield markets are now experiencing a blow up because of unsustainable loss assumptions and the covenant-lite transactions, which is the corporate equivalent of low-documentation, subprime residential mortgages.

At the highest level, what this shows is that there are risks associated with using analytics to create new financial institutions and strategies to exploit the inefficiencies in a market. In the process of financial engineering, you change the environment so that it longer matches the one modeled. This risk has been understood by the rating agencies and others, who generally are conservative in the early days of a new market, but it seems they have been less conservative in allowing ongoing adjustments in markets with patterns which change from historical norms.

In a world of seemingly imperfect models, senior managers in financial services firms must renew their attention to traditional management tools: checks, balances, and controls, and, behind them, a strong risk culture. Recent events in the subprime mortgage market should be sounding an alarm in executive offices. Players in the new capital markets, particularly those that survive the current market will have learned some important lessons on what practices work and which do not. In the first edition of *Managing Credit Risk*, the cultural problems that appeared to be threatening some players in the financial industry was largely a lack of control and improper incentives for traders and other risk takers. While some problems still exist, good practices have eliminated most of them. What is now challenging the industry is more insidious and difficult to control. The markets are more volatile, complex, and harder to predict. In these circumstances, it is extremely important for the firm to have a clear understanding of what their risk tolerances are and how they plan to manage those risks. Capital adequacy for nonbank financial institutions will undoubtedly be a topic for analysis and some adjustment. Already the U.S. Congress and European Commissions are calling for reviews and suggesting regulatory responses. Lending practices and processes will need to be reengineered. Model validation and recalibration cannot wait. We are in the midst of the first serious test of the new financial technology, and we are finding gaps and problems that need attention and some solutions.

But there is no turning back. The banking industry cannot and will not be the primary source of finance in the United States or in Europe. Nor will it be for most of the rest of the world. Banking has an important role to play, but modern economies need to have modern capital markets capable of understanding and financing the businesses those economies create. When the current crisis has run its course, as Hemingway pointed out, those who learned from the experience will probably be the majority and they should be better at what they do from the experiences they have had. There are good reasons to be optimistic about the future sophistication of the credit markets.

Meanwhile, one thing that has not changed is that a key to a strong risk culture is to have the CEO make his or her risk appetite known to every employee. Business strategies need to be consistent with risk tolerances and reward systems. Management needs to model good practice and get involved in risk decisions. There is plenty of evidence to support the concept that market savvy, informed, experienced, well-capitalized, and disciplined financial players can prosper in these markets. It will not be so easy for those who are not.

REFERENCES

BNP Paribas. 2007. "Liquidity Crisis: Central Banks Doing More," *BNP Paribas Market Economics*, 30 November, 5.

———. 2007. "Liquidity Crisis Globalisation," *BNP Paribas Market Economics*, pp 4–9, 30 November.

Bright, L.S., E.A. Fahey, and D. Barile. 2007. "Liquidity Analysis of US Securities Firms," *Fitch Ratings Financial Institutions Special Report*, August.

Cecchetti, S.G. 2007. Market Liquidity and Short Term Credit: The Financial Crisis of August 2007. Working Paper Brandeis International Business School, 3 September.

Gallagher, S., and A. Markowska. 2007. "Shocks and Aftershocks: 2007 Crisis of Confidence and Liquidity." *Societe Generalte Economic Research*, 26 November.

Greenberg, H. 2007. "How NovaStar Held Clues to Mortgage Mess." *Wall Street Journal*, November 24.

Hillard, B. 2007. "Alternative Economic Scenarios in the Light of the Liquidity Crisis," *Societe Generale Economic Research*, 31 August.

Lewis, R. 2007. Robert Lewis, AIG, interviewed by authors.

Mehren, A. M. 2007. "Mechanics behind the Liquidity Crisis," *Danskebank Research*, 13 August.

Rappaport, L. 2007. "Liquidity Crisis Goes Global." *TheStreet.com*, 9 August.

Tuckett, D. 2007. "Emotion's Role in Investment." *Financial Times*, September 20.

Notes

INTRODUCTION

1. Hammurabi's Code, circa 1800 BCE is said to include many sections relating to the regulation of credit in Babylon (see Homer and Sylla 1996). There is evidence that the Indus Valley Civilization, a riverine civilization possibly of greater antiquity than Babylonia, had trade contact with it through neighboring Melukha (see Sasson 1995). So it is possible that concerns about credit risk go even further back history than 1800 BCE.
2. Sienna and Piacenza are credited with being the main banking centers of Europe, preceding Florence by as many as 75 years. The Bardi, the Peruzzi, and the Acciaiulli families dominated the banking scene between 1300 and 1345. All of them collapsed due to the overextension of credit, probably the first victims of cross-border lending. Their place was eventually taken over by the Medici, the Pazzi, and others, of which the Medici of Florence are the best remembered (see de Roover 1963).
3. Municipal bond insurance and municipal bond banks have existed for many years, reducing credit risk through pooling and guarantees.

CHAPTER 3

1. SDRs are *special drawing rights* issued by the International Monetary Fund and represent an international reserve asset allocated to IMF member countries proportional to their quotas.
2. W. Edward Deming's work led Japanese industry into principles of process management which revolutionized their quality and productivity. His work is the precursor to Total Quality Management (TQM).
3. Interestingly, Household Finance was itself the product of an earlier merger between two leading finance companies, Beneficial Finance and Household International
4. GSEs are a group of financial service organizations, some privately held, with public purposes created by the U.S. Congress to reduce the cost of capital for certain borrowing sectors of the economy. Principal examples are the Federal Home Loan Banks, Federal Home Mortgage Corporation (Freddie Mac) and Federal National Mortgage Association (Fannie Mae.)

CHAPTER 7

1. "Cash flow analysis is a powerful tool. It is powerful because it almost unfailingly succeeds in exposing the key mechanism by which a company lives or dies. Cash flows cannot be manipulated by accounting convention and there is virtually no way in which a company can hide significant flows from an analyst who knows how to use cash flow analysis skillfully, except by outright fraud. Cash flow analysis is for these reasons not much liked by companies or their accountants and there is considerable hostility to it in most published work on corporate finance." (Boyadjian and Warren 1987, 158)
2. George Scott (in Mayer 1974, 240) of First National City Bank (now Citigroup) summarized his approach as follows: "I have been up and down this business, and there is still no substitute for, 'What do you want the loan for? How are you going to pay me back? And what are you going to do if your theory doesn't work?'"
3. The ideas on industry analysis are drawn from Porter (1985).

CHAPTER 9

1. This is based on the property of the normal distribution, which states that 68 percent of the realized values will within standard deviation and 96 percent will fall within standard deviations.
2. A variable has a log-normal distribution if the natural logarithm of the variable is normally distributed. Saying that stock price is log-normally distributed is equivalent to saying that the rate of return from a stock, which is a function of the logarithm of stock price, is normally distributed.

CHAPTER 10

1. The use of averages to distinguish between two groups is a decision process that is commonplace in credit analysis. For instance, in commercial real estate, the debt service coverage ratio should exceed 1.5 as a general rule. This value is modest relative to coverage requirements for unsecured corporate debt because of the existence of real estate collateral.
2. Stratification was achieved by matching a failed firm with a healthy firm of comparable size from the same industry. Since there could be several healthy firms fitting the criteria, the pairing firm was randomly chosen from this subgroup.

3. The authors conclude that the two approaches give very similar results but they favor discriminant analysis model outputs due to their continuous and finer gradients of credit quality.
4. The illustration and description are drawn from Altman, Marco, and Varetto (1994).
5. Linear discriminant analysis is a special case of a neural network consisting of a single neuron that receives signals from a set of indicators and generates an output which is the discriminant score.
6. CASA stands for Center for Adaptive Systems Applications and is based in Los Alamos, New Mexico. The authors gratefully acknowledge the inputs from Drs. Camilo Gomez and José Hernadez on the neural network model described here.
7. Compustat is a company that provides quarterly and annual financial statement data in machine-readable form for publicly traded companies. BARRA factors are fundamental drivers of security returns. In the fixed income world, they include parallel shifts of the yield curve, as well as yield curve twists and butterfly movements. In addition, they include various security-specific factors such as credit quality, industry sector, call features, and the like. These factor weights are estimated using historical return data. The basic idea is that for each security, you can statistically estimate its sensitivity to each of the fundamental factors. Then if you can predict which way the factors will move, you can estimate price behavior of each security and of the overall portfolio. BARRA is based in Berkeley, California.
8. This is not to say that AI has been a failure in this area; just that it has not been absorbed by the credit management community as rapidly as one would have expected. For some examples, see Duchessi, Shawky, and Seagle (1988); Srinivasan and Kim (1988); and Shaw and Gentry (1988).
9. For example, following the failure of Herstatt bank in 1974, money center banks implemented systems to monitor daylight overdraft.
10. Credit, debit and Smart cards are examples of technology as an enabling agent for extending credit.

CHAPTER 11

1. KMV is a San Francisco based firm that sells credit analysis software and information products to financial institutions. KMV was acquired by Moody's in 2002 and the successor fim is now known as Moody's KMV or MKMV. The EDF Model of KMV is now known as Credit Monitor.

2. A similar option theory based model to measure credit risk called Helix is marketed by Helix Investment Partners, L.P. Los Angeles, CA. It employs the same inputs as KMV and produces a risk score for corporate bonds.

3. Strictly speaking, this function should also include the riskless rate of return for borrowing and lending

4. Based on private communication with Steve Kealhofer and Peter Crosbie, Moody's KMV Corporation.

5. KMV maintains a large database of defaulted public firms and reports to have upwards of 2,500 defaults.

6. The authors benefited from discussions with Stephen Kealhofer and Peter Crosbie of KMV Corporation and Jan Nicholson of CapMAC in the exposition of the model, and also received written comments from them on an earlier version of this chapter. However, full blame cannot be shifted to their shoulders for any remaining errors or omissions.

7. Spearman rank correlation is similar to the more commonly known Pearson correlation coefficient, both of which are used to measure the degree of association between pairs of numerical values. Spearman's correlation is used for comparison where the numerical value is more indicative of rank than of any absolute measure. Both ZETA and KMV values, though expressed in numerical quantities indicate the relative likelihood of default of a set of companies than the absolute likelihood. For more details on rank correlation see Lehmann (1975).

8. *Unconditional* means that no other conditions must be attached, for example, industry membership or bond rating; that is, no other information other than what the model uses as input.

9. Using the option-adjusted yield spreads on a universe of 108 bonds (Vasicek 1995), KMV has found that forming portfolios using EDFs to determine under or overpricing generates significant excess returns. However, the authors caveat the results due to potential error in the reported bond prices and spreads.

10. The EDF may often signal frequent changes to the risk ratings, which may be viewed as a negative; KMV's position is that indeed the credit risk of the borrower continually changes.

CHAPTER 12

1. Sample design to eliminate sample bias is an extremely important step to ensure that the model designed is statistically valid. Among other factors there may be groups exhibiting differences based on geography, gender and age some of which may be discernable from the data set and some may not be either because it was not collected or because it is a prohibited

type of data. The sample should be as random as possible and the sample sizes need to be large.

2. Sample design to eliminate sample bias is an extremely important step to ensure that the model designed is statistically valid. Among other factors there may be groups exhibiting differences based on geography, gender and age some of which may be discernable from the data set and some may not be either because it wasn't collected or because it is a prohibited type of data. The sample should be as random as possible and the sample sizes need to be large.

3. For a technical discussion of these techniques see Han and Kamber (2001) and Lee (1990).

4. Two test statistics that are used are the Kolmogorow-Smirnow two-sample statistic and the Chi square statistic. For a description of these methods, see Sachs (1984).

5. The D statistic is nonparametric, that is, it distribution free. For a table of critical values see Sachs (1984, 291–292).

6. *Truly creditworthy* is a conditional definition. Even the truly creditworthy may go to charge-off if impacted by severe adversity. Here the term is taken to mean that these accounts exhibited no delinquency in the period of observation. The good sample is called a censored sample because its long-term outcomes are unknown.

7. According R. W. Johnson's 1989 article, "The Consumer Banking Problem: Causes and Cures," which appeared in the *Journal of Retail Banking* (volume 11 (Winter), pages 39–44), Hibernia National Bank, Wells Fargo Bank, and Chemical Banking Corporation, now Chase, are using computer models to approve small-business loans for as much as $250,000. Most variables in these models are of the same kind as used in consumer credit models because business financial statements are the exception rather than the rule in loans.

CHAPTER 13

1. Dunn & Bradstreet measures the timely payment by a company through the *"paydex"* score, which is a measure of the payment behavior relative to the credit terms. Higher scores indicate better payment behavior.

2. Campbell and Dietrich (1983) point out that delaying payment and default are really sequential events and account for this in the classification procedure.

3. A dummy variable is one that will take on a value of 1 or 0. For example, the New Home dummy will be 1 for a new home, and 0 for a pre-owned home.

CHAPTER 14

1. *Unconditional* means that no other conditions must be attached, for example, industry membership or bond rating; that is, no other information other than what the model uses as inputs.
2. Real change is defined as a material change, either positive or negative, in the financial condition of the borrower determined on an ex post basis.
3. There are other problems with the calculated correlations; for one thing, they tend to be unstable.
4. Another name for directional error is turning point error such as when a positive change was predicted whereas the actual change was negative.

CHAPTER 16

1. In the current version of the KMV model, default occurs when the firm's asset value goes below a threshold represented by the sum of the total amount of short-term liabilities and half of the amount of long-term liabilities.
2. The standard reference is Jones, Mason, and Rosenfeld (1984), who found that, even for firms with very simple capital structures, a Merton-type model is unable to price investment-grade corporate bonds better than a naive model that assumes no risk of default.
3. One of the earliest studies based on this framework is Black and Cox (1976). However, this is not included in the second generation models in terms of the treatment of the recovery rate.
4. Using Moody's corporate bond yield data, they find that credit spreads are negatively related to interest rates.
5. See Eom, Helwege, and Huang (2001) for an empirical analysis of structural-form models.
6. As discussed in Jones and Mingo (1998), reserves are used to cover expected losses.
7. For a comprehensive analysis of these models, see Crouhy, Galai, and Mark (2000) and Gordy (2000).
8. Because of this simplifying assumption the model can be implemented using an exogenous PD, so that the firm asset value parameters need not be estimated. In this respect, the model combines features of both structural-form and reduced-form models.
9. Data for the 1970–1981 period have been eliminated from the sample period because of the low number of default prices available for the computation of yearly recovery rates.

10. Hamilton, Gupton, and Berthault (2001) and Altman, Brady, Resti, and Sironi (2003 and, 2005) provide clear empirical evidence of this phenomenon.
11. Demand mostly comes from niche investors called "vultures," who intentionally purchase bonds in default. These investors represented a relatively small (perhaps $100 billion) and specialized segment of the debt market. This hedge fund sector grew considerably, however, in the 2003–2006 period, perhaps more than doubling in size (author estimates).
12. Available at federalreserve.gov/GeneralInfo/Basel2/NPR_20060905/ NPR.
13. Procyclicality involves the sensitivity of regulatory capital requirements to economic and financial market cycles. Since ratings and default rates respond to the cycle, the new IRB approach proposed by the Basel Committee risks increasing capital charges, and limiting credit supply, when the economy is slowing (the reverse being true when the economy is growing at a fast rate).
14. Both expected losses and VaR measures associated with different confidence levels tend to be underestimated by approximately 30 percent.
15. Interestingly, the comparable median for defaults through 2003 was about 4.5 percent lower (54.5 percent), showing the considerable increase in default recovery rates on bonds in the period 2004–2006.

CHAPTER 17

1. See Oleksin (1997) for a description of a survey of credit migration procedures of the 100 largest U.S. bank holding companies. Oleksin's objective was to learn which institutions were conducting credit migration analysis and how they were doing it. Out of the 100, 80 responded, with the majority of banks analyzing migration in some manner on all loans or only on loans that have been charged off.
2. Carty (1997) is an update and covers Moody's rating changes from 1938 to 1996, while Moody's (2007) covers rating transitions of structured finance securities from 1993 to 2006.
3. This is also true for both rating agencies' cumulative default analyses, for example, Carty and Lieberman (1996a) and Standard & Poor's (2007). Altman and Ramayanam's (2007) mortality rate results (see Chapter 15) trace the cumulative default/mortality rate of all bonds from initial issuance. This is consistent with Altman and Kao's (1991a) rating migration method discussed in this chapter.

4. A Markov chain is a stochastic process where the conditional probability of a future event given any past event and the present state, is independent of the past event and depends only on the present state of the process.
5. This is the approach suggested by CreditMetrics (Gupton, Finger, and Bhatia 1997).

CHAPTER 18

1. Regulations and search for new funding sources are also behind these innovations. Chapters 18 through 24 describe the industry's responses.
2. Collateral limits are common, for example, in commercial real estate. A bank may set limits on office buildings, shopping malls, light-manufacturing buildings, warehouses, and the like.
3. The number of correlations for an N-asset portfolio is $\frac{N(N-1)}{2}$.
4. *Intertemporal* refers to the ability of the algorithm to look forward and backward in time when seeking the optimum solution. For example, should a bond be sold in period t or $t + 1$ or $t + 2$? The effect of these choices can be modeled only in a multi-period model.
5. Please see Chapter 13 for bond default and mortality data. The development of the loan securitization market has led now to more tracking data on defaults and recoveries. Please see also Altman and Suggitt (1997) referred to in Chapter 15 for data on syndicated loan defaults.
6. CreditMetrics (1997), a portfolio theory-based approach to valuing credit risk, for example, uses the probability of default from bond rating data.
7. The *Sharpe Ratio* (Sharpe 1994) is defined as the ratio of portfolio expected excess return divided by portfolio standard deviation. Excess return is the return in excess of the risk free rate.
8. Notice that unexpected loss (95 percent value) is simply expected loss + 2 standard deviations for a normal distribution. There is no unexpected gain; we do not have a symmetrical term on the positive side. The minimum loss is just 0.
9. Possibly because the rating criteria themselves have drifted; there is no guarantee that the rating agency criteria are applied consistently because of the human factor and subjectivity involved.
10. See Chirinko and Guill (1991) on the impact of default covariation and Lucas (1995) for data on bond default correlations.

CHAPTER 19

1. Instead of the loss at a given confidence level, some people use the average of the losses to the right of the probability value. This quantity is called the *expected shortfall* or the *conditional tail expectation*.

2. RAROC was initially applied to the trading portfolio. Bankers Trust used to be a full service bank but in the 1970s withdrew completely from retail banking to concentrate entirely on wholesale banking and trading. It used the RAROC approach in the derivatives market as well. It is notable that the origins of risk-adjusted metrics such as RAROC, RiskMetrics and CreditMetrics are all in 100 percent wholesale banks (Bankers Trust and JPMorgan). Wholesale banks which lend to corporations is more exposed to concentration risk than retail banks. Bankers Trust was acquired by Deutsche Bank and JPMorgan by the successor to Chemical Bank which prior to this acquisition had absorbed two other money center banks Manufacturers Hanover, and Chase Manhattan Bank. The successor bank is now called JPMorgan Chase.

3. It is important to distinguish between linear and nonlinear risks. In most cases the pay off (or loss) changes linearly with the asset. For example, if you owned a Treasury bill, a drop of 1 percent in value of the bill will directly equate to a 1 percent drop of the Treasury bill you own. For derivatives and some securities such as mortgages, the value of the product may change by more or less than the change in the underlying risk factor. Additional risk factors with options are: change in value due to change in volatility (*vega risk*) and nonlinear change in value due to change in price (*gamma risk*). This terminology is associated with market risk, not credit risk, although credit risk may be a contributory factor of these variables.

4. *No-arbitrage argument* is used, for example, in deriving the fair value of an option in the Black-Scholes model. If you can not arbitrage, such as when there is a discontinuity in the market, the fair value derived is no longer applicable. For comments on pricing model risk see Wilson (1995).

5. Basel I and II are discussed further in this chapter.

6. With mathematical programming techniques such as optimization it is readily possible to impose multiple constraints and solve for the optimum mix of assets. A simple example is presented in Chapter 17.

7. The standard portfolio optimization method is called *asset normal* because it assumes that asset returns are jointly normally distributed. When the asset returns are not normal, then optimization may be carried out using the delta (small changes in price of assets in response to small changes in the underlying variables). When the payoffs are not linear,

then delta-gamma methods are used. These methods are progressively more complex, and yet cannot handle event risk. See Wilson (1995).

CHAPTER 20

1. Loss given default was considered only for credit-impaired loans for setting credit reserves.
2. The term *asset* here refers to the assets of a firm, not the asset held by the investor in the form of debt or equity.
3. Strictly speaking, default is not an absorbing state because a firm can return to a functioning state even after default.
4. The zero-coupon rate is used to discount the cash flows because this rate does not have a reinvestment component, and each promised cash flow from the bond may be treated as a zero-coupon security. Note that the Treasury yield curve expresses the interest rates on a yield to maturity basis with semiannual coupon payments and a balloon payment for principal. To derive the value of a BBB bond with a 6 percent coupon and five year maturity, the cash flows of $6, $6, $6, $6, and $106 by the zero coupon rate of 4.10, 4.67, 5.25, and 5.63 respectively to result in the value of $107.55.
5. While this is the assumption made in CreditMetrics, it may not be true if recoveries are jointly distributed with the rating. Altman and Kishore (1996), however found that the rating when adjusted for seniority, has no effect on recoveries.
6. This is similar to the market value-at-risk concept. The major difference being that the value at risk is derived from actual observed market prices. Also VaR does not explicitly deal with defaults. In market VaR, all the ramifications of credit migration and default are handled through the observed, realized return. Another difference is that VaR has an overnight horizon whereas CreditMetrics uses a one-year horizon.
7. The probability of n defaults experienced in one year is expressed in the Poisson distribution as $\frac{e^{-\mu}\mu^n}{n!}$, where T is the long term expected number of defaults per year. This is a fairly common way to represent component failure rates in engineering.
8. One way of handling the holding period problem is to optimize a portfolio of zero-coupon securities, representing all the available maturities.
9. The measurement of expected defaults for existing bonds compared to newly issued ones is basically the same for bonds with maturities of at least five years. Moody's and S&P publish data on existing baskets of bonds by rating without regard to age. Their results and Altman's essentially converge after year 4 (see Altman, 1992).

10. For updated data through 1995, see Altman and Kishore (1997) and Chapter 15 on mortality rates.
11. This is changing, however. In 1997, Moody's had rated $200 billion in outstanding bank loans, representing 891 facilities and 494 borrowers.
12. Systems such as ZETA Services, Moody's, Helix, or neural network-based bond rating replication techniques are available to assign ratings and/or expected defaults to all companies, whether or not they have public debt outstanding. Please see our earlier discussions of these models in Chapters 9–14.
13. The Z''-Score model is a four variable version of the Z-Score approach. It was designed to reduce distortions in credit scores for firms in different industries or different countries. We have also found this model extremely effective in assessing the credit risk of corporate bonds in the emerging market arena, see Altman, Hartzell, and Peck (1995).
14. Altman recognized that the measure of covariance is potentially biased in two ways. First, estimates of individual firms' debt unexpected losses are derived from empirical data on bonds from a given bond rating class and as such will probably understate the risk of loss from individual firm defaults. On the other hand, the covariance of default losses between two firms' debt is based on the joint probability of both defaulting at the same time. If the default decision of each firm is viewed as 0,1 (i.e., as a binomial distribution), then the appropriate covariance or correlation should be calculated from a joint density function of two underlying binomial distributions. Altman's measure, however, assumes a normal density function for returns and thus returns are jointly, normally distributed for each firm which could result in a higher aggregate measure of portfolio risk. As such, the two biases neutralize each other to some extent although it is difficult to assess the relative magnitude of each.
15. Using a *double precision, linear constrained optimization program* (DLCONG).
16. To quote from remarks by Sheila C. Bair, Chairman, Federal Deposit Insurance Corporation before the Global Association of Risk Professionals in New York City on February 26, 2007:

> *Into this already highly leveraged global banking landscape we have introduced a BIS II regulatory capital regime that appears likely to deliver substantial double digit reductions in minimum bank capital requirements. I emphasize substantial. Half of the banks participating in the latest U.S. impact survey reported that their minimum risk-based tier 1 capital requirements would be reduced by 31 percent or more. In the U.S., the agencies*

agreed such results would be unacceptable if produced under an up-and-running capital regulation, and that we could not responsibly proceed without safeguards.

I understand the concerns of our large banks, but as a regulator, I am convinced we need those safeguards. I remain very concerned about what would happen under this proposed regulation when the floors come off. The safety-and-soundness of the U.S. banking system would not be well-served by unconstrained double digit reductions in bank capital requirements. In my judgment, the same could be said of the global banking system.

CHAPTER 21

1. *Asset concentration* refers to both an unacceptably high and/or unprofitable exposure. The exposure may be to single obligor or to a group of obligors sharing common risk factors such as industry group or geographic location, such as a country, state, or region. Concentration is the consequence of a bank's desire to specialize in certain industries and/or geographic areas. As to be expected, when concentration increases, there is an increase in the severity of default. The antidote for concentration is diversification, that is, replacing highly correlated assets with uncorrelated or negatively correlated assets. This concept was formalized by Harry Markowitz as modern portfolio theory in the 1950s. See also Chapter 17.

2. "For guarantor banking organizations, the examiners should review the credit quality of individual reference assets in derivative contracts in the same manner as other credit instruments such as standby letters of credit. Thus the examiners should evaluate a credit derivative . . . based upon the overall financial condition and resources of the reference obligor, the obligor's credit history; and any secondary source of payment such as collateral." (Board of Governors of the Federal Reserve System 1996, 12) Note the similarity to traditional credit analysis.

3. "Under New York law entities have to be specifically licensed under the Federal Financial Guarantee Insurance Program to write financial insurance guarantee contracts. Only sever institutions are authorized and noe of thme have any connection with Wall Street." (Credit Derivatives 1996, 26)

4. Unexpected loss may also be adjusted upward by using the "high" estimate of the default probability and the "low" estimate of recovery rate.

Unexpected loss is thus influenced not only by the correlation of default risk with other assets but also the degree of ignorance associated with the estimate of the unconditional probabilities of default and recoveries. These are subtle but extremely important points to understand.

5. Refer to Chapters 17 to 20 for methodologies used in portfolio management, including the development of loan portfolio optimization strategies.

6. A term made famous by the Hechscher-Ohlin theorem that held that economic welfare is maximized when countries produce things in which they have an advantage in cost and quality and trade these with other countries, who should do otherwise.

7. See Chapter 24 for more discussion about this as it relates to securitization.

8. See, Remarks by Chairman Alan Greenspan at Lancaster House, London, U.K., September 25, 2002, concluding that credit derivatives "appear to have effectively spread losses from defaults by Enron, Global Crossing, Railtrack, WorldCom and Swissair in recent months from financial institutions with large short-term leverage to insurance firms pensions funds or others." Howard Davies, the outgoing head of Britain's Financial Services Authority called synthetic collateralized default obligations "the most toxic element of the financial markets."

9. See Lucas (1995) for the derivation of this relationship.

10. Intrinsic value and price are not the same thing. The former is an estimate of what it is worth, and the latter is what one is willing to pay for it.

CHAPTER 22

1. A high leverage is behind the recent collapse of Amaranth, the Connecticut-based hedge fund that lost 2/3 of its value betting on energy derivatives.

2. Professor Roy Davies at the University of Exeter has compiled a list of recent derivatives fiascos.

3. The risk in currency swaps is greater, though it tends to remain constant.

4. Some of the rating agencies are starting to rate the operational dimension of hedge funds.

5. In some instances the increase in short-term rates may flatten or invert the yield curve, thereby indicating lower future short-term rates. Typically, this sort of behavior is modeled in the interest rate scenarios used to estimate exposure.

6. *Replacement cost* is defined as the dollar amount that would cost to replace an asset at current prices.

7. This section draws from Duffee (1996).

8. The credit spreads and default probabilities shown in Table 21.4 and Table 21.5 are merely illustrative.

9. Stochastic models owe their name to *stochastic calculus,* a subfield in calculus that deals with random movements in the variables modeled. According to a random movement, typically known in the mathematical jargon *Brownian motion,* a variable is equally likely to move up or down over the next infinitesimal increase in time. The best-known example of random motion is a stock's movement over time, which indeed follows a random walk.

10. Please refer to Chapter 13 for more on financial institution risk.

11. For example, the International Swap Dealers Association (ISDA) has a standard master agreement to separate deal-specific confirmations that are added. The U.S. Bankruptcy Code has been amended expressly to permit the exercise of rights of termination, and in particular, closeout netting. This was to allay concerns that a bankruptcy trustee would cherry pick the contracts to continue depending on financial impact (Hendricks 1994).

12. It is assumed here that the closeout netting is consistent with the legal jurisdiction relevant for the counterparty.

13. The Ho-Lee model generates a future interest by modeling it as the previous interest rate plus or minus a random shock. It assumes that at any time the interest rate is normally distributed. It uses only two parameters: interest rate volatility σ and drift term m.

14. The Black-Derman-Toy model, unlike the Ho-Lee model, allows the short-term volatility to vary over time and makes the drift term a function of the level of rates.

15. The Heath, Jarrow, and Morton (HJM) model is the most general form of term structure models. It focuses on instantaneous forward rates in the yield curve. A wide variety of volatility structures can be chosen in the HJM model to match either the historical or observable volatility in the term structure. Being able to model each forward rate independently allows each of them to depend on external shocks differently and exhibit a richer correlation structure than was possible with other models. It has demonstrated that all the previous term structure models are special cases of HJM. HJM is actually an approach, not a model. In many of its variations, it is becoming the standard method of term structure modeling. Please see Baxter and Rennie (1997) and van Deventer and Imai (1997).

CHAPTER 24

1. In some cases, the institution may also securitize not-so-good assets but wrap the around with various credit enhancements.
2. In the U.S. *mortgage-backed securities* (MBS) have developed as a separate category of investment from asset-backed securities, which developed after the mortgage market was reaching maturity. This distinction continues, although the techniques used in the markets are quite similar. In this chapter, we combine the two under the term securitization.
3. There exists a secondary market for syndicated bank loans and the Section 144A private placements that are trade in the over-the-counter market. See Chapter 25 for further discussion about these markets.
4. The asset weight for a C&I loan is 100 percent, whereas for securities guaranteed by U.S.-sponsored agencies such as FNMA, FHLMC, and SLMA it is 20 percent. For one dollar of capital, a bank can hold five times as much in these securities as in C&I loans, or in individual mortgages without the guarantee. Note that within an asset class the capital requirement does not change whether it is a real estate loan or a loan to a major corporation. For life insurance companies, the reserve factors are 10 percent for commercial and other mortgages and 1 percent for BBB-rated securities.
5. U.S. insurance companies are regulated by states. The New York Department of Insurance, because of the size, experience, stature, and stringent regulations, has led insurers to regard New York as the de facto insurance regulatory authority. To promote a convergence of state regulatory standards, state insurance commissioners formed the National Association of Insurance Commissioners (NAIC) more than a century ago in 1871. NAIC proposes model investment laws, which the states may choose to adopt. See Santamero and Babbel (1997).

CHAPTER 25

1. Moody's (2007) defines the type of program as follows:
   - *Multi-seller*. Diversified portfolios of term and trade receivables that have typically been structured for APCP programs. The sellers of the assets are usually, but not always, customers of the bank.
   - *Credit arbitrage*. A way for banks to fund portfolios of highly rated securities off balance sheet at lower regulatory capital cost.
   - *Hybrid*. A program that funds term and trade receivables like a multiseller, but also have a facility that funds purchased, rated securities like an arbitrage vehicle.

2. Primus was the first CDCP established in 2003. Athilon was established in 200. Both are public companies (get some further details)

CHAPTER 26

1. The following is reported in "Mattel Seeks to Placate China With Apology, by Nicholas Casey, Nicholas Zamiska and Andy Pasztor, *Wall Street Journal*, 22 September 2007, A1.

> *Mattel has recalled more than 21 million toys world-wide in recent weeks.... The biggest recall, affecting 18 million toys, involved tiny magnets that can fall off toys and be deadly if swallowed. The recall of those toys, Mattel is now stressing, had nothing to do with a failure of Chinese manufacturing but rather stemmed from Mattel's own flawed designs for everything from Barbie accessories to Batman action figures.*

See also "Accident Raises Safety Concerns on Chinese Tires" by Timothy Aeppel, *Wall Street Journal*, 26 June 2007, A1.
2. For the rest of this discussion on what caused the credit bubble, see "Emotion's Role in Investment" (*Financial Times*, 20 September 2007) for an interview with Richard Taffer, professor at the University of Edinburgh and David Tuckett, visiting professor in psychoanalysis at UCL.

Sources of Information for Credit Analysts

This appendix summarizes and reviews a large number of information sources related to the analysis of credit risk of individual corporate entities. The analyst engaged in this task has an ever increasing number of sources available due to the communication industry's explosion. Whereas the electronic media has become the major source of credit information, the print media's importance has not diminished. Indeed, if anything, there are many new sources as well as the venerable ones. Many of the sources listed here can be accessed (and purchased when applicable) through the Internet. Almost all major vendors of data have established web sites and may be contacted very easily. Search engines such as Yahoo! or Google also make it possible to obtain data somewhat more readily than in the past. As most people would agree, using the Internet may be either enormously productive or quite useless, depending partly upon the user's agility on the system. *AAII Journal*, in *The Individual's Investor's Guide to Investment Web Sites,* contains a list of sites that provide substantial investing information or interactions. These may be of interest also to financial institutions.

We have organized our listings in several ways. First, we proceed from the general macroeconomic and financial sources to industry and sector trend analysis. These aggregated sources are a useful jumping-off point for the analyst who should understand the economic and financial environments that the individual firm functions within. Company-specific sources, while the main focus of our attention, need to be utilized and compared to many benchmarks, including aggregated sector data, market- and product-line

---

The authors would like to thank Jaime Pozuelo-Monfort for his assistance on this appendix. An up-to-date version can be found on http://j.pozuelo-monfort.com/mcr.

comparable data, and historic time series data. Another critical benchmark of companies is the aggregated statistics of credit risk categories of bond ratings. The rating agency designations play an important role in both individual credit and portfolio analysis. A second organizing method for credit source discussion is the aforementioned electronic versus print media dichotomy.

The Internet has opened the world of financial information and provides financial statements to the casual as well as the professional observer. In addition, online services complement the stored data for a variety of credit-related sources. Most of these online services involve four types of databases: (1) directories, (2) indexes, (3) full-text databases, and (4) statistical databases. Some sources are hybrids of more than one of these distinctions. Although much of what is available is oriented toward stock market investors, analysis of credit risk is also relevant in most cases.

Inevitably we incorporated links launching basic, extensive portals, recommending elaborated sources, information deemed essential. Nonetheless the organization for the herein epilogue, establishes unique resources on practically every aspect needed, ultimately neglecting inaccurate, obsolete numbers.

Extremely relevant sources of credit risk data are the several reports that document the default risk and loss severity of aggregated credit risk classes, such as credit quality ratings. These default and credit risk migration studies and their sources are noted here but are reviewed in depth in two chapters of this book.

Every source mentioned comes along its website, whenever available.

GENERAL ECONOMIC AND FINANCIAL ANALYSIS

A number of factors such as capacity utilization, monetary and fiscal policies, level of disposable personal income, inflation, interest rates, and GDP growth influence the economy and labor cost. In general, the economy undergoes periods of expansion and contraction, although the length of the periods varies. This business cycle pattern is also a fundamental determinant of the performance of the economy, which in turn affects the performance of the industry and company. Hence, the study of the economy is often the starting point in analyzing the expected performance of companies. The following sources provide information on the economy.

U.S. Government Publications on Macroeconomic Data

The primary source of macroeconomic information is published by the U.S. government. The following are the most important ones.

Administrative Office of the U.S. Bankruptcy Courts

http://pacer.psc.uscourts.gov This agency reports monthly and annual data on corporate and personal bankruptcies throughout the U.S. District Court system. The data are in aggregate form and sorted by chapter, type, and so on. The data can be used for statistical purposes. This publication does not provide information on individual companies.

Bureau of Labor Statistics (BLS)

http://www.bls.gov BLS provides information on employment, unemployment, consumer expenditures, prices, productivity, and economic growth. Its most important publication is *Employment and Earnings,* which is published monthly. It covers employment development and provides data on national, regional, and area unemployment, hours worked, and earnings. Following are its other publications:

- Consumer Expenditure Survey
- Consumer Price Index
- CPI Detailed Report
- Producer Price Indexes
- Compensation and Working Conditions

Economic Indicators

http://www.economicindicators.gov This is a monthly publication prepared by the Council of Economic Advisors and contains monthly and annual data on prices, money and credit, output, income, spending, employment, and production.

Economic Report of the President

http://www.gpoaccess.gov/eop/index.html In January of each year, the President of the United States presents an economic report on the United States to the Congress. This report discusses the economy in the past year and is published in the *Annual Report of the Council of Economic Advisors*. This report has a wealth of historical information on income, employment, production, inflation, and so forth.

Federal Reserve Banks

http://www.federalreserveonline.org   There are 12 Federal Reserve banks in the Federal Reserve System. They represent 12 geographical areas in the United States, as shown here:

1. Federal Reserve Bank of Boston
2. Federal Reserve Bank of New York
3. Federal Reserve Bank of Philadelphia
4. Federal Reserve Bank of Cleveland
5. Federal Reserve Bank of Richmond
6. Federal Reserve Bank of Chicago
7. Federal Reserve Bank of Atlanta
8. Federal Reserve Bank of St. Louis
9. Federal Reserve Bank of Minneapolis
10. Federal Reserve Bank of Kansas City
11. Federal Reserve Bank of Dallas
12. Federal Reserve Bank of San Francisco

These banks publish monthly reviews or letters that provide economic data on their region, or commentary on various economic issues, and at times on accounting issues also. The Federal Reserve Bank of St. Louis publishes statistics on various economic factors on a weekly and monthly basis. Statistical data on interest rates and yields of short-term and long-term securities in particular are important to the credit analyst because they serve as benchmarks for the borrowing costs of companies. These banks also maintain websites on the Internet.

Federal Reserve Bulletin

http://www.federalreserve.gov/pubs/bulletin/default.htm   The *Federal Reserve Bulletin* is published by the Board of Governors of the Federal Reserve System, Washington, D.C. This monthly publication is the primary source for most of the data on the U.S. banking system and for the monetary data. It also provides historical data on financial markets, industrial production, assets and liabilities of corporations, and GNP, among other items.

Quarterly Financial Report

http://www.census.gov/csd/qfr This quarterly report provides information on the financial condition of U.S. corporations. It is published by the Federal Trade Commission (FTC). FTC estimates income, expenses, and balance-sheet and related financial statements for all manufacturing and mining corporations. The statistics are classified by industry and size.

Statistical Abstract of the United States

http://www.census.gov/compendia/statab This publication, also available on a CD-ROM, is prepared by the *Economics and Statistical Administration of the Bureau of the Census* and provides statistical data covering all subjects. It provides information on population, employment, earnings, cost of living, purchasing power, and a host of other subjects.

Survey of Current Business

http://bea.gov/scb/index.htm This monthly periodical is published by the Bureau of Economic Analysis (BEA) of the U.S. Department of Commerce. It provides raw data on monthly updates on a broad spectrum of economic information such as GNP, manufacturers' shipments, business inventories, the labor market, fixed investment, and gross state product. This periodical provides voluminous data on various industries that are useful to the analyst in studying a particular industry and is perhaps the most important economic publication by the U.S. Government. In addition, BEA publishes *Weekly Business Statistics,* a weekly update. This publication has provided economic statistics for close to 2,000 data series on a monthly basis for the past four years, and annual statistics for the last 25 years. The data include general business indicators, production, sales, inventory, and other sources. Additionally, it provides quarterly and annual data on new plant and equipment expenditures.

EUROPEAN UNION MACROECONOMIC DATA

European Central Bank

http://www.ecb.int The Central Bank of the European Monetary Union (sometimes referred as *Euroland*) has further links to each of the national centrals of the 13 member states of the monetary union. The European Central Bank has its headquarters in Frankfurt, Germany, and is an independent institution responsible for fixing interest rates in Euroland, and for establishing the monetary policy. There are 13 Central Banks in the Eurosystem, representing 13 different countries: Belgium, Germany, Ireland, Greece, Spain, France, Italy, Luxembourg, The Netherlands, Austria, Portugal, Slovenia, and Finland.

Nongovernmental Macroeconomic Publications

Global Insight®

http://www.globalinsight.com Formerly known as DRI/McGraw-Hill, Global Insight provides a comprehensive economic, financial, and political coverage of countries, regions, covering over 200 countries and spanning more than approximately 170 industries, using a combination of expertise, models, data, and software within a common analytical framework to support planning and decision making.

Morningstar®

http://www.mornigstar.com Ibbotson Associates is now integrated in Morningstar. Morningstar is one of the leading providers of independent investment research in the United States and in major international markets. Its mission is to create products that help investors reach their financial goals, offering an extensive line of Internet, software, and print-based products for individual investors, financial advisors, and institutional clients.

Standard & Poor's Statistical Service This publication provides an exhaustive array of statistical data on a monthly and annual basis covering the economy, industries, production, the labor market, and the stock market.

The S&P publication, Standard & Poor's Statistical Service, is still published in print format and consists of the following sections:

- *Current Statistics*, published monthly
- *Security Price Index Record*, published biannually
- *Basic Statistical Sections*, published on different topics at variable dates

INDUSTRY ANALYSIS

After studying economic and financial conditions, the analyst can examine the relevant industry. The following sources provide information on industries.

Almanac of Business and Industrial Financial Ratios 2003 Edition   Published by Aspen/Wolters Kluwer in Amsterdan, The Netherlands, this annual study provides financial data on several industries. It provides 22 financial indicators, and companies are segmented by asset size. The data is derived from tax returns of 4 million companies filed with the Internal Revenue Service.

Annual Survey of Manufacturers

http://www.census.gov/mcd/asmhome.html   This study prepared by the WEFA Group in Eddystone, Pennsylvania, uses government data to provide over 5,000 time series of industry data. The data, based on *standard industrial classification* (SIC) code, presents raw material cost, value added by manufacturers, value of shipments, employment, payroll, and capital expenditures.

Industry Magazines

Industry magazines provide continuous coverage of particular industries. These magazines provide developments in the industry, performance of companies, products coming to the market, government regulations, and so forth. These are some examples:

- *Automotive News*, http://www.autonews.com
- *Beverage World*, http://www.beverageworld.com
- *Chemical Week*, http://www.chemweek.com
- *Coal Age*, http://www.mining-media.com/publications/coal_age.asp
- *Electric Utility Week*, http://www.platts.com
- *Modern Plastics*, http://www.modplas.com
- *Pulp and Paper*, http://www.pulpandpaper.net
- *Supermarket News*, http://www.supermarketnews.com

Industry Norms and Key Business Ratios (Dun & Bradstreet)

http://kbr.dnb.com   Dun & Bradstreet (D&B) provides operating financial norms and key business ratios for more than 800 lines of businesses and over 19 million public and privately owned U.S. companies. It provides industry balance sheet, short income statement and working capital, solvency, and efficiency and profitability ratios for a total of 14 key business ratios for each industry for up to three years. The industry norms are published separately for the following five major industry segments:

1. Agriculture, mining, construction, transportation, communication, and utilities
2. Manufacturing
3. Wholesaling
4. Retailing
5. Finance, real estate, and services

The data are provided based on SIC codes as well as geographic region (east, west, north, and south). The publication is available in hard copy or on the Internet. The following publications are available:

■ *Industry Norms and Key Business Ratios*, three-year edition
■ *Industry Norms and Key Business Ratios*, one-year edition
■ *Key Business Ratios*, one-year edition

D&B can provide industry studies as well as company analysis in comparison with its industry. Its V.I.P. service provides customized service to the client that includes an overview of the company's structure and business background, financial analysis compared with its peers, trend and comparative information, and an outlook on the industry specifics and a description of world events that have shaped the industry's past and will impact the future.

Manufacturing, U.S.A.: Industry Analyses, Statistics, and Lending Companies (Gale Research)

http://www.gale.com   Published by Gale Research in two volumes, this set provides data on 458 industries and over 21,000 manufacturing corporations. The presentation includes the following:

■ 17-year data, including 4-year projections
■ Financial ratios for companies and industries
■ More than 21,000 listed companies, ranked by sales volume and other relevant data
■ Material consumption for each industry showing volume and raw materials and their cost
■ Industry data by state
■ Inputs and outputs

Moody's Investors Service

http://www.moodys.com   In addition to providing ratings on bond issues and company information, Moody's performs annual default/mortality studies based on the number of issuers defaulted, and periodic reports on rating migration patterns. This is discussed in a later section.

RMA Annual Statement Studies (Risk Management Association)

http://www.rmahq.org/RMA   This is an annual study of more than 350 industries in terms of 17 financial and operating ratios. The data are presented for total industry as well as stratified by asset size. The studies provide current and historical analysis of an industry's assets, liabilities and income, classified according to the size of the company assets. The data are provided in six parts as shown:

1. Manufacturing industries
2. Wholesale industries
3. Retailing, service, agricultural and other industries
4. Contractor industries
5. Construction Financial Management Association (CFMA) data.These are excerpts from *Construction Industry Annual Financial Survey,* published by CFMA.
6. The First National Bank of Chicago Consumer and Diversified Finance Company Ratios

The publications provide the balance sheet, condensed income statement, and 16 ratios, which are grouped into three categories: upper quartile, median quartile, and lower quartile. The quartile ratios are strong ratios in the top 25 percent of the ratios. An explanation of ratios is included.

Service Industries, U.S.A.: Industry Analyses, Statistics, and Leading Companies

http://www.gale.com   Published by Gale Research in two volumes, it provides data on 2,100 services grouped into 151 industries, and over 3,500 service corporations and 700 nonprofit organizations. The presentation includes the following:

- Statistical data by firms, employment, payroll, revenues, and type of ownership by SIC code

- Statistical data by firms, employment, payroll, revenues, and type of ownership by city
- Financial and operating ratios
- List of leading companies
- Occupations employed by the industry

Standard & Poor's Industry Surveys The surveys are published annually and updated every week. The annual study is presented in terms of the following:

- Current environment
- Industry profile
- Industry trends
- How the industry operates
- Key industry ratios and statistics
- How to analyze the industry
- Glossary
- Industry references
- Composite industry data
- Comparative company analysis

In addition, S&P publishes *Industry Surveys Monthly,* which covers performance and valuation statistics for all industries in the S&P 500 Index, industry outlook and charts on various aspects of the industries, and an earnings supplement. The surveys cover 52 industries. The *Trade and Security Statistics* provides historical data on various industries and security prices. In addition to providing ratings of bond issues and company information, Standard & Poor's publishes annual default/mortality and rating migration studies based on the number of issuers defaulted and utilizes a static-pool analysis. This is discussed in a later section.

Trade Associations

These provide a wealth of information on the industry they represent. Some of the trade associations are:

- Steel Institute, http://www.steel.org
- Insurance Information Institute, http://www.iii.org
- Paper Institute, http://www.tappi.org
- American Bankers Association, http://www.aba.com

These associations provide extensive statistical data on the industry and also information that affects the industry. Some of them publish fact books annually, which provide industry shipments, pricing, operating costs, companies in the industry, historical trends, foreign competition, and latest developments. The publication *Encyclopedia of Associations* provides a comprehensive list of associations.

U.S. Department of Commerce

http://www.commerce.gov The department publishes industry studies every five years. Partial updates are published as Annual Survey of Manufacturers:

- *Census of Manufactures,* http://www.census.gov/econ/www/mancen. html
- *Census of Construction Industries,* http://www.census.gov/const/www/cci/fintro.html
- *Census of New Retail and Wholesale Trade,* http://www.census.gov/econ/www/retmenu.html *Census of Service Industries,* http://www.census.gov/econ/www/se0200.html

Census of Manufacturers provides reports on manufacturing activity every five years. Statistics on the industry are provided by SIC codes and geographic regions ranging from places with a population as low as 2,500 to the entire United States. This is updated annually in the *Annual Survey of Manufacturers.*

Census of Construction Industries provides data on different segments of the industry. The data are reported for the entire United States, states, and selected *standard metropolitan statistical areas* (SMAs). The census covers receipts, employment, hours worked, payments for materials and supplies, and other data.

Census of Retail Trade provides data by SIC code. The data include sales volume, operating costs, capacity, operating ratios, and other data of the retail industry. In addition, it provides descriptive data on shopping centers, malls, and neighborhood business districts. The data are extensive and useful to the analyst studying the retail industry. The data are presented by geographic region ranging from places with 2,500 people to the total United States.

Census of Wholesale Trade provides data by SIC code. The data include sales volume, operating costs, capacity, operating ratios, and other data of the wholesale trade industry. The data are presented by geographic region ranging from places with 2,500 people to the total United States.

Census of Service Industries provides data on service industries arranged by SIC code. The data include the number of service establishments, receipts, payroll, and expenses, and selected operating ratios. The data are presented by geographic region ranging from places with 2,500 people to the total United States.

INDEXES

Periodical indexes make the analyst's job easier. They provide titles of articles published periodically. The analyst can search for appropriate sources and then go to the articles relevant to the analysis.

The Business Periodicals Index

http://www.hwwilson.com/reviews/business_review.htm   Published by H. W. Wilson, this index provides articles from approximately 400 periodicals on subjects relating to business, economics, and finance. It is available online through WILSONLINE as well as CD-ROM. Although most of the coverage is general, the index cites articles on specific industries as well.

Journal of Economic Literature Index

http://www.aeaweb.org/journal.html   The *Journal of Economic Literature* (*JEL*) began publication in 1969 under the auspices of the American Economic Association with quarterly issues appearing in March, June, September, and December. *JEL* contains survey and review articles, book reviews, an annotated bibliography of newly published books, and a list of current dissertations in North American universities.

New York Times Index

http://www.nytimes.com   This is an annual index that is updated every two weeks. Subjects are arranged in chronological order. The *New York Times* provides articles on current business topics and features extensive market data.

Wall Street Journal Index

http://www.wsj.com   This index provides reference to articles that have appeared in the *Wall Street Journal*. The index is presented in two parts: corporate news (which lists companies) and general news. In addition, the index references *Barron's* articles as well.

DIRECTORIES

Directory of Corporate Affiliations (LexisNexis)

http://www.lexisnexis.com/dca Directory of Corporate Affiliations (DCA) database covers more than 180,000 of the most prominent parent companies, affiliates, subsidiaries, and divisions worldwide that help to research corporate ownership. DCA covers major U.S. and international public and private businesses—more than 180,000 companies. DCA enables the user to search for a parent company and subsidiary of large corporations.

Dun & Bradstreet's Million Dollar Database

http://www.dnbmdd.com/mddi/ Dun's Million Dollar Database allows you to look up companies by geographic location and by industry. This database also lists many smaller private companies. Dun's North American Million Dollar Database provides the information professional, marketer and sales executive with information on approximately 1,600,000 U.S. and Canadian leading public and private businesses. Company information includes industry information with up to 24 individual 8-digit SICs, size criteria (employees and annual sales), type of ownership, principal executives, and biographies.

The International Directory of Company Histories
Published by Gale/St. James Press, this 16-volume collection of over 2,650 company profiles includes historical developments, acquisitions and mergers, and a company perspective. Volumes 1–6 are organized alphabetically by major industries. Volume 7 and subsequent volumes are arranged alphabetically by company name within each volume. Each volume includes a cumulative index to companies and personal names. Volume 7 and subsequent volumes include a cumulative index to industries.

Harvard Business School (HBS) Publishing

http://www.hbsp.harvard.edu This is a renowned university press publisher of books on a wide range of disciplines in the realm of business administration, including communication, finance and accounting, global business, innovation and entrepreneurship, leadership, management, organizational development, sales and marketing, strategy, and technology and operations.

Market Share Reporter (Gale Research)   Presenting comparative business statistics in a clear, straightforward manner, *Market Share Reporter* affords an immediate overview of companies, products and services and cites original sources. A convenient arrangement by four-digit SIC code helps business decision makers and researchers easily access needed data for more than 2,000 entries. Each entry features a descriptive title, data and market description, a list of producers and products along with their market share.

Standard & Poor's Register of Corporations, Directors, and Executives
This publication covers 56,000 companies in three volumes. The first volume, Corporate Listings, provides the address, telephone number, officers, directors, lines of business, SIC code, and other relevant data in alphabetical order. The second volume, Individual Listings, provides biographies of officers and directors. The third volume is an assortment of indexes. Companies are arranged by SIC code and geography, and in an index that links parents and subsidiaries.

Thomas's Register of American Manufacturers

http://www.thomasnet.com   This directory is published in 26 volumes. Volumes 1 through 15 list over 150,000 U.S. manufacturers by products and service. Volume 16 contains a product index. Volumes 17 and 18 contain the list of companies arranged alphabetically with the following information:

- Name and address of the company
- Branch offices
- Subsidiaries
- Products
- Brand names of products
- Principal officers

An *American Trademark Index* is included in volume 18. Volumes 19 through 26 provide descriptions of products made by nearly 3,000 of these companies.

Ward's Business Directory of U.S. Private and Public Companies (Gale Research)

http://www.gale.com/pdf/facts/wards.pdf This directory is a leading source of information on 120,000 private and public companies. It provides complete company listings to companies with national and state ranking by sales within SIC codes. The publication consists of seven volumes. The first three volumes present company profiles in alphabetical order. Up to 20 items of information are presented, including the following:

- Financial data
- Number of employees
- Up to four-digit SIC codes, with description of products and services offered
- Executive officers' names and titles
- Year founded
- Ticker symbol and stock exchange where traded
- Name of immediate parent
- Description of products and services
- Import/export status
- Company type: private, public, subsidiary, division, joint venture, or investment fund

The fourth volume is a geographical listing of companies listed in the first three volumes. The companies are organized by state. In addition, it contains a special feature section that presents various tables based on company sales and includes the following information:

- 1,000 largest privately held companies
- 1,000 largest publicly held companies
- 1,000 largest employers
- Analysis of private and public companies by state
- Analysis by revenue per employee of top 1,000 companies
- Analysis of private and public companies by four-digit SIC code

The fifth volume presents companies listed in the first three volumes by the four-digit SIC code and ranks them according to sales. Other financial data are also included. The sixth and seventh volumes derive from the first five volumes, presenting companies by state, then by the four-digit SIC code, and then by sales ranking. In addition, there is a special features section that presents the following information:

- 100 largest privately held companies for each state
- 100 largest publicly held companies for each state
- 100 largest employers for each state

In addition, the seventh volume has a list of companies ranked alphabetically, with assigned state rank number, state, and primary SIC code.

In addition to these directories, there are directories based on industries published by associations, individuals, or Dun & Bradstreet.

- *Dun's Industrial Guide: the Metalworking Directory* published by Dun & Bradstreet
- *Corporate Technology Directory*
- *Davison's Textile Blue Book*
- *Thomas Grocery Register*
- *Lockwood-Post's Directory of the Pulp, Paper, and Allied Trades*
- Some trade journals publish "Buyers Guides" issues giving names and addresses of companies, for example, *Chemical Week* Buyers Guide, October issue, and *Textile World*, July issue.

PERIODICALS AND NEWSPAPERS

American Banker

http://www.americanbanker.com   This publication provides information on banking and financial services. It is a daily publication concentrating on technology, banking products, mortgages, finance, and various other subjects.

Barron's

http://www.barrons.com   This is a weekly publication. Its articles are directed toward the investor. However, there are analyses of companies in the Investment News and Views section. The Market Laboratory provides copious amounts of statistical data on bonds, stocks, economic and financial indicators, and market statistics.

Bloomberg Markets Magazine

http://wealth.bloomberg.com/news/marketsmag   This monthly magazine published by Bloomberg contains articles on market perspective, complex financings, personal wealth, new capabilities on Bloomberg, and interviews with senior officers of companies. *Bloomberg* articles cover a wide variety of cutting-edge topics.

Business Week

http://www.businessweek.com   This is a weekly publication and contains articles on the economy, industries, and companies. The articles cover products, finance, labor, production, and corporate news. It provides earnings of companies on a quarterly basis, and presents an annual survey of industry performance. In addition, it includes a weekly update on such economic variables as interest rates, electricity consumption, and market prices. Each quarter, *Business Week* publishes "*Business Week* Corporate Scoreboard" in which it provides financial data on 900 companies in 24 industries. The presentation includes sales, net profit, return on invested capital, return on common equity, growth in earnings per share, market value, and earnings per share. The quarterly earnings appear in the May, August, November, and February issues. The July issue features the *Business Week* Global 1,000, which provides information on the 1,000 largest companies in the world ranked by market value, share price, price/book value ratio, P/E ratio, sales, profits, and return on equity. All figures are translated into U.S. dollars. The April issue features the *Business Week* 1,000: America's Most Valuable Companies. Companies are ranked based on market value and the long-term outlook of the companies and their industries. The data provided include market value, sales and profit margin, return on equity and invested capital, recent share price, book value per share, and earnings per share.

Commercial Lending Review

http://www.commerciallendingreview.com   This is a publication of the American Bankers Association and provides articles on credit risk management, bank regulations, community banking, and accounting issues related to banking.

The Economist

http://www.economist.com   This magazine provides worldwide coverage of politics, business, economics, finance, science, and technology. Its articles on politics are grouped geographically as American Survey, Asia, International, Europe, and Britain. It publishes economic and financial statistics on 15 OECD countries and 25 emerging markets. Periodically it publishes surveys on countries, finance, and the economy.

Financial Times

http://www.ft.com   This international daily based in London provides news and articles on politics, economics, finance, as well as the financial, commodity, and other markets. Periodically it publishes surveys on markets, industries, and countries.

Financial World

http://www.financialworld.com   This magazine is published twice a month and contains about 10 articles on companies, industries, overall stock market performance, and stock market data.

Forbes

http://www.forbes.com   This biweekly contains 12 to 15 articles on individual companies and industries. It has columnists that write on various subjects relating to business and finance. In January, *Forbes* publishes Annual Report on American Industry in which it provides a ranking of companies in 21 industries, based on growth of sales and stock market performance. The report includes profitability, growth in sales and earnings per share, sales, net income, and profit margin.

Fortune

http://www.fortune.com   This is published biweekly. It contains in-depth articles on the economy, business, individual companies, the stock market, and personal investing. The April issue features the Fortune 500 Largest U.S. Industrial Corporations ranked by sales. The list also includes Who Did Best and Worst Among 500 section, which features companies based on return to investors, profitability, change in sales, sales per employee, and stockholders' equity. The June issue features Fortune 500 Service Companies, which ranks within each industry.

High Yield Report

http://www.highyieldreport.com   This is published by *American Banker* and includes news on high-yield markets, personnel changes in various firms, the economy, data on new issues, traded debt, and distressed bond trading.

McKinsey Quarterly

http://www.mckinseyquarterly.com   The *McKinsey Quarterly* is the business journal of McKinsey & Company. It covers a number of functions (corporate finance, economic studies, governance, information technology, marketing, operations, organization, and strategy) and industries (automotive, energy/resources/materials, financial services, food & agriculture, healthcare, high tech, media & entertainment, nonprofit, public sector, retail, telecommunications, and transportation).

RMA Journal

http://www.rmahq.org   This journal was formerly called *Journal of Lending and Credit Risk Management* and is published by Robert Morris Associates, Philadelphia, Pennsylvania. It publishes articles on banking, credit risk, lending strategies, bank regulations, and lending to various industries.

Structured Credit Investor

http://www.structuredcreditinvestor.com   A weekly magazine featuring global structured credit news, opinion, strategies and data, *Structured Credit Investor*, features the latest news and developments in the structured credit industry, on a variety of topics ranging from research pieces to current news in the credit risk industry.

Turnarounds and Workouts

http://bankrupt.com/periodicals/tw.html   This bimonthly publication by Beard Group, Inc., Washington, D.C., provides the latest news on defaulted, bankrupt, and distressed companies, a research report on companies that have filed for bankruptcy, including a profile on the officers of the company, members of the committees, the trustee, lawyers, and the judge.

Wall Street Journal

http://www.wsj.com   This is the primary daily source of information on business, economics, and finance and is the most widely circulated financial newspaper. It features articles on economy, corporate performance, company news, politics, taxes, and investing. Digest of Earnings Reports is a daily feature about updates on quarterly and annual reports of companies.

Wall Street Transcripts

http://www.twst.com This is a weekly that contains texts of speeches made in security analysts' meetings, copies of brokerage house reports on companies and industries, and interviews with corporate officers. In addition, it provides information on industries through the Round Table Discussion, where analysts discuss various aspects of an industry.

ONLINE SERVICES

Since 1998, with the publication of the first edition of this book, much has changed in the amount and quality of information available online. This is a selection of some of the best.

ABI/Inform

http://www.proquest.com/products_pq/descriptions/abi_inform.shtml
This is a database on compact disk containing indexes and abstracts of articles from over 800 business and trade journals covering the last five years.

Bloomberg News

http://www.bloomberg.com Bloomberg News is a real-time global news service that provides coverage of the world's governments, corporations, industries, commodities, and most segments of financial markets. The service is available on a dedicated computer terminal. It not only provides financial information like other online services but also processes it and presents it in tabular and/or graph form. Bloomberg provides a broad spectrum of data that includes financial news on industries and companies, debt rating actions, EDGAR filings, company analysis, equity, debt, commodities, foreign exchange, and municipal markets. The breadth and depth of coverage from Bloomberg is extensive. Its services are summarized here:

- Bloomberg analytics include beta, moving averages, money flows, volatilities, option sensitivity, deliverability, technical analysis, monitors, option modeling, option-adjusted spread, duration, convexity, derivative evaluation, risk management, and scenario analysis.

- Fundamental data provided include earnings, balance sheets, cash flows, ratio analysis, and EDGAR filings.
- Various securities including stocks, convertibles, warrants, bonds, foreign exchange, interest rates, currency swaps, synthetics, strips, mortgage- and asset-based securities, and structured products.
- Real-time prices for instruments trading on the world's exchanges. These prices include current, historical and projected bond, currency, spot energy, derivative, and over-the-counter.
- The Bloomberg Forum provides in-depth interviews with corporate executives and industry executives.
- Bloomberg Multex Research allows the user to consolidate research from hundreds of providers.
- The Bloomberg fair value model draws on real-time market prices and is based on actual market activity for similar bonds, and option-adjusted methodology provides a theoretical market price for a bond.
- Bloomberg News produces over 3,000 stories a day on companies, industries, and global markets. However, the major weakness of Bloomberg is that the information can only be printed.

Bridge Information Systems, Inc.

http://www.bridge.com   Bridge provides information on equities, fixed-income instruments, foreign exchange, derivatives, and commodities. BridgeNews (formerly Knight-Ridder Financial), a division of Bridge Information System, provides real-time news, in-depth analysis of markets, forecasts and calendars, market-focused government news, and so forth.

Center for Research in Security Prices

http://www.crsp.com   The Center for Research in Securities Prices (CRSP), located in the center of the Chicago financial district, is an integral part of the University of Chicago's Graduate School of Business. The GSB is renowned for cutting-edge financial and economic research. CRSP creates and maintains premier historical US databases for stock (Nasdaq, AMEX, NYSE), indexes, bond, and mutual fund securities.

Dun & Bradstreet

http://www.dnb.com   One of the leading information providers, Dun & Bradstreet has a wide variety of publications. *D&B Dun's Financial Record Plus* provides directory and financial information on private and public companies. The data covers company's history and operation, financial data, and SIC codes.

Business Failure Record provides a comparative statistical analysis of business failures in terms of geographic and industry trends in the United States. *Manufacturing Survey* provides a survey of 1,000 manufacturing companies regarding their production, new orders, unfilled orders, exports, finished goods, and inventories. *Construction Survey* provides a survey of 200 construction firms regarding their current conditions and expectations in the next three months. *U.S. Survey of Business expectations* provides a nationwide survey of 3,000 business executives regarding their expectations of sales, prices, inventories, exports, employment, and new orders for the coming quarter. *D&B Million Dollar Directory* provides information on public and private companies, such as address, SIC codes, ticker symbols, and in some cases, sales. This directory is a valuable addition to any library. Currently it is available in the online Dun's Market Identifier database in addition to the printed book. Dun & Bradstreet United States provides information on public and private companies in the United States. This is similar to the million dollar directory but is available only online through Information Online. Dun's Electronic Business Directory provides the names, addresses and recent information on more than 10 million U.S. businesses, and the data are arranged into eight groups based on SIC codes, as follows:

1. Construction Directory provides data on contractors.
2. Financial Services Directory provides data on banks, savings and loan institutions, insurance companies, and credit unions.
3. Manufacturers Directory provides data on manufacturers of all types.
4. Professionals Directory provides data on more than 1.2 million professionals in a variety of professions.
5. Services Directory provides data on more than 1.4 million service firms of all types and sizes.
6. Wholesale Directory provides data on over 650,000 wholesale establishments of all types and sizes.
7. Schools Directory provides data on 100,000 schools and libraries ranging from elementary schools to colleges.
8. Retailers Directory provides data on 1.9 million retail establishments of all types and sizes.

Factiva®

http://www.factiva.com   Factiva, from Dow Jones, provides essential business news and information together with the content delivery tools and services that enable professionals to make better decisions faster. Factiva's collection of more than 10,000 authoritative sources includes the exclusive combination of the *Wall Street Journal, Financial Times,* Dow Jones and Reuters newswires, and the Associated Press, as well as Reuters Fundamentals and D&B company profiles.

Guideline, Inc.®

http://www.guideline.com   Guideline, based in New York, provides its clients with customized business research and analysis including focus groups, competitive intelligence, market research, and secondary research.

LexisNexis®

http://www.lexisnexis.com   One of the most popular online services, LexisNexis provides articles published in various newspapers, periodicals, company information matter, and reports written by security analysts. In addition, it has access to the law library maintained by LexisNexis. LexisNexis Express has a service by which researchers find the information the analyst needs efficiently and send it to the analyst. Another service, Tracker, provides, at the request of the organization, automatic news updates about its clients, competition, and industry.

Reuters

http://www.reuters.com   Reuters Holdings PLC supplies the business community worldwide with a wide range of products including real-time financial data, transaction systems, and access to statistical and textual historical databases. Reuters gathers information from over 250 exchanges and OTC markets, from 4,800 subscribers who contribute data directly, and from a network of journalists. Reuters Target News delivers news stories by topic in a timely manner. It provides annual reports of companies, key facts, financial results of a company, and its 11-year history.

RGEMonitor®

http://www.rgemonitor.com   RGEMonitor.com is the leading aggregator of ahead-of-the-curve information on global economic and geostrategic information. The service delivers an up-to-the minute unbiased editorial perspective to the workflow process of business strategists, investors, researchers, academics, policy makers and regulators. With ever expanding coverage of the most relevant news, commentary, research, analysis, blogs, and data, RGE Monitor is the leading economic information hub on the Web.

Securities Data Company (SDC)

http://fisher.osu.edu/fin/sdc.htm   SDC provides a database that covers worldwide information on new issues, mergers and acquisitions, joint ventures, venture financing, and corporate restructuring. The database is updated on a daily basis and is one of the most popular. The Global New Issues database includes the following:

- Domestic common stock issues with over 14,000 offerings since 1970.
- Domestic preferred stock issues with over 2,200 offerings since 1970.
- Debt database with over 22,000 offerings since 1970, including straight debt, convertible debt, mortgage, asset-backed debt, and taxable municipals.
- Private placement database with information on over 25,000 domestic private placements since 1981, containing information on straight debt, convertible debt, common stock, and preferred stock.
- Euroequity and Eurobond databases with information on over 1,700 euro, global, and domestic issue program since 1973, covering public and private debt and common and preferred stock offerings.
- Medium-term note database with information on over 1,700 euro, global, and domestic issue programs since 1973, updated on a daily basis.
- Issues withdrawn from registration.
- Shelf registrations.
- Underwritten calls of convertibles.
- Foreign public offerings in the United Kingdom and Canada, and international warrants.
- The worldwide M&A database with coverage of more than 55,000 domestic transactions since 1980 and over 45,000 deals since 1985, covering mergers, acquisitions, partial acquisitions, leveraged buyouts, divestures, exchange offers, stock repurchases, self-tenders, squeeze outs, tender offers, and spinoffs, updated daily based on SEC filings, tender offers, major financial publications, and company press releases

In addition, SDC offers specialized databases that include the following:

- Joint Venture and Strategic Alliances database provides information on over 19,000 cross-border and intranation joint venture transactions since 1988. The database tracks over 75 data items for each transaction in which two or more companies combined existing units or assets to form a new operating business or strategic alliance. Current state of the deal, recent developments concerning the transaction, as well as coverage of the participants involved are included.

- Venture Financing database is based on research by SDC subsidiary Venture Economics and contains business and financing abstracts on more than 17,000 public and private U.S. companies since 1970.

Thomson Datastream

http://www.thomson.com/content/financial/brand_overviews/Datastream_
Advance Thomson Datastream is a historical financial numerical database that covers a number of financial instruments, equity and fixed income securities and indicators for over 175 countries and 60 markets worldwide. Datastream enables the user to access financial data on stocks, bonds, options, warrants and swaps. Moreover Datastream Equity and Bond Research cover more than 30,000 equities and 70,000 bonds. It also provides macroeconomic data from sovereigns and international financial institutions.

Thomson Dialog

http://www.dialog.com A Thomson Information service, Dialog provides access to over 450 online databases related to market research, business planning, and related areas. It provides investment analysts' reports. Dialog's Bluesheets describe and provide guidelines for searching all databases related to Dialog.

Wharton Research Data Services

http://wrds.wharton.upenn.edu Wharton Research Data Services (WRDS) is an Internet-based resource allowing the retrieval of information from a variety of financial, economic, and marketing databases. The data covers over 30,000 companies, including security prices, trading volume, income and balance sheets, and analyst projections on both earnings and sales. In addition WRDS contains stock quotes, indices, bond prices, interest rates, option as well as a number of macroeconomic series.

COMPANY ANALYSIS

After examining the economic and financial conditions and examining the industry, the analyst may now analyze the company. The following are the most important sources.

Company Reports

The best source on a company is the company itself. A company publishes press releases, which provide information on topics such as earnings and management changes. The senior officers make presentations before security analysts and are interviewed by analysts and the press. In these interviews the officers discuss current performance, company strategy, prospects for the company, business plans, and new product development. In addition, many companies have their own web site on the Internet.

Annual Reports

By far the most important source of information on the company, the annual report, provides information on the current operations and financial conditions of the company. The annual report contains two parts and must contain the following items:

Part I

- Business. If the company has multiple lines of business, those product lines that account for more than 10 percent of sales must be presented for the last two years. Gross profit or operating profit by product lines must be included.
- Summary of operations.
- Properties, location, type of property at each location, and whether each is leased or owned.
- Parents and subsidiaries.
- Legal proceedings.
- Changes in outstanding securities.
- Approximate number of equity holders.
- Executive officers of the company.
- Indemnification of officers and directors.
- Financial statements including income statements, balance sheets, and detailed footnotes.

Part II

- Principal security holders.
- Directors of the company.
- Remuneration of directors and officers of the company.
- Options granted to management to purchase.
- Ownership of the company by management and others.

Part I must be filed with the SEC within 90 days from the end of the company's fiscal year, and part II within 120 days.

Securities and Exchange Commission (SEC) Filings and Forms

http://www.sec.gov/edgar.shtml   Pursuant to the Securities and Exchange Commission Act of 1934, all firms that have publicly issued securities have to file various statements with the SEC and also distribute them to the stockholders.

- Form 10-K includes the annual report and presents the company's business and financial information in greater detail.
- Form 10-Q and quarterly reports are unaudited. Form 10-Q is filed with the SEC on a quarterly basis and must be filed within 45 days from the end of the fiscal year. The quarterly report must contain the operations for the quarter, year to date and comparison with the quarter of the previous year. The report must contain an income statement, balance sheet, and funds flow statement, as well as written analysis of the operations during the quarter.
- The proxy statement discloses information relevant to the stockholder.
- Form 8-K in an interim report filed when there is an important event that affects the corporation, such as bankruptcy filing, changes in control, and resignation of officers or directors.

S-18 Registration   S-18 registration is a simplified registration used by small companies; the offering of new securities cannot exceed $7.5 million. The following statements have to be filed with SEC:

- An audited balance sheet for one year.
- An audited income statement and statements of change in financial condition for two years.
- No management discussion or analyses of financial condition and no selected financial data.

S-1 Registration   This registration filed with the SEC is more complex and requires more information:

- Details of the offering, underwriting discounts and commission, proceeds from the issue.
- Ownership of existing shares.
- Presentation of risk factors.
- Use of proceeds.

- The company's dividend policy and a statement as to how future earnings will be used; the company's capital structure before and after the new issue.
- Management discussion of the performance of the company.
- Description of business.
- Information about the directors and officers.
- Company financial statements and auditor's opinion.

Other Sources of Company Analysis

Associations Unlimited   Associations Unlimited is a directory covering the following associations: 23,000 U.S. national associations; 21,000 national associations; 100,000 U.S. regional, state, and local associations; 2,500 materials' associations; 300,000 nonprofit organizations, agencies, and service programs (300,000).

Bank Loan Report

http://www.bankloanreport.com   This is a weekly newsletter providing information on terms and conditions of newly arranged million-dollar loans. The coverage includes fees, spreads, covenants, and participants. IDD Information Services publishes this report.

The Bankruptcy DataSource (New Generation Research)

http://www.bankruptcydata.com/DataSource2.htm   This publication provides information on companies that filed bankruptcy, asset sales, financing arrangements, law suits, claim transfers, and reorganization plans filed. New Generation Research, Inc. publishes this monthly report as well as the annual *Bankruptcy Yearbook and Almanac* . The yearbook lists companies that filed for bankruptcy, companies that came out of bankruptcy, bankrupt companies by industry, private companies that filed for bankruptcy, and other data. See also New Generation's web site, http://www.bankrupt.com.

BEA Industry Capital Stock Data Tape

http://www.bea.gov   This data tape includes capital stocks and related measures from 1925 to 2006; capital stocks and related measures by industry from 1947 to 2006; investment, fixed nonresidential private capital from 1947 to 2006; investments in residential capital from 1820 to 2006; investments in durable goods owned by consumers from 1947 to 2006; investments in government-owned, privately operated from 1917 to 2006; and investments in government enterprises and government total from 1850 to 2006.

Brokerage Reports

Most large brokerage firms periodically publish industry and company analyses written by security analysts. Stock and bond investors and credit analysts will find these publications extremely useful.

Database of Stern Stewart EVA 1000

http://www.sternstewart.com   Stern Stewart provides information on the largest 1,000 public companies. It uses a spreadsheet format that includes 20 years of historical data. The data is audited and are used to compute Stern Stewart's renowned ratios, including MVA, EVA, NOPAT, on top of the more basic return on capital and cost of capital.

Duff & Phelps Fixed Income Ratings   http://www.duffandphelps.comDuff & Phelps rates over 500 major domestic corporations. Commercial paper ratings range from Duff 1 plus (top quality) to Duff 3, and long-term debt is rated on a 17-point scale that ranges from AAA to CCC with plus and minus modifiers similar to those used by S&P. Duff & Phelps is one of four statistical rating organizations fully recognized by the SEC.

EDGAR Database of Corporations

http://www.sec.gov/edgar.shtml   EDGAR, the acronym for Electronic Data Gathering, Analysis, and Retrieval system, is the fastest growing source that provides copies of SEC filings. Companies have been phased in to EDGAR filing over a three-year period ending May 1996. As of that date all public domestic companies were required to file in EDGAR. Currently EDGAR is available through the Internet.) Any public electronic filings submitted to the SEC can be retrieved.

Federal Deposit Insurance Corporation (FDIC) http://www.fdic.gov   The FDIC database contains financial data of firms subject to file the Report of Condition and Income, as well as some savings institutions filing the OTS Thrift Financial Report. The data files provided by FDIC incorporate financial time series data, financial ratio data, and merger history data.

FDIC also provides data on banks in the United States, including the period 1920–1936.

Fitch Ratings

http://www.fitchratings.com Fitch Ratings rates debt instruments of industrial, bank, and finance companies, and municipal bonds and structured finance. Commercial paper ratings range from Fitch-1 to Fitch-4, and long-term debt is rated on a seven-point scale that ranges from AAA to CCC. Fitch IBCA is one of four statistical rating organizations fully recognized by the SEC. Fitch IBCA provides the following services:

- Corporate and government bond databases that provide financial information on securities including bond covenants.
- Rating database containing all Fitch IBCA-rated issues.
- Structured Finance Surveillance features asset-backed securities (ABS) key credit indicators.
- Market risk ratings to gauge comparative risk for CMO tranches.
- Research reports detailing Fitch's IBCA credit opinions.
- Real-time rating news.

Global Business Insight

http://www.globalbusinessinsight.com Business Insights develops a series of reports on a variety of industries including consumer goods, energy, finance, healthcare, and technology. Working in association with numerous experts, Business Insights is able to provide with more incisive market analysis specific to an industry sector.

Hoover's®

http://www.hoovers.com Hoover's, based in Austin, Texas, covers more than 23 million companies and 30 million decision makers worldwide, with comprehensive company overviews, plus extensive financial data. the Hoover's database spreads over 600 industries, with in-depth industry records and links to related web resources.

Hoover's also publishes the *Handbook of American Business,* which provides information on 500 of the largest and most influential companies in the United States. It is available through LexisNexis, Bloomberg, and America Online. Profiles on 500 companies are presented based on revenues and include an overview, history, key competitors, products and formation, and public visibility. These are summarized in one page. Based on its operating performance, profitability measures, financial strength, innovation, and market share in the industry, the companies are ranked from A to F. The sister product, Hoover's Company Database, provides information on approximately 3,200 foreign and domestic companies, with new entries added each month. It is available online through CompuServe Information Service.

Moody's Investors Service

http://www.moodys.com

Moody's Manuals Moody's publishes several financial databases. Its manuals are most valuable sources of information on a company and are divided into several categories as follows: (1) industrial; (2) bank and finance; (3) public utility; (4) transportation; (5) municipal and government; (6) OTC listed; (7) OTC unlisted; and (8) international.

The manuals are published annually in August of each year. They are updated with a twice-a-week supplement containing quarterly earnings, dividend announcements, mergers, and other financial news. The manuals are comprehensive and supplied in two volumes. The extent of coverage is determined by the level of coverage purchased by the company. The descriptions range from extensive to limited.

The *Industrial Manual* (two volumes) contains reports on publicly held companies that are listed in major stock exchanges. The manual provides information on the history, recent acquisitions, product lines, capital structure, financial statements ranging from 2 to 10 years, location of important properties, officers, and detailed description of securities outstanding. The *Bank and Finance Manual* (two volumes) publishes information on banks, savings and loan associations, investment companies, insurance companies, real estate companies, real estate investment trusts, and other finance-related companies. The presentation is similar to that of the *Industrial Manual*. A "Special Features" section presents summary statistics on the finance industry. The *Public Utility Manual* (two manuals) covers electric and gas utilities, gas transmission, telephone, and water companies. The presentation is similar to that of the *Industrial Manual*. A "Special Features" section presents summary statistics on the transportation industry. The *Municipal and Government Manual* (three volumes) covers federal, state, and municipal government financing. The manual describes pollution control, industrial development, revenue, and other related bonds, and financial statistics for each state. The *OTC Unlisted Manual* (one volume) covers OTC stocks that are less actively traded and those companies that are not traded on the Nasdaq. The presentation is similar to that of the industrial manual. It contains a geographical index of companies. The *International Manual* (two volumes) provides information on large international corporations and supranational institutions such as the World Bank. Corporations and institutions are arranged by country. The information includes history, subsidiaries, income statement, balance sheet, principal officers, and plant locations.

Moody's Bond Survey This publication provides ratings of commercial paper and bonds of issuers, and articles on the economy, credit analysis of companies, and ratings changes. The issuer's credit is analyzed for the purposes of rating. The rating spectrum ranges from Aaa to C, with 1, 2, or 3 used as modifiers that are similar to "plus" and "minus" used by S&P for bonds and P-1 to P-3 for commercial paper. The market sectors covered are (1) industrials; (2) sovereigns; (3) public finance; (4) structured finance; (5) insurance; and (6) project finance.

Its research activities are broken down into several major components by sector as follows:

- U.S. public finance credit research includes more than 70,000 ratings on both bonds and short-term obligations of some 20,000 municipal entities, covering more than 90 percent of bond volumes in the United States.
- Corporate credit research provides in-depth analysis of some 400 issuers in industrial, utility, and nonbank finance, and one-page analysis of some 800 issuers.
- Bank credit research provides in-depth analysis of banking institutions and security firms worldwide.
- Sovereign credit research includes reports on over 50 sovereign nations, and descriptions of economic and political factors that affect ratings.
- Speculative grade research includes monthly market commentary on over 500 issuers of non-investment-grade debt.
- Structured finance research has reports and updates on ratings of asset-backed and mortgage-backed securities.
- Insurance credit research provides credit evaluations of property-casualty companies.

Moody's Bond Record This publication is similar to S&P's *Bond Guide*. This monthly publication provides description of debt security, its month-end price, rating, date of issuance, and price range.

Moody's Handbook of Common Stocks This publication provides descriptions of stocks traded on the New York and American Stock Exchanges, with each stock described on one page. Approximately 900 stocks are covered. The coverage includes 10-year financial data, shares outstanding, earnings per share, and P/E ratio. Current condition and recent developments of the company are also presented.

OneSource®

http://www.onesource.com OneSource delivers in-depth company profiles with access to over 17 million global companies and 21 million executive profiles. It generates quality sales leads, identifies new prospects, finds key executives, manages customers effectively, researches business trends, tracks company performance, and monitors competitors.

Standard & Poor's Corporation (S&P)

http://www.ratingsdirect.com S&P has an extensive array of publications that cover most facets of finance. Many of them are discussed here.

CreditWeek *CreditWeek* presents analysis of companies, and ratings of debt issued by them. In rating a debt security, S&P takes into account the company's business risk, industry risk, financial risk, default risk, company size, management, and quality of financial statements. While rating a new security, S&P presents a complete analysis of the issuer. S&P incorporates default risk over the life of the security in assigning the rating, but financial conditions change. *Ratings Outlook* and *CreditWatch* address these situations. By placing a security in *CreditWatch,* S&P alerts the financial markets of a forthcoming change in credit rating. S&P may judge the outlook to be positive, negative, or neutral. The rating spectrum ranges from AAA to D, with ratings from AA to CCC being modified with plus and minus signs to show relative standing within the major ratings categories. The market sectors covered are (1) corporate finance; (2) sovereigns; (3) public finance; (4) structured finance; (5) insurance; and (6) project finance.

   CreditWeek presents feature articles by economists, special reports on topics of interest, selected industry and sector analyses, and assessment of key market trends. Periodically, S&P publishes several article serues on credit quality that include, among others, *Ratings Performance, Stability and Transition,* and *High Yield Bond and Bank Loan Ratings.* An offshoot of *CreditWeek,* Electronic Rating Information Service (ERIS) provides the latest database containing the ratings. The database is provided monthly.

Corporation Records This publication is a seven-volume work with companies arranged in alphabetical order in the first six volumes; the seventh volume is a daily update of companies covered in the first six volumes. *Corporation Record* is a monthly publication that provides history, financial statements, news announcements, earnings updates, and other information. The sixth volume has a statistical section covering new stock and bond offerings on a monthly basis, and a classified index of industrial companies listed by SIC code. This index is very useful in compiling a list of companies in a specific industry.

Stock Guide This is a monthly publication that provides information on stocks of several thousand companies.

Bond Guide This is a monthly publication that provides information on bonds, both rated and unrated. The *Bond Guide* lists all the outstanding bonds of the company, with the name of the bond, maturity, interest rate, price at the end of the month, amount outstanding, price range, current and former rating, date of rating change, yield to maturity, and date of issue. It has a section on convertible bonds and a section on foreign bonds. Each month it publishes rating changes, bonds called, and new offerings.

Corporate Reports One of the most popular publications, the *Corporate Reports* are a three-volume publication describing New York Stock Exchange stocks, American Stock Exchange stocks, and over-the-counter and regional exchange stocks. Current reports are published in a three-ring binder, and the annual is published in a bound form. Data is presented on product lines, 10-year historical performance, current developments, and stock performance.

Standard & Poor's Compustat® Database

http://www.compustat.com One of the most popular databases, S&P's Compustat covers 9,000+ active and 7,000+ inactive companies. The active companies have data with up to 20 years of annual, 12 years of quarterly, 7 years of business segment, and 30 years of monthly stock prices and dividend data. The active companies are divided into 270 industry groups. Compustat provides income statement, balance sheet, and statement of cash flow items, monthly price data, business segment data, geographic segment data, and company address. Compustat is estimated to contain analysts' recommendations on more than 4,000 companies. Compustat provides a more expansive database than Compustat II, which provides financial data for more companies and with SIC codes. There are specific data files that can be extracted from Compustat:

- Bank File contains financial data for approximately 150 leading U.S. banking institutions. Available in both annual and quarterly formats.
- Industrial Compustat comprises three files that can be obtained separately or merged together. These files are available in annual or quarterly format.

- Primary Industrial File has financial statement data on approximately 800 companies that include the S&P 400, S&P 40 utilities, S&P 20 transportation companies, and S&P 40 financial companies. These files are available in annual or quarterly format.
- Supplementary Industrial File provides financial statement data on approximately 800 companies traded on major exchanges but of lesser degree of investor interest.
- Tertiary Industrial File includes financial statement data on approximately 800 companies traded on major exchanges but of lesser degree of investor interest.
- Tertiary Industrial File includes financial statement data on approximately 800 companies traded on major exchanges but of lesser degree of investor interest.
- Tertiary Industrial File includes financial statement data on approximately 80 companies traded on New York and American Stock Exchanges.
- Over-the-Counter File features financial statement data on approximately 850 companies traded on the OTC. Annual format only.
- Industrial Annual Research File provides financial statement data on approximately 850 companies traded on the OTC. Annual format only.
- Industrial Annual Research File provides financial statement data on companies deleted from the primary, supplemental, tertiary, and OTC files due to acquisitions, merger, bankruptcy, liquidation, going private, or other reasons. Available in annual format.
- Full Coverage File has financial statement data on approximately 4,000 companies that file 10-K reports, primarily companies listed in Nasdaq, trading OTC, and on regional exchanges.
- Business Information Industry Segment File has SIC-code-based data on 6,250 companies for selected data items, with five-year histories.
- In addition, S&P provides a back-data companies database and the S&P Industry.
- Compustat provides investment professionals with access to information on 65,000 securities, which represent over 90% of the world's market value. The company history goes back to 1950. Compustat is used by hedge funds, money managers, analysts, quantitative reserachers, academics, and corporations. The information is organized according to three categories:
- *Essential Fundamentals* includes documents that are standardized, international data from regional providers, and key market identifiers such as CUSIP or ISIN.

- *Market data* includes pricing data, Standard & Poor's and other leading Index data, earnings data, and corporate actions and company business descriptions.
- *Propietary data* includes Standard & Poor's Stock Reports, Industry Surveys and ratings.

The Compustat Global Database offers fundamental and market data information on 65,000 global securities, up to 20 years of annual and 12 years of quarterly history, on top of precalculated ratios and concepts. In addition all Standard & Poor's indexes are classified according to the Global Industry Classification Standard (GICS), jointly developed by Standard & Poor's and MSCI Barra in 1999.

Standard & Poor's CreditPro®

http://creditpro.standardandpoors.com CreditPro allows evaluation of probabilities of default based on default data and ratings migration data covering more than 12,000 companies and 80,000 structured finance issues. It predicts future default and ratings migration scenarios, and helps to validate internal rating systems used for credit risk management purposes.

Standard & Poors NetAdvantage®

http://www.netadvantage.standardandpoors.com NetAdvantage provides searching and screening tools to facilitate academic research, case studies, strategic planning, due diligence, and MA activities. It has a database with data on 85,000 companies that are not public traded, as well as biographies of thousands of corporate executives and directors.

Standard & Poor's RatingsXpress®

http://www.ratingsdirect.com S&P RatingsXpress Credit Research provides in-depth coverage of international corporates, financial institutions, insurance companies, utilities and sovereigns. RatingsXpress data allows for determination of credit ratings of holdings and identification of key factors underlying an issuer's creditworthiness. This data can be used to distinguish the different risk exposures for new and existing deals, and attain an understanding of key regulatory, political and environmental events.

Thomson Financial

http://www.thomson.com/solutions/financial/ Thomson Financial is one of the leading providers of financial information, offering tailored solutions in a variety of asset classes including: asset management, corporations, fixed income, hedge funds, institutional equities, investment banking, private equity, and wealth management.

Value Line Investment Survey

http://www.valueline.com This survey is published in two parts. The first part provides analysis of about 1,700 stocks in 91 industries, which are updated on a quarterly basis. The analysis covers historical performance, descriptions of the company's business, current conditions, stock price data, two-year projections, and the beta of the stock. The second part is published weekly and contains stock recommendations and general investment advice.

DISTRESSED DEBT DATA

FridsonVision Distressed Debt Investor

http://www.fridsonvision.com/dd_overview.asp Distressed Debt Investor identifies opportunities in the securities of financially troubled companies. The elements of this research, updated every two weeks, include fundamental analysis and valuation of distress companies, analysis of trends within the distressed debt sector, and early identification of nondistressed companies that may be entering the distressed sector.

RATING MIGRATION DATA

The same three services discussed in the default rate section have also reported on rating migration statistics. Altman's work (with Kishore) has appeared in scholarly journals and NYU Salomon Center working papers, and Moody's and S&P report their own rating migration statistics on a regular basis (in the case of S&P, in the same report as their default statistics; in Moody's case, on an irregular, special report basis). These migration publications are of particular interest to analysts of rating stability, specific rating grade investing, credit risk deterioration, and so forth. For an in-depth discussion of the rating migration phenomenon and comparison between the three primary data sources in this area, see Chapter 17 in this book.

BOOKS

Mark J. P. Anson, Frank J. Fabozzi, Ren-Raw Chen, and Moorad Choudhry, *Credit Derivatives: Instruments, Applications and Pricing*, John Wiley & Sons, 2003.

Peter F. Bernstein, *Capital Ideas*, The Free Press, 1992.

Peter F. Bernstein, *Capital Ideas Evolving*, John Wiley & Sons, 2007.

Antulio N. Bomfim, *Understanding Credit Derivatives and Related Instruments*, Academic Press, 2004.

Geoff Chaplin, *Credit Derivatives: Risk Management, Trading and Investing*, John Wiley & Sons, 2005

Satyajit Das, *Credit Derivatives, CDOs and Structured Credit Products*, 3rd ed., John Wiley & Sons, 2005.

Satyajit Das, ed., *Credit Derivatives & Credit Linked Notes: Trading and Management of Credit and Default Risk*, 2nd ed., John Wiley & Sons, 2000.

Jon Gregory, ed., *Credit Derivatives: The Definitive Guide*, Risk Books/Application Networks, 2003.

Charles P. Kindleberger, *Maniacs, Panics and Crashes*, John Wiley & Sons, 2000.

David Lando, ed., *Derivative Credit Risk: Further Advances in Measurement and Management*, 2nd ed., Risk Books, 1999.

Roger Lowenstein, *When Genius Failed: The Rise and Fall of Long Term Capital Management*, Fourth State, 2002.

Robert J. Shiller, *The New Financial Order*, Princeton University Press, 2003.

Philipp J. Schönbucher, *Credit Derivatives Pricing Models: Model, Pricing and Implementation*, John Wiley & Sons, 2003.

Janet M. Tavakoli, *Collateralized Debt Obligations and Structured Finance*, John Wiley & Sons, 2003.

Index

Printed and bound by CPI Group (UK) Ltd, Croydon, CR0 4YY

23/04/2025

14661008-0005